Digital Speech Technology:
Processing, Recognition and Synthesis

Digital Speech Technology: Processing, Recognition and Synthesis

Edited by **Marcus Hintz**

New York

Published by Willford Press,
118-35 Queens Blvd., Suite 400,
Forest Hills, NY 11375, USA
www.willfordpress.com

Digital Speech Technology: Processing, Recognition and Synthesis
Edited by Marcus Hintz

International Standard Book Number: 978-1-68285-328-3 (Hardback)

Printed in the United States of America.

Contents

Preface

Speech technology is a rapidly advancing field of engineering. It primarily deals with processing, synthesis and recognition of human voice for various purposes. This book includes some of the vital pieces of work being conducted across the world, on various topics related to speech technology like acoustics, language modeling, speech enhancement, speaker verification and recognition, and manipulation of speech signals, etc. It strives to provide a fair idea about this discipline and to help develop a better understanding of the latest advances within this field.

After months of intensive research and writing, this book is the end result of all who devoted their time and efforts in the initiation and progress of this book. It will surely be a source of reference in enhancing the required knowledge of the new developments in the area. During the course of developing this book, certain measures such as accuracy, authenticity and research focused analytical studies were given preference in order to produce a comprehensive book in the area of study.

This book would not have been possible without the efforts of the authors and the publisher. I extend my sincere thanks to them. Secondly, I express my gratitude to my family and well-wishers. And most importantly, I thank my students for constantly expressing their willingness and curiosity in enhancing their knowledge in the field, which encourages me to take up further research projects for the advancement of the area.

Editor

Classification of speech under stress based on modeling of the vocal folds and vocal tract

Xiao Yao[1*], Takatoshi Jitsuhiro[1,2], Chiyomi Miyajima[1], Norihide Kitaoka[1] and Kazuya Takeda[1]

Abstract

In this study, we focus on the classification of neutral and stressed speech based on a physical model. In order to represent the characteristics of the vocal folds and vocal tract during the process of speech production and to explore the physical parameters involved, we propose a method using the two-mass model. As feature parameters, we focus on stiffness parameters of the vocal folds, vocal tract length, and cross-sectional areas of the vocal tract. The stiffness parameters and the area of the entrance to the vocal tract are extracted from the two-mass model after we fit the model to real data using our proposed algorithm. These parameters are related to the velocity of glottal airflow and acoustic interaction between the vocal folds and the vocal tract and can precisely represent features of speech under stress because they are affected by the speaker's psychological state during speech production. In our experiments, the physical features generated using the proposed approach are compared with traditionally used features, and the results demonstrate a clear improvement of up to 10% to 15% in average stress classification performance, which shows that our proposed method is more effective than conventional methods.

Keywords: Speech under stress; Stress classification; Physical parameters; Two-mass model; Vocal folds; Vocal tract

1. Introduction

Stress is a psycho-physiological state characterized by subjective strain, increased physiological activity, and deterioration of performance [1]. Factors inducing stress on speakers include workload, background noise, emotions, physical environmental factors (e.g., G-force), and fatigue. These factors are believed to affect voice quality and are detrimental to the performance of communication equipment, especially automated systems with speech interfaces. Therefore, it has become increasingly important to study speech under stress in order to improve the performance of speech recognition systems, to recognize when people are in a stressed state and to understand contexts in which speakers are communicating.

Researchers have attempted to probe reliable indicators of stress by analyzing acoustic variables. Some external factors (workload, background noise, etc.) and internal factors (emotional state, fatigue, etc.) may induce stress [2]. The first investigations of emotional speech were conducted in the mid-1980s, using the statistical properties of acoustic features in order to detect emotions from speech [3,4]. It has been found that fundamental frequency (F_0) has different characteristics for each emotion [5] and that respiration patterns and muscle tension also change [6]. The influence of the Lombard effect on speech recognition has also been examined [7,8]. Selected acoustic features have been analyzed, such as amplitude and distribution of spectral energy, and it was found that spectral energy shifted to higher frequencies for consonants in the presence of loud background noise. High workload stress has been proven to have a significant impact on the performance of speech recognition systems, with speech under workload sounding faster, softer, or louder than neutral speech [9,10]. Matsuo et al. examined the frequency domain and showed how differences in the spectrum of the high frequency band under stressful workload conditions could be used to catch people committing remittance fraud, and their proposed measure achieved better classification performance [11]. Furthermore, the Teager energy operator (TEO) [12] was proposed to explore variations in the energy of airflow characteristics within the glottis for the purpose of stress classification [13]. However, the features examined in these previous

* Correspondence: xiao.yao@g.sp.m.is.nagoya-u.ac.jp
[1]Graduate School of Information Science, Nagoya University, Nagoya, Aichi, Japan
Full list of author information is available at the end of the article

studies lack a physical basis, and the methods do not consider the whole process of speech production, which is believed to be essential for effective classification of speech under stress.

We propose a stressed speech classification method based on a physical model characterizing the vocal folds (VF) and the vocal tract (VT). This method can represent the process of speech production and model airflow patterns in the vocal folds and the vocal tract, which are essential for stress classification. In this physical model, changes in the physical characteristics of the vocal folds, such as muscle tension, have a modulating effect on the formants, while the shape of the vocal tract can also influence the glottal source because of the interaction between the vocal folds and the vocal tract. It is believed that the presence of stress can result in variations in the physical characteristics of physiological systems and influence the acoustic interaction between the vocal folds and the vocal tract [2]. The parameters of the physical model also help represent the influence of speaking style more directly and clearly. Therefore, a physical model is helpful to estimate the parameters of the physiological system.

An early but still prominent physical model is the source-filter model [14], which models speech as the combination of a glottal source (such as the vocal folds), and a linear acoustic filter representing the vocal tract and its radiation characteristic. An important assumption that is often made in the use of the source-filter model is independence of the source and filter. In such cases, the model should more accurately be referred to as the 'independent source-filter model'. In 1961, Wong proposed a linear model of speech production using a lossless tube model of the vocal tract [15]. In 1979, a linear source tract model was proposed to model the glottal source, the vocal tract, and radiation impedance as linear filters, using covariance analysis [16]. However, the vocal tract and vocal folds do not function independently of each other instead there is some form of interaction between them [17], which results in significant changes in fundamental frequency and formant characteristics.

The two-mass model is a physical model, which attempts to simulate the physical process of vocal fold vibration, characterizing the vocal folds and the vocal tract, and to also model the effect of glottis-vocal tract interaction [18]. Parameters affected under stressed conditions are extracted from the physical model and are used as features to identify speech under stress more precisely. We use the two-mass model as a physical model, and our proposed method estimates the values of parameters included in the model from input speech. To identify speech under stress, we evaluate parameters affected by stress.

In this paper, we propose a method for fitting a physical model to real speech in order to estimate the physical parameters which characterize the vocal folds and the vocal tract. For the physical model, a two-mass model connected to a four-tube model is used to simulate the process of speech production. The physical parameters (stiffness, vocal tract length, and cross-sectional areas of the vocal tract) are estimated by fitting the model to real speech. The estimated parameters can be further analyzed and proposed as features for the classification of neutral and stressed speech. Furthermore, different cost functions are proposed to compare classification performance. As a result, stiffness of the vocal folds and cross-sectional areas of the vocal tract are selected as features for the classification of neutral and stressed speech.

The paper is organized as follows: In Overview, an overview of our method is presented. Physical parameters, related to the vocal folds and the vocal tract, based on the two-mass model are described as features for classification in Physical parameters. This is followed by the presentation of a fitting algorithm for real speech data in Estimation method to help estimate the physical parameters. Classification describes the classification method used for evaluation. In Evaluation, experiments are performed to evaluate the obtained parameters and show their corresponding classification performances when separating neutral and stressed speech. Finally, we draw our conclusions in Conclusion.

2. Overview

An overview of our work is shown in Figure 1. It includes the three steps needed to perform stressed speech classification: proposal of physical parameters, parameter estimation by fitting them to the two-mass model, and the classification of neutral and stressed speech.

Initially, we propose physical parameters considered likely to be useful, which include stiffness parameters of the vocal folds, vocal tract length, and cross-sectional areas of the vocal tract. These parameters characterize the behavior of vocal folds and the shape of the vocal tract. Furthermore, the relationship between the selected physical parameters and acoustic parameters has been shown to represent characteristics of the interaction between the vocal folds and the vocal tract.

The proposed physical parameters are then estimated by fitting the two-mass model to real speech. An algorithm based on the analysis-by-synthesis method is proposed for fitting the model to real speech. The Nelder-Mead simplex method [19] is used as a search strategy in order to find the optimal physical parameters. An iteration method is performed for vocal fold fitting and vocal tract fitting to estimate parameters, because there is interaction between the VF and VT.

For classification, a linear classifier is trained using utterances from each speaker. Currently, a simple linear classifier based on Euclidean distance is used for classification. Also, since we only have speech data for a small number of speakers, we evaluate our proposed method as a speaker-dependent system.

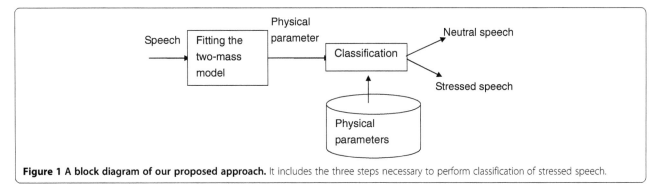

Figure 1 A block diagram of our proposed approach. It includes the three steps necessary to perform classification of stressed speech.

3. Physical parameters

A method which fits the two-mass model to real speech is proposed for classifying speech under stress. Some of the physical parameters characterizing the vocal folds and the vocal tract are estimated. The two-mass vocal fold model was originally proposed by Ishizaka and Flanagan to simulate the process of speech production [18]. We propose three types of feature parameters extracted from the two-mass model: stiffness, vocal tract length, and cross-sectional area of the entrance of the vocal tract. In the following sections, we will define these parameters and describe their characteristics.

3.1 Stiffness

The stiffness parameters are related to muscle tension in the vocal folds. Generally, the stiffness of the vocal folds is considered to depend mainly on two muscles: the cricothyroid muscle (CT) and thyroarytenoid muscle (TA) [16]. In the two-mass model, coupling stiffness k_c is relative to the tension in the TA muscle, so a high k_1 value and a low value for k_c represent the contraction of the CT muscle and relaxation of the TA muscle.

Figure 2 shows a sketch of the model. Each vocal fold is represented by a mass-spring-damper system, joined with a coupling stiffness [18]. It is represented as:

$$m_i \frac{d^2 x_1}{dt^2} + r_1 \frac{dx_1}{dt} + s_1(x_1) + k_c(x_1 - x_2) = F_1, \quad (1)$$

$$m_2 \frac{d^2 x_2}{dt^2} + r_2 \frac{dx_2}{dt} + s_2(x_2) + k_c(x_2 - x_1) = F_2. \quad (2)$$

Tissue elasticity (or 'spring') s_i represents the tension of the vocal folds, which depends on the contraction of different muscles. The equivalent tensions are given by:

$$s_i(x_i) = k_i(x_i + \eta x_i^3), \quad i = 1, 2, \quad (3)$$

whose notations and variables are documented in Table 1.

Stiffness parameters are the main factors relating to fundamental frequency, and they can also determine the amplitude of the glottal area and glottal volume velocity [20], so source excitation is significantly influenced by the degree of stiffness. During the production of speech, the natural frequency of the vocal folds is determined by both their mass and stiffness. However, in order to

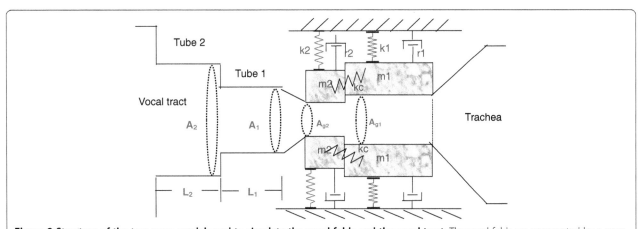

Figure 2 Structure of the two-mass model used to simulate the vocal folds and the vocal tract. The vocal folds are represented by a mass-spring-damping system, coupled with a four-tube model. In this model, m denotes a mass, k_1 and k_2 are linear stiffnesses, k_c is the coupling stiffness connecting the two masses, and r_1 and r_2 are the viscous resistances. L and A represent the length and cross-sectional area of the vocal tract, respectively.

Table 1 Notations and variables in the two-mass model for the vocal folds

Notation/variable	Description
m_i	The masses
x_i	The horizontal displacements measured from the rest (neutral) position x_0
r_i	The equivalent viscous resistances
s_i	The force related to tissue elasticity
F_i	The force of airflow, which is determined by subglottal pressure
k_i	The stiffness coefficients
k_c	The coupling stiffness
η	A coefficient of the nonlinear relations

simplify the estimation algorithm, only the stiffness parameters are estimated, with mass fixed as a constant.

3.2 Vocal tract length and cross-sectional area

The supraglottic area includes the structures that lie above the true vocal folds and below the base of the tongue. The anatomical structures present in this area that are important to speech production lie posterior to the epiglottis. They include the ventricle, false vocal folds, epiglottis, arytenoids, laryngeal aspects of the aryepiglottic folds, and vestibule [21].

The two-mass model is connected to a four-tube model representing the vocal tract [18]. The tube model is constructed using a transmission line analogy involving n cylindrical, hard-walled sections. The elemental values of the model are determined by cross-sectional areas $A_1 \cdots A_n$ and cylinder lengths $l_1 \cdots l_n$. The total length of the vocal tract is defined as L_{VT}. The tube model can be represented by an equivalent circuit, as shown in Figure 3. The inductances $L_n = \rho l_n / 2A_n$, the capacitances $C_n = l_n \cdot A_n / \rho c^2$, and the resistances $R_n = (S_n/A_n^2)\sqrt{\rho\mu\omega/2}$, where c is the velocity of sound.

Here, the tube model has been limited to four cylindrical sections of equal length, $n = 4$. In this study, the model is limited to only vowel articulation (as vowels were the subject of the experiments) and modal voice production. These assumptions greatly simplify the modeling of the vocal tract and the glottal source. In this paper, we use a four-tube model to simulate the vocal tract, which followed the original paper [18]. Furthermore, in the following analysis, we propose A_1 as one of our feature parameters because the other areas, A_2, A_3, and A_4 are less effective on classification than A_1. Thus, we currently consider the four-tube model to be sufficient.

The model is terminated in a radiation load equal to that of a circular piston in an infinite baffle. $L_n = (8\rho/3\pi)\sqrt{\pi A_n}$, $R_R = 128\rho c/9\pi^2 A_n$, where A_n is the area of the mouth. The notations and variables are documented in Table 2.

Therefore, the differential equations related to the volume velocities of the system are:

$$(R_{k1} + R_{k2})|U_g|U_g + (R_{v1} + R_{v2})U_g + (L_{g1} + L_{g2})\frac{dU_g}{dt} + L_1\frac{dU_g}{dt} + R_1 U_g + \frac{1}{C_1}\int_0^t (U_g - U_1)dt - P_s = 0$$

$$(L_1 + L_2)\frac{dU_1}{dt} + (R_1 + R_2)U_1 + \frac{1}{C_2}\int_0^t (U_1 - U_2)dt + \frac{1}{C_1}\int_0^t (U_1 - U_g)dt = 0 \qquad (4)$$
$$\vdots$$

$$L_R \frac{d}{dt}(U_R + U_L) + R_R \cdot U_R = 0,$$

where $R_{v1} = 12\frac{\mu l_g^2 d_1}{A_{g1}^3}$, $R_{v2} = 12\frac{\mu l_g^2 d_2}{A_{g2}^3}$, $L_{g1} = \frac{\rho d_1}{A_{g1}}$, $L_{g2} = \frac{\rho d_2}{A_{g2}}$, $R_{k1} = \frac{0.19\rho}{A_{g1}^2}$, and $R_{k2} = \frac{\rho\left[0.5 - \frac{A_{g2}}{A_1}\left(1 - \frac{A_{g2}}{A_1}\right)\right]}{A_{g2}^2}$.

The length of the vocal tract and its cross-sectional areas are the main parameters which determine the

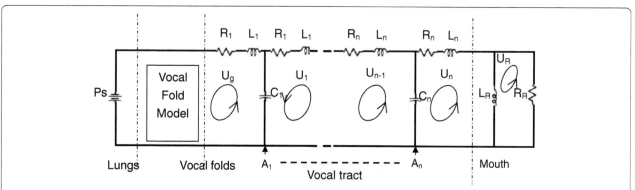

Figure 3 Circuit equivalent of the tube model, representing the production of voiced sound in the vocal tract. Current U_g denotes the velocity of airflow in the glottis. Inductance, capacitance, and resistance depend on the length and area of the vocal tract.

Table 2 Notations and variables in the two-mass model for the vocal tract

Notation/variable	Description
A_i	The cross-sectional areas in the tube model
l_i	The cylinder lengths in the tube model
d_i	The thickness of m_1 and m_2
A_{g1}, A_{g2}	The cross-sectional areas of the glottis
U_g	The average volume velocity across the glottal area
c	The velocity of sound
ρ	The air density
ω	The radian frequency

shape of the vocal tract and have a significant impact on the distribution of formants. Vocal tract length and cross-sectional areas of the tube model are computed from real speech.

3.3 Relationship between physical parameters and acoustic parameters

In this section, we describe experiments which were performed to represent the presence of acoustic interaction and show the relationship between physical and acoustic parameters. Aerodynamics in the glottis is modeled using the two-mass model. In order to clarify the relationship between physical and acoustic parameters, we will first briefly describe the main equations representing the aerodynamics of speech production.

If subglottal pressure is represented as P_s, then air pressure drops to P_{11} when air enters the glottis (at the edge of m_1) according to Bernoulli's equation. The abrupt contraction in the cross-sectional area at the inlet to the glottis causes a phenomenon called vena contracta, which causes the air pressure to undergo an even greater drop. The drop is determined by the flow measurements of van den Berg:

$$P_s - P_{11} = (1.00 + 0.37)\frac{\rho U_g^2}{2A_{g1}^2}, \tag{5}$$

where ρ is the air density, U_g is the volume velocity of glottal airflow, and A_{g1} is the cross-sectional lower glottal area, which is represented by $A_{g1} = 2l_g(x_0 + x_1)$, where l_g is the length of the vocal fold and x_0 is the displacement when the vocal folds are in the rest position.

Along masses m_1 and m_2, pressure drops as a result of air viscosity:

$$P_{i1} - P_{i2} = \frac{12\mu d_i l_g^2 U_g}{A_{gi}^3}, \quad i = 1, 2, \tag{6}$$

where μ is the air viscosity coefficient and d_1 is the width of m_1.

At the boundary between the two masses, the pressure drop can be calculated by:

$$P_{21} - P_{12} = \frac{\rho U_g^2}{2}\left(\frac{1}{A_{g1}^2} - \frac{1}{A_{g2}^2}\right), \tag{7}$$

where P_{21} is the air pressure at the lower edge of m_2 and A_{g2} is the cross-sectional lower glottal area.

At the glottal outlet, abrupt expansion causes the pressure to recover because of the relatively large area of the vocal tract. This pressure is given by:

$$P_1 - P_{22} = \frac{1}{2}\rho\frac{U_g^2}{A_{g2}^2}[2N(1-N)], \tag{8}$$

where P_1 is the pressure at the inlet of the vocal tract. Here, the parameter N is defined as $N = A_{g2} / A_1$, where A_1 is the area of the entrance to the vocal tract. N denotes the difference in area between the outlet of the vocal folds and the inlet of the vocal tract, which is significant to the acoustic interaction between the vocal folds and the vocal tract [18]. Since glottal area A_{g2} does not change significantly during the oscillation of the vocal folds, A_1 is the parameter relating to the acoustic interaction.

In Equation 4, it is shown that airflow velocity U_g depends on both the stiffness of the vocal folds and area of the entrance to the vocal tract A_1. Therefore, it is our assumption that parameters k_1, k_2, k_c, and A_1 related to velocity have an impact on acoustic interaction. In this paper, experiments are performed to represent the presence of this interaction by showing the relationship between physical and acoustic parameters. Due to the presence of these interactions, changes in the oscillation of the vocal folds affect the distribution of formants, and different shapes of the vocal tract (length and area) also influence the glottal source. Table 3 lists the physical and acoustic parameters.

We first examine how stiffness parameters impact the distribution of formants. First, we fixed the shape of the vocal tract and examined how variation in the stiffness parameters of the vocal folds affects the shift of formants. The vocal tract model was represented by a standard tube configuration for the vowels /a/ and /e/ [22]. In order to reduce the number of parameters to be estimated and simplify the proposed method, typical values were adopted for the configuration of the tube model. Therefore, as typical values, the length chosen

Table 3 Physical and acoustic parameters

Parameter	Variable
Physical	k_1, k_c, A_1, A_2, A_3, L_{VT}
Acoustic	F_0, F_1, F_2, F_3

for the vocal tract was L_{VT} = 16 cm, with each element l_i = 4 cm, and the cross-sectional area was fixed at A_1 = 0.8 cm^2, A_2 = 0.4 cm^2, A_3 = 3 cm^2, and A_4 = 8 cm^2 for /a/ and A_1 = 1 cm^2, A_2 = 8 cm^2, A_3 = 8 cm^2, and A_4 = 8 cm^2 for /e/. When a specific stiffness is checked, the other stiffness parameters are fixed at typical values. We changed stiffness parameters k_1 (20 to 240 kdyn/cm), k_2 (2 to 40 kdyn/cm), and k_c (2.5 to 70 kdyn/cm) to examine variation in formants. Formant estimation is based on modeling vocal tract frequency response using linear predictive coding (LPC) techniques. It estimates formant frequencies from the all-pole model of the vocal tract transfer function.

Figure 4 shows the relationship between the stiffness parameters and different formants. It shows that k_2 does not significantly influence formants, but that first and second formants will shift their location to a lower frequency with the increase of k_1, although there is no significant change in the third formant (F_3). A similar phenomenon occurs for k_c. When k_c decreases, F_1 also has a tendency to shift to a lower frequency, while F_2 and F_3 are less influenced by the variation of k_c. Therefore, it is shown that stiffness parameters k_1 and k_c can affect the distribution of formants and that the first and second formants are easily affected by acoustic interaction.

Next, we fixed the configuration of the vocal folds and examined how variation of the cross-sectional area of the vocal tract impacts the fundamental frequency (F_0)

of speech. Stiffness was fixed at typical values k_1 = 80,000 dyn/cm, k_2 = 8,000 dyn/cm, and k_c = 25,000 dyn/cm to check how the fundamental frequency changes with the area function. When checking the impact of a specific area, other areas and vocal tract length (VTL) were fixed at typical values for /a/ or /e/. When considering VTL, all the cross-sectional areas were fixed at typical values. We then change the cross-sectional area or VTL to examine their impact on F_0. The variation range for VTL was 13 to 19 cm, and for cross-sectional area of VT, the range was 0.1 to 20 cm. The algorithm for estimation of the fundamental frequency of speech is YIN [23]. It is based on the well-known autocorrelation method, with a number of modifications that combine to prevent error.

Figure 5 shows the relationship between the vocal tract parameters (vocal tract length and cross-sectional area) and fundamental frequency. It shows that VTL has less impact on F_0 and only determines the distribution of formants. However, an increase in cross-sectional area A_1 can cause F_0 to change significantly. While cross-sectional areas A_2 and A_3 also have an impact on F_0 to some extent, but their influence is insignificant compared to A_1.

Therefore, it is our conclusion that stiffness of the vocal folds and cross-sectional area A_1 affect both the fundamental frequency and formants and, further, the interaction between the vocal folds and the vocal tract.

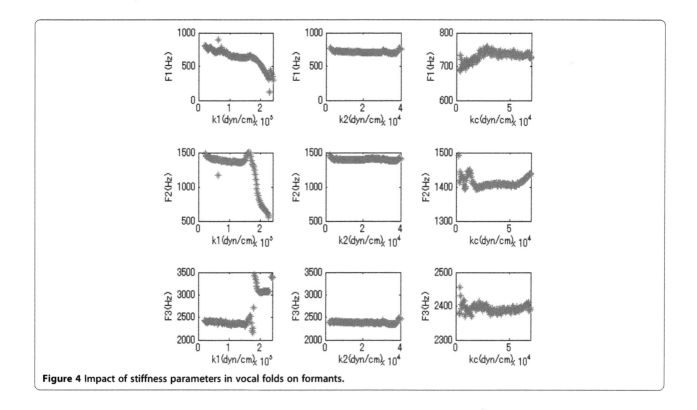

Figure 4 Impact of stiffness parameters in vocal folds on formants.

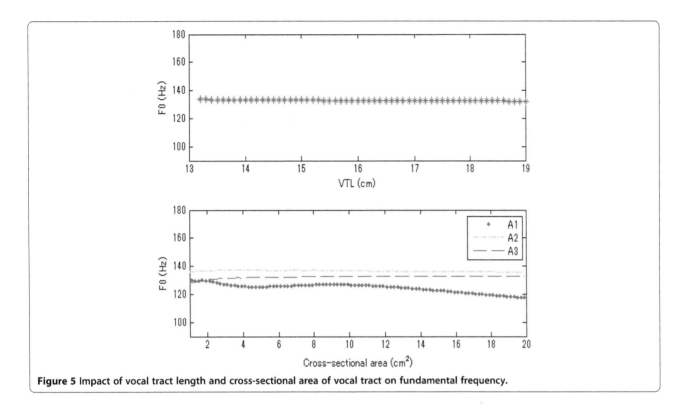

Figure 5 Impact of vocal tract length and cross-sectional area of vocal tract on fundamental frequency.

3.4 Parameters representing stress

In Relationship between physical parameters and acoustic parameters, the experimental results show that stiffness of the vocal folds and cross-sectional area A_1 have an impact on the interaction between the vocal folds and the vocal tract. It is believed that the variations in acoustic interaction differ markedly between neutral and stressed speech [2], so stiffness and A_1 should be selected as parameters for representing stress.

In theory, Equation 8 shows that both the velocity of glottal airflow and the difference between the area of the outlet of the vocal folds and the inlet of the vocal tract have an impact on the pressure difference inside and outside of the glottis. Thus, the two factors can cause variations in the airflow patterns in the glottis and thus are likely to be effective to represent the presence of stress.

Variation in the stiffness of the vocal folds influences the time span of glottal opening and closing phases and causes glottal airflow to accelerate in the glottis, thus impacting the velocity of glottal airflow. Therefore, we can also assume that stiffness parameters can be potential parameters for stress detection.

A_1 in the four-tube model is the area of the entrance to the vocal tract in the supraglottis. Narrowing A_1 facilitates phonation by decreasing the oscillation threshold pressure of the vocal folds [24]. Since glottal area A_{g2} does not change significantly during the oscillation of the vocal folds, A_1 is the main factor determining the

pressure difference between the inside and outside of the glottis and has an impact on the acoustic interaction between VF and VT. Based on these considerations, we also make the assumption that A_1 is an effective parameter for stress classification.

4. Estimation method

4.1 Algorithm for fitting

The goal of stress classification is to determine from speech data if a specific person is under stress when he or she is speaking. When speech is input to the system, it is split into several frames, and further estimation of the physical parameters is performed for each frame. VTL for each speaker is first calculated; then, the obtained VTL is input as a known parameter. Then, the two-mass model is fit to each speech sample to simulate the vocal folds and the vocal tract. An outline of our method is shown in Figure 6.

In the first step, estimation of VTL is performed. Since VTL has no impact on the glottal source, it can be estimated separately. Because VTL varies with each speaker, all of the neutral speech data for vowel /a/ from each speaker is used to estimate the vocal tract length of that speaker. Here, we mainly consider the neutral speech for each speaker in the database. During VTL estimation, real speech from a database is analyzed using LPC to obtain the spectral envelope. The stiffness parameters are fixed at typical values and are taken as an input. The two-mass model is then fit to the neutral speech of each

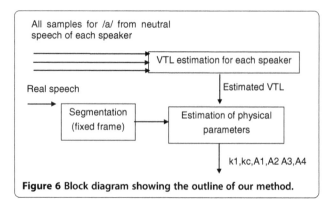

Figure 6 Block diagram showing the outline of our method.

speaker to estimate the parameters of vocal tract length and cross-sectional area. Nelder-Mead simplex method [19] is used to search for the optimal values for fitting. For each speaker i, the probability distribution $P_i(L_{VT}(i, k))$ of VTL $L_{VT}(i, k)$ for all neutral speech is calculated, and we choose the one with the highest probability as the estimated vocal tract length.

$$L_{VT}(i)^* = \arg\max_{L_{VT(i,k)}} P_i(L_{VT}(i, k)). \qquad (9)$$

The detailed fitting procedure is the same as that used for vocal tract fitting described below, which is shown in Figure 7. Equation 12 is used as the cost function.

In the next step, the estimated VTL of this speaker, which was obtained during the first step, is used, and the two-mass model is fit to the real speech to estimate the other physical parameters. Fitting the model to real speech poses a difficulty: estimation of too many parameters may make the fitting method unstable. The solution to this problem is to split the process into two main parts so that the VF and VT are fit with two different cost functions. However, the existence of interaction between VF and VT makes it impossible to fit VF and VT separately, and changes in the stiffness parameters and in A_1 in the tube model can influence both formants and the glottal source. An alternative is to perform iteration when fitting the vocal folds and the vocal tract. Thus, an iteration method is used for vocal fold and

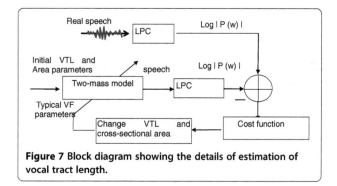

Figure 7 Block diagram showing the details of estimation of vocal tract length.

vocal tract fitting, which are accomplished as follows. Figure 8 shows the structure of the fitting algorithm.

For vocal tract fitting, stiffness parameters are fixed at typical values and are taken as an input to vocal tract fitting. The parameters for the cross-sectional areas are then estimated. Next, the obtained areas are used as an input for vocal fold fitting, and the two-mass model is fit to estimate the new stiffness parameters. When current stiffness differs significantly from the typical value, the corresponding formants are also affected, and some variations can occur. In such cases, vocal tract fitting needs to be performed again. We take iterations for the two parts until the results reach convergence.

The detailed structure of vocal tract fitting and vocal fold fitting is shown in Figures 9 and 10. Vocal tract fitting includes two steps. First, real speech from a database is analyzed using LPC to calculate the spectral envelope. In the second step, a simulation is performed using the two-mass model to produce speech using an initial area function. The same spectral envelope is calculated from the simulated speech and is compared with the one obtained in the first step to find the difference between them. The difference between the simulated spectrum and the target spectrum is represented by a cost function. The area function is then varied, and glottal flow is simulated until the cost function reaches a minimum. Optimal values of the physical parameters are then estimated using the Nelder-Mead simplex method [19]. Cost function 2 is used in vocal tract fitting. In this paper, we utilize four cost functions in order to compare classification performance, which are described in Cost functions for vocal tract fitting.

The Nelder-Mead algorithm is a simplex method for finding the minimum of a function involving several variables. It is a direct search method and does not require the calculation of a derivative. We use the Nelder-Mead method based on the comparison of the values of the cost function at the $n + 1$ vertices for n-dimensional decision variables to solve our optimization problem. Here, we select A_1, A_2, A_3, and A_4 as variables in vocal tract fitting. Each calculation will generate a new vertex for the simplex. If this new point is better than at least one of the existing vertices, it replaces the worst vertex. The simplex vertices are changed through reflection, expansion, shrinkage, and contraction operations in order to find an improved solution to estimate the parameters. Optimal values of the physical parameters are estimated using the Nelder-Mead simplex method, which is implemented to search for the optimal physical parameters to minimize the cost function.

Vocal fold fitting uses the same process as vocal tract fitting, with the difference that the residual signal is obtained using LPC analysis, and the spectrum of the residual signal is available to construct the cost function 1

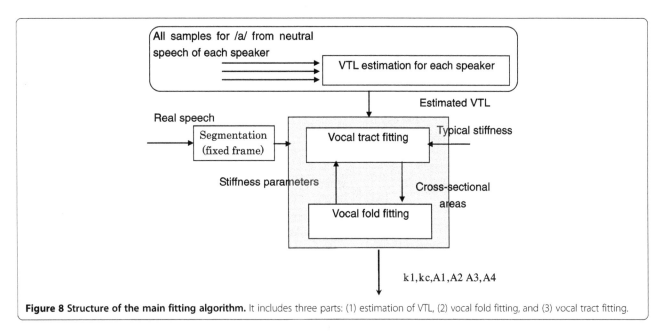

Figure 8 Structure of the main fitting algorithm. It includes three parts: (1) estimation of VTL, (2) vocal fold fitting, and (3) vocal tract fitting.

in Figure 10 for vocal fold fitting. It is used to evaluate the difference in the spectrum of the residual signal in vocal fold fitting, which is described as:

$$C = \frac{\sum_{i=1}^{fs/2} |S^*(\omega_i) - S(\omega_i)|^2}{\sum_{i=1}^{fs/2} |S(\omega_i)|^2}, \quad (10)$$

where $S(\omega)$ and $S^*(\omega)$ are the power spectrums of the residual signal for simulated and real speech, respectively. Here, we select the stiffness parameters k_1, k_2, and k_c as variables for vocal tract fitting.

Here, we use the residual signal from LPC analysis to estimate the parameters of the vocal folds. The LPC model is based on a mathematical approximation of the vocal tract. We use it to remove the effect of the vocal tract and obtain the residual signal to estimate the stiffness parameters with generated cost functions. In order

to make a comparison with the spectrum of the residual signal from real speech, an LPC inverse filter is used for the simulated speech to obtain the residual signal. Our target here is to evaluate the similarity of the spectrums of residual signals both from real and simulated speech instead of representing the source wave. The aim of this paper is to classify speech under stress. It is believed that the main differences between neutral and stressed speech are focused on the harmonic structure of the spectrum of residual signal [11]. Thus, in this study, obtaining the residual signal using LPC can work well for showing the harmonic structure of the spectrum.

4.2 Cost functions for vocal tract fitting

As for the definition of cost function 2, we utilized four different cost functions in order to compare their classification performance.

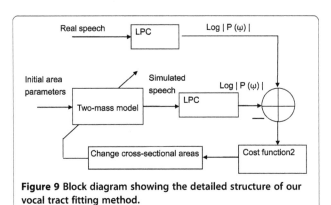

Figure 9 Block diagram showing the detailed structure of our vocal tract fitting method.

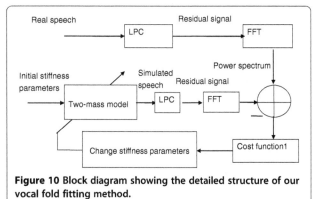

Figure 10 Block diagram showing the detailed structure of our vocal fold fitting method.

4.2.1 Formant ($C^{F_1-F_2}$)

The presence of stress causes an increase in the variability of airflow characteristics due to differences in the muscle tension of the vocal folds. This should cause changes in acoustic interaction around the false vocal folds, thus having an impact on the first and second formants (F_1 and F_2). Thus, F_1 and F_2 are calculated from the spectral envelope to define a cost function:

$$C^{F_1-F_2} = \alpha_1 \left(F_1^*-F_1\right)^2 + \alpha_2 (F_2^*-F_2)^2,$$
$$\alpha_1 = \frac{1}{\overline{F_1}}, \alpha_2 = \frac{1}{\overline{F_2}}, \tag{11}$$

where the asterisk denotes the target value for real speech. The weights are given the values α_1 and α_2 to normalize the different target parameters to the same range, and the overbar denotes mean values over the target region.

4.2.2 RMS distance of spectral envelope (C_{rms})

C_{F1-F2} only focuses on the frequency of the first two formants, which is not accurate enough to describe the spectrum. Thus, we find a set of all-pole model coefficients, the cost function of which can be defined as the root mean square (RMS) distance between the spectral envelope of simulated speech and the original speech:

$$C_{\text{rms}} = \sqrt{\frac{1}{N} \sum_{i=1}^{N} |\log P(\omega_i) - \log P^*(\omega_i)|^2}$$
$$P(\omega) = \frac{1}{|A(\omega)|^2} = \frac{1}{\left|\sum_{k=0}^{P} a_k e^{-j\omega k}\right|^2}. \tag{12}$$

4.2.3 Itakura-Saito distance of spectral envelope (C_{I-S})

The Itakura-Saito distance is a measure of the perceptual difference between an original spectrum and an approximation of that spectrum. It was proposed by Fumitada Itakura and Shuzo Saito in the 1970s and can be described as:

$$C_{\text{I-S}} = \frac{1}{N} \sum_{i=1}^{N} \frac{P(\omega_i)}{P^*(\omega_i)} - \log \frac{P(\omega_i)}{P^*(\omega_i)} - 1. \tag{13}$$

4.2.4 Envelope and formant (C_{E-F})

The cost functions C_{rms} and C_{I-S} catch the difference between the rough shapes of the spectral envelopes, but they neglect local information when locating the formant. Since only the first two formants are affected by the oscillation of the vocal folds, the characteristics of F_1 and F_2 should be the chief focus. We propose matching

the spectral envelope initially in the first iteration, and then, in the next iteration, the characteristics of the formant are fully considered:

$$C_{E\text{-}F}^{(1)} = \frac{1}{N} \sum_{i=1}^{N} |\log P(\omega_i) - \log P^*(\omega_i)|^2 \qquad n = 1,$$
$$C_{E\text{-}F}^{(n)} = \alpha_1 \left(F_1^*-F_1\right)^2 + \alpha_2 \left(F_2^*-F_2\right)^2$$
$$\qquad + w_1 \left(H_1^*-H_1\right)^2 + w_2 \left(H_2^*-H_2\right)^2 \qquad n \geq 2,$$
$$\tag{14}$$

where F_1, F_2, H_1, and H_2 refer to the frequency and amplitude of the first and second formants and n is the iteration number.

It would be helpful to evaluate the accuracy of the fitting method to show that the proposed method works well. However, it is difficult to compare the simulated values with the actual values because sensors are not available to measure the actual values for human beings. In this paper, we calculate the error in acoustic features between real and simulated speech to describe the accuracy of the fitting method.

Using the fitting method described above, the optimal simulated speech corresponding to the inputted real speech can be obtained. Some acoustic features like F_0, F_1, F_2, F_3, and F_4 can also be estimated from the simulated speech. In order to describe the accuracy of the fitting method, we calculate the error in F_0, F_1, F_2, F_3, and F_4 between real and simulated speech. Here, cost function C_{E-F} is used.

$$\begin{aligned}
\text{Err}_{F_0} &= \left(F_0-F_0^*\right) \\
\text{Err}_{F_1} &= \left(F_1-F_1^*\right) \\
\text{Err}_{F_2} &= \left(F_2-F_2^*\right) \\
\text{Err}_{F_3} &= \left(F_3-F_3^*\right) \\
\text{Err}_{F_4} &= \left(F_4-F_4^*\right),
\end{aligned} \tag{15}$$

where the asterisk denotes the target value for real speech.

We calculate the errors from simulated and real speech for all the samples for vowels /a/ and /e/ and show the distributions of the errors as shown in Figure 11. Simulated results using these four cost functions are shown in Figure 12. The errors, as shown in Figure 11, are smaller in F_0, F_1, and F_2 (±3 Hz) to obtain higher accuracy. However, the errors in F_3 and F_4 may be increasing, because the cost function chosen places more emphasis on the first and second formants, which are believed to be more important for stress classification. Thus, based on the distributions of errors, it is shown that the proposed method provides reliable accuracy for the fitting to real speech.

5. Classification

Evaluation of the physical parameters is speaker dependent. The structure of the classification method is shown in Figure 13.

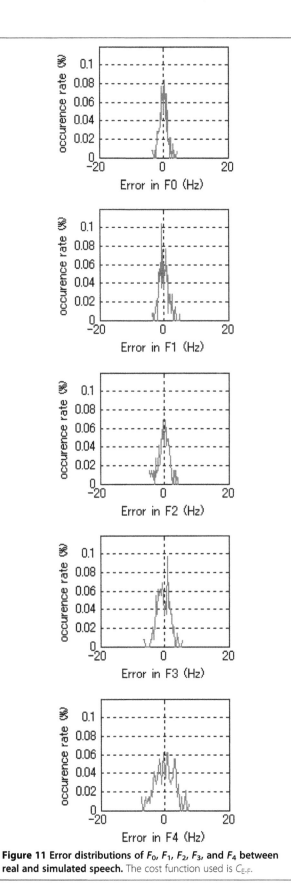

Figure 11 Error distributions of F_0, F_1, F_2, F_3, and F_4 between real and simulated speech. The cost function used is C_{E-F}.

During the training process, all of the speech samples from a specific speaker are labeled as neutral or stressed speech. The labeled speech is segmented into fixed frames, and all of the frames are fit using the two-mass model to estimate the proposed parameters. A linear classifier based on minimum Euclidean distance is trained for the classification, using the estimated physical parameters from all of the frames.

During testing, test speech is input into the system and split into frames, and the trained linear classifier then separates them into neutral or stressed speech. We use Euclidean distance to make a final decision for speech data with several frames. For a test sample with K frames, the feature vector of the ith frame is V_i. We calculate its Euclidean distance $d_i(V_i, a_N)$ $d_i(V_i, a_S)$ to the neutral and stressed classes, respectively, where a_N and a_S are the average vectors of classes for neutral and stressed speech. The final decision is made for the test sample using the following equation:

$$j = \arg\max\left(\sum_{i=1}^{K} d_1(V_i, a_N), \sum_{i=1}^{K} d_i(V_i, a_S)\right) \quad j = N \text{ or } S.$$
(16)

A K-fold cross-validation method was used in the training and testing process, and K was set to 4. Using this method, the data set was divided into four subsets, and for each classification, one of the subsets was used as a test set and the other three subsets were combined to form a training set. The final result was obtained by calculating the average classification rate across four trials.

6. Evaluation

6.1 Database and experimental setup

In the experiments, we used a database collected by the Fujitsu Corporation containing speech samples from eleven subjects (four males and seven females) [24]. To simulate mental pressure resulting in psychological stress, the speakers performed three different tasks while having telephone conversations with an operator, in order to simulate a situation involving pressure during a telephone call.

The three tasks involved (a) concentration, (b) time pressure, and (c) risk taking. For each speaker, there are four dialogues with different tasks. In two dialogues, the speaker was asked to finish the tasks within a limited amount of time, and in the other dialogues, there is relaxed chat without any task.

All of the data comes from telephone calls, so the sampling frequency was 8 kHz. Segments with the vowels /a/ and /e/ were cut from the speech and selected as samples. The experiments were conducted for each speaker, and all of the results were speaker

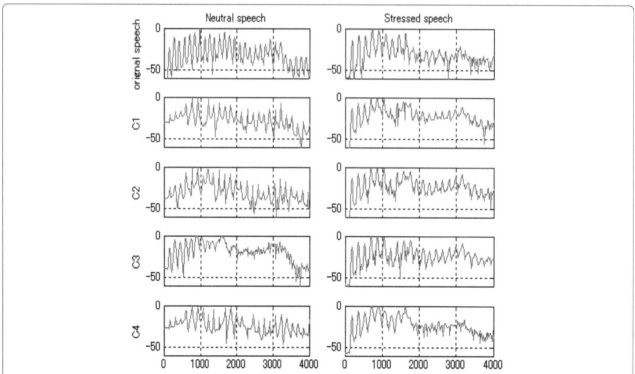

Figure 12 Simulation results of fitting for neutral and stressed speech. Spectrums for original speech (top) and simulated speech with four cost functions ($C^{F_1-F_2}$, C_{rms}, C_{I-S}, and C_{E-F}) under neutral (left column) and stressed (right column) conditions. In this figure, $C_1 = C^{F_1-F_2}$, $C_2 = C_{rms}$, $C_3 = C_{I-S}$, and $C_4 = C_{E-F}$.

dependent. The number of samples was different for each speaker. The range of the total number of samples is from 100 to 250 for each vowel from each person. We randomly chose six speakers (three males and three females) from eleven subjects to test classification performance. A K-fold cross-validation method was used in the classification experiments, in which K was set to 4. Using this method, the data set was divided evenly into four subsets, and for each classification, one of the subsets was used as a test set and the other three subsets were combined to form a training set. The final result was obtained by calculating the average classification rate across four trials. The samples were analyzed with 12-order LPC, and the frame size chosen to perform the experiment was 64 ms, with 16 ms for frame shift.

For configuration of the two-mass model, the following values were adopted, using typical values for males: $m_{1M} = 1.25 \times 10^{-4}$ kg, $m_{2M} = 2.5 \times 10^{-5}$ kg, $l_{gM} = 0.014$ m, $d_{1M} = 0.0025$ m, $d_{2M} = 5 \times 10^{-4}$ m, $\zeta_{1M} = 0.1$, $\zeta_{2M} = 0.6$, $x_0 = 2 \times 10^{-4}$ m, and $P_s = 500$ Pa. The vocal tract model was represented by a tube model, and the number of elements was limited to four cylindrical sections of equal length. Typical values used for configuration for females were as follows: $m_{1F} = 4.56 \times 10^{-5}$ kg, $m_{2F} = 9.1 \times 10^{-6}$ kg, $l_{gF} = 0.01$ m, $d_{1F} = 1.79 \times 10^{-3}$ m, $d_{2F} = 3.6 \times 10^{-4}$ m, $\zeta_{1F} = 0.1$, $\zeta_{2F} = 0.6$, $x_0 = 2 \times 10^{-4}$ m, and $P_s = 500$ Pa. Furthermore, the ranges for the control parameters were $k_1 = 10$ to 140 kdyn/cm, $k_2 = 2$ to 14 kdyn/cm, $k_c = 4$ to 45 kdyn/cm, VTL = 13 to 19 cm, and A_1, A_2, A_3, $A_4 = 0.2$ to 20 cm.

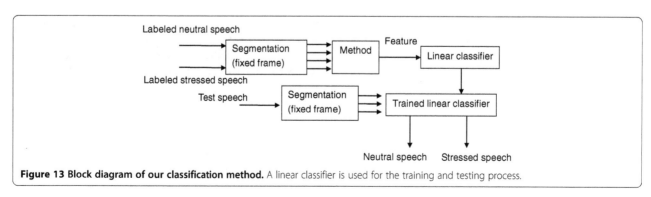

Figure 13 Block diagram of our classification method. A linear classifier is used for the training and testing process.

6.2 Results for cost functions

In the first evaluation, we estimated the vocal tract length of all of the speakers, and two comparisons were made. First, we estimated the cross-sectional area function using the vocal tract fitting method with the four proposed cost functions and then the shape of the vocal tract was fixed at the obtained values (length and area). We used $[k_1, k_c]$ to check classification performance for neutral and stressed speech using only the cost function for the vocal folds in Equation 10. In the second comparison, we estimated stiffness parameters $[k_1, k_c]$ with varied vocal tract, so cost functions both for VF and VT were used to perform the fitting, and iteration was performed. Here, varied VT denotes that the parameters for cross-sectional area are also estimated by fitting the two-mass model instead of being fixed as constants. Finally, the performance of cost functions $C^{F_1\text{-}F_2}$, C_{rms}, $C_{I\text{-}S}$, and $C_{E\text{-}F}$ was evaluated using the classification rate of $[k_1, k_c]$. We used a linear classifier for classification, and the average classification rate for all of the speakers was calculated. The results are shown in Figure 14.

The results illustrate that classification performance is improved when vocal tract values are variable. In this case, the cost functions for the vocal tract are used, and formants are also considered, which results in more information about the frequency domain of the speech being available, making the estimated results more reliable. Furthermore, we compared the performance of different cost functions. Our results show that the stress classification rate for $C_{E\text{-}F}$ is higher than for the other cost

functions. Since $C_{E\text{-}F}$ can match the rough shape of the spectral envelope and also effectively catch the characteristics of F_1 and F_2, which have been proven to be sensitive to the interaction between the VF and VT, the classification of stressed speech is improved.

6.3 Results for physical parameters

In the second evaluation, VTL was first estimated for each speaker, and further evaluations were based on the obtained vocal tract length. Here, we selected cost function $C_{E\text{-}F}$, which achieved the best performance in classification during the first evaluation. The purpose of this evaluation was to verify which parameters in the stiffness and area functions are related to stress and then check the classification performance of these parameters in comparison to traditionally used features.

6.3.1 Evaluation of vocal tract length estimation

A comparison was first made to evaluate the vocal tract length estimation for each speaker. In this experiment, segments with the vowels /a/ and /e/ were selected as samples. However, the samples for /a/ and /e/ were not mixed together. The two vowels were first used for evaluation separatelyand then the average recognition rate for the two vowels was calculated to show the experimental results. The physical parameters were estimated using the proposed fitting method, and the estimated parameters were used as features to perform the stress classification. The evaluation results for VTL estimation are shown in Figure 15. Features of physical parameters $[k_1, k_c]$ were compared for their classification performance before and after VTL estimation. Our results show that the performance of $[k_1, k_c]$ is improved by the estimation of VTL. Since a speaker's vocal tract

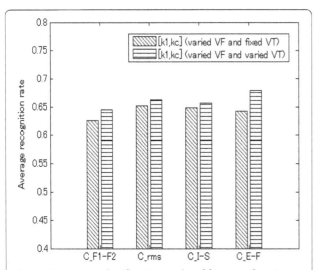

Figure 14 Average classification results of four cost functions: $C^{F_1\text{-}F_2}$, C_{rms}, $C_{I\text{-}S}$, and $C_{E\text{-}F}$. The results for varied VF and fixed VT are the classification rate when the stiffness parameters are estimated with fixed VTL and cross-sectional area. Varied VF and varied VT denote that the parameters for stiffness and cross-sectional area are estimated by fitting the two-mass model to real speech.

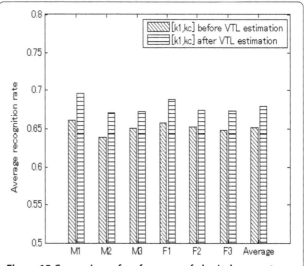

Figure 15 Comparison of performance of physical parameters k_1 **and** k_c **before and after VTL estimation.**

length is calculated from the neutral speech of that specific speaker and used as a known value for the estimation of other physical parameters, improvement in classification can be achieved by improving the accuracy of VTL estimation.

6.3.2 Evaluation of stiffness parameters of the vocal folds

In this evaluation, we focused on the stiffness parameters of the vocal folds, and the effect of each stiffness parameter on stress recognition was then examined. The physical parameters k_1, k_2, k_c, A_1, A_2, A_3, and A_4 were estimated from varied VF and varied VT values with estimated VTL, and other physical parameters were fixed at the typical values described in Database and experimental setup. We focused on the evaluation of k_1, k_2, and k_c. The classification performances of $\{[k_1]\}$, $\{[k_1, k_c]\}$, and $\{[k_1, k_2, k_c]\}$ for different speakers are shown in Figure 16. These results that stress classification performance is improved when k_c is considered. k_1 and k_c, therefore, are the parameters which are effective in stress classification. However, average classification accuracy decreases when taking k_2 into account. It suggests that k_2 is not effective in the classification of neutral and stressed speech; therefore, it is sufficient to select k_1 and k_c as feature parameters in further evaluations.

6.3.3 Evaluation of parameters of the cross-sectional areas of the vocal tract

We focused on each parameter of the cross-sectional area individually, and each area's impact on stress recognition was then examined separately. The parameters k_1, k_2, k_c, A_1, A_2, A_3, and A_4 were estimated with varied VF

and varied VT values. The parameter sets $\{[k_1, k_c]\}$, $\{[k_1, k_c, A_1]\}$, $\{[k_1, k_c, A_1, A_2]\}$, and $\{[k_1, k_c, A_1, A_2, A_3]\}$ were also evaluated. Their performance is shown in Figure 17. Among the results, we first consider sets $\{[k_1, k_c]\}$ and $\{[k_1, k_c, A_1]\}$. The results show that stiffness $[k_1, k_c]$ is a better parameter for classifying stressed speech. When A_1 is taken into account, classification performance is further improved. This suggests that A_1 is an important parameter strongly related to stress. When A_1 is increasing, it indicates that the area in the supraglottis is broadening. This results in a decrease in the pressure difference inside and outside of the glottis, causing variation in the airflow pattern and further changes in the interaction around the false vocal folds. Considering the performance of sets $\{[k_1, k_c, A_1]\}$, $\{[k_1, k_c, A_1, A_2]\}$, and $\{[k_1, k_c, A_1, A_2, A_3]\}$, we found that they have roughly the same classification accuracy. This illustrates that performance cannot be greatly improved by taking A_2 and A_3 into account and that A_2 and A_3 probably have only a small effect on acoustic interaction. It appears that A_1 is sufficient to classify stressed speech from neutral speech, which agrees with the conclusion of our first evaluation.

A_2 and A_3 do affect F_0 to some extent, which was illustrated in Figure 5, so they have some influence on acoustic interaction and, further, on stress classification; however, we believe their influence is insignificant. The characteristics of the vocal tract also affect stress classification to some extent. Since A_2 and A_3 represent the shape of the vocal tract, $[k_1, k_c, A_1, A_2, A_3]$ can achieve some improvement in the recognition rate, but the increase is very small, which suggests that A_2 and A_3 are less important for stress classification than A_1.

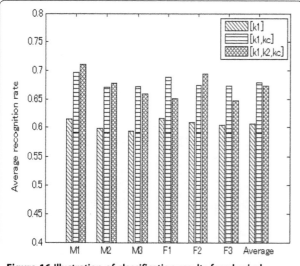

Figure 16 Illustration of classification results for physical parameters of the vocal folds. The performance of stiffness parameters k_1 and k_c shows their effectiveness for stress classification.

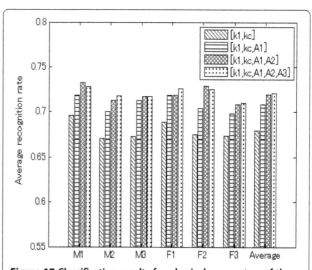

Figure 17 Classification results for physical parameters of the vocal tract. The performance of cross-sectional area parameter A_1 shows its effectiveness for stress classification.

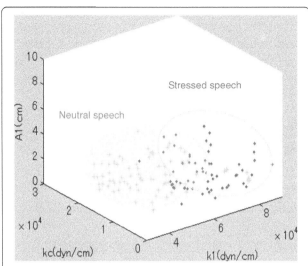

Figure 18 Distributions of estimated parameters k_1, k_c, and A_1 for neutral and stressed speech.

Table 4 Classification rates with different numbers of mixtures

	Number of mixtures					
	1	2	3	4	5	6
Classification rate (%)	61.57	66.63	71.47	71.88	71.22	71.24

6.3.4 Evaluation for proposed physical parameters

As a result of our evaluation process, parameter set $[k_1, k_c, A_1]$ was proposed. Figure 18 shows the distribution results for k_1, k_c, and A_1 with an estimated VTL. These results show that the proposed parameters are effective for stress classification. The estimated values of the parameters are limited in range, and these ranges correspond to the actual range of human beings. As this distribution shows, stiffness and area of the entrance to the vocal tract are good indicators of stressed speech. Under stressed conditions, the value of k_1 becomes relatively large, k_c smaller, and A_1 increases compared with the same parameters under neutral conditions. This indicates that stress causes variation in the muscle tension

of the vocal folds and that the area at the entrance to the vocal tract in the supraglottis becomes wider when the speaker is under stress.

We then compared the performance of proposed parameters $[k_1, k_c, A_1]$ with traditionally proposed features, namely [SFM, F_0], [TEO], and [MFCC]. The results are shown in Figure 19. As our experimental results show, [SFM, F_0], which characterizes the vocal folds, works well in classifying stressed speech. This shows that the characteristics of the vocal folds play a very important role in stress classification. MFCC, which represents vocal tract information, is also effective for stress classification, illustrating that the characteristics of the vocal tract also affect stress classification to some extent, which agrees with our previous results in Figure 17. The results shown in Figure 19 demonstrate that our proposed physical parameters outperform the features traditionally used for stress detection, which suggests that parameters estimated from a physical model are more effective at representing stress during phonation than traditional methods. Results show that $[k_1, k_c, A_1]$ has the best stress recognition performance of the physical parameter sets. This illustrates that stiffness of the vocal folds and the cross-sectional area at the entrance to the vocal tract in the supraglottis are the factors which are most impacted when a speaker is under stress.

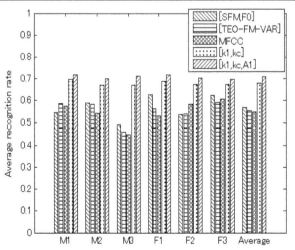

Figure 19 Performance of proposed features compared with traditional methods.

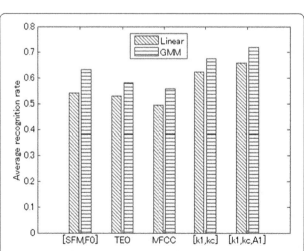

Figure 20 Performance of proposed features using Gaussian mixture models. The number of mixtures is set to 4.

6.4 Results of Gaussian mixture modeling

In this section, we modeled the features using Gaussian mixture model (GMM), which are widely used statistical classifier. Two GMM models were trained, one for neutral speech the other for stressed speech.

The data set for each speaker was divided evenly into four subsets, and for each classification, one of the subsets was used as a test set and the other three subsets were combined to form a training set. The final result was obtained by calculating the average classification rate across four trials by a K-fold cross-validation method. In order to increase the amount of training data, the GMMs were trained using training set from three male speakers. The testing set of three male speakers and all of the data from female speakers were combined to generate the testing data used in this experiment.

We performed an experiment to find the best number of mixtures which corresponds to the best performance for proposed features $[k_1, k_c, A_1]$. Table 4 shows that the best performance is obtained when the number of mixtures equals to four. When we increased the number of mixtures, the classification rate decreased, and it also makes the GMM more complicated. Therefore, the number of mixture components of the GMM was set to four, which obtained the best performance. The features for [SFM, F_0] [TEO-FM-VAR], [MFCC], $[k_1, k_c]$, and $[k_1, k_c, A_1]$ were modeled using GMMs with four mixture components. Classification performance is shown in Figure 20, which shows that improvement is achieved for each feature. However, the increase in classification rates is small because of the lack of training data. If we increase the size of training data significantly, major gains in classification rate should be achieved. Here, it is recommended that a GMM with four mixture components is acceptable for improving stress classification.

7. Conclusion

In this paper, we explored more effective features for the classification of neutral and stressed speech based on a physical model. To achieve this target, a two-mass model characterizing the properties of the vocal folds and the vocal tract was used to simulate speech production. Physical parameters including stiffness of the vocal folds, vocal tract length, and cross-sectional area of the vocal tract were investigated and estimated using a method that fits the two-mass model to real data. Cost functions were used as targets to reach more reliable results. The obtained parameters were used as physical features to classify stressed speech. We concluded that the two parameters: (1) stiffness of the vocal folds and (2) the area at the entrance to the vocal tract in the supraglottis, which is related to the velocity of glottal airflow and acoustic interaction between the vocal folds

and the vocal tract, are key indicators of stress during phonation. The average performance in the classification of speech under stress was improved by 10% to 15% using the proposed features, compared to traditional methods of stressed speech classification. In the future, our work should be focused on the exploration of parameters for a speaker-independent stressed speech classification system.

Competing interests
The authors declare that they have no competing interests.

Acknowledgments
This work has been partially supported by the 'Core Research for Evolutional Science and Technology' (CREST) project of the Japan Science and Technology Agency (JST). We are very grateful to Mr. Matsuo of the Fujitsu Corporation for allowing us to use their database and for his valuable suggestions.

Author details
[1]Graduate School of Information Science, Nagoya University, Nagoya, Aichi, Japan. [2]Department of Media Informatics, Aichi University of Technology, Gamagori, Aichi, Japan.

References
1. HJM Steeneken, JHL Hansen, Speech under stress conditions: overview of the effect on speech production and on system performance, in *Proc. ICASSP* (Atlanta, Georgia, 1996)
2. D Cairns, JHL Hansen, Nonlinear analysis and detection of speech under stressed conditions. J. Acoust. Soc. Am. **96**(6), 3392–3400 (1994)
3. RV Bezooijen, *The characteristics and recognizability of vocal expression of emotions* (Foris, Drodrecht, 1984)
4. FJ Tolkmitt, KR Scherer, Effect of experimentally induced stress on vocal parameters. J. Exp. Psychol. **12**(3), 302–313 (1986)
5. CE Williams, KN Stevens, Emotions and speech: some acoustical correlates. J. Acoust. Soc. Am. **52**(4), 1238–1250 (1972)
6. SE Bou-Ghazale, JHL Hansen, Generating stressed speech from neutral speech using a modified CELP vocoder. Speech Commun. **20**, 93–110 (1996)
7. ZS Bond, TJ Moore, *A note on loud and Lombard speech.* International Conference on Spoken Language Processing (Kobe, 1990), pp. 969–972
8. JHL Hansen, *Analysis and compensation of stressed and noisy speech with application to robust automatic recognition.* Ph.D. dissertation (Georgia Institute of Technology, Atlanta, 1988)
9. IR Murray, C Baber, A South, Toward a definition and working model of stress and its effects on speech. Speech Commun. **20**, 3–12 (1996)
10. J Whitmore, S Fisher, Speech during sustained operations. Speech Commun. **20**, 55–70 (1996)
11. A Kamano, N Washio, S Harada, N Matsuo, *A study of psychological suppression detection based on non-verbal information.* IEICE Technical Report IEICE-SP2010-64 (IEICE, Tokyo, 2010), pp. 107–110. in Japanese
12. JF Kaiser, On Teager's energy algorithm and its generalization to continuous signals, in *Proceedings of the 4th IEEE Digital Signal Processing Workshop* (New Paltz, 1990)
13. G Zhou, JHL Hansen, JF Kaiser, Nonlinear feature based classification of speech under stress. IEEE Trans. Speech Audio Process. **3**, 201–206 (2001)
14. G Fant, *Acoustic Theory of Speech Production* (Mouton, The Hague, 1960)
15. HK Dunn, Methods of measuring vowel formant bandwidths. J. Acoust. Soc. Am. **33**(12), 1737–1746 (1961)
16. DY Wong, JD Markel, AH Gray, Glottal inverse filtering from the acoustic speech waveform. IEEE Trans. Acoust. Speech Signal Process **27**(4), 350–355 (1979)
17. JF Kaiser, Some observations on vocal tract operation from a fluid flow point of view, in *Vocal Fold Physiology: Biomechanics, Acoustics, and Phonatory Control*, ed. by IR Titze, RC Scherer (Denver Center for the Performing Arts, Denver, 1983), pp. 358–386
18. K Ishizaka, JL Flanagan, Synthesis of voiced sounds from a two-mass model of the vocal cords. Bell. Syst. Tech. J. **51**, 1233–1268 (1972)

19. D Kincaid, W Cheney, *Numerical Analysis: Mathematics of Scientific Computing*, 3rd edn. (Brook/Cole, Pacific Grove, 2002), pp. 722–723

20. C Lucero, Chest- and falsetto-like oscillations in a two-mass model of vocal folds. J. Acoust. Soc. Am. **100**, 3355–3399 (1996)

21. IR Titze, Acoustic interpretation of resonant voice. J. Voice **15**, 519–528 (2001)

22. JL Flanagan, *Speech Analysis, Synthesis, and Perception* (Springer-Verlag, New York, 1972)

23. A de Cheveigne, H Kawahara, YIN, a fundamental frequency estimator for speech and music. J. Acoust. Soc. Am. **111**(4), 1917–1930 (2002)

24. IR Titze, BH Story, Acoustic interactions of the voice source with the lower vocal tract. J. Acoust. Soc. Am. **101**, 2234–2243 (1997)

2

A semisoft thresholding method based on Teager energy operation on wavelet packet coefficients for enhancing noisy speech

Tahsina Farah Sanam and Celia Shahnaz[*]

Abstract

The performance of thresholding-based methods for speech enhancement largely depends upon the estimation of the exact threshold value. In this paper, a new thresholding-based speech enhancement approach, where the threshold is statistically determined using the Teager energy-operated wavelet packet (WP) coefficients of noisy speech, is proposed. The threshold thus obtained is applied to the WP coefficients of the noisy speech by employing a semisoft thresholding function in order to obtain an enhanced speech. A number of simulations were carried out in the presence of white, car, pink, and multi-talker babble noises to evaluate the performance of the proposed method. Standard objective measures as well as subjective evaluations show that the proposed method is capable of outperforming the existing state-of-the-art thresholding-based speech enhancement approaches for noisy speech of high as well as low levels of SNR.

1 Introduction

Enhancement of noisy speech has been an important problem and has a broad range of applications, such as mobile communications, speech coding, and recognition and hearing aid devices [1]. The performance of such applications operating in noisy environments is highly dependent on the noise reduction techniques employed therein.

Various speech enhancement methods have been reported in the literature describing the know-how to solve the problem of noise reduction in speech enhancement methods. Speech enhancement methods can be generally divided into several categories based on their domains of operation, namely time domain, frequency domain, and time-frequency domain. Time domain methods include the subspace approach [2], frequency domain methods include short-time Fourier transform (STFT)-based spectral subtraction [3-6], minimum mean square error (MMSE) estimator [7-11] and Wiener filtering [12-14], and time frequency-domain methods involve the employment of the family of wavelet [15-26]. All of the methods have their own advantages and drawbacks.

In the MMSE estimator [7-11], the frequency spectrum of the noisy speech is modified to reduce the noise from noisy speech in the frequency domain. The spectral subtraction method [3-6] is simple and attempts to estimate the spectral amplitude of the clean speech by subtracting an estimate of the noise spectral amplitude from that of the observed noisy speech. Finally, the estimated amplitude is combined with the phase of the noisy speech to produce the desired estimate of the clean speech STFT. In the Wiener filter approach [12-14], the estimator of the clean speech STFT is simply the MMSE estimator when considering Gaussian-distributed clean speech and noise. In that case, the phase of the resulting estimate turns out to be that of the noisy speech. The spectral subtraction filter uses the instantaneous spectra of the noisy signal and the running average (time-averaged spectra) of the noise, whereas the Wiener filter is based on the ensemble average spectra of the signal and noise. Although the spectral subtraction method provides a trade-off between speech distortion and residual noise to some extent, its major drawback is the perceptually annoying musical nature of the residual noise characterized by tones at different frequencies that randomly appear and disappear. One of the major problems of the Wiener filter-based method is the requirement of obtaining clean speech statistics necessary

*Correspondence: celia@eee.buet.ac.bd
Department of Electrical and Electronic Engineering, Bangladesh University of Engineering and Technology, Dhaka 1000, Bangladesh

for its implementation. The use of Wiener filter in speech enhancement generally introduces little speech distortion; however, as for the spectral subtraction approach, the speech enhanced based on the Wiener filter is also characterized by residual musical noises. Among the speech enhancement methods using time-frequency analyses, the use of nonlinear techniques based on discrete wavelet transform (DWT) [15-26] is a superior alternative to the methods using STFT-based analyses, such as spectral subtraction and Wiener filtering. In the DWT, the fixed bandwidth of the STFT is replaced with one that is proportional to frequency that allows better time resolution at high frequencies than the STFT. Here, low frequencies are examined with low temporal resolution while high frequencies are observed with greater temporal resolution. Thus, the DWT gains more attractiveness in representing and preserving the signal energy in the presence of noise that needs to be removed in the speech enhancement process. Since the DWT-based speech enhancement methods exploit the superior frequency localization property of the DWT, they have more capability of reducing musical noise, thus achieving better noise reduction performance in terms of quality as well as intelligibility.

The main challenge in speech enhancement approaches based on the thresholding of the DWT coefficients of the noisy speech is the estimation of a threshold value that marks a difference between the DWT coefficients of noise and that of clean speech. Then, by using the threshold, designing a thresholding scheme to minimize the effect of DWT coefficients corresponding to the noise is another difficult task considering the fact that conventional DWT-based speech enhancement approaches exhibit a satisfactory performance only at a relatively high signal-to-noise ratio (SNR). For zero-mean, normally distributed white noise, Donoho and Johnstone proposed the Universal threshold-based method for enhancing corrupted speech [19,20]. For noisy speech, applying a unique threshold for all the DWT coefficients irrespective of the speech and silence frames may suppress noise to some extent, but it may also remove unvoiced speech frames, thus degrading the quality of the enhanced speech. The Teager energy operator (TEO) proposed by Kaiser [27] is employed to compute a threshold value that is used to threshold the wavelet packet coefficients of the noisy

speech [18,28,29]. In particular, in the wavelet packet filtering (WPF) method [18], a time-adaptive threshold value is computed and an absolute offset parameter is used to distinguish speech frames from the noise ones. Thus, the WPF method suffers from an over-thresholding problem if the speech signal is contaminated by just slight noises. Statistical modeling is another approach of thresholding-based speech enhancement, where the threshold of wavelet packet coefficients is determined using the similarity distances between the probability distributions of the signals [17].

In this paper, we develop a new speech enhancement method based on thresholding in the wavelet packet domain. Since TEO is a popular way to estimate the energy of a band-limited signal, instead of direct employment of the TEO on the noisy speech, we apply the TEO on the wavelet packet (WP) coefficients of the noisy speech (as for [18,28,29]), but we propose a statistical modeling of the Teager energy (TE)-operated WP coefficients. By exploiting the symmetric Kullback-Leibler (SKL) divergence, we then determine an appropriate threshold with respect to speech and silent subbands. The threshold thus obtained is finally employed in a semisoft thresholding function for obtaining an enhanced speech.

2 Proposed method

The block diagram of our proposed system is shown in Figure 1. It is seen from Figure 1 that WP transform is first applied to each input speech frame. Then, the WP coefficients are subject to Teager energy approximation with a view to determine a threshold value for performing thresholding operation in the WP domain. On thresholding, an enhanced speech is obtained via inverse wavelet packet (IWP) transform.

2.1 Wavelet packet analysis

A method based on the wavelet packet decomposition is a generalization of the wavelet transform-based decomposition process that offers a richer range of probabilities for the analysis of signals, namely speech. In the orthogonal wavelet decomposition procedure, the generic step splits a speech signal into sets of approximation and detail coefficients. The set of approximation coefficients is then itself split into a second-level approximation and detail

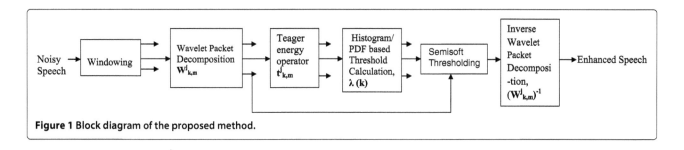

Figure 1 Block diagram of the proposed method.

coefficients, successive details are never reanalyzed, and the process is repeated. Each level of decomposition is calculated by passing only the previous wavelet approximation coefficients through discrete-time low- and high-pass quadrature mirror filters. Mallat algorithm is one of the efficient ways to construct the DWT by iterating a two-channel perfect reconstruction filter bank over the low-pass scaling function branch [30]. However, this algorithm results in a logarithmic frequency resolution, which does not work well for all signals. In order to overcome the drawback as mentioned above, it is desirable to iterate the high-pass wavelet branch of the Mallat algorithm tree as well as the low-pass scaling function branch. Such a wavelet decomposition produced by these arbitrary subband trees is known as WP decomposition.

In the WP decomposition, both the detail and approximation coefficients are decomposed to create the full binary tree. For a given orthogonal wavelet function, a library of wavelet packet bases is generated. Each of these bases offers a particular way of coding signals, preserving global energy and reconstructing exact features. It is interesting to find an optimal decomposition with respect to a convenient criterion, computable by an efficient algorithm. Simple and efficient algorithms exist for both wavelet packet decomposition and optimal decomposition selection. Functions verifying an additivity-type property are well suited for efficient searching of binary tree structures and the fundamental splitting. Classical entropy-based criteria match these conditions and describe information-related properties for an accurate representation of a given signal. In particular, the best basis algorithm by Coifman and Wickerhauser finds a set of bases that provide the most desirable representation of the data relative to a particular cost function (e.g., entropy) [31].

In DWT decomposition, by the restriction of Heisenberg's uncertainty principle, the spatial resolution and spectral resolution of high-frequency band become poor, thus limiting the application of DWT. In particular, there are some problems with the basic DWT-based thresholding method when it is applied to noisy speech for the purpose of enhancement. An important shortcoming is the shrinkage of the unvoiced frames of speech which contain many noise-like speech components leading to a degraded speech quality. On the other hand, in WP decomposition, since both the approximation and the detail coefficients are decomposed into two parts at each level of decomposition, a complete binary tree with superior frequency localization can be achieved. Thus, in the context of noisy speech enhancement, this particular feature of the WP decomposition provides better discriminability of speech coefficients among those of the noise and is indeed useful for enhancing speech in the presence of noise.

For a j-level WP transform, the noisy speech signal $y[n]$ with frame length N is decomposed into 2^j subbands. The mth WP coefficient of the kth subband is expressed as

$$W^j_{k,m} = WP[y[n],j], \quad n = 1,\ldots N, \qquad (1)$$

where $m = 1,\ldots,N/2^j$ and $k = 1,\ldots,2^j$.

2.2 Teager energy approximation

The continuous form of the TEO [27] is given as

$$\Psi_c[y(t)] = (\frac{d}{dt}y(t))^2 - y(t)\frac{d^2}{dt^2}y(t), \qquad (2)$$

where $\Psi_c[.]$ and $y(t)$ represent the continuous TEO and a continuous signal, respectively. For a given bandlimited discrete signal $y[n]$, the discrete-time TEO can be approximated by

$$\Psi_d(y[n]) = y[n]^2 - y[n+1]y[n-1]. \qquad (3)$$

The discrete-time TEO is nearly instantaneous since only three samples are required for the energy computation at each time instant as shown in (3). Due to this excellent time resolution, the output of a TEO provides us with the ability to capture the energy fluctuations and hence gives an estimate of the energy required to generate the signal [18,27–29,32–35].

In the context of the noisy speech enhancement by thresholding via WP analysis, the threshold must be adapted over time since speech is not always present in the signal. It is expected that the threshold should be larger during periods without speech and smaller for those with speech. Since the TEO provides an estimate of the signal energy over time, it can be employed to obtain an idea of speech/nonspeech activity and then decide an appropriate threshold value in the speech/nonspeech frame. But directly using the TEO on noisy speech may result in much undesired artefact and enhanced noises as TEO is a fixed-sized local operator [27]. Therefore, instead of direct employment of the TEO on the noisy speech, it is found reasonable to apply the TEO on the WP coefficients of the noisy speech [18]. The application of the discrete-time TEO on the $W^j_{k,m}$ results in a set of TEO coefficients $t^j_{k,m}$. The mth TEO coefficient corresponding to the kth subband of the WP is given by

$$t^j_{k,m} = \Psi_d[W^j_{k,m}], \quad k = 1,\ldots.2^j. \qquad (4)$$

Unlike the approach of threshold determination directly from the WP coefficients of noisy speech, the approach to determine threshold from the TE-operated WP coefficients and then employ it via a semisoft thresholding function, has more potential to eliminate as much of the noise as possible while still maintaining speech quality and intelligibility in the enhanced speech [29].

2.3 Statistical modeling of TE-operated WP coefficients

This paper proposes a new thresholding function employing a threshold value determined for each subband of the WP by statistically modeling the TE-operated WP coefficients $t^j_{k,m}$ with a probability distribution rather than choosing a threshold value directly from the $t^j_{k,m}$.

In a certain range, the probability distribution of the $t^j_{k,m}$ of the noisy speech is expected to be nearly similar to those of the noise. Also, outside that range, the probability distribution of the $t^j_{k,m}$ of the noisy speech is expected to be similar to those of the clean speech. Thus, by considering the probability distributions of the $t^j_{k,m}$ of the noisy speech, noise, and clean speech, a more accurate threshold value can be obtained using a suitable scheme of pattern matching or similarity measure between the probability distributions. It is well known that the Kullback-Leibler (K-L) divergence provides a measure of the distance between two distributions. It is an appealing approach to robustly estimate the differences between two distributions. Instead of comparing just the TE-operated WP coefficients $t^j_{k,m}$, the distribution of the $t^j_{k,m}$ of the noisy speech can be compared with the distribution of the $t^j_{k,m}$ of noise or that of clean speech using the K-L divergence. Since the K-L divergence is not a symmetric metric, we propose the use of the SKL divergence.

2.4 Optimal threshold calculation

This subsection presents our approach to obtain first the idea of speech/silent frame based on the SKL divergence and then to choose two different threshold values suitable for silent and speech frames. At first, the threshold value for a noisy speech frame is analytically obtained by solving equations either based on the SKL divergence between the probability distribution functions (pdfs) of the $t^j_{k,m}$ of the noisy speech and that of the noise or based on the SKL divergence between the pdfs of the $t^j_{k,m}$ of the noisy speech and that of the clean speech. To this end, in a frame of noisy speech/ noise/ clean speech, for each subband of WP, we formulate the histogram of the $t^j_{k,m}$ and approximate the histogram by a reasonably close pdf, namely Gaussian distribution. For this purpose, we follow the steps below:

1. The histogram of the $t^j_{k,m}$ in each subband is obtained. The number of bins in the histogram has been set equal to the square root of the number of samples divided by two.
2. Since the $t^j_{k,m}$ of clean speech, noisy speech, and noise are positive quantity, their histograms in each subband can be approximated by the positive part of

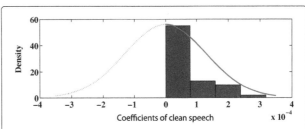

Figure 2 Probability distribution of TE-operated WP coefficients of clean speech.

a pdf following the Gaussian distribution. Such statistical modeling of the $t^j_{k,m}$ of clean speech, noisy speech, and noise is supported by experimental validation over all speech sentences of the NOIZEUS noisy speech corpus [36] at different SNR levels. Typical examples of such modeling are shown in Figures 2, 3, and 4, respectively.

The method in [17] does not employ the TE operation prior to computing the threshold value, and the threshold value for each subband of a noisy speech frame is determined by statistically modeling the WP coefficients. Since the WP coefficients are a signed quantity, their histograms in each subband are approximated by a two-sided Gaussian pdf. In the proposed method, due to the simpler approximation of the $t^j_{k,m}$ of clean speech, noisy speech, or noise by the positive part of a Gaussian pdf, the process of deriving the threshold value becomes less complex which is an additional advantage over the approach in [17]. In order to analytically determine an appropriate threshold value, we proceed as follows:

The K-L divergences are always nonnegative and zero if and only if the approximate Gaussian distribution functions of the $t^j_{k,m}$ of noisy speech and that of the noise, or the approximate Gaussian distribution functions of the $t^j_{k,m}$ of the noisy speech and that of the clean speech are exactly the same. In order to have a symmetric distance between any two approximate Gaussian distribution

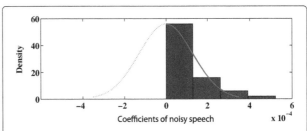

Figure 3 Probability distribution of TE-operated WP coefficients of noisy speech.

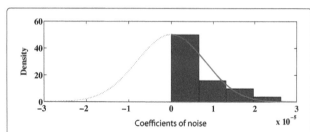

Figure 4 Probability distribution of TE-operated WP coefficients of noise.

functions as mentioned above, the symmetric K-L divergence has been adopted in this paper. The symmetric K-L divergence is defined as

$$SKL(p,q) = \frac{KL(p,q) + KL(q,p)}{2} \qquad (5)$$

where p and q are the two approximate Gaussian pdfs calculated from the corresponding histograms each having M number of bins and KL(.) is the K-L divergence given by

$$KL(p,q) = \sum_{i=1}^{M} p_i(t^j_{k,m}) \ln \frac{p_i(t^j_{k,m})}{q_i(t^j_{k,m})}. \qquad (6)$$

In (6), $p_i(t^j_{k,m})$ represents the approximate Gaussian pdf of the $t^j_{k,m}$ of the noisy speech estimated by

$$\hat{p}_i(t^j_{k,m}) = \frac{\text{Number of coefficients in the } i\text{th bin of the histogram}}{\text{Total number of coefficients in each subband}}. \qquad (7)$$

Similarly, the approximate Gaussian pdf of the $t^j_{k,m}$ of the noise and that of the $t^j_{k,m}$ of the clean speech can be estimated from (7) and denoted by $\hat{q}_i(t^j_{k,m})$ and $\hat{r}_i(t^j_{k,m})$, respectively. Below a certain value λ of the $t^j_{k,m}$ of the noisy speech, the symmetric K-L divergence between $\hat{p}_i(t^j_{k,m})$ and $\hat{q}_i(t^j_{k,m})$ is approximately zero, i.e.,

$$SKL(\hat{p}_i(t^j_{k,m}), \hat{q}_i(t^j_{k,m})) \approx 0 \qquad (8)$$

where the bins lie in the range $[1, \lambda]$ in both $\hat{p}_i(t^j_{k,m})$ and $\hat{q}_i(t^j_{k,m})$. Alternatively, above the value λ of the $t^j_{k,m}$ of the noisy speech, the symmetric K-L divergence between $\hat{p}_i(t^j_{k,m})$ and $\hat{r}_i(t^j_{k,m})$ is almost zero, i.e.,

$$SKL(\hat{p}_i(t^j_{k,m}), \hat{r}_i(t^j_{k,m})) \approx 0 \qquad (9)$$

In (9), the bins lie in the range $[\lambda+1, M]$ in both $\hat{p}_i(t^j_{k,m})$ and $\hat{r}_i(t^j_{k,m})$. Using (5) and (6) in evaluating (8) and (9), we get

$$\sum_{i=1}^{\lambda} [\hat{p}_i(t^j_{k,m}) - \hat{q}_i(t^j_{k,m})] \ln \frac{\hat{p}_i(t^j_{k,m})}{\hat{q}_i(t^j_{k,m})} \approx 0. \qquad (10)$$

$$\sum_{i=\lambda+1}^{M} [\hat{p}_i(t^j_{k,m}) - \hat{r}_i(t^j_{k,m})] \ln \frac{\hat{p}_i(t^j_{k,m})}{\hat{r}_i(t^j_{k,m})} \approx 0. \qquad (11)$$

From (10), it is apparent that the $t^j_{k,m}$ of the noisy speech lying in the range $[1, \lambda]$ can be marked as the $t^j_{k,m}$ of noise and needed to be removed. Similarly, (11) attests that the $t^j_{k,m}$ of the noisy speech residing outside $[1, \lambda]$ can be treated as similar to the $t^j_{k,m}$ of the clean speech and considered to be preserved. For obtaining a threshold value λ in each subband, (10) and (11) can be expressed as

$$\int_1^\lambda [\frac{\sqrt{\vartheta}}{\sqrt{2\pi}\sigma_S} \exp(-\frac{\vartheta x^2}{2\sigma_S^2}) - \frac{1}{2\pi\sigma_N} \exp(-\frac{x^2}{2\sigma_N^2})] \ln((1 - \sqrt{\vartheta})$$
$$\exp(-\frac{\vartheta x^2}{2\sigma_S^2} + \frac{x^2}{2\sigma_N^2})) dx \approx 0, \qquad (12)$$

$$\int_{\lambda+1}^\infty [\frac{\sqrt{\vartheta}}{\sqrt{2\pi}\sigma_S} \exp(-\frac{\vartheta x^2}{2\sigma_S^2}) - \frac{1}{2\pi\sigma_S} \exp(-\frac{x^2}{2\sigma_S^2})] \ln((\sqrt{\vartheta})$$
$$\exp(\frac{(1 - \vartheta)x^2}{2\sigma_S^2})) dx \approx 0, \qquad (13)$$

where $\vartheta = \sigma_S^2/(\sigma_N^2 + \sigma_S^2)$.

The range used for solving Equations (12) and (13) required for determining the threshold value λ in each subband is different from that used in [17]. The value of $t^j_{k,m}$ for which the threshold reaches its optimum value can be determined by minimizing (12) or (13). Since (12) is a definite integral, the derivative of the function defined in the left-hand side (L.H.S) of (12) representing the SKL divergence between $\hat{p}_i(t^j_{k,m})$ and $\hat{q}_i(t^j_{k,m})$ is calculated and set to zero. On the other hand, the derivative of the function obtained in the L.H.S of (13) representing the symmetric K-L distance between $\hat{p}_i(t^j_{k,m})$ and $\hat{r}_i(t^j_{k,m})$ is calculated and set to zero. By simplifying either derivatives, an optimum value of λ for each subband of a noisy speech frame can be obtained as

$$\lambda(k) = \sigma_N(k) \sqrt{2(\gamma_k + \gamma_k^2) \ln (\sqrt{1 + \frac{1}{\gamma_k}})}, \qquad (14)$$

where k is the subband index, σ_N is the variance of noise in each subband, and γ_k represents the segmental SNR defined as

$$\gamma_k = \sigma_S^2(k)/\sigma_N^2(k). \qquad (15)$$

Considering the facts that the threshold value $\lambda(k)$ in (14) needs to be adjusted according to the input SNR and σ_N is inversely proportional to the input SNR, a modified version of the threshold $\lambda(k)$ in each subband of a noisy speech frame can be derived as

$$\lambda(k) = [\sigma_N(k)/\sqrt{\gamma_k}] \sqrt{2(\gamma_k + \gamma_k^2) \ln (\sqrt{1 + \frac{1}{\gamma_k}})}. \quad (16)$$

In the nonspeech/silent subbands of a frame of noisy speech, the SKL divergence between the approximate Gaussian pdfs of the $t^j_{k,m}$ of the noisy speech and that of the $t^j_{k,m}$ of the noise is found to be nearly zero. An idea of speech/silent frame can thus be obtained based on the SKL divergence. Since in a silence frame only noise exists, a threshold value different from that used in a subband of a noisy speech frame should be selected for a subband of a silent frame of a noisy speech in order to remove the noise completely. Exploiting the facts above and using the threshold $\lambda(k)$ derived in (16) for each subband of a noisy speech frame, two different threshold values suitable for a subband of a silent or speech frame are proposed to be chosen as

$$\lambda'(k) = \begin{cases} \max(t^j_{k,m}), & \text{SKL}(\hat{p}_i(t^j_{k,m}),\hat{q}_i(t^j_{k,m})) \approx 0 \\ \lambda(k), & \text{otherwise.} \end{cases} \quad (17)$$

It is noteworthy that, in the context of enhancing speech under low levels of SNR, our proposed approach to determine the threshold value in a subband of a silent or speech frame is not only different but also more reasonable with simpler approximation and lesser computation in comparison to that described in [17].

2.5 Denoising by thresholding

For denoising purpose, hard thresholding sets zero to the coefficients whose absolute value is below the threshold [37-39]. This ignores the fact that there may be noise coefficients, which are bigger than the threshold value, thus resulting in time-frequency discontinuities of enhanced speech spectrum. Unlike the hard thresholding function, the soft thresholding function handles signals in a different way by making smooth transitions between the treated and the deleted coefficients based on the threshold value [20,37,38]. Noting the threshold determined by (17) as λ_1, the soft thresholding function can be applied on the mth WP coefficients of the kth subband $Y^j_{k,m}$ as

$$(\hat{Y}^j_{k,m})_S = \begin{cases} |Y^j_{k,m}| - \lambda_1(k), & |Y^j_{k,m}| \geq \lambda_1(k) \\ 0, & |Y^j_{k,m}| < \lambda_1(k). \end{cases} \quad (18)$$

The soft thresholding can be viewed as setting the components of the noise to zero and performing a magnitude subtraction on the speech plus noise components. It is evident that the soft thresholding eliminates the time-frequency discontinuity resulting in smoother signals, but

it yields the estimated coefficients that are the WP coefficients $|Y^j_{k,m}|$ of the noisy speech shifted by an amount of $\lambda_1(k)$. Employment of such a shift even when $|Y^j_{k,m}|$ stands way out of noise level creates unnecessary bias in the enhanced spectrum. The variance of the threshold values over the frames of the whole noisy speech also affects the enhanced spectrum. The variance of the threshold values over the frames of the whole noisy speech also affects the enhanced spectrum.

In order to overcome the problems as mentioned above, in the semisoft thresholding function, the shifting by the amount of the threshold value is avoided [39]. Therefore, a semisoft thresholding function is preferred over the soft thresholding function with respect to the variance and bias of the estimated threshold value. By taking into account the advantages and shortcomings of all the thresholding functions, we apply a semisoft thresholding function on the WP coefficients of the noisy speech signal. By defining $\lambda_2(k)$ as

$$\lambda_2(k) = \sqrt{2}\lambda_1(k), \quad (19)$$

the semisoft thresholding function is defined as

$$(\tilde{Y}^j_{k,m}) = \begin{cases} 0, & |Y^j_{k,m}| \leq \lambda_1(k) \\ Y^j_{k,m}, & |Y^j_{k,m}| > \lambda_2(k) \\ \text{sgn}(Y^j_{k,m})[\frac{\lambda_2(k)|Y^j_{k,m}|-\lambda_1(k)}{\lambda_2(k)-\lambda_1(k)}], & \text{otherwise,} \end{cases} \quad (20)$$

where $\tilde{Y}^j_{k,m}$ stands for the resulting semisoft thresholded WP coefficients.

2.6 Inverse wavelet packet transform

The enhanced speech frame is synthesized by performing the inverse WP transformation WP^{-1} on the resulting thresholded WP coefficients $\tilde{Y}^j_{k,m}$

$$\hat{s}[n] = WP^{-1}(\tilde{Y}^j_{k,m}), \quad (21)$$

where $\hat{s}[n]$ represents the enhanced speech frame. The final enhanced speech signal is reconstructed by using the standard overlap-and-add method.

3 Simulation results

In this section, a number of simulations are carried out to evaluate the performance of the proposed method.

3.1 Simulation conditions

Real speech sentences from the NOIZEUS noisy speech corpus [36] are employed for the experiments, where the speech data is sampled at 8 KHz. Four different types of noises, such as as white, car, pink, and multi-talker babble, are adopted from the NOISEX92 [40] and NOIZEUS databases. Noisy speech at different SNR levels ranging from 15 to −15 dB is considered for our simulations.

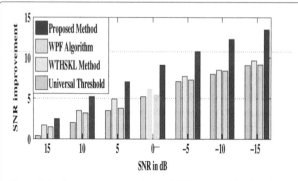

Figure 5 Performance comparison of different methods in terms of SNR improvement in decibels for white noise-corrupted speech.

Table 1 Performance comparison of different methods in terms of WSS for white noise-corrupted speech

SNR (dB)	Universal threshold	WPF algorithm	WTHSKL method	Proposed method
15	37	24.52	22.34	18.87
10	44.77	37.6	34.9	26.5
5	53.9	46.2	46.08	34.3
0	66.63	59.2	60.66	43.65
−5	83.8	71.4	76.92	52.45
−10	96	87.5	89.29	65.2
−15	104.44	91.9	90.37	77.20

In order to obtain overlapping analysis frames, Hamming windowing operation is performed, where the size of each of the frame is 512 samples with 50% overlap between successive frames. A three-level WP decomposition tree with db10 bases function is applied on the noisy speech frames, and the Teager energy operation is performed on the resulting WP coefficients. In the proposed method, for the implementation of WP decomposition, the 'wpdec' function of the Matlab wavelet toolbox is used, where in order to obtain optimal decomposition, Shanon entropy criterion is employed. For the three-level WP transform, the noisy speech signal $y[n]$ with frame length $N = 512$ samples is decomposed into eight subbands. For each subband (64 samples), a histogram is computed and variance is estimated. By computing the threshold(s), $\lambda_1(k) = \lambda'(k)$ and λ_2 from (17) and (19), respectively, a semisoft thresholding function is developed and applied on the WP coefficients of the noisy speech using (20).

3.2 Comparison metrics

Standard objective metrics, namely overall SNR improvement in decibels, Perceptual Evaluation of Speech Quality (PESQ), and Weighted Spectral Slope (WSS), are used for the evaluation of the proposed method [5,41,42]. In our simulation results, we have considered all 30 sentences of the NOIZEUS noisy speech corpus. We have taken into account the average result obtained from all 30 sentences for computing each of the objective metrics, namely SNR improvement in decibels, PESQ score, and WSS values. The proposed method is subjectively evaluated in terms of the spectrogram representations of the clean speech, noisy speech, and enhanced speech. Informal listening tests are also carried out, where the mean opinion scores (MOS) are evaluated in three dimensions, namely signal distortion (SIG), noise distortion (BAK), and overall quality (OVRL). The performance of our method is compared with some of the existing thresholding-based speech enhancement methods, such as Universal [20], Wavelet Packet Thresholding with Symmetric K-L Divergence (WTHSKL), and WPF [18] in both objective and subjective senses. In our method, while determining the threshold in (16), only time adaptation approach is incorporated through TE operation on WP coefficients as in the WPF method in [18] (time-adaptive approach), where threshold is adapted through time only and modulated depending on the speech or silent nature of the signal under an analysis frame. Unlike the time- and space-adaptive approach in [28], threshold value is not adapted

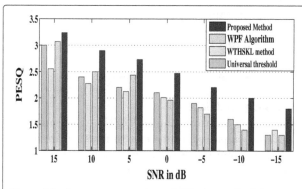

Figure 6 Performance comparison of different methods in terms of PESQ for white noise-corrupted speech.

Table 2 Performance comparison in terms of SNR improvement in decidels in the presence of white noise

SNR (dB)	MMSE	Spectral subtraction	Wiener filtering	Proposed method
15	1.93	1.84	1.1	2.45
10	3.7	2.52	2.38	5.13
5	4.6	3.2	2.9	7.2
0	5.36	4.02	3.9	9.2
−5	8	6.8	5.1	10.85
−10	9.5	8	7.2	12.42
−15	11.29	10.32	9.86	13.48

Table 3 Performance comparison in terms of PESQ scores in the presence of white noise

SNR (dB)	MMSE	Spectral subtraction	Wiener filtering	Proposed method
15	3.21	3.1	2.9	3.2374
10	2.89	2.51	2.33	2.9
5	2.4	2.2	2	2.733
0	2.1	1.82	1.68	2.47
−5	1.85	1.54	1.36	2.2
−10	2	1.4	1.31	2
−15	1.42	1.35	1.28	1.8

Table 5 Performance comparison of the SNR improvement in decibels for different methods in the presence of car noise

SNR (dB)	Universal threshold	WPF algorithm	WTHSKL method	Proposed method
15	1.2	1.3	2.7	3.1
10	3.2	3.1	4.5	5
5	5.1	5	4.99	7.89
0	6.12	5.97	6.92	9.38
−5	8	7.76	8.86	11.9
−10	9.5	9.78	10.94	12.5
−15	11.51	10.98	11.1	13.37

through scales in our proposed method. Therefore, we found it more justified and fair to compare our proposed method with the WPF method. Apart from these methods, statistical model-based method (MMSE[9]), spectral subtractive method (spectral subtraction [6]), and Wiener filtering-type algorithm (Wiener Filtering [14]) are also included for the purpose of objective and subjective comparison. We have implemented the Universal, WTHSKL, and WPF methods independently using the parameters specified therein. For implementation of the MMSE, spectral subtraction, and Weiner filtering methods, we have used publicly available Matlab codes (MMSESTSA84, WienerScalart96, and SSBoll79) from the Matlab Central website (http://www.mathworks.com/matlabcentral/).

3.3   Objective evaluation

3.3.1   Results on white noise-corrupted speech

The results for semisoft thresholding function in terms of all the objective metrics, such as SNR improvement in decibels, PESQ, and WSS, obtained using the Universal, WTHSKL, WPF, and proposed methods for white noise-corrupted speech are presented in Figures 5 and 6 and in Table 1.

Figure 5 shows the SNR improvement in decibels obtained using different methods employing semisoft thresholding function in the presence of white noise,

where the SNR varies from 15 to −15 dB. It is seen from this figure that in the SNR range under consideration, the improvement in SNR in decibels is comparable for all the comparison methods, but they show comparatively lower values relative to the proposed method at all the levels of SNR.

The PESQ scores vs SNR obtained by using different methods are portrayed in Figure 6. This figure shows that the proposed method using the semisoft function is capable of producing enhanced speech with better quality as it gives larger scores of PESQ for a wide range of SNR levels, whereas the PESQ scores resulting from all other methods are comparable and relatively lower even at a high SNR of 15 dB. It is also seen from Figure 6 that the difference in PESQ scores of the proposed method and that of the other methods increases as SNR decreases, thus indicating the effectiveness of the proposed method using semisoft thresholding function in enhancing speech even in a severely noisy environment.

The WSS values obtained by using different methods are summarized in Table 1 for varying SNR of 15 to −15 dB. For a particular method in Table 1, the WSS increases as SNR decreases. At a particular SNR, such as −15 dB, the

Table 4 Performance comparison in terms of WSS values in the presence of white noise

SNR (dB)	MMSE	Spectral subtraction	Wiener filtering	Proposed method
15	27.5	35.01	58.1	18.87
10	41.71	43.3	66.8	26.5
5	55.4	58.1	79.8	34.3
0	63.12	61.6	98.2	43.65
−5	77.6	67.9	113.8	52.45
−10	80	74	119.5	65.2
−15	91.46	85.14	123.81	77.20

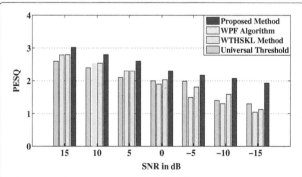

Figure 7 Performance comparison of different methods using semisoft thresholding function in terms of PESQ scores for car noise-corrupted speech.

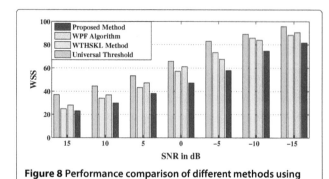

Figure 8 Performance comparison of different methods using semisoft thresholding function in terms of WSS for car noise-corrupted speech.

Table 7 Performance comparison in terms of PESQ scores in the presence of car noise

SNR (dB)	MMSE	Spectral subtraction	Wiener filtering	Proposed method
15	3	2.99	2.7	3.06
10	2.72	2.6	2.5	2.82
5	2.6	2.49	2.24	2.68
0	2.2	2.2	1.86	2.31
−5	1.9	1.8	1.6	2.19
−10	1.6	1	1.32	2.1
−15	1.42	1.39	1.26	1.94

proposed method using semisoft function is superior in a sense that it gives the lowest WSS value, whereas the other methods produce comparatively higher values of WSS.

In order to show the effectiveness of the proposed method, we have carried out another comparison here by providing the speech enhancement results of the proposed method and that of the MMSE [9], spectral subtraction [6], and Wiener filtering [14] methods in Tables 2, 3, and 4 for white noise-corrupted speech. It is clear from the results of these tables that the proposed method outperforms all the speech enhancement methods as mentioned above in the sense of higher output SNR in decibels, higher PESQ, and lower WSS values at all the SNRs ranging from high to low.

3.3.2 Results on car noise-corrupted speech

Now, we present the results in terms of all the objective metrics as mentioned above obtained by using the Universal, WTHSKL, WPF, and the proposed methods in Table 5 and in Figures 7 and 8 for car noise-corrupted speech.

In Table 5, the performance of the proposed method using semisoft thresholding function is compared with that of the other methods at different levels of SNR. For a method in Table 5, the SNR improvement in decibels

increases as SNR decreases. At a low SNR of −15 dB, the proposed method yields the highest SNR improvement in decibels. Such larger values of SNR improvement in decibels at a low level of SNR attest the capability of the proposed method in producing enhanced speech with better quality even for car noise-corrupted speech.

In the presence of car noise, the PESQ scores at different SNR levels resulting from using the other methods are compared with respect to the proposed method employing semisoft thresholding function in Figure 7. It can be seen from the figure that at a high level of SNR, such as 15 dB, Universal, WTHSKL, and WPF methods show lower values of PESQ scores, whereas the PESQ score is much higher, as expected, for the proposed method. The proposed method also yields larger PESQ scores compared to that of the other methods at lower levels of SNR. Since, at a particular SNR, a higher PESQ score indicates a better speech quality, the proposed method is indeed better in performance even in the presence of a car noise.

Figure 8 represents the WSS values as a function of SNR for the proposed method employing semisoft thresholding function and that for the other methods. As shown in the figure, the WSS values resulting from all other methods are comparable and relatively larger for a wide range of SNR levels, whereas the proposed method is capable of

Table 6 Performance comparison in terms of SNR improvement in decibels in the presence of car noise

SNR (dB)	MMSE	Spectral subtraction	Wiener filtering	Proposed method
15	1.61	2.5	2.2	3.1
10	2.74	4.1	3.74	5
5	5.63	7.5	5.4	7.89
0	6.94	8.3	6.3	9.38
−5	9.2	9.83	8.8	11.9
−10	11.74	11	12.1	12.5
−15	12.5	12.8	13.2	13.37

Table 8 Performance comparison in terms of WSS values in the presence of car noise

SNR (dB)	MMSE	Spectral subtraction	Wiener filtering	Proposed method
15	29.2	39.84	47	23
10	36.2	47.74	52.85	30.3
5	45.62	56.5	64.9	38.5
0	56.85	67.32	71.3	48.3
−5	66.85	77.7	82.51	58.4
−10	76.31	85	90.23	75
−15	89.73	92.7	101.6	81.5

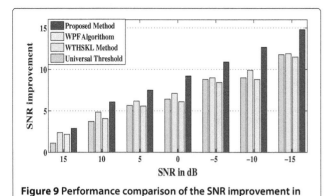

Figure 9 Performance comparison of the SNR improvement in decibels for different methods in the presence of pink noise.

Table 9 Performance comparison of PESQ scores for different methods in the presence of pink noise

SNR (dB)	Universal threshold	WPF algorithm	WTHSKL method	Proposed method
15	3.13	3	2.98	3.8
10	2.46	2.62	2.82	3.4
5	2.2	2.5	2.6	3
0	2.00	2.04	2.2	2.5
−5	1.82	1.51	1.4	2.3
−10	1.45	1.59	1.2	2.114
−15	1.31	1.14	1	1.8

producing enhanced speech with better quality as it gives lower values of WSS at a low SNR of −15 dB.

For car noise-corrupted speech, the results of the objective experiments comparing the proposed method with the MMSE [9], spectral subtraction [6], and Wiener filtering [14] methods are shown in Tables 6, 7, and 8. These results attest that even in the presence of car noise, the proposed method remains better in speech enhancement performance in terms of SNR improvement in decibels, PESQ scores, and WSS values for a wide range of SNR.

3.3.3 Results on pink noise-corrupted signal

All the objective metrics for evaluating the performance of the proposed method relative to the other methods for pink noise-corrupted speech are computed and depicted in Figures 9 and 10 and in Table 9.

The SNR improvement in decibels resulting from using different methods are summarized in Figure 9. It is vivid from this figure that the other methods produce comparatively lower improvement in SNR in decibels in the whole SNR range, while the proposed method using semisoft thresholding function remains superior in a sense that it

gives the highest improvement in SNR in decibels even at an SNR as low as −15 dB of pink noise.

The PESQ scores of the proposed method and that obtained using different comparison methods are shown in Table 9 with respect to SNR levels varying from high (15 dB) to low (−15 dB). It is clear from the table that the other methods continue to provide lower PESQ scores, while the proposed method maintain comparatively higher PESQ scores even in the presence of severe pink noise of −15 dB.

The variation of the output WSS with respect to SNR levels for different methods and that for the proposed method using semisoft thresholding function is portrayed in Figure 10. It is evident from analyzing each of these figures that, in the whole SNR range, the other methods continue to produce much higher WSS values with respect to the proposed method using the semisoft thresholding function. Note that the proposed method performs best in a sense that it yields the lowest WSS values almost at different SNR levels.

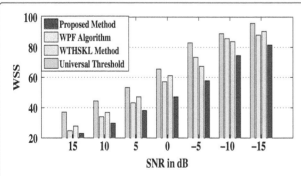

Figure 10 Performance comparison of different methods using semisoft thresholding function in terms of WSS values for pink noise-corrupted speech.

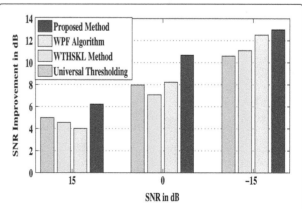

Figure 11 Performance comparison of different methods in terms of SNR improvement in decibels for babble noise-corrupted speech.

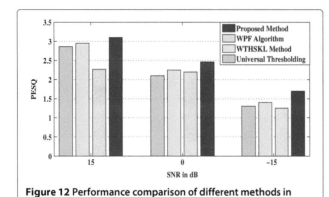

Figure 12 Performance comparison of different methods in terms of PESQ scores for babble noise-corrupted speech.

3.3.4 Results on multi-talker babble noise-corrupted speech

The results obtained from the multi-talker babble noise-corrupted speech in terms of the SNR improvement in decibels, PESQ scores, and WSS values for the proposed method using semisoft thresholding function and that of the other methods are depicted in Figures 11, 12, and 13 at particular SNR levels of 15, 0, and −15 dB. It is noticeable from these figures that the performance of all the methods degrades in the presence of multi-talker babble noise compared to that in the pink or car or white noise, but the proposed method retains its superiority with respect to all the levels of SNRs.

Figure 11 provides a plot for the SNR improvement in decibels obtained from all the methods for babble noise-corrupted speech. It is seen that the proposed method maintains better performance at all the SNR levels considered. Also, the proposed method still remains the best, thus showing higher capability of producing enhanced speech with better quality at a very low SNR level of 0 dB or even lower than that.

In a similar babble noisy condition, the PESQ scores resulting from using the speech enhancement methods under consideration are shown in Figure 12. As seen, the proposed method continues to provide better results for low levels of SNR, such as −15 dB.

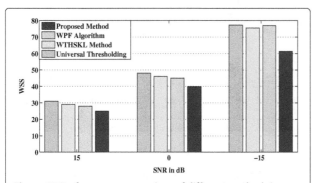

Figure 13 Performance comparison of different methods in terms of WSS values for babble noise-corrupted speech.

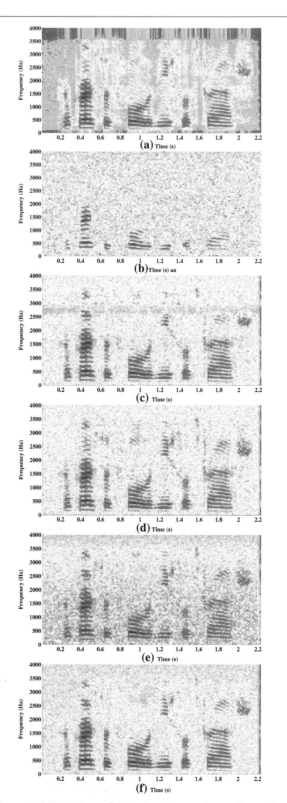

Figure 14 Spectrogram of sp03.wav utterance by a male speaker from the NOIZEUS database. (a) Clean speech, **(b)** noisy speech (white noise from NOISEX92 database of 5-dB SNR), **(c, d, e, f)** enhanced speech signals obtained using the Universal, WPF, WTHSKL, and the proposed methods, respectively.

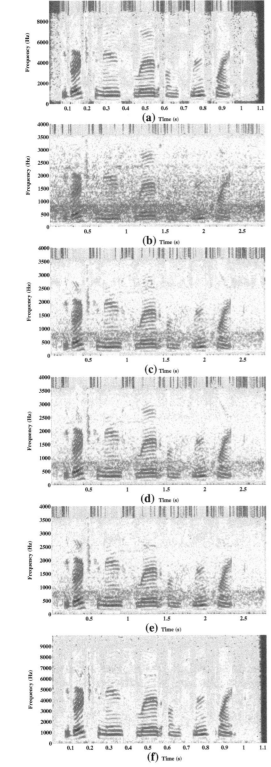

Figure 15 Spectrogram of sp01.wav utterance by a male speaker from the NOIZEUS database. (a) Clean speech, **(b)** noisy speech (car noise from NOIZEUS database of −5-dB SNR), **(c, d, e, f)** enhanced speech signals obtained using the Universal, WPF, WTHSKL, and the proposed methods, respectively.

Table 10 Mean scores of SIG scale for different methods in the presence of car noise at a 5-dB SNR

Listener	Spectral subtraction	Wiener filtering	MMSE	Proposed method
1	3.7	3.1	4.3	4.8
2	3	2	4	3.5
3	3.5	3	3.5	5
4	1.5	1.5	3.5	5
5	3	2.5	4	5

Performance comparison of the mean scores of SIG scale evaluated for different methods in the presence of car noise at a SNR of 5 dB.

Also, the WSS values obtained from all the methods as a function of SNR are plotted in Figure 13 for babble noise-corrupted speech. This figure illustrates that, as expected, the WSS values of the proposed method are somewhat increased in comparison to the other noisy cases, but its performance still remains better than that provided by the other methods for a wide range of SNR values from 15 to −15 dB.

We have tested our proposed method in a wide range of SNRs and reported the results in the SNR range of 15 to −15 dB, where a significant difference in performance is noticed for the proposed method relative to the other methods in comparison. Our main focus was to show the capability of the proposed method at very low SNR levels, such as −15 dB, where the other comparison methods produce less accurate results but the proposed method successfully enhances speech with higher accuracy. On the other hand, in the case of very high SNR, such as that above 15 dB, although the proposed method consistently demonstrates better performance, the performance becomes competitive with respect to the other methods in comparison. Therefore, the range of SNR used to present the comparative performance analysis is chosen from 15 to −15 dB.

3.4 Subjective evaluation

In order to evaluate the subjective observation of the enhanced speech obtained by using the proposed method,

Table 11 Mean scores of BAK scale for different methods in the presence of car noise at a 5-dB SNR

Listener	Spectral subtraction	Wiener filtering	MMSE	Proposed method
1	2.4	3.8	2.9	4.3
2	1.5	3	1	1.5
3	3	3	3	4
4	1.5	2.5	3	4
5	4	4	4.5	4

Performance comparison of the mean scores of BAK scale evaluated for different methods in the presence of car noise at a SNR of 5 dB.

Table 12 Mean scores of OVRL scale for different methods in the presence of car noise at a 5-dB SNR

Listener	Spectral subtraction	Wiener filtering	MMSE	Proposed method
1	3.2	3.4	3.7	4.6
2	2	2	3	3.5
3	3	2.5	4	5
4	1	1.5	3.5	5
5	4	3.5	5	5

Performance comparison of the mean scores of OVRL scale evaluated for different methods in the presence of car noise at a SNR of 5 dB.

Table 14 Mean scores of BAK scale for different methods in the presence of babble noise at a 10-dB SNR

Listener	Spectral subtraction	Wiener filtering	MMSE	Proposed method
1	3.5	3.3	3.8	4.0
2	2.6	2.5	3.3	3.9
3	3	2.8	3.5	3.8
4	3	2.9	3.6	3.7
5	3.2	3.2	3.6	3.9

Performance comparison of the mean scores of BAK scale evaluated for different methods in the presence of babble noise at a SNR of 10 dB.

spectrograms of the clean speech, noisy speech, and enhanced speech signals obtained using the Universal [20], WTHSKL [17], WPF [18], and proposed methods are presented in Figure 14 for white noise-corrupted speech at an SNR of 5 dB and in Figure 15 for car noise-corrupted speech at an SNR of −5 dB for clean speech (a), noisy speech (b), enhanced speech signals obtained using the Universal, WPF, WTHSKL, and the proposed methods, respectively (c, d, e, f). It is evident from these figures that the harmonics are preserved and the amount of distortion is greatly reduced in the proposed method no matter how corrupted the speech is by white or car noise and regardless of its level. Thus, the spectrogram observations with lower distortion also validate our claim of better speech quality as obtained in our objective evaluations in terms of higher SNR improvement in decibels, higher PESQ score, and lower WSS in comparison with the other methods.

Informal listening tests are also conducted, where the listeners were allowed and arranged to perceptually evaluate the enhanced speech signals. In order to reduce the length and cost of the subjective evaluations, only a subset of the NOIZEUS corpus was processed by MMSE [9], spectral subtraction [6], Wiener filtering [14], and the proposed methods for subjective evaluation. A total of ten sentences spoken by two male and two female speakers and corrupted in two background noises (car and babble)

at SNR levels of 5 and 10 dB were processed and presented to five listeners for evaluation.

Subjective tests were performed according to ITU-T recommendation P.835 [36,43]. The P.835 methodology is designed to reduce the listener's uncertainty in a subjective test about the basis of their ratings on overall quality of a noisy speech signal. In this test, a listener is instructed to successively attend and rate the enhanced speech signal based on (a) the speech signal alone using a scale of SIG (1 = very unnatural, 5 = very natural), (b) the background noise alone using a scale of background conspicuous/intrusiveness (BAK) (1 = very conspicuous, very intrusive; 5 = not noticeable), and (c) the overall effect using the scale of the mean opinion score (OVRL) (1 = bad, 5 = excellent). More details about the testing methodology can be found in [36].

The mean scores of SIG, BAK, and OVRL scales for the four speech enhancement methods evaluated in the presence of car noise at an SNR of 5 dB are shown in Tables 10, 11, and 12 . For the four methods examined using babble noise-corrupted speech at an SNR of 10 dB, the mean scores of SIG, BAK, and OVRL scales are summarized in Tables 13, 14, and 15. The mean scores in the presence of both car and babble noises demonstrate that the lower signal distortion (i.e., higher SIG scores) and the lower noise distortion (i.e., higher BAK scores) are obtained with the proposed method relative to that

Table 13 Mean scores of SIG scale for different methods in the presence of babble noise at a 10-dB SNR

Listener	Spectral subtraction	Wiener filtering	MMSE	Proposed method
1	4.1	3.1	4.2	4.5
2	3.9	3.9	4.4	5
3	4.2	4.1	4.7	4.8
4	4.1	3.7	4	4.4
5	4.2	3.9	4.3	5

Performance comparison of the mean scores of SIG scale evaluated for different methods in the presence of babble noise at a SNR of 10 dB.

Table 15 Mean scores of OVRL scale for different methods in the presence of babble noise at a 10-dB SNR

Listener	Spectral subtraction	Wiener filtering	MMSE	Proposed method
1	3.6	3.9	4.3	4.8
2	4.5	3.8	4.1	4.9
3	3	3.5	4.2	4.6
4	3.2	4.2	4	4.7
5	4.0	3.8	4.1	5

Performance comparison of the mean scores of OVRL scale evaluated for different methods in the presence of babble noise at a SNR of 10 dB.

obtained by MMSE [9], spectral subtraction [6], and Wiener filtering [14] methods in most of the conditions. It is also shown that a consistently better performance in OVRL scale is offered by the proposed method not only in car but also in babble noisy conditions at both SNR levels of considered in comparison to that provided by all the methods mentioned above. Overall, it is found that the proposed method possesses the highest subjective sound quality in comparison to that of the other methods in case of different noises at various levels of SNR. The performance of the proposed system can be validated following the web link https://sites.google.com/site/celiatahsinaresearchwork/research/important-research-links that includes the noisy and enhanced files.

4 Conclusions

An improved WP-based approach to solve the problems of speech enhancement has been presented in this paper. We develop a statistical model-based technique, where TE-operated WP coefficients are employed to obtain a suitable threshold based on the SKL divergence. To solve the equations required for threshold determination, the TE-operated WP coefficients of noisy speech, clean speech, or noise is well approximated by the positive part of a Gaussian distribution. Instead of using a unique threshold for all frames, the threshold value here is adapted with respect to speech and silence frames based on the SKL divergence. Then, by employing a semisoft thresholding function, the WP coefficients of the noisy speech are thresholded in order to obtain a cleaner speech. Standard objective and subjective evaluations on the simulation results show that the proposed method is capable of consistently yielding enhanced speech with better quality and intelligibility compared to that obtained from the existing thresholding-based methods. However, there are some scopes for possible future research. In the proposed speech enhancement method, we have formulated the histogram of the Teager energy-operated WP coefficients and approximated the histogram by a reasonably close probability distribution function, namely Gaussian distribution. But other types of distributions, such as logistic, T-scale, extreme value, and generalized extreme value can also be explored to approximate the histograms of the WP coefficients. Moreover, in our method, both the threshold determination and the thresholding operation are performed in the WP domain. Same operations can be employed in perceptual wavelet packet domain, where the use of a perceptually weighted filter would be able to mask the residual noise, making it audibly imperceptible.

Competing interests
The authors declare that they have no competing interests.

Acknowledgements
The authors would like to express their sincere gratitude towards the authorities of the Department of Electrical and Electronics Engineering and Bangladesh University of Engineering and Technology (BUET) for providing constant support throughout this research work.

References
1. D O'Shaughnessy, *Speech Enhancement: Theory and Practice* (IEEE Press, New York, 2000)
2. F Jabloun, B Champagne, Incorporating the human hearing properties in the signal subspace approach for speech enhancement. IEEE Trans. Speech Audio Process. **11**, 700–708 (2003)
3. H Gustafsson, S Nordholm, I Claesson, Spectral subtraction using reduced delay convolution and adaptive averaging. IEEE Trans. Speech Audio Process. **9**(8), 799–807 (2001)
4. S Kamath, P Loizou, A multi-band spectral subtraction method for enhancing speech corrupted by colored noise, in *Proceedings of the IEEE International Conference on Acoustics, Speech, and Signal Processing (ICASSP)*, vol.4 (IEEE, Piscataway, 2002), pp. IV–4164
5. K Yamashita, T Shimamura, Nonstationary noise estimation using low-frequency regions for spectral subtraction. IEEE Signal Process. Lett. **12**, 465–468 (2005)
6. S Boll, Suppression of acoustic noise in speech using spectral subtraction. IEEE Trans. Acoustics Speech Signal Process. **27**(2), 113–120 (1979)
7. B Chen, PC Loizou, A Laplacian-based MMSE estimator for speech enhancement. Speech Commun. **49**, 134–143 (2007)
8. P Loizou, Speech enhancement based on perceptually motivated Bayesian estimators of the magnitude spectrum. IEEE Trans. Speech Audio Process. **13**(5), 857–869 (2005)
9. Y Ephraim, D Malah, Speech enhancement using a minimum mean-square error log-spectral amplitude estimator. IEEE Trans. Acoustics Speech Signal Process. **33**(2), 443–445 (1985)
10. H Sameti, H Sheikhzadeh, L Deng, R Brennan, HMM-based strategies for enhancement of speech signals embedded in nonstationary noise. IEEE Trans. Speech Audio Process. **6**(5), 445–455 (1998)
11. J Hansen, V Radhakrishnan, K Arehart, Speech enhancement based on generalized minimum mean square error estimators and masking properties of the auditory system. IEEE Trans. Audio Speech Lang. Process. **14**(6), 2049–2063 (2006)
12. I Almajai, B Milner, Visually derived wiener filters for speech enhancement. IEEE Trans. Audio Speech Lang. Process. **19**(6), 1642–1651 (2011)
13. S Ben Jebara, A perceptual approach to reduce musical noise phenomenon with Wiener denoising technique, in *IEEE International Conference on Acoustics, Speech and Signal Processing, (ICASSP)*, vol.3 (IEEE, Piscataway, 2006), p. III
14. A Papoulis, SU Pillai, *Probability, Random Variables and Stochastic Processes* (McGraw-Hill, New York, 2002)
15. S Chang, Y Kwon, Si Yang, Ij Kim, Speech enhancement for non-stationary noise environment by adaptive wavelet packet, in *Proceedings of the IEEE International Conference on Acoustics, Speech, and Signal Processing (ICASSP)*, vol.1 (IEEE, Piscataway, 2002), pp. I-561–I-564
16. Y Hu, P Loizou, Speech enhancement based on wavelet thresholding the multitaper spectrum. IEEE Trans. Speech Audio Process. **12**, 59–67 (2004)
17. S Tabibian, A Akbari, B Nasersharif, A new wavelet thresholding method for speech enhancement based on symmetric Kullback-Leibler divergence, in *Proceedings of the 14th International CSI Computer Conference, (CSICC)* (IEEE, Piscataway, 2009), pp. 495–500
18. M Bahoura, J Rouat, Wavelet speech enhancement based on the Teager energy operator. IEEE Signal Process. Lett. **8**, 10–12 (2001)
19. DL Donoho, IM Johnstone, Ideal spatial adaptation by wavelet shrinkage. Biometrika. **81**, 425–455 (1994)
20. D Donoho, De-noising by soft-thresholding. IEEE Trans. Inf. Theory. **41**, 613–627 (1995)
21. Y Ghanbari, MRK Mollaei, A new approach for speech enhancement based on the adaptive thresholding of the wavelet packets. Speech Commun. **48**(8), 927–940 (2006)

22. H Sheikhzadeh, HR Abutalebi, An improved wavelet-based speech enhancement system, in *EUROSPEECH* (ICSA, France, 2001), pp. 1855–1858

23. Q Fu, E Wan, Perceptual Wavelet Adaptive Denoising of Speech, in *EUROSPEECH* (ICSA, France, 2003), pp. 1937–1940

24. SH Chen, JF Wang, Speech enhancement using perceptual wavelet packet decomposition and Teager energy operator. J. VLSI Signal Process. Syst. **36**(2/3), 125–139 (2004)

25. Y Shao, CH Chang, A generalized time-frequency subtraction method for robust speech enhancement based on wavelet filter banks modeling of human auditory system. IEEE Trans. Syst. Man Cybern. **37**(4), 877–889 (2007)

26. MT Johnson, X Yuan, Y Ren, Speech signal enhancement through adaptive wavelet thresholding. Speech Commun. **49**, 123–133 (2007)

27. J Kaiser, Some useful properties of Teager's energy operators, in *IEEE International Conference on Speech, and Signal Processing, (ICASSP)*, vol.3 (IEEE, Piscataway, 1993), pp. 149–152

28. M Bahoura, J Rouat, A new approach for wavelet speech enhancement, in *EUROSPEECH* (ICSA, France, 2001), pp. 1937–1940

29. M Bahoura, J Rouat, Wavelet speech enhancement based on time-scale adaptation. Speech Commun. **48**(12), 1620–1637 (2006)

30. S Mallat, WL Hwang, Singularity detection and processing with wavelets. IEEE Trans. Inf. Theory. **38**(2), 617–643 (1992)

31. R Coifman, M Wickerhauser, Entropy-based algorithms for best basis selection. IEEE Trans. Inf. Theory. **38**(2), 713–718 (1992)

32. A Dimitriadis, P Maragos, A comparison of the squared energy and Teager-Kaiser operators for short-term energy estimation in additive noise. IEEE Trans. Signal Process. **57**(7), 2569–2581 (2009)

33. J Kaiser, International Conference on Acoustics, Speech, and Signal Processing, (ICASSP) vol.1 (IEEE, Piscataway, 1990), pp. 381–384

34. P Maragos, T Quatieri, J Kaiser, Speech nonlinearities, modulations, and energy operators, in *International Conference on Acoustics, Speech, and Signal Processing, (ICASSP)*, vol.1 (IEEE, Piscataway, 1991), pp. 421–424

35. J Rouat, *Nonlinear operators for speech analysis, in Visual representations of speech signals* (Wiley, New York, 1992), pp. 335–340

36. Y Hu, PC Loizou, Subjective comparison and evaluation of speech enhancement algorithms. Speech Commun. **49**(7-8), 588–601 (2007)

37. WH Abdulla, HMM-based techniques for speech segments extraction. Sci. Program. **10**(3), 221–239 (2002)

38. M Bahoura, J Rouat, Wavelet noise reduction: application to speech enhancement. J. Can. Acoustical Assoc. **28**(3), 158–159 (2000)

39. S Ayat, M Manzuri, R Dianat, Wavelet based speech enhancement using a new thresholding algorithm, in *Proceedings of the International Symposium on Intelligent Multimedia, Video and Speech Processing* (IEEE, Piscataway, 2004), pp. 238–241

40. A Varga, HJM Steeneken, Assessment for automatic speech recognition: II. NOISEX-92: a database and an experiment to study the effect of additive noise on speech recognition systems. Speech Commun. **12**, 247–251 (1993)

41. Y Lu, PC Loizou, Estimators of the magnitude-squared spectrum and methods for incorporating SNR uncertainty. IEEE Trans. Audio Speech Lang. Process. **19**(5), 1123–1137 (2011)

42. ITU, P56 IT: objective measurement of active speech level. ITU-T Recommendation (ITU, Geneva, 1993), p. 56

43. ITU, P835 IT: subjective test methodology for evaluating speech communication systems that include noise suppression algorithms. ITU-T Recommendation (ITU, Geneva, 2003), p. 835

3

Single-channel dereverberation by feature mapping using cascade neural networks for robust distant speaker identification and speech recognition

Aditya Arie Nugraha[1*], Kazumasa Yamamoto[1,2] and Seiichi Nakagawa[1]

Abstract

We present a feature enhancement method that uses neural networks (NNs) to map the reverberant feature in a log-melspectral domain to its corresponding anechoic feature. The mapping is done by cascade NNs trained using Cascade2 algorithm with an implementation of segment-based normalization. Experiments using speaker identification (SID) and automatic speech recognition (ASR) systems were conducted to evaluate the method. The experiments of SID system was conducted by using our own simulated and real reverberant datasets, while the CENSREC-4 evaluation framework was used as the evaluation for the ASR system. The proposed method could remarkably improve the performance of both systems by using limited stereo data and low speaker-variant data as the training data. From the evaluation using SID, we reached 26.0% and 34.8% of error rate reduction (ERR) relative to the baseline by using simulated and real data, respectively, by using only one pair of utterances for matched condition cases. Then, by using combined dataset containing 15 pairs of utterances by one speaker from three positions in a room, we could reach 93.7% of average identification rate (three known and two unknown positions), which was 42.2% of ERR relative to the use of cepstral mean normalization (CMN). From the evaluation using ASR, by using 40 pairs of utterances as the NN training data, we could reach 78.4% of ERR relative to the baseline by using simulated utterances by five speakers. Moreover, we could reach 75.4% and 71.6% of ERR relative to the baseline by using real utterances by five speakers and one speaker, respectively.

Keywords: Dereverberation; Feature enhancement; Cascade neural network; Stereo training data; Speech recognition; Speaker identification

1 Introduction

The use of distant-talking microphones for automatic speech recognition (ASR) system or automatic speaker identification (SID) system can improve user convenience. The use of such microphones is essential for certain applications, e.g., the application of ASR and/or SID for smart home, where it will be not practical if the users have to hold or wear microphone anytime they want to interact with the system. However, the use of distant-talking microphones will make the captured signal be vulnerable to the phenomenon known as reverberation, where the signal not only travels directly from the speaker to the microphone but also through reflections, which can be seen as delayed and attenuated versions of the direct signal. Thus, reverberation will cause *smearing effect* because the microphone captures the currently spoken utterance along with other utterance spoken in the past [1]. Because of this signal degradation, the use of reverberant signal captured by the microphone will degrade the ASR or SID system performance, which is usually trained using anechoic speech data.

Several approaches already proposed to deal with this reverberation problem from ASR point of view.

*Correspondence: arie@slp.cs.tut.ac.jp
[1] Department of Computer Science and Engineering, Toyohashi University of Technology, Toyohashi, Aichi 441-8580, Japan
Full list of author information is available at the end of the article

According to [2] in which the state-of-the-art in reverberant speech processing is discussed, there are two classes of approaches in dealing with reverberation problem, i.e., front-end-based and back-end-based approaches. The front-end-based approaches attempt to remove the effect of reverberation from the observed feature vectors. It can be divided into linear filtering, spectrum enhancement, and feature enhancement. The linear filtering dereverberates time-domain signals or STFT coefficients, e.g., [3,4], the spectrum enhancement dereverberates the corrupted power spectra of signal, e.g., [5-7], and the feature enhancement dereverberates the corrupted feature vectors, e.g., [8-10]. Meanwhile, the back-end-based approaches attempt to modify the acoustic model and/or decoder so that they are suitable for reverberant environment, e.g., [11,12].

Among the front-end-based approaches, there are single-channel approaches (by using single microphone) and multi-channel approaches (by using microphone array). Many recently proposed dereverberation researches focus on the use of microphone array, e.g., multi-channel linear prediction [13], minimum variance distortionless response (MVDR) beamformer [14], multi-channel least mean squares (LMS) [15]. Comparing to the use of single microphone, the main benefit of microphone array is the spatial information it can provide. Despite the benefits of microphone array, the use of single microphone is much easier and cheaper to be implemented for real applications. Thus, the research on single-channel dereverberation method is still worth to be considered.

Many works focused on feature enhancement approach. Several single-channel feature enhancement methods have been proposed. Some of them do not need stereo data at all, e.g., cepstral mean normalization (CMN) [16,17], long-term feature normalization [18], vector Taylor series (VTS) [19], particle filter [8,20], and extended Kalman filter [9,21]. Meanwhile, some of them assume that *stereo training data* can be acquired. In the context of distant SID or ASR system, stereo data are simultaneously recorded pairs of close-talking and distant-talking utterances. In general, the stereo training data is used to train a mapping function from the distant-talking utterance to its corresponding close-talking utterance. Several existing approaches which need stereo training data will be reviewed in Section 2.

This research focused on developing a single-channel dereverberation method for automatic speaker identification and speech recognition under real environmental conditions by doing feature enhancement and assuming that stereo data can be acquired. In order to increase its feasibility for real-world applications, the method should have good performance by using a limited number of stereo data.

We proposed a single-channel non-linear regression-based dereverberation method using cascade neural networks (NNs). The NNs were trained on stereo data to compensate the reverberation effect by mapping a segment of reverberant 24-dimensional log-melspectral feature vectors to its corresponding anechoic feature vector. Two most important parts of the proposed method are the segment-based normalization and the feature mapping using NN. The segment-based normalization is done by normalizing the current frame of the anechoic and the reverberant feature and also preserving the power envelope of reverberant input segment. For the feature mapping, cascade NNs trained using the Cascade2 algorithm with the Resilient Backpropagation (RPROP) weight update algorithm, which is a variation of batch backpropagation algorithm, were used. These two most important parts are most likely the reason why the proposed method could generalize and perform remarkably well for a limited number of stereo data (one or five pairs of utterances; corresponds to less than 1 min of utterance).

The proposed method was evaluated on SID and ASR systems. Both evaluations were done by using simulated and real data. The evaluation using SID system used our own simulated and real data, while the evaluation using ASR system used simulated and real data from CENSREC-4 [22]. The proposed method could perform very well by using only few stereo data and also low speaker-variant data as the NN training data.

The experimental result of SID using simulated data shows that in matched condition cases, the error rate reduction (ERR) relative to the baseline by using only *one pair of utterances* could reach 26.0% when single NN ('1 NNs') configuration was used. Meanwhile, by using 15 pairs of utterances and multiple NNs ('24 NNs') configuration, the ERR reached 62.6%. Also in matched condition cases, the experimental result using real data shows that by using '6 NNs' configuration and only *one pair of utterances* for the NN training data, we could reach 34.8% of ERR relative to the use of CMN. Then, by combining the training data from known positions in a room, we could train NNs which performed well for unknown positions in the same room. By using multiple NNs ('24 NNs') and 15 pairs of utterances by one speaker from three positions, we could reach 93.7% of average identification rate over three known and two unknown positions, which was 42.2% of ERR relative to the use of CMN.

The experimental result of ASR using simulated data shows that we could reach 78.4% of ERR relative to the baseline by using dataset containing 40 pairs of utterances by five speakers as the NN training data. Meanwhile, by using the same number of real reverberant data, we could reach 75.4% and 71.6% of ERR relative to the baseline by using dataset containing utterances by five speakers and one speaker, respectively.

2 Related works

The most popular feature enhancement method using stereo data is stereo-based piece-wise linear compensation for environments (SPLICE), which estimates the clean cepstral feature from the noisy feature using a Gaussian mixture model (GMM) of noisy feature [23]. In general, SPLICE tries to represent a non-linear relation by using piece-wise linear relation in each subspace of noisy feature. SPLICE could perform well for both simulated and real noisy data [24]. However, SPLICE is designed specifically for dealing with the noise problem.

For the reverberation problem, in [25], 13 multi-layer perceptron (MLP) NNs were trained using stereo data to map the 13-dimensional reverberant cepstral feature, where one NN was used for one dimension of feature, to its corresponding anechoic feature. The input of each NN was a sequence of cepstral feature coefficients from nine consecutive frames, and the output was a cepstral feature coefficient. The approach was evaluated using vector quantization (VQ)-based speaker identification method and could reach 80.2% of ERR relative to baseline.

In [26], a linear regression by least squares method (LSM) was used to do a mapping of melspectral feature vectors from a four-frame sequence of reverberant speech to a frame of clean speech. Several schemes of dynamic time warping (DTW) were introduced because there was only non-stereo dataset for the experiments. The non-stereo dataset contained close-talking utterances recorded from the distance of 25 cm and distant-talking utterances recorded from various positions in a room. These close- and distant-talking utterances were not recorded simultaneously, although the speakers and the utterances were the same. The DTW was used to align frames of a distant-talking utterance to frames of its corresponding close-talking utterance before they were used as the training data. Nonetheless, the approach should be also worked on stereo dataset.

In [10,27], a joint sparse representation (JSR) technique was used to capture the relationship between clean and reverberant speech. The dictionary for clean feature space and the dictionary for reverberant feature space were jointly trained using the stereo data in order to have common representation coefficients. Basically, the approach did a mapping of log-melspectral feature vectors from N frames of reverberant speech to N frames of estimated clean speech. In [27], besides the 24-dimensional log-melspectral feature vectors, the mapping included the log-energy coefficients. In the same paper, the sequence of N frames included the use of left and right context (past, current, and future frames).

Stereo data also found to be used in linear filtering approaches. In [28], the dereverberation was done using linear and binary-weighted least squares techniques on time and fast Fourier transform (FFT) domain. The stereo data was needed to calculate the inverse filter coefficients, which then was used to transform N frames of reverberant complex-valued FFT coefficient vectors to N frames of estimated clean FFT coefficient vectors. The experiments were done using 512-, 1,024-, and 2,048-dimensional vectors. The length of vector corresponds to the length of DFT.

Recently, in [29,30], a denoising autoencoder (DAE), which is one of deep neural network (DNN) approaches, was used to do a mapping of coefficient vectors from a sequence of reverberant speech to a sequence of clean speech. They also introduced the use of short and long window. The short window is used to extract 256 dimensions of power spectral coefficients and the log energy. On the other hand, the long window is used to extract 24 dimensions of melspectral coefficients and the log energy. Thus, by using both windows, the DNN was used to map from and to 2,538-dimensional vectors, which are constructed by power spectral, melspectral, and log-energy coefficients of a nine-frame segment. In addition, DAE was also used for speech enhancement by mapping the power spectral coefficients [31] and the melspectral coefficients [32]. These DNN-based approaches are effective, but they require much training data for training a huge number of parameters.

In summary, the approaches proposed in [25,26] did a mapping from a N-frame segment to a one-frame segment. Meanwhile, the approaches proposed in [10,27-30] did a mapping from a N-frame segment to a N-frame segment. The method proposed in this work does a mapping from a N-frame segment to a one-frame segment of log-melspectral coefficients by using cascade NNs and requires only few training data. The NN is used because it should be able to capture a non-linear relation across the frames, which is caused by the insufficiency of analysis window (frame) length in capturing the reverberation effect and other complex factors.

3 Overview of neural network

3.1 Artificial neural network

NN, or more properly called artificial neural network (ANN), is a computational model inspired by the biological nervous systems, such as the brain. In a simple way, a biological nervous system consists of interconnected webs of neurons, where each neuron has dendrites, soma, and axon. The dendrites receive input signals and when the soma feels that the input signals are strong enough, it emits an output signal through the axon. This signal then can be sent to other neuron's dendrites through the synapses, which are the end points of axon's branches.

How a biological neuron works is modeled by an artificial neuron, as depicted by Figure 1. The neuron has inputs x_n with their associated weights w_n. The weighted

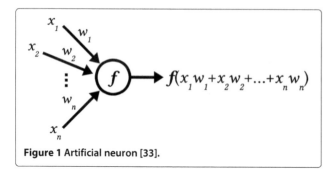

Figure 1 Artificial neuron [33].

inputs are integrated in the neuron, which in most cases is simply done by summation, and then evaluated by an activation function f, e.g., hyperbolic tangent function, to determine the output. An ANN is simply a network that consists of interconnected artificial neurons and has three important elements, i.e., the structure of the nodes/neurons (how the inputs are integrated, the activation function), topology/architecture (the way artificial neurons interconnected), and the training algorithm (to determine the weights in the network) [33].

Various types of NN are defined based on their architectures. The architecture itself is a combination of their framework and their interconnection scheme [34].

The framework is defined by the number of clusters and the number of neurons in each cluster. The clusters are called layers if they are ordered and are called slabs otherwise. There are input, hidden, and output clusters, where each cluster contains one or more neurons. The neurons within a cluster are not necessarily ordered.

The interconnection scheme is mainly defined by the connectivity (describes which neurons are connected) and the types of connections. In layered NN, connections can be divided into interlayer, intralayer, and supralayer connections. Interlayer connection connects neurons from adjacent layers, intralayer connection connects neurons within a layer, and supralayer connection connects neurons from different (non-adjacent) layers. In slabbed NN, where the clusters are not ordered, there are only interslab connection, which connects neurons from different slabs, and intraslab connection, which connects neurons within a slab. Further, in regard to the directionality, connections can be divided into symmetric (bidirectional) and asymmetric (unidirectional) connections.

3.2 Conventional multi-layer perceptron and cascade networks

Both conventional MLP and the cascade networks used in the proposed method may use the same structure of neurons. The main differences between them are in the architecture and how to build the architecture, which then cause a difference in the training algorithm.

3.2.1 Conventional MLP network

In conventional MLP approach, the NN is fully defined in advance before the training is started. The NN is a layered NN with asymmetric interlayer connections (Figure 2A). The NN contains an input layer, one or more hidden layers, and an output layer. Except the output layer, each layer commonly contains more than one neuron. The training (weight update) algorithm is then used to update the previously initialized weights and determine the most appropriate weights based on the training data. Backpropagation can be regarded as the most popular weight update algorithm for training MLP. It propagates an input through the network, then propagates back the error and adjusts the weights to minimize the error. The algorithm can be used in both an incremental training, in which the weights are updated for each training datum in the training set, and a batch training, in which the weights are updated only after all training data in the training set are presented.

3.2.2 Cascade network

Besides the common approach above, there are dynamic approaches in which the architecture of NN is altered during the training by adding neurons and/or clusters. Thus, the training algorithm not only consists of the weight update algorithm but also consists of the architecture algorithm, e.g., cascade. Two most common cascade algorithms are Cascade-Correlation (CasCor) and Cascade2 [35]. Cascade2 algorithm is a variation of CasCor algorithm. Instead of using covariance maximization as in CasCor, Cascade2 uses direct error minimization. By doing so, Cascade2 is better algorithm for regression task, while CasCor is better for classification task [36].

In cascade algorithm, the NN can be regarded as layered NN with asymmetric interlayer and supralayer connections (Figure 2B). Usually, the NN contains an input layer,

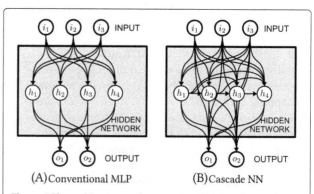

(A) Conventional MLP   (B) Cascade NN

Figure 2 The architectures of conventional MLP and cascade NN depicted in conventional MLP representation. **(A)** Conventional MLP: layered NN with asymmetric interlayer connections. **(B)** Cascade NN: layered NN with asymmetric interlayer and supralayer connections.

many hidden layers, and an output layer. Different from conventional MLP approach, each hidden layer in cascade algorithm contains one hidden neuron. The other difference is that in the cascade NN, every hidden neuron and also the output neurons are directly connected to the input neurons. Meanwhile, in a conventional MLP, only hidden neurons of the first hidden layer are directly connected to the input neurons and the output neurons are directly connected only to the hidden neurons of the last hidden layer.

Before the training of a cascade NN is started, the NN only contains an input layer and an output layer with interlayer connections connect neurons from these two layers. The NN is then grown by adding hidden neurons/layers during the training. Each newly added hidden neuron connects to the neurons from input layer and output layer. The newly added hidden neuron also connects to the previously added hidden neuron. The hidden neuron addition is controlled by the cascade algorithm and done after the weight update algorithm cannot find a proper weight to generate the correct output by using the existing architecture. The same backpropagation weight update algorithm as for conventional MLP training can also be used for cascade NN training.

According to [37] and [35], the cascade algorithm offers several advantages, including:

- The algorithm will automatically build a reasonably small network, so there is no need to define the NN in advance,
- The algorithm learns fast because it employs weight freezing to overcome moving target problem by training one unit at a time instead of training the whole network at once as in conventional MLP, and
- The algorithm can build deep network (high-order feature representation) without dramatic slowdown as seen in conventional MLP with more than one hidden layers.

The deep network generated by cascade algorithm can represent very strong non-linearity. It is good for some problems but may be bad for other problems. It can be regarded as overfitting problem caused by the use of too many layers and neurons. As explained in [37], CasCor employs 'patience' parameter to stop the training when the error has not changed significantly for a period of time. However, according to [35], overfitting will still occurr if the NN is allowed to grow too much. Therefore, we need to define the proper maximum number of hidden neurons. Besides using less hidden neurons, we can also use more training data to minimize the overfitting possibility.

For further details of cascade NN in general and Cascade2 algorithm in particular, please refer to [35].

4 The estimation function

4.1 Reverberation model

On the time domain, the relation between anechoic and reverberant signal (regardless the noise) can be expressed as

$$y(t) = s(t) * h(t), \tag{1}$$

where $s(t)$ and $y(t)$ are the clean and reverberant signals, respectively, and $h(t)$ is the room impulse response (RIR), which defines the room transfer function (RTF).

The relation between anechoic and reverberant signal in log-melspectral domain should be represented as a nonlinear model as shown in [12,21]. However, for simplicity, we defined it as

$$Y(t) = \sum_{i=0}^{N} \alpha_i S(t - i) \tag{2}$$

$$= \alpha_0 S(t) + \sum_{i=1}^{N} \alpha_i S(t - i), \tag{3}$$

where $S(t)$ and $Y(t)$ represent the log-melspectral coefficients of anechoic and reverberant signal, respectively, for frame index t. While, $\alpha_0, \alpha_1, \ldots, \alpha_N$ represent the RTF. This formulation was introduced in [26] and also employed in [38-40].

The first term of Equation 3 corresponds to the direct-path signal captured by the microphone and is represented by the solid line in Figure 3. Meanwhile, the second term corresponds to the sum of signal reflections and are represented by the dotted lines in Figure 3. The reflection can be regarded as an attenuated and delayed version of the direct signal.

4.1.1 Causal model

From Equation 3, $S(t)$ could be expressed as

$$S(t) = \frac{1}{\alpha_0} Y(t) - \sum_{i=1}^{N} \frac{\alpha_i}{\alpha_0} S(t - i), \tag{4}$$

and by recursively substituting the last term, $S(t)$ could be expressed as

$$S(t) = \frac{1}{\alpha_0} Y(t) - \sum_{i=1}^{N} \frac{\alpha_i}{\alpha_0} \frac{1}{\alpha_0} Y(t - i)$$
$$+ \sum_{i=1}^{N} \frac{\alpha_i}{\alpha_0} \sum_{j=1}^{N} \frac{\alpha_j}{\alpha_0} S(t - i - j), \tag{5}$$

$$S(t) = \frac{1}{\alpha_0} Y(t) - \sum_{i=1}^{N} \frac{\alpha_i}{\alpha_0^2} Y(t - i)$$
$$+ \sum_{i=1}^{N} \sum_{j=1}^{N} \frac{\alpha_i \alpha_j}{\alpha_0^3} Y(t - i - j) - \ldots . \tag{6}$$

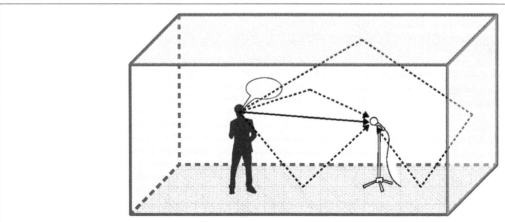

Figure 3 Illustration of reverberation in a closed room. The solid line represents the direct-path signal. The dotted lines represent the reflections.

The first term of Equation 6 considers only the current frame $Y(t)$, while the succeeding terms consider the left context. The second term considers $Y(t-N)$ until $Y(t-1)$, the third term considers $Y(t-2N)$ until $Y(t-2)$, the fourth term considers $Y(t-3N)$ until $Y(t-3)$, and so on.

RIR is characterized by reverberation time (T_{60}), which is the time required for reflections of a direct-path signal to decay by 60 dB or one-millionth of the original energy. If N is selected such that the N-segment covers the T_{60}, we may limit the calculation up to the frame N because the energy of reflections in the frames after N is very low and negligible. If the practicality is considered, N should be a trade-off between the dereverberation performance and the computational cost for processing this segment will be higher. A longer segment may capture the reverberation effect better which then potentially improve the dereverberation, but the computational cost for processing this segment will be higher. In order to simplify the equation, β_i is used for representing the variables formed by the combination of α_i, e.g. $\beta_0 = \alpha_0^{-1}$, $\beta_1 = -\alpha_1\alpha_0^{-2}$, $\beta_2 = -\alpha_2\alpha_0^{-2} + \alpha_1^2\alpha_0^{-3}$, $\beta_3 = -\alpha_3\alpha_0^{-2} + (2\alpha_1\alpha_2 - \alpha_1^3)\alpha_0^{-3}$, and so on. Thus, the estimated anechoic coefficient $\hat{S}(t)$ could be expressed as a function of reverberant signal $Y(t)$

$$\hat{S}(t) = \beta_0 Y(t) + \sum_{k=1}^{L} \beta_k Y(t-k) + \varepsilon, \quad (7)$$

$$\hat{S}(t) \approx \sum_{k=0}^{L} \beta_k Y(t-k), \quad (8)$$

where $\beta_0, \beta_1, \ldots, \beta_L$ denotes the weights which are used to compensate the RTF and L denotes the number of past frames in the segment. L is used to substitute N in order to indicate that the frames are the left context. By using Equation 8, we could estimate current source signal $S(t)$ by using an $(L+1)$-frame segment of observed signal consisting of current observed signal $Y(t)$ and L frame(s) of past observed signal.

4.1.2 Non-causal model

By considering a typical RIR, intuitively, we know that the information of current frame will remain in its reflections in the future, especially in its early reflections part where the reflections still have considerable amount of energy.

Let $0 < n < N$ and $N > 1$, Equation 3 can be rewritten as

$$Y(t) = \sum_{i=0}^{n-1} \alpha_i S(t-i) + \alpha_n S(t-n)$$
$$+ \sum_{i=n+1}^{N} \alpha_i S(t-i), \quad (9)$$

and $S(t-n)$ could be expressed as

$$S(t-n) = \frac{1}{\alpha_n} Y(t) - \sum_{i=0}^{n-1} \frac{\alpha_i}{\alpha_n} S(t-i)$$
$$- \sum_{i=n+1}^{N} \frac{\alpha_i}{\alpha_n} S(t-i). \quad (10)$$

Then, by substituting $S(t-i)$ using the causal model on Equation 8, $S(t-n)$ could be expressed as

$$S(t-n) = \frac{1}{\alpha_n} Y(t) - \sum_{i=0}^{n-1} \frac{\alpha_i}{\alpha_n} \sum_{j=0}^{N} \beta_j Y(t-i-j)$$
$$- \sum_{i=n+1}^{N} \frac{\alpha_i}{\alpha_n} \sum_{j=0}^{N} \beta_j Y(t-i-j). \quad (11)$$

Equation 11 comprises three terms. The first term considers only $Y(t)$. The second term considers the left context, which is $Y(t)$ until $Y(t-n+1)$; the current frame, which is $Y(t-n)$; and the right context, which is $Y(t-n-1)$ until $Y(t-n-N+1)$. Meanwhile, the third term considers only the right context, which is $Y(t-n-1)$ until $Y(t-2N)$. In order to simplify the equation, γ_i is used to substitute the variables formed by the combination of α_i

and βi. Thus, the estimated anechoic coefficient $\hat{S}(t - n)$ could be expressed as

$$\hat{S}(t - n) = \sum_{k=0}^{n-1} \gamma_k Y(t - k) + \gamma_n Y(t - n)$$

$$+ \sum_{k=n+1}^{2N} \gamma_k Y(t - k) + \varepsilon. \qquad (12)$$

Then, by making generalization on Equation 12, the estimated anechoic coefficient $\hat{S}(t)$ could be expressed as

$$\hat{S}(t) = \sum_{k=-R}^{-1} \gamma_k Y(t - k) + \gamma_0 Y(t)$$

$$+ \sum_{k=1}^{L} \gamma_k Y(t - k) + \varepsilon, \qquad (13)$$

$$\hat{S}(t) \approx \sum_{k=-R}^{L} \gamma_k Y(t - k), \qquad (14)$$

where $\gamma_K, \ldots, \gamma_{-1}, \gamma_0, \gamma_1, \ldots, \gamma_L$ denotes the weights which are used to compensate the RTF, L denotes the number of past frames in the segment, and R denotes the number of future frames in the segment. L and R are used to indicate that the frames are the left context and right context, respectively. By using Equation 14, we could estimate current source signal $S(t)$ by using an $(L+1+R)$-frame segment of observed signal consisting of current observed signal $Y(t)$, L frame(s) of past observed signal (left context), and R frame(s) of future observed signal (right context).

Equation 14 could be seen as the general form of reverberation model. We could get Equation 8 from Equation 14 by setting $R = 0$.

Hereafter, we refer to Equation 8 as causal reverberation model and Equation 14 as non-causal reverberation model (for $R > 0$). For the causal reverberation model, the estimation of $\hat{S}(t)$ can be seen as removing the unwanted information (reflections of previous frames) which is estimated from the left context. While, for the non-causal reverberation model, besides removing the unwanted information, the estimation can be seen as gathering more information about the current frame to be processed, which is estimated from the right context.

4.2 Frame selection
Inspired by the use of window skipping in [41], besides Equation 14 we also defined

$$\hat{S}(t) \approx \sum_{k=-R}^{L} \gamma_k Y(t - 2k). \qquad (15)$$

Hereafter, we refer to Equation 8 as 'linear' frame selection and Equation 15 as 'skip1' frame selection.

In this work, we named the frame selection used in the experiments using *L-C-R* notation. *L*, *C*, and *R* show the number of left context (past), current, and right context (future) frames, respectively. For example, frame selection *4-1-0* means that four past and one current frames of reverberant speech are used to estimate the dereverberated version of current frame, and frame selection *4-1-4* means that four past, one current, and four future frames are used to do the dereverberation.

The use of skipping frame selection could be regarded as dimensionality reduction strategy by minimizing the redundant parts caused by the windowing. Therefore, we could get a representation of longer context of time-domain signal using smaller number of frames, which is beneficial for the NN training. For example, if we use 25 ms window with 10 ms shift, 145 ms of context can be represented by using 13-frame linear frame selection, e.g., 12-1-0 or 6-1-6, or 7-frame skip1 frame selection, e.g., 6-1-0 or 3-1-3.

4.3 Assumptions on the log-melspectral feature
In our works, we made several assumptions on the log-melspectral feature. The first assumption is about the dependency of certain feature dimension to the other feature dimensions, and the second is about the RTF of feature dimension.

On the dependency of feature dimension, we defined several *channel selection*, as follows:

- All-dimension selection, where the dimensions are assumed to be fully dependent on each other.
- Single-dimension selection, where the dimensions are assumed to be independent on each other and certain dimension is only affected by the same dimension.
- Neighboring-dimension selection, where certain dimension is assumed to be affected by the same dimension and its neighbor dimension.

The estimation function above was derived using the assumption used in *all-dimension selection*. However, our experiments mainly used the *single-dimension selection*, which can be expressed as

$$\hat{S}_d(t) \approx \sum_{k=-R}^{L} \gamma_{d,k} Y_d(t - k), \text{ for } d = 1, 2, \ldots, D, \qquad (16)$$

where d is the feature dimension number and D is the total number of feature dimension.

By using the single-dimension selection, we could define several assumptions on the transformation of feature dimension caused by the RTF. In our case, the assumptions on the transformation affects the number of NNs that should be used. Thus, we defined several *NN configurations* as follows:

- *Single NN* configuration, where it is assumed that the transformation on each dimension is the same as each other, so one NN is used to transform all dimensions of feature.
- *Basic multiple NNs* configuration, where it is assumed that the transformation on each dimension is different from each other, so one NN is used to transform one specific dimension.
- *Modified multiple NNs* configuration, where it is assumed that the transformation on certain several neighboring dimensions are the same, one NN is used to transform *more than* one dimension (neighboring dimensions).

The basic multiple NNs configuration, in which one transformation function (in the form of NN) is used to transform one dimension, corresponds to Equation 16. Meanwhile, the single NN configuration, in which one transformation function (in the form of NN) is used to transform all dimensions, corresponds to Equation 17. Note that Equations 16 and 17 are linear mapping functions, while transformation by NN is a non-linear mapping. As shown in [26], the use of linear mapping is not good enough to do dereverberation.

$$\hat{S}_d(t) \approx \sum_{k=-R}^{L} \gamma_k Y_d(t - k), \text{ for } d = 1, 2, \ldots, D. \quad (17)$$

5   The proposed dereverberation method

Figure 4 shows the block diagram of proposed dereverberation method. In general, the method can be divided into segment-based normalization, feature scaling, and feature mapping using NNs. The inputs of the method are $Y(t - L), \ldots, Y(t - 1), Y(t), Y(t + 1), \ldots, Y(t + R)$, which are past frames, current frame, and future frames of reverberant log-melspectral coefficient vector, and the output is $\hat{S}(t)$, which is the estimated current anechoic log-melspectral coefficient vector.

5.1   Segment-based normalization

Segment-based normalization is employed to deal with the power difference between the anechoic speech signal and the reverberant signal captured by a distant-talking microphone and to normalize the loudness of speech utterance. In the NN training stage, it is done by normalizing the current reverberant feature vector and the current anechoic feature vector (which is the target of training) to the normalization target. Besides, the segment-based normalization is employed to preserve the relative variation of power envelope in a segment by normalizing the past frames relative to the current frame. The normalization is done using Equations 18 and 19 below.

$$\delta(t) = \Delta - \frac{1}{D} \sum_{d=1}^{D} Y_d(t), \quad (18)$$

$$\bar{Y}_d(t - k) = Y_d(t - k) + \delta(t), \text{ for } d = 1, 2, \ldots, D,$$
$$\text{for } -R \leq k \leq L, \quad (19)$$

where $\delta(t)$ is the normalization factor, $\bar{Y}_d(t)$ is the normalized log-melspectral coefficient for feature dimension d and time index t, D is the number of feature dimensions, and Δ is the normalization target.

The mean of NN output $\bar{S}(t)$ should be equal to the normalization target because the target of NN training was also normalized. Therefore, the denormalization (Equation 20) is used to recover its original mean of power.

$$\hat{S}_j(t) = \bar{S}_j(t) - \delta(t). \quad (20)$$

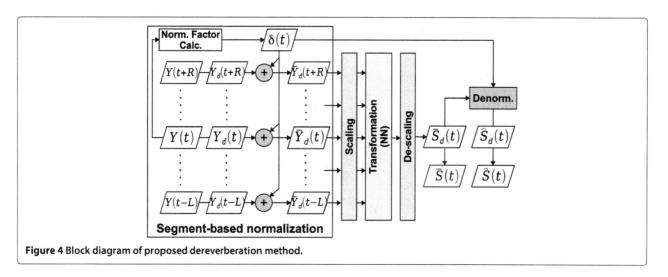

Figure 4 Block diagram of proposed dereverberation method.

Actually, the use of normalization factor $\delta(t)$ calculated from the reverberant feature vector (distant-talking speech utterance) is not the best way to calculate the estimation of clean feature vector (close-talking speech utterance) because the power levels of clean and reverberant signals are most likely not identical due to the influence of the RIR. However, the distant-talking speech utterance is the only input for the dereverberation method, and we assume that the distance is unknown, so the use of normalization factor $\delta(t)$ is the most reasonable way we can do to recover the power level of a frame relative to its surrounding frame. Thus, the estimation $\hat{S}(t)$ in Equation 20 can be regarded as an attenuated close-talking speech utterance. Although, it is not the best approach, the denormalization could remarkably improve the output, as can be seen in Figure 5.

Figure 5 shows spectrograms of an input and outputs of a dereverberation process. Utterance-based normalization (based on maximum value) was done in creating the spectrogram to ease the observation because there is power difference between close-talking speech utterance (clean feature vectors) and distant-talking speech utterance (reverberant feature vectors). Figure 5A shows the feature vectors of close-talking utterance, which was recorded from the distance of 25 cm. Figure 5B shows the feature vector of corresponding distant-talking utterance, which was recorded from the distance of about 4.0 m. Figure 5C,D are the dereverberated feature vectors without denormalization and with denormalization, respectively. We can observe that by using denormalization, we could get better estimation of the clean feature vectors, especially for non-speech segments. In Figure 5C,D, the difference of non-speech segments can be easily observed, for example, between frames 290 and 330 (in frames).

5.2 Feature scaling

The feature scaling consists of scaling and de-scaling processes. In general, the scaling and de-scaling can be regarded as the pre-processing and post-processing for the NNs. The scaling is done so that the NN input and output have values ranging from *about* -1 until 1. The constants τ and κ were used for this purpose, and the value of these constants were determined empirically from preliminary experiments. In contrast, the de-scaling is used to recover the log-melspectral coefficient value from its scaled value. The scaling and de-scaling are done using Equations 21 and 22, respectively.

$$\bar{Y}_d'(t-k) = \frac{\bar{Y}_d(t-k) + \tau}{2^\kappa}, \text{ for } -R \le k \le L, \quad (21)$$

$$\bar{S}_d(t) = \bar{S}_d'(t) * 2^\kappa - \tau. \quad (22)$$

5.3 Feature mapping using neural networks

In matrix form, Equation 14 could be written as

$$\hat{S} = G\,Y, \quad (23)$$

where $\hat{S}$ denotes the estimated anechoic feature vector, Y denotes the supervector which consists of reverberant feature vectors, and G denotes the transformation matrix which represents the RTF compensation. In our works, a non-linear regression is done to determine the function G such that

$$\underset{G}{\text{argmin}} \|S - (G \otimes Y)\|^2, \quad (24)$$

where S is the anechoic (reference) feature vector and $\otimes$ denotes a non-linear transformation. The regression is done by NN training algorithm and the NNs resulted from the training are used as the transformation function G. Thus, the NNs are the functions for mapping the reverberant feature vectors Y to the anechoic feature vector S.

We use cascade NNs trained using the Cascade2 algorithm. The algorithm is chosen because our task is a regression task and Cascade2 is better algorithm for the task than CasCor [36].

Figure 6 shows an illustration of cascade NN that we used in our works, with N input neurons, M hidden neurons, and one output neuron. Figure 7 shows the same NN in conventional MLP representation. The input neurons are represented by $y_1, y_2, \ldots, y_N$, the hidden neurons are represented by $h_1, h_2, \ldots, h_M$, and the output neuron is represented by s. Besides, we also use one bias neuron b. The neurons y_i and b are connected to $h_1, h_2, \ldots, h_M, s$ and the neuron s is connected to $y_1, y_2, \ldots, y_N, h_1, h_2, \ldots, h_M, b$. The connection weight between neuron n_1 and n_2 is represented by $w(n_1, n_2)$.

The NN input $y_1, y_2, \ldots, y_N$ in Figure 6 correspond to $\bar{Y}_d'(t-L), \ldots, \bar{Y}_d'(t-1), \bar{Y}_d'(t), \bar{Y}_d'(t+1), \ldots, \bar{Y}_d'(t+R)$ in Figure 4, which are the scaled value of the dereverberation input segment. While, the NN output s corresponds to $\bar{S}_d'(t)$, which is the scaled value of the estimated clean log-melspectral coefficient for frame t and dimension d.

We use the implementation of the Cascade2 algorithm with RPROP (resilient propagation) weight update algorithm, which is an advanced variation of batch backpropagation algorithm [35,42], in Fast Artificial Neural Network library (FANN) [43,44]. A linear activation function is used for the output neuron, while the hidden neurons use a symmetric sigmoid (tanh) function. For defining these hidden neurons, we use four options of steepness value, i.e., 0.25, 0.50, 0.75, and 1.00. The training algorithm will choose the best steepness value for each hidden neuron. Equation 25 expresses the linear activation function and Equation 26 expresses the tanh activation function, where

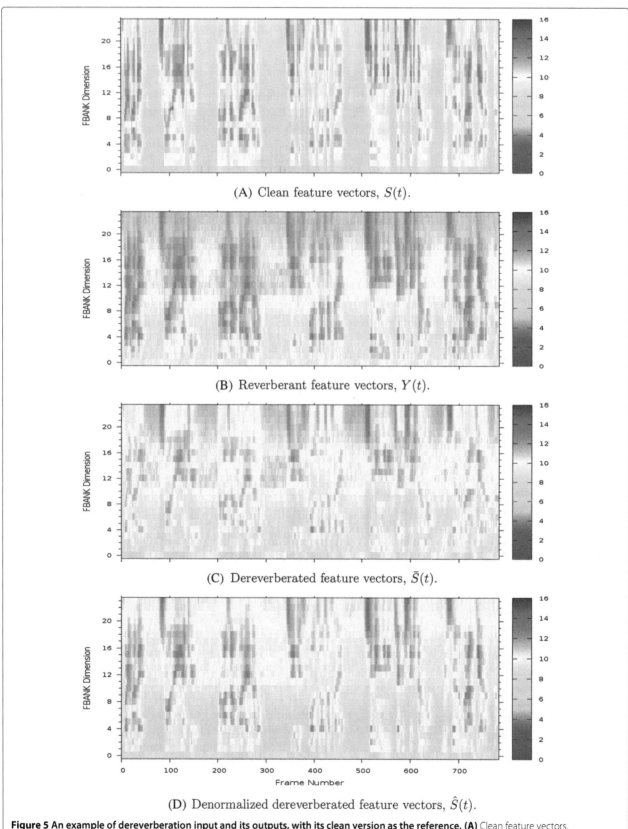

(A) Clean feature vectors, $S(t)$.

(B) Reverberant feature vectors, $Y(t)$.

(C) Dereverberated feature vectors, $\bar{S}(t)$.

(D) Denormalized dereverberated feature vectors, $\hat{S}(t)$.

Figure 5 An example of dereverberation input and its outputs, with its clean version as the reference. (A) Clean feature vectors.
(B) Reverberant feature vectors. **(C)** Dereverberated feature vectors. **(D)** Denormalized dereverberated feature vectors.

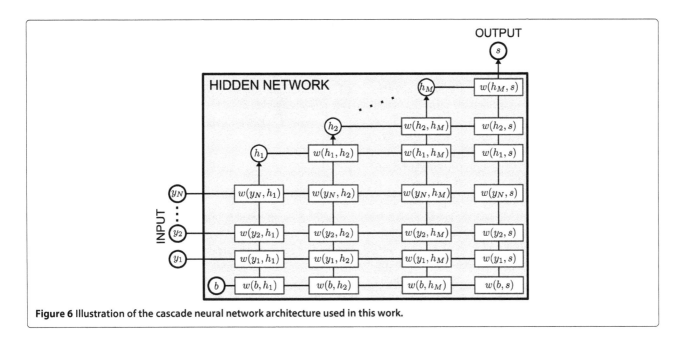

Figure 6 Illustration of the cascade neural network architecture used in this work.

x_{af} and y_{af} are the input and output of activation function, respectively, and z is the steepness.

$$y_{af} = zx_{af}, \tag{25}$$

$$y_{af} = \tanh(zx_{af}) = \frac{2}{1 + \exp(-2zx_{af})} - 1. \tag{26}$$

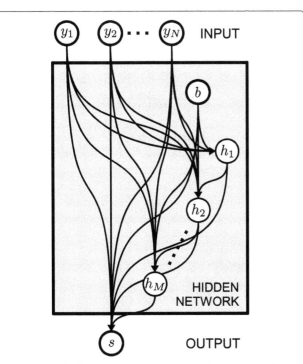

Figure 7 Illustration of the cascade neural network architecture used in this work depicted in conventional MLP representation.

Thus, the function of our output neuron s, which corresponds to $\hat{S}$, can be expressed as

$$s = z \left(\sum_{i=1}^{N} y_i w(y_i, s) + \sum_{j=1}^{M} h_j w(h_j, s) + w(b, s) \right), \tag{27}$$

where z is the activation function steepness, y_i are the input neurons, which corresponds to Y, $w(n1, n2)$ are the connection weights between neurons n_1 and n_2, b is the bias neuron, and h_j are the hidden neurons, whose function can be expressed as

$$h_j = \begin{cases} \tanh(zp) & \text{for } j = 1, \\ \tanh(zq) & \text{else,} \end{cases} \tag{28}$$

in which

$$p = \sum_{i=1}^{N} y_i w(y_i, h_j) + w(b, h_j), \tag{29}$$

$$q = \sum_{i=1}^{N} y_i w(y_i, h_j) + \sum_{k=1}^{j-1} h_k w(h_k, h_j) + w(b, h_j). \tag{30}$$

By using a linear activation function for the output neuron in the CasCor algorithm, it means that, initially, we use a linear regression to fit the transformation function. Then, it becomes a non-linear regression when the training process starts to add hidden neuron to the network.

We use several termination criteria for the training, i.e., maximum number of hidden neurons, maximum and minimum epochs for candidates and output training, and mean squared error. The number of hidden neurons is set proportionally to the number of NN inputs (neurons). Therefore, the size of network depends on the length of input segment. For the default configuration, we set the maximum number of hidden neurons to be equal to twice of the number of NN inputs ($M \leq 2N$). The number of hidden layers will be equal to the number of hidden neurons.

By using the above termination criteria of hidden neuron number, our NN will be compact. For example, if we use nine-frame segment of input, we use in total 29 neurons, consisting of 9 input neurons, 1 bias neuron, 18 hidden neurons, and 1 output neuron. In addition, from our experiments, we could have good performance by training this compact NN using relatively few training samples. It fits the statement in [37] that the CasCor algorithm can learn fast while still create a reasonably small network that *generalizes* well.

6 Evaluation using automatic speaker identification system

6.1 Overview of the automatic speaker identification system

Figure 8 depicts the general experimental setup used in the evaluation using the SID system. The NN training and feature mapping used 24-dimensional log-melspectral feature, while the speaker model training and identification used 12-dimensional melcepstral feature (MFCC). For these experiments, we needed to create three datasets, i.e., speaker model training dataset, NN training dataset, and testing dataset.

The figure also shows the use of CMN after cepstral feature extraction. For the experiments using real dataset, it is necessary to use CMN because we need to remove the noise and reverberation in the close-talking utterances used to train the speaker models. However, it may not necessary for the experiments using simulated dataset because we have anechoic utterances to train the speaker models. Nevertheless, we used CMN in the experiments using simulated dataset. For the experiments using real dataset, we experimented on the use of speaker models trained using original MFCC and also normalized MFCC (by CMN). Meanwhile, for the experiments using simulated dataset, we experimented on the use of speaker models trained using normalized MFCC only.

The SID system used speaker-specific GMMs as the speaker models [45]. Each speaker was represented by a D-variate GMM as

$$\lambda = \{c_i, \mu_i, \Sigma_i\}, \quad \text{for } i = 1, 2, \dots, M, \qquad (31)$$

where c_i is the mixture weight, μ_i is the mean vector, Σ_i is the covariance matrix, and M is the component number. In our experiments, $M = 32$ was used. GMM parameters were estimated using the standard maximum likelihood (ML) estimation method via the expectation maximization (EM) algorithm. For a sequence of T test vectors $X = x_1, x_2, \dots, x_T$, the GMM likelihood can be calculated using

$$L(X|\lambda) = \log p(X|\lambda) = \sum_{t=1}^{T} \log p(x_t|\lambda). \qquad (32)$$

GMM is used to model the speaker identity because the Gaussian components can represent some general speaker-dependent spectral shapes and the Gaussian mixtures can model arbitrary densities [46]. In this work, we focused on developing a dereverberation approach, instead of improving the identification accuracy based on discriminative classification approach, so the use of GMM approach should be sufficient for our purpose in evaluating the proposed dereverberation method. Consideration of the state-of-the-art in speaker identification is beyond the scope of this work.

Voice activity detection (VAD) was also employed to remove the silence parts in the beginning and ending of recordings. For the simulated reverberant data, the VAD was done automatically on the melcepstral domain based on the frame log-energy coefficients. While, for the real reverberant data, the VAD was done manually by hand because the SNRs were low in utterances recorded from very distant position, e.g., from 4.0 m, and made our current automatic VAD unreliable.

6.2 Experiments using simulated reverberant data

6.2.1 Dataset description

The clean speech data was taken from the newspaper reading part of JNAS database [47]. The speech data of 100 male speakers were used. In average, each speaker has 105 utterances. The RIR and noise data were taken from Aurora-5 [48], while the simulation program was SImulation of REal Acoustics (SIREAC) [49,50]. The simulation program was used to generate the reverberant speech data from the clean speech and the RIR. The program can also add additive noise to the signal.

We created the simulated reverberant data by using the RIR of 'office' and 'livingroom' with reverberation time (T_{60}) of 400 ms. Besides, we also created a simulated noisy reverberant data by adding noise of 'office' with signal-to-noise ratio (SNR) of 20 and 10 dB to the 'office' reverberant data.

6.2.2 Experimental setup

The GMMs for the speaker identification system was trained using 500 clean utterances (100 speakers, 5 utterances for each speaker). The utterances were selected

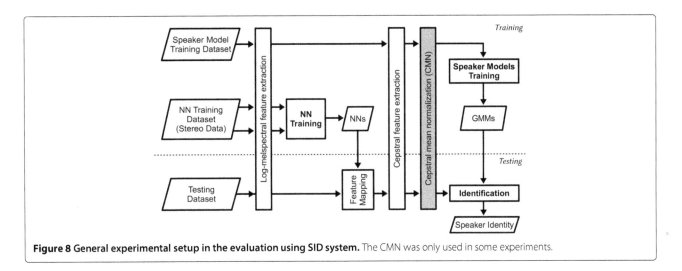

Figure 8 General experimental setup in the evaluation using SID system. The CMN was only used in some experiments.

randomly but constrained by the file size requirement so that the average duration of the utterances after VAD was about 3 s. CMN was also employed as pre-processing of GMM training data.

A pool of training data was created for each environment. This pool of data consisted of 25 pairs of clean utterance and simulated (noisy) reverberant utterance. The utterances were selected randomly but constrained by the file size requirement so that the average duration of the utterances after VAD was about 7 s. From this pool of training data, '1u' (1 pair of utterances by 1 speaker), '5u' (5 pairs of utterances by 5 speakers), '10u' (10 pairs of utterances by 10 speakers), and '15u' (15 pairs of utterances by 15 speakers) NN training datasets were created.

A testing dataset was also created for each type of simulated (noisy) reverberant data. Each dataset consisted of 1,000 simulated (noisy) reverberant utterances (100 speakers, 10 utterances for each speaker). The utterances were selected randomly but constrained by the file size requirement so that the average duration of the utterances after VAD was about 5 s. Note that the utterances in the testing dataset contained different contents (sentences) from the utterances used to train the GMMs.

The experiments were done by using causal reverberation model (using left context only) and non-causal reverberation model (using left and right context) on known environments (matched conditions). We did experiments on the use of single NN (1 NN for 24 feature dimensions) and multiple NNs (1 NN for 1 feature dimension) configurations. In addition, we did experiments using linear and skip1 frame selection.

The NN training used random weight initialization, and variations in the final NN were not unexpected. All experimental results below show the average of three experimental results, where each experiment consists of training phase and testing phase.

6.2.3 Experimental results

The baseline for each type of simulated (noisy) reverberant data is shown in Table 1. For the noisy reverberant, we only experimented on the RIR of 'office', so the baseline for the RIR of 'livingroom' is not available. The identification rate for the clean version of testing dataset was 98.0%. Note that we can regard this baseline as the result of enhancement using CMN because it was used as pre-processing of GMM training data.

We used several frame selection numbers in the experiments. In the experimental result tables, we divided the frame selection numbers into three groups, i.e., (1) left context only (L), (2) left and right context (L+R), and (3) left and shorter right context (L+sR). Group L represents the causal reverberation model, while group L+R and group L+sR represent the non-causal reverberation model. Our hypothesis in deriving the non-causal model was that the early reflections part still has considerable amount of energy. That was why the addition of short right context to the left context should be enough. The italicized text in Tables 2 and 3 represents the best performance for each training data number in a frame selection number group. The bold and italicized text represents the best performance for each training data number regardless the frame selection number group.

For a limited number of stereo data, we believed that the performance of feature mapping depends on the context

Table 1 Speaker identification baseline for each type of simulated (noisy) reverberant data

RIR			Speaker identification rate (%)		
			Reverb.	Noisy reverberant	
Type	T_{60} (ms)	Clean	SNR = ∞	SNR = 20 dB	SNR = 10 dB
Office	400	98.0	74.3	55.3	20.6
Livingroom			70.9	–	–

Table 2 Experimental results by using simulated reverberant data

				Speaker identification rate (%)													
			Left context only (L)					Left+right context (L+R)					Left+short right context (L+sR)				
NN conf.	RIR	Frame sel. type	Frame sel.	Training data				Frame sel.	Training data				Frame sel.	Training data			
				1u	5u	10u	15u		1u	5u	10u	15u		1u	5u	10u	15u
Multiple NNs	Office	Linear	3-1-0	71.6	76.7	76.8	77.0	–	–	–	–	–	–	–	–	–	–
			7-1-0	59.9	79.6	81.7	81.9	3-1-3	70.0	82.3	82.7	83.1	–	–	–	–	–
			15-1-0	33.4	65.3	78.8	80.9	7-1-7	55.5	76.9	83.3	85.1	7-1-3	56.2	81.3	85.4	85.8
		Skip1	3-1-0	**74.4**	79.5	79.4	80.1	–	–	–	–	–	–	–	–	–	–
			7-1-0	57.1	81.3	82.4	84.0	3-1-3	69.2	**83.8**	**85.8**	86.1	–	–	–	–	–
			–	–	–	–	–	7-1-7	52.7	72.0	82.2	85.0	7-1-3	59.1	83.1	85.7	**87.1**
	Livingroom	Linear	3-1-0	60.1	69.6	70.6	70.8	–	–	–	–	–	–	–	–	–	–
			7-1-0	52.3	76.0	78.1	78.9	3-1-3	52.3	75.4	75.8	75.7	–	–	–	–	–
			15-1-0	23.6	58.4	72.2	76.5	7-1-7	35.5	62.4	74.4	78.4	7-1-3	32.5	74.1	79.4	81.1
		Skip1	3-1-0	**63.2**	74.0	74.1	74.5	–	–	–	–	–	–	–	–	–	–
			7-1-0	39.8	75.5	78.8	79.7	3-1-3	52.4	**77.8**	79.5	79.1	–	–	–	–	–
			–	–	–	–	–	7-1-7	25.6	61.3	74.6	79.2	7-1-3	32.5	72.2	79.6	**82.1**
Single NN	Livingroom	Linear	3-1-0	64.9	71.6	70.6	71.3	–	–	–	–	–	–	–	–	–	–
			7-1-0	71.8	75.4	75.4	75.4	3-1-3	72.0	75.4	74.9	74.0	–	–	–	–	–
			15-1-0	70.5	77.0	77.2	77.7	7-1-7	73.6	77.5	79.2	78.4	7-1-3	**76.9**	77.8	78.8	78.6
		Skip1	3-1-0	71.1	73.4	74.3	74.4	–	–	–	–	–	–	–	–	–	–
			7-1-0	72.6	75.9	76.1	76.2	3-1-3	73.7	76.2	76.2	77.0	–	–	–	–	–
			–	–	–	–	–	7-1-7	71.4	79.3	79.5	**79.9**	7-1-3	74.6	**79.6**	**79.7**	79.7

Table 3 Experimental results by using simulated noisy reverberant data (RIR = 'office')

			Speaker identification rate (%)														
			Left context only (L)					Left+right context (L+R)					Left+short right context (L+sR)				
			Frame sel.	Training data				Frame sel.	Training data				Frame sel.	Training data			
NN conf.	RIR	Frame sel. type		1u	5u	10u	15u		1u	5u	10u	15u		1u	5u	10u	15u
	20 dB	Linear	3-1-0	**53.0**	59.0	63.5	61.8	–	–	–	–	–	–	–	–	–	–
			7-1-0	38.9	60.5	62.9	64.6	3-1-3	42.3	**64.9**	**66.6**	65.4	–	–	–	–	–
			15-1-0	15.3	40.7	55.1	60.5	7-1-7	24.7	50.8	61.8	65.7	7-1-3	27.8	58.6	65.8	67.0
		Skip1	3-1-0	48.6	58.8	63.4	62.2	–	–	–	–	–	–	–	–	–	–
			7-1-0	32.1	60.5	61.8	62.9	3-1-3	46.3	63.1	66.0	67.0	–	–	–	–	–
			–	–	–	–	–	7-1-7	22.7	45.8	57.3	62.9	7-1-3	27.6	54.1	66.2	**67.1**
Multiple NNs	10 dB	Linear	3-1-0	20.7	34.8	32.0	35.7	–	–	–	–	–	–	–	–	–	–
			7-1-0	18.3	34.1	37.6	38.4	3-1-3	25.6	**37.4**	38.6	41.1	–	–	–	–	–
			15-1-0	3.2	20.4	31.7	33.9	7-1-7	6.1	25.2	36.9	41.0	7-1-3	10.1	32.3	**40.8**	**42.8**
		Skip1	3-1-0	**31.9**	32.1	34.1	35.1	–	–	–	–	–	–	–	–	–	–
			7-1-0	13.2	32.0	36.5	37.0	3-1-3	20.7	37.3	39.8	41.3	–	–	–	–	–
			–	–	–	–	–	7-1-7	6.2	19.8	31.4	37.2	7-1-3	8.1	32.5	37.5	41.2

length represented by the frame selection. Based on the context length it represents, the frame selection numbers used in these experiments could be divided into:

- Short context (<100 ms): linear 3-1-0 (55 ms of context), linear 7-1-0 (95 ms), linear 3-1-3 (85 ms), and skip1 3-1-0 (85 ms).
- Medium context (100 to 200 ms): linear 15-1-0 (175 ms), linear 7-1-7 (165 ms), linear 7-1-3 (125 ms), skip1 7-1-0 (165 ms), and skip1 3-1-3 (145 ms).
- Long context (>200 ms): skip1 7-1-7 (305 ms), skip1 7-1-3 (225 ms).

In general, the feature mapping using short context could perform well. It could be improved by using medium or long context as long as the NN training data is sufficient because the use of longer context will make the NN vulnerable to high variance (overfitting) problem, where the use of more NN training data might help.

We can observe that the skip1 frame selection could almost always outperform the linear frame selection for the simulated noiseless reverberant data (Table 2). While for the simulated noisy reverberant data (Table 3), the linear frame selection was better, although the skip1 frame selection could be better for some cases.

We can also observe that we could get better performance by adding the right context. The use of left context only (group L) was the best for the small training dataset ('1u'), but for the other training datasets, the use of right context (group L+R and L+sR) could perform better. When multiple NNs configuration is used, the group L+sR could always be the best for the '15u' dataset and almost always be the best for the '10u' dataset.

In Table 2, we can observe that the single NN (1 NN) configuration was better than the multiple NNs (24 NNs) configuration for the '1u' and '5u' training datasets. For the bigger datasets, the best performance of single NN configuration could not surpass the best performance of multiple NNs configuration. In fact, the addition of training data number did not affect the performance of single NN configuration and we can observe it on each frame selection number. By using single NN configuration, it means that the NN training dataset contains the data of 24 dimensions of log-melspectral features and the NN training generalized the RTF of these 24 feature dimensions. For small training dataset, it is beneficial because we could have sufficient training dataset for training an NN. At least, it could prevent us from overfitting problem. However, if we have much more training data, the RTF generalization over 24 dimensions is not good enough because the RTF should be frequency-dependent. Consequently, the performance of single NN can not surpass the performance of multiple NNs when many

training data were used. Therefore, the multiple NNs configuration should be the best choice, especially if the NN training data is sufficient. For the single NN configuration, the combination of the use of left and right context with skip1 frame selection was almost always give the best performance for each NN training data size.

6.3 Experiments using real reverberant data
6.3.1 Dataset description

The real reverberant data used in these experiments was recorded in a recording room whose dimensions were about $5 \times 6.4 \times 2.65$ m, as depicted in Figure 9 [51,52]. There were eight T-shape microphone arrays installed in the room, and each array was consisted of four microphones. Half of the arrays were installed on the ceiling, and the other half were on the wall. There was no material that was intentionally installed to reduce reverberation or noise, except the materials for microphone array that was used to place the microphones. The reverberation time was approximately 330 ms and the background noise was approximately 35 dBA, measured from the middle of the room (denoted by 'RIR' in Figure 9). The recording process was done using 32-channel recording system with 16 kHz sampling rate.

We created two real reverberant datasets in the recording room as described above. Both datasets consisted of close-talking utterances, which were recorded from the distance of 25 cm, and distant-talking utterances, which uttered from five different positions (P01 to P05) and captured by eight microphone arrays. However, for the experiments which are presented here, we only considered the first microphone of microphone array A (hereafter, simply referred as microphone A). Figure 9 shows the speaker positions, the microphone A position, and also rough distance between the speaker and the microphone.

The distances from P01, P02, P03, P04, and P05 to microphone A were about 4.0, 2.5, 2.2, 2.2, and 1.5 m, respectively. Theoretically, the direct-to-reverberant ratios (DRRs) of these distant-talking recordings were small because the distances were greater than the critical distance for the room, which is around 0.9 m (calculated using approximation of Sabine's formula [53]).

The first dataset was a non-stereo dataset. It contained two sessions of 20 speakers' recordings where each speaker uttered 10 utterances from each position in each session. In this dataset, there were also close-talking utterances (25 cm), but they were not simultaneously recorded with the distant-talking utterances. Besides, there were also utterances recorded from the distance of 50 cm, but we did not use this data. Thus, for these experiments, there were 2,000 distant-talking utterances (2 sessions $\times$ 20 speakers $\times$ 10 utterances $\times$ 5 positions) and 400 close-talking utterances (2 sessions $\times$ 20

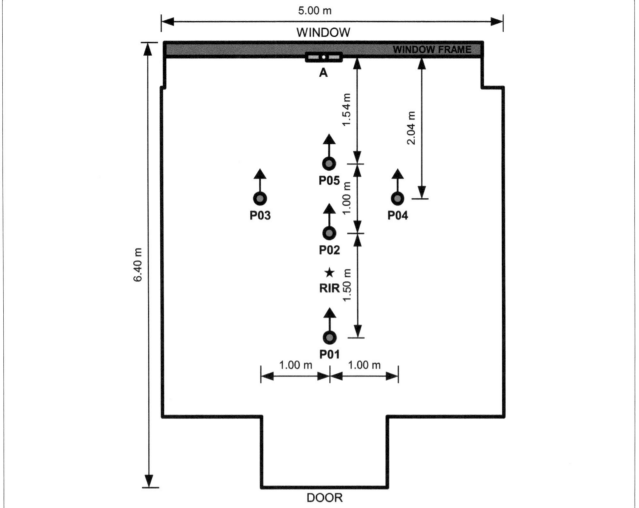

Figure 9 Illustration of the recording room used in acquiring the real reverberant data. 'P01' until 'P05' denote the speaker positions, while 'A' denotes the microphone position. The arrows represent the face direction of the speakers.

speakers × 10 utterances). This dataset was also used in [26].

The second dataset was a stereo dataset, where the close-talking and distant-talking utterances were recorded simultaneously. It contains one session of three speakers' recordings where each speaker uttered 10 utterances from each position. Thus, for these experiments, there were 150 pairs of distant-talking and close-talking utterances (1 session × 3 speakers × 10 utterances × 5 positions).

6.3.2 Experimental setup

The GMMs for the SID system were trained using 10 close-talking utterances from the non-stereo dataset for each speaker. We used two schemes for training the GMMs. Consequently, there were also two schemes in creating the testing dataset which consisted of 200 distant-talking utterances (20 speakers × 10 utterances) for each position.

- First scheme: the training data for GMMs consisted of the first five utterances (utterance A0-A4) from two sessions, while the testing data consisted of the second five utterances (utterance A5-A9) from two sessions.
- Second scheme: the training data for GMMs consisted of 10 utterances (utterance A0-A9) from the first session, while the testing data consisted of 10 utterances (utterance A0-A9) from the second session.

By using the first scheme, we could show that the SID system was text-independent because the sentences of the training dataset and testing dataset were completely different. However, the second scheme could represent a real application better, where the data of an earlier session was used as the training dataset and the later session was used as the testing dataset, although the contents of training and testing utterances are the same.

The NN training datasets were created using utterances from the stereo dataset. Although they were recorded from the distance of 25 cm, we regarded the close-talking utterances as our clean speech signals and tried to map the distant-talking utterances to close-talking utterances using NNs. The NN training datasets were created for each position and consisted of one or five pairs of utterances (utterance A0-A4) from each speaker. We defined three kinds of dataset, i.e., '1s.1u' (1 pair of utterances, 1 speaker), '1s.5u' (5 pairs, 1 speaker), and '3s.15u' (15 pairs, 3 speakers). The average duration of the training utterances after VAD was about 6.3 s. Thus, the '1s.1u', '1s.5u', and '3s.15u' datasets correspond to about 6.3, 32, and 94 s of speech signal, respectively.

We did preliminary experiments by using small NN training dataset, including '1s.1u' dataset, which contained only one pair of utterances. By using this constraint, we experimented on modified multiple NN by modifying our assumptions on the transformation of each feature dimension. In these experiments, we only considered position P01, P02, and P05.

In the next experiments, we divided the data into known conditions/positions (P01, P03, P05) and unknown conditions/positions (P02 and P04). By using the known conditions, we created position-specific and combined NN training data. Then, the NNs were used to dereverberate the known conditions and also the unknown conditions.

Besides, we tried to employ a decision-making process on which known condition was the most similar to the condition of particular input (utterance) by using environment models (GMMs), which were trained using the same data for training the position-specific NNs. It can also be seen as a way to choose the best NN sets to be used. Let $Y_t = [Y_{t,1} \ Y_{t,2} \ \cdots \ Y_{t,d}]^T$ be a d-dimensional log-melspectral feature vector for frame t. We created supervector $\hat{Y}_t = [Y_{t+N-1} \ Y_{t+N-2} \ \cdots \ Y_t]^T$ and then normalized it using segment-based normalization (as in Subsection 5.1) relative to the latest frame (Y_{t+N-1}). In the experiments, we used $d = 24$ and $N = 8$. Thus, the supervector $\hat{Y}_t$ was a 192-dimensional feature vector and the environment models (GMMs) were trained using this supervector. By using 32-mixture GMM λ for each known condition (position), the likelihood of an utterance $Y = Y_1, Y_2, \ldots, Y_T$ was determined using $\hat{Y} = \hat{Y}_1, \hat{Y}_2, \ldots, \hat{Y}_{T-N+1}$ as

$$L(Y|\lambda) = \log p(\hat{Y}|\lambda) = \sum_{t=1}^{T-N+1} \log p(\hat{Y}_t|\lambda). \qquad (33)$$

Thus, for each input utterance, we calculate the GMM likelihood of each known condition (position). Then, we selected the condition (position) having the highest likelihood from the likelihood calculation result and used

its position-specific NN sets to do feature mapping on the input.

In other words, we tried to determine the most appropriate position-specific NNs to be used by evaluating segments of the input utterance using the environment models (GMMs). The GMM itself tried to model the RTF for each known reverberant environment (position). It is impossible to capture the characteristic of reverberant environment (RTF) by using a single frame, so we used the GMM to model segments (eight-frame, corresponds to 95 ms of context) of reverberant utterances. However, by using segment, the approach will be text-dependent because the segment is long enough to capture one or more phonemes, which are also affected by the adjacent phonemes beyond the segment length. Therefore, it is important to do the experiment using the first scheme of training and testing, where the spoken utterances of training and testing were different. In addition, it is possible to improve the approach by training and evaluating using segments which are ended by silence only.

As comparison, we tried to implement the mapping method on *melcepstrum (MFCC) domain* using MLP network proposed in [25]. Because we only use 12-dimensional MFCC for the identification, we only created 12 MLPs, instead of 13 MLPs. Moreover, there was no further explanation about the frame selection used in [25], so we did two implementations, i.e., by using linear frame selection 8-1-0 and 4-1-4.

All experimental results below show the average performance of several experiments. For the preliminary experiments (**Fundamental results**), the experimental results of '1s.1u' represent the average of 45 experiments (3 speakers × 5 utterances/speaker × 3 experiment sets) and the experimental results of '1s.5u' represent the average of 9 experiments (3 speakers × 3 experiment sets). For the use of '1s.5u' dataset in the other experiments (**Position-dependent/independent results**), we calculated the average of three experimental results for each training speaker, and then we average them. Thus, they also represent the average of nine experiments. While for all use of '3s.15u' dataset, we calculated the average of three experimental results. Thus, they represent the average of three experiments.

6.3.3 Experimental results

Fundamental results Table 4 shows the baseline for the first and second scheme of GMM training and testing. The tables also show the result of CMN enhancement.

The baselines for both schemes were quite low. Note that the speaker model trained using utterances recorded from the distance of 25 cm, which most likely contained noise and reverberation. The CMN was very effective to

Table 4 Baseline for the speaker identification experiments using the real reverberant data

Experiment scheme	Method	Speaker identification rate (%)							
		P01	P03	P05	P02	P04	Avg. known	Avg. unknown	Avg. all
I	Baseline	45.0	49.0	45.5	44.0	46.0	46.5	45.0	45.9
	CMN	83.0	88.0	91.5	93.0	90.0	87.5	91.5	89.1
II	Baseline	45.0	50.5	54.0	55.5	49.5	49.8	52.5	50.9
	CMN	84.0	89.5	91.0	91.5	89.5	88.2	90.5	89.1

The known environments include P01, P03, and P05, while the unknown environments include P02 and P04.

remove that distortions and improve the speaker identification rate. The CMN could reach 79.9% and 77.8% of ERR relative to the baseline for the first and second testing schemes, respectively. By using CMN, the identification rates for the close-talking version of testing dataset were 99.5% and 100% for the first and second schemes, respectively. For the evaluation using SID system, our proposed method could also perform very well when combined with CMN and was not effective when it worked alone, as shown later.

Table 5 shows our first experimental results using the real reverberant data. The experiments used the first scheme on creating the GMM training dataset and testing dataset. Besides, we only considered the utterances from positions P01, P02, and P05, because these three positions and microphone A were in-line and the speakers' utterances were directed to microphone A.

Similar to the experiment results using the simulated reverberant data, the multiple NNs configuration showed better performance for the '3s.15u' dataset but worse for the '1s.1u' and '1s.1u' datasets. Therefore, we tried to look for a good performance trade-off for all datasets by using

modified multiple NNs configuration, where one NN was used for more than one dimension of feature. In our experiments, the number of dimension in each NN was divided evenly. For example, in six NNs configuration, the first NN was for the dimension 1-4 of 24-dimensional log-melspectral feature, the second NN was for 5-8, and so on. It meant that we assumed that the RTF for the dimension 1-4 was the same, the RTF for the dimension 5-8 was the same, and so on.

Table 5 shows the experimental results in terms of ERR relative to the CMN for the use of causal skip1 3-1-0 frame selection (corresponds to 85 ms of context). '1 NN' represents the single NN configuration, and '24 NNs' represents the *original* multiple NNs configuration.

We can observe that the use of modified multiple NNs configuration ('6 NNs' and '12 NNs') could be better than single NN configuration ('1 NN') and also original multiple NNs configuration ('24 NNs'). The averages of ERR (relative to the CMN) across the types of dataset for the '6 NNs' and '12 NNs' configuration were 41.7% and 41.1%. So, the '6 NNs' configuration gave us the best trade-off. Comparing to '1 NN' configuration, '6 NNs' significantly

Table 5 Experimental results on the use of modified multiple NNs configuration for known positions (matched conditions)

Method	Dataset	Error rate reduction (%)			
		P01	P02	P05	Avg.
Proposed (1 NN) + CMN	1s.1u	30.8	19.4	21.7	24.0
	1s.5u	34.7	27.8	23.5	28.7
	3s.15u	35.4	33.3	23.5	30.8
Proposed (6 NNs) + CMN	1s.1u	40.8	44.0	19.7	**34.8**
	1s.5u	45.5	62.7	16.3	41.5
	3s.15u	51.0	71.4	23.5	48.7
Proposed (12 NNs) + CMN	1s.1u	33.0	33.7	22.9	29.8
	1s.5u	40.6	54.0	32.0	**42.2**
	3s.15u	55.2	71.4	27.5	**51.4**
Proposed (24 NNs) + CMN	1s.1u	17.9	2.5	10.5	10.3
	1s.5u	30.2	31.0	22.2	27.8
	3s.15u	46.9	42.9	13.7	34.5

The experiments were done by using the first testing scheme and skip1 3-1-0 frame selection. The results are shown in term of ERR relative to the 'CMN'. The bold text represents the best average performance for each training data number.

improved the performance of '1s.5u' and '1s.1u' datasets. Surprisingly, comparing to '24 NNs' configuration, it also improved the performance of '3s.15u' dataset. The averages of ERR (relative to the CMN) for '1s.1u', '1s.5u', and '3s.15u' were 34.8%, 41.5%, and 48.7%, respectively. In ddition, we could get better performance for '3s.15u' dataset by using '12 NNs' configuration, where its average ERR was 51.4%.

Position-dependent/independent results For the next experiments, we considered the utterances from all positions but divided the data into known conditions/positions (P01, P03, P05) and unknown conditions/positions (P02, P04). The data of known conditions is used for training and/or testing, while the data of unknown conditions is used for testing only.

Table 6 shows the experimental results by using position-specific training data for the first testing scheme. In these experiments, the NN sets were trained using the utterances from one position and then were used to dereverberate the utterances from all positions (including the position used for training).

Table 6 shows that by using '1s.5u' datasets, the average identification rates of '24 NNs', '12 NNs', and '6 NNs' configurations for matched conditions were 88.4%, 90.3%, and 90.3%. While, by using '3s.15u' datasets, the

average identification rates were 93.2%, 93.7%, and 92.2%. Besides the experiment using the first scheme, we also did it using the second scheme. For the '1s.5u' datasets, the '6 NNs' configuration performed best in the first and second schemes. Meanwhile, for the '3s.15u' datasets, the '12 NNs' configuration performed best in the first scheme and the '24 NNs' performed best in the second scheme.

From Table 6, we can also observe that the use of utterances from one position could perform reasonably well for the other (unknown) positions in the room. We can observe that by using more training data, we could improve the performance. Comparing to the identification rate of CMN (Table 4), the total averages of identification rate were often worse for '1s.5u' datasets but always better for the '3s.15u' datasets. It is similar as the experimental results for the matched conditions as discussed above. Besides, we can observe that the use of utterances from position P05 as NN training data could perform better than, or at least could perform as good as, the use of utterances from other positions. Moreover, by using a small dataset ('1s.5u') of position P05, we could get a reasonably good performance.

For Tables 7 and 8, we combined the utterances from known positions (P01, P03, P05) into a training dataset. Therefore, we created '1s.15u' dataset ('1s.5u' dataset × 3

Table 6 Experimental results by using position-specific training data

Method	Dataset		Speaker identification rate (%)							
			P01	P03	P05	P02	P04	Avg. known	Avg. unknown	Avg. all
Proposed (24 NNs) + CMN	P01	1s.5u	85.8*	86.0	85.9	87.1	85.5	85.8	86.1	86.1
		3s.15u	91.8*	91.8	92.0	93.2	90.0	91.8	91.8	91.8
	P03	1s.5u	84.0	86.8*	85.2	88.1	88.6	86.8	86.5	86.5
		3s.15u	90.3	92.7*	93.5	94.8	92.8	92.7	92.9	92.8
	P05	1s.5u	88.8	91.2	92.7*	93.3	89.7	92.7	90.8	91.1
		3s.15u	90.3	93.0	95.0*	96.2	91.7	95.0	92.8	93.2
Proposed (12 NNs) + CMN	P01	1s.5u	88.8*	88.6	88.6	89.9	90.4	88.8	89.4	89.3
		3s.15u	93.5*	94.3	94.2	95.0	93.3	93.5	94.2	94.1
	P03	1s.5u	87.8	89.6*	89.3	90.7	92.3	89.6	90.0	89.9
		3s.15u	91.5	94.7*	94.3	95.0	94.2	94.7	93.8	**93.9**
	P05	1s.5u	89.9	92.5	92.4*	94.2	92.7	92.4	92.3	**92.3**
		3s.15u	91.5	93.2	92.8*	96.5	92.7	92.8	93.5	93.3
Proposed (6 NNs) + CMN	P01	1s.5u	89.5*	88.4	87.9	90.9	91.7	89.5	89.7	89.7
		3s.15u	92.2*	91.7	91.0	94.7	93.3	92.2	92.7	92.6
	P03	1s.5u	89.1	89.7*	88.4	91.0	92.7	89.7	90.3	90.2
		3s.15u	91.5	92.0*	92.0	95.0	93.8	92.0	93.0	92.9
	P05	1s.5u	90.1	91.4	91.7*	94.7	93.4	91.7	92.4	**92.3**
		3s.15u	92.5	93.2	92.3*	96.3	94.2	92.3	94.0	93.7

The known environments include P01, P03, and P05, while the unknown environments include P02 and P04. The experiments were done by using the first testing scheme and skip1 7-1-0 frame selection. The asterisks (*) indicate known positions (matched conditions). The bold text represents the best average performance for each training data number.

Table 7 Experimental results by using combined training data (three known positions) on the first testing scheme

Method	Dataset		Speaker identification rate (%)							
			P01	P03	P05	P02	P04	Avg. known	Avg. unknown	Avg. all
Prop. (24 NNs) + CMN	combd	1s.15u	88.9	90.4	93.9	93.8	90.2	91.1	92.0	91.4
		3s.45u	90.5	93.7	94.5	96.2	92.0	92.9	94.1	93.4
Prop. (12 NNs) + CMN	combd	1s.15u	90.9	92.5	93.0	94.2	92.2	92.1	93.2	**92.6**
		3s.45u	93.5	94.8	94.2	96.2	93.2	94.2	94.7	**94.4**
Prop. (6 NNs) + CMN	combd	1s.15u	90.8	91.2	91.6	94.4	93.8	91.2	94.1	92.4
		3s.45u	92.7	92.2	92.5	96.0	94.0	92.4	95.0	93.5

The known environments include P01, P03, and P05, while the unknown environments include P02 and P04. The experiments were done by using skip1 7-1-0 frame selection. The bold text represents the best average performance for each training data number.

positions) and '3s.45u' dataset ('3s.15u' dataset × 3 positions). From Table 6, the use of 15 pairs of utterances as NN training data ('15u') seems enough for our method to perform well. So, one possibility that may make a difference of performance between '1s.15u' and '3s.45u' datasets is speaker variation in the NN training data. However, these two types of combined datasets could perform well, and the performance difference between both datasets was not significant. For the first scheme, the total average identification rates were 91.4% to 94.4%, which is 21.1% to 48.6% of ERR relative to the CMN. Meanwhile, for the second scheme, the total average identification rates were 92.6% to 94.8%, which corresponds to 32.1% to 52.3% of ERR relative to the CMN. Thus, eventually, the similarity of utterances' content between training and testing data was affecting the performance. In addition, similar as experimental results shown in Table 6, the '12 NNs' and '24 NNs' configurations performed best in the first and second schemes, respectively.

The identification rates for unknown conditions were also improved. It shows that by combining the training data from known positions in a room, we could train NN sets which generalize well, so that the NN sets could also perform well for unknown positions in the same room.

Table 9 shows the performance of GMM as position-specific NNs selector. We can compare it to the performance of combining training data approach (Table 7). For '6 NNs' configuration, both approaches showed similar performance. However, for '12 NNs' and '24 NNs' configuration, the combining training data approach could perform better. Besides, we could also compare it to the results of matched condition cases in Table 6.

Table 9 shows that by using '1s.5u' datasets, the average identification rates of '24 NNs', '12 NNs', and '6 NNs' configurations for known conditions were 90.5%, 91.4%, and 91.1%. Meanwhile, by using '3s.15u' datasets, the average identification rates were 92.4%, 93.0%, and 92.2%. Thus, we could see that the use of environment models (GMMs) as NNs selector could actually perform well because it could perform as good as the matched condition case, especially for the small datasets ('1s.5u'). However, the combining training data approach (Table 7) was slightly better than the use of environment models (GMMs).

Comparison to the feature mapping on MFCC domain
In addition, we implemented the mapping method on melcepstrum (MFCC) domain by MLP network as proposed in [25] and experimented by using position-specific training data. For the first testing scheme, the average identification rates of 'linear 8-1-0' and 'linear 4-1-4' frame selections for matched conditions were 69.7% and 76.2% by using '1s.5u' datasets and 78.5% and 82.1% by using '3s.15u' datasets. Meanwhile, for the second scheme, they were 74.1% and 78.9% by using '1s.5u' datasets and 79.2% and 83.0% by using '3s.15u' datasets. Thus, our proposed

Table 8 Experimental results by using combined training data (three known positions) on the second testing scheme

Method	Dataset		Speaker identification rate (%)							
			P01	P03	P05	P02	P04	Avg. known	Avg. unknown	Avg. all
Prop. (24 NNs) + CMN	combd	1s.15u	89.7	92.4	94.6	96.9	91.0	92.2	94.0	**92.9**
		3s.45u	91.5	92.8	95.8	99.0	92.7	93.4	95.8	**94.4**
Prop. (12 NNs) + CMN	combd	1s.15u	89.5	92.4	93.6	96.1	91.6	91.8	93.9	92.6
		3s.45u	90.5	92.2	94.5	98.0	92.5	92.4	95.3	93.5
Prop. (6 NNs) + CMN	combd	1s.15u	90.5	90.8	93.7	94.8	93.5	91.7	94.2	92.7
		3s.45u	91.5	92.0	95.0	96.0	93.0	92.8	94.5	93.5

The known environments include P01, P03, and P05, while the unknown environments include P02 and P04. The experiments were done by using skip1 8-1-0 frame selection. The bold text represents the best average performance for each training data number.

Table 9 Experimental results by using environment models (GMMs) as NNs selector

Method	Dataset		Speaker identification rate (%)							
			P01	P03	P05	P02	P04	Avg. known	Avg. unknown	Avg. all
GMM32 + Prop. (24 NNs) + CMN	P01/3/5	1s.5u	88.6	90.2	92.8	93.4	90.0	90.5	91.7	91.0
		3s.15u	89.5	93.3	94.3	95.3	91.0	92.4	93.2	92.7
GMM32 + Prop. (12 NNs) + CMN	P01/3/5	1s.5u	89.4	92.3	92.4	93.5	92.5	91.4	93.0	92.0
		3s.15u	91.7	93.5	93.8	96.5	93.5	93.0	95.0	**93.8**
GMM32 + Prop. (6 NNs) + CMN	P01/3/5	1s.5u	90.4	90.9	91.9	94.3	93.7	91.1	94.0	**92.2**
		3s.15u	92.0	92.7	92.0	96.7	94.2	92.2	95.4	93.5

The known environments include P01, P03, and P05, while the unknown environments include P02 and P04. The experiments were done by using the first testing scheme and skip1 7-1-0 frame selection. The bold text represents the best average performance for each training data number.

method is much better. In fact, the mapping method by MLP network could not be better than the use of CMN alone. Nevertheless, these experiments also show that the use of right context is beneficial.

7 Evaluation using automatic speech recognition system

7.1 Overview of CENSREC-4

CENSREC-4 is an evaluation framework for distant-talking speech recognition in reverberant environments [22]. The task in CENSREC-4 is grammar-based connected digit recognition. The vocabulary consists of eleven Japanese numbers: 'ichi', 'ni', 'san', 'yon', 'go', 'roku', 'nana', 'hachi', 'kyu', 'zero', and 'maru'. All recordings are sampled at 16 kHz.

CENSREC-4 data is divided into 'basic dataset' and 'extra dataset'. The basic dataset contains simulated reverberant data made by convolving eight kinds of RIRs with the clean speech, as shown in Table 10 [22]. In this dataset, there are two sets of testing data and two sets of training data. The testing data is divided into test set A (office, elevator hall, in car, living room) and test set B (lounge, Japanese-style room, meeting room, Japanese-style bath). In total, each testing dataset consists of 4,004 utterances by 104 speakers (52 females and 52 males). Thus, there are 1,001 utterances for each reverberant environment.

The training data is divided into clean and multi-condition datasets. The clean dataset consists of 8,440 utterances by 110 speakers (55 females and 55 males). The multi-condition dataset consists of simulated reverberant data generated by convolving four kinds of RIRs from test set A with the utterances from clean dataset. Thus, there are 2,110 utterances for each reverberant environment. Because of the availability of multi-condition training data, test set A can be regarded as *known* reverberant environments and test set B can be regarded as *unknown* environments.

The extra dataset contains two sets of testing data. The testing data is divided into test set C, which contains simulated reverberant data with multiplicative and additive noise, and test set D, which contains real reverberant data. The utterances of test set D were recorded in a car, lounge, meeting room, and office (Table 10) by 10 speakers (five females and five males) using close- and distant-talking microphones. The close-talking microphone was using headset, while the distant-talking microphone was 50 cm away from the speaker. For each environment, the data is divided into testing dataset (493 utterances) and adaptation dataset (110 utterances). Thus, the testing dataset of set D contains 1,972 utterances by 10 speakers.

Test sets A and B were used to evaluate the proposed method on simulated reverberant environments, while

Table 10 Environment conditions for CENSREC-4 data acquisition

Room	Test set	Room size	Mic. distance	Reverb. time (T_{60})	Ambient noise (dBA)
Office	A/D	9.0 × 6.0 m	0.5 m	0.25 s	36.5 dB
Elevator hall	A	11.5 × 6.5 m	2.0 m	0.75 s	39.0 dB
In car	A/D	Middle-sized sedan	0.4 m	0.05 s	32.0 dB
Living room	A	7.0 × 3.0 m	0.5 m	0.65 s	34.0 dB
Lounge	B/D	11.5 × 27.0 m	0.5 m	0.50 s	52.5 dB
Japanese-style room	B	3.5 × 2.5 m	2.0 m	0.40 s	30.0 dB
Meeting room	B/D	7.0 × 8.5 m	0.5 m	0.65 s	48.5 dB
Japanese-style bath	B	1.5 × 1.0 m	0.3 m	0.60 s	29.5 dB

test set D was used to evaluate the proposed method on real reverberant environments. For both evaluations, the acoustic models were trained using clean and/or multi-condition training datasets. The acoustic models consist of 18 phoneme models (5 states; 20-mixture GMM), silence 'sil' (5 states; 36-mixture GMM), and short pause 'sp' (3 states; 36-mixture GMM).

7.2 Experiments using simulated reverberant data

7.2.1 Experimental setup

The experimental setup for the simulated reverberant data is depicted by Figure 10. The NN training and the feature mapping were done using 24-dimensional log-melspectral feature vectors, while the acoustic model (AM) training and the recognition were done using 39-dimensional melcepstral feature vectors consisting of 12-dimensional MFCC parameters and the log energy, with their delta and delta-delta parameters. The benefit of CMN use *after* our proposed method (feature mapping) was also investigated.

Some pairs of utterances from set A were used as the NN training data. We created multi-condition five-speaker datasets ('5s') as described in Table 11. We selected 5 speakers (2 females and 3 males) from the 110 available speakers, then randomly selected some pairs of utterances from each environment (4 environments) for each selected speaker (5 speakers) and combined them to make the dataset.

We also created cross validation dataset consisting of randomly selected 400 utterances from simulated reverberant data by 104 speakers. The NN training used random weight initialization and variations in the final NN were not unexpected. Therefore, in our experiments, we did the NN training five times which resulted five NNs

for each dimension of feature. Then, we selected the NNs which yielded the lowest MSE for the cross validation dataset. Finally, the best set of NNs was used in the feature mapping.

In all experimental results below, the original AMs (refer to [22]) trained using only clean data and only multi-condition data are denoted by 'clean' and 'multi', respectively. The retrained AM is denoted by '-rt'. For example, 'multi-rt' denotes the AM retrained using dereverberated multi-condition data, and 'cln+mlt-rt' denotes the AM retrained using clean and processed multi-condition data. The experiments were done by using causal reverberation model and skip1 frame selection only.

7.2.2 Experimental results

Table 12 shows the upper bound and the baseline for set A and set B. In the table, 'close' denotes the clean utterances and represents the upper bound. The table shows that the use of multi-condition AM and CMN were effective. By using that combination, we could reach 44.9% of average ERR relative to the baseline. The baseline (by using clean and multi-condition AMs) is the same as shown in [22,54].

The experimental results on the simulated reverberant data of CENSREC-4 by using Hybrid Delta [55] reached 95.7% and 94.7% of average digit accuracy for sets A and B. Thus, it reached 95.2% of total average digit accuracy, or 71.3% of average ERR relative to the baseline. Meanwhile, the DAE-based approach proposed in [29,30] reached 98.4% and 97.0% of average digit accuracy for sets A and B. Thus, it reached 97.7% of total average digit accuracy, or 86.2% of average ERR relative to the baseline, which was better than the ideal case (upper bound) for multi-condition AM (96.2% of digit accuracy). Both works used retrained multi-condition AM.

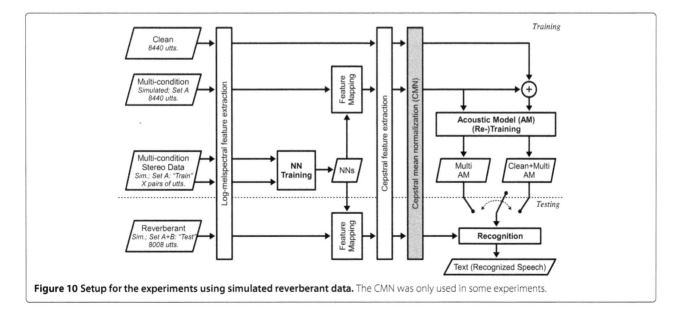

Figure 10 Setup for the experiments using simulated reverberant data. The CMN was only used in some experiments.

Table 11 Multi-condition (combined) NN training datasets for the experiments using simulated reverberant data

Dataset name	Speaker number	Utterances num. per spk. per env. (pairs of utts.)	Total duration of utterances (seconds)
5s.20u	5	1	61
5s.40u	5	2	110

The total duration of utterances is after removing the silence parts in the beginning and ending of each recording.

Table 13 shows the experimental results of our proposed approach on set A and set B using '5s.20u'. The table shows the performance of skip1 frame selection with segment length of nine frames ('8-1-0'). We can observe that the use of CMN after our proposed method is not effective. We can also observe that the use of 'multi-rt' AM was effective and the use of 'cln+mlt-rt' AM, which used more training data, could not improve the performance further. The best average performance of our proposed method shown in Table 13 is 96.1%, or 76.6% of ERR relative to the baseline, which was almost the same as the ideal case (upper bound) for multi-condition AM. It is better than the performance of Hybrid Delta approach, but worse than the DAE approaches.

We tried to double the number of NN training data ('5s.40u') and also the context length (17 frames, '16-1-0'). By using more training data, the performance could be improved, but the DAE approaches were still better. The best average performance of our proposed method shown is 96.4%, which is 78.4% of ERR relative to the baseline. Comparing to our approach, besides using different NN architecture, DAE used a bigger neural network, which was trained using more advanced training algorithm and also much more NN training data (2,110 pairs of utterances).

7.3 Experiments using real reverberant data

7.3.1 Experimental setup

The experimental setup for the real reverberant data is depicted by Figure 11. The features used in these experiments were the same as in the experiments using simulated reverberant data (Subsubection 7.2.1).

Some pairs of utterances from the adaptation set of set D were used as the NN training data. We created *multi-condition (combined)* five-speaker datasets ('5s') and one-speaker datasets ('1s') as described in Table 14. We selected 5 speakers (2 females and 3 males) from the 10 available speakers. For the five-speaker datasets, we randomly selected some pairs of utterances from each environment (four environments) *for each selected speaker (five speakers)* and then combined them to make the dataset. For the one-speaker datasets, we randomly selected some pairs of utterances from each environment (four environments) and then combined them to make the dataset *for each selected speaker (five speakers in total)*. The total duration of utterances for each speaker varies from 37 to 84 s (20-utterance datasets) and 75 to 166 s (40-utterance datasets). We also created a multi-condition (combined) cross validation dataset consists of randomly selected 200 utterances (50 utterances for each environment) of 10 speakers.

In addition, slightly different from the experimental setup shown in Figure 11, we also used *environment-specific* five-speaker ('5s') and one-speaker ('1s') datasets as described in Table 15 for training the NNs and environment-specific cross validation datasets for selecting the best set of NNs. In fact, the environment-specific datasets were the datasets which compose the multi-condition (combined) datasets, for example the multi-condition (combined) '5s.20u' datasets were composed by environment-specific '5s.5u' datasets of four environments. The environment-specific cross validation datasets were also the datasets which compose the multi-condition (combined) cross validation dataset.

Table 12 Upper bound and baseline for the experiments using the simulated reverberant data

Method	Acoustic model	Digit accuracy (%)								Avg. set A	Avg. set B	Avg.
		Set A				Set B						
		Office	EvHall	InCar	LivingR	Lounge	JPstyR	ConfR	BathR			
Close (Ideal)	Clean	99.5	99.4	99.5	99.3	99.5	99.4	99.5	99.3	99.4	99.4	99.4
	Multi	96.2	96.5	96.1	96.2	96.2	96.5	96.1	96.2	96.2	96.2	96.2
Baseline	Clean	97.5	57.9	95.6	84.4	74.0	89.5	89.8	78.0	83.8	82.8	83.3
	Multi	94.3	90.5	94.7	91.5	79.6	93.5	93.4	84.2	92.8	87.7	90.2
CMN	Clean	97.8	66.0	98.7	83.5	87.3	92.2	93.3	81.7	86.5	88.6	87.6
	Multi	92.8	91.9	92.5	90.0	92.6	91.9	93.1	81.3	91.8	89.7	90.8

Table 13 Experimental results on the simulated reverberant data by using NN training dataset '5s.20u'

Method	Frame selection	Acoustic model	Digit accuracy (%)										
			Set A				Set B				Avg. set A	Avg. set B	Avg.
			Office	EvHall	InCar	LivingR	Lounge	JPstyR	ConfR	BathR			
Proposed (24 NNs)	skip1 8-1-0	Clean	98.6	66.3	98.8	89.8	90.1	95.2	92.7	91.5	88.4	92.4	90.4
		Multi-rt	97.4	95.6	97.8	97.4	92.1	97.3	96.1	94.5	97.1	95.0	96.1
		Cln+mlt-rt	97.6	94.2	98.0	97.0	93.5	97.7	96.5	94.2	96.7	95.5	96.1
Proposed (24 NNs) + CMN	skip1 8-1-0	Clean	97.7	67.8	98.4	86.0	93.3	93.4	92.4	86.6	87.5	91.4	89.5
		Multi-rt	96.6	94.7	96.8	96.2	94.7	96.5	95.9	93.6	96.1	95.2	95.7
		Cln+mlt-rt	97.1	94.7	97.1	95.2	94.1	96.2	96.2	92.5	96.0	94.7	95.4

We used clean and multi-condition datasets to train the new acoustic models. The multi-condition dataset was dereverberated first using the feature mapping method. Because of the multi-condition dataset is noiseless while NN training data is noisy, we implemented log-melspectral channel mean normalization (hereafter, referred as LMCN) before the NN training and the feature mapping to deal with the mismatch. The LMCN, which works the same as CMN, can be expressed as

$$c'_{t,d} = c_{t,d} - \frac{1}{T} \sum_{t=1}^{T} c_{t,d}, \quad \text{for } d = 1, 2, \ldots, D, \quad (34)$$

where $c'_{t,d}$ and $c_{t,d}$ are the normalized and original coefficients of frame index t and feature dimension d, T is the number of frames, and D is the number of feature dimension.

In all experimental results below, the original AMs (refer to [22]) trained using only clean data and only multi-condition data are denoted by 'clean' and 'multi', respectively. The retrained AM is denoted by '-rt'. Besides

'multi-rt' AM, we have 'clean+multi-rt' AM, which is the same as 'cln+mlt-rt' AM in the experiments using the simulated reverberant dataset, and we also create 'clean-rt' AM specifically for the experiments using the real reverberant dataset. The difference between 'clean' and 'clean-rt' AMs was in the cepstal feature (MFCCs) extraction. The cepstral feature for 'clean' was extracted from the log-melspectral feature (as in standard MFCC extraction), while the MFCCs for 'clean-rt' were extracted from the *normalized* log-melspectral feature. The experiments were done by using causal reverberation model only. Besides, we mainly used skip1 frame selection.

7.4 Experimental results

7.4.1 Fundamental results

Table 16 shows the upper bound and the baseline for set D. In the table, 'close' denotes close-talking utterances and represents the upper bound. The table shows that the use of multi-condition AM and CMN were effective. By using that combination, we could reach 40.9% of ERR relative to

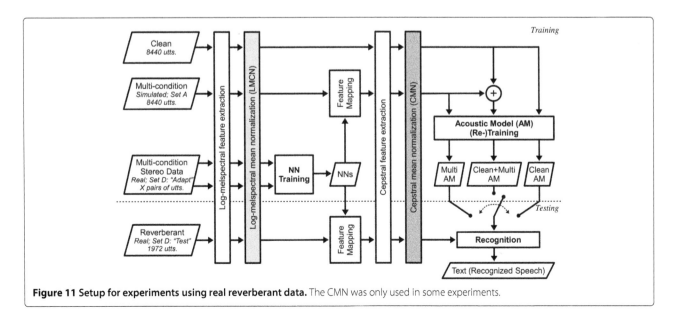

Figure 11 Setup for experiments using real reverberant data. The CMN was only used in some experiments.

Table 14 *Multi-condition (combined)* **NN training datasets for the experiments using real reverberant data**

Dataset name	Speaker number	Utterances num. per spk. per env. (pairs of utts.)	Total duration of utterances (seconds)
5s.20u	5	1	54
5s.40u	5	2	108
5s.60u	5	3	162
5s.80u	5	4	213
1s.20u	1	5	70
1s.40u	1	10	138

The total duration of utterances is after removing the silence parts in the beginning and ending of each recording. For the one-speaker datasets ('1s'), the total duration is the average from five speakers' datasets.

the baseline. The baseline (by using clean AM) is the same as shown in [10,54].

As a comparison, we show the experimental results from [10] in Table 17. It shows the performance of generalized spectral subtraction (GSS) and joint sparse representation (JSR) on the real reverberant dataset of CENSREC-4. In the GSS approach, the AM was retrained using processed (dereverberated) multi-condition reverberant data. Meanwhile, the JSR approach worked on clean AM, assumed that the environment is known, and used 110 pairs of utterances in training the sparse representation for each environment. The best performances for both approaches were when the CMN was employed. The performance of 'GSS+CMN' and 'JSR+CMN' reached 56.3% and 53.4%, respectively, of ERR relative to the baseline.

Besides, we also compare our experimental results to the performance of Hybrid Delta, which is a new scheme for calculating the delta and delta-delta coefficients of static MFCC coefficients by using linear-logarithmic hybrid domain [55]. A multi-condition AM was retrained using the proposed features. The performance of Hybrid Delta reached 31.4% of ERR relative to the baseline.

Table 18 shows the experimental results of our proposed approach on set D using '5s.20u' dataset. The table shows the performance of linear and skip1 frame selection with segment length of 9 frames ('8-1-0'), 17 frames ('16-1-0'), and 33 frames ('32-1-0'). Note that the segment of skip1 8-1-0 represents the same context length to linear 16-1-0, which is 185 ms, and skip1 16-1-0 represents the same context length to linear 32-1-0, which is 345 ms.

We can observe the performance difference caused by the difference of AM used in the recognition. The 'clean+multi-rt' AM could perform much better than the 'multi-rt' AM. We can observe that the frame selection used in the feature mapping was affecting the performance. The differences of performance between the use of linear 16-1-0 and the use of skip1 8-1-0 were not significant, except when we used 'multi-rt' AM. Meanwhile, the use of skip1 16-1-0 was better than the use of linear 32-1-0. Because of the long segment it used, the use of linear 32-1-0 most likely had high variance (overfitting) problem. That was also why the use of linear 32-1-0 was worse than the use of linear 16-1-0. We can observe that the use of longer segment for linear frame selection was not effective. However, we can see the benefit of using longer segment for skip1 frame selection. The use of 17-frame segment (skip 16-1-0) could perform better than the use of nine-frame segment (skip1 8-1-0). As an additional information, the CMN is not effective when it was used for the retrained AMs, which may be caused by the fact that the LMCN works the same as CMN. The difference is only the domain they work on. LMCN works on log-melspectral domain, while CMN works on melcepstral domain.

The best average performance of our proposed method shown in Table 18 is 93.2%, or 74.2% of ERR relative to the baseline, which is better than the ideal case (upper bound) for multi-condition AM. It is better than the performance of GSS and JSR approaches, where both approaches employ CMN. Comparing to our approach,

Table 15 *Environment-specific* **NN training datasets for the experiments using real reverberant data**

Dataset name	Speaker number	Utterances num. per spk. per env. (pairs of utts.)	Total duration of utterances (seconds)
5s.5u	5	1	14
5s.10u	5	2	27
1s.5u	1	5	17
1s.10u	1	10	35

The total duration of utterances is after removing the silence parts in the beginning and ending of each recording.

Table 16 Upper bound and baseline for the experiments using the real reverberant data

Method	Acoustic model	Digit accuracy (%)				
		InCar	Lounge	MeetR	Office	Average
Close (ideal)	Clean	97.3	96.5	97.3	98.1	97.3
	Multi	90.0	88.7	91.6	89.1	89.9
Baseline	Clean	76.4	43.8	89.2	85.1	73.6
	Multi	82.9	74.3	93.3	85.6	84.0
CMN	Clean	84.9	59.8	90.7	93.5	82.2
	Multi	80.1	83.1	89.9	84.4	84.4

JSR worked on clean AM, assumed that the environment is known, and used more training data (110 pairs of utterances). Our best performance is also better than Hybrid Delta approach. However, we should notice that comparing to our approach, Hybrid Delta do not need stereo data.

Table 19 shows the experimental results of our proposed approach on set D using '1s.20u' datasets. We had five '1s.20u' datasets (one dataset for each selected speaker), and Table 19 shows the average performance of these five datasets. The table shows that by using only one speaker, the proposed method could still perform relatively well. The best average performance of our proposed method shown in Table 19 is 91.8%, which is 68.9% of ERR relative to the baseline. It is also better than the performance of other approaches which were already presented above.

7.4.2 Further results and analyses

Figure 12 tries to analyze the performance by using five-speaker datasets ('5s'), 'clean+multi-rt' AM, various numbers of NN training data, various lengths of segment, and the use of CMN. The lengths of frame segment range from 5-frame until 33-frame. Because of the use of skip1 frame selection, it means that the context length we considered varies from 145 ms (5-frame) until 985 ms (33-frames).

In general, CMN did not improve the performance. We can observe that the use of CMN gave lower performance in most cases, although it was not significant. If we only observe this experimental results (using real reverberant data), we may think that the CMN was not effective because we included the function of CMN as

LMCN. However, the experimental results for simulated reverberant data (Subsubsection 7.2.2) also show that the use of CMN after the feature mapping was not effective. Note that in the experiments using simulated reverberant data, we did not employ LMCN. This lack of performance is also confirmed and shown in [54]. Because of this lack of performance, Hybrid Delta also did not employ CMN [55].

We can observe that by limited stereo data, we could get good performance, as long as we use appropriate segment length. The small dataset ('20u') tends to give the best performance when we used frame selections of skip1 12-1-0 and 16-1-0, while the large dataset ('80u') tends to give the best performance when we used longer frame selection (skip1 24-1-0). The best average performance of our proposed method shown in Figure 12 is 93.5%, which is 75.4% of ERR relative to the baseline, reached by using skip1 24-1-0 on '60u' and '80u' datasets.

Figure 13 tries to analyze the performance by using one-speaker datasets ('1s'), 'clean+multi-rt' AM, various numbers of NN training data, various lengths of segment, and the use of CMN. We can also observe that the limited stereo data ('20u' and '40u') tends to give the best performance when we used frame selections of skip1 12-1-0. The best average performance of our proposed method shown in Figure 13 is 92.5%, which is 71.6% of ERR relative to the baseline, reached by using skip1 12-1-0 on '40u' datasets.

In a real application, the use of one-speaker dataset is more practical because it is easier to acquire stereo data of many utterances by one speaker. The performance was not as good as the performance of five-speaker

Table 17 Experimental results on the real reverberant data using GSS and JSR [10]

Method	Acoustic model	Digit accuracy (%)				
		InCar	Lounge	MeetR	Office	Average
GSS	Multi-rt	86.32	76.67	85.65	83.29	82.98
GSS + CMN	Multi-rt	88.88	83.07	89.32	92.52	88.45
JSR	Clean	84.71	67.32	92.55	95.23	84.95
JSR + CMN	Clean	87.62	79.74	90.19	93.30	87.71

Table 18 Experimental results on the real reverberant data by using NN training data '5s.20u' (combined)

Method	Frame selection	Acoustic model	Digit accuracy (%)				
			InCar	Lounge	MeetR	Office	Average
LMCN + Proposed (24 NNs)	Linear 8-1-0	Clean	69.4	38.5	78.9	75.3	65.6
		Clean-rt	85.9	60.9	90.3	93.7	82.7
		Multi-rt	82.4	85.1	90.9	86.0	86.1
		Clean+multi-rt	89.6	91.0	94.4	93.5	92.1
	Linear 16-1-0	Clean	67.8	35.1	79.4	78.0	65.1
		Clean-rt	85.7	58.8	90.7	94.7	82.5
		Multi-rt	82.6	84.2	90.2	89.3	86.6
		Clean+multi-rt	89.2	90.9	94.4	93.5	92.0
	Linear 32-1-0	Clean	67.0	30.0	74.6	77.6	62.3
		Clean-rt	84.7	53.0	89.2	94.1	80.3
		Multi-rt	78.4	82.0	88.4	87.9	84.2
		Clean+multi-rt	86.5	89.2	93.1	92.0	90.2
	Skip1 8-1-0	Clean	69.1	38.0	78.4	75.6	65.3
		Clean-rt	85.3	61.3	90.9	93.5	82.8
		Multi-rt	81.0	82.5	91.2	84.2	84.7
		Clean+multi-rt	89.2	90.7	95.1	93.4	92.1
	Skip1 16-1-0	Clean	67.2	34.7	75.8	77.6	63.8
		Clean-rt	85.2	58.5	89.6	93.6	81.7
		Multi-rt	83.2	84.8	91.5	87.1	86.6
		Clean+multi-rt	90.0	92.9	95.5	94.3	**93.2**

The bold text represents the best average performance.

dataset because the lack of speaker variation in the training data may cause the NNs become speaker-dependent. However, the experimental results show that by using one-speaker dataset, we could still get a good robust speaker-independent system. Figures 12 and 13 show that the best performance for one-speaker and five-speaker datasets were 92.3% and 93.2%, respectively, for the dataset containing 20 pairs of utterances. Meanwhile, for the dataset containing 40 pairs, the best performance for one-speaker and five-speaker datasets were 92.5% and 93.5%, respectively.

8 Conclusions

In this work, we propose a single-channel non-linear regression-based dereverberation method using cascade NNs. The NNs were trained on stereo data to compensate the reverberation effect by mapping the reverberant feature in a log-melspectral domain to its corresponding anechoic feature.

In Section 6, we present the evaluation using SID system and the proposed method could perform very well by using only few stereo data (five pairs of utterances) as the NN training data. In Subsection 6.2, we did

Table 19 Experimental results on the real reverberant data by using NN training dataset '1s.20u' (combined)

Method	Frame selection	Acoustic model	Digit accuracy (%)				
			InCar	Lounge	MeetR	Office	Average
LMCN + Proposed (24 NNs)	Skip1 8-1-0	Clean-rt	84.9	58.5	90.7	93.6	81.9
		Multi-rt	80.9	82.7	90.4	83.6	84.4
		Clean+multi-rt	89.1	90.7	94.7	93.0	**91.8**
	Skip1 16-1-0	Clean-rt	84.5	55.4	89.5	93.7	80.7
		Multi-rt	78.2	80.5	88.5	84.5	82.9
		Clean+multi-rt	88.5	90.6	94.0	93.9	91.7

The bold text represents the best average performance.

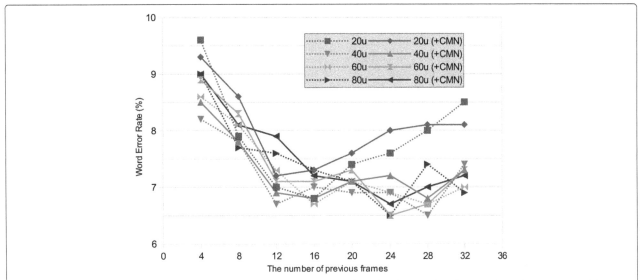

Figure 12 Performance analysis on the real reverberant data of CENSREC-4 by using five-speaker datasets ('5s'). The acoustic model was retrained by using clean and dereverberated multi-condition data ('clean+multi-rt').

experiments using various frame selection types, frame selection numbers, and training data numbers on several simulated noiseless and noisy reverberant environments. In general, the skip1 frame selection could perform better than the linear one. The use of longer context (frame selection number) could improve the performance, but the data for NN training should be sufficient. The non-causal reverberation model could perform better than the causal reverberation model. However, the use of left context only is still reasonable on a theoretical point of view. The single NN configuration could perform better for small training dataset, but the performance could not

surpass the multiple NNs when much more training data was used, which is most likely because of channel transformation overgeneralization problem. Note that the RTFs, which are represented by the NNs, should be frequency-dependent. For example, the best ERR (regardless the frame selection) for RIR type of 'living room' by using only 1 pair of utterances and single NN reached 26.0%, while by using 15 pairs of utterances and multiple NN reached 62.6% (Table 2).

In Subsection 6.3, we did experiments on modified multiple NNs (by modifying our assumptions on the channel transformation) and using NNs trained using combined

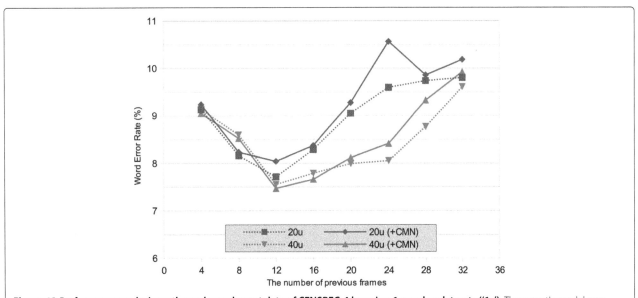

Figure 13 Performance analysis on the real reverberant data of CENSREC-4 by using 1-speaker datasets ('1s'). The acoustic model was retrained by using clean and dereverberated multi-condition data ('clean+multi-rt').

training data of known conditions in a room for dereverberating utterances from unknown condition in the same room. For a very limited stereo data (e.g., one or five pairs of utterances), the use of *modified* multiple NNs configuration could improve the performance. By using the '6 NNs' configuration, the skip1 3-1-0 frame selection, and only one pair of utterances for the NN training data, we could reach 34.8% of ERR relative to the use of CMN. Our results also show that by combining the training data from known positions in a room, we could train NNs which generalize well, so that the NNs could also perform well for unknown positions in the same room. In addition, the use of utterances from one position could perform reasonably well for other unknown positions in the same room. By using multiple NNs and 15 pairs of utterances by 1 speaker from 3 positions, we could reach 93.7% of average identification rate, which was 42.2% of ERR relative to the use of CMN.

In Section 7, we present the evaluation using ASR system, where CENSREC-4 framework [22] was used. In the experiments using simulated reverberant data, we could reach 78.4% of ERR relative to the baseline by using '5s.40u' dataset (5 speakers, 40 pairs of utterances). By using the same number of utterances (40 pairs of utterances) in the experiments using real reverberant data, we could reach 75.4% and 71.6% of ERR relative to the baseline by using '5s.40u' (5 speakers) and '1s.40u' (1 speaker).

Our experimental results could show that by using limited numbers of stereo data, our proposed method could perform remarkably well. However, the need of stereo data in implementing the method could be regarded as troublesome. Thus, possible future research directions are omitting the need of stereo data and developing unsupervised dereverberation method.

Competing interests
The authors declare that they have no competing interests.

Author details
[1]Department of Computer Science and Engineering, Toyohashi University of Technology, Toyohashi, Aichi 441-8580, Japan. [2]Department of Information and Computer Engineering, Toyota National College of Technology, Toyota, Aichi 471-8525, Japan.

References
1. B Raj, T Virtanen, R Singh, The problem of robustness in automatic speech recognition, in *Techniques for Noise Robustness in Automatic Speech Recognition*, ed. by T Virtanen, R Singh, and B Raj (Wiley West Sussex, 2013)
2. T Yoshioka, A Sehr, M Delcroix, K Kinoshita, R Maas, T Nakatani, W Kellermann, Making machines understand us in reverberant rooms: robustness against reverberation for automatic speech recognition. IEEE Signal Process. Mag. **29**(6), 114–126 (2012)
3. T Nakatani, T Yoshioka, K Kinoshita, M Miyoshi, B-H Juang, Speech dereverberation based on variance-normalized delayed linear prediction. IEEE Trans. Audio Speech Lang. Process. **18**(7), 1717–1731 (2010)
4. T Yoshioka, T Nakatani, M Miyoshi, HG Okuno, Blind separation and dereverberation of speech mixtures by joint optimization. IEEE Trans. Audio Speech Lang. Process. **19**(1), 69–84 (2011)
5. K Lebart, JM Boucher, A new method based on spectral subtraction for speech dereverberation. Acta Acustica. **87**, 359–366 (2001)
6. EAP Habets, Single-channel speech dereverberation based on spectral subtraction, in *Proceedings of the 15th Annual Workshop on Circuits, Systems and Signal Processing (ProRISC)* (STW Technology Foundation Utrecht, Netherlands, 250)
7. JS Erkelens, R Heusdens, Correlation-based and model-based blind single-channel late-reverberation suppression in noisy time-varying acoustic environments. IEEE Trans. Audio Speech Lang. Process. **18**(7), 1746–1765 (2010)
8. A Mushtaq, C-H Lee, An integrated approach to feature compensation combining particle filters and hidden Markov models for robust speech recognition, in *Proceedings of IEEE ICASSP* (IEEE Piscataway, NJ, USA, 2012), pp. 4757–4760
9. V Leutnant, A Krueger, R Haeb-Umbach, Bayesian feature enhancement for reverberation and noise robust speech recognition. IEEE Trans. Audio Speech Lang. Process. **21**(8), 1640–1652 (2013)
10. W Li, L Wang, F Zhou, Q Liao, Joint sparse representation based cepstral-domain dereverberation for distant-talking speech recognition, in *Proceedings of IEEE ICASSP* (IEEE Piscataway, NJ, USA, 2013), pp. 7117–7120
11. H-G Hirsch, H Finster, A new approach for the adaptation of HMMs to reverberation and background noise. Speech Comm. **50**(3), 244–263 (2008)
12. A Sehr, R Maas, W Kellermann, Reverberation model-based decoding in the logmelspec domain for robust distant-talking speech recognition. IEEE Trans. Audio Speech Lang. Process. **18**(7), 1676–1691 (2010)
13. M Delcroix, T Hikichi, M Miyoshi, Dereverberation and denoising using multichannel linear prediction. IEEE Trans. Audio Speech Lang. Process. **15**(6), 1791–1801 (2007)
14. E Habets, J Benesty, I Cohen, S Gannot, J Dmochowski, New insights into the MVDR beamformer in room acoustics. IEEE Trans. Audio Speech Lang. Process. **18**(1), 158–170 (2010)
15. L Wang, K Odani, A Kai, Dereverberation and denoising based on generalized spectral subtraction by multi-channel LMS algorithm using a small-scale microphone array. EURASIP J. Adv. Signal Process. **2012**(1) (2012)
16. BS Atal, Effectiveness of linear prediction characteristics of the speech wave for automatic speaker identification and verification. J. Acoust. Soc. Am. **55**(6), 1304–1312 (1974)
17. S Furui, Cepstral analysis technique for automatic speaker verification. IEEE Trans. Acoust. Speech Signal Process. **29**(2), 254–272 (1981)
18. C Avendaño, S Tibrewala, H Hermansky, Proceedings of EUROSPEECH (ISCA Baixas, France, 1997), pp. 1107–1110
19. PJ Moreno, B Raj, RM Stern, A vector Taylor series approach for environment-independent speech recognition, in *Proceedings of IEEE ICASSP*, vol. 2 (IEEE Piscataway, NJ, USA, 1996), pp. 733–736
20. M Wolfel, Enhanced speech features by single-channel joint compensation of noise and reverberation. IEEE Trans. Audio Speech Lang. Process. **17**(2), 312–323 (2009)
21. A Krueger, R Haeb-Umbach, Model-based feature enhancement for reverberant speech recognition. IEEE Trans. Audio Speech Lang. Process. **18**(7), 1692–1707 (2010)
22. T Fukumori, T Nishiura, M Nakayama, Y Denda, N Kitaoka, T Yamada, K Yamamoto, S Tsuge, M Fujimoto, T Takiguchi, C Miyajima, S Tamura, T Ogawa, S Matsuda, S Kuroiwa, K Takeda, S Nakamura, CENSREC-4: an evaluation framework for distant-talking speech recognition in reverberant environments. Acoust. Sci. Tech. **32**(5), 201–210 (2011)
23. L Deng, A Acero, L Jiang, J Droppo, X Huang, High-performance robust speech recognition using stereo training data, in *Proceedings of IEEE ICASSP*, vol. 1 (IEEE Piscataway, NJ, USA, 2001), pp. 301–304
24. J Droppo, L Deng, A Acero, Evaluation of SPLICE on the Aurora 2 and 3 tasks, in *Proceedings of ICSLP* (ISCA Baixas, France, 2002), pp. 29–32
25. Y Pan, A Waibel, *The effects of room acoustics on MFCC speech parameter* (ISCA, Baixas, France, 2000), pp. 129–132
26. K Shimada, K Yamamoto, S Nakagawa, Consideration of robust speaker recognition for reverberation in distant speech, in *Proceedings of the Spring Meeting of Acoustical Society of Japan* (ASJ Tokyo, Japan, 2012), pp. 199–202. (in Japanese)

27. W Li, Y Zhou, N Poh, F Zhou, Q Liao, Feature denoising using joint sparse representation for in-car speech recognition. E Signal Process. Lett. **20**(7), 681–684 (2013)

28. P Jinachitra, RE Prieto, Towards speech recognition oriented dereverberation, in *Proceedings of IEEE ICASSP* (IEEE Piscataway, NJ, USA, 2005), pp. 437–440

29. T Ishii, T Shinozaki, Y Horiuchi, S Kuroiwa, Reverberant speech recognition based on denoising autoencoder using multiple analysis window lengths, in *Proceedings of the Spring Meeting of Acoustical Society of Japan* (ASJ Tokyo, Japan, 2013), pp. 65–66. (in Japanese)

30. T Ishii, H Komiyama, T Shinozaki, Y Horiuchi, S Kuroiwa, Reverberant speech recognition based on denoising autoencoder, in *Proceedings of INTERSPEECH* (ISCA Baixas, France, 2013), pp. 3512–3516

31. Xia B-y, Bao C-c, Speech enhancement with weighted denoising auto-encoder, in *Proceedings of INTERSPEECH* (ISCA Baixas, France, 2013), pp. 3444–3448

32. X Lu, Y Tsao, S Matsuda, C Hori, Speech enhancement based on deep denoising autoencoder, in *Proceedings of INTERSPEECH* (ISCA Baixas, France, 2013), pp. 436–440

33. Rojas R (ed.), *Neural Networks: A Systematic Introduction*. (Springer, Berlin, 1996)

34. E Fiesler, Neural network classification and formalization. Comput. Stand. Interfac. **16**, 1994

35. S Nissen, *Large scale reinforcement learning using q-sarsa(λ) and cascading neural networks*. (PhD thesis, University of Copenhagen, Denmark, 2007)

36. L Prechelt, Investigation of the CasCor family of learning algorithms. Neural Netw. **10**, 885–896 (1996)

37. SE Fahlman, C Lebiere, The cascade-correlation learning architecture, in *Advances in Neural Information Processing Systems 2*, ed. by Touretzky DS (Morgan Kaufmann San Francisco, 1990), pp. 524–532

38. AA Nugraha, S Nakagawa, Proceedings of the Autumn Meeting of Acoustical Society of Japan (ASJ Tokyo, Japan, 2012), pp. 163–166

39. AA Nugraha, K Yamamoto, S Nakagawa, Single channel dereverberation method in log-melspectral domain using limited stereo data for distant speaker identification, in *Proceedings of APSIPA Annual Summit and Conference* (IEEE Piscataway, NJ, USA, 2013)

40. AA Nugraha, K Yamamoto, S Nakagawa, Single channel dereverberation method by feature mapping using limited stereo data. Technical Report. **113**(161), 7–12 (2013). SP2013-54, IEICE

41. L Wang, N Kitaoka, S Nakagawa, Distant-talking speech recognition based on spectral subtraction by multi-channel LMS algorithm. IEICE Trans. Inf. Syst. **E94-D**(3), 659–667 (2011)

42. M Riedmiller, H Braun, A direct adaptive method for faster backpropagation learning: the RPROP algorithm, in *Proceedings of IEEE International Conference on Neural Networks*, vol. 1 (IEEE Piscataway, NJ, USA, 1993), pp. 586–591

43. S Nissen, FANN: Fast Artificial Neural Network Library (2013). http://leenissen.dk/fann. Accessed 8 September 2013

44. S Nissen, Implementation of a fast artificial neural network library (FANN). Technical report, University of Copenhagen, Denmark (2007)

45. KP Markov, S Nakagawa, Text-independent speaker recognition using non-linear frame likelihood transformation. Speech Commun. **24**(3), 193–209 (1998)

46. S Nakagawa, L Wang, S Ohtsuka, Speaker identification and verification by combining MFCC and phase information. IEEE Trans. Audio Speech Lang. Process. **20**(4), 1085–1095 (2012)

47. K Itou, M Yamamoto, K Takeda, JNAS: Japanese speech corpus for large vocabulary continuous speech recognition research. J. Acoust. Soc. Jpn. **20**(3), 199–206 (1999)

48. HG Hirsch, D Pearce, Aurora-5 (2007). http://aurora.hsnr.de/aurora-5.html. Accessed 8 September 2013

49. HG Hirsch, SIREAC - SImulation of REal ACoustics (Web Demo) (2005). http://dnt.kr.hs-niederrhein.de/wwwsim. Accessed 8 September 2013

50. HG Hirsch, H Finster, Proceedings of INTERSPEECH (ISCA Baixas, France, 2005), pp. 2697–2700

51. AY Nakano, S Nakagawa, K Yamamoto, Automatic estimation of position and orientation of an acoustic source by a microphone array network. J. Acoust. Soc. Am. **126**(6), 3084–3094 (2009)

52. AY Nakano, *Exploring spatial information for distant speech recognition under real environmental conditions*. (PhD thesis, Toyohashi University of Technology, Japan, 2010)

53. PA Naylor, EAP Habets, JY-C Wen, ND Gaubitch, Models, measurement and evaluation, in *Speech Dereverberation*, ed. by Naylor PA, Gaubitch ND (Springer London, 2010), pp. 21–56

54. M Nakayama, T Nishiura, Y Denda, N Kitaoka, K Yamamoto, T Yamada, S Tsuge, C Miyajima, M Fujimoto, T Takiguchi, S Tamura, T Ogawa, S Matsuda, S Kuroiwa, K Takeda, S Nakamura, CENSREC-4: development of evaluation framework for distant-talking speech recognition under reverberant environments, in *Proceedings of INTERSPEECH* (ISCA Baixas, France, 2008), pp. 968–971

55. O Ichikawa, T Fukuda, M Nishimura, Dynamic features in the linear-logarithmic hybrid domain for automatic speech recognition in a reverberant environment. IEEE J. Sel. Top. Signal. Process. **4**(5), 816–823 (2010)

4

RNN language model with word clustering and class-based output layer

Yongzhe Shi[1*], Wei-Qiang Zhang[1], Jia Liu[1] and Michael T Johnson[2]

Abstract

The recurrent neural network language model (RNNLM) has shown significant promise for statistical language modeling. In this work, a new class-based output layer method is introduced to further improve the RNNLM. In this method, word class information is incorporated into the output layer by utilizing the Brown clustering algorithm to estimate a class-based language model. Experimental results show that the new output layer with word clustering not only improves the convergence obviously but also reduces the perplexity and word error rate in large vocabulary continuous speech recognition.

Keywords: Brown word clustering; RNN language model; Speech recognition

1 Introduction

Statistical language models estimate the probability of a word occurring in a given context, which plays an important role in many natural language processing applications such as speech recognition, machine translation, and information retrieval. Standard n-gram back-off language models (LMs) are widely used for their simplicity and efficiency. However, in this approach, words are modeled as discrete symbols with richer linguistic information, such as syntax and semantic, ignored completely. Additionally, large numbers of parameters need to be estimated, and due to the sparsity characteristics of natural language, the probability of low- and zero-frequency events is estimated crudely and inaccurately using various smoothing algorithms.

The distributional hypothesis in linguistics states that words occurring in the same context tend to have similar meanings. It is a reasonable assumption that similar words occur in the same context with similar probability, for example, 'America', 'China', and 'Japan' which usually come after the same preposition or as the subject of a sentence. Based on this assumption, neural network language models (NNLMs) [1,2] project the discrete word indices into a continuous space where similar words occur close together. The predicted probability of the next word is returned by a smooth function of the context representation, which alleviates the sparsity issue to some extent and leads to better generalization for unseen n-grams. In 2010, Elman's recurrent neural network was first used for language modeling by Mikolov [3] and then an extension of this model was proposed in 2011 [4,5]. The recurrent neural network language model (RNNLM) has a longer memory and has recently performed better than other modeling methods [3,4,6]. Accordingly, we select the RNNLM as our baseline approach in this paper.

One key issue is the heavy computational cost for the RNNLM. As the output layer contains one unit for each word in the vocabulary, it is infeasible to train the model for large vocabulary with hundreds of thousands of words. Therefore, reducing the complexity of neural network language models has been an important topic. Perhaps one method is to estimate the several thousand most frequent words (the shortlist) via NNLMs, while other words are estimated via n-gram back-off models. Unfortunately, it has been shown that this technique causes severe degradation of performance for a small shortlist [1]. Other tree-structured output layer methods have also been proposed to speed up the NNLMs [7,8]. In these

*Correspondence: shiyz09@gmail.com
[1]Tsinghua National Laboratory for Information Science and Technology, Department of Electronic Engineering, Tsinghua University, 100084 Beijing, China
Full list of author information is available at the end of the article

methods, the tree structure of the output layer needs to be constructed carefully using linguistic knowledge such as WordNet [9] or word continuous representation. In general, speed and performance need to be balanced so that training and testing process is accelerated as much as possible, without deteriorating the performance of the model.

In this paper, we introduce a new method for constructing a class-based output layer using the Brown clustering algorithm. The closest previous work to this is a simple frequency-based word factorizing algorithm used to construct the output layer [4]. Words are roughly clustered according to their frequencies in this method, with training speed increasing but performance degraded. We extend this work to improve the performance of RNNLM and speed up the training. Words are clustered off-line and then the word classes are embedded into the output layer to estimate the class-based language model, where the RNN is used to estimate the conditional probability of classes and words.

This paper is organized as follows: In Section 2, we introduce our baseline RNNLM and the proposed Brown clustering method for constructing the output layer. Perplexity evaluation on a public corpus is performed in Section 3. Our proposed model is further evaluated on the Wall Street Journal (WSJ) and Switchboard speech-to-text tasks in Sections 4 and 5. Finally, Section 6 concludes this paper and gives the future work.

2 Model description

2.1 RNN language model

An Elman recurrent neural network (RNN) [10] is shown in Figure 1. The hidden state is a function of the entire input history. RNNs are well known for their long memory and are widely used for dynamic system modeling and sequence prediction. Let V denotes the vocabulary with

'1-of-$|V|$' coding used in the input layer, so that the ith word of the vocabulary is encoded as a binary $|V|$-dim vector, where the ith element is set as 1 and all others are 0. Let $h_t = \text{sigmoid}(W_{ih}x_t + W_{hh}h_{t-1})$, where x_t and h_t denote the input and the hidden activation at the current time step, respectively. The hidden state h_t is activated by the current input x_t and the previous hidden activation h_{t-1}. Define $P(w_t|w_1^{t-1}) = o_t = \text{softmax}(W_{ho}h_t)$, where w_t and w_1^{t-1} denote the next word and the context. The output layer o_t corresponds to the predicted probability of all words in the vocabulary. To speed up the training of RNNLM, a frequency-based extension of RNNLM is introduced in [4], which is a class-based model as shown in Figure 2. Let $P(w_t|w_1^{t-1}) = P(C(w_t)|w_1^{t-1})P(w_t|C(w_t), w_1^{t-1})$, where $C(w_t)$ denotes the class of the word w_t. The predicted probabilities of classes and specific words are estimated to decrease the computational complexity.

To speed this up, a simple frequency-based factorizing method is used to construct the equivalence class of words in the class-based model. Compared with RNNLM without a class-based layer, the perplexity (PPL) of the model shown in Table 1 is 10% higher for the Penn Treebank Corpus (one million words). Details can be found in Section 3.

2.2 Word clustering for output layer

2.2.1 Frequency-based clustering

Frequency-based word clustering is referred to as the frequency binning factorization method [4], where words are assigned to classes proportionally. Figure 3 gives the unigram cumulative probability distribution for the Penn Treebank Corpus, which describes the well-known phenomenon of Zipf's law in natural language. This method divides the cumulative probability into K partitions to form K frequency binnings which correspond to K clusters, a very rough word partition which only considers frequency. Zipf's law states that given some corpus of natural language utterances, the frequency of any word is inversely proportional to its rank in the frequency table. This means that the very few high-frequency words occupy most of the text corpus. It can be seen in Figure 3 that the most frequent 150 words and 2,800 words occupy more than 50% and 80% of the text corpus, respectively. In order to have 100 equal clusters, the top 150 words make up the first 50 clusters and the top 2,800 words make up the first 80 clusters, which means the last 7,200 words form 20 clusters. Therefore, clusters containing high-frequency words are very small, possibly even containing one word. In contrast, most words are in the remaining clusters, each containing hundreds or even thousands of words. Thus, the clustering results of this method depend severely on frequency distribution of the training corpus, leading to unsatisfactory clustering results.

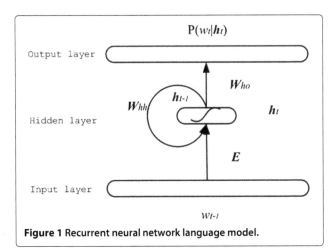

Figure 1 Recurrent neural network language model.

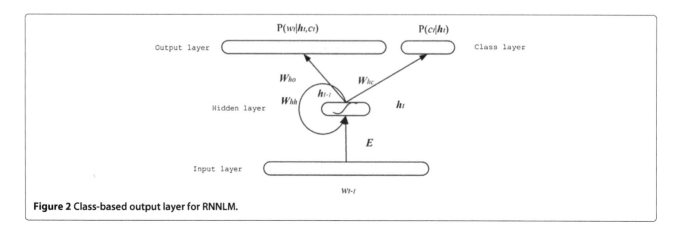

Figure 2 Class-based output layer for RNNLM.

2.2.2 Brown clustering

Brown clustering is a data-driven hierarchical word clustering algorithm [11,12], which is widely used in natural language processing. The input to this algorithm is text, which is a sequence of words $w_1, w_2, ..., w_n$, and the output of the clustering algorithm is a binary tree, the leaves of which are words. In this paper, we interpret all leaves with the same parent node as a cluster in the tree. The Brown clustering algorithm was first proposed to estimate a class-based language model [11]. Let V, C, and T denote the vocabulary, the word clusters and the text corpus, respectively. The optimization object is the cross entropy of the text corpus:

$$
\begin{aligned}
loss(C) &= -\frac{1}{|T|} \log \mathrm{P}(w_1...w_{|T|}) \\
&= -\frac{1}{|T|} \log \prod_{i=1}^{|T|} \mathrm{P}(C(w_i)|C(w_{i-1})\mathrm{P}(w_i|C(w_i)))
\end{aligned}
\tag{1}
$$

where $|T|$ denotes the length of text and $C(\cdot)$ maps the words to the specific clusters. $\mathrm{P}(C(w_i)|C(w_{i-1}))$ and $\mathrm{P}(w_i|C(w_i))$ can be estimated by frequency. Therefore, the object loss function can be rewritten as follows:

$$
\begin{aligned}
loss(C) &= -\frac{1}{|T|} \sum_{i=1}^{|T|} \log \frac{n_{c_i,c_{i-1}}}{n_{c_{i-1}}} * \frac{n_{w_i}}{n_{c_i}} \\
&= -\sum_{c,c' \in C} \mathrm{P}(c,c') \log \frac{\mathrm{P}(c,c')}{\mathrm{P}(c)\mathrm{P}(c')} \\
&\quad - \sum_{w \in V} \mathrm{P}(w) \log \mathrm{P}(w),
\end{aligned}
\tag{2}
$$

Table 1 Perplexities on test set of Penn Treebank Corpus

Model	Perplexity
RNNLM (class 100)	135.49
RNNLM (no class layer)	123.00

where n_{w_i} denotes the occurrence count of pattern w_i that occurs in the corpus.

Initially, the algorithm starts with each word in its own cluster. As long as there are more than one cluster left, the algorithm merges the two clusters that minimizes the loss of the clustering result as shown in Equation 2. The naive algorithm has time complexity $O(|V|^3)$ [11] and is impractical for hundreds of thousands of words. Fortunately, a variant algorithm with time complexity $O(|V|K^2 + |T|)$ was proposed in [13], where K denotes the number of clusters. The algorithm is described as follows with details available in [13].

Input: text corpus **T**, the number of clusters K
Output: K word clusters

- Take the K most frequent words, put each into its own cluster $c_1, c_2, ..., c_K$
- For $i = K + 1 : |V|$

  1. Create a new cluster c_{K+1} for the ith most frequent word, giving $K + 1$ clusters.

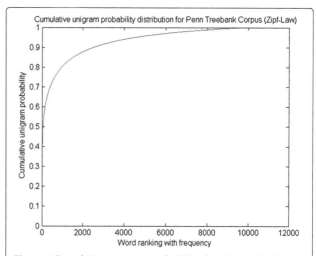

Figure 3 Cumulative unigram probability distribution for Penn Treebank Corpus with about one million words (Zipf's law).

2. Choose two clusters from $c_1, c_2, ..., c_{K+1}$ to merge, selecting these that minimize Equation 2.

- Implement $|V| - K$ merges to create a full hierarchical word clusters.

In this paper, we partition the words into clusters using this algorithm and demonstrate its effectiveness for RNN language modeling in terms of both perplexity and word error rate.

3 Penn Treebank Corpus evaluation

The proposed language model is evaluated on the Wall Street Journal portion of the Penn Treebank which is preprocessed by lowercasing words, removing punctuation and replacing numbers with the 'N' symbol. Sections 00-20 (930K words) are used as training sets, sections 21-22 as validation sets (74K words), and sections 23-24 as test sets (82K words). The vocabulary size is 10K, including a special token for unknown words.

We compare the proposed model with the baseline RNNLM model [5,6]. We denote our proposed model as RNNLM-Brown and the baseline as RNNLM-Freq for convenience, where the 'Brown' and 'Freq' mean the Brown clustering and the frequency-based clustering, respectively. Both models have the same basic configuration (200 hidden units) for comparisons in the following experiments. The truncated backpropagation through time algorithm (BPTT) is used for training the RNNLMs using ten time steps. When the perplexity decreases very slowly or increases, the learning rate is halved. The basic 5-gram back-off language model (LM-KN5) is trained with the modified Kneser-Ney smoothing algorithm. Figure 4 shows the convergence process of the

Table 2 Comparisons of perplexities on test set of Penn Treebank Corpus with different sizes of class layer

Class	RNNLM-Freq / +KN5 (words per second)	RNNLM-Brown / +KN5 (words per second)
30	135.57 / 113.13 (744)	131.46 / 110.83 (567)
50	136.39 / 113.53 (938)	129.79 / 109.96 (862)
100	135.49 / 113.07 (1,047)	128.36 / 109.33 (970)
200	136.03 / 112.89 (1,013)	128.52 / 109.13 (1,000)
400	135.75 / 113.04 (847)	128.03 / 109.09 (906)
800	134.98 / 112.51 (645)	128.09 / 109.23 (710)
1,600	133.44 / 111.93 (367)	128.67 / 109.47 (480)
10,000 (full)	123.00 / 106.00 (65)	123.00 / 106.00 (65)

The full model use the whole 10K vocabulary as the class layer, which is the same for both models. Perplexity of LM-KN5 on test set is 141.46.

validation set's perplexity for RNNLM-Freq and RNNLM-Brown, where RNNLM-Brown with 13 epochs obtains the same perplexity as RNNLM-Freq with 24 epochs. We can see that the proposed RNNLM-Brown converges twice faster and obtains lower perplexity on the validation set. Accordingly, appropriate word clustering for the output layer can speed up the convergence, which is especially important for a large training corpus.

In the following experiments, perplexity and training speed are evaluated with different sizes of class layers, as shown in Table 2. The first two columns refer to the baseline (RNNLM-Freq) and the interpolated model with LM-KN5 (RNNLM-Freq + KN5), respectively, which is consistent with the results reported in [4]. The last two columns correspond to the proposed language model (RNNLM-Brown) and the interpolated version with LM-KN5 (RNNLM-Brown + KN5). The full model uses the entire vocabulary for the class layer, in which each word

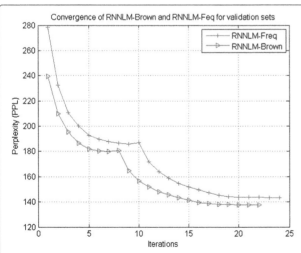

Figure 4 PPL convergence of RNNLM-Freq/Brown on validation sets.

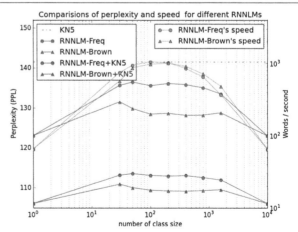

Figure 5 Detailed comparisons of perplexity and speed for different RNNLMs on Penn Treeback Corpus.

Table 3 Comparisons of perplexities on test set of five million training corpus with different sizes of class layer

Class	RNNLM-Freq / +KN5	RNNLM-Brown / +KN5
50	218.13 / 178.10	206.19 / 172.08
100	220.47 / 178.50	208.37 / 172.06
200	219.60 / 178.21	206.54 / 171.21
400	219.73 / 178.09	205.02 / 170.56

Perplexity of LM-KN5 with the same training text (five million words) on test set is 231.02.

corresponds to a separate cluster. The interpolated coefficients are determined according to the validation set. To make the observation easier, we plot the test perplexity and the speed of training in Figure 5, where the blue and red lines correspond to the left y-axis for perplexity and the green lines correspond to the right y-axis for the training speed. The training speed is evaluated by the number of words processed per second on a machine with an Intel® Core™2 Quad CPU Q9400 at 2.66 GHz, 8-GB RAM. In practice, the training speed first increases and then decreases with the increasing number of clusters. There is a trade-off between the perplexity and the training speed, especially for a larger corpus. From Figure 5, 100 or 200 clusters are the best choices balancing this, and the training speed is 15 times faster than that of the full model. Empirically, the best number of clusters is around $\sqrt{|V|}$, where $|V|$ denotes the size of vocabulary. In the experiments, the perplexity is reduced by about 5% for both single and interpolated models without reducing the speed of training, compared with the baseline. Moreover, the performance of the proposed RNNLM-Brown is much closer to that of the full model without the class layer.

4   WSJ speech recognition experiment

To evaluate the performance of the proposed language model for speech recognition, we use the WSJ task which is a standard task for language model evaluation. The acoustic model is a 6,000-tied-state continuous model with 32 Gaussians, trained on the WSJ1 Corpus; the details of which can be found in [14]. The LM training text contains 26 million words from the entire NYT-1994 section of the English Gigaword Corpus. The top 64,000 most frequent words are selected as the vocabulary

Table 4 WER for development set rescored with different RNNLMs and LM-KN5

Model	Class			
	50	100	200	400
LM-KN5 + RNNLM-Freq (%)	11.7	11.6	11.6	11.7
LM-KN5 + RNNLM-Brown (%)	11.5	11.5	11.5	11.4

The WER of 1-best hypothesis is 13.4% and the WER for LM-KN5 is 12.9%.

Table 5 WER for evaluation set rescored with different RNNLMs and LM-KN5

Model	Class			
	50	100	200	400
LM-KN5 + RNNLM-Freq (%)	13.0	13.1	13.0	13.1
LM-KN5 + RNNLM-Brown (%)	12.7	12.7	12.7	12.4

The WER of 1-best hypothesis is 14.1% and the WER for LM-KN5 is 13.8%.

and other words are mapped to a special token. Trigram (LM-KN3) and 5-gram (LM-KN5) models are trained on the text using the MITLM toolkit [15] with the modified Kneser-Ney smoothing algorithm for decoding and rescoring.

In the experiment, we use the NIST 1993 CSR Hub and Spoke Benchmark Test Corpora [16] as our test bed. We select the hub 1 and spoke 1, 2 and 4 sections for evaluations, which contain 1,251 utterances (about 25K words, 2.5 h of voice data) All the utterances are divided equally into two parts as the development set and the evaluation set.

Due to the complexity of training the neural network language model, this requires several days or an even longer time period to converge for several million training words. Thus, we randomly select about five million words from the NYT-1994 section of English Gigaword Corpus as the training data, 500K words as the validation data for early stopping and 500K words as the test data for perplexity evaluation. The top 30K frequent words are selected as the vocabulary. The truncated BPTT is used for training the different RNNLMs with ten time steps. Two hundred hidden units are used. The learning rate is initially set to 0.1 and halved when the perplexity of the validation data is increased. The detailed results are given

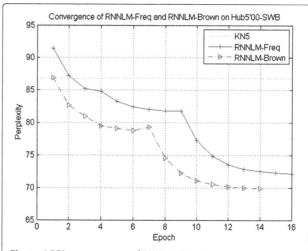

Figure 6 PPL convergence of RNNLM-Freq/Brown on Hub5'00-SWB set.

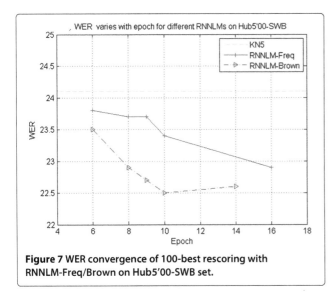

Figure 7 WER convergence of 100-best rescoring with RNNLM-Freq/Brown on Hub5′00-SWB set.

in Table 3, where consistent improvements are observed with different class sizes for the larger training corpus. The perplexity is reduced by approximately 5%, compared with the baseline.

In the following experiments, the 200-best hypotheses are generated using back-off trigram trained on the entire 26 million words and then rescored with different language models for comparisons. The interpolated coefficient of RNNLM and LM-KN5 is determined on the development set. Detailed results can be found in Tables 4 and 5. We can see that the word error rate (WER) for evaluation set is consistently reduced by 0.3% to 0.7% absolutely, compared with that of RNNLM-Freq, and 1.4% to 1.7% compared with the 1-best hypothesis (i.e. more than 10% relative reduction of WER).

5 Switchboard speech recognition experiment
In this section, the effectiveness of our proposed model on the task of speech-to-text transcription is evaluated on the 309h Switchboard-I training set [17], a larger corpus than WSJ Corpus. The system uses 13-dimensional PLP features with rolling-window mean-variance normalization

and up to third-order derivatives, reduced to 39 dimensions by HLDA. The speaker-independent three-state cross-word triphones share 9,308 CART-tied states. The GMM-HMM baseline system has 40-Gaussian mixtures per state, trained with maximum likelihood and refined discriminatively with the boosted maximum-mutual-information criterion.

The data for system development is the 1831-segment SWB part of the NIST 2000 Hub5 evaluation set (Hub5′00-SWB). The FSH half of the 6.3 h Spring 2003 NIST Rich Transcription set (RT03S-FSH) acts as the evaluation set. Based on Kneser-Ney smoothing, a back-off trigram language model (LM-KN3) was trained on the 2000h Fisher transcripts containing 20 million tokens for decoding, where the vocabulary is limited to 53K words and unknown words are mapped into a special token <unk>. Note that no other unkown text is used to train LMs for interpolations so that the following experimental results are easily repeatable. The pronouncing dictionary comes from the CMU pronouncing dictionary [18].

Two models (RNNLM-Freq/Brown) with 300 hidden units are trained on the entire training text for comparisons. The perplexity convergence of RNNLM-Freq and RNNLM-Brown on Hub5′00-SWB set is shown in Figure 6. It can be seen that waiting long enough, the RNNLM with brown clustering converges better than that with frequency partitions. Moreover, the perplexity of RNNLM-Brown with 9 epochs competes with that of RNNLM-Freq with 16 epochs; it means that RNNLM-Brown converges twice faster than RNNLM-Freq.

Subsequently, these models are further compared to rescore N-best hypotheses. For convenience, 100-best hypotheses are generated from Hub5′00-SWB and RT03S-FSH and rescored by different LMs. The interpolation weights are tuned on Hub5′00-SWB, and the performances of these LMs are evaluated on RT03S-FSH. These intermediate models during the training are used for rescoring, and the performance of these models in word error rate is plotted in Figure 7 for comparisons, where the RNNLM-Brown converges much faster and better than

Table 6 100-Best rescoring with different LMs on Hub5′00-SWB and RT03S-FSH

Model	Perplexity		WER (%, absolute change)	
	Hub5′00-SWB	RT03S-FSH	Hub5′00-SWB	RT03S-FSH
LM-KN3	89.40	66.76	24.5	27.5
LM-KN5	86.78	63.80	24.1 (−0.4)	27.1 (−0.4)
RNNLM-Freq	72.47	55.76	22.9 (−1.6)	25.9 (−1.6)
RNNLM-Freq + LM-KN5	67.66	52.15	22.4 (−2.1)	25.5 (−2.0)
RNNLM-Brown	69.91	54.48	22.6 (−1.9)	25.7 (−1.8)
RNNLM-Brown + LM-KN5	*66.00*	*51.24*	*22.2 (−2.3)*	*25.3 (−2.2)*

Values in italics indicate the lowest perplexity and WER on Hub5′00-SWB and RT03S-FSH.

RNNLM-Freq. We can see that RNNLM-Brown with 9 epochs obtains the same WER as RNNLM-Freq with 16 epochs.

The performances of different LMs in perplexity and word error rate are shown in Table 6, where Hub5'00-SWB and RT03S-FSH are used for validation and evaluation, respectively. We can see that the WER of our proposed model RNNLM-Brown interpolated with LM-KN5 obtains the lowest perplexity 51.24 and word error rate 25.3% on the evaluation set. In a word, our proposed RNNLM-Brown converges faster and better in the experiment.

6 Conclusions

In this paper, the Brown word clustering algorithm is proposed to construct a class layer for the RNNLM. Experimental results show that our proposed RNNLM-Brown improves the perplexity and decreases the word error rate obviously. The performance of our proposed RNNLM-Brown is much closer to that of the full model without a class layer. Moreover, our proposed RNNLM-Brown converges twice faster than RNNLM-Freq, which is critical for a large-scale dataset. Additionally, we notice that the outputs of the brown clustering algorithm include a binary tree structure of clusters, which is not used in this paper. In future work, we will further investigate this tree-structured output layer according to the hierarchical word cluster results. Additionally, we will also investigate whether soft clustering of words [19] can be incorporated into the RNNLM to further improve its performance.

Abbreviations
ASR: Automatic speech recognition; BPTT: Backpropagation through time algorithm; LM: Standard back-off n-gram language model; NNLM: Neural network language model; RNNLM: Recurrent neural network language model; Freq: Freq-based word clustering; Brown: Brown word clustering; KN: Kneser-Ney smoothing algorithm; LM-KN5: 5-gram based on Kneser-Ney smoothing algorithm; PPL: Perplexity; WER: Word error rate; WSJ: Wall Street Journal.

Competing interests
The authors declare that they have no competing interests.

Acknowledgements
This work was supported by the National Natural Science Foundation of China under grant nos. 61273268, 61005019 and 90920302, and in part by Beijing Natural Science Foundation Program under grant no. KZ201110005005.

Author details
[1]Tsinghua National Laboratory for Information Science and Technology, Department of Electronic Engineering, Tsinghua University, 100084 Beijing, China. [2]Department of Electrical Engineering, Marquette University, WI 53201, Milwaukee, USA.

References
1. F Balado, NJ Hurley, EP Mccarthy, GCM Silvestre, Continuous space language models. Comput. Speech. Lang. **21**(3), 492–518 (2007)
2. LH Son, R Allauzen, G Wisniewski, F Yvon, in *Proceedings of the Conference on Empirical Methods in Natural Language Processing (EMNLP)*. Training continuous space language models: some practical issues. Massachusetts, 9–11 October 2010, pp. 778–788
3. M Tomas, K Martin, B Lukas, HG Jan, K Sanjeev, in *Proceedings of the Annual Conference of International Speech Communication Association (INTERSPEECH)*. Recurrent neural network based language model. Chiba, 26–30 September 2010, pp. 1045–1048
4. M Tomas, K Stefan, B Lukas, HG Jan, K Sanjeev, in *Proceedings of IEEE International Conference on Acoustic, Speech and Signal Processing (ICASSP)*. Extensions of recurrent neural network language model. Prague, 22–27 May 2011
5. M Tomas, D Anoop, K Stefan, B Lukas, HG Jan, in *Proceedings of Automatic Speech Recognition and Understanding Workshop (ASRU)*. RNNLM - recurrent neural network language modeling toolkit. Waikoloa, 11–15 December 2011
6. M Tomas, D Anoop, K Stefan, B Lukas, HG Jan, in *Proceedings of the Annual Conference of International Speech Communication Association (INTERSPEECH 2011)*. Empirical evaluation and combination of advanced language modeling techniques. Florence, 27–31 August 2011
7. F Morin, Y Bengio, in *Proceedings of AISTATS*. Hierarchical probabilistic neural network language model. Christchurch, 6–8 January 2005, pp. 246–252
8. HS Le, I Oparin, A Allauzen, JL Gauvain, F Yvon, in *Proceedings of IEEE International Conference on Acoustic, Speech and Signal Processing (ICASSP)*. Structured Output Layer neural network language model. Prague, 22–27 May 2011, pp. 5524–5527
9. C Fellbaum, *WordNet: An Electronic Lexical Database*. (MIT Press, Cambridge, 1998)
10. JL Elman, Finding structure in time. Cogn. Sci. **14**(2), 179–211 (1990)
11. PF Brown, PV deSouza, RL Mercer, VJD Pietra, JC Lai, Class-based n-gram models for natural language. Comput. Linguist. **18**(4), 467–479 (1992)
12. S Martin, J Liermann, H Ney, Algorithms for bigram and trigram word clustering. Speech Commun. **24**, 1253–1256 (1998)
13. P Liang, Semi-supervised learning for natural language processing. Master's thesis, MIT, 2005. http://dspace.mit.edu/handle/1721.1/33296
14. K Vertanen, *Baseline WSJ acoustic models for HTK and Sphinx: training recipes and recognition experiments*, (2006). http://keithv.com/software/
15. BJP Hsu, MIT language modeling toolkit (2009). http://code.google.com/p/mitlm/
16. 1993 ARPA CSR Hub and Spoke Benchmark Tests Corpora (1993). http://www.ldc.upenn.edu/Catalog/readme_files/csr2.readme.html
17. J Godfrey, E Holliman, *Switchboard-1 Release*, vol. 2. (Linguistic Data Consortium, Philadelphia, 1997)
18. The CMU Pronouncing Dictionary Release 0.7a (2007). http://www.speech.cs.cmu.edu/cgi-bin/cmudict
19. Y Su, in *Proceedings of IEEE International Conference on Acoustic, Speech and Signal Processing (ICASSP)*. Bayesian class-based language models. Prague, 22–27 May 2011

5

Context-dependent acoustic modeling based on hidden maximum entropy model for statistical parametric speech synthesis

Soheil Khorram[1*], Hossein Sameti[1], Fahimeh Bahmaninezhad[1], Simon King[2] and Thomas Drugman[3]

Abstract

Decision tree-clustered context-dependent hidden semi-Markov models (HSMMs) are typically used in statistical parametric speech synthesis to represent probability densities of acoustic features given contextual factors. This paper addresses three major limitations of this decision tree-based structure: (i) The decision tree structure lacks adequate context generalization. (ii) It is unable to express complex context dependencies. (iii) Parameters generated from this structure represent sudden transitions between adjacent states. In order to alleviate the above limitations, many former papers applied multiple decision trees with an additive assumption over those trees. Similarly, the current study uses *multiple decision trees* as well, but instead of the additive assumption, it is proposed to train the smoothest distribution by *maximizing entropy* measure. Obviously, increasing the smoothness of the distribution improves the context generalization. The proposed model, named *hidden maximum entropy model (HMEM)*, estimates a distribution that maximizes entropy subject to multiple moment-based constraints. Due to the simultaneous use of multiple decision trees and maximum entropy measure, the three aforementioned issues are considerably alleviated. Relying on HMEM, a novel speech synthesis system has been developed with maximum likelihood (ML) parameter re-estimation as well as maximum output probability parameter generation. Additionally, an effective and fast algorithm that builds multiple decision trees in parallel is devised. Two sets of experiments have been conducted to evaluate the performance of the proposed system. In the first set of experiments, HMEM with some heuristic context clusters is implemented. This system outperformed the decision tree structure in small training databases (i.e., 50, 100, and 200 sentences). In the second set of experiments, the HMEM performance with four parallel decision trees is investigated using both subjective and objective tests. All evaluation results of the second experiment confirm significant improvement of the proposed system over the conventional HSMM.

Keywords: Hidden Markov model (HMM)-based speech synthesis; Context-dependent acoustic modeling; Decision tree-based context clustering; Maximum entropy; Overlapped context clusters; Statistical parametric speech synthesis

1 Introduction

Statistical parametric speech synthesis (SPSS) has dominated speech synthesis research area over the last decade [1,2]. It is mainly due to SPSS advantages over traditional concatenative speech synthesis approaches; these advantages include the flexibility to change voice characteristics [3-5], multilingual support [6-8], coverage of acoustic space [1], small footprint [1], and robustness [4,9]. All of the above advantages stem from the fact that SPSS provides a statistical model for acoustic features instead of using original speech waveforms. However, these advantages are achieved at the expense of one major disadvantage, i.e., degradation in the quality of synthetic speech [1]. This shortcoming results from three important factors: vocoding distortion [10-13], accuracy of statistical models [14-25], and accuracy of parameter generation algorithms [26-28]. This paper is an attempt to alleviate the second factor and improve the accuracy of statistical models. Most of the researches carried out to improve the acoustic modeling performance aimed to develop systems that generate natural and high-quality speech using large training speech databases (more than 30 min) [18,21,22]. Nevertheless,

* Correspondence: khorram@ce.sharif.edu
[1]Department of Computer Engineering, Sharif University of Technology, Tehran, Iran
Full list of author information is available at the end of the article

there exist a great number of under-resourced languages (such as Persian) for which only limited amount of data are available. To alleviate this shortcoming, we target developing a statistical approach that leads to an appropriate speech synthesis system not only with large but also with small training databases.

Every SPSS system consists of two distinct phases, namely training and synthesis [1,2]. In the training phase, first acoustic and contextual factors are extracted for the whole training database using a vocoder [12,29,30] and a natural language pre-processor. Next, the relationship between acoustic and contextual factors is modeled using a context-dependent statistical approach [14-25]. Synthesis phase starts with a parameter generation algorithm [26-28] that exploits trained context-dependent statistical models and aims to generate realistic acoustic feature trajectories for a given input text. Acoustic trajectories are then fed into the same vocoder used during the training phase in order to generate the desired synthesized speech.

In the most predominant statistical parametric approach, spectrum, excitation, and duration of speech are expressed concurrently in a unified framework of *context-dependent multi-space probability distribution hidden semi-Markov model (HSMM)* [14]. More specifically, a multi-space probability distribution [17] is estimated for each leaf node of decision trees [31]. These decision tree-based structures split contextual space into a number of non-overlapped clusters which form multiple groups of context-dependent HMM states, and each group shares the same output probability distribution [31]. In order to capture acoustic variations accurately, the model has to be able to express a large number of robust distributions [19,20]. Decision trees are not efficient for such expression because increasing the number of distributions by growing the tree reduces the population of each leaf and consequently reduces the robustness of the distributions. This problem stemmed from the fact that decision tree assigns each HMM state to an only one cluster (small region in contextual space), therefore, each state contributes in modeling just one distribution. In other words, the decision tree structure makes the models match training data just in non-overlapped regions which are expressed through decision tree terminal nodes [31]. In the case of limited training data, the decision tree would be small, so it cannot split contextual factor space sufficiently. In this case, the accordance between model and data is not sufficient, and therefore, the speech synthesis system generates unsatisfactory output. Accordingly, it is clear that by extending the decision tree in such a way that each state affects multiple distributions (larger portion of the contextual space), the generalization to unseen models will be improved. The main idea of this study is to extend non-overlapped regions of one decision tree to overlapped regions of multiple decision trees and hence exploit contextual factors more efficiently.

A large number of research works have already been performed to improve the quality of basic decision tree-clustered HSMM. Some of them are based on a model adaptation technique. This latter method exploits an invaluable prior knowledge attained from an average voice model [3], and adapts this general model using an adaptation algorithm such as *maximum likelihood linear regression (MLLR)* [32], *maximum a posteriori (MAP)* [33], and *cluster adaptive training (CAT)* [21]. However, working with average voice models is difficult for under-resourced languages since building such general model needs remarkable efforts to design, record, and transcribe a thorough multi-speaker speech database [3]. To alleviate the data sparsity problem in under-resourced languages, speaker and language factorization (SLF) technique can be used [34]. SLF attempts to factorize speaker-specific and language-specific characteristics in training data and then model them using different transforms. By representing the speaker attributes by one transform and language characteristics by a different transform, the speech synthesis system will be able to alter language and speaker separately. In this framework, it is possible to exploit the data from different languages to predict speaker-specific characteristics of the target speaker, and consequently, the data sparsity problem will be alleviated. Authors in [15,16] also developed a new technique by replacing maximum likelihood (ML) point estimate of HSMM with a *variational Bayesian* method. Their system was shown to outperform HSMM when the amount of training data is small. Other notable structures used to improve statistical modeling accuracy are *deep neural networks (DNNs)* [18]. The decision tree structure is not efficient enough to model complicated context dependencies such as XORs or multiplexers [18]. To model such complex contextual functions, the decision tree has to be excessively large, but DNNs are capable to model complex contextual factors by employing multiple hidden layers. Additionally, a great number of overlapped contextual factors can be fed into a DNN to approximate output acoustic features, so DNNs are able to provide efficient context generalization. Speech synthesis based on Gaussian process regression (GPR) [35] is another novel approach that has recently been proposed to overcome HMM-based speech synthesis limitations. The GPR model predicts frame-level acoustic trajectories from frame-level contextual factors. The frame-level contextual factors include the relative position of the current frame within the phone and some articulatory information. These frame-level contextual factors are employed as the explanatory variable in GPR. The frame-level modeling of GPR removes the inaccurate stationarity assumption of state output distribution in HMM-based speech synthesis. Also, GPR can directly represent the complex context dependencies without using parameter tying by decision tree clustering; therefore, it is capable of improving context generalization.

Acoustic modeling with *contextual additive* structure has also been proposed to represent dependencies between contextual factors and acoustic features more precisely [19,20,23,32,36-40]. In this structure, acoustic trajectories are considered to be a sum of independent acoustic components which have different context dependencies (different decision trees have to be trained for those components). Since the mean vectors and covariance matrices of the distribution are equal to the sum of mean vectors and covariance matrices of additive components, the model would be able to exploit contextual factors more efficiently. Furthermore, in this structure, each training data sample contributes to modeling multiple mean vectors and covariance matrices. Many papers applied the additive structure just for F0 modeling [37-40]. Authors in [37] proposed an additive structure with multiple decision trees for mean vectors and a single tree for variance terms. In this paper, for different additive components, different sets of contextual factors were used and multiple trees were built simultaneously. In [40], multiple additive decision trees are also employed, but they train this structure using minimum generation error (MGE) criterion. Sakai [38] defines an additive model with three distinct layers, namely intonational phrase, word-level, and pitch-accent layers. All of these components were trained simultaneously using a regularized least square error criterion. Qian et al. [39] propose to use multiple additive regression trees with a gradient-based tree-boosting algorithm. Decision trees are trained in successive stages to minimize the error squares. Takaki et al. [19,20] applied additive structure for spectral modeling and reported that the computational complexity of this structure is extremely high for full context labels as used in speech synthesis. To alleviate this issue, they proposed two approaches: covariance parameter tying and a likelihood calculation algorithm using matrix inversion lemma [19]. Despite all the advantages, this additive structure may not match training data accurately because once training is done, the first and second moments of the training data and model may not be exactly the same in some regions.

Another important problem of conventional decision tree-clustered acoustic modeling is difficulty in capturing the effect of weak contextual factors such as word-level emphasis [23,36]. It is mainly because weak contexts have less influence on the likelihood measure [23]. One clear approach to address this issue is to construct the decision tree in two successive steps [36]. In the first step, all selections are done among weak contextual factors, and in the second step, the remaining questions are adopted [36]. This procedure can effectively exploit weak contextual factors, but it leads to a reduction in the amount of training

data available for normal contextual factors. Context adaptive training with factorized decision trees [23] is another approach that can exploit weak context questions efficiently. In this system, a canonical model is trained using normal contextual factors and then a set of transforms is built by weak contextual factors. In fact, canonical models and transforms, respectively, represent the effects of normal and weak contextual factors [23]. However, this structure also improves context generalization of conventional HMM-based synthesis by exploiting adaptation techniques.

This paper introduces a *maximum entropy model* (*MEM*)-based speech synthesis. MEM [41] has been demonstrated to be positively effective in numerous applications of speech and natural language processing such as speech recognition [42], prosody labeling [43], and part-of-speech tagging [44]. Accordingly, the overall idea of this research is to improve HSMM context generalization by taking advantage of a distribution which not only matches training data in many overlapped contextual regions but also is optimum in the sense of an entropy criterion. This system has the potential to model the dependencies between contextual factors and acoustic features such that each training sample contributes to train multiple sets of model parameters. As a result, context-dependent acoustic modeling based on MEM could lead to a promising synthesis system even for limited training data.

The rest of the paper is organized as follows. Section 2 presents HSMM-based speech synthesis. The hidden maximum entropy model (HMEM) structure and the proposed HMEM-based speech synthesis system are explained in Section 3. Section 4 is dedicated to experimental results. Finally, Section 5 concludes this paper.

2 HSMM-based speech synthesis

This section aims to explain the predominant statistical modeling approach applied in speech synthesis, i.e., *context-dependent multi-space probability distribution left-to-right without skip transitions HSMM* [3,14] (simply called HSMM in the remainder of this paper). The discussion presented in this section provides a preliminary framework which will be used as a basis to introduce the proposed HMEM technique in Section 3. The most significant drawback of HSMM, namely inadequate context generalization, is also pointed out.

2.1 HSMM structure

HSMM is a hidden Markov model (HMM) having explicit state duration distribution instead of self-state transition probabilities. Figure 1 illustrates the standard HSMM. As it can be observed, HSMM initially partitions acoustic parameter (observation) trajectories into a fixed number of time slices (so-called states) in order to moderate the undesirable influence of non-stationarity. Note that state durations are latent variables and have to be trained in an

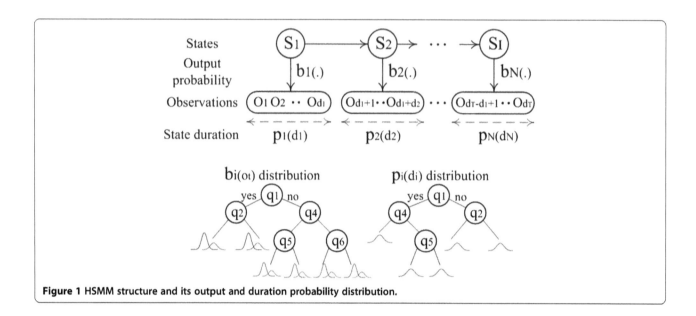

Figure 1 HSMM structure and its output and duration probability distribution.

unsupervised manner. An N-state HSMM λ is specified by a set of state output probability distributions $\{b_i(\cdot)\}_{i=1}^N$ and a complementary set of state duration probability distributions $\{p_i(\cdot)\}_{i=1}^N$. To model these distributions, a number of distinct decision trees are used for output and duration probability distributions. Conventionally, different trees are trained for different states [31]. These trees cluster the whole contextual factor space into a large number of tiny regions which are expressed by terminal nodes. Thereafter, in each terminal node, the output distribution $b_i(\cdot)$ is modeled by a multi-space probability distribution, and similarly, a typical Gaussian distribution is considered for the duration probability $p_i(\cdot)$ [14].

To handle the absence of fundamental frequency in unvoiced regions, multi-space probability distribution (MSD) is used for output probability distribution [17]. In accordance with commonly used synthesizers, this paper assumes that acoustic sample space consists of G spaces. Each of these spaces, specified by an index g, represents an n_g dimensional real space, i.e., $\mathscr{R}^{n_g}$. Each observation vector o_t has a probability w_g to be generated by the gth space iff the dimensionality of o_t is identical to n_g. In other words, we have

$$b_i(o_t) = \sum_{g \in S(o_t)} w_{ig} b_{i|g}(o_t),$$

$$b_{i|g}(o_t) = \mathcal{N}_{n_g}\left(o_t; \mu_{ig}, \Sigma_{ig}\right), \tag{1}$$

$$p_i(d) = \mathcal{N}_1\left(d; m_i, \sigma_i^2\right), \tag{2}$$

where $S(o_t)$ represents a set of all space indexes with the same dimensionality of o_t, and where $\mathcal{N}_l(.; \mu, \Sigma)$ denotes an l-dimensional Gaussian distribution with mean μ, and covariance matrix Σ ($\mathcal{N}_0$ is defined to be 1). Furthermore,

the output probability distribution of the ith state and gth space is denoted by $b_{i|g}(o_t)$ which is a Gaussian distribution with mean vector μ_{ig} and covariance matrix Σ_{ig}. Also, m_i and σ_i^2 represent mean and variance of the state duration probability.

Regarding the method for providing context dependency, it should be noted that HSMM normally offers binary decision trees and acoustic models are established for each leaf of these trees, separately [45,46]. Suppose f and L are contextual functions based on a decision tree Y and are defined as

$$f_l(i; Y) \stackrel{\text{def}}{=} \begin{cases} 1 \text{ if context of the } i\text{th state} \in l\text{th leaf of } Y \\ 0 \text{ if context of the } i\text{th state} \notin l\text{th leaf of } Y \end{cases},$$

$$L(Y) \stackrel{\text{def}}{=} \text{number of leaves in } Y \tag{3}$$

Applying the above functions, all model parameters of Equations 1 and 2 can be expressed by linear combinations of model parameters defined for each terminal node. More precisely,

$$\Sigma_{ig} = \sum_{l=1}^{L(Y_o)} f_l(i; Y_o) \Sigma_{ig}^l,$$

$$\mu_{ig} = \sum_{l=1}^{L(Y_o)} f_l(i; Y_o) \mu_{ig}^l,$$

$$w_{ig} = \sum_{l=1}^{L(Y_o)} f_l(i; Y_o) w_{ig}^l, \tag{4}$$

$$\sigma_i = \sum_{l=1}^{L(Y_o)} f_l(i; Y_d) \sigma_i^l,$$

$$m_i = \sum_{l=1}^{L(Y_o)} f_l(i; Y_d) m_i^l,$$

where Y_o and Y_d are decision trees trained for modeling output observation vectors and state durations. All symbols with superscript l indicate model parameters defined for the lth leaf.

2.2 HSMM likelihood

Having described the HSMM structure, we can now probe the exact expression for model likelihood or the probability of the observation sequence $O = [o_1, o_2, ..., o_T]$ as [14]:

$$P(O|\lambda) = \sum_{i=1}^{N} \sum_{j=1, j\neq i}^{N} \sum_{d=1}^{t} \alpha_{t-d}(j) p_i(d) \prod_{s=t-d+1}^{t} b_i(o_s) \beta_t(i)$$

(5)

where this equality is valid for every value of $t \in [1, T]$. Also, $\alpha_t(i)$ and $\beta t(i)$ are partial forward and backward probability variables that are calculated successively from their previous or next values as follows [3,14]:

$$\alpha_t(i) = \sum_{d=1}^{t} \sum_{j=1, j\neq i}^{N} \alpha_{t-d}(j) p_i(d) \prod_{s=t-d+1}^{t} b_i(o_s),$$

(6)

$$\beta_t(i) = \sum_{d=1}^{T-t} \sum_{j=1, j\neq i}^{N} p_j(d) \prod_{s=t+1}^{t+d} b_j(o_s) \beta_{t+d}(j),$$

(7)

where the initial forward and backward variables for every state indexes i are $\alpha_0(i)$-1 and $\beta_T(i) = 1$.

2.3 HSMM parameter re-estimation

The ML criterion is commonly used to estimate model parameters of HSMM. However, we are not aware of latent variables, i.e., state durations and space indexes; therefore, an expectation maximization (EM) algorithm has to be adopted. Applying EM algorithm leads to the following re-estimation formulas [14]:

$$\hat{\mu}_{ig}^l = \frac{\sum_k f_l(i; Y_o) \sum_{t=1}^{T} \gamma_t(i, g) o_t}{\sum_k f_l(i; Y_o) \sum_{t=1}^{T} \gamma_t(i, g)},$$

$$\hat{\sum}_{ig}^l = \frac{\sum_k f_l(i; Y_o) \sum_{t=1}^{T} \gamma_t(i, g) \left(o_t - \hat{\mu}_{ig}^l\right)\left(o_t - \hat{\mu}_{ig}^l\right)^T}{\sum_k f_l(i; Y_o) \sum_{t=1}^{T} \gamma_t(i, g)},$$

$$\hat{w}_{ig}^l = \frac{\sum_k f_l(i; Y_o) \sum_{t=1}^{T} \gamma_t(i, g)}{\sum_{h=1}^{G} \sum_k f_l(i; Y_o) \sum_{t=1}^{T} \gamma_t(i, h)},$$

$$\hat{m}_i^l = \frac{\sum_k f_l(i; Y_d) \sum_{t=1}^{T} \sum_{d=1}^{t} \chi_t^d(i) d}{\sum_k f_l(i; Y_d) \sum_{t=1}^{T} \sum_{d=1}^{t} \chi_t^d(i)},$$

$$\hat{\sigma}_i^{l2} = \frac{\sum_k f_l(i; Y_d) \sum_{t=1}^{T} \sum_{d=1}^{t} \chi_t^d(i)(d - \hat{m}_i^l)^2}{\sum_k f_l(i; Y_d) \sum_{t=1}^{T} \sum_{d=1}^{t} \chi_t^d(i)},$$

(8)

where $\gamma_t(i,g)$ denotes the posterior probability of being in state i and space g at time t, and $\chi_t^d(i)$ is the probability of occupying the ith state from time $t-d+1$ to t. The following equations calculate the above probabilities:

$$\gamma_t(i, g) = \frac{1}{P(o|\lambda)} \sum_{t0=1}^{t-1} \sum_{t1=t}^{T} \sum_{j=1, j\neq i}^{N} \alpha_{t-d}(j) p_i(d) b_{i|g}(o_t)$$

$$\prod_{s=t0, s\neq t}^{t1} b_i(o_s) \beta_{t_1}(i), \chi_t^d(i) = \frac{1}{p(o|\lambda)}$$

$$\sum_{j=1, j\neq i}^{N} \alpha_{t-d}(j) p_i(d) \prod_{s=t-d+1}^{t} b_i(o_s) \beta_t(i).$$

(9)

2.4 Inefficient context generalization

A major drawback of decision tree-clustered HSMM can now be clarified. Suppose we have only two real contextual factors, f_1 and f_2. Figure 2 shows a sample decision tree and the regions represented by its terminal nodes. By training HSMM, the model matches training data in all non-overlapped regions expressed by the terminal nodes. However, there is no guarantee that this accordance is held for overlapped regions such as the region R in Figure 2.

It can be noticed from the definition of function $f_i(c;Y)$ in Equation 3 that this function can be viewed as a set of $L(Y)$ *non-overlapped* binary contextual factors. The fact that these contextual factors are non-overlapped leads to the insufficient context generalization, because this fact makes each training sample contribute to the model of only one leaf and only one Gaussian distribution. Hence, by extending $f_i(c;Y)$ to *overlapped* contextual factors, more efficient context generalization capabilities could be achieved. Section 3 proposes an approach which enables the conventional structure to model the overlapped contextual factors and thus improves the modeling performance of unseen contexts.

3. Hidden maximum entropy model

The goal of this section is to develop a context-dependent statistical model for acoustic parameters with adequate context generalization. The previous section on HSMM revealed that inappropriate generalization stemmed from the application of *non-overlapped* features only. Consequently, relating acoustic parameters to contextual information by incorporating *overlapped* features could improve generalization efficiency. This section proposes *HMEM* to establish this relation.

3.1 HMEM structure

The proposed HMEM technique exploits exactly the same structure and graphical model as the original HSMM, and thus, the model likelihood expression given by Equation 5 is also valid for HMEM. The only difference between HSMM and HMEM is the way they incorporate contextual factors in output and duration probability distributions

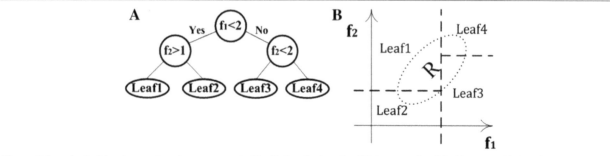

Figure 2 Sample decision tree and regions represented by its terminal nodes. (A) An example of decision tree with just three questions. **(B)** Regions that are classified by the tree and an arbitrary region (named R).

(i.e., $\{b_i(\cdot)\}_{i=1}^{N}$, $\{p_i(\cdot)\}_{i=1}^{N}$). HSMM builds a decision tree and then trains a Gaussian distribution for each leaf of the tree. On the contrary, HMEM obeys the maximum entropy modeling approach which will be described in the next subsection.

3.1.1 Maximum entropy modeling

Let us now derive a simple maximum entropy model. Suppose an ℓ-dimensional random vector process with output x that may be influenced by some contextual information c. Our target is to construct a stochastic model that precisely predicts the behavior of x, when c is given, i.e., $P(x|c)$. Maximum entropy principle first imposes a set of constraints on $P(x|c)$ and then chooses a distribution as close as possible to a uniform distribution by maximizing the entropy criterion [41]. In fact, this method will find the least biased distribution among all distributions that satisfy our constraints. In other words,

$$\hat{P}(x|c) \stackrel{\text{def}}{=} \operatorname{argmax}_P \mathcal{H}(P) \text{ subject to a set of constraint,}$$

(10)

employed constraints make the model preserve some context-dependent statistics of the training data. $\mathcal{H}(P)$ represents entropy criterion [41] that is calculated as

$$\mathcal{H}(P) \stackrel{\text{def}}{=} -\int_x \sum_{\text{all possible } c} P(x,c) \log P(x,c) \mathrm{d}x.$$

(11)

Computing the above expression is extremely complex because there are a large number of contextual factors and all possible values of c are not calculable. However, authors in [41] applied the following approximation for $P(x,c)$:

$$P(x,c) = \tilde{P}(c)P(x|c).$$

(12)

where $\tilde{P}(c)$ denotes empirical probability which can be calculated directly using the training database [41].

The above approximation simplifies the entropy expression as

$$\mathcal{H}(P) = -\int_x \sum_{\text{all } c \text{ in database}} \tilde{P}(c)P(x|c) \log P(x|c)dx$$
$$-\sum_{\text{all } c \text{ in database}} \tilde{P}(c) \log \tilde{P}(c),$$

(13)

where the second term is constant and does not affect the optimization problem. Therefore, we have

$$\mathcal{H}(P) = -\sum_{\text{all } c \text{ in database}} \tilde{P}(c) \int_x P(x|c) \log P(x|c)dx.$$

(14)

Additionally, we adopt a set of L_f predefined binary contextual factors, $f_l(c)$, and another set of L_g binary contextual factors, $g_l(c)$, that both of them may be highly overlapped. In order to obtain a Gaussian distribution for $\hat{P}(x|c)$ and extend the conventional HSMM distribution, first- and second-order context-dependent moments expressed in Equation 14 are considered for the constraints.

$$\hat{P}(x|c) \stackrel{\text{def}}{=} \operatorname{argmax}_P \mathcal{H}(P)$$

(15)

subject to following constraints:

$$\left\{ \begin{array}{c} \forall 1 \leq l \leq L_f \ E\{f_l(c)x\} = \tilde{E}\{f_l(c)x\} \\ \forall 1 \leq l \leq L_g \ E\{g_l(c)x\,x^T\} = \tilde{E}\{g_l(c)x\,x^T\} \\ \text{For all possible } c \int_x P(x|c)dx = 1 \end{array} \right\},$$

where E and $\hat{E}$ indicate real and empirical mathematical expectations given in the following equations:

$$\tilde{E}\{f_l(c)x\} = \sum_{\text{all } c \text{ in database}} \tilde{P}(c)f_l(c)x(c),$$

(16)

$$E\{f_l(c)x\} = \sum_{\text{all } c \text{ in database}} \tilde{P}(c)f_l(c) \int_x xP(x,c)dx$$

where $x(c)$ denotes the realization of ℓ-dimensional random vector x for the context c in the database. If there are multiple realizations for x, $x(c)$ will be obtained by taking the average over those values. In sum, the proposed context-dependent acoustic modeling approach obtains the smoothest (maximum entropy) distribution that captures first-order moments of training data in L_f regions indicated by $\{f_l(c)\}_{l=1}^{L_f}$ and second-order moments of data computed in $\{g_l(c)\}_{l=1}^{L_g}$.

In order to solve the optimization problem expressed by Equation 10, the Lagrange multipliers method is applied. This method defines a new optimization function as follows:

$$\hat{P}(x|c) = \text{argmax}_P \mathcal{H}(P) + \sum_{l=1}^{L_f} u_l^T \left(E\{f_l(c)x\} - \tilde{E}\{f_l(c)x\} \right)$$
$$+ \sum_{l=1}^{L_g} \left(E\{g_l(c)x^T H_l x\} - \tilde{E}\{g_l(c)x^T H_l x\} \right), \quad (17)$$

where u_l denotes a vector of Lagrange multipliers for satisfying the lth first-order moment constraints and H_l is a matrix of Lagrange multipliers for satisfying the lth second-order moment constraints. Taking derivatives of the above function with respect to P leads to the following equality.

$$\sum_{\text{all } c} \tilde{P}(c) \int_x \left(-\log P(x|c) + u^T x + x^T H x + \text{const.} \right) dx = 0$$
$$H \overset{\text{def}}{=} \sum_{l=1}^{L_g} g_l(c) H_l, u \overset{\text{def}}{=} \sum_{l=1}^{L_f} f_l(c) u_l. \quad (18)$$

Therefore, one possible solution that maximizes entropy with the constraint of Equation 15 using Lagrange multipliers can be expressed as:

$$\hat{P}(x|c) = \frac{1}{\left(\det(2\pi H^{-1}) \right)^{0.5}} \exp$$
$$\times \left[-\frac{1}{2} \left(x + \frac{1}{2} H^{-1} u \right)^T H \left(x + \frac{1}{2} H^{-1} u \right) \right],$$
$$H \overset{\text{def}}{=} \sum_{l=1}^{L_g} g_l(c) H_l, u \overset{\text{def}}{=} \sum_{l=1}^{L_f} f_l(c) u_l, \quad (19)$$

where H_l and u_l are model parameters related to the lth contextual factors $g_l(c)$ and $f_l(c)$, respectively. H_l is an ℓ-by-ℓ matrix and u_l is an ℓ-dimensional vector. When $f_l(c)$ becomes 1 (i.e., it is active), u_l affects the distribution; otherwise, it has no effect on the distribution. In fact, Equation 19 is nothing but the well-known Gaussian

distribution with mean vector $-0.5H^{-1}u$, and covariance matrix H^{-1}, both calculated from a specific context-dependent combination of model parameters. Indeed, the main difference of MEM in comparison with other methods such as spectral additive structure [19,20] is that mean and variance in MEM are not a linear combination of other parameters. This type of combination enables MEM to match training data in all overlapped regions.

This form of context-dependent Gaussian distribution presents a promising flexibility in utilizing contextual information. On one hand, using detailed and non-overlapped contextual factors such as features defined by Equation 3 (decision tree terminal node indicators) generates context-dependent Gaussian distributions which are identical to those used in conventional HSMM. These distributions have straightforward and efficient training procedure but suffer from insufficient context generalization capabilities. On the other hand, incorporating general and highly overlapped contextual factors overcomes the latter shortcoming and provides efficient context generalization, but its training procedure becomes more computationally complex. In the case of highly overlapped contextual factors, an arbitrary context activates several contextual factors, and hence, each observation vector is involved in modeling several model parameters.

3.1.2 ME-based modeling vs. additive modeling

At first glance, the contextual additive structure [19,20,32,37] seems to have the same capabilities as the proposed ME-based context-dependent acoustic modeling. Therefore, to clarify their differences, this section compares HMEM with the additive structure through a very simple example.

In this example, the goal is to model a one-dimensional observation value using both ME-based modeling and a contextual additive structure. Due to the prime importance of mean parameters in HMM-based speech synthesis [47], we investigate the difference between mean values predicted by two systems.

Figure 3A shows a three-dimensional contextual factor space (c_1-c_2-c_3) which is clustered by an additive structure. The additive structure consists of three different additive components with three different decision trees, namely Q_1, Q_2, and Q_3. Each tree has a simple structure with just one binary question that splits a specific dimension of the contextual factor space into two regions. Each region is represented by a leaf node, and inside that leaf node, a mean parameter of each additive component is written. As it is depicted in the figure, these trees split contextual factor space into eight different cubic clusters. Mean values estimated for these cubic clusters are computed by adding mean values of additive components.

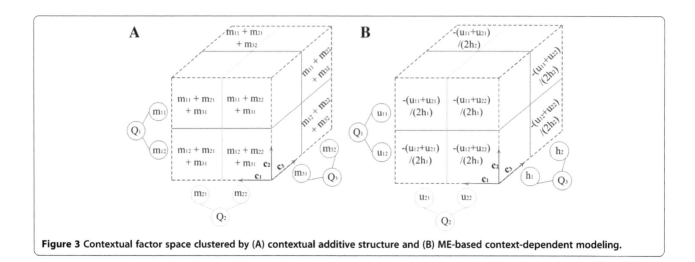

Figure 3 Contextual factor space clustered by (A) contextual additive structure and (B) ME-based context-dependent modeling.

In contrast, Figure 3B shows the corresponding ME-based modeling approach. In the previous subsection, it is described that ME-based context-dependent modeling needs two sets of regions, $\{f_l(c)\}_{l=1}^{L_f}$ and $\{g_l(c)\}_{l=1}^{L_g}$. This example assumes that the leaves of Q_1 and Q_2 are defined as the first set of regions $\{f_l(c)\}_{l=1}^{L_f}$, and the leaves of Q_3 are defined as the second set $\{g_l(c)\}_{l=1}^{L_g}$. Therefore, according to the explanation of the previous subsection, first empirical moments of Q_1 and Q_2, in addition to the second empirical moments of Q_3, are captured by ME-based modeling. Figure 3B shows the estimated model mean values for all eight cubic clusters. As it is realized from the figure, model mean values estimated by ME-based modeling is a combination of adding parameters live in the regions $\{f_l(c)\}_{l=1}^{L_f}$ divided by the parameters defined for the regions $\{g_l(c)\}_{l=1}^{L_g}$. In fact, the proposed ME-based modeling is an extension to the additive structure that ties all covariance matrices [19]. This extension is clear because if $\{g_l(c)\}_{l=1}^{L_g}$ is defined with one region containing all contextual feature space, the ME-based modeling converts to the additive structure that ties all covariance matrices [19].

3.1.3 HMEM-based speech synthesis

HMEM improves both state duration distribution $\{p_i(\cdot)\}_{i=1}^N$ and output observation distribution $\{b_i(\cdot)\}_{i=1}^N$ using maximum entropy modeling. According to the discussion presented in Section 3.1.1, MEM requires two sets of contextual factors. In this section, for the sake of simplicity, it is assumed that the contextual regions defined for first-order moment constraints $\{f_l(c)\}_{l=1}^{L_f}$ are identical to the regions defined for second-order moment constraints

$\{g_l(c)\}_{l=1}^{L_g}$. All equations presented in this section is based on this assumption; however, their extension to the general case (different $\{f_l(c)\}_{l=1}^{L_f}$ and $\{g_l(c)\}_{l=1}^{L_g}$) is straightforward. Therefore, we define $f_l^d(i)$ and $f_l^o(i)$ as L^d and L^o contextual factors which are designed carefully for the purpose of modeling duration and acoustic parameters of the ith state. Maximum entropy criterion leads to the following duration and output probability distributions.

$$b_i(o_t) = \sum_{g \in S(o_t)} w_{ig} b_{i|g}(o_t),$$

$$b_{i|g}(o_t) = \mathcal{N}_{n_g}\left(o_t; -\frac{1}{2} u_{ig} H_{ig}, H_{ig}^{-1}\right),$$

$$P_i(d) = \mathcal{N}_1\left(d; -\frac{1}{2} u_i h_i, \frac{1}{h_i}\right),$$

$$u_i = \sum_{l=1}^{L^d} f_l^d(i) u_i^l, \qquad h_i = \sum_{l=1}^{L^d} f_l^d(i) h_i^l,$$

$$u_{ig} = \sum_{l=1}^{L^o} f_l^o(i) u_{ig}^l, \qquad H_{ig} = \sum_{l=1}^{L^o} f_l^o(i) H_{ig}^l,$$

$$w_{ig} = \frac{\exp\left(\sum_{l=1}^{L^o} f_l^o(i) w_{ig}^l\right)}{\sum_{g=1}^{G} \exp\left(\sum_{i=1}^{L^o} f_l^o(i) w_{ig}^l\right)}.$$

$$(20)$$

In these equations, $S(o_t)$ is a set of all possible spaces defined for o_t. u_i^l and h_i^l are the duration model parameters, and w_{ig}^l, u_{ig}^l, and H_{ig}^l denote the output model parameters related to the lth contextual factor, gth space, and ith state.

We can now probe the differences between HSMM and HMEM context-dependent acoustic modeling. These two modeling approaches are dramatically close to each other, so that defining HMEM contextual factors based on the decision trees described by Equation 3 would reduce HMEM to HSMM. Accordingly, HMEM extends HSMM and enables its structure to exploit overlapped contextual factors.

Moreover, another significant conclusion that could be drawn from this section is that several HSMM concepts are transposable within the HMEM framework. These concepts involve Viterbi algorithm, methods which calculate forward/backward variables and occupation probabilities, and even all parameter generation algorithms [26-28]. It just needs to define mean vectors, covariance matrices, and space probabilities of HSMM in accordance with Equation 20.

3.2 HMEM parameter re-estimation

In the training phase, we are given a set of K i.i.d. training data $\{O^k\}_{k=1}^{K}$; the goal is to find the best set of model parameters $\hat{\lambda}$, which maximizes the log likelihood:

$$\hat{\lambda} \overset{\text{def}}{=} \text{argmax}_{\lambda} L(\lambda),$$
$$L(\lambda) \overset{\text{def}}{=} \frac{1}{K}\sum_{k=1}^{K} \ln P(O^{(k)}|\lambda).$$

$$(21)$$

Substituting Equation 5 for the likelihood $P(O^{(k)}|\lambda)$ leads to an excessively complex optimization problem with seemingly impossible direct solution. The major issue is that the distribution wholly depends upon the latent variables which are unknown. The expectation maximization (EM) technique offers an iterative algorithm which overcomes this problem and accurately solves the issue:

$$\lambda^{n+1} = \text{argmax}_{\lambda}\, \mathcal{Q}(\lambda;\lambda^n),$$
$$\mathcal{Q}(\lambda;\lambda^n) = \sum_{k}\sum_{\text{all } d,\text{all } q} P(d,q|O^{(k)};\lambda^n)\ln P(O^{(k)},d,q|;\lambda),$$

$$(22)$$

where d and q represent possible state durations and space indexes for the kth training utterance and the second summation is calculated over all possible values of d and q. In general, these functions cannot be minimized in a closed-form expression. Therefore, a numerical optimization technique such as the Broyden-Fletcher-Goldfarb-Shanno (BFGS) [48] method or Newton algorithm has to be derived to find one of the local optima. This paper proposes to exploit the outstanding BFGS algorithm, due to its favorable characteristics. However,

BFGS needs solely the first partial derivatives of the cost functions calculated as follows:

$$\frac{\partial \mathcal{Q}}{\partial u_i^l} = -\frac{1}{2}\sum_{k}f_l^d(i)\sum_{t=1}^{T}\sum_{d=1}^{t}\chi_t^d(i)\left[d+\frac{u_i}{2h_i}\right],$$
$$\frac{\partial \mathcal{Q}}{\partial h_i^l} = -\frac{1}{2}\sum_{k}f_l^d(i)\sum_{t=1}^{T}\sum_{d=1}^{t}\chi_t^d(i)\left[d^2-\frac{1}{h_i}-\left(\frac{u_i}{2h_i}\right)^2\right],$$
$$\frac{\partial \mathcal{Q}}{\partial w_{ig}^l} = \sum_{k}f_l^o(i)\sum_{t=1}^{T}\gamma_t(i,g)[1-w_{ig}],$$
$$\frac{\partial \mathcal{Q}}{\partial u_{ig}^l} = -\frac{1}{2}\sum_{k}f_l^o(i)\sum_{t=1}^{T}\gamma_t(i,g)\left[o_t+\frac{H_{ig}^{-1}u_{ig}}{2}\right],$$
$$\frac{\partial \mathcal{Q}}{\partial H_{ig}^l} = -\frac{1}{2}\sum_{k}f_l^o(i)\sum_{t=1}^{T}\gamma_t(i,g)\left[o_t o_t^T - H_{ig}^{-1} - \frac{H_{ig}^{-1}u_{ig}u_{ig}^T H_{ig}^{-1}}{4}\right],$$

$$(23)$$

where $\gamma_t(i,g)$ and $\chi_t^d(i)$ are defined in Section 2.3. Therefore, at every iteration of BFGS, we need to find the above gradient values and BFGS estimates new parameters which are closer to the optimum ones.

At first glance, calculating the above gradient expressions seems to be computationally expensive, but they can be calculated efficiently if we rewrite them in terms of sufficient statistics as in the following equations. By doing this, the computational complexity no longer depends on the number of training observation vectors, but rather on the total number of states. Furthermore, storing sufficient statistics instead of all observation vectors reduces the amount of main memory usage of the training procedure. These equations are expressed as

$$\frac{\partial \mathcal{Q}}{\partial u_i^l} = -\frac{1}{2}\sum_{k}f_l^d(i)\,\tilde{X}_i\left(\tilde{m}_i+\frac{u_i}{2h_i}\right),$$
$$\frac{\partial \mathcal{Q}}{\partial h_i^l} = -\frac{1}{2}\sum_{k}f_l^d(i)\,\tilde{X}_i\left(\tilde{r}_i-\frac{1}{h_i}-\left(\frac{u_i}{2h_i}\right)^2\right),$$
$$\frac{\partial \mathcal{Q}}{\partial w_{ig}^l} = \sum_{k}f_l^o(i)\tilde{\gamma}(i,g)[1-w_{ig}],$$
$$\frac{\partial \mathcal{Q}}{\partial u_{ig}^l} = -\frac{1}{2}\sum_{k}f_l^o(i)\tilde{\gamma}(i,g)\left[\tilde{\mu}(i,g)+\frac{H_{ig}^{-1}u_{ig}}{2}\right],$$
$$\frac{\partial \mathcal{Q}}{\partial u_{ig}^l} = -\frac{1}{2}\sum_{k}f_l^o(i)\tilde{\gamma}(i,g)\left[\tilde{R}(i,g)+\frac{H_{ig}^{-1}u_{ig}}{2}\right],$$

$$(24)$$

where $\tilde{X}_i$, $\tilde{m}_i$, and $\tilde{r}_i$ are sufficient statistics required to train duration distribution and are calculated as

$$\tilde{X}_i = \sum_{t=1}^{T}\sum_{d=1}^{t}\chi_t^d(i),$$
$$\tilde{m}_i = \frac{1}{\tilde{X}_i}\sum_{t=1}^{T}\sum_{d=1}^{t}\chi_t^d(i)d,$$
$$\tilde{r}_i = \frac{1}{\tilde{X}_i}\sum_{t=1}^{T}\sum_{d=1}^{t}\chi_t^d(i)d^2.$$

$$(25)$$

Also, $\tilde{\gamma}(i,g)$, $\tilde{\mu}(i,g)$, and $\tilde{R}(i,g)$ are sufficient statistics related to output probability distribution:

$$\tilde{\gamma}(i,g) = \sum_{t=1}^{T} \gamma_t(i,g),$$

$$\tilde{\mu}0(i,g) = \frac{1}{\tilde{\gamma}(i,g)} \sum_{t=1}^{T} \sum_{d=1}^{t} \chi_t^d(i)o_t, \qquad (26)$$

$$\tilde{R}(i,g) = \frac{1}{\tilde{\gamma}(i,g)} \sum_{t=1}^{T} \sum_{d=1}^{t} \chi_t^d(i)o_t^2.$$

These equations prove that regardless of calculating sufficient statistics, an EM iteration in HMEM is just

equivalent to train three maximum entropy models for state duration distribution, state output distribution for each subspace, and subspace probability.

Having introduced HMEM parameter estimation procedure, we can now proceed to explain the overall structure of HMEM. Figure 4 shows the whole architecture illustrating the HMEM-based speech synthesis system. Just like other statistical parametric approaches, it consists of two phases, training and synthesis. In the training phase, we first extract a parametric representation of the speech signal (i.e., acoustic features) including both spectral and excitation features from training speech database. In parallel, contextual factors are obtained for all states of the database.

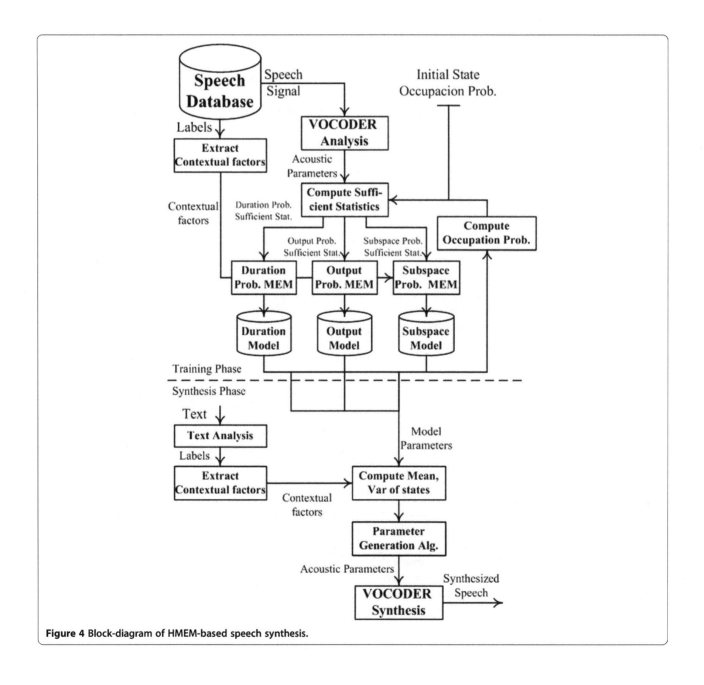

Figure 4 Block-diagram of HMEM-based speech synthesis.

Thereafter, both acoustic and contextual factors are applied for HMEM training. The training procedure is performed by iterating through three steps: computing sufficient statistics, training all maximum entropy distributions, and calculating occupation probabilities. However, the training procedure needs prior information about state occupation probabilities for the first iteration. This paper proposes to utilize a trained HMM for this purpose. Training procedure continues until an amount of increase in likelihood falls below a specific threshold. The synthesis phase is completely identical to a typical HSMM-based speech synthesis system. The only difference is that in HMEM state, mean and covariance parameters are estimated in accordance with Equation 20 instead of tracing a binary decision tree.

3.3 Decision tree-based context clustering

Statistical parametric speech synthesis systems typically exploit around 50 different types of contextual factors [23]. For such system, it is impossible to prepare tanning data covering all context-dependent models, and there are a large number of unseen models that have to be predicted in synthesis phase. Therefore, a context clustering approach such as decision tree-based clustering has to be used to decide about unseen contexts [31,45]. Due to the critical importance of context clustering algorithms in HMM-based speech synthesis systems, this section focuses on designing a clustering algorithm for HMEM.

As it is realized from the discussion in this section, In order to implement the proposed architecture, we initially need to define two sets of contextual regions. These regions are represented by two sets, namely $\{f_l(c)\}_{l=1}^{L_f}$ and $\{g_l(c)\}_{l=1}^{L_g}$. First- and second-order moment constraints have to be satisfied for all regions in $\{f_l(c)\}_{l=1}^{L_f}$ and $\{g_l(c)\}_{l=1}^{L_g}$, respectively. Before training, the first empirical moments of all regions in $\{f_l(c)\}_{l=1}^{L_f}$ and the second empirical moments of all regions in $\{g_l(c)\}_{l=1}^{L_g}$ are computed using training data. Then, HMEM is trained to be consistent with these empirical moments. The major difficulty in defining these regions is to find a satisfactory balance between model complexity and the availability of training data. For limited training databases, a model with a small number of parameters, i.e., small number of regions has to be defined. In this case, bigger (strongly overlapped) contextual regions seem to be more desirable, because they can alleviate the problem of weak context generalization. On the other hand, for large training databases, larger number of contextual regions has to be defined to escape from under-fitting model to training data. In this case, smaller contextual regions can be applied to capture the details of acoustic features. This section introduces an algorithm that defines multiple contextual regions for first- and second-order moments by considering HMEM structure.

Due to the complex relationship between acoustic features and contextual factors, it is extremely difficult to find the optimum sets of contextual regions that maximize likelihood for HMEM. For the sake of simplicity, we have made some simplifying assumptions to find a number of suboptimum contextual regions. These assumptions are expressed as follows:

- We have used conventional binary decision tree structures to define $\{f_l(c)\}_{l=1}^{L_f}$ and $\{g_l(c)\}_{l=1}^{L_g}$. This is a common approach in many former papers [19,20,23]. It should be noted that the decision tree structure is not the only possible structure to express the relationship between acoustic features and contextual factors. For example, other approaches such as neural networks or soft-clustering methods can be applied as well. However, in this paper, we limit our discussion to the conventional binary decision tree structure.

- Multiple decision trees are trained for $\{f_l(c)\}_{l=1}^{L_f}$, and just one decision tree is constructed for $\{g_l(c)\}_{l=1}^{L_g}$. In this way, the final HMEM preserves the first empirical moments of multiple decision trees, and the second moments of just one decision tree. This assumption is a result of the fact that first-order moments seem to be more important than second-order moments [32,47].

- The discussion of current section shows that the ML estimates of parameters defined for $\{f_l(c)\}_{l=1}^{L_f}$ and $\{g_l(c)\}_{l=1}^{L_g}$ significantly depend on each other. Therefore, in each step of decision tree construction, a BFGS optimization algorithm has to be executed to re-estimate both sets of parameters simultaneously, and this procedure leads to an extreme amount of computational complexity. To alleviate this problem, it is proposed to borrow $\{g_l(c)\}_{l=1}^{L_g}$ from a baseline system (conventional HMM-based speech synthesis system) and construct $\{f_l(c)\}_{l=1}^{L_f}$ independently.

- In HMEM structure, $\{f_l(c)\}_{l=1}^{L_f}$ is responsible to provide satisfactory clustering of first-order moments (mean vectors). Similarly, contextual additive structures [19,20,37] that tie all covariance matrices offer multiple overlapped clustering of mean vectors based on the likelihood criterion; therefore, an appropriate method is to borrow $\{f_l(c)\}_{l=1}^{L_f}$ from the contextual additive structure.

- However, training a contextual additive structure using algorithms proposed in [19,20] is still computationally expensive for large training databases (more than 500 sentences). Three modifications are applied to the algorithm proposed by Takaki et al. [19] for computational complexity reduction: (i) The number of decision trees is considered to be fixed (in our experiments, an additive structure with four decision trees is built). (ii) Questions are selected one by one for different decision trees. Therefore, all trees are grown simultaneously, and the size of all trees would be equal. (iii) In the process of selecting the best pair of question and leaf, it is assumed that just the parameters of candidate leaf will be changed and all other parameters remain unchanged. It should be noted that the selection procedure is repeated until the total number of free parameters reaches the number of parameters trained for the baseline system (HSMM-based speech synthesis system).

In sum, the final algorithm of determining $\{f_l(c)\}_{l=1}^{L_f}$ and $\{g_l(c)\}_{l=1}^{L_g}$ can be summarized as follows. $\{g_l(c)\}_{l=1}^{L_g}$ is simply borrowed from a conventional HMM-based speech synthesis system. $\{f_l(c)\}_{l=1}^{L_f}$ also resulted from an independent context clustering algorithm that is a fast and simplified version of contextual additive structure [19]. This clustering algorithm builds four binary context-dependent decision trees, simultaneously. It should be noted that when the number of clusters reaches the number of leaves of the decision tree trained for an HSMM-based system, the clustering algorithm is finished.

The following algorithm shows the overall procedure of the proposed context clustering.

4 Experiments

We have conducted two sets of experiments. First, the performance of HMEM with heuristic context clusters is examined; second, the impact of the proposed method for decision tree-based context clustering presented in the Section 3.3 is evaluated.

4.1 Performance evaluation of HMEM with heuristic context clusters

This subsection aims to compare HMEM-based acoustic modeling with conventional HSMM-based method. In this subsection, contextual regions of HMEM are defined heuristically and it is fixed for different sizes of training database.

4.1.1 Experimental conditions

A Persian speech database [49] consisting of 1,000 utterances from a male speaker was used throughout our experiments. Sentences were between 5 and 20 words long and have an average duration of 8 s. This database was specifically designed for the purpose of speech synthesis. Sentences in the database covered most frequent Persian words, all bi-letter combinations, all bi-phoneme combinations, and most frequent Persian syllables. In the modeling of the synthesis units, 31 phonemes were used, including silence. As presented in Section 4.1.2, a large variety of phonetic and linguistic contextual factors was considered in this work.

Speech signals were sampled at a rate of 16 kHz and windowed by a 25-ms Blackman window with a 5-ms

Inputs:
- $\{t_l(c)\}_{l=1}^{L_t}$: Context clusters trained for HSMM-based synthesis
- Acoustic features and contextual factors of untied state models
- N: Predefined number of decision trees for $\{f_l(c)\}_{l=1}^{L_f}$

Outputs:
- $\{f_l(c)\}_{l=1}^{L_f}$: Context clusters for first-order moment constraints
- $\{g_l(c)\}_{l=1}^{L_g}$: Context clusters for second-order moment constraints

Context clustering algorithm:
1. Initialize N trees for $\{f_l(c)\}_{l=1}^{L_f}$:
2. While true
    For $n = 1 \dots N$ (for each tree)
      1'. For all leaf nodes r and questions q
        $\Delta L(r,q)$ = delta-likelihood by spiting node r using q (assume parameters of all other nodes are fixed):
      2'. $\hat{r}, \hat{q} = \mathrm{argmax}_{r,q}\Delta L(r,q)$;
      3'. Split the rth leaf node of the nth tree in $\{f_l(c)\}_{l=1}^{L_f}$ with question q:
      4'. Train an additive structure for $\{f_l(c)\}_{l=1}^{L_f}$ (assume all covariance matrices are tied):
      5'. If $L_f = L_t$ then exit:
3. $\{g_l(c)\}_{l=1}^{L_g} = \{t_l(c)\}_{l=1}^{L_t}$:

shift. 40 Mel-cepstral coefficients, 5 bandpass aperiodicity and fundamental frequency, and their delta and delta-delta coefficients extracted by STRAIGHT [11] were employed as our acoustic features. In this experiment, the number of states was 5, and multi-stream left-to-right with no skip path MSD-HSMM was trained as the traditional HSMM system. Decision trees were built using maximum likelihood criterion, and the size of decision trees was determined by MDL principle [46]. Additionally, global variance (GV)-based parameter generation algorithm [20,26] and STRAIGHT vocoder were applied in the synthesis phase.

Both subjective and objective tests were carried out to compare HMEM that uses some heuristic contextual regions with the traditional HSMM system. In our experiments, two different synthesis systems named HMEM1 and HMEM2 were developed based on the proposed approach. HMEM1 employs a small number of general highly overlapped contextual factors that are designed carefully for each stream, while HMEM2 uses a larger number of contextual factors.

More precisely, a set of 64 initial contextual factors were extracted for each segment (phoneme) of the Persian database. These factors contain both segmental and suprasegmental contextual features. From these contextual factors, a set of approximately 8,000 contextual questions were designed and the HSMM system was trained using these questions. Each question can form two regions; therefore, these 8,000 questions can be converted to 16,000 regions. For each stream of HMEM1, a small number of these contextual regions that seem to be more important for that stream were selected and HMEM1 was trained using them. Contextual factors of HMEM2 contain all contextual factors of HMEM1 in addition to a number of detailed ones. The number of contextual regions in HMEM2 is twice the number of regions in HMEM1. Regions of both HMEM1 and HMEM2 were selected based on the linguistic knowledge of the Persian language. Table 1 shows the number of contextual regions for different synthesis systems (namely HSMM with different training data sizes, HMEM1 and HMEM2).

Experiments were conducted on five different training sets with 50, 100, 200, 400, and 800 utterances. Additionally, a fixed set of 200 utterances, not included in the training sets, was used for testing.

4.1.2 Employed contextual factors

In our experiments, contextual factors contained phonetic, syllable, word, phrase, and sentence level features. In each of these levels, both general and detailed features were considered. Features such as phoneme identity, syllable stress pattern, or word part-of-speech tag are examples of general features, and a question like the position of the current phoneme is a sample of a detailed one. Specific information with regard to contextual features is presented in this subsection.

Contextual factors play a significant role in the proposed HMEM method. As a consequence, they have been designed carefully and are now briefly presented:

➢ Phonetic-level features
- Phoneme identity before the preceding phoneme; preceding, current, and succeeding phonemes; and phoneme identity after the next phoneme
- Position of the current phoneme in the current syllable (forward and backward)
- Whether this phoneme is 'Ezafe' [50] or not (Ezafe is a special feature in Persian pronounced as a short vowel 'e' and relates two different words together. Ezafe is not written but is pronounced and has a profound effect on intonation)

➢ Syllable-level features
- Stress level of this syllable (five different stress levels are defined for our speech database)
- Position of the current syllable in the current word and phrase (forward and backward)
- Type of the current syllable (syllables in Persian language are structured as CV, CVC, or CVCC, where C and V denote consonants and vowels, respectively)
- Number of the stressed syllables before and after the current syllable in the current phrase
- Number of syllables from the previous stressed syllable to the current syllable
- Vowel identity of the current syllable

➢ Word-level features
- Part-of-speech (POS) tag of the preceding, current and succeeding word
- Position of the current word in the current sentence (forward and backward)

Table 1 The number of leaf nodes for each stream in different speech synthesis systems

		Various speech synthesis systems					
		HSMM-100	HSMM-200	HSMM-400	HSMM-800	HMEM1	HMEM2
Streams of acoustic features	bap	239	392	581	958	565	1,130
	dur	124	193	319	512	256	512
	log F0	590	904	1,425	2,487	565	1,130
	mgc	267	416	736	1,279	695	1,390
Total parameters		75,628	118,314	204,683	354,133	188,217	377,834

- Whether the current word contains 'Ezafe' or not
- Whether this word is the last word in the sentence or not
➢ Phrase-level features
- Number of syllables in the preceding, current, and succeeding phrase
- Position of the current phrase in the sentence (forward and backward)
➢ Sentence-level features
- Number of syllables, words, and phrases in the current sentence
- Type of the current sentence

4.1.3 Illustratory example

Before going further with the objective and subjective evaluations, the superiority of HMEM over HSMM when few training data are available can be already illustrated. Although the improvement will be shown in Sections 4.1.4 and 4.1.5 to be achieved for all speech characteristics (log F0, duration, and spectral features), it is here emphasized for the prediction of log F0 trajectories. Figure 5 shows the trajectory of log F0 generated by HSMM and HMEM1 with 100 training utterances, in contrast to the natural contour. This plot confirms the superiority of HMEM over HSMM in modeling fundamental frequency when the amount of training data is small, as the generated contour by HMEM is far closer to the natural one compared to HSMM.

In limited training sets, HSMM produces sudden transitions between adjacent states. This drawback is the result of decision tree-clustered context-dependent modeling. More specifically, when few data are available for training, the number of leaves in the decision tree is reduced. As a result, the distance between the mean vectors of adjacent states can be large. Even the parameter generation algorithm proposed by [26-28] cannot compensate such jumps. In such cases, the quality of synthetic speech with HSMM is expected to deteriorate.

On the opposite, if we let adjacent states contain common active contextual factors, then the variation of mean vectors in state transitions will be smoother. This is the key idea of HMEM which makes it possible to outperform HSMM when the data are limited. However, the use of overlapped contextual factors in HMEM will result in over-smoothing problem when the size of the training data is increased. Therefore, the detailed contextual factors are additionally considered in HMEM2 to alleviate the over-smoothing issue.

4.1.4 Objective evaluation

The average mel-cepstral distortion (MCD) [51] and root-mean-square (RMS) error of phoneme durations (expressed in terms of number of frames) were selected as relevant metrics for our objective assessment. For the calculation of both average mel-cepstral distance and RMS error of phoneme durations, the state boundaries (state durations) were determined using Viterbi alignment with the speaker's real utterance.

The MCD measure is defined by:

$$\text{MCD} = \frac{10}{\ln(10)} * \sqrt{2\sum_{i=1}^{40}\left(mc_i^t - mc_i^p\right)^2}, \qquad (27)$$

where mc_i is the ith mel-cepstral coefficients in a frame, mc^t is the target coefficient we are comparing against, and mc^p is the generated coefficient. In addition, RMS is defined as the following function:

$$\text{RMS} = \sqrt{\sum_{s=1}^{N}\left(d_s^t - d_s^p\right)^2 / N}, \qquad (28)$$

where N is the total number of states in a sentence, d_s is the duration of the sth state, d_s^t is the original duration, and d_s^p is the estimated duration.

Figure 6 shows the average mel-cepstral distance between spectra generated from the proposed method and

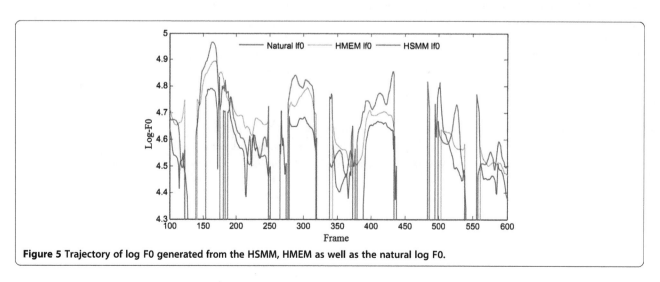

Figure 5 Trajectory of log F0 generated from the HSMM, HMEM as well as the natural log F0.

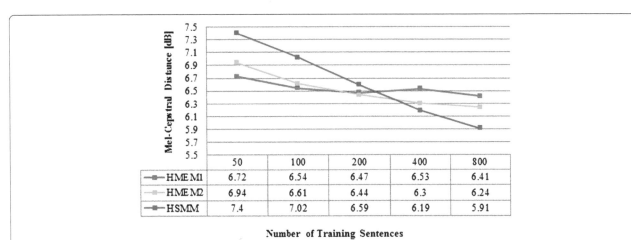

	50	100	200	400	800
HMEM1	6.72	6.54	6.47	6.53	6.41
HMEM2	6.94	6.61	6.44	6.3	6.24
HSMM	7.4	7.02	6.59	6.19	5.91

Number of Training Sentences

Figure 6 Comparison of average MCD as an objective measure between the proposed method and the HSMM-based one.

spectra obtained by analyzing the speaker's real utterance. For comparison, we also present the average distance of spectra generated from the HSMM-based method and the real spectra. In this figure, it is clearly observed that the proposed HMEM systems outperform the standard HSMM approach for limited training datasets. Nonetheless, this advantage disappears when more than 200 utterances are available for training. It can be noticed that a reduction of the size of the training set has a dramatic impact on the performance of HSMM, contrary to HMEM-based systems.

The same conclusions are observed for Figure 7 in which the generated duration of proposed systems is compared against that of HSMM. It can be again noticed that the proposed systems outperform HSMM in small databases. However, when the size of the database increases, HSMM gradually surpasses the proposed HMEM systems. Furthermore, detailed features added in HMEM2 affect the proposed method constructively when the synthesis units model by large databases. Thus, we expect that the proposed method could be comparable with HSMM or

outperform it even for large databases if we apply more detailed and well-designed features.

In summary, from these figures and the illustratory example presented before, we can see that when the available data are limited, all features (log F0, duration, and spectra) of synthetic speech generated by HMEM are closer to the original features than those obtained with HSMM. However, when the training database is large, the HSMM-based method performs better than HMEM. Nevertheless, employing more detailed features can assist the proposed method in becoming closer to the HSMM-based synthetic speech.

In addition to the abovementioned objective measurements, we have compared the accuracy of voiced/unvoiced detection in the proposed system with its counterpart in HSMM-based synthesis. Table 2 shows information about the false negative (FN), false positive (FP), true negative (TN), and true positive (TP) rates. Moreover, the data in Table 2 are summarized in Table 3 in which the accuracy of detecting voice/unvoiced regions is presented. As

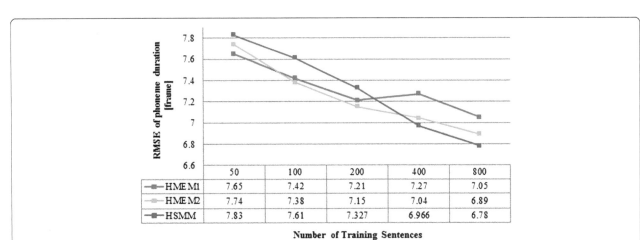

	50	100	200	400	800
HMEM1	7.65	7.42	7.21	7.27	7.05
HMEM2	7.74	7.38	7.15	7.04	6.89
HSMM	7.83	7.61	7.327	6.966	6.78

Number of Training Sentences

Figure 7 Comparison of RMS error of phoneme durations as objective measure between the proposed method and HSMM one.

Table 2 FN, FP, TN, and TP rates of detecting voiced/unvoiced regions through HMEM2 and the HSMM-based method

# training data	Implemented systems		Really voiced (%)	Really unvoiced (%)
50	HMEM2	Voiced	77.00	3.70
		Unvoiced	7.09	12.21
	HSMM	Voiced	78.23	5.79
		Unvoiced	5.86	10.12
100	HMEM2	Voiced	75.78	2.75
		Unvoiced	8.31	13.16
	HSMM	Voiced	78.07	5.34
		Unvoiced	6.02	10.57
200	HMEM2	Voiced	77.25	1.54
		Unvoiced	6.84	14.37
	HSMM	Voiced	78.43	4.43
		Unvoiced	5.66	11.48
400	HMEM2	Voiced	77.18	1.34
		Unvoiced	6.91	14.57
	HSMM	Voiced	76.09	2.70
		Unvoiced	8.00	13.21
800	HMEM2	Voiced	77.10	0.83
		Unvoiced	6.99	15.08
	HSMM	Voiced	77.17	2.66
		Unvoiced	6.92	13.25

realized from these tables, the proposed method detects voiced/unvoiced regions more accurately than HSMM regardless of the size of the database. In other words, not only in small databases but also for larger ones, HMEM outperforms HSMM in terms of detecting voiced/unvoiced regions.

4.1.5 Subjective evaluation

Two different subjective methods are employed in order to show the effectiveness of the proposed system and assess the effect of the size of the training database. A comparative mean opinion score (CMOS) test [52] with a 7-point scale, ranging from –3 (meaning that method A is much better than method B) to 3 (meaning the opposite), and a preference scoring [53] are used to evaluate the subjective quality of the synthesized speech. The results of this evaluation are respectively shown in Figures 8 and 9.

Table 3 Accuracy of voiced/unvoiced detector

# training data	HMEM2 accuracy (%)	HSMM accuracy (%)
50	89.21	88.35
100	88.94	88.64
200	91.62	89.91
400	91.75	89.30
800	92.18	90.42

Twenty native participants were asked to listen to ten randomly chosen pairs of synthesized speech samples generated by two different systems (selected arbitrarily among HMEM1, HMEM2, and HSMM).

Remarkably, the proposed systems are noticed to be of a great interest when the training data are limited (i.e., for 50, 100, and 200 utterances) and are in line with the conclusions of the objective assessments. The superiority of HMEM1 over HSMM and HMEM2 is clear in the training sets containing 50 and 100 utterances. In other words, general contextual factors lead the proposed system to a better performance when the amount of training

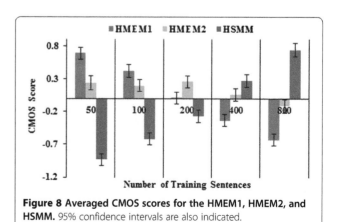

Figure 8 Averaged CMOS scores for the HMEM1, HMEM2, and HSMM. 95% confidence intervals are also indicated.

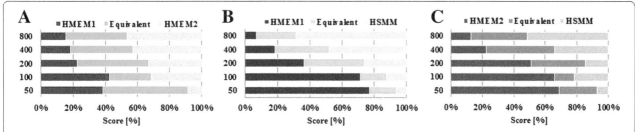

Figure 9 Preference scores as a function of the number of utterances used for training. (A) Comparison between HMEM1 and HMEM2. **(B)** Comparison between HMEM1 and HSMM. **(C)** Comparison between HMEM2 and HSMM.

data is very small. Gradually, as the number of utterances in the training set increases, detailed features assist the proposed system in achieving more effective synthetic speech. Therefore, HMEM2 surpasses HMEM1 for training sets with 200 and more utterances. However, for relatively large training sets (400 and 800), the use of HSMM is recommended.

Table 1 compares the number of leaf nodes in different speech synthesis systems. It can be seen from the table that to model mgc stream, HMEM2 exploits more parameters than HSMM-400 and HSMM-800, but the objective evaluations presented in Figure 6 show that HSMM-400 and HSMM-800 results in better mel-cepstral distances. The above argument shows that HMEM with some heuristic contextual clusters cannot exploit model parameters efficiently. In fact, a great number of contextual regions in HMEM1 and HMEM2 are redundant; therefore, their corresponding parameters are not useful. The next section evaluates the performance of HMEM with the suboptimum context clustering algorithm proposed in Section 3.3. This proposed clustering algorithm selects appropriate contextual regions and consequently solves the aforementioned problem.

4.2 Performance evaluation of HMEM with decision tree-based context clustering

This section is dedicated to the second set of experiments conducted to evaluate the performance of HMEM with decision tree construction algorithm proposed in Section 3.3. As it is realized from the first set of experiments, HMEM with heuristic and naïve contextual regions cannot outperform HSMM in large training databases. This section proves that by employing appropriate sets of $\{f_l(c)\}_{l=1}^{L_f}$ and $\{g_l(c)\}_{l=1}^{L_g}$, HMEM outperforms HSMM even for large databases.

4.2.1 Experimental conditions

Experiments were carried out on Nick [54], a British male database collected in Edinburgh University. This database consists of 2,500 utterances from a male speaker. We considered five sets including 50, 100, 200, 400, and 800

utterances for training, and 200 sentences that were not included in training sets were used as test data. Each sentence in the database is about 5 s of speech. Speech signals are sampled at 48 kHz, windowed by a 25-ms Blackman window with 5-ms shift. This database was specifically designed for the purpose of speech synthesis research, and utterances in the database covered most frequent English words. Also, different segmental and suprasegmental contextual factors were extracted for this database.

The speech analysis conditions and model topologies of CSTR/EMIME HTS 2010 [54] were used in this experiment. Bark cepstrum was extracted from smooth STRAIGHT trajectories [11]. Also, instead of log F0 and five frequency sub-bands (0 to 1, 1 to 2, 2 to 4, 4 to 6, and 6 to 8 kHz), pitch in mel and auditory-scale motivated frequency bands for aperiodicity measure were applied [54]. The analysis process resulted in 40 bark cepstrum coefficients, 1 mel in pitch value, and 25 auditory-scale motivated frequency bands aperiodicity parameters for each frame of training speech signals. These parameters incorporated with their delta and delta-delta parameters considered as the observation vectors of the statistical parametric model.

A five-state multi-stream left-to-right with no skip path MSD-HSMM was trained as the baseline system. Conventional maximum likelihood-based decision tree clustering algorithm was used to tie HMM states, but MDL criterion is used to determine the size of decision trees.

In order to have a fair comparison, the proposed system (HMEM with decision tree structure) was trained with the same number of free model parameters as the baseline system. HMEM was trained based on the decision tree construction algorithm presented in Section 3.3 and parameter re-estimation algorithm proposed in Section 3.2. It should be noted that four decision trees were built for $\{f_l(c)\}_{l=1}^{L_f}$ and one decision tree for $\{g_l(c)\}_{l=1}^{L_g}$. After training acoustic models, in the synthesis phase, GV-based parameter generation algorithm [20,26] and STRAIGHT synthesis module generated synthesized speech signals. Both subjective and objective tests were conducted to compare HMEM that uses decision tree-based clusters with traditional HSMM-based synthesis.

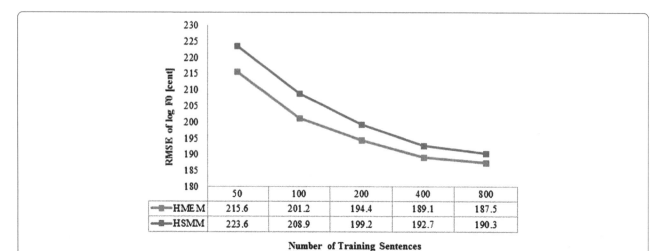

Figure 10 RMSE as objective measure to compare log F0 trajectories generated by decision tree-based HMEM and conventional HSMM.

It is useful to mention that training the proposed HMEM structure with decision tree-based context clustering took approximately 5 days for 800 training sentences, while training its corresponding HSMM-based synthesis system took approximately 16 h.

4.2.2 Employed contextual factors

In this experiment, employed contextual factors contained phonetic, syllable, word, phrase, and sentence level factors. In each of these levels, all important features were considered. Specific information about these features is presented in this subsection.

➢ Phonetic-level features
- Phoneme identity before the preceding phoneme; preceding, current, and succeeding phonemes; and phoneme identity after the next phoneme
- Position of the current phoneme in the current syllable, word, phrase, and sentence

➢ Syllable-level features
- Stress level of previous, current, and next syllable (three different stress levels are defined for this database)
- Position of the current syllable in the current word, phrase, and sentence
- Number of the phonemes of the previous, current, and next syllable
- Whether the previous, current, and next syllable is accented or not
- Number of the stressed syllables before and after the current syllable in the current phrase
- Number of syllables from the previous stressed syllable to the current syllable
- Number of syllables from the previous accented syllable to the current syllable

➢ Word-level features
- Part-of-speech (POS) tag of the preceding, current, and succeeding word

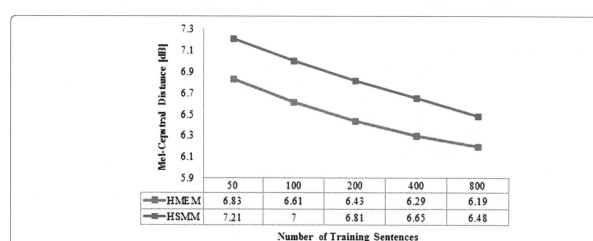

Figure 11 Result of the MCD measure that compares decision tree-based HMEM and conventional HSMM.

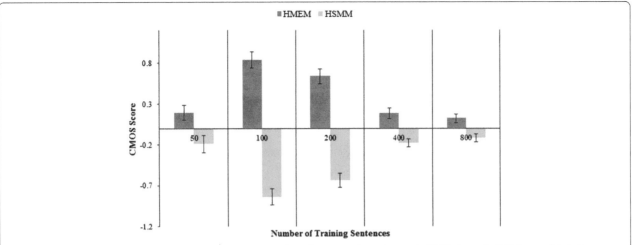

Figure 12 Subjective evaluation of HMEM with decision tree-based context clustering and HSMM through CMOS test with 95% confidence intervals.

- Position of the current word in the current phrase and sentence (forward and backward)
- Number of syllables of the previous, current, and next word
- Number of content words before and after current word in the current phrase
- Number of words from previous and next content word
➢ Phrase-level features
- Number of syllables and words of the preceding, current, and succeeding phrase
- Position of the current phrase in the sentence
- Current phrase ToBI end tone
➢ Sentence-level features
- Number of phonemes, syllables, words, and phrases in the current utterance
- Type of the current sentence

4.2.3 Objective evaluation

Two well-known measures were applied for objective evaluation of the proposed decision tree-based HMEM in comparison with conventional HSMM. The first measure computes RMS error of generated log F0 trajectories, and the second one compares synthesized spectrograms using average MCD criterion. The results of these measures are shown in Figures 10 and 11. As it is realized from Figure 10 that shows the RMS error of the log F0 in terms of cent for different sizes of training data, the log F0 trajectories generated from the proposed approach are more similar to the natural log F0 trajectories, and therefore, HMEM improves the performance of log F0 modeling. However, by increasing the size of the database, the amount of this improvement is slightly reduced. Hence, it can be implied from this figure that in log F0 modeling, the effect of applying overlapped regions for small databases

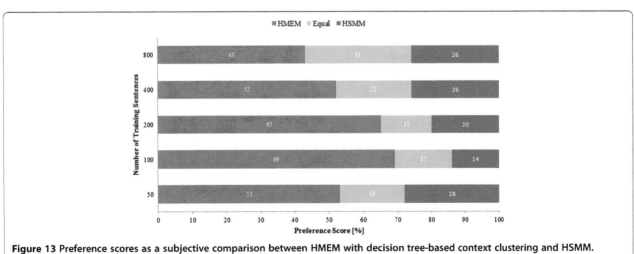

Figure 13 Preference scores as a subjective comparison between HMEM with decision tree-based context clustering and HSMM.

is relatively more than its effect on big databases. Additionally, Figure 11 shows the result of average MCD test. This result also confirms the improvement of HMEM performance in contrast to conventional HSMM for all training databases. As it is clear from the figure, the improvement in average MCD test is fixed for all databases.

4.2.4 Subjective evaluation

We conducted paired comparison tests and reported comparative mean opinion score (CMOS) and preference score as subjective evaluations. Fifteen non-professional native listeners were presented with 30 randomly chosen pairs of synthesized speech generated by HMEM and HSMM. Listeners selected the synthesized speech which sounds better and determined how much is better (much better, better, slightly better, or about the same). The results are shown in Figures 12 and 13.

Both CMOS test and preference score confirm the superiority of the proposed method over HSMM in all databases. Thus, if context clusters are determined through an effective approach, the proposed HMEM will outperform HSMM.

5. Conclusions

This paper addressed the main shortcomings of HSMM in context-dependent acoustic modeling, namely inadequate context generalization. HSMM uses decision tree-based context clustering that does not provide efficient generalization, because each acoustic feature vector is associated with modeling only one context cluster. In order to alleviate this problem, this paper proposed HMEM as a new acoustic modeling technique based on maximum entropy modeling approach. HMEM improves HSMM by enabling its structure to take advantage of overlapped contextual factors, and therefore, it can provide superior context generalization. Experimental results using objective and subjective criteria showed that the proposed system outperforms HSMM.

Despite the advantages, which enabled our system to outperform HSMM, a drawback of computationally complex training procedure is noticed in large databases.

Competing interests
The authors declare that they have no competing interests.

Author details
[1]Department of Computer Engineering, Sharif University of Technology, Tehran, Iran. [2]Centre for Speech Technology Research, University of Edinburgh, Edinburgh EH8 9LW, UK. [3]TCTS Lab, Faculte Polytechnique de Mons, Mons, Belgium.

References
1.   H Zen, K Tokuda, AW Black, Statistical parametric speech synthesis. Speech Comm. **51**(11), 1039–1064 (2009)

2.   AW Black, H Zen, K Tokuda, *Statistical parametric speech synthesis, in IEEE International Conference on Acoustics*, vol. 4 (Speech and Signal Processing (ICASSP), Honolulu, Hawaii, USA, 2007), pp. IV1229–IV1232

3.   J Yamagishi, T Kobayashi, Average-voice-based speech synthesis using HSMM-based speaker adaptation and adaptive training. IEICE - Trans. Info. Syst. **90**(2), 533–543 (2007)

4.   J Yamagishi, T Nose, H Zen, ZH Ling, T Toda, K Tokuda, S King, S Renals, Robust speaker-adaptive HMM-based text-to-speech synthesis, In IEEE Transactions on Audio, Speech, and Language Processing. **17**(6), 1208–1230 (2009)

5.   J Yamagishi, T Kobayashi, Y Nakano, K Ogata, J Isogai, Analysis of speaker adaptation algorithms for HMM-based speech synthesis and a constrained SMAPLR adaptation algorithm, IEEE Transactions on Audio, Speech, and Language Processing. **17**(1), 66–83 (2009)

6.   YJ Wu, Y Nankaku, K Tokuda, State mapping based method for cross-lingual speaker adaptation in HMM-based speech synthesis, in *INTERSPEECH* (Brighton, UK, 2009), pp. 528–531

7.   H Liang, J Dines, L Saheer, A comparison of supervised and unsupervised cross-lingual speaker adaptation approaches for HMM-based speech synthesis, in *IEEE International Conference on Acoustics Speech and Signal Processing (ICASSP)* (Dallas, Texas, USA, 2010), pp. 4598–4601

8.   M Gibson, T Hirsimaki, R Karhila, M Kurimo, W Byrne, Unsupervised cross-lingual speaker adaptation for HMM-based speech synthesis using two-pass decision tree construction, in *IEEE International Conference on Acoustics Speech and Signal Processing (ICASSP)* (Dallas, Texas, USA, 2010), pp. 4642–4645

9.   J Yamagishi, Z Ling, S King, Robustness of HMM-based speech synthesis, in *INTERSPEECH* (Brisbane, Australia, 2008), pp. 581–584

10. T Yoshimura, K Tokuda, T Masuko, T Kobayashi, T Kitamura, Mixed excitation for HMM-based speech synthesis, in *INTERSPEECH* (Aalborg, Denmark, 2001), pp. 2263–2266

11. H Kawahara, I Masuda-Katsuse, A de Cheveigné, Restructuring speech representations using a pitch-adaptive time–frequency smoothing and an instantaneous-frequency-based F0 extraction: possible role of a repetitive structure in sounds. Speech Comm. **27**(3), 187–207 (1999)

12. T Drugman, G Wilfart, T Dutoit, A deterministic plus stochastic model of the residual signal for improved parametric speech synthesis, in *INTERSPEECH* (Brighton, United Kingdom, 2009), pp. 1779–1782

13. T Drugman, T Dutoit, The deterministic plus stochastic model of the residual signal and its applications. IEEE Trans. Audio. Speech. Lang. Process **20**(3), 968–981 (2012)

14. H Zen, K Tokuda, T Masuko, T Kobayasih, T Kitamura, A hidden semi-Markov model-based speech synthesis system. IEICE - Trans. Info. Syst **90**(5), 825 (2007)

15. K Hashimoto, Y Nankaku, K Tokuda, *A Bayesian approach to hidden semi Markov model based speech synthesis, in Proceedings of INTERSPEECH* (Brighton, United Kingdom, 2009), pp. 1751–1754

16. K Hashimoto, H Zen, Y Nankaku, T Masuko, K Tokuda, *A Bayesian approach to HMM-based speech synthesis, in IEEE International Conference on Acoustics, Speech and Signal Processing (ICASSP)* (Taipei, Taiwan, 2009), pp. 4029–4032

17. K Tokuda, T Masuko, N Miyazaki, T Kobayashi, Multi-space probability distribution HMM. IEICE Trans. on Info. Syst **85**(3), 455–464 (2002)

18. H Zen, A Senior, M Schuster, Statistical parametric speech synthesis using deep neural networks, in *IEEE International Conference on Acoustics, Speech and Signal Processing (ICASSP)* (Vancouver, British Columbia, Canada, 2013), pp. 7962–7966

19. S Takaki, Y Nankaku, K Tokuda, Spectral modeling with contextual additive structure for HMM-based speech synthesis, in *Proceedings of 7th ISCA Speech Synthesis Workshop* (Kyoto, Japan, 2010), pp. 100–105

20. S Takaki, Y Nankaku, K Tokuda, Contextual partial additive structure for HMM-based speech synthesis, in *IEEE International Conference on Acoustics, Speech and Signal Processing (ICASSP)* (Vancouver, British Columbia, Canada, 2013), pp. 7878–7882

21. MJ Gales, Cluster adaptive training of hidden Markov models. IEEE Trans. Speech. Audio. Process. **8**(4), 417–428 (2000)

22. H Zen, MJ Gales, Y Nankaku, K Tokuda, Product of experts for statistical parametric speech synthesis, IEEE Trans. Audio. Speech. Lang. Process. **20**(3), 794–805 (2012)

23. K Yu, H Zen, F Mairesse, S Young, Context adaptive training with factorized decision trees for HMM-based statistical parametric speech synthesis. Speech Comm. **53**(6), 914–923 (2011)

24. T Toda, S Young, Trajectory training considering global variance for HMM-based speech synthesis, in *IEEE International Conference on Acoustics, Speech and Signal Processing (ICASSP)* (Taipei, Taiwan, 2009), pp. 4025–4028

25. L Qin, YJ Wu, ZH Ling, RH Wang, LR Dai, Minimum generation error criterion considering global/local variance for HMM-based speech synthesis, in *IEEE International Conference on Acoustics, Speech and Signal Processing (ICASSP)* (Las Vegas, Nevada, USA, 2008), pp. 4621–4624

26. T Toda, K Tokuda, Speech parameter generation algorithm considering global variance for HMM-based speech synthesis. IEICE - Trans. Info. Syst. Arch **E90-D**(5), 816–824 (2007)

27. K Tokuda, T Yoshimura, T Masuko, T Kobayashi, T Kitamura, *Speech Parameter Generation Algorithms for HMM-based Speech Synthesis, in ICASSP*, vol. 3 (Istanbul, 2000), pp. 1315–1318

28. K Tokuda, T Kobayashi, S Imai, Speech parameter generation from HMM using dynamic features, in *International Conference on Acoustics, Speech, and Signal Processing (ICASSP)*, vol. 1 (Detroit, Michigan, USA, 1995), pp. 660–663

29. Comparing glottal-flow-excited statistical parametric speech synthesis methods, in *IEEE International Conference on Acoustics, Speech and Signal Processing (ICASSP)* (Vancouver, British Columbia, Canada, 2013), pp. 7830–7834

30. T Yoshimura, K Tokuda, T Masuko, T Kobayashi, T Kitamura, Simultaneous modeling of spectrum, pitch and duration in HMM-based speech synthesis, in *Proceedings of Eurospeech* (1999), pp. 2347–2350

31. SJ Young, JJ Odell, PC Woodland, Tree-based state tying for high accuracy acoustic modeling, in *Proceedings of the workshop on Human Language Technology, Association for Computational Linguistics* (1994), pp. 307–312

32. CJ Leggetter, PC Woodland, Maximum likelihood linear regression for speaker adaptation of continuous density hidden Markov models. Comput. Speech. Lang. **9**(2), (1995)

33. VV Digalakis, LG Neumeyer, Speaker adaptation using combined transformation and Bayesian methods. IEEE Trans. Speech. Audio. Process. **4**(4), 294–300 (1996)

34. H Zen, N Braunschweiler, S Buchholz, MJ Gales, K Knill, S Krstulovic, J Latorre, Statistical parametric speech synthesis based on speaker and language factorization. IEEE Transactions. Audio. Speech. Lang. Process. **20**(6), 1713–1724 (2012)

35. T Koriyama, T Nose, T Kobayashi, *Statistical parametric speech synthesis based on Gaussian process regression, IEEE Journal of Selected Topics in Signal Processing* (2013), pp. 1–11

36. K Yu, F Mairesse, S Young, Word-level emphasis modeling in HMM-based speech synthesis, in *IEEE International Conference on Acoustics Speech and Signal Processing (ICASSP)* (Dallas, Texas, USA, 2010), pp. 4238–4241

37. H Zen, N Braunschweiler, Context-dependent additive log f_0 model for HMM-based speech synthesis, in *INTERSPEECH* (Brighton, United Kingdom, 2009), pp. 2091–2094

38. S Sakai, *Additive modeling of English f0 contour for speech synthesis, in Proceedings of ICASSP* (Las Vegas, Nevada, USA, 2008), pp. 277–280

39. Y Qian, H Liang, FK Soong, Generating natural F0 trajectory with additive trees, in *INTERSPEECH* (Brisbane, Australia, 2008), pp. 2126–2129

40. YJ Wu, F Soong, Modeling pitch trajectory by hierarchical HMM with minimum generation error training, in *IEEE International Conference on Acoustics, Speech and Signal Processing (ICASSP)* (Kyoto, Japan, 2012), pp. 4017–4020

41. AL Berger, VJD Pietra, SAD Pietra, A maximum entropy approach to natural language processing. Computer Ling **22**, 39–71 (1996)

42. A Borthwick, *A maximum entropy approach to named entity recognition, PhD dissertation (New York University)*, 1999

43. V Rangarajan, S Narayanan, S Bangalore, *Exploiting acoustic and syntactic features for prosody labeling in a maximum entropy framework, in Proceedings of NAACL HLT*, 2007, pp. 1–8

44. A Ratnaparkhi, A maximum entropy model for part-of-speech tagging, in Proceedings of the conference on empirical methods in natural language processing. **1**, 133–142 (1996)

45. JJ Odell, *The use of context in large vocabulary speech recognition, PhD dissertation (Cambridge University)*, 1995

46. K Shinoda, W Takao, MDL-based context-dependent subword modeling for speech recognition. J. Acoust. Soc. Jpn **21**(2), 79–86 (2000)

47. K Oura, H Zen, Y Nankaku, A Lee, K Tokuda, A covariance-tying technique for HMM-based speech synthesis. J. IEICE **E93-D**(3), 595–601 (2010)

48. J Nocedal, JW Stephen, *Numerical Optimization* (Book of Springer, USA, 1999)

49. M Bijankhan, J Sheikhzadegan, MR Roohani, Y Samareh, C Lucas, M Tebiani, The speech database of Farsi spoken language, in *Proceedings of 5th Australian International Conference on Speech Science and Technology (SST)* (1994), pp. 826–831

50. J Ghomeshi, Non-projecting nouns and the ezafe: construction in Persian. Nat. Lang. Ling. Theor. **15**(4), 729–788 (1997)

51. R Kubichek, Mel-cepstral distance measure for objective speech quality assessment, in *IEEE Pacific Rim Conference on Communications, Computers and Signal Processing*, vol. 1, 1993, pp. 125–128

52. B Picart, T Drugman, T Dutoit, *Continuous control of the degree of articulation in HMM-based speech synthesis, 12th Annual Conference of the International Speech Communication Association (ISCA)* (INTERSPEECH, Florence, Italy, 2011), pp. 1797–1800

53. J Yamagishi, *Average-Voice-Based Speech Synthesis, PhD dissertation* (Tokyo Institute of 1362 Technology, Yokohama, 2006)

54. J Yamagishi, O Watts, *The CSTR/EMIME HTS system for Blizzard challenge, in Proceedings of Blizzard Challenge 2010* (Kyoto, Japan, 2010), pp. 1–6

6

Empirically combining unnormalized NNLM and back-off *N*-gram for fast *N*-best rescoring in speech recognition

Yongzhe Shi[*], Wei-Qiang Zhang, Meng Cai and Jia Liu

Abstract

Neural network language models (NNLM) have been proved to be quite powerful for sequence modeling, including feed-forward NNLM (FNNLM), recurrent NNLM (RNNLM), etc. One main issue concerned for NNLM is the heavy computational burden of the output layer, where the output needs to be probabilistically normalized and the normalizing factors require lots of computation. How to fast rescore the *N*-best list or lattice with NNLM attracts much attention for large-scale applications. In this paper, the statistic characteristics of normalizing factors are investigated on the *N*-best list. Based on the statistic observations, we propose to approximate the normalizing factors for each hypothesis as a constant proportional to the number of words in the hypothesis. Then, the unnormalized NNLM is investigated and combined with back-off *N*-gram for fast rescoring, which can be computed very fast without the normalization in the output layer, with the complexity reduced significantly. We apply our proposed method to a well-tuned context-dependent deep neural network hidden Markov model (CD-DNN-HMM) speech recognition system on the English-Switchboard phone-call speech-to-text task, where both FNNLM and RNNLM are trained to demonstrate our method. Experimental results show that unnormalized probability of NNLM is quite complementary to that of back-off *N*-gram, and combining the unnormalized NNLM and back-off *N*-gram can further reduce the word error rate with little computational consideration.

Keywords: Neural network language model; *N*-best rescoring; Speech recognition

1 Introduction

The output of the speech-to-text (STT) system is usually a multi-candidate form encoded as lattice or *N*-best list. Rescoring via more accurate models, as a second pass of the STT system, has been widely used to further improve the performance. Fast rescoring with neural network language models is investigated in the paper.

Neural network language models (NNLMs), including feed-forward NNLM (FNNLM) [1,2] and recurrent NNLM (RNNLM) [3-5], have achieved very good results on many tasks [6-8], especially for RNNLM. Distributed word representations and the associated probability estimates are jointly computed in a feed-forward or recurrent neural network architecture. This approach provides

automatic smoothing and leads to better generalization for unseen *N*-grams. The main drawback of NNLM is the great computational burden of the output layer that contains tens of thousands of nodes corresponding to the words in the vocabulary, where the output needs to be probabilistically normalized for each word with the softmax function and this softmax-normalization requires lots of computations. Thus, *N*-best list for its simplicity is usually rescored and reranked by NNLM, and the evaluation speed of NNLM needs to be improved further for large-scale applications.

Most of the previous work focuses on the speedup of the training of NNLM via word clustering to structure the output layer [4,9,10]. One typical method, the class-based output layer method, was proposed, recently, for speeding up RNNLM training [4], based on word frequency. This method divides the cumulative probability into *C* partitions to form *C* frequency binnings which correspond

*Correspondence: shiyz09@gmail.com
Tsinghua National Laboratory for Information Science and Technology, Department of Electronic Engineering, Tsinghua University, Beijing 100084, China

to C clusters. The words are assigned to classes proportionally. Based on the frequency clustering method, the closed-form solution of the output layer complexity can be written as $O((C + |\mathbf{V}|/C)H)$, where $|\mathbf{V}|$ and H denote the number of nodes in the output layer and the hidden layer, respectively. Another method [9,11,12] is to factorize the output layer with a tree structure that needs to be carefully constructed based on expert knowledge [13] or other clustering method [14]. Although the structure-based methods can speed up the evaluation of NNLM, the complexities of these methods are still quite high in real-time systems.

In this paper, the statistic characteristics of normalizing factors are investigated for the N-best hypotheses. Based on the statistic observations, we proposed to approximate the normalizing factors for each hypothesis as a constant proportional to the number of words in the hypothesis, and the normalizing factors can be easily absorbed into the word penalty. Then, the unnormalized NNLM is investigated and combined with back-off N-gram for fast rescoring, which can be computed very fast without the normalization in the output layer, with the complexity reduced significantly.

We apply our proposed method to a well-tuned context-dependent deep neural network hidden Markov model (CD-DNN-HMM) speech recognition system on the English-Switchboard speech-to-text task. Both feedforward NNLM and recurrent NNLM are well-trained to verify the effectiveness of our method. Experimental results show that unnormalized probability of NNLM is quite complementary to that of back-off N-gram, and combining the unnormalized NNLM and back-off N-gram can further improve the performance of speech recognition with little computational resource.

As our method is theoretically founded on the statistic observations, we first introduce the experimental setup, including the speech recognizer, N-best hypotheses, NNLM structure, and NNLM training, in Section 2 for convenience. The remainder of this paper is organized as follows: The statistics of the normalizing factors on the hypotheses are investigated and the constant normalizing factor approximation is proposed in Section 3. How to combine the unnormalized NNLM and back-off N-gram is presented in Section 4, followed by complexity analysis and speed comparisons in Section 5. Detailed experimental evaluations for N-best rescoring are presented in Section 6. Discussions on the related work are given in Section 7, followed by the conclusions in Section 8.

2 Experimental setup

The experimental setup for the speech recognizer, N-best hypotheses, the NNLM structure, and the NNLM training in our work was introduced here, since our method is theoretically founded on statistical observations.

2.1 Speech recognizer and N-best hypotheses

The effectiveness of our proposed method is evaluated on the STT task with the 309-hour Switchboard-I training set [15]. The 13-dimensional perceptual linear prediction features (PLP) with rolling-window mean-variance normalization and up to third-order derivatives are reduced to 39 dimensions by heteroscedastic linear discriminant analysis (HLDA). The speaker-independent three-state cross-word triphones share 9,308 tied states. The GMM-HMM baseline system has 40-Gaussian mixtures per state, trained with maximum likelihood (ML), and refined discriminatively (DT) with the minimum phone error (MPE) criterion. The well-tuned CD-DNN-HMM system replaces the Gaussian mixtures with scaled likelihoods derived from DNN posteriors. The input to the DNN contains 11 (5-1-5) frames of 39-dimensional features, where the DNN uses the architecture of 429-2048×7-9308. The data for system development is the 1831-segment Switchboard part of the NIST 2000 Hub5 eval set (Hub5'00-SWB). The Fisher half of the 6.3h Spring 2003 NIST rich transcription set (RT03S-FSH) acts as the evaluation set.

The 2000h Fisher transcripts, containing about 23 million words, are taken as our training corpus for language modeling. Based on Kneser-Ney smoothing, a back-off trigram language model (KN3) was trained on the 2000h Fisher transcripts for decoding, where the vocabulary is limited to 53K words and unknown words are mapped into a special token <unk>. Note that no additional text is used to train LMs for interpolations to ensure the repeatability. The out-of-vocabulary rate is 0.80% for the training corpus, 0.53% for the development corpus, and 0.017% for the evaluation corpus. The pronouncing dictionary comes from CMU [16]. The HDecode[a] command is used to decode the utterance with KN3 to output the lattice, and then the N-best hypotheses are extracted from the lattice using the lattice-tool[b] command. In the setup, top 100-best hypotheses are rescored and reranked by other language models, such as back-off 5-gram, FNNLM, and RNNLM, to improve the performance.

2.2 Structure and training of NNLM

The typical structures of NNLMs are shown in Figures 1 and 2, corresponding to FNNLM and RNNLM, respectively. We also define $\mathbf{V}$, H and N as the vocabulary, the size of hidden layer and the order of FNNLM, respectively. The projection matrix $\mathbf{E} \in \Re^{|\mathbf{V}| \times H}$ maps each word to the feature vector as the distributional representation and fed into the hidden layer.

Based on the structures of NNLM, the hidden state $\mathbf{h}_t$ of FNNLM can be computed as $\mathbf{h}_t = \tanh\left(\sum_{o=1}^{N-1} \mathbf{W}_{iho}\mathbf{v}_{t-o}\right)$, while that of RNNLM can be computed as $\mathbf{h}_t = \text{sigmoid}(\mathbf{W}_{hh}\mathbf{h}_{t-1}+\mathbf{v}_t)$, where tanh and sigmoid are the activation functions. The probability of the next word is computed via the softmax function in the

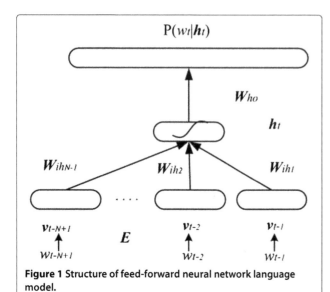

Figure 1 Structure of feed-forward neural network language model.

output layer, where $W_{ho} \in \Re^{|V| \times H} = [\theta_1, \theta_2, \ldots, \theta_{|V|}]^T$ is the predicting matrix and $\theta_{\forall i} \in \Re^{H \times 1}$ corresponds to each output node.

The transcripts of the Hub5'00-SWB set and the RT03S-FSH set act the development set and the evaluation set, respectively, for NNLM training. One FNNLM and one RNNLM are well-trained on the training corpus with the open source toolkits, CSLM [17] and RNNLM [18], respectively, where both of the hidden layers contain 300 nodes.

To speed up the training of the RNNLM, a frequency-based partition method [4] is used to factorize the output layer with 400 classes. The truncated backpropagation through time algorithm (BPTT) [19] is used to train the RNNLM with 10 time steps, with the initial learning rate set to 0.1. The learning rate is halved, when the perplexity decreases very slowly or increases. On the contrary, the training of FNNLM can be speeded up with

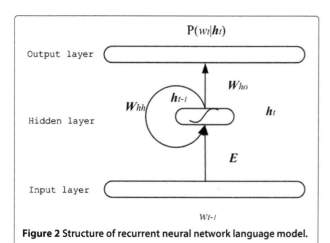

Figure 2 Structure of recurrent neural network language model.

128 context-word pairs as a mini-batch based on GPU implementation, so that no class layer was used, as the class layer usually sacrifices the performance of NNLM for speedup. The learning rate is empirically set as $lr = lr_0/(1 + \text{count} \times \text{wdecay})$, where the initial learning rate lr_0 is set to 1.0, the weight decay 'wdecay' is set to 2×10^{-8}, and the parameter 'count' denotes the number of samples processed, so that the learning rate will decay with the training of model. The basic back-off 5-gram language model (KN5) is also trained with the modified Kneser-Ney smoothing algorithm.

3 Statistics of normalizing factors on N-best hypotheses

3.1 Review of N-best rescoring

The output from the first decoding pass is usually a multi-candidate form encoded as lattice or N-best list. Each path in lattice or N-best list is a candidate time-aligned transcript $W = w_1, w_2, \ldots, w_n$ of the speech utterance X. N-best list for its simplicity is widely used, and N-best rescoring in LVCSR is reviewed here.

Given the acoustic model Λ, the language model L, and a speech utterance X_i, N-best hypotheses from ASR's decoding are denoted as $H_i = W_{i1}, W_{i2}, \ldots, W_{iN}$, where the score of each hypothesis W_{ij} is computed as

$$g(X_i, W_{ij}|\Lambda, L) = \log P(X_i|W_{ij}, \Lambda) + \alpha \cdot \log P(W_{ij}|L) + n_{ij} \cdot \text{wdpenalt}, \tag{1}$$

where the first two items correspond to acoustic scores and language scores, respectively, and the last one denotes the word penalty that balances insertions and deletions. Also, α denotes a scaling factor for language scores and n_{ij} denotes the number of words in the hypothesis W_{ij}. The global score for each hypothesis in H_i is computed and reranked. The top hypothesis is selected as the output for evaluation. Generally, better performance is expected with more accurate models.

3.2 Normalizing factor for one word

Given a word sequence $\bar{s}$, denote the t-th word as w_t. The identity of word w_t is denoted as $q(w_t) = y_i \in V$, where the subscript i of y_i is the word index in the vocabulary V. The structures of FNNLM and RNNLM are shown in Figures 1 and 2, respectively, where $W_{ho} \in \Re^{|V| \times H} = [\theta_1, \theta_2, \ldots, \theta_{|V|}]^T$ is the prediction matrix and $\theta_{\forall i} \in \Re^{H \times 1}$ corresponds to each output node.

The predicted probability of NNLM is computed as

$$P(q(w_t) = y_j|h_t) = \frac{\exp(s_t)}{z_t}$$

$$\text{with} \quad s_t = \theta_j^T h_t \quad \text{and} \quad z_t = \sum_{i=1}^{|V|} \exp\left(\theta_i^T h_t\right), \tag{2}$$

where $\exp(s_t)$ and z_t respectively correspond to the unnormalized probability and the softmax-normalizing factor. Computing this factor z_t results in heavy computational burden for normalization.

We evaluated our well-trained FNNLM and RNNLM on the 100-best hypotheses generated from the Hub5'00-SWB set (1,812 utterances), containing 147,454 hypotheses and 2,125,315 words. The $\log(z_t)$ for each word is computed and the probability density functions (PDFs) of the $\log(z_t)$ for FNNLM and RNNLM are plotted and shown in Figure 3. It shows that the log normalizing factor is widely distributed, ranging from 13 to 20 for FNNLM and from 7 to 20 for RNNLM, respectively. It seems that the variance of $\log(z_t)$ is so large that the normalizing factor $\log(z_t)$ can't be simply approximated as a constant for N-best rescoring. However, several findings from our firsthand experience have been noticed to help us approximate the normalizing factor, and we also conclude that some discriminative information of NNLM exists in the unnormalized probability for N-best rescoring in the next two sub-sections.

3.3 Normalizing factor for one hypothesis
The output of speech recognizer is usually encoded as N-best hypotheses, and the better hypothesis can be selected via rescoring with more accurate models. The language score for the hypothesis $W_{ij} = w_{ij1}, w_{ij2}, \ldots, w_{ijn_{ij}}$ is computed as

$$\begin{aligned}
\log P(W_{ij}|L) &= \sum_{t=1}^{n_{ij}} \log(P(w_{ijt}|\boldsymbol{h}_{ijt})) \\
&= \sum_{t=1}^{n_{ij}} s_{ijt} - \sum_{t=1}^{n_{ij}} \log(z_{ijt}),
\end{aligned} \tag{3}$$

where n_{ij} denotes the number of words in hypothesis W_{ij}, s_{ijt} can be efficiently computed with the dot product of two vectors, while z_{ijt} requires a lot of computing consideration.

We randomly selected one utterance from Hub5'00-SWB set and decoded it with HDecode for recognition. Top ten hypotheses are shown in Table 1. We notice that there are lots of similar contexts in N-best hypotheses, especially for the hypotheses with a low word error rate (WER), and differences usually exist in local. As a matter of fact, the normalizing factor z_{ijt} is completely determined by the context via a smooth function in Equation 2, and similar contexts will result in similar normalizing factors close to each other in value. Thus, lots of normalizing factors in the N-best hypotheses are the same or similar as for lots of the same or similar contexts, so that we roughly approximate $\sum_{t=1}^{n_{ij}} \log(z_{ijt})$ for hypothesis W_{ij} as a constant proportional to n_{ij} in this case, shown as

$$\mu_{ij} = \frac{1}{n_{ij}} \sum_{t=1}^{n_{ij}} \log(z_{ijt}) \approx \mu_i, \tag{4}$$

where μ_i is the constant corresponding to utterance X_i and μ_i can be estimated as $\mu_i \approx \overline{\mu_{ij}} = \frac{1}{N} \sum_{j=1}^{N} \mu_{ij}$.

This approximation for utterance X_i can be evaluated with the variance of μ_{ij} as $\text{Var}(\mu_{ij}) = \frac{1}{N} \sum_{j=1}^{N} (\mu_{ij} - \overline{\mu_{ij}})^2$, and $\overline{\mu_{ij}}$ denotes the mean of μ_{ij} in H_i. As a matter of fact, many utterances need to be approximated with Equation 4, and these approximations can be evaluated as mean of $\text{Var}(\mu_{ij})$ and variance of $\text{Var}(\mu_{ij})$ for all utterances. The statistically smaller the $\text{Var}(\mu_{ij})$, the more accurate the approximations.

We evaluated the well-trained FNNLM and RNNLM on the 100-best hypotheses generated from Hub5'00-SWB

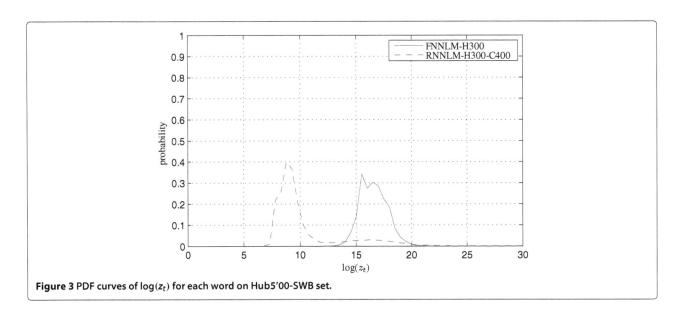

Figure 3 PDF curves of $\log(z_t)$ for each word on Hub5'00-SWB set.

Table 1 Ten hypotheses decoded from one utterance in Hub5'00-SWB set

	Hypotheses
1	No no it doesn't work on every issue
2	No no it doesn't work in every issue
3	No no it doesn't work and every issue
4	No no it doesn't work out every issue
5	Oh no no it doesn't work on every issue
6	No no it doesn't work then every issue
7	No no he doesn't work on every issue
8	Oh no no it doesn't work in every issue
9	On no no it doesn't work on every issue
10	No no he doesn't work in every issue

Lots of contexts are similar and differences usually exist in local.

set (1,812 utterances). The μ_{ij} for each hypothesis and the $\mathrm{Var}(\mu_{ij})$ for each 100-best list are computed, and the PDFs of $\mathrm{Var}(\mu_{ij})$ for FNNLM and RNNLM are shown in Figure 4. It shows that the PDFs are quite sharp and close to zero, just like an impulse function, and the constant approximation in Equation 4 for each utterance is accurate and reasonable to some extent.

3.4 Number of words in hypothesis

We also notice that the number of words for one hypothesis is similar with each other in the N-best list. As a matter of fact, N-best hypotheses are rescored and reranked according to the relative scores. If all the hypotheses for utterance X_i contain the same number of words, then the second item in Equation 3 for one hypothesis will be

the same as that of others in the N-best list, based on Equation 4, shown as

$$n_{ij}\mu_{ij} \approx n_{ik}\mu_{ik}, \quad \forall i,j,k$$
$$\text{s.t.} \quad n_{ij} \approx n_{ik} \quad \text{and} \quad \mu_{ij} \approx \mu_i \approx \mu_{ik} \quad \forall i,j,k, \tag{5}$$

That is to say, the normalizing factors for one hypothesis will not affect the ranking in the N-best rescoring, and μ_i for utterance X_i can be arbitrary. We further approximate the constant μ_i to a global constant, irrelevant with the utterance, shown as

$$\mu_{ij} \approx \mu_i \approx \mu, \tag{6}$$

where μ is the global constant and can be estimated as $\mu = \frac{1}{MN}\sum_{i=1}^{M}\sum_{j=1}^{N}\mu_{ij}$ on the validation set. M and N denote the number of utterances and the number of hypotheses for each utterance, respectively.

Please note that the approximations in Equation 5 depend on the assumption that the hypotheses for each utterance are equal in length. We count the number of words n_{ij} for each hypothesis W_{ij} and compute the variance of n_{ij} for each utterance X_i as

$$\mathrm{Var}(n_{ij}) = \frac{1}{N}\sum_{j=1}^{N}(n_{ij} - \overline{n_{ij}})^2) \quad \text{with} \quad \overline{n_{ij}} = \frac{1}{N}\sum_{j=1}^{N}n_{ij} \tag{7}$$

The statistically smaller the $\mathrm{Var}(n_{ij})$, the more accurate the approximation in Equations 5 and 6. The PDF of $\mathrm{Var}(n_{ij})$ on the 100-best hypotheses generated from Hub5'00-SWB set is shown in Figure 5. It shows that the PDF of $\mathrm{Var}(n_{ij})$ is sharp and most of the $\mathrm{Var}(n_{ij})$

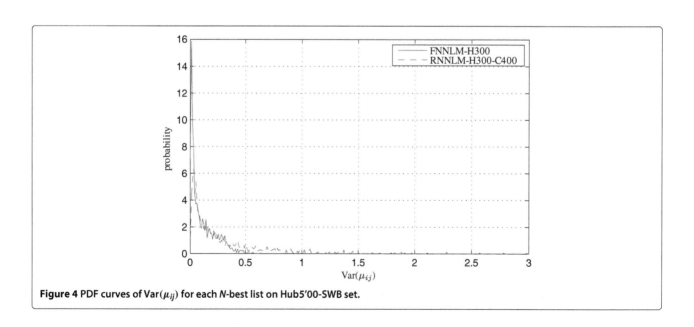

Figure 4 PDF curves of $\mathrm{Var}(\mu_{ij})$ for each N-best list on Hub5'00-SWB set.

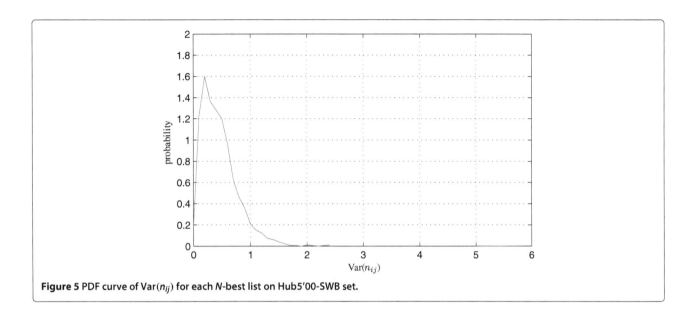

Figure 5 PDF curve of $\mathrm{Var}(n_{ij})$ for each N-best list on Hub5'00-SWB set.

are smaller than 1.0. The difference of N-best hypotheses in length is small, and the approximation for N-best hypotheses in Equation 5 is reasonable to some extent.

3.5 Normalizing factor approximation

Based on the approximation in Equations 4, 5, and 6, the LM scores in Equation 3 can be simplified as

$$\mathrm{logP}(W_{ij}|L) \approx \sum_{t=1}^{n_{ij}} s_{ijt} - n_{ij} \cdot \mu, \tag{8}$$

where only the first item needs to be estimated, while the second item can be estimated on validation set for rescoring. The complexity of the output layer is significantly reduced form $\mathrm{O}(|\mathbf{V}|H)$ to $\mathrm{O}(H)$ with the constant approximation of the normalizing factor.

We also notice that the discriminative information of NNLM for N-best rescoring exists in the unnormalized probability in Equation 8 and the LM scores from back-off N-gram, especially for the KN3 in decoding, usually are available for rescoring. We will investigate the discriminative information in unnormalized NNLM (UP-NNLM), combined with back-off N-gram, to further improve the performance of speech recognizer in the next section.

4 Combining unnormalized NNLM and back-off N-gram

The UP-NNLM combined with back-off N-gram in the logarithmic domain is presented in detail. Generally, the performance of STT systems can be further improved with interpolation of NNLM and back-off N-gram. Since exact probability of NNLM is unavailable in Equation 8, the linear interpolation is performed in logarithmic domain for the entire hypothesis, shown as

$$
\begin{aligned}
&\mathrm{log}\tilde{P}(W_{ij}|L)\\
&= \lambda \cdot \mathrm{logP}(W_{ij}|L) + (1-\lambda) \cdot \mathrm{logP}_{\mathrm{Ngram}}(W_{ij}|L)\\
&= \lambda \cdot \sum_{t=1}^{n_{ij}} (s_{ijt} - \mu) + (1-\lambda) \cdot \mathrm{logP}_{\mathrm{Ngram}}(W_{ij}|L),
\end{aligned}
\tag{9}
$$

where $\mathrm{P}_{\mathrm{Ngram}}(W_{ij}|L)$ is the language score of back-off N-gram for hypothesis W_{ij}. By substituting Equation 9 into Equation 1, the global score for each hypothesis is computed as

$$
\begin{aligned}
&g(X_i, W_{ij}|\Lambda, L)\\
&= \alpha \cdot \lambda \cdot \sum_{t=1}^{n_{ij}} s_{ijt} + \alpha \cdot (1-\lambda) \cdot \mathrm{logP}_{\mathrm{Ngram}}(W_{ij}|L)\\
&\quad + \mathrm{logP}(X_i|W_{ij}, \Lambda) + n_{ij} \cdot \mathrm{wdpenalty}'\\
&\text{with}\quad \mathrm{wdpenalty}' = \mathrm{wdpenalty} - \alpha \cdot \lambda \cdot \mu,
\end{aligned}
\tag{10}
$$

where the normalizing factor is absorbed into the word penalty. The unnormalized probability only needs to be computed. The computational complexity of the output layer is reduced significantly without explicit normalization.

5 Complexity analysis and speed comparisons

The complexities of NNLM and UP-NNLM are analyzed, and the evaluation speeds of NNLM and UP-NNLM are also measured, shown in Table 2 for detailed comparisons.

The class-based output layer method was based on the frequency partition [4], and the computational complexity of the output layer is given as $O((C + |\mathbf{V}|/C)H)$, shown in Table 2. This method is usually used to speed up the training of NNLM while the evaluation of NNLM is also speeded up. Compared with the class-based method, the unnormalized probability of NNLM (UP-NNLM) in our

Table 2 Complexity and speed comparisons of UP-NNLMs and NNLMs for word predictions

Model	Complexity	Speed × 10^3 (words/second)
RNNLM[a]	$O(H^2 + |\mathbf{V}|H)$	0.041
+Class layer	$O(H^2 + (|\mathbf{V}|/C + C)H)$	4.21
UP-RNNLM	$O(H^2 + H)$	11.95
FNNLM[a]	$O((N-1)DH + |\mathbf{V}|H)$	0.214
+Class layer	$O((N-1)DH + (|\mathbf{V}|/C + C)H)$	9.55
UP-FNNLM	$O((N-1)DH + H)$	17.77
fast-UP-FNNLM	$O(H)$	240.38

[a]The implementations of RNNLM and FNNLM are based on the open source toolkits, CSLM and RNNLM. The matrix and vector operations in CSLM toolkit are optimized via MKL Library, so that the evaluation of FNNLM is faster than RNNLM with the same size of hidden layer.

method is required with the complexity $O(H)$ in the output layer. Especially, the complexity of the hidden layer in FNNLM can be further reduced by lookup in the position-dependent projection matrix $\widehat{E}_k \in \Re^{|\mathbf{V}| \times H}, k = 1, 2, \cdots, N-1$, where the $\widehat{E}_k = EW_{\mathrm{ih}k}$ can be computed off-line. We denote the fast version of UP-FNNLM as fast-UP-FNNLM in Table 2.

The evaluation speed is measured by the number of words processed per second on a machine with an Intel(R) Xeon(R) 8-core CPU E5520 at 2.27 GHz and 8-G RAM, shown in Table 2. The implementations are based on the open source toolkits, CSLM [17] and RNNLM [18], to ensure the repeatability. To compare clearly, the speed of NNLM without a class layer is also measured. One million words are randomly selected from training data and evaluated by the FNNLM and NNLM, where the word is fed into the FNNLM and RNNLM one by one. Experimental results show that UP-FNNLM and UP-RNNLM are about 2~3 times faster than 'FNNLM + class layer' and 'RNNLM + class layer' for evaluation. Note that the com-

plexity of the hidden layer in UP-FNNLM or UP-RNNLM is comparable with that of class-based output layer in FNNLM + class layer or RNNLM + class layer, so that this speedup factor is reasonable. Also, it is worthy to notice that the fast-UP-FNNLM is more than 25 times faster than FNNLM + class layer and more than 1,100 times faster than FNNLM. To clearly show the speedup, the evaluation speed is also compared with different hidden layers, shown in Table 3. The larger the hidden layer, the slower the evaluation, and the 'fast-UP-FNNLM' is the fastest of all.

6 N-best rescoring evaluation

The NNLM and UP-NNLM are applied to N-best rescoring to demonstrate the performance of our method in this section. According to our experimental setup described in Section 2, the perplexities of our trained language models, including KN3, KN5, FNNLM, and RNNLM-C400, are presented in Table 4 for comparisons, where KN3 is used for decoding. It shows that the RNNLM-C400 interpolated with KN5 performs best of all on the Hub5'00-SWB set and the RT03S-FSH set. Also, RNNLM-C400 performs slightly better than FNNLM with the same setup in perplexity. The Hub5'00-SWB set and the RT03S-FSH set act the validation set and evaluation set, respectively. The 100-best hypotheses for these two sets are rescored and reranked by different language models, shown in Table 5, where 1-best denotes the output of HDecode with KN3. The results for 1-best hypothesis on these two sets as our baseline are comparable with other reported results [20,21].

The UP-FNNLM and UP-RNNLM, combined with back-off N-gram, are used for fast rescoring in this section. Note that the output layer of our trained RNNLM-C400 is divided into many small softmax output layers in order to speed up the training on the large corpus. Thus, the unnormalized probability comes from the activations of the class layer and the specific softmax output layer, while the entire normalizing factor is also approximated as Equation 6. The UP-NNLM is linearly interpolated with KN5 in the logarithmic domain. The

Table 3 Testing speed comparisons of UP-NNLMs and NNLMs for different hidden layers

Model	Speed × 10^3 (words/second)					
	10	50	100	200	300	400
RNNLM[a]	0.78	0.23	0.11	0.056	0.041	0.029
+Class layer	70.87	28.5	13.94	7.39	4.21	3.10
UP-RNNLM	400.01	197.75	80.30	26.93	11.95	7.20
FNNLM[a]	2.72	1.63	0.35	0.291	0.214	0.14
+Class layer	124.89	66.83	36.02	16.16	9.55	5.75
UP-FNNLM	678.48	209.16	83.95	25.33	17.77	11.63
fast-UP-FNNLM	746.43	557.18	406.47	291.35	240.38	201.75

[a]The implementations of RNNLM and FNNLM are based on the open source toolkits, CSLM and RNNLM. The matrix and vector operations in CSLM toolkit are optimized via MKL Library, so that the evaluation of FNNLM is faster than RNNLM with the same size of hidden layer.

Table 4 Perplexity of Hub5'00-SWB and RT03S-FSH set for different LMs

Model	Perplexity	
	Hub5'00-SWB	RT03S-FSH
KN3	89.40	66.76
KN5	86.78	63.80
+FNNLM	71.84	53.98
+RNNLM-C400	66.67	51.34
FNNLM	76.17	56.99
RNNLM-C400	70.83	54.39

Table 5 Word error rates (WERs) of Hub5'00-SWB and RT03S-FSH for 100-best/1,000-best rescoring with NNLM and UP-NNLM

Model	100-best WER (%)		1,000-best WER (%)	
	Hub5'00-SWB	RT03S-FSH	Hub5'00-SWB	RT03S-FSH
1-best (KN3)	17.3	20.2	17.3	20.2
+UP-FNNLM	16.6 (−0.7)	19.0 (−1.2)	16.5 (−0.8)	19.0 (−1.2)
+UP-RNNLM-C400	16.5 (−0.8)	19.0 (−1.2)	16.4 (−0.9)	19.1 (−1.1)
+FNNLM	15.7 (−1.6)	18.4 (−1.8)	15.6 (−1.7)	18.4 (−1.8)
+RNNLM-C400	15.4 (−1.9)	18.2 (−2.0)	15.2 (−2.1)	18.4 (−1.8)
KN5	17.1 (−0.2)	19.5 (−0.7)	16.9 (−0.4)	19.4 (−0.8)
+UP-FNNLM	16.4 (−0.9)	18.6 (−1.6)	16.2 (−1.1)	18.6 (−1.6)
+UP-RNNLM-C400	_16.1_ (−1.2)	_18.5_ (−1.7)	_16.0_ (−1.3)	_18.5_ (−1.7)
+FNNLM	15.6 (−1.7)	18.3 (−1.9)	15.4 (−1.9)	18.2 (−2.0)
+RNNLM-C400	_15.3_ (−2.0)	_18.1_ (−2.1)	_15.2_ (−2.1)	_18.1_ (−2.1)
FNNLM	15.9 (−1.4)	18.7 (−1.5)	15.8 (−1.5)	18.7 (−1.5)
RNNLM-C400	15.4 (−1.9)	18.4 (−1.8)	15.5 (−1.8)	18.6 (−1.6)

weight for interpolation, the scale of LM scores, and the word penalty are all individually tuned on Hub5'00-SWB set, and then the final performance is evaluated on RT03S-FSH set, shown in Table 5. Significant reductions in WER are observed on the validation and evaluation sets. The language scores of KN3 is usually available in the lattice or N-best list, so that the UP-RNNLM combined with the KN3 reduces WER by 0.8% and 1.2% absolute on Hub5'00-SWB and RT03S-FSH sets, respectively. 'KN5 + UP-RNNLM-C400' further reduces the WER by 1.2% and 1.7% absolute on these two sets. Also, we notice that UP-RNNLM performs slightly better than UP-FNNLM, while UP-FNNLM can be evaluated much faster than UP-RNNLM. It can be seen that the 'UP-NNLM + KN5' can obtain about 1/2 to 2/3 gains of 'NNLM + KN5' with little computation. Experimental results show that the unnormalized probability of NNLMs, including FNNLM and RNNLM, is quite complementary to that of back-off N-gram, and the performance is further improved via the combination of back-off N-gram and NNLM.

7 Discussions with related work

Fast rescoring with NNLM has attracted much attention in the field of speech recognition [9,10,22-24]. Many methods [9,10,22] for factorizing the output layer were proposed to reduce the complexity of NNLM and to speed up the training and the evaluation. Other techniques [22,24] were proposed to avoid redundant computations existing in N-best or lattice rescoring. Our proposed method can be easily combined with these methods to further improve the speed of rescoring. Also, a good work on fast training of NNLM with noise-contrastive estimation (NCE) [25] was proposed in [26], where the normalizing factor for each context was treated as a parameter

to learn during the training. The training of NNLM was speeded up without the explicit normalization. As a matter of fact, the normalizing factor for each context needs to be learned separately, and these normalizing factors for different contexts will be different, so that the evaluation of NNLM needs to be normalized explicitly. Interestingly, we noticed that the normalizing factors can be manually fixed to one instead of learning them during the training of NNLM, as mentioned in [26]. We believe this findings will be helpful to further improve our current work, since if the variance of the normalizing factor could be constrained in a small range the approximation will be further improved in Equation 6. In this work, the distribution of normalizing factors on the N-best list is investigated, and the normalizing factor for each hypothesis is approximated as a constant for fast rescoring without considering the variance of the normalizing factor. Based on the findings mentioned in [26], we will investigate how to constrain the variance of normalizing factors during the training to further improve our method in the next work.

Table 6 Word error rates (WERs) of Hub5'00-SWB and RT03S-FSH for lattice rescoring with UP-FNNLM

Model	WER	
	Hub5'00-SWB	RT03S-FSH
1-best (KN3)	17.3	20.2
KN5 (100-best)	17.1	19.5
KN5 (1,000-best)	16.9	19.4
KN5 (lattice)	17.0	19.4
UP-FNNLM + KN5 (100-best)	16.4	18.6
UP-FNNLM + KN5 (1,000-best)	16.2	18.6
UP-FNNLM + KN5 (lattice)	_16.2_	_18.5_

Furthermore, an alternative method to speed up the rescoring is to use the word lattice instead of N-best list. The word lattice can compactly represent much more hypotheses than the N-best list, as the output of STT. We wonder whether our proposed method can be extended to lattice rescoring. As we all know, the N-best list is close to the lattice with the size of N-best list increased. Two experiments are designed to validate our method. On the one hand, we investigate whether the performance of N-best rescoring will be degraded with the size of N-best list increased. 1,000-best list instead of 100-best list is extracted for each utterance and rescored by our proposed method, shown in Table 5. Experimental results show that our proposed method still works well for 1,000-best list, and similar improvements are obtained for 1,000-best rescoring. On the other hand, we directly rescore the lattice with 'lattice-tool' [27] command to evaluate our proposed method. In consideration of the easy implementation and fast rescoring, the 'UP-FNNLM + KN5' is integrated into lattice-tool command, where the computation of the LM score is replaced with Equation 9 for convenience. The experimental results show that the rescoring of lattice obtains a slightly lower WER than that of N-best list in Table 6. All the results also mean that our proposed approximations based on our firsthand observations are reasonable and effective for fast N-best rescoring.

8 Conclusions

Based on the observed characteristics of N-best hypotheses, the normalizing factors of NNLM for each hypothesis are approximated as a global constant for fast evaluation. The unnormalized NNLM combined with back-off N-gram is empirically investigated and evaluated on the English-Switchboard speech-to-text task. The computation complexity is reduced significantly without explicit softmax normalization. Experimental results show that UP-NNLM is about 2~3 times faster than 'NNLM + class layer' for evaluation. Moreover, the fast-UP-FNNLM is more than 25 times faster than FNNLM + class layer and more than 1,100 times faster than FNNLM. The N-best hypotheses from STT's output are approximately rescored and reranked by unnormalized NNLM combined with back-off N-gram model in the logarithmic domain. Experimental results show that the unnormalized probability of NNLM, including FNNLM and RNNLM, is quite complementary to that of back-off N-gram, and UP-NNLM is discriminative for N-best rescoring, even though UP-NNLM is not so accurate. The performance of STT system is improved significantly by 'KN5 + UP-NNLM' with little computational resource.

Endnotes

^{a}HDecode -A -D -T 1 -s 12.0 -p -6.0 -n 32 -t 150.0 150.0 -v 105.0 95.0 -u 10000 -l lat/ -z lat -C CF -H

models/HMM -w models/LM -S xa.scp -i xa.mlf models/DICT models/LIST (http://htk.eng.cam.ac.uk/extensions/).

^{b}lattice-tool -nbest-decode 100 -read-htk -htk-logbase 2.718 -htk-lmscale 12.0 -htk-wdpenalty -6.0 -in-lattice-list xa.lst -out-nbest-dir nbest/ (http://www.speech.sri.com/projects/srilm/manpages/lattice-tool.1.html).

Abbreviations

ASR: automatic speech recognition; DNN: deep neural network; FNNLM: feed-forward neural network language model; KN: Kneser-Ney smoothing algorithm; KN3: back-off 3-gram based on KN smoothing; KN5: back-off 5-gram based on KN smoothing; LM: back-off N-gram language model; NNLM: neural network language model; PDF: probability density function; PPL: perplexity; RNNLM: recurrent neural network language model; STT: speech-to-text; WER: word error rate.

Competing interests

The authors declare that they have no competing interests.

Acknowledgements

The authors are grateful to the anonymous reviewers for their insightful and valuable comments. This work was supported by the National Natural Science Foundation of China under Grant Nos. 61273268, 61005019, and 90920302, and in part by the Beijing Natural Science Foundation Program under Grant No. KZ201110005005.

References

1.   Y Bengio, R Ducharme, P Vincent, C Jauvin, A neural probabilistic language model. Mach. Learn. Res. (JMLR), 1137–1155 (2003)
2.   E Arisoy, TN Sainath, B Kingsbury, B Ramabhadran, Deep neural network language models, in *Proceedings of NAACL-HLT Workshop* (Montreal, 2012), pp. 20–28. http://www.aclweb.org/anthology/W12-2703
3.   T Mikolov, M Karafiat, L Burget, JH Cernocky, S Khudanpur, Recurrent neural network based language model, in *Proceedings of InterSpeech* (Makuhari, 2010), pp. 1045–1048
4.   T Mikolov, S Kombrink, L Burget, JH Cernocky, S Khudanpur, Extensions of recurrent neural network language model, in *Proceedings of ICASSP* (Prague, 2011)
5.   M Sundermeyer, R Schluter, H Ney, LSTM neural networks for language modeling, in *Proceedings of InterSpeech* (Portland, 2012)
6.   T Mikolov, A Deoras, S Kombrink, L Burget, JH Cernocky, Empirical evaluation and combination of advanced language modeling techniques, in *Proceedings of InterSpeech* (Florence, 2011)
7.   S Kombrink, T Mikolov, M Karafiat, L Burget, Recurrent neural network based language modeling in meeting recognition, in *Proceedings of InterSpeech* (Florence, 2011)
8.   T Mikolov, Statistical language models based on neural networks. PhD thesis, Brno University of Technology (BUT), 2012. http://www.fit.vutbr.cz/~imikolov/rnnlm/thesis.pdf.
9.   HS Le, I Oparin, A Allauzen, JL Gauvain, F Yvon, Structured output layer neural network language models for speech recognition. IEEE Trans. Audio Speech Lang. Process. **21**, 197–206 (2013)
10. Y Shi, WQ Zhang, J Liu, MT Johnson, RNN language model with word clustering and class-based output layer. EURASIP J. Audio Speech Music Process. **22** (2013). doi:10.1186/1687-4722-2013-22
11. F Morin, Y Bengio, Hierarchical probabilistic neural network language model, in *Proceedings of AISTATS* (Barbados, 2005), pp. 246–252
12. A Mnih, G Hinton, A scalable hierarchical distributed language model. Adv. Neural Inf. Process. Syst. **21**, 1081–1088 (2008)
13. C Fellbaum, *WordNet: an Electronic Lexical Database* (MIT, Cambridge, 1998)
14. PF Brown, PV deSouza, RL Mercer, VJD Pietra, JC Lai, Class-based N-gram models for natural language. Comput. Linguist. **18**(4), 467–479 (1992)
15. J Godfrey, E Holliman, *Switchboard-1 Release 2* (Linguistic Data Consortium, Philadelphia, 1997)

16. The CMU pronouncing dictionary release 0.7a (2007). http://www.speech. cs.cmu.edu/cgi-bin/cmudict.

17. H Schwenk, CSLM: Continuous space language model toolkit (2010). http://www-lium.univ-lemans.fr/cslm/

18. T Mikolov, A Deoras, S Kombrink, L Burget, JH Cernocky, RNNLM - Recurrent Neural Network Language Modeling Toolkit, in *Proceedings of ASRU* (Hawaii, 2011). http://www.fit.vutbr.cz/imikolov/rnnlm/

19. DE Rumelhart, GE Hinton, RJ Williams, Learning representations by back-propagating errors. Nature **323**, 533–536 (1986)

20. F Seide, G Li, X Chen, D Yu, Feature engineering in context-dependent deep neural networks for conversational speech transcription, in *Proceedings of ASRU* (Hawaii, 2011)

21. M Cai, Y Shi, J Liu, Deep maxout neural networks for speech recognition, in *Proceedings of ASRU* (Olomouc, 2013)

22. H Schwenk, Continuous space language models. Comput. Speech Lang. **21**(3), 592–518 (2007)

23. M Auli, M Galley, C Quirk, G Zweig, Joint language and translation modeling with recurrent neural networks, in *Proceedings of EMNLP* (Seattle, 2013), pp. 1044–1054

24. Y Si, Q Zhang, T Li, J Pan, Y Yan, Prefix tree based n-best list re-scoring for recurrent neural network language model used in speech recognition system, in *Proceedings of InterSpeech* (Lyon, 2013), pp. 3419–3423

25. M Gutmann, A Hyvarinen, Noise-contrastive estimation: a new estimation principle for unnormalized statistical models, in *Proc. of AISTATS* (Sardinia, 2010), pp. 297–304

26. A Mnih, YW Teh, A fast and simple algorithm for training neural probabilistic language models, in *Proceedings of ICML* (Edinburgh, 2012)

27. A Stolcke, SRILM – an extensible language modeling toolkit, in *Proceedings of ICSLP*, (2002), pp. 901–904

7

Classification of heterogeneous text data for robust domain-specific language modeling

Ján Staš*, Jozef Juhár and Daniel Hládek

Abstract

The robustness of *n*-gram language models depends on the quality of text data on which they have been trained. The text corpora collected from various resources such as web pages or electronic documents are characterized by many possible topics. In order to build efficient and robust domain-specific language models, it is necessary to separate domain-oriented segments from the large amount of text data, and the remaining out-of-domain data can be used only for updating of existing in-domain *n*-gram probability estimates. In this paper, we describe the process of classification of heterogeneous text data into two classes, to the in-domain and out-of-domain data, mainly used for language modeling in the task-oriented speech recognition from judicial domain. The proposed algorithm for text classification is based on detection of theme in short text segments based on the most frequent key phrases. In the next step, each text segment is represented in vector space model as a feature vector with term weighting. For classification of these text segments to the in-domain and out-of domain area, document similarity with automatic thresholding are used. The experimental results of modeling the Slovak language and adaptation to the judicial domain show significant improvement in the model perplexity and increasing the performance of the Slovak transcription and dictation system.

Keywords: Document similarity; Language modeling; Speech recognition; Term weighting; Text classification; Topic detection

1 Introduction

With an increasing amount of the text data gathered from various web pages or electronic documents and growing need for more accurate and robust models of the Slovak language [1], a question of how to classify the text data according to their content arises even more than expected. This question is getting on importance with using heterogeneous text corpora, in which we do not have any knowledge about the document boundaries. In the case of the *task-oriented speech recognition* and *domain-specific language modeling* [2], these heterogeneous text data bring many ambiguities caused by the overestimating such *n*-gram probabilities that are typically unrelated with the area of speech recognition into the process of the training language models. Therefore, we were looking for a way of classification of the text data into predefined domains

as good way as possible and adjustment of the parameters of language modeling for effective *large vocabulary continuous speech recognition* (LVCSR).

There are two ways existing for assigning text data into domains; using text classification or document clustering with topic detection. The difference between them is that the *text classification* is based on assigning the text data into two or more predefined classes, whereas *document clustering* tries to group similar documents into a number of classes and find some relationship between them. The similarity of two documents represented by their feature vectors is usually based on computing cosine of the angle between them [3]. After clustering, the topic detection for every cluster of documents is needed [4]. Unlike clustering, the classification is supervised learning technique and requires the training data for classifying new documents. Considering fact that we need to group text documents only into two classes, we focused our research on the text classification techniques.

A growing number of statistical methods have been applied to the problem of text classification in recent

*Correspondence: jan.stas@tuke.sk
Department of Electronics and Multimedia Communications, Technical University of Košice, Park Komenského 13, 041 20 Košice, Slovakia

years, including *naïve Bayes classifier* and *probabilistic language models* [5,6], similarity-based approaches using *k-nearest neighbor classifier* [5,7], *decision trees* and *neural networks* [8], *support vector machines* [5,9], or *semi-supervised clustering* [10]. When large amount of documents is used, these algorithms usually suffer from a very high computational complexity. Moreover, for correct estimation of parameters of these classification algorithms, a training corpus is needed. Therefore, we proposed an algorithm based on computing similarity between two documents and decision, which one will appertain to the domain and one which will not, using a threshold value calculated automatically on a development data set. This simple and effective algorithm classifies short text segments (such as paragraphs) from heterogeneous text corpora gathered from various resources to the in-domain and out-of-domain data. Classified text data are then used in statistical language modeling for enhancing its quality and robustness in the task-oriented speech recognition.

The rest of this paper is organized as follows. Section 2 starts with a short overview about the source data used either for text classification, training acoustic and language models, and testing the Slovak LVCSR system. Our proposed approach for text classification based on the key phrase identification, term weighting, measuring similarity between two documents, and automatic thresholding is introduced in the Section 3. Section 4 presents the speech recognition setup used for evaluating language models trained on classified text corpora. The experimental results with adapted models of the Slovak language into the selected domain are discussed in the Section 5. Finally, Section 6 summarizes the contribution of our work and concludes this article with future directions.

2 Source data

2.1 Acoustic database

For testing language models using speech recognition system, the Slovak acoustic database was created, on which acoustic models have been trained. Speech database consists of three subsets (see the Table 1):

- The first part is characterized by gender-balanced speakers, contains 250 h of speech recordings obtained from 250 speakers together and consists of two parts: APD1 and APD2 databases. The APD1 database includes 100 h of readings of real adjustments from the court with personal data changed, recorded in sound studio conditions. The APD2 database consists of 150 h of read phonetically rich sentences, web texts, newspaper articles, short phrases, and spelled items, recorded in conference rooms using table and close-talk headset microphones [2].
- The second PAR database includes 90 h of 90% male and 10% female speech recordings realized in the main conference hall of the Slovak Parliament using conference gooseneck condenser microphones [11].
- The mixture of Broadcast news (BN) databases consists of 145 h of speech recordings acquired from main and morning TV shows and 35 h from broadcast news and TV and radio shows, together realized with TV DVB-S PCI card [12].

All speech recordings were downsampled to 16-kHz 16-bit PCM mono format for training and testing. The whole acoustic database was manually annotated by our team of trained annotators using the Transcriber tool [12], double checked, and corrected.

2.2 Text corpora

The main part of text corpora used for text classification and statistical language modeling was created by using our proposed *system for gathering text data* from various web pages and electronic resources written in Slovak language [1]. From the retrieved text data, there was a large amount of numerals, symbols, or grammatically incorrect words filtered out and the rest of the data were normalized into their pronounced form by additional processing, such as word tokenization, sentence segmentation, numerals transcription, and abbreviations expanding. The processed text corpora were later divided into smaller domain-specific subcorpora ready for the training language models. Contemporary text corpora consists of following subsets:

Table 1 Acoustic database description

Acoustic database	Hours	Sampling (kHz)	Resolution (bit)	Microphone type	Sound environment and conditions
APD1 database	100	48	16	Close-talk headset	Sound studio conditions
APD2 database	150	48	16	Close-talk headset	Offices and conference rooms
PAR database	90	44	24	Gooseneck condenser	Main conference hall of the Slovak Parliament
BN1 database	145	48	16	TV DVB-S PCI card	Sound studio, telephone, and degraded speech
BN2 database	35	48	16	TV DVB-S PCI card	Sound studio, telephone, and degraded speech
Evaluation data set	5.25	48	16	Close-talk headset	Sound studio, offices, and conference rooms

- *Slovak web corpus* was collected by crawling whole web pages from various Slovak domains saved with information about date, title, URL, extracted text, and HTML source code.
- *Corpus of newspapers* is a collection of articles that have been gathered from the most popular online news portals, magazines, and journals in the Slovak Republic. This corpus was extended by a large amount of newspaper articles downloaded via RSS channels and collection of manually corrected speech transcriptions of four main TV broadcast news and five radio shows.
- *Corpus of legal texts* (judicial corpus) was obtained from the Ministry of Justice of the Slovak Republic in order to develop the automatic dictation system for their internal purpose [2].
- *Corpus of fiction texts* was created from $1,625$ electronic books and other stories freely available on the Internet written in Slovak language.
- *Corpus of contemporary blogs* consists of web-extracted blog texts from main news portals in the Slovak Republic saved without contribution's comments.
- *Development data set* (held-out data) was created from 10% randomly selected sentences from (in-domain) corpus of legal texts that were not used in the process of training language models.
- *Speech annotations* (transcriptions) of data obtained from acoustic database are a special portion of the text corpus. Transcriptions also contain a large amount of filled pauses and additional disfluent speech events together with useful text. We have discovered that filled pauses have a positive effect on the quality of language modeling, both for dictated or spontaneous speech. Therefore, we decided to include these speech transcriptions into the process of language modeling.

The complete statistics on the total number of tokens and sentences for particular text subcorpus are summarized in the Table 2.

Table 2 Statistics on the text corpora

Text corpus	Tokens	Sentences	Documents
Slovak web corpus	748,854,697	50,694,708	2,803,412
Corpus of newspapers	554,593,113	36,326,920	2,022,483
Corpus of legal texts	565,140,401	18,524,094	1,503,271
Corpus of fiction texts	101,234,475	8,039,739	367,956
Corpus of contemporary blogs	55,711,674	4,071,165	211,533
Development data set	55,163,941	1,782,333	165,577
Speech annotations	4,434,217	485,800	5,520
Total	2,085,132,518	119,924,759	7,079,752

Moreover, each text corpus was annotated using our proposed *Slovak morphological classifier* [13] based on a hidden Markov model (HMM) together with suffix-based word clustering function and restricted by *manually morphologically annotated lexicon of words*. The HMM has been trained on trigram statistics generated from *morphologically annotated corpus* together with the lexicon delivered by the Slovak National Corpus [14]. Note that the morphologically annotated corpus were then used in the process of extraction of key phrases from development data set of the proposed algorithm for classification of heterogeneous text data.

3 Proposed text classification approach

As it was mentioned before, we proposed an effective approach for classification of heterogeneous text corpora into the two data sets, the in-domain and out-of-domain data, to increase the robustness of domain-oriented statistical language modeling in the Slovak LVCSR system. Our algorithm is based on identifying key phrases with their occurrences in short text segments. Each text document is represented as a vector of key phrases in a vector space (a key phrase/document matrix). For reducing the influence of frequent key phrases in documents, term weighting was applied. The next step includes measuring the similarity between reference and examined document to determine the closeness between them. Based on the automatic thresholding, the algorithm then decides which text document belongs or does not belong to the examined domain (in our case to the judicial one). The block scheme of the proposed text classification approach is depicted in Figure 1.

In the following sections, the proposed text classification approach is described in more detail.

3.1 Key phrase extraction

The first step in the process of classification of the text data is to propose an algorithm for extracting key phrases from examined domain (from development data). Based on morphologically annotated corpora, described in the Section 2.2, we created a set of 14 *morpho-syntactic patterns* for extracting bigrams, trigrams, and quadrigrams from this corpora, summarized in the Table 3. Morphosyntactic patterns take into account part of speech of the corresponding words and syntactic dependency between them, unlike other statistical approaches based on computing pointwise mutual information, t score or χ^2 score between n words. In order to prevent any occurrence of key phrases from other domains in this list, we filtered out all key phrases from the other out-of-domain corpora, except corpus of legal texts. Using this approach, we created a list of $5,210$ in-domain key phrases that are later used in the block key phrase identification and measuring similarity between two documents. More details and

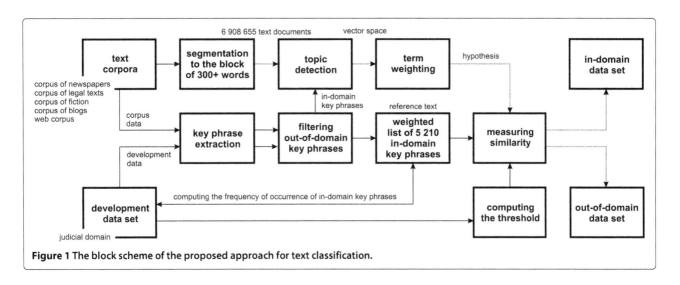

Figure 1 The block scheme of the proposed approach for text classification.

background on how the set of morpho-syntactic patterns were created can be found in [15].

3.2 Text segmentation
In general, text data gathered from the Internet are characterized by a large variety of domains or topics that are contained in the web articles, from which the text corpus is composed. Moreover, in case of large-scale text documents, they may also contain more than one theme within. As it was mentioned earlier, this problem is gaining on importance when using heterogeneous text corpora, in which we have no knowledge about the document boundaries. Therefore, the next step in the text classification process includes segmentation of the used text corpora into the *small segments* (paragraphs) *with at least 300 words*. This value was determined empirically from the

statistical observation and expresses the average number of words contained in one paragraph of a web-based article. By application of segmentation rules, we obtained a total of $6,908,655$ short (300+ words) text segments - documents - entering to the process of text classification. The statistics on the number of documents after text segmentation for particular subcorpus are resumed in the Table 2.

3.3 Key phrase identification
In the next step, the key phrases were used in *computing the frequency of their occurrence* in examined text segments of 300+ words. The key phrase identification process is similar to any topic detection approach. However, in this process we have not considered removal of stop-words, because key phrases extracted using proposed morpho-syntactic patterns contained such part-of-speech classes as prepositions or conjunctions (see the Table 3). Also lemmatization (or stemming) is very time-consuming and would cause high memory requirements, therefore it has not been introduced into this process of text classification. Note that text segments that did not contain any key phrases were automatically classified as out-of-domain data.

3.4 Vector space modeling
One of the simplest way how to represent the occurrence of terms (key words or key phrases) in any text document is to use a *vector space model* (VSM). In each ith document, $\bar{d}_i$ is represented as a feature vector of the terms t_j that appear in this document as follows [5]:

$$\bar{d}_i = (t_{i,1}, t_{i,2}, \ldots, t_{i,N}). \tag{1}$$

Using this approach, each short text segment was represented by a vector of $5,210$ key phrases. With respect to the number of documents in the collection (see the

Table 3 Morpho-syntactic patterns

Type	Characterization	Scheme
2-gram	Adjective + noun	AS
	Numeral + noun	NS
	Noun + noun	SS
	Abbreviation + noun	WS
3-gram	Adjective + adjective + noun	AAS
	Adjective + noun + noun	ASS
	Adverb + adjective + noun	DAS
	Numeral + adjective + noun	NAS
	Noun + adjective + noun	SAS
	Noun + preposition + noun	SES
	Noun + numeral + noun	SNS
4-gram	Noun + preposition + adjective + noun	SEAS
	Noun + preposition + noun + noun	SESS
	Noun + noun + conjunction + noun	SSOS

Section 3.2), we have received the matrix with $5,210$ columns and $6,908,655$ rows. However, the main disadvantage of such representation is a very high dimension of this matrix and sparsity of values in the vector space, resulting in very high requirements on its storage.

3.5 Term weighting

As it was mentioned earlier, term weighting was applied as a feature selection algorithm for reducing the influence of frequently occurring terms in a collection of documents. In this research, we have tested three different weighting schema: (a) tf-idf, (b) Okapi BM25, and (c) Ltu factors.

The conventional term weighting came from the computing frequency of a term in a document using the *term frequency* and the frequency in the collection of documents in which the term appears, which is expressed as the *document frequency*. A number of term weighting schemes based on these two frequency functions exist such as idf - *inverse document frequency*, expressed by the negative reciprocal value of the document frequency; ridf - *residual* idf, defined as the difference between actual idf and logarithm of idf predicted by Poisson distribution in a term distribution model; tf-idf and tf-ridf that combines term frequency and document frequency into one algorithm, which can be scaled *logarithmically* or normalized by *augmented* version [5]. Moreover, term weighting does not have to be performed on the entire collection of documents. It can be calculated on a small training corpus and used in clustering dynamic data streams using tf-icf weighting [16].

Based on the previous research [17] focused on a comparative study of term weighting schemes, we observed that standard tf-idf achieved the best results in clustering of the Slovak text documents obtained from Wikipedia. Therefore, we used this weighting scheme in the proposed classification too.

The tf-idf is a standard term weighting scheme used in information retrieval or data mining and combines term frequency and inverse document frequency together. The importance of tf-idf increases proportionally to the occurrence of a word in the document and is offset by the frequency of the word in the collection of documents according to formula [5]

$$w_{i,j} = \text{tf}_{i,j} \times \text{idf}_i = \frac{f_{i,j}}{\sum_k f_{k,j}} \times \log \frac{N}{\text{df}_i}, \qquad (2)$$

where $f_{i,j}$ is the number of occurrence of a term t_i in a document d_j and sum in the denominator of $\text{tf}_{i,j}$ component expresses the number of occurrences of all terms t_i in d_j. Then, N is the total number of documents, and the denominator of idf_i component expresses the total number of documents in a collection that t_i occurs in well-known as document frequency df_i.

Contemporary term weighting schemes take into account additional factors such as *maximum of term frequency* $\max(\text{tf}_{i,j})$ in a document, *length of a document* dl_i, or *average document length* dl_{avg} in a collection of documents. Between these, we can fit a simple *automated text classification* (ATC), which uses the idf as the term importance factor and Euclidean vector length as the document length normalization factor, either Okapi BM25 or Ltu scoring [18] that were used in our experiments.

The Okapi BM25 score is defined as a bag-of-words retrieval function that ranks a collection of documents regardless of the inter-relationship between the terms within a document [5]. It is based on computing BM25-tf score and idf component derived from the binary independence model that is well-known from the probabilistic theory in the information retrieval [19]:

$$w_{i,j} = \text{BM25} - \text{tf}_{i,j} \times \text{idf}_i^* = \frac{\text{tf}_{i,j}}{0.5 + 1.5 \times \frac{\text{dl}_i}{\text{dl}_{avg}} + \text{tf}_{i,j}}$$
$$\times \log \frac{N - \text{df}_i + 0.5}{\text{df}_i + 0.5}, \qquad (3)$$

where $\text{tf}_{i,j}$ means term frequency, N is a total number of documents in the collection, df_i presents the document frequency, dl_i document length and dl_{avg} the average document length for the collection. In addition, we can put the Okapi BM25 scoring into the tf-idf scheme, which was presented in [20].

In Ltu term weighting scheme, L factor expresses the *logarithm of the term frequency*, t factor the *inverse document frequency*, and u the *length normalization* factor as follows [21]:

$$w_{i,j} = \text{L} \times \text{t} \times \text{u} = (\log \text{tf}_{i,j} + 1) \times \log \frac{N}{\text{df}_i} \times \frac{1}{0.8 + 0.2 \times \frac{\text{dl}_i}{\text{dl}_{avg}}}. \qquad (4)$$

As we can see from these equations, both the Okapi BM25 and Ltu scores are only a certain variation of the conventional tf-idf weighting.

The problem of data sparsity and high dimension of VSM after term weighting can be efficiently eliminated using *latent semantic analysis/indexing* (LSA/LSI) or its *probabilistic* (pLSA) version that projects terms and documents into a space of co-occurring terms, also by *principal component analysis* (PCA), based on a *singular value* or *eigen-value decomposition* of a term/document matrices [22]. However, this space reduction is very time-consuming and computationally intensive considering a large amount of documents in our collection. Therefore, they were not implemented into the process of text classification.

3.6 Document similarity measurement

The next step involves measuring similarity of two documents. In this approach, we measured the document similarity between reference and examined texts, not between all documents in a collection, commonly used in the tasks oriented on the document clustering. The reference text contained weighted form of all key phrases which occurred in a development data set. Both reference and examined text documents were represented by the vector of $5,210$ key phrases weighted according to the selected weighting scheme, described in the Section 3.5, so they could be compared.

By empirical study of numerous similarity measures described in [23], we have chosen three different measures: (a) Bhattacharyya coefficient, (b) Jaccard correlation index, and (c) Jensen-Shannon divergence, satisfying the conditions of *non-negativity, symmetricity, triangle inequality*, and *identity*, when distance is equal to 0.

For clustering phonemes in the process of training acoustic models, the *Bhattacharyya coefficient* is often used. In general, it can be used as a classification criterion in many other tasks oriented on clustering in information theory. Therefore, we used this coefficient as one classification criterion. Bhattacharyya coefficient comes from the *sum of geometric means* between two probability density functions and specifies the separability of two classes x and y as follows:

$$d_{\text{Bha}} = -\ln \sum_{i=1}^{N} \sqrt{x_i y_i}. \tag{5}$$

On the contrary, *Jaccard correlation index* is defined as a *harmonic mean* between two probability density functions and expresses a scalar sum of two vectors. It comes from equation on computing cosine similarity [5], normalized by absolute deviation of two distributions x and y according to the formula

$$d_{\text{Jac}} = \frac{\sum_{i=1}^{N}(x_i + y_i)^2}{\sum_{i=1}^{N} x_i^2 + \sum_{i=1}^{N} y_i^2 - \sum_{i=1}^{N} x_i y_i}. \tag{6}$$

Jensen-Shannon divergence comes from the principle of uncertainty. It is often used in information theory and natural language processing as a special case of *relative entropy approach* similar to the averaged Kullback-Leibler divergence, satisfying the condition of symmetry in the entire range of values. For two probability density functions x and y, it is computed as

$$d_{\text{JS}} = \frac{1}{2} \sum_{i=1}^{N} x_i \ln\left(\frac{2x_i}{x_i + y_i}\right) + \frac{1}{2} \sum_{i=1}^{N} y_i \ln\left(\frac{2y_i}{x_i + y_i}\right). \tag{7}$$

3.7 Automatic thresholding

The last step in the classification process is to correctly adjust the threshold that determines which documents will appertain to the in-domain and which to the out-of-domain area. In general, this value is usually determined empirically from long-term observation or can be adjusted automatically based on a set of statistic values derived from development data. There are many algorithms for automatic thresholding. A comprehensive study about those can be found in [24].

We used the *median* (centroid) of a sequence of coefficients derived from a set of values determining the similarity of two documents as a method of automatic thresholding (see the Section 3.6). The threshold value was calculated on a development data set and its acquisition shares the same process with classification of the text data described in the previous sections. This means that the development data were divided into short text segments consisting of at least 300 words, represented by VSM through the key phrases, and weighted, and each document was compared with the reference text (weighted list of key phrases) using one of the presented similarity measure. Using this process, we get a list of the coefficients (one coefficient for each document in development data set) expressing distance to the target domain. This list was sorted and the median value was selected as a threshold.

In the Table 4, we can find the statistics of the number of in-domain and out-of-domain documents after applying the proposed classification approach to the segmented text corpora for different term weighting scheme and distance measure used in the step of measuring similarity between the reference and examined documents with automatic thresholding.

The performance between in-domain and out-of-domain language models is summarized in the Table 5. Model perplexity evaluated on a development data set was used for testing the quality of the language models. Its calculation will be introduced in the next section.

4 Speech recognition setup

4.1 Decoding

For evaluation of the quality of language modeling after text classification and performance of the Slovak LVCSR,

Table 4 The number of documents after text classification

Similarity/weighting	tf-idf	Okapi	Ltu
In-domain data set			
Bhattacharyya coefficient	1,166,806	607,004	698,061
Jaccard correlation index	1,258,169	537,729	699,033
Jensen-Shannon divergence	2,305,230	956,243	698,062
Out-of-domain data set			
Bhattacharyya coefficient	5,741,849	6,301,651	6,210,594
Jaccard correlation index	5,650,486	6,370,926	6,209,622
Jensen-Shannon divergence	4,603,425	5,952,412	6,210,593

Table 5 Model perplexity for particular language models computed on development data

Similarity/weighting	tf-idf	Okapi	Ltu
In-domain data set			
Bhattacharyya coefficient	14.1223	15.7542	17.2876
Jaccard correlation index	14.0815	14.8402	17.2872
Jensen-Shannon divergence	15.0343	15.4863	17.2878
Out-of-domain data set			
Bhattacharyya coefficient	90.6770	25.7417	183.670
Jaccard correlation index	75.0398	20.7094	162.901
Jensen-Shannon divergence	99.8450	24.3595	187.167

we configured a speech recognition setup based on Julius, an open-source continuous speech recognition engine [25]. Julius uses *two-level Viterbi search algorithm*, when input speech is processed in the forward search with bigram model, and the final backward search is performed again using the result obtained from the first search to narrow the search space with reverse language model of the highest order (in our case with trigram model). Proposed speech recognition setup is depicted in the Figure 2.

4.2   Acoustic modeling
The speech recognition setup involves a set of *triphone context-dependent acoustic models* based on HMMs. All models have been generated from feature vectors containing 39 *mel-frequency cepstral* (MFC) *coefficients*, where each of four states had been modeled by 32 Gaussian mixtures. Acoustic models have been trained on four databases of annotated speech recordings, described in the Section 2.1, using HTK Toolkit. The training set also involves model of silence, short pause, and additional

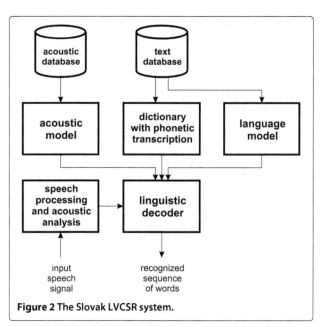

Figure 2 The Slovak LVCSR system.

noise events. Rare triphones have been modeled by the *effective triphone mapping algorithm* [11].

4.3   Language modeling
The experimental results have been performed taking an advantage of *trigram models* created using the SRI LM Toolkit [26], restricted by the vocabulary size of 325, 555 unique words and smoothed by the *Witten-Bell back-off algorithm*. All models have been trained on the processed text corpora size of about 2 billion of tokens in 120 million of sentences (see the Table 2) and divided into two parts, to the in-domain and out-of-domain data, after text classification (see the Table 4). Particular models trained on in-domain and out-of-domain data were combined with a model trained on the small portion of text data obtained from speech transcriptions (see the Table 2). Finally, the resulting trigram model was composed from three independent models and *adapted to the judicial domain* using *linear interpolation* with computing interpolation weights by our proposed algorithm based on the *minimization of perplexity* on a development data set. The complete process of building the Slovak language models is depicted on the Figure 3 and described in [1].

In this article we have compared the contribution of changes performed in the vocabulary, also using better text preprocessing steps, adding new text data, or introducing new principles into the Slovak language modeling during the recent time periods. These contributions and differences between language models are summarized in the Table 6.

During this period, the named entities such as people names, surnames, and geographical items were assigned into the word classes in recognition dictionary. The vocabulary has been continually updated with the new words, checked, and corrected. We have introduced filled pauses into the language modeling as transparent words and model some geographically named entities as multi-words. We have also tested a number of methods for language model adaptation to the ted domain and algorithms for text classification and clustering.

4.4   Evaluation
For evaluation of the Slovak language models after text classification, three standard measures have been used.

Accuracy (Acc) and *Correctness* (Corr) are the standard extrinsic measures for evaluating the performance of the LVCSR system. If N is the total number of words in an evaluation data set (reference), S, I, and D reflect the total number of substituted, inserted, and deleted words in recognized hypothesis, respectively, and $H = N - (S + D)$ is the total number of words in hypothesis, then

$$\text{Acc} = \frac{H - I}{N} \quad \text{and} \quad \text{Corr} = \frac{H}{N}. \tag{8}$$

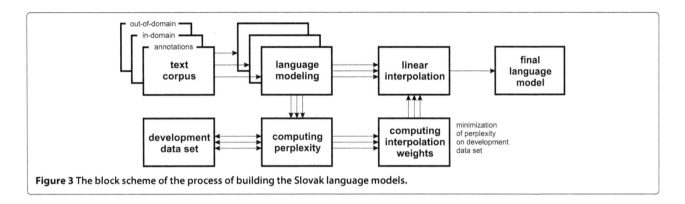

Figure 3 The block scheme of the process of building the Slovak language models.

For intrinsic evaluation of the quality of language modeling, the model perplexity has been used. *Model perplexity* (PPL) is defined as the reciprocal value of the weighted (geometric) probability assigned by the language model to each word in the test set and is related to cross-entropy $H(W)$ by the equation

$$\mathrm{PPL} = 2^{H(W)} = \frac{1}{\sqrt[n]{P(W)}}, \tag{9}$$

where $P(W)$ is the probability of sequence of n words in a language model.

The *evaluation data set* used for testing the performance of the LVCSR system and the quality of the Slovak language modeling after text classification were represented by randomly selected segments from the APD databases (see the Section 2.1, Table 1) containing $1,950$ male and $1,476$ female speech utterances with total length of about 5.25 h. These speech segments were not used in the training of acoustic models and contain $41,868$ words in $3,426$ sentences and short phrases. We have decided to include also short phrases in the test set because people make pauses in real conditions not only on the sentence

boundaries, but also on phrase boundaries, usually before conjunctions.

5 Experimental results

The experiments have been oriented on the evaluation of the model perplexity and performance of the Slovak LVCSR system on the evaluation (test) data after text classification and statistical modeling of the Slovak language from judicial domain. The selection of this domain was intentional concerning our research oriented on development of the Slovak automatic dictation and transcription system for the Ministry of Justice of the Slovak Republic in recent years [2]. The same approach for text classification and statistical language modeling can be also used for several other domains, in the task of broadcast news transcription, meeting speech recognition, etc.

As it was mentioned in the Section 3, the statistics on the numbers of in-domain and out-of-domain documents after text classification regarding the used term weighting scheme in combination with selected similarity measure are resumed in the Table 4.

Table 6 Differences in the text processing and language modeling during the recent time periods

	Period				
	Dec 2011	Jul 2012	Dec 2012	Apr 2013	May 2013
No. of pronunciation variants	475,156	475,357	474,456	474,453	474,453
No. of unique word forms	326,299	326,295	325,555	325,555	325,555
No. of words under classes	97,471	97,680	97,678	97,678	97,678
No. of classes of words	20	22	22	22	22
No. of transparent words	4	5	5	5	5
Vocabulary extension	•	•	•	•	-
Word classes extension	•	•	-	-	-
Adding new text data	•	-	-	•	•
Additional text processing	•	-	•	•	•
Filled pause modeling	-	•	•	•	•
New text classification	•	-	-	-	•

• Change was performed.

Table 7 Language model perplexity and performance of Slovak LVCSR system with different acoustic models

PPL	Text classification		APD1+APD2 250 h (table mic.) sp. adapt.: no eval. set: gender-bal.		APD1+APD2 250 h (close-talk mic.) sp. adapt.: no eval. set: gender-bal.		APD1+APD2 +PAR 340 h sp. adapt.: no eval. set: gender-bal.		APD1+APD2 +PAR+BN 520 h sp. adapt.: no eval. set: gender-bal.	
	Weighting	Similarity	Acc %	Corr %	Acc %	Corr %	Acc %	Corr %	Acc %	Corr %
40.4302	Reference language model		91.84	93.08	93.61	94.51	94.36	95.13	94.06	94.89
36.0428	tf-idf	Bhattacharyya	92.44	93.64	93.99	94.85	94.70	95.46	94.36	95.13
35.9444		Jaccard index	92.46	93.65	93.97	94.85	94.72	95.47	94.37	95.16
38.1756		Jensen-Shannon	92.23	93.39	93.78	94.70	94.50	95.25	94.21	94.99
38.1289	Okapi	Bhattacharyya	92.17	93.34	93.77	94.65	94.61	95.34	94.27	95.02
39.9782		Jaccard index	92.10	93.31	93.60	94.54	94.48	95.21	94.11	94.89
39.2267		Jensen-Shannon	92.27	93.42	93.77	94.67	94.61	95.36	94.18	94.95
40.1325	Ltu	Bhattacharyya	91.86	93.12	93.57	94.51	94.42	95.16	94.05	94.87
40.1439		Jaccard index	91.87	93.12	93.56	94.50	94.40	95.16	94.04	94.87
40.1319		Jensen-Shannon	91.87	93.12	93.57	94.51	94.42	95.16	94.05	94.87

As we can see from this results, we achieved the best class separation of in-domain and out-of-domain data in combination of Okapi BM25 weighting with similarity based on computing Jaccard correlation index. Using this combination, we yielded the in-domain data with the best possible concentration of key phrases in it. On the contrary, the worst separation of classes was observed when using tf-idf weighting and Jensen-Shannon divergence. Although this combination gives the largest number of text documents in the in-domain corpus, it has a much weaker concentration of key phrases in it. If we review the Ltu weighting, similar results of class

separation were noticed for any similarity measure we have chosen. It would be interesting to discover the overlap between classes for the same term weighting and different distance/similarity measure. Their intersection or union could produce more interesting results in the future.

However, if we look at the performance between in-domain and out-of-domain language models using perplexity evaluated on development data summarized in the Table 5, the text classification using tf-idf weighting with measuring similarity based on computing Jaccard correlation index or Bhattacharyya coefficient predetermines the

Table 8 Language model perplexity and performance of the Slovak LVCSR system with gender-dependent acoustic models

PPL	Text classification		APD1+APD2 +PAR 340 h sp. adapt.: female eval. set: gender-bal.		APD1+APD2 +PAR 340 h sp. adapt.: male eval. set: gender-bal.		APD1+APD2 +PAR 340 h sp. adapt.: female eval. set: female sp.		APD1+APD2 +PAR 340 h sp. adapt.: male eval. set: male sp.	
	Weighting	Similarity	Acc %	Corr %	Acc %	Corr %	Acc %	Corr %	Acc %	Corr %
40.4302	Reference language model		90.15	91.68	92.72	93.80	95.72	96.48	94.10	94.87
36.0428	tf-idf	Bhattacharyya	91.23	92.50	93.23	94.18	95.97	96.68	94.34	95.06
35.9444		Jaccard index	91.26	92.55	93.24	94.22	95.98	96.68	94.73	95.11
38.1756		Jensen-Shannon	90.71	92.10	92.92	93.94	95.81	96.54	94.23	94.94
38.1289	Okapi	Bhattacharyya	90.95	92.23	93.03	94.01	95.88	96.59	94.25	94.96
39.9782		Jaccard index	90.59	91.99	92.82	93.84	95.81	96.53	94.17	94.90
39.2267		Jensen-Shannon	90.93	92.27	93.00	93.97	95.94	96.65	94.17	94.89
40.1325	Ltu	Bhattacharyya	90.19	91.70	92.72	93.78	95.73	96.49	94.10	94.85
40.1439		Jaccard index	90.18	91.70	92.73	93.78	95.76	96.51	94.11	94.86
40.1319		Jensen-Shannon	90.18	91.70	92.72	93.78	95.73	96.49	94.10	94.85

Table 9 Model perplexity and performance of Slovak LVCSR system with different language and acoustic models

PPL	Language model (period)	APD1+APD2 250 h (table mic.) sp. adapt.: no eval. set: gender-bal.		APD1+APD2 250 h (close-talk mic.) sp. adapt.: no eval. set: gender-bal.		APD1+APD2 +PAR 340 h sp. adapt.: no eval. set: gender-bal.		APD1+APD2 +PAR+BN 520 h sp. adapt.: no eval. set: gender-bal.	
		Acc %	Corr %	Acc %	Corr %	Acc %	Corr %	Acc %	Corr %
44.9254	Dec. 2011	91.89	93.09	93.44	94.39	94.21	94.98	93.90	94.68
38.9688	Jul. 2012	92.33	93.55	93.78	94.69	94.46	95.26	94.30	95.11
40.2543	Dec. 2012	92.47	93.66	93.86	94.77	94.65	95.43	94.38	95.19
44.3262	Apr. 2013	92.35	93.56	93.76	94.69	94.53	95.33	94.30	95.12
35.9444	May 2013	92.46	93.65	93.97	94.85	94.72	95.47	94.37	95.16

optimal combination in terms of the quality the text segments used only for in-domain language modeling. Using Ltu factor, we observed significant degradation in the perplexity of language models trained not only on in-domain, but also on out-of-domain text data for each selected similarity measure. This is probably caused by inappropriate setting of a threshold in the last step of the proposed algorithm.

As regards the overall results performed on the randomly selected speech utterances from judicial domain, the first part of the experiments presented in the Tables 7 and 8 were oriented on the computing of model perplexity and performance of the Slovak LVCSR system after language modeling trained on classified text corpora using proposed approach.

The first table summarizes the performance of the Slovak language modeling using acoustic models trained on different speech databases, described in the Section 2.1. The results have shown that increasing the amount of acoustic data that were close to the examined domain with similar recording environment improved the recognition accuracy. On the other hand, the BN database degraded the results because the recording environment was quite different to the evaluation data selected from the APD databases.

The second table presents the quality of language modeling using gender-dependent acoustic models (optimized

to male and female speech) trained on the APD1, APD2 and PAR databases, giving the best results in previous experiment.

In the first two columns of the Table 8, the experimental results with acoustic models adapted to the male and female gender of speaker evaluated on the whole test data set are presented. The next two columns show the performance of language models in combination of gender-dependent acoustic models evaluated on the test speech utterances per gender.

As we can see from these results, gender-dependent acoustic modeling can significantly improve the recognition accuracy. If we look at the language model perplexity, we have achieved significant reduction about 11% relatively in comparison with the reference model trained on unclassified text corpora, if we applied combination of tf-idf weighting with similarity based on Jaccard correlation index in the text classification process. Similar results were obtained in the accuracy and correctness evaluated by the LVCSR system. Slightly worse results were noticed when using the Okapi BM25 and Ltu weighting in combination with one of the selected similarity measure. However, we can say that the proposed text classification approach had a significant impact on the overall robustness of the Slovak language modeling.

The second part of the experiments presented in the Tables 9 and 10 show the progress of acoustic and

Table 10 Model perplexity and performance of the Slovak LVCSR system with different language and gender-dependent acoustic models

PPL	Language model (period)	APD1+APD2 +PAR 340 h sp. adapt.: female eval. set: gender-bal.		APD1+APD2 +PAR 340 h sp. adapt.: male eval. set: gender-bal.		APD1+APD2 +PAR 340 h sp. adapt.: female eval. set: female sp.		APD1+APD2 +PAR 340 h sp. adapt.: male eval. set: male sp.	
		Acc %	Corr %	Acc %	Corr %	Acc %	Corr %	Acc %	Corr %
44.9254	12/2011	90.34	91.70	92.68	93.72	95.77	96.48	93.93	94.72
38.9688	07/2012	91.23	92.53	93.18	94.24	95.85	96.61	94.21	95.00
40.2543	12/2012	91.28	92.60	93.22	94.25	95.93	96.70	94.30	95.05
44.3262	04/2013	91.26	92.58	93.24	94.22	95.92	96.67	94.21	94.99
35.9444	05/2013	91.26	92.55	93.25	94.27	95.97	96.68	94.73	95.11

language modeling in development of the Slovak transcription and dictation system from the judicial domain, observed during the recent time periods.

With increasing amount of acoustic and linguistic data from the judicial domain, using gender-dependent acoustic modeling and speaker adaptation based on maximum likelihood linear regression (MLLR) as well as much better text preprocessing and classification for robust domain-specific language modeling, we achieved the speech recognition accuracy nearly 95% with a significant decrease in language model perplexity. Besides the better text processing and classification of training data, this result was achieved either by introducing classes of names, surnames, and other named entities into the recognition dictionary; representation of geographically named entities and technical terms by multiword expressions; by modeling of filled pauses in a language; or by effective adaptation of language models to the ted domain (see the Table 6).

In the future, we want to build also a new evaluation data set containing different acoustic environments to compare the performance of the Slovak LVCSR system for mixed end-user environments.

6 Conclusions

This paper proposed an algorithm for classification of heterogeneous text corpora to the in-domain and out-of-domain data with the aim of increasing robustness and quality of the statistical language modeling in task-oriented continuous speech recognition. By combining straightforward and effective methods used for text classification and document clustering based on topic detection with key phrases in short text segments, term weighting, measuring similarity between documents and automatic thresholding, we have achieved significant improvement in the quality of modeling of the Slovak language and performance of the Slovak automatic transcription and dictation system. The proposed algorithm can also be used in classification of heterogeneous text corpora into the other domains depending on the used development data.

Further research should be also focused on a better key phrase extraction in fully unsupervised manner without using morphologically annotated corpora or application of dimensionality reduction based on singular value decomposition and using latent semantic indexing or principal component analysis for better representation of text documents in the vector space despite of very high time and memory requirements of this process. Based on the initial tests with document clustering using the latent Dirichlet allocation, our proposed classification approach gives the similar results in the model perplexity as well as the recognition accuracy of the Slovak LVCSR system.

Besides the better text preprocessing and classification of the training data, the robustness and quality of

modeling of the Slovak language can be enhanced by addition of large amount of text data from transcripts of real speech recordings, introducing modeling of disfluent speech in a language, or by adaptation of language models to a specific user, group of users, or conversation, depending on the speech recognition task in which they will be used, for example, broadcast news transcription or meeting speech recognition.

Competing interests
The authors declare that they have no competing interests.

Acknowledgements
The research presented in this paper was partially supported by the Ministry of Education, Science, Research and Sport of the Slovak Republic under the research projects MS SR 3928/2010-11 (20%) and VEGA 1/0386/12 (30%) and the Research and Development Operational Program funded by the ERDF under the project ITMS-26220220141 (50%).

References
1. J Juhár, J Staš, D Hládek, in *New Technologies - Trends, Innovations and Research*, ed. by C Volosencu. Recent progress in development language model for Slovak large vocabulary continuous speech recognition (InTech Open Access, Rijeka, 2012), pp. 261–276
2. Rusko M, J Juhár, M Trnka, Staš J, S Darjaa, D Hládek, R Sabo, M Pleva, Ritomský M, Ondáš S, in *Proceedings of the 6th Language and Technology Conference on HLT*. Recent advances in the Slovak dictation system for the judicial domain (Poznań, LTC, 2013), pp. 555–560
3. A Huang, in *Proceedings of the 6th New Zealand Computer Science Research Student Conference*. Similarity measures for text document clustering (Christchurch, NZCSRSC, 2008), pp. 49–56
4. L Yue, S Xiao, X Lv, T Wang, in *Proceedings of 2011 International Conference on Mechatronic Science, Electric Engineering and Computer*. Topic detection based on keyword (Jilin, MEC, 2011), pp. 464–467
5. CD Manning, P Raghavan, H Schütze, *Introduction to Information Retrieval*. (Cambridge University Press, Cambridge, 2009)
6. F Peng, D Schuurmans, S Wang, Augmenting naïve Bayes classifiers with statistical language models. Inf. Retr. **7**(3–4), 317–345 (2004)
7. S Tan, An effective refinement strategy for KNN text classifier. Expert Syst. Appl. **30**(2), 290–298 (2006)
8. N Remeikis, I Skučas, Melninkaité V, Text categorization using neural networks initialized with decision trees. Informatica. **15**(4), 551–564 (2004)
9. T Joachims, in *Proceedings of the 10th European Conference on ML*. Text categorization with support vector machines: learning with many relevant features (Chemnitz, ECML, 1998), pp. 137–142
10. W Zhang, T Yoshida, X Tang, in *Proceedings of the 2nd International Conference on Business Intelligence and Financial Engineering*. Text classification using semi-supervised clustering (Beijing, BIFE, 2009), pp. 197–200
11. S Darjaa, M Cerňak, M Trnka, M Rusko, in *Proceeding of INTERSPEECH 2011*. Effective triphone mapping for acoustic modeling in speech recognition (Florence, INTERSPEECH, 2011), pp. 1717–1720
12. M Pleva, J Juhár, Building of broadcast news database for evaluation of the automated subtitling service. Communications. **15**(2A), 124–128 (2013)
13. D Hládek, Staš J, J Juhár, Dagger, in *Proceedings of the 54th International Symposium ELMAR 2012*. the Slovak morphological classifier (Zadar, ELMAR, 2012), pp. 195–198
14. R Garabík, in *Proceedings of the 1st Workshop on Intelligent and Knowledge Oriented Technologies*. Slovak morphology analyzer based on Levenshtein edit operations (Bratislava, WIKT, 2006), pp. 2–5
15. Staš J, D Hládek, J Juhár, M Ološtiak, in *Proceedings of the 7th International Conference on Natural Language Processing, Corpus Linguistics and E-learning*. Automatic extraction of multiword units from Slovak text corpora (Bratislava, SLOVKO, 2013), pp. 228–237
16. JW Reed, Y Jiao, TE Potok, BA Klump, MT Elmore, AR Hurson, TF-ICF, in *Proceedings of the 5th International Conference on Machine Learning and*

Applications. a new term weighting scheme for clustering dynamic data sets (ICMLA Orlando, 2006), pp. 258–263

17. Zlacký D, Staš J, J Juhár, A Čižmár, *Term weighting schemes for Slovak text document clustering*. (J. Electr. Electron. Eng, ed.), vol. 6, (2013), pp. 163–166

18. R Jin, C Falusos, AG Hauptmann, in *Proceedings of the 24th Annual International ACM Conference on Research and Development in Information Retrieval*. Meta-scoring: automatically evaluating term weighting schemes in IR without precision-recall (New Orleans, USA, SIGIR ACM, New York, 2001), pp. 83–89

19. SE Robertson, S Walker, S Jones, MM Hancock-Beaulieu, M Gatford, in *Proceedings of the 3rd Text Retrieval Conference*. Okapi at TREC-3 (Gaithersburg, TREC-3, 1996), pp. 109–126

20. JS Whissell, Clarke ChLA, Improving document clustering using Okapi BM25 feature weighting. Inf. Retr. **14**(5), 466–487 (2011)

21. A Singhal, in *Proceedings of the 6th Text Retrieval Conference*. AT&T at TREC-6 (Gaithersburg, TREC-6, 1998), pp. 215–226

22. S Lee, J Song, Y Kim, An empirical comparison of four text mining methods. J. Comp. Inf. Sys. **51**(1), 1–10 (2010)

23. SH Cha, Comprehensive survey on distance/similarity measures between probability density functions. Intl. J. Math. Model. Methods Appl. Sci. **1**(4), 300–307 (2007)

24. PL Rosin, Edges: saliency measures and automatic thresholding. Technical Note No. I.95.58: Institute for Remote Sensing Applications (1995)

25. A Lee, T Kawahara, in *em Proceedings of the 2009 Asia-Pacific Signal and Information Processing Association Annual Summit and Conference*. Recent development of open-source speech recognition engine Julius (Sapporo, APSIPA ASC, 2009), pp. 131–137

26. A Stolcke, J Zheng, W Wang, V Abrash, in *Proceedings of IEEE Automatic Speech Recognition and Understanding Workshop*. SRILM at sixteen: update and outlook (Waikoloa, ASRU, 2011), p. 5 pages

8

Recognizing emotion from Turkish speech using acoustic features

Caglar Oflazoglu and Serdar Yildirim[*]

Abstract

Affective computing, especially from speech, is one of the key steps toward building more natural and effective human-machine interaction. In recent years, several emotional speech corpora in different languages have been collected; however, Turkish is not among the languages that have been investigated in the context of emotion recognition. For this purpose, a new Turkish emotional speech database, which includes 5,100 utterances extracted from 55 Turkish movies, was constructed. Each utterance in the database is labeled with emotion categories (happy, surprised, sad, angry, fearful, neutral, and others) and three-dimensional emotional space (valence, activation, and dominance). We performed classification of four basic emotion classes (neutral, sad, happy, and angry) and estimation of emotion primitives using acoustic features. The importance of acoustic features in estimating the emotion primitive values and in classifying emotions into categories was also investigated. An unweighted average recall of 45.5% was obtained for the classification. For emotion dimension estimation, we obtained promising results for activation and dominance dimensions. For valence, however, the correlation between the averaged ratings of the evaluators and the estimates was low. The cross-corpus training and testing also showed good results for activation and dominance dimensions.

Keywords: Turkish emotional speech database; Emotion recognition; Emotion primitives estimation; Cross-corpus evaluation

1 Introduction

Recognizing the emotional state of the interlocutor and changing the way of communicating accordingly play a crucial role for the success of human-computer interaction. However, many technical challenges need to be resolved before integrating a real-time emotion recognizer into human-computer interfaces. These challenges include, as in any pattern recognition problem, data acquisition and annotation, feature extraction and finding the most salient features, and building a robust classifier. In this paper, we address each of these problems in the context of emotion recognition from Turkish speech and perform a cross-corpus evaluation.

The lack of data is a major challenge in emotion recognition. Even though great efforts have been made to collect emotional speech data in recent years, there is still a need for emotional speech recordings to cope with the problem of data sparseness. One way to obtain emotional speech data is to use human subjects reading utterances, generally with a certain number of pre-determined and emotionally neutral sentences, in specified emotional states. Berlin database of emotional speech [1], Danish Emotional Speech [2], LDC Emotional Prosody Speech and Transcripts [3], and Geneva Multimodal Emotion Portrayals (GEMEP) [4] are examples of studio-recorded emotional speech databases.

Even though studio-recorded (acted) databases provide us more balanced data in terms of the number of utterances per emotion, emotions are less natural and realistic compared to those we encounter in real life. One way to overcome this problem is to create environments so that the subjects produce the desired emotions. Sensitive Artificial Listener (SAL) [5], Airplane Behaviour Corpus (ABC) [6], Speech Under Simulated and Actual Stress (SUSAS) [7], TUM Audiovisual Interest Corpus (AVIC) [6], Interactive Emotional Dyadic Motion Capture (IEMOCAP) [8], the SEMAINE database [9], and the FAU Aibo emotion corpus [10] are examples of such

*Correspondence: serdar@mku.edu.tr
Computer Engineering Department, Mustafa Kemal University, Iskenderun, 31200, Hatay, Turkey

databases. For example, the FAU Aibo emotion corpus consists of 9 h of German spontaneous speech of 51 children interacting with Sony's pet robot Aibo. A Wizard-of-Oz technique was used for data collection and then the speech data was annotated with 11 emotion categories by five annotators at word level [10]. Audio-visual recordings obtained from TV shows and movies are also used for data acquisition, e.g., Vera-Am-Mittag (VAM) database [11], Situation Analysis in Fictional and Emotional Corpus (SAFE) [12], and the Belfast Naturalistic Database [13]. For example, the VAM corpus consists of audio-visual recordings taken from German TV talk show called Vera-Am-Mittag. The corpus contains 946 spontaneous speech from 47 participants of the show. The SAFE corpus [12] contains 7 h of audio-visual data extracted from English fiction movies and is mainly constructed for the purpose of fear-type emotion recognition system. In this paper, we utilized Turkish movies and TV shows to obtain speech data since the emotional speech extracted from movies is more realistic than studio-recorded emotions expressed by actors reading some pre-defined sentences.

An important requirement of most data-driven systems is the availability of annotated data. The goal of annotation is to assign a label to data. For the emotion recognition task, the annotation is needed to determine the true emotion expressed in the collected speech data. Largely motivated from psychological studies, two approaches were employed within the emotion recognition research for emotion annotation. The classical approach is to use set of emotion words (categories) to describe emotion-related states. Even though there are ongoing debates concerning how many emotion categories exist, the emotion categories (fear, anger, happiness, disgust, sadness, and surprised) defined by Ekman [14] are commonly used in most of the studies on automatic emotion recognition. However, the main disadvantage of the categorical approach is that it fails to represent a wide range of real-life emotions. The second approach is to use continuous multidimensional space model to describe emotions. In this approach, the emotion is defined as points in multi-dimensional space rather than a small number of emotion categories. Dimensions in this approach are called emotion primitives. The most commonly used dimensions are *valence*, *activation*, and *dominance*. Valence represents negative to positive axis, activation represents calm to excited axis, and dominance represents weak to strong axis in 3D space. The most common databases such as the FAU Aibo emotion corpus, Situation Analysis in Fictional and Emotional Corpus (SAFE), Airplane Behaviour Corpus (ABC), and TUM Audiovisual Interest Corpus (AVIC) were annotated with the categorical approach. Only a few databases exist where emotions are represented by emotion primitives. Sensitive Artificial Listener (SAL) [5] and

Vera-Am-Mittag (VAM) [11] are labeled with the dimensional approach. To our knowledge, among the common databases, only a few of them includes both categorical and dimensional labeling such as IEMOCAP [8] and Belfast Naturalistic Database [15].

Many previous efforts have addressed emotion recognition by employing pattern recognition techniques using segmental and/or supra-segmental information obtained from speech [6,16-26]. Acoustic parameters of speech signal have been used extensively to separate emotional coloring present in the speech. Acoustic features are obtained from low-level descriptors (LLDs) such as pitch, energy, duration, Mel-frequency cepstral coefficients (mfcc), and voice quality parameters by applying functionals (mean, median, percentiles, etc.). Comprehensive list of LLDs and functionals is given in [27]. Linguistic information can also be used for emotion recognition especially when the speech data is spontaneous [16,18,22,25,28-31]. In this study, we only considered acoustic features and used the same feature set given in the INTERSPEECH 2010 Paralinguistic Challenge [32].

In this paper, we also performed cross-corpus evaluations where the system is trained on one corpus and tested on another. Only a few studies provide such cross-corpus results [33,34]. In [34], cross-corpus evaluation results of six well-known emotional speech databases were provided. In this work, we provided cross-corpus results using the VAM database.

This paper is organized as follows. Section 2 describes Turkish emotional speech database. Section 3 explains the feature extraction and selection procedures. Experimental setup and results are given in Section 4. Section 5 concludes the paper.

2 Turkish emotional speech database

In recent years, several corpora in different languages have been collected; however, Turkish is not among the languages that has been investigated in the context of emotion recognition. As an attempt to create a TURkish Emotional Speech database[a] (TURES), we have recently extracted and annotated a large amount of speech data from 55 Turkish movies [35].

2.1 Acquisition

Collecting real-life utterances is a challenging task; hence, most of the previous studies have used speech data with studio-recorded emotions. In this study, we decided to use Turkish movies from various genres for data collection because the speech extracted from movies is more realistic than studio-recorded emotions expressed by speakers reading some pre-defined sentences. The data collection process has been done in several stages. First, the audio tracks were extracted from each movie and saved as a separate file. The movies were originally in video object (vob)

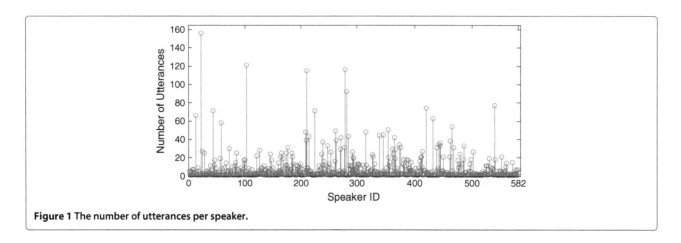

Figure 1 The number of utterances per speaker.

format that contains audio data in Dolby Digital (AC-3) (six channel) format. Then, the audio channel that contains the dialogues was separated from other audio channels for each movie and saved as a separate file at 48 kHz, 16 bit, mono, PCM-wave format. In the final stage of the data acquisition process, the audio data containing dialogue sequences were segmented into utterances manually by two native Turkish speakers. During the segmentation procedure, the utterances that are affected by background noise/music were removed from the database, resulting in 5,303 utterances. The utterances that have low intelligibility were also removed from the database. As a result, 5,100 utterances from 582 (188 females, 394 males) speakers were obtained. The average length of the utterances is 2.34 s. The distribution of the utterances over the speakers is given in Figure 1 and Table 1. Note that having 448 of the speakers with less than ten utterances shows how diverse the database is, thus introduces a difficulty to the emotion recognition.

2.2 Annotation of emotional content

The annotation is needed to determine the true emotion expressed in the speech data. In this study, we employed both categorical and dimensional approaches for emotion annotation. In categorical approach, a set of emotion words are used to describe emotion-related states. On the other hand, in the dimensional approach, the emotion is defined as points in multidimensional space rather than a small number of emotion categories.

The emotion in each utterance was evaluated in a listener test by a large number of annotators (27 university students) independently of one another. The annotators were asked to listen to the entire speech recordings (randomly permuted) and assign an emotion label (both categorical and dimensional) for each utterance. The annotators only took audio information into consideration.

2.2.1 Categorical annotation

Utterances were labelled in seven emotional states: *happy, surprised, sad, angry, fear, neutral,* and *others.* For each utterance, the final emotion label was computed from the majority label of the 27 annotators. The distribution of the utterances over emotion classes is given in Figure 2, and the distributions of the utterances over speakers for each emotion class are given in Figure 3. As expected, neutral is the majority of the expressed emotions.

For assessing the quality of the annotations (i.e., inter-annotator reliability), we used the Fleiss' kappa metric [36]. The kappa, κ, is defined as,

$$\kappa = \frac{P_a - P_c}{1 - P_c}, \tag{1}$$

Table 1 Distribution of utterances over speakers

Number of utterances	Number of speakers
≥ 100	4
50 to 99	10
25 to 49	39
10 to 24	81
2 to 9	279
1	169

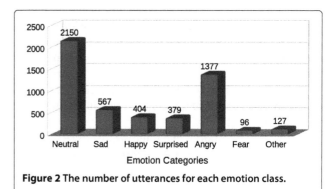

Figure 2 The number of utterances for each emotion class.

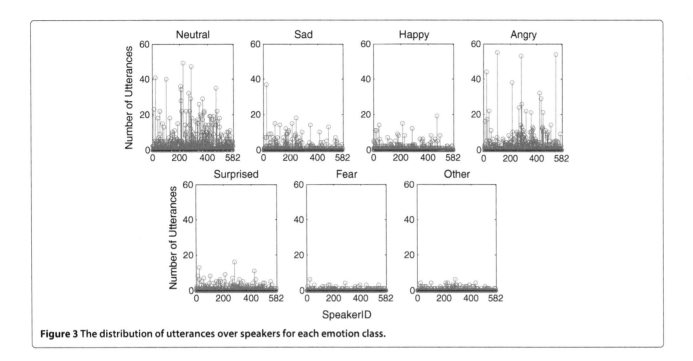

Figure 3 The distribution of utterances over speakers for each emotion class.

where P_a is the proportion of times that the n evaluators agree, and P_c is the proportion of times we would expect the n evaluators to agree by chance. The details of how P_a and P_c can be calculated are as in [36]. If there is no agreement among the evaluators, $\kappa = 0$, and $\kappa = 1$ when there is full agreement. The kappa score computed for the agreement level of the emotion categories between the 27 annotators is 0.32. A score between 0.2 and 0.4 may be considered moderate inter-evaluator agreement.

2.2.2 Annotation in 3D space

For the emotion labelling in 3D space, we followed the same procedure proposed in [11] for emotion primitives evaluation. Self-assessment manikins (SAMs) [37] (Figure 4) were used for measuring the emotional content of each audio clip with ratings on a five-level scale between one and five for valence, activation, and dominance. Valence represents negative to positive axis, activation represents calm to excited axis, and dominance

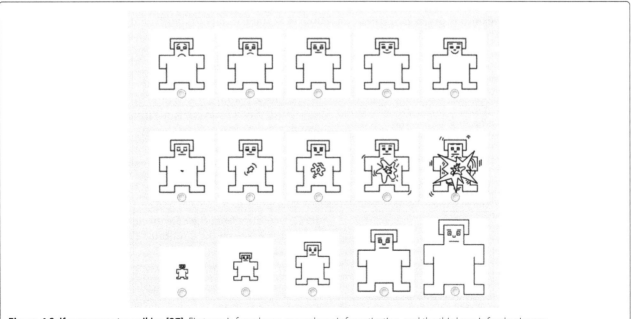

Figure 4 Self-assessment manikins [37]. First row is for valence, second row is for activation, and the third row is for dominance.

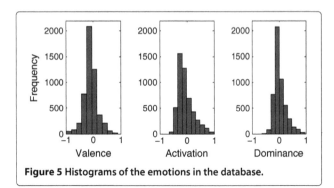

Figure 5 Histograms of the emotions in the database.

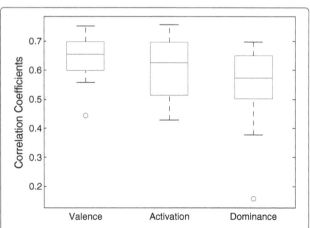

Figure 7 The distribution of the correlation coefficients between the annotator's ratings and the average ratings. High correlation coefficients show high inter-annotator agreement.

represents weak to strong axis of three-dimensional emotion space. For each utterance in the database, annotators were asked to select one of the iconic image from the corresponding row for each of three dimensions. The ratings for each emotion dimension were later transformed to unity space [-1,1] [11]. To estimate the true emotion (ground truth) of each utterance based on 27 annotators, we simply took the mean of the annotator's ratings. Figure 5 shows the histograms of the emotions based on the mean of the annotator's ratings.

To measure the agreement among the annotators, the standard deviations can be calculated for each utterance. The correlation coefficients between the annotator's ratings and the average ratings of all annotators can also be used to describe the inter-annotator reliability. In Figure 6, the distributions of the standard deviations are given in terms of box plots. The averages of standard deviations are 0.28, 0.43, and 0.39 for valence, activation, and dominance, respectively, indicating good agreement between annotators. The distribution of the correlation coefficients is given in Figure 7, and the related statistics are shown in Table 2. As can

be observed from Table 2, the mean values of correlations between the annotator's ratings and the average ratings for all dimensions show also high agreement (0.65, 0.61, and 0.56 for valence, activation, and dominance, respectively).

The distribution of categorical emotions in 3D space is shown in Figure 8. The class centroid, the mean, and the standard deviation of valence, activation, and dominance values of each emotion category are given in Table 3. The results show that angry speech data is negative and strong, and has high activation. Sad speech data is very negative, whereas happy speech data is very positive compared to other emotions. It is worth to note that the standard deviation values of emotion classes are high, and this might be the reason for the moderate inter-evaluator agreement in the categorical space.

3 Acoustic features

In this study, we used the same feature set, a set of 1,532 acoustic features based on several acoustic low-level descriptors (LLDs) and statistics (functionals), used in the INTERSPEECH 2010 Paralinguistic Challenge [32]. We extracted these features using the openSMILE toolkit [27]. The LLDs include fundamental frequency (F0), loudness, voicing probability, 0-14 mfcc, 0 to 7 logarithmic power

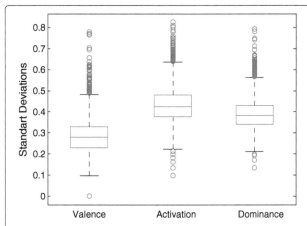

Figure 6 The distributions of the standard deviations for each emotion primitives. Utterances with low standard deviation show high inter-annotator agreement.

Table 2 Statistics from the distribution of the correlation coefficients between the annotator's ratings and the average ratings

	Mean	Stdv	Min	Max
Valence	0.65	0.08	0.44	0.75
Activation	0.61	0.10	0.43	0.76
Dominance	0.56	0.12	0.16	0.70

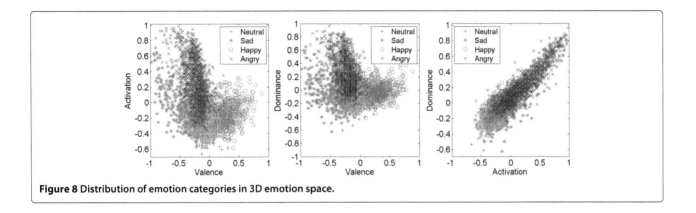

Figure 8 Distribution of emotion categories in 3D emotion space.

of Mel-frequency bands (logMelFreqBand), 0 to 7 line spectral pair frequencies computed from 8 LPC coefficients (lspFreq), and the voice quality measures (shimmer and jitter). Delta coefficients of each these LLDs are also included.

Functionals applied to descriptors are absolute position (frame) of the maximum value (maxPos), absolute position (frame) of the minimum value (minPos), arithmetic mean of the contour (amean), slope of a linear approximation of the contour (linregc1), onset of a linear approximation of the contour (linregc2), linear error computed as the difference of the linear approximation and the actual contour (linregerrA), quadratic error computed as the difference of the linear approximation and the actual contour (linregerrQ), standard deviation of the values in the contour (stddev), skewness, kurtosis, three first quartiles (quartile1: 25% percentile, quartile2: 50% percentile, and quartile3: 75% percentile), three inter-quartile ranges (iqr1-2: quartile1-quaritle2, iqr2-3: quartile2-quaritle3, and iqr1-3: quartile1-quaritle3), outlier-robust minimum value of the contour (percentile1.0), outlier-robust maximum value of the contour (percentile99.0), outlier robust signal range (pctlrange0-1), percentage of time the signal is above 75% × range + minimum value (upleveltime75), and percentage of time the signal is above 90% × range + minimum signal value

(upleveltime90). A summary of the acoustic features is given in Table 4.

3.1 Feature selection

To identify the most salient features and thus reduce the number of feature size, we performed feature selection. For this purpose, we used correlation-based feature selection (CFS) [38]. The idea behind the correlation-based feature selection technique is to find a subset in which features are uncorrelated with each other but highly correlated to the class [38]. CFS is a filter-based subset feature evaluation algorithm that evaluates each feature subset using simple objective functions. The algorithm computes a heuristic measure of the 'merit' of the feature subset S using Equation 2.

$$\text{Merit}_S = \frac{k r_{\text{cf}}}{\sqrt{k + k(k-1) r_{\text{ff}}}}, \tag{2}$$

where k is the number of features in subfeature space S, r_{cf} is the average class-feature correlation, and r_{ff} is the average feature-feature inter-correlation. CFS calculates r_{cf} and r_{ff} using a symmetric information gain.

Since exhaustive search through all possible feature subsets is not feasible, sub-optimal but faster search functions such as hill climbing, genetic, best first, and random are

Table 3 Comparison of emotion class centroids, mean, and standard deviations (stdv) in the 3D emotion space

	Valence			Activation			Dominance		
	Centroid	Mean	Stdv	Centroid	Mean	Stdv	Centroid	Mean	Stdv
Neutral	-0.02	-0.02	0.12	-0.24	-0.23	0.14	-0.09	-0.08	0.11
Sad	-0.35	-0.37	0.21	-0.11	-0.10	0.21	-0.07	-0.07	0.16
Happy	0.37	0.37	0.16	-0.13	-0.13	0.16	-0.02	-0.02	0.13
Surprised	-0.07	-0.06	0.15	-0.13	-0.12	0.17	-0.04	-0.04	0.13
Angry	-0.22	-0.23	0.14	0.26	0.27	0.28	0.26	0.28	0.22
Fear	-0.22	-0.24	0.17	0.04	0.05	0.21	0.04	0.04	0.14
Others	-0.04	-0.03	0.14	-0.09	-0.08	0.20	0.02	0.04	0.19

Table 4 Overview of low-level descriptors and functionals

Low-level descriptors	Functionals
Pitch (F0)	maxPos, minPos
Loudness	amean, stddev, skewness, kurtosis
mfcc	linregc1, linregc2, linregerrA, linregerrQ
logMelFreqBand	quartile1, quartile2, quartile3, iqr1-2, iqr2-3, iqr1-3
lspFreq	percentile1.0, percentile99.0, pctlrange0-1
Shimmer and jitter	upleveltime75, upleveltime90

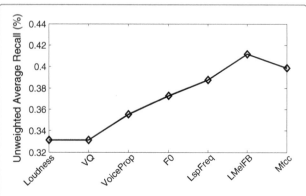

Figure 9 The classification performances of each LLD in terms of unweighted average recall. VQ, voice quality (jitter and shimmer); LMelFB, log mel frequency band.

usually chosen. In this work, we used best-first search method.

4   Emotion classification

In this paper, we focused on four major emotion classes *neutral, sad, happy,* and *angry,* and did not include *surprised, fear,* and *other* classes in the classification experiments. We evaluated performances of support vector machine (SVM) with radial basis kernel function (SVM-RBF) implemented in the LIBSVM library [39] and Bayesian Networks (BayesNet) provided by the Weka pattern recognition tool [40,41]. The performance of SVM highly depends on the parameters used. In order to optimize the SVM performance, we used grid search with fivefold cross validation to select the penalty parameter for mislabeled examples C and Gaussian parameter γ. We also linearly scaled each attribute to the range [0,1]. The scaling parameters for each attribute were calculated from the training data of each fold, and same scaling factors are applied to both corresponding training and testing data.

The performance of the classifiers was evaluated by tenfold cross-validation. To ensure the speaker independence, no instance of a test subject is allowed to be in the train dataset of each fold. For each experiment, the feature selection is performed using CFS to the training set of each fold. The results are presented in terms of confusion matrix, weighted average (WA) recall, and unweighted average (UA) recall. WA recall is defined as the ratio of the number of correctly classified instances to the total number of instances in the database. As classes are unbalanced in the databases, we also reported UA recall. UA recall is the average of per-class accuracies and more useful than WA recall when the distribution of classes is highly skewed.

4.1   Categorical classification results

First, we evaluated the relative importance of the seven low-level descriptors of acoustic features using BayesNet classifier. The performances are shown in Figure 9 in terms of UA recall. It can be seen that logarithmic power of Mel-frequency bands and mfcc seem to have more discriminative power than other LLDs.

The classification results are given in Table 5 in terms of confusion matrix. We obtain 70.9%, 26.8%, 13.1%, and 62.4% recall rates using SVM and 48.5%, 41.4%, 22.5%, and 69.7% recall rates using BayesNet for *neutral, sad, happy,* and *angry* classes, respectively. Overall, we obtain good recall rates for *neutral, sad,* and *angry* classes. However, the recognition accuracy for the *happy* class is about chance level.

4.2   Emotion primitives estimation

Support vector regression (ϵ-SVR) with the radial basis kernel function [42] is used in this paper as it has shown promising results in performing emotion primitives estimation [19]. The ϵ-SVR design parameters, the complexity C, ϵ, and the kernel parameter γ are selected using grid-search with fivefold cross validation. For all regression experiments, LIBSVM [39] implementation of ϵ-SVR was used. The performance of the estimators was evaluated in terms of correlation coefficient (CC), mean absolute error (MAE), and root-mean-square error (RMSE).

Table 5 Performances for categorical emotion classification

	SVM-RBF				BayesNet			
	Neutral	Sad	Happy	Angry	Neutral	Sad	Happy	Angry
Neutral	*1,524*	205	133	288	*1,042*	485	271	352
Sad	289	*152*	42	84	172	*235*	72	88
Happy	218	39	*53*	94	122	66	*91*	125
Angry	381	63	74	*859*	209	65	143	*960*
WA recall	57.5%				51.8%			
UA recall	43.3%				45.5%			

The results are given in terms of confusion matrix, WA recall and UA recall for SVM (RBF kernel) and BayesNet classifiers. The diagonal elements (the values in italics) of confusion matrix represent the number of correctly predicted emotion labels.

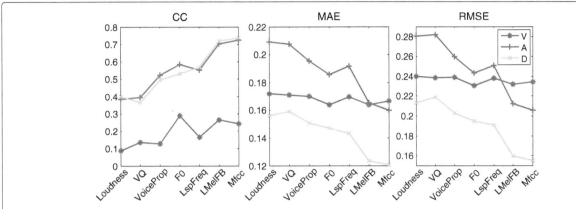

Figure 10 Performance comparisons of different acoustic feature groups for each emotion primitive for TURES database. Results are shown in terms of correlation coefficient (CC), mean absolute error (MAE), and root-mean-square error (RMSE).

$$CC = \frac{\sum_{i=1}^{N}(x_i - \bar{x})(y_i - \bar{y})}{\sqrt{\sum_{i=1}^{N}(x_i - \bar{x})^2}\sqrt{\sum_{i=1}^{N}(y_i - \bar{y})^2}} \qquad (3)$$

$$MAE = \frac{1}{N}\sum_{i=1}^{N}|x_i - y_i| \qquad (4)$$

$$RMSE = \sqrt{\frac{1}{N}\sum_{i=1}^{N}(x_i - y_i)^2}, \qquad (5)$$

where N is the number of speech data in the database, x is the true value, and y is the predicted value.

For the cross-corpus experiments, we employed the VAM database [11]. The VAM corpus consists of audio-visual recordings taken from German TV talk show called Vera-Am-Mittag. The corpus contains 946 spontaneous utterances from 47 participants of the show, and each utterance was labeled using a discrete five-point scale for three-dimensional emotion space of valence, activation, and dominance by 6 to 17 labelers.

4.2.1 Estimation results

First, we evaluated the relative importance of each LLD in emotion estimation. The performance comparisons of different acoustic feature groups for each emotion primitives using support vector regression are given for the TURES

database in Figure 10. For this task, the ϵ-SVR parameters C, γ, and ϵ were set to 1, 0.01, and 0.001, respectively. The results are based on tenfold cross validation. As can be seen from Figure 10, for activation and dominance, mfcc are the most informative low-level descriptors followed by logarithmic power of Mel-frequency bands (LogMelFreqBand). For valence, F0, LogMelFreqBand and mfcc have more discriminative power than other LLD groups.

The regression results for emotion primitives are given in Table 6. The results show that all emotion primitives are estimated with a small mean absolute error, 0.166, 0.156, and 0.119 for TURES database and 0.149, 0.160, and 0.153 for the VAM database, for valence, activation, and dominance, respectively. The regression results in terms of correlation coefficient show good results for activation and dominance for both databases. For valence, however, the correlation between the averaged ratings of the annotators (reference values) and the SVR estimates was low (only 0.288 for TURES and 0.310 for VAM).

Research shows that language and culture play an important role in how vocal emotions are perceived [43]. Recently, a few studies present results on cross-corpus evaluations, i.e., training on one and testing on a different one [34]. However, most of the work employed either different databases of the same language or Germanic

Table 6 The estimation performances for TURES and VAM databases

Train	Test	Valence			Activation			Dominance		
		CC	MAE	RMSE	CC	MAE	RMSE	CC	MAE	RMSE
TURES	TURES	0.288	0.166	0.232	0.739	0.156	0.201	0.743	0.119	0.153
VAM	TURES	0.131	0.204	0.275	0.624	0.191	0.246	0.649	0.165	0.208
VAM	VAM	0.310	0.149	0.196	0.810	0.160	0.202	0.761	0.153	0.196
TURES	VAM	0.289	0.170	0.219	0.743	0.189	0.238	0.717	0.178	0.225

Results are given in terms of correlation coefficient (CC), mean absolute error (MAE), and root-mean-square error (RMSE). The cross-corpus results for each primitive are also given.

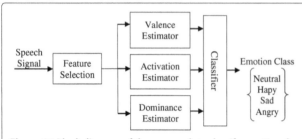

Figure 11 Block diagram of the approach to classify emotional classes using emotion primitives.

languages. Turkish is an agglutinative language, i.e. new words can be formed from existing words using a rich set of affixes. In this study, we performed cross-corpus experiments between the Turkish emotional speech database and the VAM corpus. The cross-corpus results were given in Table 6. It can be seen from the table that the cross-corpus training and testing seems to work especially for activation and dominance dimensions. For example, when TURES is chosen for training and VAM for testing, the correlation coefficients of 0.743 and 0.717 with 0.189 and 0.178 mean absolute errors were obtained for activation and dominance, respectively. For valence, like intra-corpus experiments, the cross-corpus results were not promising. This result indicates that acoustic information alone is not enough to discriminate emotions in valence dimension. These results are consistent with previous research [44]. Other sources of information, such as linguistic information, are needed in order to obtain better discrimination results in valence dimension [31].

4.2.2 Emotion classification from the emotion primitives

As a final experiment, we used the emotion primitives to classify emotion classes. A block diagram of the approach is shown in Figure 11. We used SVR to estimate the emotion primitives from acoustic features, and for the classification, BayesNet classifier is employed. First, we assumed perfect primitive estimation and used true labels as a feature set for training and testing the classifier. This

experiment will show the upper bound of the classification performance. Table 7 shows that a recognition rate of 77.6% in terms of UA recall can be achieved using true emotion primitive values. However, when we used regression estimates, the classification performance is about random. The underlying reason is the low regression performance for the valence dimension.

5 Conclusion

In this work, we carried out a study on emotion recognition from Turkish speech using acoustic features. In recent years, several corpora in different languages have been collected; however, Turkish is not among the languages that has been investigated in the context of emotion recognition. In this paper, we presented the Turkish Emotional Speech Database and reported the baseline results. Categorical representations and dimensional descriptions are two common approaches to define emotion present in speech. In categorical approach, a fixed set of words is used to describe an emotional state, whereas in the dimensional approach, emotion is defined as points in the multidimensional space. The three most common dimensions used are valence, activation, and dominance which represent the main properties of emotional states. In this work, both categorical evaluation and emotion primitive estimation were performed. An unweighted average recall of 45.5% was obtained for the classification. For emotion dimension estimation, the regression results in terms of correlation coefficient are promising for activation and dominance, with 0.739 and 0.743, respectively. For valence, however, the correlation between the averaged ratings of the evaluators (reference values) and the SVR estimates was low (only 0.288). In this study, we also performed cross-corpus evaluations, and the results were promising especially for activation and dominance dimensions. This result indicates that acoustic information alone is not enough to discriminate emotions in valence dimension. Future work includes the use of linguistic information to improve the classification and regression results especially for valence.

Table 7 Emotion classification results from three-dimensional emotion primitives

	Neutral	Sad	Happy	Angry	Neutral	Sad	Happy	Angry
Neutral	*1,955*	53	57	85	*1,430*	24	0	696
Sad	114	*342*	1	110	371	*11*	0	185
Happy	93	0	*302*	9	262	6	*1*	135
Angry	163	50	2	*1,162*	947	13	0	*417*
WA recall			83.6%				41.3%	
UA recall			77.6%				24.8%	

Left confusion matrix: emotion classification from the ground truth emotion primitives. Right confusion matrix: emotion classification from the estimates of emotion primitives. SVR is used to estimate the three emotion primitives. For classification, BayesNet classifier is used. The values in italics of the confusion matrices represent the number of correctly predicted emotion labels.

Endnotes

[a] The Turkish emotional speech database is available to the research community through the website http://www.turesdatabase.com.

Competing interests

The authors declare that they have no competing interests.

Acknowledgements

This work was supported by the Turkish Scientific and Technical Research Council (TUBITAK) under project no. 109E243.

References

1. F Burkhardt, A Paeschke, M Rolfes, W Sendlmeier, B Weiss, A database of, German emotional speech. Paper presented at the Interspeech 9th European conference on speech, communication and technology. Lisbon, Portugal, 4–8 Sept 2005
2. IS Engberg, AV Hansen, Documentation of the Danish Emotional Speech Database. (Aalborg University, Aalborg, 1996)
3. M Liberman, K Davis, M Grossman, N Martey, J Bell, Emotional Prosody, Speech and Transcripts. (Linguistic Data Consortium, Philadelphia, 2002)
4. T Banziger, M Mortillaro, K Scherer, Introducing the Geneva multimodal expression corpus for experimental research on emotion perception. Emotion. 12, 1161–1179 (2012)
5. E Douglas-Cowie, R Cowie, I Sneddon, C Cox, O Lowry, M Mcrorie, J Claude Martin, L Devillers, S Abrilian, A Batliner, N Amir, K Karpouzis, in Affective Computing and Intelligent Interaction: Lecture Notes in Computer Science, ed. by ACR Paiva, R Prada, and RW Picard. The HUMAINE Database: addressing the collection and annotation of naturalistic and induced emotional data, vol. 4738 (Springer Berlin, 2007), pp. 488-500
6. B Schuller, B Vlasenko, F Eyben, G Rigoll, A Wendemuth, in IEEE Workshop on Automatic Speech Recognition Understanding. Acoustic emotion recognition: a benchmark comparison of performances (IEEE Merano, Italy, 13 Nov–17 Dec 2009)
7. JHL Hansen, S Bou-Ghazale, Getting started with SUSAS: a speech under simulated and actual stress database. Paper presented at the fifth European conference on speech communication and technology, EUROSPEECH 1997. Rhodes, Greece 22–25 Sept 1997
8. C Busso, M Bulut, CC Lee, A Kazemzadeh, E Mower, S Kim, J Chang, S Lee, S Narayanan, IEMOCAP: Interactive emotional dyadic motion capture database. J. Lang. Resour. Eval. 42(4), 335–359 (2008)
9. G McKeown, M Valstar, R Cowie, M Pantic, in IEEE ICME. The SEMAINE corpus of emotionally coloured character interactions (Suntec City, 19–23 Jul 2010)
10. S Steidl, Automatic Classification of Emotion Related User States in Spontaneous Children's Speech. (University of Erlangen-Nuremberg, Germany, 2009)
11. M Grimm, K Kroschel, S Narayanan, in IEEE International conference on multimedia and expo (ICME). The Vera am Mittag German audio-visual emotional speech database (IEEE Hannover, Germany, 23 Jun–26 Apr 2008)
12. C Clavel, I Vasilescu, L Devillers, T Ehrette, G Richard, in LREC. The SAFE Corpus: fear-type emotions detection for surveillance applications (Genoa, Italy, 24–26 May 2006)
13. E Douglas-Cowie, N Campbell, R Cowie, P Roach, Emotional speech: towards a new generation of databases. Speech Commun. Spec. Issue, Speech and Emotion. 40, 33–60 (2003)
14. P Ekman, in Handbook of Cognition and Emotions, ed. by L Dalgleish, M Power. Basic emotions (Wiley New York, 1999), pp. 409–589
15. E Douglas-Cowie, R Cowie, M Schroder, in ISCA Workshop on speech and emotion. A new emotion database: considerations, sources and scope (Newcastle UK, 5–7 Sept 2000)
16. J Ang, R Dhillon, A Krupski, E Shriberg, A Stolcke, in ICSLP 2002. Prosody-based automatic detection of annoyance and frustration in human-computer dialog (ISCA Denver, Colorado, 16–20 Sept 2002)
17. TL Nwe, SW Foo, L De Silva, Speech emotion recognition using hidden Markov models. Speech Commun. 41(4), 603–623 (2003)
18. CM Lee, S Narayanan, Towards detecting emotions in spoken dialogs. IEEE T Speech Audi. P. 13(2), 293–303 (2005)
19. M Grimm, K Kroschel, E Mower, S Narayanan, Primitives-based evaluation and estimation of emotions in speech. Speech Commun. 49, 787–800 (2007)
20. BS Schuller, A Batliner, D Seppi, S Steidl, T Vogt, J Wagner, L Devillers, L Vidrascu, N Amir, L Kessous, V Aharonson, in eighth conference on InterSpeech. The relevance of feature type for the automatic classification of emotional user states: low level descriptors and functionals (ISCA Antwerp, Belgium, 27–31 Aug 2007)
21. C Clavel, I Vasilescu, L Devillers, G Richard, T Ehrette, Fear-type emotion recognition for future audio-based surveillance systems. Speech Commun. 50(6), 487–503 (2008)
22. S Yildirim, S Narayanan, A Potamianos, Detecting emotional state of a child in a conversational computer game. Comput. Speech and, Lang. 25, 29–44 (2011)
23. EM Albornoz, DH Milone, HL Rufiner, Spoken emotion recognition using hierarchical classifiers. Comput. Speech and Lang. 25(3), 556–570 (2011)
24. CC Lee, E Mower, C Busso, S Lee, S Narayanan, Emotion recognition using a hierarchical binary decision tree approach. Speech Commun. 53(9-10), 1162–1171 (2011). [Special issue: Sensing Emotion and Affect - Facing Realism in Speech Processing]
25. T Polzehl, A Schmitt, F Metze, M Wagner, Anger recognition in speech using acoustic and linguistic cues. Speech Commun. 53(9-10), 1198–1209 (2011)
26. A Batliner, S Steidl, B Schuller, D Seppi, T Vogt, J Wagner, L Devillers, L Vidrascu, V Aharonson, L Kessous, N Amir, Whodunnit - searching for the most important feature types signalling emotion-related user states in speech. Comput. Speech Lang. 25, 4–28 (2011)
27. F Eyben, M Wöllmer, B Schuller, in international conference on multimedia. openSMILE: the Munich versatile and fast open-source audio feature extractor (ACM Firenze, Italy, 25–29 Oct 2010)
28. S Arunachalam, D Gould, E Andersen, D Byrd, S Narayanan, in InterSpeech. Politeness and frustration language in child-machine interactions (Aalborg Denmark, 3–7 Sept 2001)
29. A Batliner, S Steidl, B Schuller, D Seppi, K Laskowski, T Vogt, L Devillers, L Vidrascu, N Amir, L Kessous, V Aharonson, in fifth Slovenian and first international language technologies conference. Combining efforts for improving automatic classification of emotional user states (IS-LTC'06 Ljubljana, Slovenia, 9–10 Oct 2006)
30. B Schuller, A Batliner, S Steidl, D Seppi, in IEEE international conference on acoustics, speech, and signal processing. Emotion recognition from speech: putting ASR in the loop (IEEE Taipei, Taiwan, 19–24 Apr 2009)
31. B Schuller, Recognizing affect from linguistic information in 3D continuous space. IEEE Trans. Affect. Comput. 2(4), 192–205 (2012)
32. B Schuller, S Steidl, A Batliner, F Burkhardt, L Devillers, C Muller, S Narayanan, in InterSpeech. The INTERSPEECH 2010 paralinguistic challenge (Makuhari Japan, 26–30 Sept 2010)
33. M Shami, W Verhelst, in Speaker Classification II LNCS, ed. by C Müller. Automatic classification of expressiveness in speech: a multi-corpus study (Springer Berlin, 2007), pp. 43–56
34. B Schuller, B Vlasenko, F Eyben, M Wollmer, A Stuhlsatz, A Wendemuth, G Rigoll, Cross-corpus acoustic emotion recognition: variances and strategies. IEEE Trans. Affect. Comput. 1(2), 119–131 (2010)
35. C Oflazoglu, S Yildirim, in IEEE 19th conference signal processing and communications applications. Turkish emotional speech database (IEEE Antalya, Turkey, 20–22 Apr 2011)
36. J Fleiss, Measuring nominal scale agreement among many raters. Psychol. Bull. 76(5), 378–382 (1971)
37. M Bradley, PJ Lang, Measuring emotion: the self-assessment manikin and the semantic differential. J. Behav. Ther. Exp. Psychiatry. 25, 49–59 (1994)
38. M Hall, Correlation-based feature selection for machine learning. (PhD thesis, University of Waikato, New Zealand, 1999)
39. CC Chang, CJ Lin, LIBSVM: a library for support vector machines. ACM Trans. Intell. Syst. Technol. 2, 1–27 (2011)
40. M Hall, E Frank, G Holmes, B Pfahringer, P Reutemann, IH Witten, The WEKA data mining software: an update. SIGKDD Explor. Newsl. 11, 10–18 (2009)
41. R Bouckaert. Bayesian Network Classifiers in Weka for Version 3-5-7, Technical Report (Waikato University Hamilton, NZ, 2008)

42. AJ Smola, B Schölkopf, A tutorial on support vector regression. Stat. Comput. **14**(3), 199–222 (2004)

43. KR Scherer, R Banse, H Wallbott, Emotion inferences from vocal expression correlate across languages and cultures. J Cross Cult, Psychol. **32**, 76–92 (2001)

44. M Grimm, K Kroschel, S Narayanan, in *IEEE international conference on acoustics, speech and signal processing*. Support vector regression for automatic recognition of spontaneous emotions in speech (Honolulu, HI, 15–20 Apr 2007)

9

Robust Bayesian estimation for context-based speech enhancement

Devireddy Hanumantha Rao Naidu[1*] and Sriram Srinivasan[2]

Abstract

Model-based speech enhancement algorithms that employ trained models, such as codebooks, hidden Markov models, Gaussian mixture models, etc., containing representations of speech such as linear predictive coefficients, mel-frequency cepstrum coefficients, etc., have been found to be successful in enhancing noisy speech corrupted by nonstationary noise. However, these models are typically trained on speech data from multiple speakers under controlled acoustic conditions. In this paper, we introduce the notion of context-dependent models that are trained on speech data with one or more aspects of context, such as speaker, acoustic environment, speaking style, etc. In scenarios where the modeled and observed contexts match, context-dependent models can be expected to result in better performance, whereas context-independent models are preferred otherwise. In this paper, we present a Bayesian framework that automatically provides the benefits of both models under varying contexts. As several aspects of the context remain constant over an extended period during usage, a memory-based approach that exploits information from past data is employed. We use a codebook-based speech enhancement technique that employs trained models of speech and noise linear predictive coefficients as an example model-based approach. Using speaker, acoustic environment, and speaking style as aspects of context, we demonstrate the robustness of the proposed framework for different context scenarios, input signal-to-noise ratios, and number of contexts modeled.

Keywords: Bayesian; Codebook; Context; Noise reduction; Speech enhancement

1 Introduction

Speech enhancement pertains to the processing of speech corrupted by noise, echo, reverberation, etc. to improve its quality and intelligibility. In this paper, by speech enhancement, we refer to the problem of noise reduction. It is relevant in several scenarios, for example, mobile telephony in noisy environments, such as restaurants and busy traffic, suffers from unclear communication. Also, speech recognition units [1] and hearing aids [2] require speech enhancement as a preprocessing algorithm.

Speech enhancement algorithms can be broadly classified into single- and multi-channel algorithms based on the number of microphones used to acquire the input noisy speech. Multi-channel algorithms exhibit superior performance because of the additional spatial information available about the noise and speech sources. However, the need for single-channel speech enhancement cannot

be ignored. For example, single microphone systems are preferred in low-cost mobile units. In addition, multi-channel methods include a single-channel algorithm as a post-processing step to suppress diffuse noise. In this paper, we focus on single-channel speech enhancement.

Single-channel speech enhancement has been a challenging research problem for the last four decades. Several techniques have been devised to arrive at efficient solutions for the problem. Among these, spectral subtraction is one of the earliest and simplest techniques [3]. Herein, an estimate of the noise magnitude spectrum is subtracted from the observed noisy magnitude spectrum to obtain an estimate of the clean speech magnitude spectrum. Several variations of this technique have been developed over the years [4-7]. Methods based on a statistical model of speech to estimate the speech spectral amplitude such as the minimum mean square error short-time spectral amplitude estimator (MMSE-STSA) method have been found to be successful [8-10]. The statistical approach explicitly uses the probability density function (pdf) of the speech and noise DFT coefficients. Also, it

*Correspondence: dhanumantharao@sssihl.edu.in
[1] Department of Mathematics and Computer Science, Sri Sathya Sai Institute of Higher Learning, Prasanthi Nilayam, Anantapur, Andhra Pradesh 515134, India
Full list of author information is available at the end of the article

allows consideration of non-Gaussian prior distributions [11] and different ways of modeling the spectral data [12,13]. Subspace-based algorithms [14] assume the clean speech to be confined to a subspace of the noisy space. The noisy vector space is decomposed into noise-only and speech-plus-noise subspaces. The noise subspace components are suppressed, and the speech-plus-noise subspace components are further processed. A comprehensive survey of these techniques is provided in [15]. However, most of these methods depend on an accurate estimate of the noise power spectrum, for example, estimation of the noise magnitude spectrum during silent segments in [3], or *a priori* signal-to-noise ratio (SNR) estimation in [9], or estimation of the noise covariance matrix in the subspace-based methods.

Noise estimation algorithms mainly include voice activity detector (VAD) [16,17] and buffer-based methods [18-20]. While VADs are unreliable at low SNRs, the buffer-based methods are not fast enough to track the quickly varying noise in nonstationary noise conditions. Thus, while these algorithms perform well in stationary noise, their accuracy deteriorates under nonstationary conditions. An improvement over these algorithms is provided in [21] wherein a recursive approach is employed for online noise power spectral density (PSD) tracking by analytically retrieving the prior and posterior probabilities of speech absence, and noise statistics, using a maximum likelihood-based criterion. A low-complexity, fast noise tracking algorithm is proposed in [22,23].

Speech enhancement algorithms which employ trained models, such as codebooks [24-28], hidden Markov models (HMM) [29-31], Gaussian mixture models (GMM) [32], non-negative matrix factorization (NMF) models [33], dictionaries [34], etc., for speech and noise data are able to process noisy speech with sufficient accuracy even under nonstationary noise conditions. For example, codebook-based speech enhancement (CBSE) algorithms [25,26] estimate the noise power spectrum for short segments of noisy speech, thus tracking nonstationary noise better than the buffer-based methods [18]. However, model-based methods typically employ *a priori* speech models which are trained on speech data from multiple speakers. For applications where the input noisy speech is more frequent from a particular speaker, such as in mobile telephony, it is desirable to exploit the speaker dependency for better speech enhancement. Similarly, it might be beneficial to consider models trained on or adapted to a specific acoustic environment or language. In this paper, we introduce the notion of context-dependent (CD) models, where by the word 'context', we refer to one or more aspects such as the speaker, acoustic environment, emotion, language, speaking style, etc. of the input noisy speech. By employing CD models, improved enhancement of noisy speech can be expected. These models can

be adapted online from a context-independent (CI) model during high SNR regions of the input signal. In this paper, we assume the availability of such adapted CD models and focus on the enhancement using the converged models.

When the context of the noisy input matches the context of the data used to train the model, CD models are expected to result in better speech enhancement than CI models. We refer to such scenarios as context match scenarios. However, in practice, the modeled and observed contexts may not always match, leading to a context mismatch. In such scenarios, a CD model may lead to poorer results, and so the CI model would be preferred. Thus, what is required is a method that retains the benefits of both the CD and CI models and provides robust results irrespective of the scenario at hand.

In this paper, we introduce a Bayesian framework to optimally combine the estimates from the CD and CI models to achieve robust speech enhancement under varying contexts. As different aspects of context can be expected to remain constant for an extended duration in the input noisy signal, the framework considers past information to improve the estimation process. Also, in practice, different aspects of context may occur at the same time. So, the framework is designed to include several codebooks at the same time.

As an example of the model-based algorithm, we use the CBSE technique that employs trained models of speech and noise linear predictive (LP) coefficients as priors [26]. A part of this work has been presented in [35]. This papers extends [35] by incorporating memory-based estimation, considers the use of multiple CD models, and presents a detailed experimental analysis for different noise types, input SNRs, and aspects of context. The framework developed is general and can be used for other representations such as mel-frequency cepstrum coefficients, higher resolution PSDs, as well as other models such as GMMs, HMMs, and NMF.

The remainder of the paper is organized as follows. In the next section, a brief outline of the CBSE techniques [25,26] is provided. Following this, we derive the memory-based Bayesian framework to optimally combine estimates from several codebooks (CD/CI). Thereafter, we present the experimental results for the proposed framework under varying contexts, noise types, and input SNRs. Finally, we summarize the conclusions.

2 Codebook-based speech enhancement

Consider an additive noise model of the observed noisy speech $y(n)$:

$$y(n) = x(n) + w(n), \tag{1}$$

where n is the time index, $x(n)$ is the clean speech signal, and $w(n)$ is the noise signal.

We assume that speech and noise are statistically independent and follow zero-mean Gaussian distribution. Under these assumptions, Equation 1 leads to the following relation in the frequency domain:

$$P_y(\omega) = P_x(\omega) + P_w(\omega), \tag{2}$$

where $P_y(\omega)$, $P_x(\omega)$, and $P_w(\omega)$ are PSDs of the observed noisy speech, clean speech, and noise respectively, and ω is the angular frequency.

Consider a short-time segment of the observed noisy speech given by a vector $\mathbf{y} = [y(1), \ldots, y(N)]^T$, where N is the size of the segment. Let the vectors $\mathbf{x}$ and $\mathbf{w}$ be defined analogously. Let $\mathbf{a}_x = (a_{x_0}, \ldots, a_{x_p})$ denote the vector of LP coefficients for the short-time speech segment $\mathbf{x}$ corresponding to $\mathbf{y}$, with $a_{x_0} = 1$ and p the speech LP model order. Similarly, let $\mathbf{a}_w = (a_{w_0}, \ldots, a_{w_q})$ denote the LP coefficient vector for the short-time noise segment $\mathbf{w}$ corresponding to $\mathbf{y}$, with $a_{w_0} = 1$ and q being the noise LP model order. Then, the speech and noise PSDs can be written as:

$$P_x(\omega) = \frac{g_x}{|A_x(\omega)|^2} \text{ and } P_w(\omega) = \frac{g_w}{|A_w(\omega)|^2}, \tag{3}$$

where g_x and g_w denote the variance of the prediction error for speech and noise, respectively; $A_x(\omega) = \sum_{k=0}^{p} a_{x_k} e^{-j\omega k}$; and $A_w(\omega) = \sum_{k=0}^{q} a_{w_k} e^{-j\omega k}$. Let

$$m_x = [\mathbf{a}_x, g_x],$$
$$m_w = [\mathbf{a}_w, g_w]. \tag{4}$$

m_x is a model describing the speech PSD, and m_w describes the noise PSD. Codebook-driven speech enhancement techniques [25,26] estimate m_x and m_w for each short-time segment: $\mathbf{a}_x$ and $\mathbf{a}_w$ are selected from trained codebooks of vectors of speech and noise LP coefficients, C_x and C_w, respectively, and the gain terms g_x and g_w are computed online, resulting in good performance in nonstationary noise. A maximum likelihood approach is adopted in [25] and a Bayesian minimum mean squared error (MMSE) approach in [26].

The estimates $\hat{m}_x$ and $\hat{m}_w$ are used to construct a Wiener filter to enhance the noisy speech in the frequency domain:

$$H(\omega) = \frac{\hat{P}_x(\omega)}{\hat{P}_x(\omega) + \hat{P}_w(\omega)}, \tag{5}$$

where $\hat{P}_x(\omega)$ and $\hat{P}_w(\omega)$ are estimates of the speech and noise PSDs, respectively, described by $\hat{m}_x$ and $\hat{m}_w$. The Wiener filter is one example of a gain function, and any other gain function can be employed using the obtained speech and noise PSD estimates.

3 Bayesian estimation under varying contexts

In this section, we develop a Bayesian framework to obtain estimates of the speech and noise LP parameters,

m_x and m_w, using one or more CD codebooks and a CI speech codebook. The CD codebooks improve estimation accuracy in the event of a context match, and the CI codebook provides robustness in the event of a context mismatch. The Bayesian framework needs to optimally combine the estimates from the various codebooks with no prior knowledge on whether or not the observed context matches the context modeled by the codebooks.

Consider K speech codebooks $[C_x^1, \ldots, C_x^K]$, which include one or more CD codebooks and a CI codebook, depending on the contexts modeled. We consider a single noise codebook, C_w, corresponding to the encountered noise type. Robustness to different noise types can be provided by extending the notion of context dependency to the noise codebooks as well. To maintain the focus on context dependency in speech, we only consider a single noise codebook.

As m_x is a model for the speech PSD and m_w is a model for the noise PSD, $m = [m_x, m_w]$ is a model for the noisy PSD, given by the sum of the corresponding speech and noise PSDs. We consider m to be a random variable and seek its MMSE estimate, given the noisy observation, the speech codebooks, and the noise codebook. Let $\mathcal{M}_1$ denote the collection of all models of the noisy PSD corresponding to the speech codebook C_x^1 and the noise codebook C_w. The set $\mathcal{M}_1$ consists of quadruplets $[\mathbf{a}_x^{1i}, g_x, \mathbf{a}_w^j, g_w]$, where $\mathbf{a}_x^{1i}$ is the ith vector from the speech codebook C_x^1, $\mathbf{a}_w^j$ is the jth vector from the noise codebook C_w, and the gain terms g_x and g_w are computed online for each combination of $\mathbf{a}_x^{1i}$ and $\mathbf{a}_w^j$. Thus, $\mathcal{M}_1$ contains $N_x^1 \times N_w$ vectors, where N_x^1 is the number of vectors in C_x^1 and N_w is the number of vectors in C_w. The sets $\mathcal{M}_2, \ldots, \mathcal{M}_K$ are similarly defined, corresponding to the speech codebooks $C_x^2, \ldots, C_x^K$. Let $\mathcal{M}$ be a collection of all the models m contained in all the K speech codebooks and the noise codebook, i.e.,

$$\mathcal{M} = \mathcal{M}_1 \cup \mathcal{M}_2 \cup \ldots \cup \mathcal{M}_K. \tag{6}$$

We consider the following K hypotheses:

- H_k: speech codebook C_k best models the speech context for the current segment, $1 \leq k \leq K$.

At a given time T, one of the K hypotheses is valid. This corresponds to a state, and we write $S_T = H_k$ to denote that at time T, the most appropriate speech codebook for the observed noisy segment is C_k.

As mentioned in the introductory section, various aspects of context such as speaker, language, etc. can be expected to remain constant over multiple short-time segments, which can be exploited to improve estimation accuracy. The MMSE estimate of m for the Tth short-time segment is thus obtained using not just the current noisy segment $\mathbf{y}_T$ but a sequence that includes the current as well as past noisy segments, $[\mathbf{y}_1, \ldots, \mathbf{y}_T]$, where t is the segment index and $\mathbf{y}_t$, $1 \le t \le T$ is a vector containing N noisy speech samples. The MMSE estimate of m can be written as

$$
\begin{aligned}
\hat{m} &= E\left[m|\mathbf{y}_1, \mathbf{y}_2 \ldots, \mathbf{y}_T\right] \\
&= \sum_{k=1}^{K} p\left(S_T = H_k|\mathbf{y}_1, \mathbf{y}_2, \ldots, \mathbf{y}_T\right) \\
&\quad \times E\left[m|\mathbf{y}_1, \mathbf{y}_2 \ldots, \mathbf{y}_T, S_T = H_k\right].
\end{aligned}
\tag{7}
$$

The two terms in the last line of (7) lend themselves to an intuitive representation. The second term $E\left[m|\mathbf{y}_1, \mathbf{y}_2 \ldots, \mathbf{y}_T, S_T = H_k\right]$ corresponds to an MMSE estimate of m assuming that the context is best described by H_k. The first term provides a relative importance score to this estimate, based on the likelihood that C_x^k is indeed the most appropriate speech codebook. The weighted summation corresponds to a soft estimation, which allows the coexistence of multiple contexts, e.g., speaker and language, each being modeled by a separate codebook. Next, we derive expressions for both these terms.

First, we consider the term $p\left(S_T = H_k|\mathbf{y}_1, \mathbf{y}_2, \ldots, \mathbf{y}_T\right)$. Let

$$
\alpha_T(k) = p\left(\mathbf{y}_1, \mathbf{y}_2 \ldots, \mathbf{y}_T, S_T = H_k\right),\ k = 1, 2, \ldots, K
\tag{8}
$$

represent the forward probability as in standard HMM theory [36]. It can be recursively obtained as follows:

Basis step:

$$
\alpha_1(k) = p\left(H_k\right) p\left(\mathbf{y}_1|H_k\right),\ k = 1, 2, \ldots, K.
\tag{9}
$$

The prior probabilities in the absence of any observation can be assumed to be equal in Equation 9. Thus, $p\left(H_k\right) = \frac{1}{K}$, i.e., all hypotheses are equally likely.

Induction step: The state S_T of the current noisy observation $\mathbf{y}_T$ could have been reached from any of the states from the previous frame with a particular transition probability. This can be modeled as

$$
\alpha_{t+1}(k) = \left[\sum_{l=1}^{K} \alpha_t(l) a_{lk}\right] p\left(\mathbf{y}_{t+1}|H_k\right),
\tag{10}
$$

where $1 \le t \le T - 1$ and $l, k = 1, 2, \ldots, K$, and a_{lk} represent the transition probability of reaching state k from state l. We assume the *a priori* transition probabilities to be known beforehand for a given set of speech codebooks. In this paper, we assume them to be fixed such that a_{lk} takes higher values when $l = k$ than otherwise, to capture

the intuition that we typically do not rapidly switch between contexts such as speaker and language. Note that only the *a priori* transition probabilities are assumed to be fixed. The data-dependent part in Equation 10 is captured by the term $p(\mathbf{y}_{t+1}|H_k)$, whose computation is addressed in the following. Using Equation 8,

$$
\begin{aligned}
p\left(S_T = H_k|\mathbf{y}_1, \mathbf{y}_2, \ldots, \mathbf{y}_T\right) &= \frac{p\left(\mathbf{y}_1, \mathbf{y}_2, \ldots, \mathbf{y}_T, S_T = H_k\right)}{p\left(\mathbf{y}_1, \mathbf{y}_2, \ldots, \mathbf{y}_T\right)} \\
&= \frac{\alpha_T(k)}{\sum_{k=1}^{K} \alpha_T(k)}.
\end{aligned}
\tag{11}
$$

Next, we consider the term $E\left[m|\mathbf{y}_1, \mathbf{y}_2 \ldots, \mathbf{y}_T, S_T = H_k\right]$ in Equation 7. In this section, we are interested in exploiting memory to ensure that the codebook that is most relevant to the current context at hand receives a high likelihood, and this is captured by Equation 11. For a given codebook, $E\left[m|\mathbf{y}_1, \mathbf{y}_2 \ldots, \mathbf{y}_T, S_T = H_k\right]$ provides an improved estimate of m by exploiting not only the current noisy observation $\mathbf{y}_T$ but also the past noisy segments. An expression for this term can be derived as in [26], where memory was restricted to the previous frame in view of the signal nonstationarity. Here, to retain the focus on selecting the appropriate context, we assume

$$
E\left[m|\mathbf{y}_1, \mathbf{y}_2 \ldots, \mathbf{y}_T, S_T = H_k\right] = E\left[m|\mathbf{y}_T, S_T = H_k\right].
\tag{12}
$$

In the following, we ignore the term S_T and write $E[m|\mathbf{y}_T, S_T = H_k]$ as $E[m|\mathbf{y}_T, H_k]$ for brevity. For a given hypothesis H_k, we have

$$
\begin{aligned}
E\left[m|\mathbf{y}_T, H_k\right] &= \sum_{m \in \mathcal{M}} m\, p\left(m|\mathbf{y}_T, H_k\right) \\
&= \sum_{m \in \mathcal{M}} m\, \frac{p\left(\mathbf{y}_T|m, H_k\right)\, p\left(m|H_k\right)}{p\left(\mathbf{y}_T|H_k\right)}.
\end{aligned}
\tag{13}
$$

Under a Gaussian LP model, m corresponds to an autocorrelation matrix R_y for $\mathbf{y}_T$, which fully characterizes the pdf $p\left(\mathbf{y}_T|m\right)$ as in

$$
\begin{aligned}
p\left(\mathbf{y}_T|m\right) &= \frac{1}{(2\pi)^{N/2}|R_x + R_w|^{1/2}} \\
&\quad \times \exp\left(-\frac{\mathbf{y}_T^\dagger (R_x + R_w)^{-1} \mathbf{y}_T}{2}\right),
\end{aligned}
\tag{14}
$$

where $\dagger$ represents transpose, $R_y = R_x + R_w$, $R_x = g_x(B_x^\dagger B_x)^{-1}$, $R_w = g_w\left(B_w^\dagger B_w\right)^{-1}$, B_x is an $N \times N$ lower triangular Toeplitz matrix with $[\mathbf{a}_x, 0, \ldots, 0]^\dagger$ as the first column, and B_w is an $N \times N$ lower triangular Toeplitz matrix with $[\mathbf{a}_w, 0, \ldots, 0]^\dagger$ as the first column. Thus, given a model m, $\mathbf{y}_T$ is conditionally independent of H_k, and we have

$$p(\mathbf{y}_T|m, H_k) = p(\mathbf{y}_T|m), \ k = 1, 2, \ldots, K. \qquad (15)$$

The logarithm of the likelihood $p(\mathbf{y}_T|m)$ in the Equation 14 can be efficiently computed in the frequency domain following the approach of [26]. The gain terms that maximize the likelihood can be computed as in [26].

Next, we consider the term $p(m|H_k)$ in Equation 13. Under hypothesis H_k, the speech signal in the observed segment is best described by the codebook C_x^k. We assume all the models resulting from a given codebook are equally likely. This assumption is valid, in general, if the codebook size is large and derived from a phonetically balanced large training set.

Thus, assuming all the models resulting from C_x^k are equally likely, we have

$$p(m|H_k) = \frac{1}{|\mathcal{M}_k|}, \ \forall m \in \mathcal{M}_k$$
$$= 0, \text{otherwise}, \qquad (16)$$

where $|\mathcal{M}_k|$ is the cardinality of $\mathcal{M}_k$. From Equations 13 and 16, we have

$$E\left[m|\mathbf{y}_T, H_k\right] = \frac{1}{|\mathcal{M}_k|} \sum_{m \in \mathcal{M}_k} m \frac{p(\mathbf{y}_T|m)}{p(\mathbf{y}_T|H_k)}, \qquad (17)$$

where

$$p(\mathbf{y}_T|H_k) = \frac{1}{|\mathcal{M}_k|} \sum_{m \in \mathcal{M}_k} p(\mathbf{y}_T|m) \qquad (18)$$

and $p(\mathbf{y}_T|m)$ is given by Equation 14. Equation 18 is used in Equations 9 and 10 to obtain the forward probabilities. Finally, the required MMSE estimate $\hat{m}$ is obtained by using Equations 11 and 17 in Equation 7. The speech and noise PSDs corresponding to $\hat{m}$ can be obtained using Equation 3 and the Wiener filter from Equation 5. To ensure stability of the estimated LP parameters, the weighted sum in Equation 7 can be performed in the line spectral frequency domain. Note that the weights are non-negative and add up to unity as is evident from Equation 11. Alternatively, as we are finally interested in the speech and noise PSDs to be used in a Wiener filter, the weighted sum can be performed in the power spectral domain.

We conclude this section with some remarks on the calculation of the forward probabilities α_T which for a codebook captures how well that codebook matches the context of the Tth input segment. As mentioned earlier, the proposed framework can be used to model context in speech as well as noise. When context is modeled by the speech codebooks, it was found to be beneficial to

calculate α_T during speech-dominated segments, and during noise-dominated segments when modeling the noise context. The goal in computing α_T is to assess how well a given speech codebook matches the underlying context for a given input segment. If this computation is performed during speech-dominated frames, we obtain accurate values for α_T. However, inaccurate weight values may result when the computation is based on segments that lack sufficient information about the speech, such as silence or low-energy segments dominated by noise. In such situations, it is preferable to use the value of α_T computed in the last speech-dominated segment. This, in other words, assumes that the context of the current segment is the same as that of the past segment. This assumption is valid in general as the context of speech is not expected to rapidly change from one speech burst to another. Thus, updating α_T only during speech-dominated segments does not affect performance. However, estimating α_T only during speech-dominated segments suffers from the disadvantage that there may not be a sufficient number of such segments in highly noisy conditions. Introducing a preliminary noise reduction step, e.g., using the long-term noise estimate from [18], and estimating α_T from the enhanced signal was seen to address this problem. Importantly, the estimation of the speech and noise PSDs and the resulting Wiener filter occurs for each short-time segment, providing good performance under nonstationary noise conditions.

4 Experimental results

Experiments were performed to verify the robustness of the proposed framework under varying contexts. The contexts modeled by a trained CD codebook may or may not match with that of the observed noisy input signal, leading to two scenarios:

- Context match: the best-case scenario for a CD codebook
- Context mismatch: the worst-case scenario for a CD codebook

The robustness of the proposed framework, employing both CD and CI codebooks, was tested under both scenarios. Two different sets of experiments were performed, which differed in terms of number of codebooks employed and the aspects of contexts modeled. The first set consisted of experiments with two speech codebooks, a CI speech codebook and a CD speech codebook, modeling the speaker and acoustic environment as aspects of context. The second set consisted of experiments with three speech codebooks: a CI speech codebook and two CD speech codebooks to study the performance of the proposed framework with an increase in the number of codebooks employed. This set modeled, apart from speaker and acoustic environment, the speech type (normal, whisper, loud, etc.) of the input speech as aspects of context.

In the following, we first describe the experimental setup and, thereafter, the various experiments along with the corresponding results.

4.1 Experimental setup

In all the experiments, the input noisy test utterances were enhanced under different context scenarios, using the CBSE technique [26] applied using the CD codebook alone, the CBSE technique applied using the CI codebook alone, and the proposed Bayesian scheme. We expect that in the context match scenarios, employing the CD codebook alone should lead to the best results. On the other hand, in the context mismatch scenarios, employing the CI codebook alone should lead to results better than those obtained using the CD codebook. The proposed method, however, is expected to provide robust results under varying contexts, i.e., results close to the best results in all scenarios. To serve as a reference for comparisons, we also include results when applying the Wiener filter (5) with a noise estimate obtained from a state-of-the-art noise estimation scheme [37].

The performance of these four processing schemes was compared using two measures: the improvement in segmental SNR (SSNR) referred to as ΔSSNR (in dB) and the improvement in the perceptual evaluation of speech quality (PESQ) [38] measure, referred to as ΔPESQ, averaged over all the enhanced utterances considered under a particular experiment.

The speech codebooks used in the experiments were trained using the Linde-Buzo-Gray (LBG) algorithm [39]. First, the clean speech training utterances, resampled at 8 kHz, were segmented into 50% overlapped Hann windowed frames of size 256 samples each, corresponding to a duration of 32 ms wherein the speech signal can be assumed stationary. Then, LP coefficient vectors of dimension 10, extracted using these frames, were clustered using the LBG algorithm to generate speech codebooks of size 256 each using the Itakura-Saito (IS) distortion [40] as the error criterion.

For training the CI speech codebook, 180 English language utterances of duration 3 to 4 seconds each were used, from 25 male and 25 female speakers from the WSJ speech database [41]. This codebook served as the CI codebook for all the experiments described in this section. The speakers whose utterances were used to train the CI codebook were not used in the test utterances. The different experiments use different CD codebooks and input noisy test data, which are discussed later along with the description of each experiment.

The different CD and CI speech codebooks considered in the experiments are of large size (256) and are derived

from a large number of phonetically balanced sentences from the WSJ database. Moreover, the LBG algorithm used to generate the speech codebooks computes cluster centroids in an optimal fashion. All these factors ensure the validity of the assumption about equal probability of models in Equation 16.

Two noise codebooks for two different noise types, traffic and babble, with eight entries each were trained similarly using LP coefficient vectors. For the traffic noise codebook, LP coefficient vectors of order 6 extracted from 2 min of nonstationary traffic noise were used. Since babble noise is speech-like, a higher LP model order of 10 was used while extracting LP coefficient training vectors from approximately 3 min of nonstationary babble noise. The same noise types were also used in the creation of test utterances at 0, 5, and 10 dB SNR for all the experiments. The actual samples were different from those used in training. The active speech level was computed using ITU-T P.56 method B in [42], and noise was scaled and added to obtain a desired SNR.

When processing the noisy files for a particular noise type, the appropriate noise codebook was used. In practice, a classified noise codebook scheme as discussed in [25] can be used. This scheme employs multiple noise codebook, each trained for a particular noise type. A maximum likelihood scheme is used to select the appropriate noise codebook for each short-time frame. This method was shown in [25] to perform as well as the case when the ideal noise codebook was used. We choose to use the ideal noise codebook to retain the focus on the performance of the proposed framework with regard to various aspects of the speech context.

4.2 Experiments with a single CD codebook

In this experiment, we test the proposed framework when two speech codebooks are employed, a CI and a CD codebook. The CD codebook models two aspects of context, 'speaker' and 'acoustic environment'.

4.2.1 CD codebook training

For training the CD codebook, 180 English language utterances from a *single* speaker, of 3 to 4 s duration each, were used from the WSJ speech database. These utterances were convolved with an impulse response recorded at a distance of 50 cm from the microphone, in a reverberant room (T60 = 800 ms). This corresponds, for example, to hands-free mode on a mobile phone. In practice, this codebook is adapted during hands-free usage, making it dependent on both the speaker and acoustic environment.

4.2.2 Test utterances for the experiment

Two sets of ten clean speech utterances each were used to generate the noisy test data. Utterances for the first set were from the same speaker and acoustic environment as the data used to train the CD codebook, corresponding to the context match scenario and thus the best case for the CD codebook. The utterances themselves were different from those used in the training set.

The second set of clean utterances were from a speaker different from the one involved in training the CD codebook. These utterances were not convolved with the recorded impulse response (e.g., corresponding to handset mode in a mobile phone). Thus, both the speaker and acoustic environment were different from those used to train the CD codebook, corresponding to the context mismatch scenario and thus the worst case for the CD codebook.

4.2.3 Enhancement results

The test utterances were enhanced using the four schemes, mentioned in Section 4.1. The transition probabilities a_{lk} were set to 0.99 when $l = k$ and to 0.01 when $l \neq k$, with $l, k = 1, 2$. Tables 1 and 2 provide the results for the best- and worst-case scenarios, respectively, in babble noise.

As can be observed from Table 1, the best results are obtained for the CD codebook, as expected in a context match scenario. There is a significant difference between the results corresponding to the CD and CI codebooks, e.g., 0.19 for ΔPESQ and 1.3 dB for ΔSSNR, at 5 dB input SNR. Moreover, the standard deviation values indicate that the observed differences between the CD and CI results are statistically significant. This illustrates the benefit of employing CD codebooks. On the other hand, Table 2 demonstrates poorer performance when using the CD codebook compared to using the CI codebook, in a context mismatch scenario. The difference between their results is significant for ΔSSNR at all input SNRs, e.g., 1 dB at 0 dB input SNR, and for ΔPESQ at higher SNR, e.g., 0.22 at 10 dB input SNR. These results demonstrate the need for a scheme that appropriately combines the estimates obtained from the CD and CI codebooks, depending on the context at hand.

In Table 1, with increasing input SSNR, there is an increase in ΔPESQ but a decrease in ΔSSNR for all schemes except the reference method. This can be explained by considering the trade-off between speech distortion and noise reduction.

In general, enhancement using a Wiener filter involves applying a gain (also called attenuation) function. When applying this gain function to the noisy speech, both speech and noise components are attenuated. At lower input SNRs, the SSNR measure is dominated by the benefit of noise reduction while ignoring the penalty due to speech distortion. So in these scenarios, applying a greater attenuation than is optimal can increase the output SSNR values as it results in more noise attenuation (it also results in more speech attenuation but that is not captured by the SSNR measure). This situation occurs when using a mismatched codebook, where the clean speech PSD is underestimated, resulting in more severe attenuation of the noisy speech. PESQ is more closer to human perception, and we believe that the effect of speech distortion is better captured by PESQ, resulting in negative delta PESQ values for these scenarios. At higher input SNRs, the SSNR measure also captures the effect of speech distortion. Since ΔPESQ captures well the decrease in speech distortion with increasing input SSNR, there is an increase in ΔPESQ with increasing input SSNR in Table 1. On the other hand, SSNR measure is dominated at lower input SNRs by the benefit of noise reduction ignoring the penalty due to speech distortion. As a result, there is larger ΔSSNR at lower input SNRs than at higher input SNRs.

In contrast to the results obtained when using the CD and CI codebooks alone, the proposed framework achieves robust performance regardless of the observed context. For the best-case scenario (Table 1), its results are close to the CD results. For the worst-case scenario (Table 2), its results are close to the CI results. Thus, the proposed framework achieves results close to the best results for a given scenario, as desired. The reference scheme performs poorly due to the nonstationary nature of the noise. It may be noted that even using a mismatched codebook outperforms the reference scheme, highlighting the benefit of using *a priori* information for speech enhancement in nonstationary noise.

Tables 3 and 4 provide the results for the best- and worst-case scenarios, respectively, for the traffic noise case. Similar observations can be made as from the Tables 1 and 2 regarding the need for both the CI and CD codebooks for better performance and the robust performance of the proposed framework under varying

Table 1 Best-case scenario for a single CD codebook under babble noise

Input SSNR	ΔPESQ			ΔSSNR (in dB)		
	0 dB	5 dB	10 dB	0 dB	5 dB	10 dB
CBSE with CD	0.12 ± 0.06	0.18 ± 0.06	0.20 ± 0.07	6.44 ± 0.72	6.01 ± 0.70	4.50 ± 0.88
CBSE with CI	-0.04 ± 0.07	-0.01 ± 0.06	-0.02 ± 0.09	5.59 ± 0.97	4.76 ± 0.92	2.82 ± 1.09
Proposed	0.12 ± 0.06	0.18 ± 0.06	0.20 ± 0.07	6.44 ± 0.72	6.00 ± 0.70	4.49 ± 0.88
Reference	-0.11 ± 0.02	-0.11 ± 0.02	-0.10 ± 0.04	2.08 ± 0.46	2.42 ± 0.47	2.17 ± 0.53

The CD codebook is modeling two aspects of context, speaker and acoustic environment. Both mean and standard deviation values are reported.

Table 2 Worst-case scenario for a single CD codebook under babble noise

Input SSNR	ΔPESQ			ΔSSNR (in dB)		
	0 dB	5 dB	10 dB	0 dB	5 dB	10 dB
CBSE with CD	0.14 ± 0.09	0.12 ± 0.05	0.07 ± 0.05	4.52 ± 0.90	3.72 ± 0.69	1.75 ± 0.68
CBSE with CI	0.17 ± 0.07	0.20 ± 0.06	0.23 ± 0.05	5.51 ± 0.78	5.01 ± 0.74	3.53 ± 0.63
Proposed	0.17 ± 0.07	0.20 ± 0.06	0.21 ± 0.06	5.52 ± 0.79	4.98 ± 0.73	3.47 ± 0.62
Reference	0.09 ± 0.02	0.12 ± 0.03	0.15 ± 0.05	2.40 ± 0.40	2.99 ± 0.40	3.09 ± 0.44

The CD codebook is modeling two aspects of context, speaker and acoustic environment. Both mean and standard deviation values are reported.

contexts. Again, the reference method performs poorly due to the nonstationary nature of noise.

Comparing ΔPESQ values for the best-case scenarios in Tables 1 and 3 for the two noise types shows that there is a sharper drop in values from 5 to 0 dB input SNR in the case of traffic noise results (0.2) compared to babble noise results (0.06). A similar observation can be made for the ΔPESQ values for the worst-case scenarios in Tables 2 and 4 for the two noise types. These observations indicate that the traffic noise case is more difficult to handle than babble noise at 0 dB input SNR. This occurred because the traffic noise considered for the experiments is highly nonstationary compared to the babble noise used for the experiments.

4.2.4 Comparison of the proposed method with the MMSE-STSA method

In the above experiments, the reference method chosen for comparison with the proposed method uses the Wiener gain, as described by (5), computed using a state-of-the-art noise estimator [37]. This choice provides an even comparison as the proposed method too employs the Wiener gain function. The two approaches, however, differ in the computation of the speech and noise PSDs for computing the Wiener gain.

Also of interest is a comparison of the proposed method with a popular statistical approach such as the MMSE-STSA method [9], the results of which are provided in Tables 5 and 6 for the Babble noise case. Table 5 corresponds to the context match scenario wherein the context of the CD codebook matches with that of the input noisy speech. Here, the performance of the proposed method is superior, especially for the PESQ values, to that of

the MMSE-STSA technique. The advantage with the proposed approach is higher at lower SNR values. For the mismatch scenario, the performance of both the methods is comparable as shown in Table 6. Note that the Wiener filter is just one example of a gain function that can use the speech and noise PSDs estimated using the proposed method. The estimated speech and noise PSDs can also be used to compute the *a priori* and *a posteriori* SNRs for use in the MMSE-STSA gain function. This is however beyond the scope of this paper and is a topic for future work.

4.3 Experiments with multiple CD codebooks

In the previous subsection, we tested the proposed framework under conditions when a single CD codebook was employed along with a CI codebook. Multiple aspects of context were modeled by the single CD codebook. In practice, different contexts will be modeled by different CD codebooks. In this subsection, we experiment with the case of two CD codebooks along with one CI codebook.

4.3.1 CD codebook training

The first CD codebook, referred to as CD-1, models a particular speaker and a speech type. The speech type considered is 'whisper' speech. The speech produced in the case of certain speech disorders (dysphonic speech) is similar to whispered speech. CD-1 was trained using around 10 min of whispered speech data from a single speaker from the CHAINS database [43].

The second CD codebook employed, referred to as CD-2, models normal speech in reverberant conditions for the same speaker as modeled by CD-1. CD-2 was trained using training utterances of duration around 10 min,

Table 3 Best-case scenario for a single CD codebook under traffic noise

Input SSNR	ΔPESQ			ΔSSNR (in dB)		
	0 dB	5 dB	10 dB	0 dB	5 dB	10 dB
CBSE with CD	0.00 ± 0.30	0.19 ± 0.06	0.25 ± 0.11	7.84 ± 1.08	6.97 ± 1.11	5.40 ± 1.35
CBSE with CI	−0.21 ± 0.29	−0.05 ± 0.10	0.00 ± 0.14	6.67 ± 1.37	5.57 ± 1.29	3.64 ± 1.49
Proposed	0.01 ± 0.30	0.19 ± 0.06	0.26 ± 0.11	7.83 ± 1.09	6.96 ± 1.11	5.39 ± 1.35
Reference	−0.04 ± 0.31	0.08 ± 0.05	0.08 ± 0.06	2.75 ± 0.49	2.82 ± 0.54	2.21 ± 0.79

The CD codebook is modeling two aspects of context, speaker and acoustic environment. Both mean and standard deviation values are reported.

Table 4 Worst-case scenario for a single CD codebook under traffic noise

Input SSNR	ΔPESQ			ΔSSNR (in dB)		
	0 dB	5 dB	10 dB	0 dB	5 dB	10 dB
CBSE with CD	−0.13 ± 0.10	−0.02 ± 0.11	−0.01 ± 0.07	5.98 ± 1.78	5.28 ± 1.65	3.45 ± 1.63
CBSE with CI	0.09 ± 0.09	0.32 ± 0.09	0.42 ± 0.09	7.35 ± 1.25	7.12 ± 1.25	5.81 ± 1.07
Proposed	0.08 ± 0.09	0.29 ± 0.07	0.39 ± 0.08	7.34 ± 1.24	7.05 ± 1.22	5.75 ± 1.07
Reference	0.21 ± 0.08	0.28 ± 0.10	0.34 ± 0.09	3.21 ± 0.65	3.65 ± 0.65	3.35 ± 0.58

The CD codebook is modeling two aspects of context, speaker and acoustic environment. Both mean and standard deviation values are reported.

convolved with the same impulse response as used in the previous experiments (corresponding to a distance of 50 cm from the microphone, in a reverberant room with T60 = 800 ms).

The two codebooks differ in terms of speaking style, whispered and normal, and also the acoustic environment. The separation in terms of acoustic environment is useful, e.g., to have different CD models for a particular user of the mobile phone to cater to hand-set and hands-free modes of operation. Note that the CI codebook is speaker-independent and corresponds to hand-set mode.

4.3.2 Test utterances for the experiment

Two sets of experiments were performed pertaining to the matching codebook being CD-1 or CD-2. The first set consisted of test utterances generated by adding noise to ten clean 'whispered' speech utterances from the same speaker as in generation of the CD-1 codebook. Similarly, the second set of experiments had test utterances generated using ten clean 'normal' speech utterances from the same speaker as in CD-2, convolved with the same recorded impulse response as used in training CD-2 to constitute the context match scenario for CD-2. In both sets of experiments, the test utterances considered were different from those used in the training of the codebooks. The noisy test utterances were generated as described in the beginning of the section.

4.3.3 Enhancement results

Enhancement using multiple CD codebooks was performed by setting transition probabilities a_{lk} to 0.9 when $l = k$ and to 0.05 when $l \neq k$, with $l, k = 1$ to 3. Tables 7 and 8 present the matching scenario results for CD-1 and CD-2, respectively, for the babble noise case. Similarly,

Tables 9 and 10 present the matching scenario results for CD-1 and CD-2, respectively, for traffic noise case. As can be observed from these tables, the best results for all the scenarios occur for the matching CD codebook. The difference between context match and mismatch (between CD-1 and CD-2/CI, and between CD-2 and CD-1/CI) is significant, especially in the ΔPESQ scores. The differences in ΔSSNR values are significant at higher input SNRs. As the number of codebooks employed by the proposed framework increases, there is a possibility of a negative influence from the inappropriate codebooks in the estimation of the model estimate. But from Tables 7, 8, 9, and 10, we observe that for the case of two CD codebooks and one CI codebook, the results for the proposed framework are close to those of the matched codebook at all input SNRs and for both noise types, confirming the robustness of the proposed framework under varying contexts.

5 Conclusions

In this paper, we have introduced the notion of context-dependent (CD) models for speech enhancement methods that use trained models of speech and noise parameters. CD speech models can be trained on one or more aspects of speech context such as speaker, acoustic environment, speaking style, etc., and CD noise models can be trained for specific noise types. Using CD models results in better speech enhancement performance compared to using context-independent (CI) models when the noisy speech shares the same context as the trained codebook. The risk, however, is degraded performance in the event of a context mismatch. Thus, the CD and CI models need to co-exist in a practical implementation. The Bayesian speech enhancement framework proposed

Table 5 Comparison of the proposed method with the MMSE-STSA technique for context match scenario corresponding to Table 1

Input SSNR	ΔPESQ			ΔSSNR (in dB)		
	0 dB	5 dB	10 dB	0 dB	5 dB	10 dB
Proposed	0.12 ± 0.06	0.18 ± 0.06	0.20 ± 0.07	6.44 ± 0.72	6.00 ± 0.70	4.49 ± 0.88
MMSE-STSA	−0.14 ± 0.06	−0.06 ± 0.08	0.04 ± 0.05	5.21 ± 1.28	5.01 ± 0.96	4.21 ± 0.62

Table 6 Comparison of the proposed method with the MMSE-STSA technique for context mismatch scenario corresponding to Table 2

Input SSNR	ΔPESQ			ΔSSNR (in dB)		
	0 dB	5 dB	10 dB	0 dB	5 dB	10 dB
Proposed	0.17 ± 0.07	0.20 ± 0.06	0.21 ± 0.06	5.52 ± 0.79	4.98 ± 0.73	3.47 ± 0.62
MMSE-STSA	0.14 ± 0.04	0.18 ± 0.03	0.23 ± 0.05	5.60 ± 1.14	5.60 ± 0.77	5.03 ± 0.75

Table 7 Results using two CD codebooks and on CI codebook, for context match scenario for CD-1 under babble noise

Input SNR	ΔPESQ			ΔSSNR (in dB)		
	0 dB	5 dB	10 dB	0 dB	5 dB	10 dB
CBSE with CD-1	0.18 ± 0.14	0.18 ± 0.16	0.12 ± 0.14	5.87 ± 1.16	4.88 ± 1.14	2.81 ± 1.27
CBSE with CD-2	0.08 ± 0.18	0.05 ± 0.16	−0.03 ± 0.12	5.69 ± 1.30	4.52 ± 1.17	2.18 ± 1.31
CBSE with CI	0.04 ± 0.17	0.02 ± 0.15	−0.11 ± 0.17	5.41 ± 1.20	4.39 ± 1.16	1.98 ± 1.28
Proposed	0.17 ± 0.13	0.16 ± 0.14	0.07 ± 0.16	5.81 ± 1.14	4.87 ± 1.10	2.58 ± 1.33
Reference	−0.03 ± 0.07	−0.03 ± 0.06	−0.07 ± 0.07	1.76 ± 0.50	1.93 ± 0.43	1.66 ± 0.57

Both mean and standard deviation values are reported.

Table 8 Results using two CD codebooks and one CI codebook, for context match scenario for CD-2 under babble noise

Input SNR	ΔPESQ			ΔSSNR (in dB)		
	0 dB	5 dB	10 dB	0 dB	5 dB	10 dB
CBSE with CD-1	0.11 ± 0.13	0.09 ± 0.09	0.06 ± 0.12	4.15 ± 1.02	3.25 ± 1.18	1.55 ± 1.44
CBSE with CD-2	0.24 ± 0.12	0.21 ± 0.13	0.21 ± 0.12	5.22 ± 1.07	4.64 ± 1.17	3.02 ± 1.32
CBSE with CI	0.18 ± 0.11	0.16 ± 0.10	0.17 ± 0.12	4.77 ± 0.91	4.24 ± 1.02	2.61 ± 1.29
Proposed	0.24 ± 0.12	0.22 ± 0.11	0.21 ± 0.11	5.08 ± 1.12	4.51 ± 1.20	2.93 ± 1.39
Reference	0.08 ± 0.09	0.10 ± 0.07	0.08 ± 0.05	2.59 ± 0.49	3.06 ± 0.51	2.71 ± 0.52

Both mean and standard deviation values are reported.

Table 9 Results using two CD codebooks and one CI codebook, for context match scenario for CD-1 under traffic noise

Input SNR	ΔPESQ			ΔSSNR (in dB)		
	0 dB	5 dB	10 dB	0 dB	5 dB	10 dB
CBSE with CD-1	0.07 ± 0.17	0.24 ± 0.17	0.25 ± 0.18	6.67 ± 1.67	5.70 ± 1.62	3.76 ± 1.50
CBSE with CD-2	−0.16 ± 0.16	−0.03 ± 0.17	−0.03 ± 0.19	6 ± 1.78	4.49 ± 1.82	1.88 ± 2.00
CBSE with CI	−0.1 ± 0.18	0.01 ± 0.16	0.03 ± 0.17	5.85 ± 1.76	4.53 ± 1.87	2.06 ± 1.84
Proposed	0.06 ± 0.16	0.20 ± 0.19	0.22 ± 0.21	6.58 ± 1.68	5.44 ± 1.65	3.19 ± 1.61
Reference	0.05 ± 0.07	0.11 ± 0.09	0.17 ± 0.11	2.54 ± 0.85	2.96 ± 0.91	2.71 ± 1.02

Both mean and standard deviation values are reported.

Table 10 Results using two CD codebooks and one CI codebook, for context match scenario for CD-2 under traffic noise

Input SNR	ΔPESQ			ΔSSNR (in dB)		
	0 dB	5 dB	10 dB	0 dB	5 dB	10 dB
CBSE with CD-1	−0.05 ± 0.13	0.08 ± 0.15	0.13 ± 0.12	6.39 ± 1.40	5.87 ± 0.98	4.4 ± 0.95
CBSE with CD-2	0.01 ± 0.12	0.21 ± 0.15	0.25 ± 0.15	6.69 ± 1.35	6.21 ± 0.91	4.62 ± 0.96
CBSE with CI	−0.07 ± 0.14	0.09 ± 0.16	0.19 ± 0.16	6.48 ± 1.37	5.80 ± 1.02	4.17 ± 1.03
Proposed	0.01 ± 0.12	0.20 ± 0.15	0.27 ± 0.14	6.69 ± 1.36	6.21 ± 0.95	4.70 ± 0.96
Reference	0.07 ± 0.07	0.12 ± 0.10	0.13 ± 0.10	2.76 ± 0.84	3.17 ± 0.83	2.78 ± 0.69

Both mean and standard deviation values are reported.

in this paper obtains estimates of speech and noise parameters based on all available models, requires no prior information on the context at hand, and automatically obtains results close to those obtained when using the appropriate codebook for a given context scenario as seen from experiments with various aspects of speech context.

The improved performance of the proposed method is at the cost of increased computational complexity. As opposed to employing a single CI model, the proposed method involves computations with multiple models. The computations related to each model can, however, occur simultaneously, which allows for a parallel implementation.

The proposed method has been developed using the codebook-based speech enhancement system as an example of a data-driven model-based speech enhancement system. Other model-based schemes, such as those using HMMs, GMMs, and NMF, can benefit in a similar manner, and the extension is a topic for future work. The theory developed in this paper is directly applicable to context-dependent noise codebooks and can be used for robust noise estimation under varying noise conditions.

In this paper, context-dependent models are assumed to be available. In practice, they need to be trained online. For several aspects of context, a separate enrollment stage may not be meaningful and the models need to be progressively adapted during usage when the SNR is high. Distinguishing between different aspects of context and training separate models for them online is another topic for future work.

The codebooks considered in this paper consist of vectors of tenth-order LP coefficients, which model the smoothed spectral envelope. It will be worthwhile to investigate the suitability of other spectral representations such as higher resolution PSDs, mel-frequency cepstral coefficients, etc., to capture context-dependent information. Different features may be employed depending on which aspects of context are to be modeled and depending on the application, e.g., whether the enhancement is for speech communication, speaker identification, or for speech recognition.

Competing interests

The authors declare that they have no competing interests.

Authors' information

This work was performed when SS was with Philips Research Laboratories, Eindhoven, The Netherlands.

Acknowledgements

The authors would like to thank Prof. G. V. Prabhakara Rao, Head, Department of Information Technology, Rajiv Gandhi Memorial College of Engineering and Technology, Nandyal, Andhra Pradesh, India, for valuable discussions on this topic.

Author details

[1]Department of Mathematics and Computer Science, Sri Sathya Sai Institute of Higher Learning, Prasanthi Nilayam, Anantapur, Andhra Pradesh 515134, India. [2]Microsoft Corporation, Redmond, WA 98052, USA.

References

1. B Schuller, M Wöllmer, T Moosmayr, G Rigoll, Recognition of noisy speech: a comparative survey of robust model architecture and feature enhancement. EURASIP J. Audio Speech Music Process. **2009**, 1–17 (2009)
2. V Hamacher, J Chalupper, J Eggers, E Fischer, U Kornagel, H Puder, U Rass, Signal processing in high-end hearing aids: state of the art, challenges, and future trends. EURASIP J. Appl. Signal Process. **2005**(18), 2915–2929 (2005)
3. SF Boll, Suppression of acoustic noise in speech using spectral subtraction. IEEE Trans. Acoust. Speech Signal Process. **27**(2), 113–120 (1979)
4. M Berouti, M Schwartz, J Makhoul, Enhancement of speech corrupted by acoustic noise, in *Proceedings of the IEEE Int. Conf. Acoust. Speech Signal Processing (ICASSP)* (Washington D. C., 2–4 April 1979), pp. 208–211
5. S Kamath, P Loizou, A multi-band spectral subtraction method for enhancing speech corrupted by colored noise, in *Proceedings of the IEEE Int. Conf. Acoust. Speech Signal Processing (ICASSP)* (Orlando, 13–17 May 2002), pp. IV-4164
6. Y Lu, PC Loizou, A geometric approach to spectral subtraction. Speech Commun. **50**(6), 453–466 (2008)
7. K Paliwal, B Schwerin, K Wojcicki, Speech enhancement using a minimum mean-square error short-time spectral modulation magnitude estimator. Speech Commun. **54**(2), 282–305 (2012)
8. RJ McAulay, ML Malpass, Speech enhancement using a soft-decision noise suppression filter. IEEE Trans. Acoust. Speech Signal Process. **28**(2), 137–145 (1980)
9. Y Ephraim, D Malah, Speech enhancement using a minimum mean square error short-time spectral amplitude estimator. IEEE Trans. Acoust. Speech Signal Process. **32**(6), 1109–1121 (1984)
10. E Plourde, B Champagne, Multidimensional STSA estimators for speech enhancement with correlated spectral components. IEEE Trans. Sig. Proc. **59**(7), 3013–3024 (2011)
11. BJ Borgstrom, A Alwan, A unified framework for designing optimal STSA estimators assuming maximum likelihood phase equivalence of speech and noise. IEEE Trans. Audio Speech Language Process. **19**(8), 2579–2590 (2011)
12. Y Andrianakis, PR White, Speech enhancement algorithm based on a Chi MRF of the speech STFT amplitudes. IEEE Trans. Acoust. Speech Signal Process. **17**(8), 1508–1517 (2009)
13. M McCallum, B Guillemin, Stochastic-deterministic MMSE STFT speech enhancement with general a priori information. IEEE Trans. Audio Speech Language Process. **21**(7), 1445–1457 (2013)
14. Y Ephraim, HL Van Trees, A signal subspace approach for speech enhancement. IEEE Trans. Acoust. Speech Signal Process. **3**(4), 251–266 (1995)
15. P Loizou, *Speech Enhancement: Theory and Practice.* (CRC Press, Boca Raton, 2007)
16. K Srinivasan, A Gersho, Voice activity detection for cellular networks, in *Proceedings of the IEEE Speech Coding Workshop* (Sainte-Adèle, 13–15 October 1993), pp. 85–86
17. J Gorriz, J Ramirez, E Lan, C Puntonet, Jointly Gaussian pdf-based likelihood ratio test for voice activity detection. IEEE Trans. Audio Speech Language Process. **16**(8), 1565–1578 (2009)
18. R Martin, Noise power spectral density estimation based on optimal smoothing and minimum statistics. IEEE Trans. Speech Audio Process. **9**(4), 504–512 (2001)
19. I Cohen, Noise spectrum estimation in adverse environments: improved minima controlled recursive averaging. IEEE Trans. Acoust. Speech Signal Process. **11**(5), 466–475 (2003)
20. JS Erkelens, R Heusdens, Tracking of nonstationary noise based on data-driven recursive noise power estimation. IEEE Trans. Audio, Speech, Language Process. **16**(6), 1112–1123 (2008)

21. M Souden, M Delcroix, K Kinoshita, T Yoshioka, T Nakatani, Noise power spectral density tracking: a maximum likelihood perspective. IEEE Sig. Process. lett. **19**(8), 495–498 (2012)

22. R Hendriks, R Heusdens, J Jensen, MMSE based noise PSD tracking with low complexity, in *Proc. of IEEE International Conf. on Acoustics Speech and Signal Processing (ICASSP), 2010* (Dallas, 14–19 March 2010), pp. 4266–4269

23. T Gerkmann, R Hendriks, Unbiased MMSE-based noise power estimation with low complexity and low tracking delay. IEEE Trans. Audio, Speech, Language Process. **20**(4), 1383–1393 (2012)

24. TV Sreenivas, P Kirnapure, Codebook constrained Wiener filtering for speech enhancement. IEEE Trans. Acoust. Speech Signal Process. **4**(5), 383–389 (1996)

25. S Srinivasan, J Samuelsson, WB Kleijn, Codebook driven short-term predictor parameter estimation for speech enhancement. IEEE Trans. Audio Speech Language Process. **14**(1), 163–176 (2006)

26. S Srinivasan, J Samuelsson, WB Kleijn, Codebook-based Bayesian speech enhancement for nonstationary environments. IEEE Trans. Audio Speech Language Process. **15**(2), 441–452 (2007)

27. X Xiao, RM Nickel, Speech enhancement with inventory style speech resynthesis. IEEE Trans. Audio, Speech Language Process. **18**(6), 1243–1257 (2010)

28. T Rosenkranz, H Puder, Improving robustness of codebook-based noise estimation approaches with delta codebooks. IEEE Trans. Audio Speech Language Process. **20**(4), 1177–1188 (2012)

29. H Sameti, H Sheikhzadeh, L Deng, HMM-based strategies for enhancement of speech signals embedded in nonstationary noise. IEEE Trans. Acoust. Speech Signal Process. **6**(5), 445–455 (1998)

30. DY Zhao, WB Kleijn, HMM-based gain-modeling for enhancement of speech in noise. IEEE Trans. Audio Speech Language Process. **15**(3), 882–892 (2007)

31. H Veisi, H Sameti, Speech enhancement using hidden Markov models in Mel-frequency domain. Speech Commun. **55**(2), 205–220 (2013)

32. J Hao, T-W Lee, TJ Sejnowski, Speech enhancement using Gaussian scale mixture models. IEEE Trans. Audio Speech Language Process. **18**(6), 1127–1136 (2010)

33. N Mohammadiha, P Smaragdis, A Leijon, Supervised and unsupervised speech enhancement using nonnegative matrix factorization. IEEE Trans. Audio Speech Language Process. **21**(10), 2140–2151 (2013)

34. C Sigg, T Dikk, J Buhmann, Speech enhancement using generative dictionary learning. IEEE Trans. Audio, Speech, Language Process. **20**(6), 1698–1712 (2012)

35. DHR Naidu, S Srinivasan, A Bayesian framework for robust speech enhancment under varying contexts, in *Proceedings of the IEEE Int. Conf. Acoust. Speech Signal Processing (ICASSP)* (Kyoto, 25–30 March 2012), pp. 4557–4560

36. LR Rabiner, A tutorial on hidden Markov models and selected applications in speech recognition. Proc. IEEE. **77**(2), 257–286 (1989)

37. S Rangachari, P Loizou, A noise estimation algorithm for highly nonstationary environments. Speech Commun. **28**, 220–231 (2006)

38. A Rix, J Beerends, M Hollier, A Hekstra, Perceptual evaluation of speech quality (PESQ) - a new method for speech quality assessment of telephone networks and codecs, in *Proceedings of the IEEE Int. Conf. Acoust. Speech Signal Processing (ICASSP)* (Salt Lake City, 7–11 May 2001), pp. 749–752

39. Y Linde, A Buzo, RM Gray, An algorithm for vector quantizer design. IEEE Trans. Commun. **28**(1), 84–95 (1980)

40. R Gray, A Buzo, A Gray, Y Matsuyama, Distortion measures for speech processing. IEEE Trans. Acoust. Speech Signal Process. **28**(4), 367–376 (1980)

41. CSR-II (WSJ1) Complete LDC94S13A. DVD. Philadelphia: Linguistic Data Consortium (1994)

42. ITU-T Rec. P.56, Objective measurement of active speech level. International Telecommunication Union, CH-Geneva (1993)

43. F Cummins, M Grimaldi, T Leonard, J Simko, The CHAINS corpus: characterizing individual speakers, in *Proceedings of the International Conference on Speech and Computer (SPECOM)* (St Petersburg, 2006), pp. 431–435

10

Intra-frame cepstral sub-band weighting and histogram equalization for noise-robust speech recognition

Jeih-weih Hung[*] and Hao-teng Fan

Abstract

In this paper, we propose a novel noise-robustness method known as weighted sub-band histogram equalization (WS-HEQ) to improve speech recognition accuracy in noise-corrupted environments. Considering the observations that high- and low-pass portions of the intra-frame cepstral features possess unequal importance for noise-corrupted speech recognition, WS-HEQ is intended to reduce the high-pass components of the cepstral features. Furthermore, we provide four types of WS-HEQ, which partially refers to the structure of spatial histogram equalization (S-HEQ). In the experiments conducted on the Aurora-2 noisy-digit database, the presented WS-HEQ yields significant recognition improvements relative to the Mel-scaled filter-bank cepstral coefficient (MFCC) baseline and to cepstral histogram normalization (CHN) in various noise-corrupted situations and exhibits a behavior superior to that of S-HEQ in most cases.

Keywords: Sub-band division; Speech recognition; Robust speech features; Histogram equalization

1 Introduction

The performance of speech recognition systems is often degraded due to noise in application environments. A significant number of noise-robustness techniques have been proposed to address the noise problem, and one prevailing subset of these techniques is focused on reducing the statistical mismatch of speech features in the training and testing conditions of the recognizer. Typical examples are perceptual masking [1], empirical mode decomposition [2], optimally modified log-spectral amplitude estimation [3], wavelet packet decomposition with AR modeling [4], cepstral mean and variance normalization (MVN) [5], cepstral histogram normalization (CHN) [6,7], MVN with ARMA filtering (MVA) [8], higher order cepstral moment normalization (HOCMN) [9], and temporal structure normalization (TSN) [10]. In some of these methods, the compensation is performed on each individual cepstral channel sequence of an utterance by assuming that these channels are mostly uncorrelated [7].

Recently, certain studies have investigated the use of cepstral frame-based processing to compensate for the noise effect to achieve better recognition accuracy. For example, the work in [11] revealed that in the CHN method, even though each cepstral channel is processed by histogram equalization (HEQ), a significant histogram mismatch still exists among the training and testing cepstral features for the low-pass filtered (LPF) and high-pass filtered (HPF) portions of the intra-frame cepstra. Thus, the method of spatial HEQ in [11] further performs HEQ on the LPF and HPF portions to eliminate the aforementioned mismatch for the CHN-preprocessed cepstra. Compared with conventional CHN that processes each individual cepstral channel, spatial HEQ (S-HEQ) additionally takes the neighboring cepstral channels into consideration collectively and produces superior noise robustness. Furthermore, for a frame signal, the LPF and HPF portions of the cepstral vector just correspond to the logarithmic filter-bank (LFB) components at lower and higher frequencies, respectively. However, compensation performed directly on LPF and HPF is more helpful than that applied to the LFB components, most likely because the LFB components are significantly correlated [11].

*Correspondence: jwhung@ncnu.edu.tw
Department of Electrical Engineering, National Chi Nan University, Nantou 545, Taiwan

Partly inspired by S-HEQ, here we develop a novel scheme known as the weighted S-HEQ (WS-HEQ) to improve the recognition performance and operation efficiency of S-HEQ in three directions. First, because the LPF and HPF portions of the original or CHN-preprocessed cepstra possess different characteristics in noisy environments and provide unequal contributions to the recognition accuracy, we tune the portion of HPF produced in the original S-HEQ and show that this adjustment can outperform S-HEQ in recognition accuracy. Second, we change the order of the procedures in S-HEQ by first splitting the original intra-frame cepstra (not the CHN-preprocessed cepstra) into LPF and HPF, subsequently compensating LPF and HPF individually, and finally, normalizing the full-band cepstra. This new structure can reduce the effect of noise on the LPF and HPF portions in the plain cepstra more directly in comparison with S-HEQ. Finally, because S-HEQ requires three HEQ operations, we use the simpler process of MVN to replace any of the three HEQ processes in S-HEQ to improve the computational efficiency. The experimental results show that some variants of WS-HEQ, which require fewer HEQ operations, provide a similar or even better recognition accuracy relative to S-HEQ.

The remainder of this paper is organized as follows. Section 2 reviews S-HEQ, and the basic concept and detailed procedures of the proposed WS-HEQ are presented in Section 3. Section 4 describes the experimental setup, and Sections 5 and 6 contain a series of recognition experiments for WS-HEQ together with their corresponding discussions. Finally, the concluding remarks are summarized in Section 7.

2   Brief review of S-HEQ

If we consider using the Mel-scaled filter-bank cepstral coefficients (MFCC) as the baseline features for speech recognition, then the cepstral feature vector stream associated with an arbitrary utterance is represented by a matrix $\mathbf{C}$:

$$\mathbf{C} = \{c(m, n); 0 \leq m \leq M - 1, 0 \leq n \leq N - 1\}, \quad (1)$$

where m is the cepstral channel index within a frame and n is the frame index, and M and N are the total number of channels and frames within the utterance, respectively. In the temporal processing methods as MVN and CHN, the compensation is often directly performed on the individual channel stream (i.e., the sequence $\{c(\tilde{m}, n); 0 \leq n \leq N - 1\}$ with respect to the $\tilde{m}$th channel), and therefore, all of the channel streams of the features are treated independently. According to the general concept that the cepstral coefficients within a frame are mostly uncorrelated [7], such a process is quite reasonable.

Recently, a novel method known as the spatial HEQ (S-HEQ) was suggested to decompose each frame of a CHN-preprocessed cepstral vector into two parts, a high-pass filtered and low-pass filtered portion (denoted hereafter as HPF and LPF), such that the temporal sequences of HPF and LPF can be processed separately and then the updated HPF and LPF can be combined to form the new feature vector stream. The work in [11] shows that S-HEQ outperforms the conventional CHN by providing better recognition accuracy. The overall procedure of S-HEQ is depicted in Figure 1.

3   Proposed approach: WS-HEQ

S-HEQ [11] offers additional insight into the possible distortions left unprocessed by CHN and a method for achieving even better noise robustness for speech features. In this section, we further examine S-HEQ to assess whether it can be further improved. The following two observations can be made about S-HEQ:

1. S-HEQ divides each CHN-preprocessed cepstral vector into HPF and LPF and subsequently treats the temporal stream of these two parts in the same manner (i.e., with HEQ processing). Therefore, S-HEQ does not consider the characteristic differences between HPF and LPF. According to [11], the plain HPF (from the original cepstra, not the CHN-preprocessed cepstra) is often more vulnerable to noise and displays more mismatch than the plain LPF, whereas S-HEQ compensates for the CHN-preprocessed HPF and LPF directly. Additionally, HPF and LPF possess unequal importance in speech recognition, which will be shown later.

2. In S-HEQ, the HEQ operation is repeated up to three times: one for the original feature stream set and the other two for the HPF and LPF stream sets. Thus, S-HEQ requires twice more computational effort than the conventional CHN method, which only processes the original stream set once via HEQ.

In this work, we design a simple experiment to evaluate the relative importance of different sub-bands of the cepstral features in speech recognition. With the Aurora-2

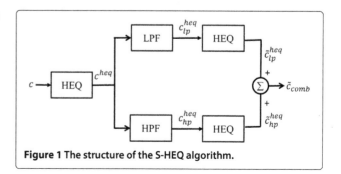

Figure 1 The structure of the S-HEQ algorithm.

database [12], we select 8,440 clean utterances for the clean-condition training task as the data used to train the acoustic models and 8,440 noisy utterances (corrupted by any of four types of noise at five signal-to-noise ratios) originally for the multi-condition training task as the testing data. Each utterance in the training and testing sets is first converted into a sequence of 13-dimensional cepstral vectors ($c0$, $c1$ to $c12$). The obtained cepstra are either kept unchanged or processed by CHN. Next, for each original/CHN-processed cepstral vector, we obtain its 'sub-band' version with the following two steps:

Step 1. Find the spectrum of the cepstral vector via discrete Fourier transform (DFT):
Let $\mathbf{c} = [c_0\, c_1\, c_2\, \ldots\, c_{12}]^T$ denote an arbitrary cepstral vector, and its spectrum is obtained by

$$C[k] = \sum_{m=0}^{12} c_m e^{-j\frac{2\pi mk}{13}}, 0 \le k \le 12. \quad (2)$$

Due to the conjugate symmetry of $\{C[k]\}$, we only need to retain the first seven points, which correspond to $\{k\frac{2\pi}{13}; 0 \le k \le 6\}$ in normalized frequency.

Step 2. Retain a contiguous portion of the spectral points and transform them (together with their conjugate symmetric parts) into a new cepstral vector via inverse DFT. For example, if we retain the first to fifth spectral points unchanged and set the zeroth and the sixth spectral points to zero, then the resulting new cepstral vector is a sub-band version of the original cepstral vector and corresponds approximately to the band range of $[\frac{2\pi}{13}, \frac{10\pi}{13}]$.

The recognition accuracy rates for different cepstral features obtained from the above sub-band processing are shown in Figures 2a and 3a, the former being for the original cepstra and the later being for the CHN-processed cepstra (Please note that the testing data undergo the same process as the training data in the recognition experiment. Therefore, the original testing cepstra are recognized by the acoustic models trained from the original training cepstra, and the CHN-processed testing cepstra are recognized by the acoustic models trained from the CHN-processed training cepstra). The vertical axis in Figures 2a and 3a denotes the word accuracy rate, and the other two axes indicate the initial and final spectral points, k_L and k_H, of the assigned sub-band, respectively. Obviously, the CHN-processed cepstra outperform the original cepstra in recognition results. Besides, for both types of cepstra the full-band features are always able to achieve the highest accuracy, and decreasing the bandwidth of the sub-band worsens the accuracy. However, we can further evaluate the relative importance of different spectral points in the sub-band from the two figures using the following equation:

$$r_m = \frac{1}{N_r}\left(\sum_{k>m+1}(R_{m,k} - R_{m+1,k}) + \sum_{k<m-1}(R_{k,m} - R_{k,m-1})\right), \quad (3)$$

where r_m denotes the averaged contribution of the mth spectral points, $R_{m,k}$ is the recognition rate using the cepstra within the sub-band including the mth to kth spectral points, and N_r is the total number of items in the summation of Equation 3. (The term 'relative importance' and its definition shown in Equation 3

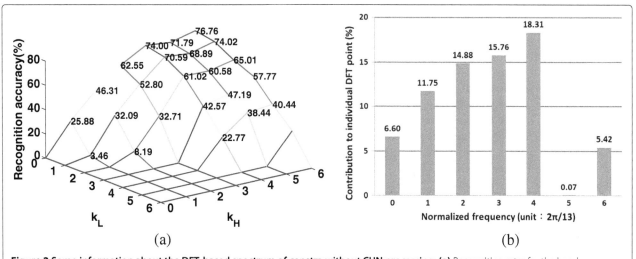

Figure 2 Some information about the DFT-based spectrum of cepstra without CHN processing. (a) Recognition rates for the band-pass filtered cepstra. **(b)** The contribution of each individual spectral point.

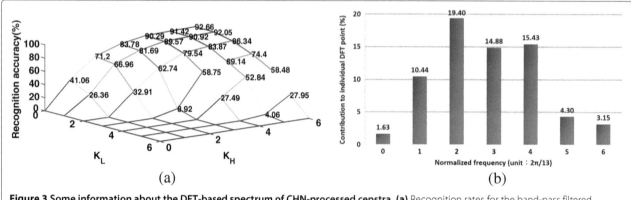

Figure 3 Some information about the DFT-based spectrum of CHN-processed cepstra. **(a)** Recognition rates for the band-pass filtered cepstra. **(b)** The contribution of each individual spectral point.

are borrowed from [13], in which a series of band-pass filters are used to evaluate the various *modulation* spectral components in their contribution to the recognition accuracy.) The obtained results from the original and the CHN-processed cepstra are shown in Figures 2b and 3b, respectively. Note that in Equation 3, the number of spectral points in the assigned sub-band range is always greater than or equal to 2 because the cepstra associated with a single spectral point quite often result in a rather poor (even negative) recognition accuracy.

From Figures 2b and 3b, the seven spectral points possess unequal importance in noisy speech recognition. The middle and lower frequency points (except for the DC point) seem to contribute more to the recognition accuracy than the upper points. These results suggest that alleviating the higher frequency components in the cepstra more likely results in better recognition performance in a noisy environment. Besides, comparing Figure 3b with Figure 2b, we find that the CHN process helps the higher frequency points to reinforce their importance in speech recognition, especially for the point at frequency $\frac{10\pi}{13}$.

The spectrum of the cepstra in the aforementioned evaluation experiment is created via the DFT, with the main reason that low-pass and high-pass filters are to be applied to the cepstra in later discussions, and we often evaluate the effect of a filter on the processed signal in the Fourier-based frequency domain. Also, in most cases, the characteristics of a filter are investigated by its frequency response; the Fourier transform, of its impulse response. However, since each frame-wise cepstral vector is the truncated version of the inverse discrete cosine transform (IDCT) of the logarithmic spectrum of the corresponding frame, here we reconduct the preceding evaluation experiment based on the 'DCT-based' spectrum of the original/CHN-processed cepstra. That is, in step 1 of the experiment, we obtain the 13-point spectrum

of any arbitrary cepstral vector $\mathbf{c} = [c_0 \, c_1 \, c_2 \, \ldots \, c_{12}]^T$ via DCT:

$$\tilde{C}[k'] = \sum_{m=0}^{12} c_m \cos\left(\frac{\pi (m + \frac{1}{2})k'}{13}\right), \quad 0 \leq k' \leq 12,$$

(4)

and then in step 2, a contiguous portion of the DCT-based spectral points is retained and transformed into a new cepstral vector via IDCT.

Some differences between the DCT-based spectrum $\{\tilde{C}[k']\}$ in Equation 4 and DFT-based spectrum $\{C[k]\}$ in Equation 2 are as follows:

1. Unlike the DFT-based spectrum $\{C[k]\}$ which is complex-valued and conjugate symmetric, in general, the real-valued DCT-based spectrum $\{\tilde{C}[k']\}$ is not symmetric in any sense. Thus, we cannot discard the second half points of $\{\tilde{C}[k']\}$ as we do on $\{C[k]\}$.

2. $\{\tilde{C}[k']\}$ possesses a higher frequency resolution than $\{C[k]\}$. Comparing Equation 4 with Equation 2, the frequency difference between any two adjacent bins of $\{\tilde{C}[k']\}$ is $\frac{\pi}{13}$, while it is $\frac{2\pi}{13}$ for $\{C[k]\}$.

3. Referring to [14], the N-point DCT, $\{\tilde{C}[k']\}$, of a length-N sequence $\{c[n], 0 \leq n \leq N-1\}$ (here $N = 13$), can be computed via a $2N$ DFT of another length-$2N$ sequence $\{\tilde{c}[n], 0 \leq n \leq 2N-1\}$, denoted by $\{D[k']\}$, in which $\tilde{c}[n]$ is the even extension of $c[n]$ satisfying $\tilde{c}[n] = c[n]$ for $0 \leq n \leq N-1$ and $\tilde{c}[n] = x[2N-1-n]$ for $N \leq n \leq 2N-1$. $\{\tilde{C}[k']\}$ and $\{D[k']\}$ are related by:

$$\tilde{C}[k'] = 0.5e^{-j\frac{\pi k}{2N}}D[k'] \text{ for } 0 \leq k \leq N-1. \quad (5)$$

Generally speaking, the DCT-based spectrum $\{\tilde{C}[k']\}$ is more concentrated at low frequencies than the DFT-based spectrum $\{C[k]\}$, which is well known as the 'energy compaction property' of DCT. An underlying reason for this phenomenon is that

DFT implicitly assumes the periodic extension of the processed signal and often causes the artificial discontinuities at the signal boundary, which adds high frequency contents in the DFT-based spectrum. To show this, a length-N sequence $\{x[n], 0 \leq n \leq N - 1\}$ is treated by N-point DFT as an N-periodic signal, denoted by $x_e[n]$, in which $x_e[n] = x[n]$ for $0 \leq n \leq N - 1$ and $x_e[n + N] = x_e[n]$. Thus, $x_e[n]$ is generally discontinuous at the (original) boundary positions:

$$x_e[0] = x[0] \neq x[N - 1] = x_e[-1], \tag{6}$$

$$x_e[N - 1] = x[N - 1] \neq x[0] = x_e[N]. \tag{7}$$

However, as mentioned earlier, the N-point DCT of a length-N sequence $\{x[n]\}$ (starting at $n = 0$) can be obtained from the $2N$-point DFT of the even extension of $\{x[n]\}$, and the corresponding $2N$-periodic signal, denoted by $\tilde{x}_e[n]$, remains continuous at the boundary positions:

$$\tilde{x}_e[0] = \tilde{x}[0] = \tilde{x}[2N - 1] = \tilde{x}_e[2N - 1] = \tilde{x}_e[-1], \tag{8}$$

$$\tilde{x}_e[2N - 1] = \tilde{x}[2N - 1] = \tilde{x}[0] = \tilde{x}_e[0] = \tilde{x}_e[2N]. \tag{9}$$

As a result, the (N-point) DCT-based spectrum does not contain the high frequency artifacts as the (N-point) DFT-based spectrum, and it appears more compact at low frequencies.

With the cepstra from the IDCT of sub-band DCT-based spectra, the corresponding evaluation experiment is performed to obtain the recognition accuracy rates, which are shown in Figures 4a and 5a, and the relative

importance of different spectral points are shown in Figures 4b and 5b. Figure 4a,b is for the original cepstra and Figure 5a,b is for the CHN-processed cepstra. These two figures roughly reveal that the lower and middle DCT-based spectral points contribute to the recognition more than the upper ones in recognition, which some-what coincides our observations from Figures 2a,b and 3a,b associated with the DFT-based spectra. In addition, comparing Figure 4b with Figure 2b and Figure 5b with Figure 3b, we find that the higher DCT-based spectral points reveal more importance than the higher DFT-based spectral points. which partially agrees with our previous statement that the DFT-based spectrum contains some artificial high frequency contents, which distort the higher spectral points and reduce the corresponding contribution.

In light of the aforementioned discussions, we developed a novel method known as the WS-HEQ to enhance the speech features in noise robustness. The initial concept of WS-HEQ is to apply a weighting factor to the HPF portion in S-HEQ (as shown in Figure 1) to reduce the intra-frame higher frequency components, and we further provide several variations on the presented WS-HEQ. First, according to the order of the HEQ processing for the full-band cepstra and sub-band cepstra, we describe two structures:

Structure I. HEQ first operates on the plain (intra-frame) *full-band* cepstra and subsequently on the *sub-band* cepstra.

Structure II. HEQ first operates on the plain (intra-frame) *sub-band* cepstra and subsequently on the *full-band* cepstra.

Please note that in the above two structures, the two sub-band cepstral portions, LPF and HPF, are obtained with

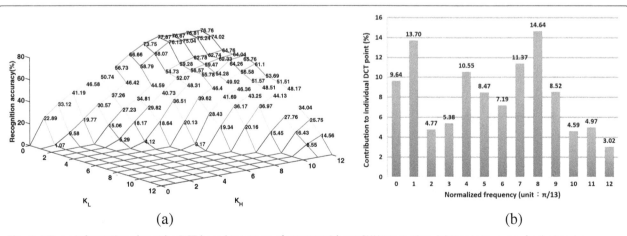

(a)   (b)

Figure 4 Some information about the DCT-based spectrum of cepstra without CHN processing. (a) Recognition rates for the band-pass filtered cepstra. **(b)** The contribution of each individual spectral point.

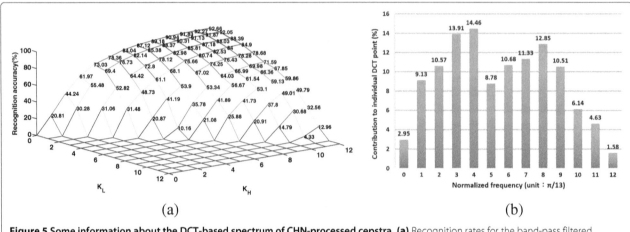

Figure 5 Some information about the DCT-based spectrum of CHN-processed cepstra. (a) Recognition rates for the band-pass filtered cepstra. **(b)** The contribution of each individual spectral point.

simple two-point FIR filters operating on the full-band cepstra [11]:

$$\text{LPF:} c_{lp}(m,n) = \frac{c(m,n) + c(m-1,n)}{2}, \quad (10)$$

$$\text{HPF:} c_{hp}(m,n) = \frac{c(m,n) - c(m-1,n)}{2}, \quad (11)$$

where $c_{lp}(m,n)$ and $c_{hp}(m,n)$ denote the low-pass and high-pass filtered parts of the nth cepstral frame.

Next, according to different treatments (i.e., the compensation methods, HEQ, and MVN) of LPF and HPF in Equations 10 and 11, each structure of WS-HEQ has the following four types of variations:

$$\text{Type 1:} \tilde{c}_{lp} = \textbf{HEQ}[c_{lp}], \tilde{c}_{hp} = \alpha \textbf{HEQ}[c_{hp}], \quad (12)$$

$$\text{Type 2:} \tilde{c}_{lp} = \textbf{MVN}[c_{lp}], \tilde{c}_{hp} = \alpha \textbf{HEQ}[c_{hp}], \quad (13)$$

$$\text{Type 3:} \tilde{c}_{lp} = \textbf{HEQ}[c_{lp}], \tilde{c}_{hp} = \alpha \textbf{MVN}[c_{hp}], \quad (14)$$

$$\text{Type 4:} \tilde{c}_{lp} = \textbf{MVN}[c_{lp}], \tilde{c}_{hp} = \alpha \textbf{MVN}[c_{hp}], \quad (15)$$

where $\textbf{HEQ}[\cdot]$ and $\textbf{MVN}[\cdot]$ denote the operators of the HEQ and MVN processes, respectively; $\tilde{c}_{lp}$ and $\tilde{c}_{hp}$ are the updated LPF and HPF, respectively (we omit the indices

(m,n) for simplicity); and the parameter α with a range of [0, 1] is the scaling factor selected specifically for the HPF component. The flowcharts of the various structures and types of WS-HEQ are depicted in Figure 6a,b.

For clarity, in the following discussions, the term 'WS-HEQ' is written with an additional subscript of 'I' or 'II', and a superscript of '(1)', '(2)', '(3)', or '(4)' to identify different structures and different processing schemes for LPF and HPF in the presented WS-HEQ method. For example, WS-HEQ$_{II}^{(3)}$ indicates that the WS-HEQ method applying the second structure shown in Figure 6b and uses HEQ and MVN for the LPF and HPF portions, respectively. Additional discussions on the various forms of WS-HEQ are given:

1. Because the HEQ operation is nonlinear, WS-HEQ$_{II}^{(1)}$ with $\alpha = 1.0$ (no attenuation for HPF) as shown in Equation 12 in which HEQ is first performed on the sub-band cepstra and subsequently on the full-band cepstra, is different from S-HEQ (equivalent to WS-HEQ$_{I}^{(1)}$ with $\alpha = 1.0$) shown in Figure 1, in

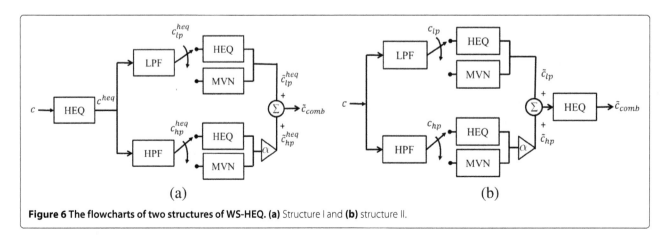

Figure 6 The flowcharts of two structures of WS-HEQ. (a) Structure I and **(b)** structure II.

which the full-band cepstra are HEQ-processed in advance.

2. In the first type of WS-HEQ$_{II}$, (*viz.* WS-HEQ$_{II}^{(1)}$), both LPF and HPF (of the original MFCC) are processed by HEQ. The resulting new HPF is attenuated by a factor of α and then combined with the new LPF to form the full-band cepstra, which are further processed by HEQ in the final stage. Therefore, WS-HEQ$_{II}^{(1)}$ requires three HEQ operations, the same as S-HEQ, demonstrating that S-HEQ and WS-HEQ$_{II}^{(1)}$ are similar in computational complexity.

3. The other three types of WS-HEQ as shown in Equations 13 to 15 differ from the first type in that they compensate either or both of the LPF and HPF portions via MVN instead of HEQ. MVN can be implemented more efficiently than HEQ because MVN involves only the operations of addition and multiplication, whereas a sorting algorithm is required in HEQ. We expect that the cost savings of HEQ on HPF/LPF will not affect the prospective recognition accuracy.

4 Experimental setup

The performance of our proposed WS-HEQ scheme is examined in two databases. One is the Aurora-2 database [12] corresponding to a connected English-digit recognition task, and the other is a subset of the TCC-300 database [15] for the recognition of 408 Chinese syllables. Briefly speaking, we conduct more comprehensive experiments with the Aurora-2 database for analysis and comparison upon the various forms of the presented WS-HEQ together with some other robustness algorithms, and a smaller number of experiments conducted on the subset of the TCC database are simply to examine if the presented WS-HEQ can be extended to work well in a median-size vocabulary recognition task which is more complicated than Aurora-2. Furthermore, in order to avoid the ambiguity and confusion in discussion, the remainder of this section and Section 5 are specially for the Aurora-2 evaluation task, while the detailed discussions about the TCC-300 subset task will given in Section 6.

As for the Aurora-2 database, the test data consist of 4,004 utterances, and three different subsets are defined for the recognition experiments: test sets A and B are both affected by four types of noise, and test set C is affected by two types. Each noise instance is artificially added to the clean speech signal at seven SNR levels (ranging from 20 to −5 dB). The signals in test sets A and B are filtered with a G.712 filter, and those in Set C are filtered with an MIRS filter. In the 'clean-condition training, multi-condition testing' evaluation task defined in [12],

the training data consist of 8,440 noise-free clean utterances filtered with a G.712 filter. Thus, compared with the training data, test sets A and B are distorted by additive noise, and test set C is affected by additive noise and a channel mismatch.

In the experiments, each utterance in the clean training set and the three testing sets is first converted to a 13-dimensional MFCC ($c0$, $c1$ to $c12$) sequence. Next, the MFCC features are processed by either S-HEQ [11] or the various forms of WS-HEQ noted in Section 3. In addition, the selected target distribution of the HEQ operation applied to any of the full-band, LPF, and HPF cepstra is the standard normal (Gaussian), with a zero mean and unity variance. (Please note that, given the full-band cepstral sequences being standard normal and approximately mutually uncorrelated, the corresponding LPF and HPF via the operations in Equations 10 and 11 are also standard normal. Similarly, if the HPF and LPF are both standard normal and approximately mutually uncorrelated, then the corresponding full-band cepstra are normally distributed with a zero mean and a variance of less than 1 since we scale down the HPF portion.)

The resulting 13 new features, in addition to their first- and second-order derivatives, are the components of the final 39-dimensional feature vector. With the new feature vectors in the clean training set, the hidden Markov models (HMMs) for each digit and for silence are trained with the scripts provided by the Aurora-2 CD set [16]. Each HMM digit contains 16 states, with three Gaussian mixtures per state.

In particular, the 8,440 noisy utterances (corrupted by four types of noise at five signal-to-noise ratios) originally for the multi-condition training task [12], which has been mentioned earlier in Section 3, are served as the *development set* here in order to obtain an appropriate selection of the scaling factor α for the HPF portion in Equations 12 to 15. The value of α is varied from 0.0 to 1.0 with an interval of 0.1 in each form of WS-HEQ, and then the one that achieves the optimal recognition accuracy for the development set is chosen for the corresponding WS-HEQ in practice. The selected values of α for different forms of WS-HEQ are listed in Table 1.

Table 1 Scaling factor α for each type of WS-HEQ

Structure I		Structure II	
Method	Optimal α	Method	Optimal α
WS-HEQ$_I^{(1)}$	0.6	WS-HEQ$_{II}^{(1)}$	0.6
WS-HEQ$_I^{(2)}$	0.6	WS-HEQ$_{II}^{(2)}$	0.6
WS-HEQ$_I^{(3)}$	0.5	WS-HEQ$_{II}^{(3)}$	0.7
WS-HEQ$_I^{(4)}$	0.7	WS-HEQ$_{II}^{(4)}$	0.6

It gives the optimal recognition accuracy for each WS-HEQ variant in the development set as to the Aurora-2 database.

Table 2 The recognition accuracy results (%) of the MFCC baseline, CHN, S-HEQ, and WS-HEQ with structure I

Method		Set A	Set B	Set C	Average	RR
MFCC		59.24	56.37	67.53	59.75	-
CHN		79.28	81.53	79.98	80.32	51.11
WS-HEQ$_I^{(1)}$	$\alpha = 1.0$ (S-HEQ)	81.56	84.51	80.78	82.58	56.73
	$\alpha = 0.6$	83.36	85.37	83.89	84.27	60.92
WS-HEQ$_I^{(2)}$	$\alpha = 1.0$	80.88	83.64	80.46	81.90	55.04
	$\alpha = 0.6$	82.29	83.22	82.82	82.76	57.16
WS-HEQ$_I^{(3)}$	$\alpha = 1.0$	79.66	82.51	79.33	80.73	52.13
	$\alpha = 0.5$	83.57	85.15	83.93	84.27	60.92
WS-HEQ$_I^{(4)}$	$\alpha = 1.0$	80.20	82.82	80.18	81.24	53.39
	$\alpha = 0.7$	82.88	84.70	82.78	83.59	59.23

They are for different test sets while averaged over five SNR conditions (20 to 0 dB) as to the Aurora-2 database. RR (%) is the relative error rate reduction compared with the MFCC baseline.

5 Experimental results and discussions for the Aurora-2 task

5.1 Recognition accuracy

The presented WS-HEQ is evaluated in terms of recognition accuracy. Tables 2 and 3 show the individual set recognition accuracy rates averaged over five SNR conditions (0 to 20 dB, with a 5-dB interval) for the MFCC baseline, CHN, S-HEQ (equivalent to WS-HEQ$_I^{(1)}$ with $\alpha = 1.0$), and various forms of the presented WS-HEQ, while Table 4 further lists the recognition accuracy rates for each individual SNR situations but averaged over ten noise situations. In addition, Figure 7 depicts the overall averaged word error rates achieved by several methods, including MVA, HOCMN, TSN, CHN, S-HEQ, WS-HEQ$_I^{(1)}$($\alpha = 0.6$), and WS-HEQ$_{II}^{(1)}$($\alpha = 0.6$). From Tables 2,3,4 and Figure 7, we have the following findings:

1. Compared with the MFCC baseline, all of the HEQ-related methods provide very similar accuracy rates for the clean situation, and they are able to provide significant improvement in recognition accuracy for various noise-corrupted situations, showing that HEQ is quite helpful for speech features in terms of noise robustness.

2. S-HEQ (WS-HEQ$_I^{(1)}$ with $\alpha = 1.0$) outperforms CHN by around 2.3% in the averaged accuracy, and thus, further manipulation of the mismatch in LPF and HPF with two extra HEQ operations can benefit the recognition performance.

3. WS-HEQ$_{II}^{(1)}$ with $\alpha = 1.0$ produces results similar to those of S-HEQ, and thus, the proposed structure II (shown in Figure 6b) performs quite well. Additionally, provided that no attenuation exists for HPF by setting $\alpha = 1.0$, using structure II in the other three types of WS-HEQ, i.e., WS-HEQ$_{II}^{(2)}$, WS-HEQ$_{II}^{(3)}$, and WS-HEQ$_{II}^{(4)}$ as shown in Equations 13 to 15, outperforms the respective

Table 3 The recognition accuracy results (%) of the MFCC baseline, CHN, and WS-HEQ with structure II

Method		Set A	Set B	Set C	Average	RR
MFCC		59.24	56.37	67.53	59.75	-
CHN		79.28	81.53	79.98	80.32	51.11
WS-HEQ$_{II}^{(1)}$	$\alpha = 1.0$	81.75	84.61	80.81	82.70	57.03
	$\alpha = 0.6$	84.13	86.16	84.39	84.99	62.71
WS-HEQ$_{II}^{(2)}$	$\alpha = 1.0$	82.59	84.93	82.03	83.41	58.79
	$\alpha = 0.6$	83.54	85.75	83.83	84.48	61.44
WS-HEQ$_{II}^{(3)}$	$\alpha = 1.0$	80.55	83.99	79.80	81.77	54.72
	$\alpha = 0.7$	83.25	85.10	83.50	84.04	60.35
WS-HEQ$_{II}^{(4)}$	$\alpha = 1.0$	80.83	83.44	80.37	81.78	54.73
	$\alpha = 0.6$	82.30	83.45	82.90	82.88	57.47

They are for different test sets while averaged over five SNR conditions (20 to 0 dB) as to the Aurora-2 database. RR (%) is the relative error rate reduction compared with the MFCC baseline.

Table 4 The recognition accuracy results (%) of the MFCC baseline, CHN, and eight forms of WS-HEQ

Method		Clean	20 dB	15 dB	10 dB	5 dB	0 dB	−5 dB
MFCC		99.12	95.33	86.62	65.93	36.01	14.86	8.16
CHN		98.97	96.30	93.89	88.48	74.81	48.10	19.94
WS-HEQ$_I^{(1)}$	$\alpha = 1.0$ (S-HEQ)	99.02	97.24	94.99	90.09	77.88	52.73	22.68
	$\alpha = 0.6$	98.99	97.60	95.72	91.54	80.62	55.87	23.26
WS-HEQ$_I^{(2)}$	$\alpha = 1.0$	99.02	97.34	95.14	90.10	77.38	49.57	18.40
	$\alpha = 0.6$	99.09	97.68	95.64	91.30	79.23	49.97	17.69
WS-HEQ$_I^{(3)}$	$\alpha = 1.0$	98.96	96.89	94.45	89.02	75.55	47.78	17.26
	$\alpha = 0.5$	98.99	97.51	95.71	91.59	80.59	55.95	23.88
WS-HEQ$_I^{(4)}$	$\alpha = 1.0$	98.93	97.20	95.01	89.75	76.57	47.68	16.92
	$\alpha = 0.7$	99.07	97.87	96.18	91.98	79.99	51.94	19.83
WS-HEQ$_{II}^{(1)}$	$\alpha = 1.0$	98.84	96.86	94.61	89.76	78.00	54.30	24.91
	$\alpha = 0.6$	99.05	97.53	95.75	91.99	81.35	58.35	26.98
WS-HEQ$_{II}^{(2)}$	$\alpha = 1.0$	98.87	97.41	95.50	91.15	79.06	53.96	22.29
	$\alpha = 0.6$	99.04	97.60	95.70	91.68	80.83	56.61	24.45
WS-HEQ$_{II}^{(3)}$	$\alpha = 1.0$	98.89	96.76	94.29	88.97	76.42	52.44	23.69
	$\alpha = 0.7$	99.05	97.87	95.98	91.86	80.62	53.88	20.51
WS-HEQ$_{II}^{(4)}$	$\alpha = 1.0$	98.92	97.13	94.84	90.07	76.92	49.96	19.89
	$\alpha = 0.6$	98.96	97.49	95.54	91.17	79.00	51.23	19.37

They are for different SNR cases while averaged over ten noise situations as to the Aurora-2 database.

methods under structure I. In particular, WS-HEQ$_{II}^{(2)}$ behaves better than WS-HEQ$_{II}^{(1)}$, whereas WS-HEQ$_I^{(2)}$ behaves worse than WS-HEQ$_I^{(1)}$, revealing that applying structure II can make WS-HEQ less costly in computation and can obtain improved recognition results simultaneously.

4. Reducing the HPF component by setting the factor α as less than 1.0 as in Table 1 significantly improves the recognition accuracy, regardless of the different structures and types of WS-HEQ. WS-HEQ$_{II}^{(1)}$ gives an averaged accuracy of 84.99%, which is optimal among all of the methods and corresponds to error

reduction rates of 62.71%, 23.73%, and 13.83% relative to the MFCC baseline, CHN, and S-HEQ, respectively. These results support the aforementioned observations that HPF is more extensively contaminated by noise and that lo wering HPF is beneficial.

5. Among the four types of WS-HEQ listed in Equations 12 to 15, by assigning α as less than 1.0, WS-HEQ$^{(1)}$, which requires three HEQ operations, displays the best behavior, regardless of the selected structure. However, the two types that require only two HEQ operations (i.e., WS-HEQ$^{(2)}$ and

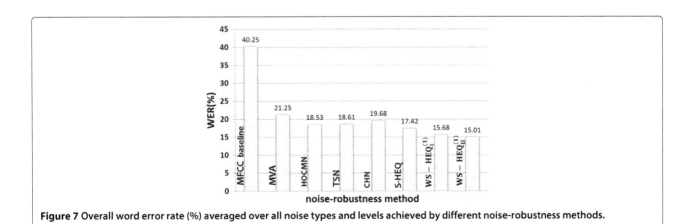

Figure 7 Overall word error rate (%) averaged over all noise types and levels achieved by different noise-robustness methods.

WS-HEQ$^{(3)}$) perform quite similarly to WS-HEQ$^{(1)}$ when structure II is used. Finally, WS-HEQ$^{(4)}$ performs worse than the other three types, possibly because it applies only one HEQ operation. Even so, WS-HEQ$_I^{(4)}$ and WS-HEQ$_{II}^{(4)}$ with $\alpha = 0.6$ can behave very close to S-HEQ (WS-HEQ$_I^{(1)}$ with $\alpha = 1.0$).

6. The presented WS-HEQ$_{II}^{(1)}$ with $\alpha = 0.6$ behaves better in the overall averaged word error rate when compared with several well-known noise-robustness methods: TSN, HOCMN, MVA, CHN, and S-HEQ. The absolute error rate reduction of WS-HEQ$_{II}^{(1)}$ with $\alpha = 0.6$ relative to the MFCC baseline is as high as 25.24%.

Taking a step further, among the methods used for comparison, MVA and TSN explicitly applies a temporal filter, and in most cases, the used filter is low pass so as to perform a 'temporal' smoothing on the cepstral time series. In contrast, the presented WS-HEQ lowers HPF (the high-pass filtered portion) of each cepstral vector and is analogous to a 'spatial' smoothing operation. Such an observation leads to the idea of combining either MVA or TSN with WS-HEQ in order to achieve a two-dimensional smoothing. To realize this idea, the cepstra are first processed with any of the eight forms of WS-HEQ and then further compensated by MVA or TSN. The obtained recognition results are shown in Tables 5 and 6, in which the applied WS-HEQ uses the scaling factor α listed in Table 1. As we look into the results shown in Tables 5 and 6, it can be found that the pairing of WS-HEQ and MVA/TSN consistently achieves better performance than the individual component method, regardless of the various forms of WS-HEQ. For example, the method 'WS-HEQ$_{II}^{(1)}$+TSN' obtains the averaged accuracy of 86.25%, better than TSN (81.39%) and

Table 5 The recognition accuracy results (%) achieved by the combination of MVA and WS-HEQ

Method	Set A	Set B	Set C	Average
MVA	78.15	79.17	79.12	78.75
WS-HEQ$_I^{(1)}$	83.36	85.37	83.89	84.27
WS-HEQ$_I^{(1)}$+MVA	84.95	85.60	84.97	85.21
WS-HEQ$_I^{(2)}$	82.29	83.22	82.82	82.76
WS-HEQ$_I^{(2)}$+MVA	85.34	85.89	85.69	85.63
WS-HEQ$_I^{(3)}$	83.57	85.15	83.93	84.27
WS-HEQ$_I^{(3)}$+MVA	84.84	85.59	85.38	85.25
WS-HEQ$_I^{(4)}$	82.88	84.70	82.78	83.59
WS-HEQ$_I^{(4)}$+MVA	84.62	85.70	84.90	85.11
WS-HEQ$_{II}^{(1)}$	84.13	86.16	84.39	84.99
WS-HEQ$_{II}^{(1)}$+MVA	85.08	86.43	85.40	85.69
WS-HEQ$_{II}^{(2)}$	83.54	85.75	83.83	84.48
WS-HEQ$_{II}^{(2)}$+MVA	85.81	86.69	86.17	86.23
WS-HEQ$_{II}^{(3)}$	83.25	85.10	83.50	84.04
WS-HEQ$_{II}^{(3)}$+MVA	84.18	85.69	84.48	84.84
WS-HEQ$_{II}^{(4)}$	82.30	83.45	82.90	82.88
WS-HEQ$_{II}^{(4)}$+MVA	85.14	85.41	85.87	85.40

They are for different test sets while averaged over five SNR conditions (20 to 0 dB) as to the Aurora-2 database. The scaling factor α listed in Table 1 is adopted for each WS-HEQ.

Table 6 The recognition accuracy results (%) achieved by the combination of TSN and WS-HEQ

Method	Set A	Set B	Set C	Average
TSN	80.86	82.39	80.46	81.39
WS-HEQ$_I^{(1)}$	83.36	85.37	83.89	84.27
WS-HEQ$_I^{(1)}$+TSN	85.32	86.77	85.01	85.84
WS-HEQ$_I^{(2)}$	82.29	83.22	82.82	82.76
WS-HEQ$_I^{(2)}$+TSN	85.06	86.21	84.75	85.46
WS-HEQ$_I^{(3)}$	83.57	85.15	83.93	84.27
WS-HEQ$_I^{(3)}$+TSN	85.35	86.54	85.15	85.78
WS-HEQ$_I^{(4)}$	82.88	84.70	82.78	83.59
WS-HEQ$_I^{(4)}$+TSN	84.41	85.81	83.96	84.88
WS-HEQ$_{II}^{(1)}$	84.13	86.16	84.39	84.99
WS-HEQ$_{II}^{(1)}$+TSN	85.59	87.41	85.26	86.25
WS-HEQ$_{II}^{(2)}$	83.54	85.75	83.83	84.48
WS-HEQ$_{II}^{(2)}$+TSN	85.77	87.08	85.34	86.21
WS-HEQ$_{II}^{(3)}$	83.25	85.10	83.50	84.04
WS-HEQ$_{II}^{(3)}$+TSN	84.68	86.75	84.25	85.42
WS-HEQ$_{II}^{(4)}$	82.30	83.45	82.90	82.88
WS-HEQ$_{II}^{(4)}$+TSN	84.59	85.32	84.59	84.88

They are for different test sets while averaged over five SNR conditions (20 to 0 dB) as to the Aurora-2 database. The scaling factor α listed in Table 1 is adopted for each WS-HEQ.

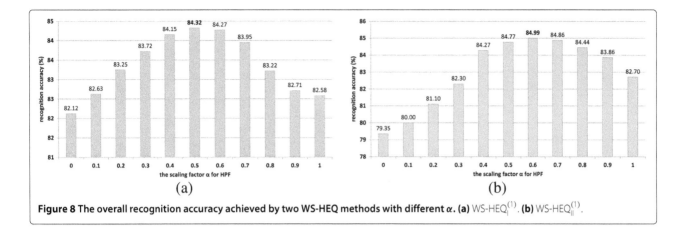

Figure 8 The overall recognition accuracy achieved by two WS-HEQ methods with different α. **(a)** WS-HEQ$_{\text{I}}^{(1)}$. **(b)** WS-HEQ$_{\text{II}}^{(1)}$.

WS-HEQ$_{\text{II}}^{(1)}$ (84.99%). These results indicate that the joint spatial-temporal smoothing can provide the cepstral features with better noise robustness in comparison with either spatial smoothing or temporal smoothing in isolation. In particular, different forms of WS-HEQ behave very similar and can give around 85% in averaged accuracy when TSN/MVA is integrated, implying that when employing TSN/MVA as a post-processing technique, simpler versions of WS-HEQ, such as WS-HEQ$_{\text{I}}^{(4)}$ and WS-HEQ$_{\text{II}}^{(4)}$, are relatively more appropriate in practical applications due to their high recognition performance and relatively low computation complexity in comparison with S-HEQ, WS-HEQ$_{\text{I}}^{(1)}$, and WS-HEQ$_{\text{II}}^{(1)}$.

5.2 The influence of the parameter α in WS-HEQ

As stated previously, the parameter α in WS-HEQ determines the degree of attenuation for the HPF portion of the processed cepstra. Here, we would like to investigate how the value of α in WS-HEQ influences the recognition accuracy of the test sets. For simplicity, we vary the parameter α from 0.0 to 1.0 in two types of WS-HEQ: WS-HEQ$_{\text{I}}^{(1)}$ and WS-HEQ$_{\text{II}}^{(1)}$, and the corresponding recognition accuracy rates averaged over all noise types and levels in three test sets are shown in Figure 8a,b. These two figures reveal that

1. Lowering the HPF part by tuning α from 1.0 to 0.4 in both WS-HEQ$_{\text{I}}^{(1)}$ and WS-HEQ$_{\text{II}}^{(1)}$ achieves better results consistently relative to these two WS-HEQ methods using $\alpha = 1.0$. However, further reducing the HPF part can ruin the recognition accuracy, which implies that the HPF part also contains information helpful for recognition.

2. The optimal accuracy for WS-HEQ$_{\text{I}}^{(1)}$ and WS-HEQ$_{\text{II}}^{(1)}$ occurs when α is assigned to 0.5 and 0.6, respectively, while the results from the development

Table 7 Recognition accuracy results (%) of WS-HEQ$_{\text{I}}^{(1)}$ using the optimal scaling factor α (in parentheses)

SNR	Set A					Set B			Set C	
	Subway	Babble	Car	Exhibition	Restaurant	Street	Airport	Train	MIRS subway	MIRS street
Clean	99.14 (0.5)	99.06 (0.5)	98.96 (0.9)	99.04 (0.9)	99.14 (0.5)	99.06 (0.5)	98.96 (0.9)	99.04 (0.9)	99.14 (0.6)	99.21 (1.0)
20 dB	96.87 (0.4)	97.61 (0.8)	98.51 (1.0)	97.41 (0.5)	97.73 (0.7)	98.07 (0.5)	98.27 (0.7)	97.90 (0.6)	97.33 (0.5)	97.91 (0.5)
15 dB	94.69 (0.4)	95.77 (0.6)	96.87 (0.6)	94.79 (0.5)	95.70 (0.7)	96.46 (0.5)	96.99 (1.0)	96.51 (0.5)	94.87 (0.4)	96.43 (0.7)
10 dB	89.84 (0.4)	91.38 (0.6)	92.93 (0.7)	89.57 (0.4)	91.74 (0.8)	92.53 (0.6)	93.89 (0.8)	93.58 (0.6)	90.24 (0.4)	92.08 (0.5)
5 dB	79.80 (0.3)	79.66 (0.6)	82.11 (0.5)	78.90 (0.4)	80.32 (0.7)	81.17 (0.5)	84.61 (0.7)	82.91 (0.5)	80.29 (0.2)	81.17 (0.5)
0 dB	57.69 (0.3)	50.00 (0.6)	55.41 (0.7)	57.42 (0.4)	55.30 (0.7)	56.77 (0.5)	62.69 (0.7)	58.04 (0.7)	58.12 (0.3)	56.77 (0.4)
−5 dB	26.74 (0.4)	20.16 (1.0)	20.16 (0.0)	28.85 (0.0)	23.76 (1.0)	24.76 (0.4)	27.65 (1.0)	21.97 (1.0)	26.71 (0.1)	24.15 (0.2)

This is with respect to each noise type and level (SNR) as to the Aurora-2 database.

Table 8 The recognition accuracy results (%) of WS-HEQ$_{II}^{(1)}$ using the optimal scaling factor α (in parentheses)

SNR	Set A					Set B			Set C	
	Subway	Babble	Car	Exhibition	Restaurant	Street	Airport	Train	MIRS subway	MIRS street
Clean	99.36 (0.7)	99.06 (0.8)	99.05 (0.8)	99.11 (0.4)	99.36 (0.7)	99.06 (0.8)	99.05 (0.8)	99.11 (0.4)	99.17 (0.7)	99.15 (0.4)
20 dB	96.56 (0.7)	97.52 (0.6)	98.12 (0.8)	96.98 (0.8)	97.54 (0.7)	97.94 (0.8)	98.42 (0.5)	98.36 (0.8)	96.96 (0.4)	97.76 (0.8)
15 dB	94.60 (0.4)	95.71 (0.7)	97.17 (0.7)	94.60 (0.5)	95.52 (0.6)	96.55 (0.6)	96.90 (0.6)	97.25 (0.8)	94.41 (0.6)	96.28 (0.6)
10 dB	89.65 (0.5)	92.14 (0.6)	93.83 (0.7)	89.48 (0.5)	91.83 (0.7)	93.05 (0.6)	94.72 (0.8)	94.32 (0.6)	89.75 (0.4)	92.62 (0.6)
5 dB	79.89 (0.5)	80.11 (0.6)	84.28 (0.8)	78.22 (0.5)	80.07 (0.7)	82.56 (0.5)	85.51 (0.8)	84.33 (0.6)	79.83 (0.4)	81.65 (0.6)
0 dB	58.27 (0.4)	53.42 (0.7)	61.65 (0.7)	57.27 (0.4)	56.77 (0.7)	58.92 (0.5)	65.49 (0.7)	61.65 (0.8)	57.72 (0.4)	58.74 (0.6)
−5 dB	28.43 (0.5)	22.76 (0.8)	28.81 (0.9)	30.48 (0.4)	25.85 (0.9)	27.33 (0.6)	31.26 (0.9)	29.28 (0.9)	29.60 (0.5)	27.42 (0.8)

This is with respect to each noise type and level (SNR) as to the Aurora-2 database.

set suggest the parameter α to be 0.6 for these two WS-HEQ methods (as shown in Table 1). However, WS-HEQ$_I^{(1)}$ with $\alpha = 0.6$ gives the recognition rate of 84.27%, very close to the optimal one (84.32%). Therefore, it assures us that the development set can help to determine the nearly optimal parameter in the test sets.

3. The performance of WS-HEQ$_I^{(1)}$ and WS-HEQ$_{II}^{(1)}$ is not very sensitive to the parameter α, which is based on the observation that the accuracy difference is below 1.0% provided the value of α is within the range [0.4, 0.7].

Next, we explore the best possible recognition results for each testing situation achieved by WS-HEQ with various assignments of the scaling parameter α. Please note that, in the preceding experiments the scaling parameter α in WS-HEQ is determined by the development set and then uniformly applied to the every test set. Here, we would like to investigate whether the optimal choice of α (which gives rise to the highest recognition accuracy) depends on the noise type and level (viz. the SNR) of the testing utterances. To do this, we vary the value of α from 0.0 to 1.0 with an interval of 0.1 in each form of WS-HEQ to process the features in the training and testing sets and then perform the experiment. The optimal recognition accuracy rate and the associated α with respect to each noise type and level in the testing set achieved by WS-HEQ$_I^{(1)}$ and WS-HEQ$_{II}^{(1)}$ are respectively shown in Tables 7 and 8. Some contents of the tables together with the data obtained from the other six forms of WS-HEQ (which are not listed here due to their huge amount) are further summarized in

Table 9 The recognition accuracy results (%) of various forms of WS-HEQ for different test sets

Method		Set A	Set B	Set C	Average
WS-HEQ$_I^{(1)}$	$\alpha = 0.6$	83.36	85.37	83.89	84.27
	Optimal α	83.86	85.56	84.52	84.67
WS-HEQ$_I^{(2)}$	$\alpha = 0.6$	82.29	83.22	82.82	82.76
	Optimal α	83.04	84.08	83.32	83.51
WS-HEQ$_I^{(3)}$	$\alpha = 0.5$	83.57	85.15	83.93	84.27
	Optimal α	83.86	85.46	84.43	84.62
WS-HEQ$_I^{(4)}$	$\alpha = 0.7$	82.88	84.70	82.78	83.59
	Optimal α	83.52	84.86	83.85	84.12
WS-HEQ$_{II}^{(1)}$	$\alpha = 0.6$	84.13	86.16	84.39	84.99
	Optimal α	84.47	86.39	84.57	85.26
WS-HEQ$_{II}^{(2)}$	$\alpha = 0.6$	83.54	85.75	83.83	84.48
	Optimal α	84.25	86.04	84.52	85.02
WS-HEQ$_{II}^{(3)}$	$\alpha = 0.7$	83.25	85.10	83.50	84.04
	Optimal α	83.84	85.85	84.05	84.69
WS-HEQ$_{II}^{(4)}$	$\alpha = 0.6$	82.30	83.45	82.90	82.88
	Optimal α	82.92	84.18	83.17	83.47

These results are obtained by using (1) the scaling factor α listed in Table 1 (2) the scaling factor α that achieves the optimal recognition accuracy with respect to the individual noise type and level (SNR), both of which are for different Test Sets while averaged over 5 SNR conditions (20 dB to 0 dB) as to the Aurora-2 database.

Tables 9 and 10, which also contain a portion of the data in Tables 2 and 3 for the purpose of comparison. Observing these tables, we find that the value of the factor α that achieves the optimal recognition accuracy indeed depends on the noise type and level of the utterances. However, there seems no general rule for selecting a better α with respect to any specific noise situation. Furthermore, as seen in Table 9, in most cases, the accuracy rates obtained with the optimal α associated with the individual noise situation are very close to the accuracy rates using a fixed α which gets the optimal results for the development set. The maximum difference between the above two types of accuracy rates is 0.75%, which occurs at the method of WS-HEQ$_{\mathrm{I}}^{(2)}$. As a result, we can roughly conclude that using the α recommended by the development set suffices to provide WS-HEQ with nearly optimal performance.

5.3 The feature distortion reduced by WS-HEQ

Apart from the recognition performance, in this subsection, we evaluate WS-HEQ in the capacity of reducing the

feature distortion caused by noise. The incoherent feature distortion [7] defined by

$$\varphi = \frac{\Sigma_k(|X[k]| - |\tilde{X}[k]|)^2}{\Sigma_k|\tilde{X}[k]|^2} \tag{16}$$

is measured for the feature streams processed by the noise-robustness method, where $\tilde{X}[k]$ and $X[k]$ denote the DFT of the noise-free clean feature stream and its noise-corrupted counterpart, respectively. Figure 9 depicts the feature distortion associated with any cepstral channel at the SNR of 10 dB, averaged over the 1,001 utterances in test set A of the Aurora-2 database, with respect to the feature streams processed by any of S-HEQ, WS-HEQ$_{\mathrm{I}}^{(1)}$ with $\alpha = 0.6$, and WS-HEQ$_{\mathrm{II}}^{(1)}$ with $\alpha = 0.6$. From Figure 9, two observations are made: first, WS-HEQ$_{\mathrm{I}}^{(1)}$ with $\alpha = 0.6$ results in smaller distortions than S-HEQ irrespective of the cepstral channel, implying that to lower the HPF portion of the cepstra can further reduce the

Table 10 The recognition accuracy results (%) of various forms of WS-HEQ at different SNRs

Method		Clean	20 dB	15 dB	10 dB	5 dB	0 dB	−5 dB
WS-HEQ$_{\mathrm{I}}^{(1)}$	$\alpha = 0.6$	98.99	97.60	95.72	91.54	80.62	55.87	23.26
	Optimal α	99.08	97.76	95.91	91.78	81.09	56.82	24.29
WS-HEQ$_{\mathrm{I}}^{(2)}$	$\alpha = 0.6$	99.09	97.68	95.64	91.30	79.23	49.97	17.69
	Optimal α	99.10	97.86	95.94	91.66	79.87	52.22	19.62
WS-HEQ$_{\mathrm{I}}^{(3)}$	$\alpha = 0.5$	98.99	97.51	95.71	91.59	80.59	55.95	23.88
	Optimal α	99.08	97.67	95.88	91.81	81.03	56.69	24.64
WS-HEQ$_{\mathrm{I}}^{(4)}$	$\alpha = 0.7$	99.07	97.87	96.18	91.98	79.99	51.94	19.83
	Optimal α	99.10	97.87	96.23	92.14	80.51	53.86	23.00
WS-HEQ$_{\mathrm{II}}^{(1)}$	$\alpha = 0.6$	99.05	97.53	95.75	91.99	81.35	58.35	26.98
	Optimal α	99.15	97.62	95.90	92.14	81.65	58.99	28.12
WS-HEQ$_{\mathrm{II}}^{(2)}$	$\alpha = 0.6$	99.04	97.60	95.70	91.68	80.83	56.61	24.45
	Optimal α	99.13	97.80	96.09	92.15	81.44	56.68	24.40
WS-HEQ$_{\mathrm{II}}^{(3)}$	$\alpha = 0.7$	99.05	97.87	95.98	91.86	80.62	53.88	20.51
	Optimal α	99.13	97.51	95.68	91.66	80.94	57.64	27.09
WS-HEQ$_{\mathrm{II}}^{(4)}$	$\alpha = 0.6$	98.96	97.49	95.54	91.17	79.00	51.23	19.37
	Optimal α	99.08	97.58	95.69	91.30	79.41	53.39	21.84

These results are obtained using (1) the scaling factor α listed in Table 1 (2) the scaling factor α that achieves the optimal recognition accuracy with respect to the individual noise type and level (SNR), both of which are for different SNR conditions while averaged over ten noise types as to the Aurora-2 database.

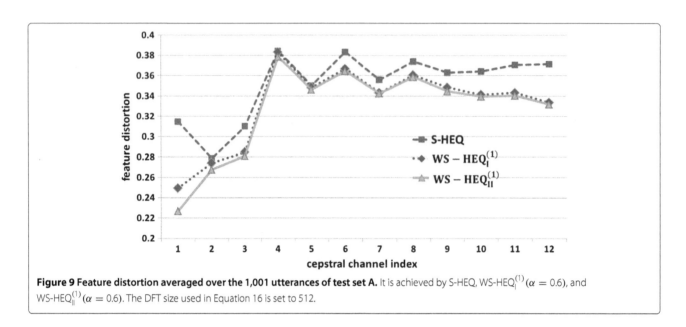

Figure 9 Feature distortion averaged over the 1,001 utterances of test set A. It is achieved by S-HEQ, WS-HEQ$_I^{(1)}$ ($\alpha = 0.6$), and WS-HEQ$_{II}^{(1)}$ ($\alpha = 0.6$). The DFT size used in Equation 16 is set to 512.

effect of noise; second, by setting the parameter α to 0.6, the distortions provided by WS-HEQ$_{II}^{(1)}$ are slightly smaller than those by WS-HEQ$_I^{(1)}$ for most of the cepstral channels, which agrees with the finding that WS-HEQ$_{II}^{(1)}$ slightly outperforms WS-HEQ$_I^{(1)}$ in recognition accuracy.

5.4 The effect of lowering HPF in different schemes
In order to further examine the effect of attenuating HPF in recognition accuracy, here we additionally design three schemes to process the cepstra in training and testing sets:

Scheme 1. The original (full-band) cepstra is split into LPF and HPF, and then the HPF portion is scaled by a factor α. Finally, the original LPF and the attenuated HPF are combined to constitute the new cepstra. This scheme is to remove all three HEQ processes in WS-HEQ$_I^{(1)}$ or WS-HEQ$_{II}^{(1)}$ shown in Figure 6a,b, and its flowchart is depicted in Figure 10a.

Scheme 2. The original (full-band) cepstra is preprocessed by HEQ, and then the

HEQ-preprocessed cepstra is split into LPF and HPF. We scale LPF by a factor α and finally combine LPF and attenuated HPF to obtain the new cepstra. This scheme is to remove the two HEQ processes for LPF and HPF in WS-HEQ$_I^{(1)}$ shown in Figure 6a, and its flowchart is depicted in Figure 10b.

Scheme 3. The original cepstra is split into LPF and HPF, and then the HPF portion is tuned with the scaling factor α. Next, we combine LPF and attenuated HPF to obtain the full-band cepstra, which are further post-processed by HEQ to obtain the new cepstra. This scheme is to remove the two HEQ processes for LPF and HPF in WS-HEQ$_{II}^{(1)}$ shown in Figure 6b, and its flowchart is depicted in Figure 10c.

The scaling factor α in the above three schemes is varied from 0.6 to 1.4 with an interval of 0.2. Please note that the case with $\alpha > 1$ corresponds to amplifying HPF and thus reducing the proportion of LPF in the overall cepstra. The recognition results for the three schemes are

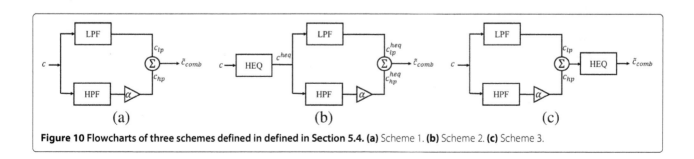

Figure 10 Flowcharts of three schemes defined in defined in Section 5.4. (a) Scheme 1. **(b)** Scheme 2. **(c)** Scheme 3.

shown in Table 11. From this table, we have the following observations:

1. At the clean noise-free case in all three schemes, the recognition accuracy remains as high as around 99% nearly irrespective of the varied scaling factor α, which implies that neither lowering nor raising the HPF portion of the cepstra can significantly influence the recognition performance. The possible explanation for this result is that the back-end acoustic modeling with HMMs compensates well for the variation of the front-end speech features.

2. From the results for scheme 1, reducing HPF (using $\alpha < 1$) without pre- or post-processing with HEQ produces degraded performance under noise-corrupted situations compared with the case using $\alpha = 1$, which disagrees with the results for various forms of WS-HEQ as shown in the preceding sub-sections. Under the same situations, setting $\alpha > 1$ to amplify HPF (and thus to reduce the proportion of LPF) cannot improve the accuracy, either. Therefore, the relative importance of LPF and HPF in noise-corrupted cepstra discussed in Section 3 cannot be reflected in recognition accuracy when there is no noise-robust processing such as HEQ. In other words, merely emphasizing LPF or HPF fails to result in more noise-robust cepstra and produces worse recognition accuracy.

3. Different from the results for scheme 1, the results associated with schemes 2 and 3 show that when the cepstra are pre- or post-processed by HEQ, reducing the HPF part by setting $\alpha < 1$ can promote the recognition accuracy under noise-corrupted situations (except for the case of -5-dB SNR). On

the other hand, the cases corresponding to $\alpha > 1$ in which HPF is raised produce worse results. The underlying reason is probably that the noise effect of HPF is relatively difficult to alleviate, and simply lowering HPF can benefit HEQ to give better performance. Similar situations can be also found in Tables 2 and 3 by comparing the results of WS-HEQ$_I^{(2)}$, WS-HEQ$_I^{(3)}$, WS-HEQ$_{II}^{(2)}$ and WS-HEQ$_{II}^{(3)}$ with $\alpha = 1$. WS-HEQ$_I^{(2)}$ and WS-HEQ$_{II}^{(2)}$ outperform WS-HEQ$_I^{(3)}$ and WS-HEQ$_{II}^{(3)}$, respectively, indicating a stronger normalization strategy like HEQ is required to compensate the distortion in HPF, while a relatively simple MVN process suffices to improve LPF well. Furthermore, comparing Table 11 with Tables 2 and 3 we find that the effect of lowering HPF in recognition accuracy appears a lot more significant when we further compensate the sub-band cepstra (*viz.* HPF and LPF) by HEQ/MVN, again in agreement with the statements about S-HEQ [11] that additionally normalizing HPF and LPF can reduce the environmental mismatch caused by noise.

6 The experiment on the TCC-300 Mandarin dataset

Besides the evaluation on the Aurora-2 dataset as described in the previous two sections, here the recognition experiments with the presented WS-HEQ are further carried out in another dataset, the eleventh group of the TCC-300 microphone speech database from the Association for Computational Linguistics and Chinese Language Processing in Taiwan [15]. This dataset includes 7,009 Mandarin character strings uttered by 50 male and 50 female adult speakers. The corresponding read

Table 11 The recognition accuracy results (%) of the three schemes defined in Section 5.4

	SNR	The scaling factor α				
		0.6	0.8	1.0	1.2	1.4
Scheme 1 (MFCC)	Clean	99.08	99.16	99.12	99.14	99.09
	20 ~ 0 dB	52.84	59.15	59.75	59.42	56.48
	−5 dB	6.13	7.67	8.16	7.70	6.87
Scheme 2 (pre-HEQ)	clean	98.95	99.00	98.97	98.92	99.00
	20 ~ 0 dB	81.84	81.41	80.32	80.16	80.04
	−5 dB	17.58	17.27	19.94	15.12	14.39
Scheme 3 (post-HEQ)	clean	98.97	99.00	98.97	98.99	98.84
	20 ~ 0 dB	81.19	80.42	80.32	79.72	79.35
	−5 dB	16.73	14.62	19.94	14.05	18.34

They are for the clean condition, the average of five SNR conditions (20, 15, 10, 5, and 0 dB), and the −5 dB SNR condition but averaged over the ten noise types as to the Aurora-2 database.

speaking-style speech signals were recorded with a microphone at the sampling rate of 16 kHz. The Mandarin characters included in the utterances of this dataset correspond to 408 different Mandarin syllables. In the experiment, the syllable recognition is performed on this dataset without any language model or grammar constraint at the back end so that the recognition performance can be more related to the used front-end acoustic features. As a result, in comparison with the 11-digit recognition on the Aurora-2 telephone-band dataset in the previous sections, here we conduct a more complicated task of medium-vocabulary recognition (408 syllables) on the broad-band speech data. Among the 7,009 Mandarin utterances in the TCC-300 subset, 6,509 strings are selected in acoustic model training, while the other 500 are in testing. The utterances in the training set are kept noise-free, while the utterances in the testing set are artificially added with noise at four SNR levels (20, 15, 5, and 0 dB) to produce noise-corrupted speech data. The

noise types include white (broad-band) and pink (narrow-band), both taken from the NOISEX 92 database [17]. These utterances for training and testing are first converted into 13-dimensional MFCCs ($c0$, $c1 - c12$), and then processed by various kinds of noise-robustness algorithms. Similar to the feature parameter settings for the Aurora-2 database, the resulting 13 new features plus their first- and second-order derivatives constitute the finally used 39-dimensional feature vector.

As for the acoustic modeling, we train the HMMs of INITIAL and FINAL units, which corresponds to the semi-syllables in Mandarin Chinese. In most cases, a Mandarin Chinese syllable can be split into INITIAL/FINAL parts analogous to the consonant/vowel pair in English. There are totally 112 right-context-dependent INITIAL HMMs and 38 context-independent FINAL HMMs to be trained. Each INITIAL HMM consists of five states and eight Gaussian mixtures per state, while each FINAL HMM contains ten states and eight

Table 12 Recognition accuracy results (%) of WS-HEQ for different SNR conditions at *white* noise environment

Method		Clean	20 dB	15 dB	10 dB	5 dB	Average
MFCC		76.38	30.08	14.72	6.23	3.52	13.64
CHN		76.52	55.22	43.56	30.90	18.84	37.13
WS-HEQ$_I^{(1)}$	$\alpha = 1.0$	77.15	56.48	46.81	33.05	19.40	38.94
	$\alpha = 0.6$	76.94	59.28	49.81	36.80	22.74	42.16
WS-HEQ$_I^{(2)}$	$\alpha = 1.0$	77.50	56.30	47.62	33.75	19.82	39.37
	$\alpha = 0.6$	76.07	59.63	49.88	36.73	23.74	42.50
WS-HEQ$_I^{(3)}$	$\alpha = 1.0$	77.08	55.92	44.94	32.09	19.36	38.08
	$\alpha = 0.6$	76.84	58.68	48.44	36.22	23.11	41.61
WS-HEQ$_I^{(4)}$	$\alpha = 1.0$	76.91	54.71	45.29	32.02	19.22	37.81
	$\alpha = 0.6$	76.59	58.14	48.95	35.89	23.11	41.52
WS-HEQ$_{II}^{(1)}$	$\alpha = 1.0$	77.96	56.88	47.46	33.82	20.94	39.78
	$\alpha = 0.6$	76.54	59.75	49.79	36.89	23.72	42.54
WS-HEQ$_{II}^{(2)}$	$\alpha = 1.0$	77.31	57.79	47.83	33.91	20.85	40.10
	$\alpha = 0.6$	76.33	59.86	49.72	37.24	24.37	42.80
WS-HEQ$_{II}^{(3)}$	$\alpha = 1.0$	77.92	57.18	46.36	33.70	20.64	39.47
	$\alpha = 0.6$	77.01	59.98	49.11	36.26	23.53	42.22
WS-HEQ$_{II}^{(4)}$	$\alpha = 1.0$	77.10	57.11	46.46	34.40	20.90	39.72
	$\alpha = 0.6$	77.24	60.07	49.91	36.85	23.65	42.62

These recognition accuracy results (%) of the MFCC baseline, CHN, and eight forms of WS-HEQ are for different SNR conditions at the white noise environment as to the subset of the TCC database.

Gaussian mixtures per state. The HMM for each of the 408 Mandarin syllables is then constructed by concatenating the associated INITIAL and FINAL HMMs.

Tables 12 and 13 list the syllable recognition accuracy rates of the MFCC baseline and the various robustness methods including CHN, S-HEQ (equivalent to WS-HEQ$_I^{(1)}$ with $\alpha = 1.0$), and seven forms of the presented WS-HEQ for the white and pink noise environments, respectively. The scaling parameter α in WS-HEQ is set to 0.6, which is not optimized but just to clarify whether lowering HPF can give rise to performance improvement. From these two tables, we have the following findings:

1. Due to the simple free-syllable decoding framework in the recognition procedure, the recognition accuracy of MFCC baseline features at the clean noise-free condition is just around 75%. Besides, the noise robustness methods used here result in similar or even better performance compared with the MFCC baseline when the testing utterances contain no noise.

2. Both types of noise degrade the performance of MFCC seriously as the SNR gets worse, while CHN and all of the other HEQ-related algorithms benefit the recognition accuracy significantly. In particular, the various forms of WS-HEQ with $\alpha = 1$ outperforms CHN, indicating that additionally processing LPF and HPF with HEQ or MVN can further enhance CHN to produce better results.

3. Reducing the scaling factor α from 1.0 to 0.6 in the eight forms of WS-HEQ consistently brings about better results by significant margins in all noise-corrupted situations. This result reconfirms the capability of the presented HPF lowering operation in boosting noise robustness of CHN-processed features. Furthermore, when α is set to 0.6, the performance difference among various

Table 13 Recognition accuracy results (%) of WS-HEQ for different SNR condition at the _pink_ noise environment

Method		Clean	20 dB	15 dB	10 dB	5 dB	Average
MFCC		76.38	59.44	44.24	22.34	5.85	32.97
CHN		76.52	61.40	52.71	38.06	24.30	44.12
WS-HEQ$_I^{(1)}$	$\alpha = 1.0$	77.15	62.83	53.96	39.62	25.09	45.38
	$\alpha = 0.6$	76.94	63.48	54.99	40.76	27.10	46.58
WS-HEQ$_I^{(2)}$	$\alpha = 1.0$	77.50	63.62	54.45	39.79	25.91	45.94
	$\alpha = 0.6$	76.07	63.11	55.22	40.35	26.94	46.41
WS-HEQ$_I^{(3)}$	$\alpha = 1.0$	77.08	61.38	51.89	38.06	24.44	43.94
	$\alpha = 0.6$	76.84	62.55	54.34	40.60	26.61	46.03
WS-HEQ$_I^{(4)}$	$\alpha = 1.0$	76.91	62.38	53.15	38.43	23.81	44.44
	$\alpha = 0.6$	76.59	63.15	54.50	40.14	26.14	45.98
WS-HEQ$_{II}^{(1)}$	$\alpha = 1.0$	77.96	63.04	54.15	39.83	25.63	45.66
	$\alpha = 0.6$	76.54	63.62	55.27	41.51	26.84	46.81
WS-HEQ$_{II}^{(2)}$	$\alpha = 1.0$	77.31	63.27	54.24	39.65	25.75	45.73
	$\alpha = 0.6$	76.33	62.62	55.29	40.81	26.82	46.39
WS-HEQ$_{II}^{(3)}$	$\alpha = 1.0$	77.92	62.50	53.19	39.86	24.98	45.13
	$\alpha = 0.6$	77.01	63.48	54.90	41.02	27.08	46.62
WS-HEQ$_{II}^{(4)}$	$\alpha = 1.0$	77.10	62.55	52.80	38.18	24.91	44.61
	$\alpha = 0.6$	77.24	63.13	54.52	40.88	26.91	46.36

These recognition accuracy results (%) of the MFCC baseline, CHN, and eight forms of WS-HEQ are for different SNR conditions at the pink noise environment as to the subset of the TCC database.

forms of WS-HEQ becomes relatively small in comparison with that under the condition of $\alpha = 1.0$.

7   Conclusions

In this paper, we explored the relative importance of different frequency components of the intra-frame speech features and subsequently presented a novel algorithm, WS-HEQ, to improve noisy speech recognition. WS-HEQ mainly reduces the intra-frame high-pass filtered component of the speech features, which appears more vulnerable to noise. Compared with the well-known S-HEQ method, WS-HEQ can achieve superior recognition accuracy, higher computational efficiency, or both. In future work, we will pursue new filter structures for obtaining the LPF and HPF components for WS-HEQ to achieve better results. Additionally, we will investigate how to tune the intra-frame speech features more flexibly in the corresponding DFT or DCT domains for further noise reduction.

Competing interests

The authors declare that they have no competing interests.

References

1. HK Maganti, M Matassoni, A perceptual masking approach for noise robust speech recognition. EURASIP J. Audio Speech Music Process. **2012**(29) (2012)
2. K Wu, C Chen, B Yeh, Noise-robust speech feature processing with empirical mode decomposition. EURASIP J. Audio Speech Music Process. **2011**(9) (2011)
3. I Cohen, B Berdugo, Speech enhancement for non-stationary noise environments. Signal Process. **81**(11), 2403–2418 (2001)
4. B Kotnik, Z Kačič, A noise robust feature extraction algorithm using joint wavelet packet subband decomposition and AR modeling of speech signals. Signal Process. **87**(6), 1202–1223 (2007)
5. S Tibrewala, H Hermansky, Multi-band and adaptation approaches to robust speech recognition, in *5th Eurospeech Conference on Speech Communications and Technology* (Eurospeech, Rhodes, 22–25 Sept 1997)
6. F Hilger, H Ney, Quantile based histogram equalization for noise robust large vocabulary speech recognition. IEEE Trans. Audio Lang. Process. **14**, 845–854 (2006)
7. J Benesty, MM Sondhi, Y Huang (eds.), *Springer Handbook of Speech Processing* (Springer, Heidelberg, 2008)
8. C Chen, J Bilmes, MVA processing of speech features. IEEE Trans. Audio Speech Lang. Process. **15**, 257–270 (2007)
9. C-W Hsu, L-S Lee, Higher order cepstral moment normalization for improved robust speech recognition. IEEE Trans. Audio Speech Lang. Process. **17**, 205–220 (2009)
10. X Xiao, ES Chng, H Li, Normalization of the speech modulation spectra for robust speech recognition. IEEE Trans. Audio Speech Lang. Process. **16**, 1662–1674 (2008)
11. V Joshi, R Bilgi, S Umesh, L García, MC Benítez, Sub-band level histogram equalization for robust speech recognition, in *12th International Conference on Spoken Language Processing* (Interspeech, Florence, 27–31 Sept 2011)
12. HG Hirsch, D Pearce, The AURORA experimental framework for the performance evaluations of speech recognition systems under noisy conditions, in *Proceedings of the 2000 Automatic Speech Recognition: Challenges for the new Millenium* (ISCA ITRW ASR, Paris, 18–20 Sept 2000)
13. N Kanedera, T Arai, H Hermansky, M Pavel, On the importance of various modulation frequencies for speech recognition, in *5th European Conference on Speech Communication and Technology* (Eurospeech, Rhodes, 22–25 Sept 1997)
14. X Huang, A Acero, H-W Hon, *Spoken Language Processing: A Guide to Theory, Algorithm and System Development* (Prentice Hall, New Jersey, 2001)
15. ACLCLP (1990). [http://www.aclclp.org.tw/corp.php], Accessed 10 Aug 2013
16. ELDA (1995). [http://www.elda.org/article52.html], Accessed 8 Aug 2013
17. AP Varga, HJM Steeneken, M Tomlinson, D Jones, The NOISEX-92 study on the effect of additive noise on automatic speech recognition. Technical report, DRA Speech Research Unit (1992)

11

Auditory processing-based features for improving speech recognition in adverse acoustic conditions

Hari Krishna Maganti[*] and Marco Matassoni

Abstract

The paper describes an auditory processing-based feature extraction strategy for robust speech recognition in environments, where conventional automatic speech recognition (ASR) approaches are not successful. It incorporates a combination of gammatone filtering, modulation spectrum and non-linearity for feature extraction in the recognition chain to improve robustness, more specifically the ASR in adverse acoustic conditions. The experimental results with standard Aurora-4 large vocabulary evaluation task revealed that the proposed features provide reliable and considerable improvement in terms of robustness in different noise conditions and are comparable to those of standard feature extraction techniques.

Introduction

Present technological advances in speech processing systems aim at providing robust and reliable interfaces for practical deployment. Achieving robust performance of these systems in adverse and noisy environments is one of the major challenges in applications such as dictation, voice-controlled devices, human-computer dialog systems and navigation systems. Speech acquisition, processing and recognition in non-ideal acoustic environments are complex tasks due to presence of unknown additive noise and reverberation. Additive noise from interfering noise sources and convolutive noise arising from acoustic environment and transmission channel characteristics mostly contribute to the degradation of speech intelligibility as well as the performance of speech recognition systems. This article addresses the problem of achieving robustness in large vocabulary automatic speech recognition (ASR) systems by incorporating principles inspired by cochlea processing in the human auditory system.

The human auditory processing system is a robust front-end for speech recognition in adverse conditions. In the recently conducted PASCAL CHiME challenge [1], which aimed at source separation and robust speech recognition in noisy conditions similar to that of daily life, the

performance of a human was much better than that of the ASR standard baseline for different signal-to-noise ratios (SNRs). As seen from Figure 1, the performance of a human is more robust and consistent than the ASR baseline. Further, the performance of both ASR baseline and human improved in line with the increase in SNR. This plot shows how susceptible the present systems are compared with a human listener with latest noise experimental setup.

The degradation of recognition accuracy for ASR systems in noisy environments is mostly due to the discrepancy between training and testing conditions. The training data are recorded in clean conditions, and the accuracy gets degraded when it is tested against data acquired in noisy conditions. Various speech signal enhancement, feature normalization and model parameterization techniques are applied at various phases of processing to reduce the mismatch between training and testing conditions [2,3]. Spectral subtraction-, Wiener filtering-, statistical model- and subspace-based speech enhancement techniques aim at improving the quality of speech signal captured through a single microphone or microphone array [4,5]. Feature normalization attempts to represent parameters that are less sensitive to noise by modifying the extracted features. Common techniques include cepstral mean normalization (CMN) which forces the mean of each element of the cepstral feature vector to be zero for all utterances. Other variants include

*Correspondence: maganti@ieee.org
Center for Information and Communication Technology, Fondazione Bruno Kessler, via Sommarive 18, Trento 38123, Italy

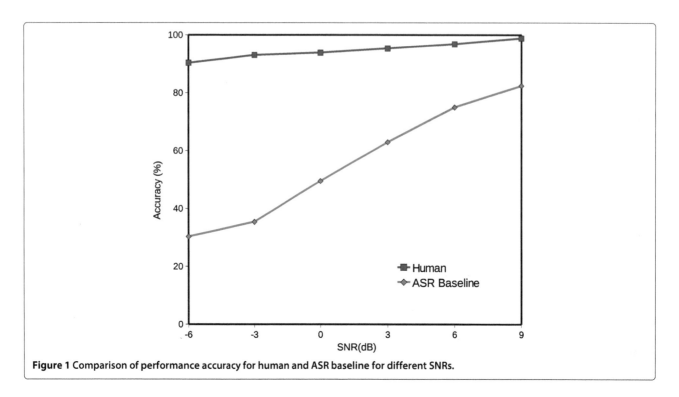

Figure 1 Comparison of performance accuracy for human and ASR baseline for different SNRs.

mean-variance normalization (MVN), cepstral mean subtraction and variance normalization (CMSVN) and relative spectral (RASTA) filtering [2,6]. Model adaptation approaches modify the acoustic model parameters' match with the observed speech features [4,7].

The auditory system-based techniques have been used in speech recognition to improve the robustness [8-15]. Examples of non-uniform frequency resolution in popular speech analysis techniques include Mel frequency-based features and perceptual linear prediction which attempt to emulate human auditory perception. The gammatone filter bank with non-uniform bandwidths and non-uniform spacing of center frequencies provided better robustness in adverse noise conditions for speech recognition tasks [12-15].

Another important characteristic, the modulation spectrum of speech, represents low temporal modulation components and is important for speech intelligibility [16,17]. Similar to the perceptual ability of human auditory system, the relative prominence of slow temporal modulations is different at various frequencies. The gammatone filter bank-derived modulation spectral features have shown to improve the robustness for far-field speaker identification [18]. Our previously described auditory-based modulation spectral feature is a combination of gammatone filtering and modulation spectral features for robust speech recognition [19].

The present paper describes an alternate approach, in which the gammatone filtering, non-linearity and modulation spectrum for feature extraction are combined. The enhanced speech signal improved the accuracy of the system by reducing the sensitivity. The features derived from the combination are used to provide robustness, particularly in the context of mismatch between training and testing in noisy environments. The studied features are shown to be reliable and robust to various noises for a large vocabulary task. For comparison purposes, the recognition results obtained by using conventional features are tested, and the usage of the proposed features is proved to be efficient.

The paper is organized as follows: Section Related work gives an overview of the auditory-inspired features including gammatone filter bank processing, modulation spectrum and non-linearity processing. Section Auditory processing-based features describes the methodology for feature extraction. Section Database description and experiments presents database description and experiments. Section Recognition results discusses the results, and finally, Section Conclusions concludes the paper.

Related work

Most state-of-the-art ASR systems perform far below the human auditory system in the presence of noise. Auditory modeling, which simulates some properties of the human auditory system, has been applied to speech recognition systems to enhance robustness. The information coded in auditory spike trains and the information transfer processing principles found in the auditory pathway are used in [20]. The neural synchrony is used for creating noise-robust representations of speech. The model parameters are fine-tuned to conform to the population discharge patterns in the auditory nerve which are then used to derive estimates of the spectrum on a frame-by-frame basis. This was extremely effective in noise and improved performance of the ASR dramatically. Various auditory processing-based approaches were proposed to improve robustness, and in particular, the works described in [13,20] were focused to address the additive noise problem. Further, in [21], a model of auditory perception (PEMO) developed by Dau et al. [22] is used as a front end for ASR, which performed better than the standard Mel-frequency cepstral coefficient (MFCC) for an isolated word recognition task. The auditory processing-related principles attempted to model human hearing to some extent have been applied for speech recognition [6,17]. The modulation spectrum is an important psychoacoustic property which represents a slow temporal modulation which is significant for determining speech intelligibility. For improving robustness, the normalized modulation spectra have been proposed in [23]. Similar work in the context of large vocabulary speech recognition such as noisy Wall Street Journal (New York, NY, USA) and GALE task as reported in [24,25].

Feature extraction at different stages of the auditory model output to determine which component has the highest impact on the accuracy of recognition has been studied [26]. The study also evaluated the contribution of each stage in auditory processing for improving robustness on the resource management database by using SPHINX-III speech recognition system (Carnegie Mellon University, Pittsburgh, PA, USA). Particularly, the effects of rectification, non-linearities, short-term adaptation and low-pass filtering were shown to contribute the most to robustness at low SNRs.

In another study [8], the techniques motivated by human auditory processing are shown to improve the accuracy of automatic speech recognition systems. It was shown that non-linearities in the representation, especially non-linear threshold effect, played important role in improving robustness. Other important aspect was the impact of time-frequency resolution based on the observations that the best estimates of attributes of noise are obtained by using relatively long observation windows and frequency smoothing provides significant improvements to robust recognition.

In the context of speaker identification, auditory-based features have been extensively studied [27]. The contrasts of MFCC and gammatone frequency cepstral coefficients (GFCC) have been compared, and the noise robust improvements by GFCC has been explained in [28].

In our earlier studies [19], several auditory processing-motivated features have shown considerably improved robustness for both additive noise and reverberation. However, all these above studies are confined to small and medium vocabulary tasks. In that direction, it is an attempt to apply these techniques for large and complex vocabulary task, namely Aurora-4, which is based on Wall Street Journal database. Artificially added noises ranged from SNRs of 5 to 15 dB with a variety of noises which include babble, car, street and restaurant. The effects at different stages of processing are analyzed to study the contribution of each stage for improving robustness. A preliminary version of our work was presented earlier [29].

Auditory processing-based features

In this section, a general overview of gammatone filter bank-, non-linearity- and modulation spectrum-based auditory features is presented.

Gammatone filter bank

Gammatone filters are linear approximation of physiologically motivated processing performed by the cochlea [30]. It is commonly used in modeling the human auditory system and consists of a series of bandpass filters. In the time domain, the filter is defined by the following impulse response:

$$g(t) = at^{n-1} cos \left(2\pi f_c t + \phi\right) e^{-2\pi bt}, \qquad (1)$$

where n is the order of the filter, b is the bandwidth of the filter, a is the amplitude, f_c is the filter center frequency, and ϕ is the phase.

The filter center frequencies and bandwidths are derived from the filter's equivalent rectangular bandwidth (ERB) as detailed in [30]. In [31], Glasberg and Moore relate center frequency and the ERB of an auditory filter as

$$\text{ERB}\left(f_c\right) = 24.7 \left(\frac{4.37 f_c}{1000} + 1\right) \qquad (2)$$

The filter output of the mth gammatone filter, X_m can be expressed by

$$X_m(k) = x(k) * h_m(k), \qquad (3)$$

where $h_m(k)$ is the impulse response of the filter.

The frequency response of the 32-channel gammatone filter bank is as shown in Figure 2.

Non-linearity

The sigmoid non-linearity that represents physiologically observed rate-level non-linearity is the same as that described in [26] and given by

$$y_i(t) = \frac{w_2}{1 + e^{(w_1 x_i[t] + w_0)}}, \qquad (4)$$

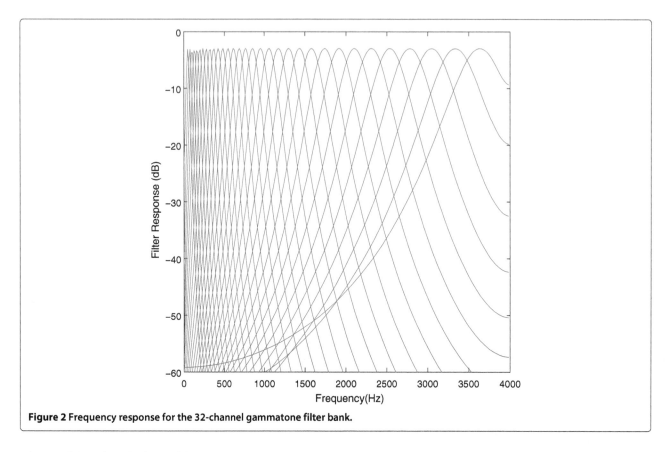

Figure 2 Frequency response for the 32-channel gammatone filter bank.

where $x_i[t]$ is the ith channel log gamma spectral value, and $y_i[t]$ is the corresponding sigmoid compressed value. The optimal parameters are derived from evaluation of resource management development set in additive noise at 10 dB [26].

Modulation spectrum

The long-term modulations examine the slow temporal evolution of the speech energy with time windows in the range from 160 to 800 ms, contrary to the conventional short-term modulations studied with time windows of 10 to 30 ms which capture rapid changes of the speech signals. The modulation spectrum $Y_m(f,g)$ is obtained by applying Fourier transform on the running spectra, obtained by taking absolute values $|Y(t,f)|$ at each frequency, where $Y(t,f)$ is the time-frequency representation after short-time Fourier analysis, expressed as

$$Y_m(f,g) = FT\left[|Y(t,f)|\right]|_{t=1,...T}, \qquad (5)$$

where T is the total number of frames, and g is the modulation frequency. The relative prominence of slow temporal modulations is different at various frequencies, similar to perceptual ability of human auditory system. Most of the useful linguistic information is in the modulation frequency components from the range between 2 and

16 Hz, with dominant component at around 4 Hz [16,17]. In [17], it has been shown that for noisy environments, the components of the modulation spectrum below 2 Hz and above 10 Hz are less important for speech intelligibility, particularly the band below 1 Hz which contains mostly information about the environment. Therefore, the recognition performance can be improved by suppressing this band in the feature extraction. Figures 3 and 4 show the spectrogram, gammatonegram and gammatonegram with non-linearity plots for two types of noise-corrupted utterance. It can be observed that the gammatonegram with non-linearity plots for babble and restaurant noises provide cleaner spectral information which is important for speech recognition.

Database description and experiments

The Aurora 4 evaluation task provides a standard database for comparing the effectiveness of robust techniques in LVCSR tasks in the presence of mis-matched channels and additive noises. It is a part of the ETSI standardization process and derived from the standard 5k WSJ0 Wall Street Journal database. It has 7,180 training utterances of approximately 15 h and 330 test utterances with an average duration of 7 s.

The acoustic data (both training and test) are also available in two different sampling frequencies (8 and 16 kHz), compressed or uncompressed. Two different

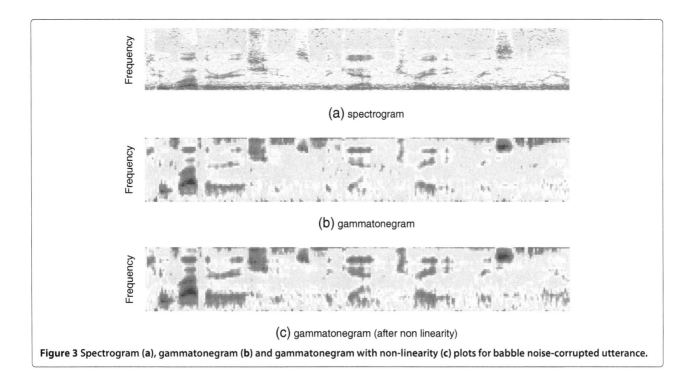

Figure 3 Spectrogram (a), gammatonegram (b) and gammatonegram with non-linearity (c) plots for babble noise-corrupted utterance.

training conditions were specified. Under clean training (clean train), the training set is the full SI-84 WSJ train set processed with no noise added. Under multicondition training (multi-train), about half of the training data were recorded using one microphone; the other half were recorded under a different channel (also used in some of the test sets) with different types of noise and different SNRs added. The noise types are similar to the noisy conditions in test.

The Aurora 4 test data include 14 test sets from two different channel conditions and six different added noises (in addition to the clean environment). The SNR was

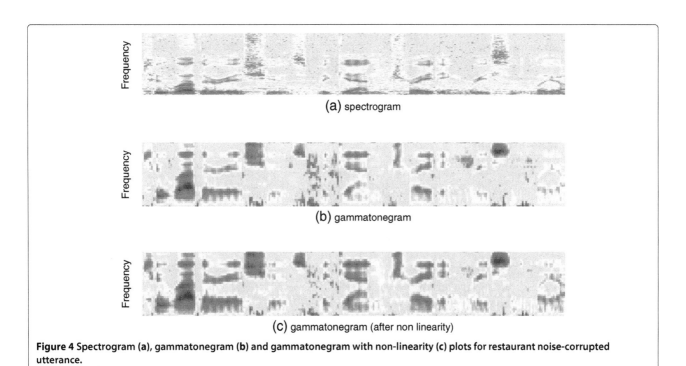

Figure 4 Spectrogram (a), gammatonegram (b) and gammatonegram with non-linearity (c) plots for restaurant noise-corrupted utterance.

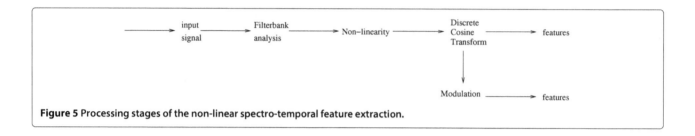

Figure 5 Processing stages of the non-linear spectro-temporal feature extraction.

randomly selected between 0 and 15 dB on an utterance-by-utterance basis. Six noisy environments and one clean environment no noise (set01), car (set02), babble (set03), restaurant (set04), street (set05), airport (set06) and train (set07) are considered in the evaluation set which comprises 5,000 words under two different channel conditions. The original audio data for test conditions 1 to 7 was recorded with a Sennheiser microphone (Lower Saxony, Germany), while test conditions 8 to 14 were recorded using a second microphone that was randomly selected from a set of 18 different microphones. These included such common types as a Crown PCC-160 (Elkhart, IN, USA), Sony ECM-50PS (New York, NY, USA) and a Nakamichi CM100 (Tokyo, Japan). Noise was digitally added to this audio data to simulate operational environments.

The block schematic for the feature extraction technique is shown in Figure 5. The speech signal first undergoes pre-emphasis (with a coefficient of 0.97), which flattens the frequency characteristics of the speech signal. The signal is then processed by a gammatone filter bank which uses 32 frequency channels equally spaced on the equivalent ERB scale as shown in Figure 2. The computationally efficient gammatone filter bank implementation as described in [32] is used. The gammatone filter bank transform is computed over L ms, and the segment is shifted by n ms. The log magnitude resulting coefficients are then decorrelated by applying a discrete cosine transform (DCT). The computations are made over all the incoming signal, resulting in a sequence of energy magnitudes for each band sampled at $1/n$ Hz. Then, frame-by-frame analysis is performed, and a N-dimensional parameter is obtained for each frame. The modulation energy of each coefficient, which is defined as the Fourier transform of its temporal evolution, is computed. In each band, the modulations of the signal are analyzed by computing FFT over the P ms Hamming window, and the segment is shifted by p ms. The energies for the frequencies between the 2 and 16 Hz, which represent the important components for the speech signal are computed. For the experiments and gammatonegrams shown in Figures 3 and 4, the values of L, n and N are 25 ms, 10 ms and 32, respectively, and modulation parameters of P and p with 160 and 10ms, respectively, are used.

Recognition results

The HTK setup followed is three-state cross-word triphone models tied to approximately 3,000 tied states, each represented by four-component Gaussian mixtures with diagonal covariance, together with the 5,000 closed vocabulary bigram language model (LM) [33]. Triphone states were tied using the linguistic-driven top-down decision-tree clustering technique, resulting in a total of 3,135 tied states in clean train and 3,068 tied states in multi-train. The CMU dictionary was used to map lexical items into phoneme strings, and the 5,000-word closed vocabulary bigram LM was used. The LM weights, pruning thresholds and insertion penalties were based on [33].

In order to analyze the effect of the non-linearity (Equation 4) on phone recognition rate, small subsets with a random number of utterances from AURORA-4 multi-condition training data are used. Experiments with training on clean condition are considered, because the purpose is precisely to test robustness in the presence of noise while retaining similar performance in clean conditions. All experiments have been performed with 16-kHz

Table 1 Accuracy rate (%) baselines for different feature extraction techniques

Channel	MFCC	PLP	GFCC
1	89.3	90.5	88.43
2	77.6	77.1	80.7
3	61.7	63.8	64.5
4	53.8	55.5	58.4
5	57.9	57.5	64.4
6	62.5	62.2	63.6
7	53.2	53.5	61.6
8	72.9	73.0	71.8
9	58.4	61.8	63.2
10	45.2	47.7	48.6
11	41.1	43.2	45.9
12	36.2	38.9	46.1
13	47.0	48.0	49.8
14	38.3	40.2	46.9
Average	56.7	58.0	61.0

Table 2 Accuracy rates (%) for the different extraction techniques

Channel	GFCC-MS	GFCC-MS-NL	GFCC-NL
1	87.3	89.9	89.6
2	80.7	83.4	81.1
3	62.6	72.8	70.9
4	56.0	69.2	65.6
5	64.5	71.6	69.4
6	62.6	73.2	70.1
7	62.0	66.9	68
8	69.7	74.4	71
9	61.7	63.8	62.4
10	48.2	52.3	51.9
11	44.5	51.2	50.1
12	43.0	50.8	48.4
13	47.2	54.3	51.6
14	46.8	50.4	50.2
Average	59.8	64.3	66.0

data of the Aurora-4 database. Table 1 shows the results in percent accuracy for the different features. The average performance for all the noise conditions for the different features is shown at the last row of the table. MFCC, perceptual linear prediction (PLP) and GFCC are the standard 39-dimensional Mel-frequency, perceptual linear prediction and gammafrequency cepstral coefficient features along with their delta and acceleration derivatives. From Table 1, it is clear that the traditional MFCC features have the lowest accuracy indicating inefficiency of these features for noisy environments. Also, it can be seen that GFCC has the best performance compared to PLP which, in turn, was better when compared to MFCC which is consistent with earlier studies [13,14].

Table 2 shows the results for gammafrequency with modulation spectrum (GFCC-MS), gammafrequency with modulation spectrum and non-linearity (GFCC-MS-NL) and gammafrequency with non-linearity (GFCC-NL) feature extraction techniques. For this task, we can see that the GFCC-MS do not provide any improvement which is contrary to our earlier study [29]. In our earlier study, the combination of GFCC and modulation spectrum was better than GFCC alone for isolated word recognition in reverberant environment of around 0.3 to 0.5 s.

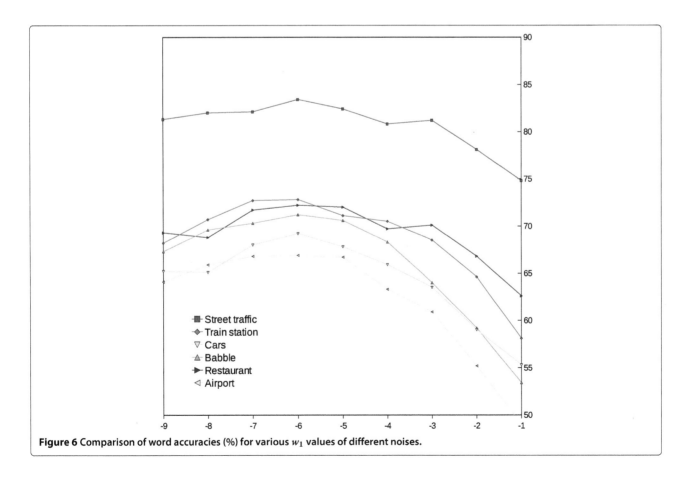

Figure 6 Comparison of word accuracies (%) for various w_1 values of different noises.

We hypothesize that we do not observe the similar effect in this case due to different task (large vocabulary with triphones) and different environment (only additive). However, from the table, we can see that the optimized non-linearity improved the performance of GFCC and GFCC-MS considerably. Further, we can also be observe that the contribution towards improved performance from the non-linearity is consistent for all types of noises. This clearly demonstrates that including a non-linearity is significantly beneficial for improving robustness in noisy environment.

The features are computed with $w_2 = 1.0$ and various w_0 and w_1 combinations. As seen from Figure 6, the selection of the weights is crucial for improving the recognition performance. It can also be observed that for w_1 ranging from -0.7 to -1.8, the performance is better than those of GFCC-MS and GFCC. The best performance for this task is obtained with $w_0 = 1$ and $w_1 = -0.9$ which are used for the experiments reported in Table 2.

Conclusions

The features proposed in the present study are derived from auditory characteristics, which include gammatone filtering, non-linear processing and modulation spectral processing, emulating the cochlear and the middle ear to improve robustness. In earlier studies, several auditory processing-motivated features have improved robustness for small and medium vocabulary tasks. The paper has studied the application of these techniques to large and complex vocabulary task, namely, the Aurora-4 database. The results have shown that the proposed features considerably improved the robustness in all types of noise conditions. However, the present study is essentially confined to handle noise effects on speech and has not considered reverberant conditions. The selected weights for the non-linearity were heuristic, and automatic selection of optimal weights from the evaluation data is desirable. For the future, we would like to investigate these issues and evaluate the performance of the proposed features for reverberant environments and large vocabulary tasks.

Competing interests

The authors declare that they have no competing interests.

References

1. J Barker, E Vincent, N Ma, C Christensen, P Green, The PASCAL CHiME speech separation and recognition challenge. Comput. Speech Lang. **27**(3), 621–633 (2013)
2. J Droppo, A Acero, robustness, Environmental, in *Springer Handbook of Speech Processing*, ed. by byJ Benesty, MM Sondhi, and Y Huang (Springer New York, 2008), pp. 653–679
3. MJF Gales, Maximum likelihood linear transformations for HMM-based speech recognition. Comput. Speech Lang. **12**(2), 75–98 (1998)
4. M Omologo, P Svaizer, M Matassoni, Environmental conditions and acoustic transduction in hands-free speech recognition. Speech Commun. **25**, 75–95 (1998)
5. R Martin, Noise power spectral density estimation based on optimal smoothing and minimum statistics. IEEE Trans. Speech Audio Process. **9**(5), 504–512 (2001)
6. H Hermansky, N Morgan, RASTA processing of speech. IEEE Trans. Speech Audio Proc. **2**(4), 578–589 (1994)
7. MJF Gales, SJ Young, A fast and flexible implementation of parallel model combination. ICASSP, **1**, 133–136 (1995)
8. C Kim, Signal processing for robust speech recognition motivated by auditory processing. Ph.D. Thesis, CMU, 2010
9. GJ Brown, KJ Palomaki, A reverberation-robust automatic speech recognition system based on temporal masking. J. Acoustical Soc. Am. **123**(5), 2978 (2008)
10. O Ghitza, Auditory models and human performance in tasks related to speech coding and speech recognition. IEEE Trans. Speech Audio Proc. SAP-2(1), 115–132 (1994)
11. D-S Kim, S-Y Lee, RM Kil, Auditory processing of speech signals for robust speech recognition in real-world noisy environments. IEEE Trans Speech Audio Proc. **7**, 55–69 (1999)
12. D Dimitriadis, P Maragos, A Potamianos, On the effects of filterbank design and energy computation on robust speech recognition. IEEE Trans. Audio Speech Lang. Proc. **19**, 1504–1516 (2011)
13. R Flynn, E Jones, A comparative study of auditory-based front-ends for robust speech recognition using the Aurora 2 database. Paper presented at the IET Irish signals and systems conference, Dublin, Ireland, 28–30, June 2006 pp. 28–30
14. R Schluter, I Bezrukov, H Wagner, H Ney, Gammatone features and feature combination for large vocabulary speech recognition. Paper presented in the IEEE international conference on acoustics, speech, and signal processing (ICASSP), Honolulu, HI, USA, 15–20 April 2007 pp. 649–652
15. Y Shao, Z Jin, DL Wang, S Srinivasan, An auditory-based feature for robust speech recognition. Paper presented at the IEEE international conference on acoustics, speech, and signal processing (ICASSP), Taipei, Taiwan, 19–24 April 2009 pp. 4625–4628
16. R Drullman, J Festen, R Plomp, Effect of reducing slow temporal modulations on speech reception. J. Acoustical Soc. Am. **95**, 2670–2680 (1994)
17. N Kanedera, T Arai, H Hermansky, M Pavel, On the importance of various modulation frequencies for speech recognition. Paper presented at the Eurospeech, Rhodes Greece, 22–25 Sept 1997 pp. 1079–1082
18. TH Falk, WY Chan, Modulation spectral features for robust far-field speaker identification. IEEE Trans. Audio Speech Lang. Process. **18**(1), 90–100 (2010)
19. HK Maganti, M Matassoni, An auditory based modulation spectral feature for reverberant speech recognition. Paper presented at the 13th annual conference of the International Speech Communication Association (Interspeech), Makuhari, Japan, 26–30 Sept 2010 pp. 570–573
20. L Deng, H Sheikhzadeh, Use of temporal codes computed from a cochlear model of speech recognition, chapter 15, in *Listening to Speech: An Auditory Perspective*, ed. by Greenberg S, W Ainsworth (Lawrence Erlbaum Mahwah, 2006), pp. 237–256
21. M Kleinschmidt, J Tchorz, B Kollmeier, Combining speech enhancement and auditory feature extraction for robust speech recognition. Speech Commun. **34**, 75–91 (2001)
22. T Dau, D Pueschel, A Kohlrausch, A quantitative model of the effective signal processing in the auditory system. J. Acoustical Soc. Am. **99**, 3615–3622 (1996)
23. X Xiong, C Eng Siong, L Haizhou, Normalization of the speech modulation spectra for robust speech recognition. IEEE Trans. Audio Speech Lang. Proc. **16**(8), 1662–1674 (2008)
24. V Mitra, H Franco, M Graciarena, A Mandal, Normalized amplitude modulation features for large vocabulary noise-robust speech recognition. Paper presented at the IEEE international conference on acoustics, speech and signal processing (ICASSP), Kyoto, Japan, 25–30 March 2012, pp. 4117–4120
25. F Valente, M Magimai-Doss, C Plahl, SV Ravuri, Hierarchical processing of the modulation spectrum for GALE Mandarin LVCSR system. Paper presented at the meeting of the International Speech Communication Association (Interspeech), Brighton, UK, 6–10 Sept 2009, pp. 2963–2966

26. Y-HB Chiu, B Raj, RM Stern, Learning-based auditory encoding for robust speech recognition. Paper presented at the IEEE international conference on acoustics, speech and signal processing (ICASSP), Dallas, TX, USA, 14–19 March 2010, pp. 4278–4281

27. X Zhao, Y Shao, DL Wang, CASA-based robust speaker identification. IEEE Trans. Audio Speech Lang. Proc. **20–25**, 1608–1616 (2012)

28. X Zhao, DL Wang, Analyzing noise robustness of MFCC and GFCC features in speaker identification. Paper presented at the IEEE international conference on acoustics, speech and signal processing (ICASSP), Vancouver, Canada, 26–31 May 2013, pp. 7204–7208

29. M Matassoni, HK Maganti, M Omologo, Non-linear spectro-temporal modulations for reverberant speech recognition. Paper presented at the joint workshop on hands-free speech communication and microphone arrays (HSCMA), Edinburgh, Scotland, 30 May–1 June 2011, pp. 115–120

30. M Slaney, *An Efficient Implementation of the Patterson-Holdsworth Auditory Filter Bank*, in Apple technical report, Perception Group, 1993

31. B Glasberg, B Moore, Derivation of auditory filter shapes from notched-noise data. Hearing Res. **47**, 103–108 (1990)

32. Ellis DPW, Gammatone-like spectrograms, http://www.ee.columbia.edu/~dpwe/resources/matlab/gammatonegram/. Accessed 6 June 2011.

33. N Parihar, J Picone, D Pearce, HG Hirsch, Performance analysis of the Aurora large vocabulary baseline system. Paper presented at the 12th European signal processing conference (EUSIPCO)n Vienna, Austria, 6–10 Sept 2004, pp. 553–556

12

The influence of speech rate on Fujisaki model parameters

Hansjörg Mixdorff[1*], Adrian Leemann[2] and Volker Dellwo[2]

Abstract

The current paper examines influences of speech rate on Fujisaki model parameters based on read speech from the BonnTempo-Corpus containing productions by 12 native speakers of German at five different intended tempo levels (very slow, slow, normal, fast, fastest possible). The normal condition was produced at an average rate of 6.34 syllables/s or 100%, the very slow version at 67%, and the fastest version at 161% of the normal rate. We extracted F0 contours and subjected them to decomposition using the Fujisaki model. We ordered all the data with respect to their actual speech rates. First, we assessed how prosodic realizations vary with speech rate and examined phrase command magnitudes, the number of phrase commands as well as the base frequency, accent command amplitudes, and the timing of accent command with respects to the underlying syllables and their nuclear vowels. Second, we analyzed between-sentence variability within and between speakers and investigated whether and how the prosodic structure is preserved at different speech rates. For very slow speech, we found for some of the speakers that the original phrase structure had disintegrated into something like a list of isolated words separated by pauses. Very fast speech became chains of uniform syllables at very high pitch and with almost flat intonation. With respect to the F0 range reflected by the amplitude of accent commands, we found strong interspeaker differences. While four of the subjects exhibited a significant reduction at higher speech rates, the others did not. As speed increases, it appears that F0 gestures commence earlier in the syllable, that is, the onset time of accent commands is located closer to the syllable/vowel onset than at lower speed.

Keywords: Speech rate; F0 contour alignment; Fujisaki model; Prosodic structure

1 Introduction

To date, there are only relatively few accounts of the effects of speech rate on fundamental frequency F0. It is well established, for example, that an increase in speaking rate correlates with a decrease in pauses and a decrease in prosodic boundary marking (cf. [1,2]). Caspers and van Heuven [3] reported that rises in Dutch are steeper at fast articulation rates. Ladd et al. [4] showed that in accentual F0 rises, rise time becomes shorter the faster the articulation rate.

In the current paper, we will employ the well-known Fujisaki model [5] to examine the dependency of F0 contour on the syllable rate. This model reproduces a given F0 contour by superimposing three components: a speaker-individual base frequency Fb, a phrase component, and an accent component. The phrase component results from impulse responses to impulse-wise phrase commands associated with prosodic breaks. Phrase commands are described by their onset time T0, magnitude Ap, and time constant alpha. The accent component results from step-wise accent commands associated with accented syllables. Accent commands are described by on- and offset times T1 and T2, amplitude Aa, and time constant beta.

Within the framework of the Fujisaki model, Fujisaki and Hirose [6] found that phrase command magnitude Ap is lower for speakers with fast articulation rates than for speakers with a normal or slow rate. Fujisaki and Hirose [5] reported that accent command amplitudes Aa, too, decrease in faster articulation rate conditions. Moreover, they showed that faster speaking rate leads to the merging of accent commands. In his D.Eng. thesis [7], the first author already addressed the influence of the speech rate on the intonational features of German, however, on a very small data set. A single trained

* Correspondence: mixdorff@beuth-hochschule.de
[1]Department of Computer Science and Media, Beuth University Berlin, Luxemburger Str. 10, Berlin 13353, Germany
Full list of author information is available at the end of the article

speaker was asked to read a short text at comfortable (henceforth 'medium'), slow, and fast speeds. Analysis showed that the fast version was produced at a speed 28% higher and the slow version at a 15% lower speed than the medium one. Ap and Aa for the N↑ and I↓ intoneme, that is, accents with rising or falling F0, respectively (see Section 2), become smaller when speed increases. This means that the F0 range is reduced. However, for these parameters, the mean difference between fast and slow versions only amounts to 17% for an overall speed difference of about 50%. Interestingly, the change between slow and medium versions was greater than between medium and fast versions, though the difference in speed was not. As explained before, increased speech rate reduces the number of prosodic phrases and also reduces the duration of pauses. It also leads to the merging of some accent commands that are separate at lower speed. In more recent work on Swiss German, Leemann [8] showed that higher articulation rates can lead to a reduction of phrase boundaries, which has an effect on the other intonation phrases, making them overall longer in duration.

Although these results seem to indicate an inherent coupling between speech rate and the F0 contour, one also has to take into account that speakers employ individual strategies when producing speech at different velocities. In their well-known cineradiographic study, Kuehn and Moll [9] performed measurements of the velocity and displacement of the tongue during speech production and found considerable intra-speaker variation of these two parameters. It has also been shown that in fast speech, segment shortening tends to cause phonetic target undershoot or spatial reduction of articulatory targets [10], which leads to reduced articulatory displacement toward the phonetic goal and slower peak velocity of participating articulators [9]. More generally speaking, speaker-specific articulatory strategies are an important factor in explaining the articulatory variations [11]. Hence, it can also be expected that the impact of speech rate on F0 gestures will to certain extent be speaker-specific.

The remainder of this paper is structured as follows: Section 2 introduces the methodology for modeling German intonation adopted in this work. Section 3 discusses the corpus employed in this study and the prosodic features we extracted from it. Section 4 then presents results of individual samples as well as statistical analyses of the entire corpus. Section 5 concludes this paper offering a discussion of the findings and conclusions.

2 The concept of intonemes and their quantitative analysis

We will discuss some of the basics of the framework adopted in this study. In the works of Isačenko and Schädlich [12] and Stock and Zacharias [13], a given F0 contour is mainly described as a sequence of communicatively motivated tone switches, major transitions of the F0 contour aligned with accented syllables. Tone switches can be thought of as the phonetic realization of phonologically distinct intonational elements, the so-called intonemes. In the original formulation by Stock, depending on their communicative function, three classes of intonemes are distinguished, namely the N↑ intoneme ('non-terminal intoneme', signaling incompleteness and continuation, rising tone switch), I↓ intoneme ('information intoneme' at declarative-final accents, falling tone switch, conveying information), and the C↑ intoneme ('contact intoneme' associated, for instance, with question-final accents, rising tone switch, establishing contact). Hence, intonemes in the original sense mainly distinguish sentence modality, although there exists a variant of the I↓ intoneme, I(E)↓ which denotes emphatic accentuation and occurs in contrastive, narrowly focused environments. Intonemes for reading style speech are predictable by applying a set of phonological rules to a string of text as to word accentability and accent group formation. Other F0 transitions - termed 'pitch interrupters' by Isačenko - will occur at phrase boundaries or in unstressed syllables where they do not have the same prominence-lending effect as tone switches (see [14]).

Based on this concept, Mixdorff and Jokisch [15] developed a model of German prosody anchoring prosodic features such as F0, duration, and intensity to the syllable as a basic unit of speech rhythm. In order to quantify the interval and timing of the tone switches with respect to the syllabic grid, the framework adopts the Fujisaki model for parameterizing F0 contours [1]. In a perception study [16] employing synthetic stimuli of identical wording but varying F0 contours created with the Fujisaki model, it was shown that information intonemes are characterized by an accent command ending before or early in the accented syllable, creating a falling contour. N↑ intonemes were connected with rising tone switches to the mid-range of the subject connected with an accent command beginning early in the accented syllable and plateau-like continuation up to the phrase boundary, whereas C↑ intonemes required F0 transitions to span a total interval of more than 10 semitones and generally starting later in the accented syllable, although the F0 interval was a more important factor than the precise alignment.

In the current study, we investigate the influence of speech rate on the realization of F0 contours. Tempo is a factor which we so far did not vary systematically within a larger range in our studies. We wish to explore how the three components of the Fujisaki model are influenced under different tempo conditions:

(1) On the utterance level: The base frequency Fb marks the floor of the F0 pattern. So far, we regard

Fb as a speaker-individual constant varying only slightly. However, we have observed that Fb can also vary depending on the emotional content of an utterance, for instance [17].

(2) On the phrase level: The phrase magnitude Ap reflects the degree of declination line reset at phrase boundaries. Earlier work suggested that Ap decreases as the tempo rises. We also expect to find fewer phrase commands at higher tempos as prosodic phrases will merge.

(3) On the syllable level: The accent command amplitude Aa corresponds to the interval of local F0 excursions associated with accented syllables and boundary tones. So far, we assume that Aa decreases with increasing tempo, and due to accent command merging or suppression of secondary accents, there will be fewer accent commands. The accent command onset times T1 and accent command offset times T2 with respect to the underlying syllable or nuclear vowel onset or offset times reflect the precise alignment of F0 excursions with the segmental tier. We hypothesize that increased speech rate also requires the F0 gesture to occur earlier in the syllable. We also wish to examine whether accent commands and hence the F0 gestures are more strongly anchored to the nuclear vowel onset than to the onset of the syllable.

3 Speech material and method of analysis

The speech material used in the current study are the recordings of the German L1 speech from the BonnTempo-Corpus [18,19]. It contains data from four male and eight female native speakers of standard German. The corpus is based on readings of a text from a novel by Schlink [20] of 76 syllables in three sentences (four main and three subordinate clauses). Versions at different tempos were elicited as follows: Subjects were provided the text and asked to familiarize with it by reading it aloud several times. Subsequently, they were recorded performing the task to read the text in a way they considered 'normal reading'. After that, subjects were recorded twice, the first time being instructed to read the text 'slowly' and the second time to read the text 'even slower'. In a third step, subjects were recorded under the instruction to read the text 'fast' and were then encouraged to read the text 'faster' until they considered themselves having reached a maximum reading speed or until their performance seriously deteriorated. From the resulting materials, five versions are examined in the current study: normal (no), slow (s1), even slower (s2), fast (f1), and fastest (f2). These were labeled on the syllabic level by the third author and his colleagues. In addition, they labeled the nuclear vowels. We are aware that the syllabic rate as a correlate of speech rate

is inferior to the perceptual local speech rate (PLSR) proposed by Pfitzinger [21], as the local syllable rate and the local phone rate are not well-correlated, since they represent different perceptual aspects of speech rate. Perception experiments with short stretches of speech being judged on a rate scale revealed that neither syllable rate nor phone rate is sufficient to predict the perception results. Subsequently, it was shown that a linear combination of the two measures yielded a correlation of $r = 0.91$ and a mean deviation of 10% which is accurate enough to successfully extract PLSR from large spoken language corpora. However, the BonnTempo-Corpus does not contain manually corrected phone labels. Since the Fujisaki model commands are anchored to the syllabic layer (see Section 2) and we did not require an exact local estimate of speech rate, but a broad classification of speech rate on the utterance level, the following investigation is performed with respect to the syllabic rate. Based on the underlying text of the utterances, we marked all lexically stressed syllables of content words.

F0 values were extracted at a step of 10 ms with F0 floors and ceilings for male (50 to 300 Hz) and female participants (120 to 400 Hz) using the *PRAAT* default method [22]. All F0 contours were then subjected to Fujisaki model parameter extraction [23], with an alpha of 2.0/s, beta of 20.0/s and variable Fb. Results were checked and if necessary corrected in the *FujiParaEditor* [24]. Evaluating the alignment between phrase and accent commands with respect to the underlying syllables, while taking into account the status of these syllables as either being lexically stressed or not, we associated each accent command with the closest syllable. As explained in Section 1, a rising tone switch is invariably connected with the onset of an accent command and a falling tone switch with an offset of an accent command. All other accent command onsets or offsets are related to pitch interrupters at unaccented syllables.

Statistical analysis of tone switch alignment indicated that rising tone switches are most closely linked to syllable onsets, whereas falling tone switches are more closely aligned with syllable offsets. It has also been observed that falling or rising tone switches related to accented syllables do not necessarily occur during those syllables but before or after, respectively. Therefore, the search for the best alignment option has to include the neighboring syllables. Once the locations of stressed syllables have been scanned for accent commands nearby, the rest of the commands are aligned with the closest syllable based on a criterion of maximum overlap, Figure 1 shows the most important alignment options taken into account.

With respect to phrase command locations, the first command in an utterance will always be associated with the first syllable of that utterance. Due to the rise-fall

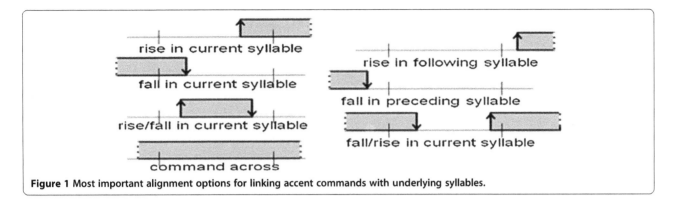

Figure 1 Most important alignment options for linking accent commands with underlying syllables.

characteristics of the phrase component, however, the phrase command usually occurs a few hundred milliseconds before utterance onset and the maximum of the phrase component ideally coincides with the segmental onset (see example in Figure 2). Subsequent phrase commands can be linked to following phrases, especially when these are preceded by short pauses. However, at many shallow boundaries, phrase commands will not appear as we will also see in the material examined in this study.

4 Results of analysis

4.1 General observations

Table 1 lists syllable rates for all speakers in all five different tempo conditions. Besides, syllable rates were expressed as percentages of the rate calculated for the normal condition for each speaker set to 100%. As can be seen, individual rates actually produced vary considerably, much more so for the decelerated and the accelerated versions than for the normal condition. On the average, the fastest condition was produced 61% faster than the normal one, whereas deceleration decreased the rate only by 33%, though individual results were much slower than that, especially for speakers 4 and 7.

Figure 2 shows results of analysis for all tempos produced by female speaker 1 uttering the sentence 1 *Am nächsten Tag fuhr ich nach Husum* - 'On the next day I went to Husum'. The figure displays the following, from the top to the bottom: the speech waveform, the F0 contour (+signs, extracted; solid line, model-based), the German SAMPA phone segmentation, the underlying phrase, and accent commands. The boundaries of underlying syllables are indicated by vertical dotted lines. Vowels carrying lexical stress are marked by bracketing, for instance (E:). Pauses are marked by underscores '_'.

As can be seen, the prosodic structure as reflected by the configuration of underlying accent commands aligned with accented syllables remains intact throughout all conditions, although the amplitudes Aa, durations, and alignments of commands vary. There is a tendency for Aa as well as for the durations of accent

commands to become smaller as speed increases. The pause after 'Tag' only disappears in the fastest condition. The declination lines in all utterances can be modeled by a single-phrase command preceding each utterance about 475 ms before the segmental onset. This is slightly smaller than the ideal value of 500 ms. It has to be taken into account that the automatic extraction method aims at pertaining a global optimum of fit for the entire phrase component. This may lead to the phrase command occurring closer to the segmental onset of the phrase.

Figure 3 shows results of analysis by male speaker 4 in the very slow (top) and normal (bottom) conditions. Speaker 4 was one of the subjects who produced his slowest version at around one third the speed of the normal one. Obviously, the sentence was chunked into single words, even syllables, associated with underlying accent commands and often separated by pauses. Comparison with the normal condition by the same speaker shows that low speed does not entail that the accent command amplitude Aa increases, only the number of accent commands rises, as well as the number of phrase commands, as each word virtually becomes a prosodic phrase.

Figure 4 displays another extreme case from the upper limit of the tempo range. It shows sentence 2 uttered by female speaker 6 at fast and very fast speeds. The prosodic structure reflected by the underlying accent commands in the fast version gives way to an almost completely flat F0 contour and a very high value of Fb in the very fast condition. Obviously, the articulation rate becomes so high that proper F0 control can no longer be executed. Overall, we find moderate correlations (Pearson's $r = 0.44$, $P < 0.001$) between Fb and the syllable rate of each utterance indicating that the F0 pattern is raised at higher tempos.

All data were analyzed using R [25] and the R packages *lme4* [26], *languageR* [27,28], and JMP [29]. If not indicated otherwise, data were analyzed using linear mixed effect models. Normality was checked by visual inspection of quantile plots. *Speaker* and *sentence* were

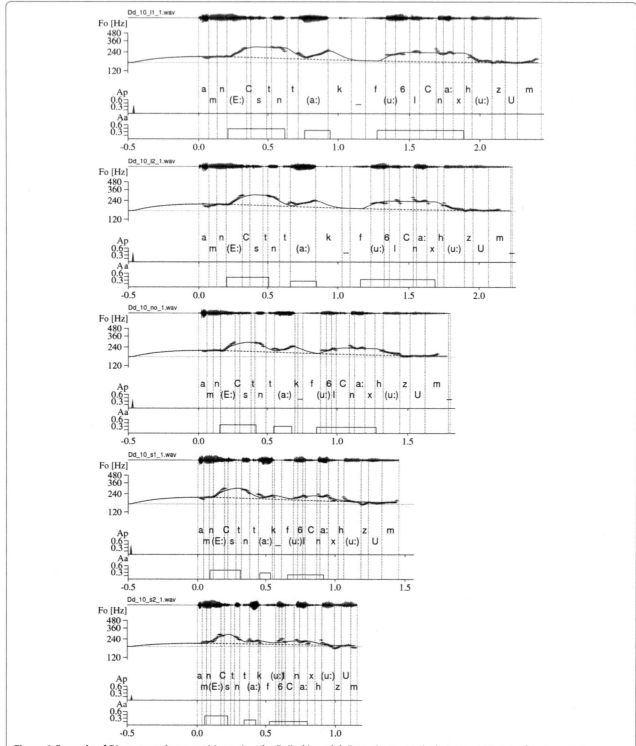

Figure 2 Example of F0 contour decomposition using the Fujisaki model. From the top to the bottom: utterances of sentence 1 *Am nächsten Tag fuhr ich nach Husum* - 'On the next day I went to Husum' produced by female speaker 1 at very slow, slow, normal, fast, and very fast tempo. Lexically stressed vowels are marked by brackets.

treated as random effects, and *intended tempo* as fixed effect. Effects were tested by model comparison between a full model in which the factor in question is entered as either a fixed or a random effect (R code example: lmer (dependent_variable ~ fixed_factor + (1|random_factor1) + (1|random_factor2), data = data)) and a reduced model in

Table 1 Overview of speaker-specific means (*M*) and standard deviations (SD) of syllable rate for the five different intended tempos

Speaker	1 Very slow			2 Slow			3 Normal			4 Fast			5 Very fast		
	M/SD/% normal			M/SD/% normal			M/SD/% normal			M/SD/% normal			M/SD/% normal		
1	4.94	1.86	76	5.57	2.24	85	6.54	2.97	100	7.48	3.33	114	8.98	3.26	137
2	4.72	2.05	67	6.02	2.95	85	7.06	2.89	100	7.29	3.16	103	9.83	3.83	139
3	4.93	1.99	83	5.57	2.40	94	5.91	2.31	100	6.16	2.51	104	9.12	3.74	154
4	2.25	0.83	33	4.63	1.85	67	6.86	2.73	100	7.49	2.84	109	12.04	4.51	176
5	3.98	1.56	85	4.44	1.70	94	4.70	1.60	100	5.61	2.22	119	7.67	2.62	163
6	6.14	2.67	89	5.28	2.55	77	6.87	3.12	100	7.55	3.41	110	11.81	5.39	172
7	1.97	0.53	31	4.58	1.79	71	6.41	2.51	100	7.10	2.64	111	11.88	4.66	185
8	5.66	2.34	82	6.00	2.79	87	6.89	3.01	100	7.30	2.89	106	10.13	4.40	147
9	4.96	1.96	73	6.07	2.74	89	6.83	3.33	100	7.76	3.87	114	10.37	5.00	152
10	3.68	1.68	64	4.73	2.09	82	5.76	2.42	100	8.40	3.43	146	12.01	5.07	209
11	4.70	1.57	71	5.69	1.91	86	6.61	2.53	100	7.51	2.98	114	10.05	4.39	152
12	2.93	1.29	52	3.95	1.86	70	5.63	2.67	100	6.34	2.62	113	8.87	3.70	158
Total	4.24	2.17	67	5.21	2.37	82	6.34	2.78	100	7.16	3.10	113	10.23	4.48	161

Each master column lists mean and standard deviation of syllable rate as well as percentage of in relationship to condition 'normal'.

which the factor in question is excluded (R code example: lmer(dependent_variable ~ 1 + (1|random_factor1) + (1|random_factor2), data = data)). *P* values were retrieved by comparing the results from the two models using ANOVAs (R code: anova(model_full, model_reduced). To assess the relative goodness of fit we indicate Akaike information criterion (AIC) values, which decrease with goodness of fit [30]. *P* values that are considered significant at the $\alpha = 0.05$ level are reported.

4.2 Phrase command parameters
Table 2 summarizes the results obtained from the model comparisons on the Fujisaki phrase level parameters, that is, phrase command magnitude Ap and *phrase duration*, the distance between subsequent phrase commands.

For phrase command magnitude Ap, comparisons between full and reduced models showed a significant difference and both full models exhibited an increased goodness of fit: between-rate variation as well as

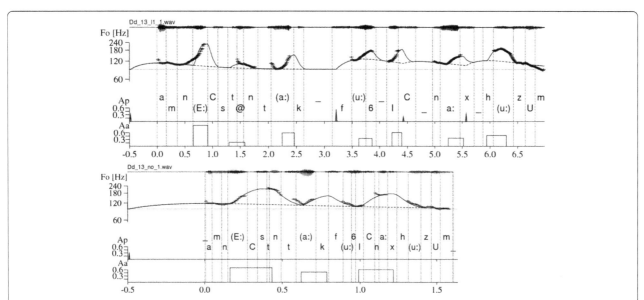

Figure 3 Analysis by male speaker 4 in the very slow and normal conditions. From the top to the bottom: utterances of sentence 1 *Am nächsten Tag fuhr ich nach Husum* - 'On the next day I went to Husum' produced by male speaker 4 at very slow and normal tempo. The time scale of the very slow version was compressed.

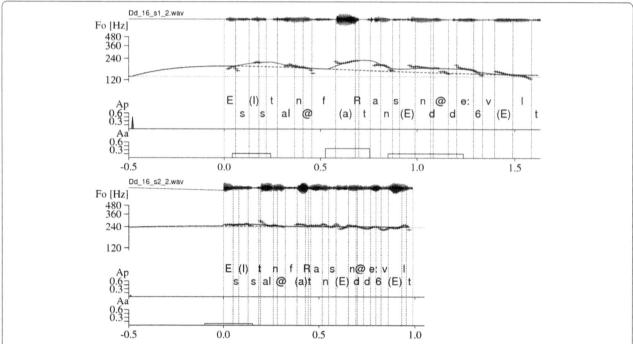

Figure 4 Extreme case from the upper limit of the tempo range. From the top to the bottom: utterances of sentence 2 *Es ist eine Fahrt ans Ende der Welt* - 'It is a journey to the end of the world' produced by speaker 6 at fast and very fast tempo.

between-speaker variation was significant. There was a small but significant interaction between the two factors, i.e., the main effect of intended tempo does not occur independently of speaker. For phrase durations, we found a significant effect of speaker and an interaction of intended tempo and speaker. Figure 5 illustrates values of phrase command magnitude Ap by intended tempo.

Figure 5 reveals that normal speech shows the highest Ap ($M = 0.266$, SD = 0.13), followed by very slow speech ($M = 0.264$, SD = 0.15), and fast intended tempo ($M = 0.263$, SD = 0.12). Very fast speech shows the lowest Ap ($M = 0.17$, SD = 0.12). Visually, if the boxes' notches do not overlap, this can be taken as strong evidence that their medians (solid black lines) differ. Results further revealed a main effect of speaker for phrase duration.

Table 2 Summary of the statistics for the phrase-level Fujisaki model parameters

Fujisaki model parameter	Factor	Result
Phrase command magnitude Ap	Intended tempo	$P < 0.0001$, AIC = −872
	Speaker	$P = 0.0009$, AIC = −872
	Intended tempo*speaker	$P = 0.033$, AIC = −860
Phrase duration	Intended tempo	Not significant
	Speaker	$P = 0.023$, AIC = 1,274
	Intended tempo*speaker	$P = 0.009$, AIC = 1,291

4.3 Accent command parameters

Table 3 summarizes the results obtained from the model comparisons on the Fujisaki accent level parameters, viz. accent command amplitude Aa, the difference between accent command onset time T1 and stressed syllable onset time (*t1relon*), as well as the difference between accent command onset time T1 and vowel onset time of a stressed syllable (*t1relvon*). For the first parameter, only stressed syllables were examined; for the latter two parameters, only stressed syllables that feature an F0 rise, that is, N↑ intonemes, were included in the analyses.

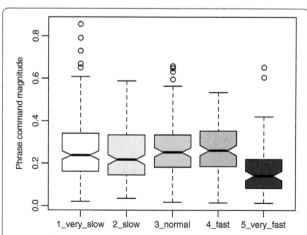

Figure 5 Boxplots of phrase command magnitude by intended tempo. Very slow (white), slow (turquoise), normal (blue), fast (gray), and very fast (dark gray). The white circles denote outliers.

Table 3 Summary of the statistics for the accent-level Fujisaki model parameters

Fujisaki model parameter	Factor	Result
Accent command amplitude Aa	Intended tempo	$P < 0.0001$, AIC = −838
	Speaker	$P < 0.0001$, AIC = −838
	Intended tempo*speaker	$P < 0.0001$, AIC = −894
t1relon (distance between T1 and syllable onset)	Intended tempo	$P < 0.0001$, AIC = −1,282
	Speaker	$P < 0.0001$, AIC = −1,282
	Intended tempo*speaker	$P < 0.0001$, AIC = −1,295
t1relvon (distance between T1 and nuclear vowel onset)	Intended tempo	$P < 0.0001$, AIC = −1,427
	Speaker	$P < 0.0001$, AIC = −1,427
	Intended tempo*speaker	Not significant

Note that the latter two parameters were correlated ($r(496) = 0.73$, $P < 0.0001$; $R^2 = 0.53$, $F(1,494) = 550$, $P < 0.001$); *t1relon* explained 53% of the variability in *t1relvon*.

As for accent command amplitude Aa, the model with intended tempo as a fixed effect provided an improved goodness of fit, which means that between-rate variation was significant. However, descriptive statistics did not reveal a straightforward connection between speech rate and accent command amplitude Aa (very slow $M = 0.33$, SD = 0.15; slow $M = 0.35$, SD = 0.16; normal $M = 0.35$, SD = 0.16; fast $M = 0.35$, SD = 0.16; very fast $M = 0.26$, SD = 0.12). There was a significant effect of speaker. Results further revealed an interaction of *intended tempo*speaker*. Figure 6 shows the box plots of the 12 speakers' accent command amplitude values.

The interaction obtained for intended tempo*speaker becomes evident in Figure 6: whereas speaker 4, for example, exhibited a trend of increasing amplitudes the faster he speaks (except for the very fast condition), speaker 11 performed conversely: the faster his speech, the lower the accent command amplitudes. Given the

interaction of *rate*speaker*, the main effects are no longer readily interpretable. To test for the simple effect of intended tempo, we processed 12 ANOVAs, one for each speaker. Only 3 of the 12 ANOVAs showed significant effects of intended tempo (Bonferroni adjusted for speaker, $\alpha = 0.0042$; speakers 2, 4, and 11). Correlation analysis between Aa and speech rate in syllables/s only yielded significant dependencies for four of the speakers with a weak Pearson's $r < -0.3$ indicating a compressed F0 range at higher rates. The syllabic distance between accent commands increases with speed: At the normal rate, subjects produce on average one accent command every 3.1 syllables, at very slow tempo every 2.7 syllables, and at very fast speed every 4.6 syllables.

As for the temporal distance between accent command onset and the onset of a stressed syllable (t1relon), the model with *speaking rate* as a fixed effect provided an improved goodness of, which means that between-rate variation was again significant. Descriptive statistics showed that the faster the speech, the smaller the distance between accent command onset and syllable onset

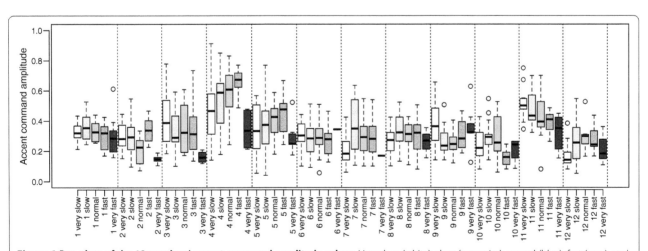

Figure 6 Box plots of the 12 speakers' accent command amplitude values. Very slow (white), slow (turquoise), normal (blue), fast (gray), and very fast (dark gray). The white circles denote outliers. The length of the whiskers (dashed lines) either indicates 1.5 times the interquartile range (IQR) or the minimum/maximum data points in cases where they are closer to the box (indicating the IQR) than 1.5 IQR.

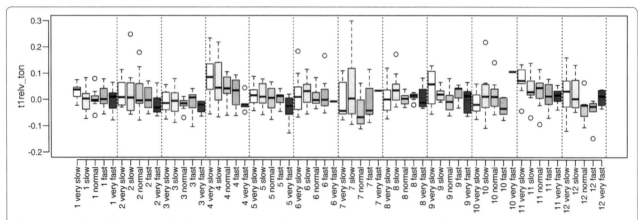

Figure 7 Box plots of the 12 speakers' *t1relvon*. Very slow (white), slow (turquoise), normal (blue), fast (gray), and very fast (dark gray) tempo. The white circles denote outliers. The length of the whiskers (dashed lines) either indicates 1.5 times the interquartile range (IQR) or the minimum/maximum data points in cases where they are closer to the box (indicating the IQR) than 1.5 IQR.

(very slow $M = 0.14$, SD = 0.09; slow $M = 0.12$, SD = 0.08; normal $M = 0.09$, SD = 0.05; fast $M = 0.08$, SD = 0.05; very fast $M = 0.05$, SD = 0.04). In other words, local rises occur earlier in the syllable the faster a person speaks. Results indicated that there was a significant effect of speaker and interaction of intended tempo*speaker. To test for the simple effect of intended tempo, we again processed 12 ANOVAs, one for each speaker. Again, only 3 of the 12 ANOVAs showed significant effects of intended tempo (Bonferroni adjusted for speaker, $\alpha = 0.0042$; speakers 4, 5, and 11).

Concerning the temporal distance between accent command, onset time T1, and the vowel onset within a stressed syllable (*t1relvon*), the model with intended tempo as a fixed effect provided an improved goodness of fit; hence, we interpret that between-rate variation was significant. Overall results showed a similar trend as for t1relon, albeit somewhat less straightforward: the faster the speech, the earlier the local F0 rises relative to the vowel onset (very slow $M = 0.023$, SD = 0.06; slow $M = 0.026$, SD = 0.073; normal $M = 0.003$, SD = 0.05; fast $M = 0.003$, SD = 0.05; very fast $M = -0.006$, SD = 0.04). There was also a significant effect of speaker. Given that intended tempo and speaker do not interact, the main effect of intended tempo occurs independently of the factor speaker. Figure 7 shows the box plots of the 12 speakers' *t1relvon* values.

Figure 7 reveals that most speakers exhibited the trend mentioned above: the faster the speech, the earlier the rise relative to the vowel onset. This is particularly evident for speakers 4, 9, and 11.

Finally, we examined whether the accent command is more strongly anchored to the syllable boundaries or the boundaries of the nuclear vowel. If we calculate correlations between T1 and T2 on the one hand and syllable or vowel onset and offset times on the other hand,

Pearson's r values are very close to unity since the accent commands are already aligned with the closest syllable. Therefore, we examined means and standard deviations of all timing difference measures, namely

- The difference between accent command onset time T1 and (1) the syllable onset time (*t1relon*), (2) the syllable offset time (*t1reloff*), (3) the vowel onset time (*t1relvon*), and (4) the vowel offset time (*t1relvoff*)
- The difference between accent command onset time T2 and (1) the syllable onset time (*t2relon*), (2) the syllable offset time (*t2reloff*), (3) the vowel onset time (*t2relvon*), and (4) the vowel offset time (*t2relvoff*).

We calculated these measures separately for rising F0 movements (N↑ intonemes) as well as falling F0 movements (I↓ intonemes) at accented syllables with results displayed in Table 4. As can be seen, rising F0 movements occur on average 104 ms after syllable onset and

Table 4 Means (*M*) and standard deviations (SD) in milliseconds for distance measures between accent commands and syllables or nuclear vowels, respectively

Distance measure	Rising F0 (N↑ intonemes)			Falling F0 (I↓ intonemes)		
	N	M [ms]	SD [ms]	N	M [ms]	SD [ms]
t1relon	513	104	76	163	−221	168
t2relon	513	435	166	163	107	88
t1reloff	513	−156	81	163	−462	214
t2reloff	513	175	118	163	−134	118
t1relvon	496	12	60	150	−287	176
t2relvon	496	344	147	150	42	89
t2relvoff	496	226	131	150	−78	96
t1relvoff	496	−106	64	150	−407	199

12 ms after vowel onset. On average, falling F0 movements start 107 ms after syllable onset and 42 ms after vowel onset. These cases are marked in red as they are the ones exhibiting the smallest standard deviations. This suggests that F0 rises and falls are most closely linked to the syllable or vowel onsets. For rising F0 movements, the alignment with the vowel seems to have only a minor advantage, that is, a lower SD. This confirms the observations made earlier in this section regarding marginal differences between *t1relon* and *t1relvon*.

5 Conclusions

The current paper examined the relationship between the F0 contour and speech rate. We employed the Fujisaki model for decomposing F0 contours into utterance level, phrase level, and syllable level components, that is, the base frequency Fb, phrase commands, and accent commands, respectively. We found that only at the extreme ends of the tempo range the prosodic structure disintegrates. Otherwise, the configuration in terms of phrase and accent command numbers and positions remains relatively unchanged, and speech rate has mostly an influence on the amplitudes and exact timings of commands.

In general, we found the following trends: The base frequency Fb increases with speech rate. The phrase duration measured as the distance between consecutive phrase commands decreased with speech rate. Although we expect phrases to contain more syllables at higher speech rate, these syllables are of shorter duration. Unless phrases are merged, phrase duration will therefore also decrease. As the examples in Figure 2 indicated, we do not necessarily see an increase in the numbers of phrase commands at low speed, unless the utterance is broken into very small chunks like in Figure 3, top. This tendency might well be due to the character of the underlying reading material which contains mostly short phrases. The deep boundaries are produced similarly at all tempos, and low speed does not give rise to new phrase commands at shallow boundaries which are rather marked by short pauses.

With respect to accent command amplitude Aa, our outcome suggests that despite a slight trend for Aa to decrease at higher tempos, the influence of the speaker on this parameter by far outweighs that of speech rate. This means that speakers have idiosyncratic ways of manipulating F0 parameters as a function of speech rate. For some speakers, for example, accent command amplitude increases the faster they speak (speaker 4, Figure 6), whereas for others, Aa decreases (speaker 11, Figure 6). We also found that speakers tend to produce fewer accent commands at higher speech rates. This indicates that a high articulatory rate imposes limitations on the frequency of F0 gestures.

As regards the alignment of F0 gestures with the syllable, our results suggest that increased tempo also leads to an early execution of F0 gestures. These observations are similar regardless of whether we anchor the accent command to the syllable onset or the nuclear vowel onset.

It is possible that the reading task underlying our data might have affected the outcome of our analyses, as people repeated the same sentences over and over again. Future work will examine other speech materials produced with more natural tempo variations.

Competing interests
The authors declare that they have no competing interests.

Author details
[1]Department of Computer Science and Media, Beuth University Berlin, Luxemburger Str. 10, Berlin 13353, Germany. [2]Phonetic Laboratory, University of Zurich, Rämistrasse 71, Zürich 8006, Switzerland.

References
1. F Goldman-Eilser, *Psycholinguistics: Experiments in Spontaneous Speech* (Academic, New York, 1968)
2. ACM Rietveld, CC Gussenhoven, Perceived speech rate and intonation. J. Phonetics **15**, 273–285 (1987)
3. J Caspers, VJ van Heuven, Effects of time pressure on the phonetic realization of the Dutch accent-lending pitch rise and fall. Phonetica **50**, 161–171 (1993)
4. DR Ladd, D Faulkner, H Faulkner, A Schepman, Constant segmental anchoring of *F0* movements under changes in speech rate. J. Acoust. Soc. Am. **106**, 1543–1554 (1999)
5. H Fujisaki, K Hirose, Analysis of voice fundamental frequency contours for declarative sentences of Japanese. J. Acoust. Soc. Japan (E) **5**(4), 233–241 (1984)
6. H Fujisaki, K Hirose, *Modeling the dynamic characteristics of voice fundamental frequency with applications to analysis and synthesis of intonation: preprints of the working group on intonation* (13th International Congress of Linguistics, Tokyo, 1982), pp. 57–70
7. H Mixdorff, *Intonation patterns of German—model-based quantitative analysis and synthesis of F0-contours* (D.Eng, Thesis, TU Dresden, 1998)
8. A Leemann, *Swiss German Intonation Patterns* (Benjamins, Amsterdam/New York, 2012)
9. DP Kuehn, KL Moll, A cineradiographic study of VC and CV articulatory velocities. J. Phonetics **23**(4), 303–320 (1976)
10. B Lindblom, Explaining phonetic variation: a sketch of the H&H theory, in *Speech production and speech modelling*, ed. by WJ Hardcastle, A Marchal (Kluwer, 1990), pp. 403–439
11. JE Flege, Effects of speaking rate on tongue position and velocity of movement in vowel production. JASA **84**, 901–916 (1988)
12. AV Isačenko, HJ Schädlich, *Untersuchungen über die deutsche Satzintonation* (Akademie-Verlag, Berlin, 1964)
13. E Stock, C Zacharias, *Deutsche Satzintonation* (VEB Verlag Enzyklopädie, Leipzig, 1982)
14. H Mixdorff, C Widera, *Perceived prominence in terms of a linguistically motivated quantitative intonation model* (Proc. Eurospeech 2001, Aalborg, Denmark, 2001), pp. 403–406
15. H Mixdorff, O Jokisch, *Building an integrated prosodic model of German, vol. 2* (Proceedings of Eurospeech 2001, Aalborg, Denmark, 2001), pp. 947–950
16. H Mixdorff, H Fujisaki, Production and perception of statement, question and non-terminal intonation in German. Proc. ICPhS, Stockholm **2**, 410–413 (1995)
17. N Amir, H Mixdorff, O Amir, D Rochman, GM Diamond, T Isserles, S Abramson, HR Pfitzinger, *Unresolved anger: prosodic analysis and classification of speech from a therapeutical setting* (Proceedings of Speech Prosody 2010, Chicago, USA, 2010)

18. V Dellwo, P Wagner, Relationships between speech rate and rhythm, in *Proceedings of the ICPhS 2003* (Barcelona, 2003)
19. V Dellwo, I Steiner, B Aschenberner, J Dankovicova, P Wagner, The BonnTempo-corpus & BonnTempo-tools: a database for the study of speech rhythm and rate, in *Proceedings of ICSLP 2005*, 2005
20. B Schlink, *Selbs Betrug* (Diogenes Verlag, Zurich, 1994)
21. HR Pfitzinger, Local speech rate perception in German speech. Proc. ICPhS **1999**, 893–896 (1999)
22. P Boersma, Praat, a system for doing phonetics by computer. Glot Int. **5**, 341–345 (2001)
23. H Mixdorff, *A novel approach to the fully automatic extraction of Fujisaki model parameters, vol 3* (Proceedings of ICASSP 2000, Istanbul Turkey, 2000), pp. 1281–1284
24. H Mixdorff, *FujiParaEditor*, 2009. http://public.beuth-hochschule.de/~mixdorff/thesis/fujisaki.html
25. R Core Team, *R, A language and environment for statistical computing, R foundation for statistical computing*, 2013. *version 3.0.0*, http://www.R-project.org
26. DM Bates, M Maechler, *lme4: linear mixed-effects models using S4 classes*, 2009. R package version 0.999375-32
27. RH Baayen, *Analyzing linguistic data: a practical introduction to statistics using R* (CUP, Cambridge, 2008)
28. RH Baayen, *LanguageR: data sets and functions with analyzing linguistic data: a practical introduction to statistics using R*, 2009. R package version 0.955
29. JMP, *Version 9.0* (SAS Institute Inc, Cary NY, 1989–2007)
30. R Kliegl, P Wei, M Dambacher, M Yan, X Zhou, Experimental effects and individual differences in linear mixed models: estimating the relationship between spatial, object, and attraction effects in visual attention. Front. Psychol. **1**(238), 1–12 (2011)

13

Improvement of multimodal gesture and speech recognition performance using time intervals between gestures and accompanying speech

Madoka Miki[1], Norihide Kitaoka[1*], Chiyomi Miyajima[1], Takanori Nishino[2] and Kazuya Takeda[1]

Abstract

We propose an integrative method of recognizing gestures such as pointing, accompanying speech. Speech generated simultaneously with gestures can assist in the recognition of gestures, and since this occurs in a complementary manner, gestures can also assist in the recognition of speech. Our integrative recognition method uses a probability distribution which expresses the distribution of the time interval between the starting times of gestures and of the corresponding utterances. We evaluate the rate of improvement of the proposed integrative recognition method with a task involving the solution of a geometry problem.

1 Introduction

Multimodal interaction, where multiple modalities sometimes play complementary roles with one another, is likely to become more widespread in human-machine communication. The semantics expressed in a modality may be ambiguous, but another modality might be able to remove these ambiguities. Combining gestures and speech is a typical example of such multimodality.

When completing a task using an interface, as task difficulty increases, users often prefer multimodal interactions rather than unimodal ones, for example, when entering data in an interface system with speech and pen modalities [1]. This implies that the smooth completion of complex transactions is facilitated by multimodality, especially by the ability to select a method capable of expressing complex intentions.

In this paper, we propose a method for improving gesture and speech recognition and use a task involving the solution of a geometry problem to test it. When performing such tasks, verbal utterances are often accompanied by pointing because individual modalities are often ambiguous.

For an automated system to understand such bimodal input, this kind of problem is generally divided into three sub-problems: independent recognition of speech and fingertip movements, matching up the utterances and fingertip movements, and simultaneous recognition (and understanding) of this bimodal input, taking into account both modalities. In this paper, we focus on the second and third issues, which, if successfully resolved, will result in what is known as 'modality fusion', which can be defined as the integration of the analysis of multiple modalities.

Although multiple feature streams from multiple modalities may be integrated and recognized simultaneously (using 'early integration' or 'data-level fusion') [2], as in bimodal audio-visual speech recognition, this approach is only successful when the modalities are well synchronized with each other. Therefore, it cannot be applied to the integration of speech and gestures. Thus, 'late integration' (or 'decision-level fusion') [2] is usually used, and thus all three of the sub-problems above need to be resolved.

To address the first issue of gesture recognition, methods using image processing have been proposed to recognize gestures, including fingertip movements. Head and hand positions have been tracked using video [3], fingertip

---

*Correspondence: kitaoka@nagoya-u.jp
[1] Department of Media Science, Nagoya University, Nagoya, Aichi Prefecture 464-8603, Japan
Full list of author information is available at the end of the article

position have been tracked using images captured by humans [4], position sensors have been used to acquire the position of a fingertip [5], and touch pens and panels have been used to interpret pointing [6,7]. In this paper, we used derivatives of position sensor data to recognize gestures. We may be able to use other methods as well to improve performance, but this is out of the scope of our current investigation.

After independently recognizing speech and gestures, correspondence must be found between them. Utterances and gestures which express identical meanings are paired. For such pairing, temporal order [6] and inclusion [8], semantic compatibility [6], and the relationship between prosodic features in speech and the speed of hand/finger movements [3] have been used. Utilizing prosodic features is an interesting approach, but extraction of F_0 features is not easy, and prosodic features include a wide range of individual variations. Thus, results using this method tend to vary widely in accuracy. Constraint by temporal order or inclusion (by overlapping the periods of modalities) is effective. However, the order constraint is relatively weak compared to the overlap constraint. On the other hand, the overlap constraint makes it difficult to determine correspondence, resulting in a lack of flexibility. We propose a soft decision method based on the statistics of the overlaps.

Finally, the information from the speech and gestures is used to construct an integrated representation. Integration/fusion methods of multimodal inputs have been well categorized, and the use of frame-based fusion has been proposed [9]. The concepts obtained from individual recognizers are put into semantic slots to represent an integrated meaning. These types of methods cannot consider temporal constraints directly, so temporal constraints are often combined, as in the method referred to above. The following schemes have also been proposed: a graph-based optimization method [10], a finite-state parsing method [11], a unification-based parsing method [12], the integration of multimodal posterior probabilities [13], and hidden Markov model-based multimodal fusion [2]. Some of these methods are able to take temporal constraints into account to some extent; however, these methods are not intended to improve single mode recognition performance as a result of the fusion.

Qu and Chai [7] proposed the use of information obtained from gestures to improve speech recognition performance. Our goal is to improve both speech and gesture recognition performance simultaneously through the modality fusion process.

In a previous study, we used the time interval between digit utterance in connected digits and accompanying finger tapping to improve digit recognition [14]. Synchronicity of speech and pen input has also been used for continuous speech recognition [15].

The rest of this paper is organized as follows. We first introduce the experimental task and explain the method of recording the multimodal inputs in Section 2. We then explain our gesture and speech recognition methods in Sections 3 and 4, respectively, and propose an integrative recognition method using multimodal time alignment in Section 5 [16]. We discuss our experimental results in Section 6 and conclude the paper in Section 7.

2 Experimental task and recording methods

An illustration of the geometry problem used to collect data for the multimodal input task is shown in Figure 1. The speech and pointing gestures of the subjects were recorded with a close-talk microphone and a 3D position sensor attached to the tip of the index finger, as shown in Figures 2 and 3, at sampling frequencies of 100 Hz and 48 kHz, respectively. Six subjects (four males and two females, all 23- to 27-year-old graduate or undergraduate students) performed a total of eight trials in a laboratory environment. Before recording, we told the subjects that they could use demonstratives such as 'this' and 'here' and point at the figure, instead of using precise explanations such as 'angle ABC'. Subjects pushed a button to start and stop the synchronized recording. The total length of the recorded data was 249.0 s (31.1 s/trial on average).

3 Gesture recognition method

In order to recognize gestures, the automated system must be able to differentiate when subjects are pointing at items such as angles, segments, vertices, etc. from the movement of their fingertips.

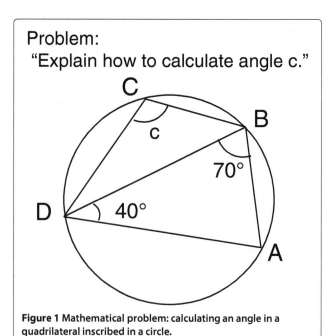

Figure 1 Mathematical problem: calculating an angle in a quadrilateral inscribed in a circle.

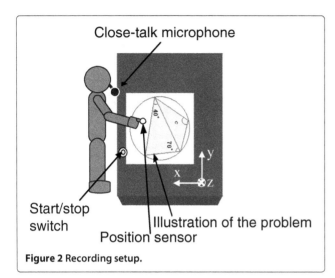

Figure 2 Recording setup.

To account for individual differences in the sizes of gestures, we used the differentials of subjects' fingertip positions in the X-Y plane as recognition features:

$$\begin{pmatrix} \Delta x[n] \\ \Delta y[n] \end{pmatrix} = \begin{pmatrix} x[n] - x[n-1] \\ y[n] - y[n-1] \end{pmatrix}, \tag{1}$$

where n indicates time, and $x[n]$ and $y[n]$ describe the fingertip position in the X-Y plane, respectively. The graph at the bottom of Figure 4 shows an example of time sequence $(\Delta x, \Delta y)^T$, indicated by arrows.

A subject's finger position in the z-axis is also important for recognizing gestures because meaningful movements can occur when a fingertip is resting on a desk, for example, so we also used absolute position in the z-axis as a

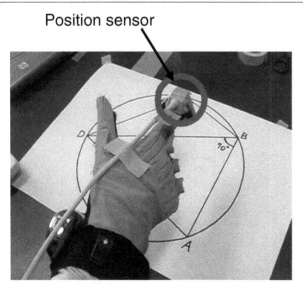

Figure 3 Position sensor apparatus.

feature. Additionally, we used the first derivatives of the features, resulting in six-dimensional features consisting of Δx, Δy, z, $\Delta \Delta x$, $\Delta \Delta y$, and Δz.

We used three-state HMMs with a single mixture to model 21 finger movements. A total of 18 of the 21 gestures corresponded to pointing at one of the 11 segments, 4 vertices, or 3 arcs between segments in the figure shown in Figure 1. The three remaining finger movements consisted of gestures which occurred during intervals between pointing gestures, pushing the start/stop switch, and touching the desk without pointing at any of the items.

We evaluated the system's gesture recognition performance using eightfold cross validation of the data recorded in Section 2 and obtained a 91.0% correct rate and 64.7% accuracy, which were defined as:

$$\mathrm{Corr} = \frac{C_g}{N_g}, \tag{2}$$

$$\mathrm{Acc} = \frac{C_g}{R_g}, \tag{3}$$

where Corr and Acc describe correct rate and accuracy, respectively, and C_g, N_g, and R_g represent the number of correctly recognized gestures, the number of gestures included in the test data, and the number of recognized gestures, respectively.

As mentioned in our introduction, we could have adopted other features and/or methods to improve recognition performance. We understand that using HMMs with the features Δx, Δy, and z may not be the best choice for gesture recognition. We did so, however, because our proposed method involves an integration, which will be described in Section 5, and each recognition method should be kept separate from the integration[a]. Improvement of the performance of individual modality recognition rates is a subject of future work, and we believe improved individual recognition methods will increase the benefits of our integrative method.

4   Speech recognition method

We also performed speech recognition experiments using the recorded explanation utterances. The Julius decoder was used for speech recognition [17]. We used a network grammar that accepted a sequence of elements, such as the expression 'angle ADB equals angle ACB', etc. Since subjects were often explaining how to solve the problem while they were still thinking about the solution, they often used fillers and disfluencies; therefore, the grammar was set up to accept fillers between any words. No other methods were used to deal with out-of-vocabulary words. The size of vocabulary was 77 words. These words and the grammar were predefined empirically and thus they could

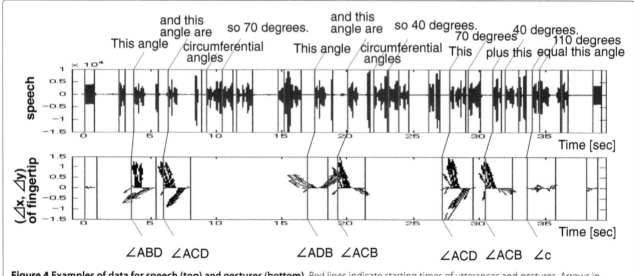

Figure 4 Examples of data for speech (top) and gestures (bottom). Red lines indicate starting times of utterances and gestures. Arrows in gesture graphs indicate $(\Delta x, \Delta y)^T$.

be used for all of the test data. Triphone HMMs were used as the acoustic models, and they were trained using the Corpus of Spontaneous Japanese (CSJ) [18], which is suitable for spontaneous speech. Each HMM had three states with output probabilities. The sampling frequency was 16 kHz, frame length and shift were 25 and 10 ms, respectively, and a 12-dimensional MFCC and its delta with delta log power were used as features. These acoustic models were also trained in advance, not using part of the test set; thus, we used the models for all of the test data. For this reason, we did not need to perform n-fold cross validation. We obtained a 75.0% speech recognition rate with a 66.7% accuracy.

5 Integrative recognition method

5.1 Relationship between speech and gestures

Some utterances could be easily paired with simultaneous gestures. However, speech, and the gestures which accompanied it, often did not occur simultaneously, as in the example given in Figure 4. In such cases, the utterances tended to begin after the corresponding gestures occurred. This was especially true at the beginning of the recordings. Figure 5 shows a histogram of the time differences, which was calculated as follows:

$$\tau = t_s - t_g, \tag{4}$$

where t_s and t_g indicate the starting time of an utterance and a gesture, respectively. We used this probabilistic tendency to match utterances and gestures. From the histogram, we can observe a symmetrical tendency towards

decay to both sides. So first, we express this histogram using the Gaussian distribution of τ:

$$p_d(\tau) = \frac{1}{\sqrt{2\pi}\sigma_\tau} \exp\left\{-\frac{(\tau - \mu_\tau)^2}{2\sigma_\tau^2}\right\}, \tag{5}$$

where μ_τ and σ_τ^2 are the mean and the variance of time difference τ, respectively. Utterances are paired with gestures with maximal probabilities of corresponding starting time differences. We could have used the discrete distribution derived directly from the histogram, but we decided to fit a parametric distribution to the histogram instead, for the purpose of generalization[b].

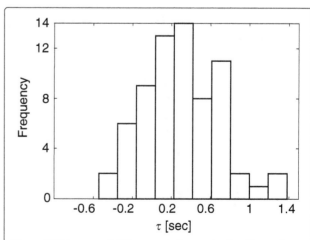

Figure 5 Histogram of differences between starting times of utterances and gestures.

To verify the effectiveness of this method, we performed a preliminary experiment in which utterances and gestures were manually segmented *a priori*. Then, each gesture was associated with an utterance including a key phrase that had its maximum probability calculated using Equation 5. Key phrases included demonstratives ('here', 'this', etc.) and parts of the figure ('angle ADB', '70 degrees', etc.). Some utterances were not associated with any gestures. The eight trials described in Section 2 were used as the test set, and μ_τ and σ_τ^2 were estimated from the data from the seven trials, not including each test trial (that is, using eightfold cross validation). Matches were considered to be 'correct' when utterances were associated with the correct gestures, and utterances without any accompanying gestures were considered 'correct' when no gestures were associated with them. Of the utterances, 93.8% was correctly associated with gestures. The nearest matching starting time strategy and longest overlapping time strategy obtained 89.7% and 83.5% association rates, respectively, and thus, our method was proven to function effectively.

5.2 Integration algorithm

We performed multimodal integration of the N-best rescorings of individual recognition results. First, we obtained the N-best lists of both speech and gesture recognition results. Each candidate in the lists was a sequence of utterances (for speech) or fingertip positions (for gestures). Then, we obtained the combined scores for all of the speech and gesture candidate pairs using dynamic programming. Local score L between utterance u_i and gesture g_j was calculated as follows using dynamic programming:

$$L(u_i, g_j)$$
$$= \begin{cases} \alpha L_s(u_i) + \beta L_g(g_j) + \gamma \log p_d(t_{s_i} - t_{g_j}), \\ \qquad\qquad\qquad\qquad\quad \text{if } M(u_i, g_j) = 1, \\ -\infty, \qquad\qquad\qquad\quad \text{if } M(u_i, g_j) = 0 \end{cases}$$
$$(6)$$

where $L_s(u_i)$ and $L_g(g_j)$ are the recognition scores for u_i and g_j, respectively, $p_d(\tau)$ is the probability of the time difference as defined by Equation 5, and $M(u_i, g_j)$ takes 1 or 0 as an indicator of the possibility of an association between u_i and g_j, based on Table 1. $L_s(u_i)$ and $L_g(g_i)$ are segment log-likelihoods for u_i and g_j, respectively, obtained using the Viterbi alignments of the HMMs. These segment log-likelihoods are not normalized using word/gesture durations. When an utterance is not associated with any gesture, it is associated with an interval between gestures, and time difference score p_d is not considered. Using local score $L(u_i, g_j)$, a candidate pair is globally aligned and scored. The candidate pair with the maximum global score in all $N \times N$ pairs[c] is selected as the final result.

Table 1 Table of possible associations between utterances and gestures (examples are excerpted)

Keyword/phrase in utterance	Example utterance(s)	Possible gesture
General demonstratives	'Here'	Pointing at an angle, a segment, or a vertex
Demonstratives for angles	'This angle'	Pointing at/tracing an angle
Demonstratives for segments	'This segment'	Tracing a segment
Demonstratives for points	'This point'	Pointing at a vertex
Expressions for angles/segment	'Angle ADB'	Pointing at/tracing a specific angle
	'70 degrees'	

6 Experiment

6.1 Experimental setup

We conducted an experiment to evaluate the improvement in speech and gesture recognition using the proposed integrative recognition method. We used the eight trials described in Section 2 as the test set and obtained the N-best results using both the speech and gesture recognition methods introduced in Sections 3 and 4. Each candidate included a word sequence and the time alignment data, i.e., the start and ending time of each word, to determine the correspondence of utterances and gestures. We set both values of N (of the N-best candidates for speech and gestures) at 20. This means that the system compared a maximum of $N \times N$ (400) pairs of speech and gesture recognition candidates per trial[d]. As for gaps between corresponding utterances and gestures, we approximated the statistics using a Gaussian distribution with the same μ_τ and σ_τ^2 used in Eqn. (5) in Section 3. To allow for dynamic ranges of likelihood for speech, gestures, and time gaps between utterances and gestures, we set α, β, and γ in Equation 6 appropriately, as the result of a preliminary experiment.

6.2 Results

The results of our experiment are shown in Table 2. '1-best' describes the ordinary 1-best recognition rate, and '20-best' describes the rate when the best candidates were selected from the 20-best candidate lists (which is the upper limit of our proposed method).

The proposed integration method achieved a 3.4% point improvement in speech recognition performance and a 3.7% percentage point improvement in gesture recognition performance. The speech recognition performance of the proposed method was near the upper bounds, and its gesture recognition performance was at the upper bounds.

Table 2 Recognition results using an integration of multiple modalities: recognition rate [%]

Modality		Recognition rate	
		Speech	Gesture
Speech	1-best	75.0	-
	20-best	80.0	-
Gesture	1-best	-	91.0
	20-best	-	94.7
Speech and gesture	-	78.4	94.7

There were many speech and gesture recognition errors. By aligning the corresponding words in utterances with gestures using dynamic programming (DP), we were able to reject pairs with low DP scores. Although this strategy was effective in our proposed method, it only aligned speech and gestures in order, and thus, its rejection ability was weak. Semantically inconsistent alignments were rejected by $M(u_i, g_j) = 0$ in Equation 6. This was a strong constraint, and some incorrect alignments were rejected, but because there were so many ambiguous words among the utterances, such as 'here' and 'this', which had many possible corresponding gestures, it was not highly effective. The distribution of time differences, however, was an effective constraint of the DP path. The start times of corresponding speech and gesture pairs should not differ greatly, and the correspondences were better identified using this strategy than by the 'nearest matching' and 'longest overlapping time' strategies described in Section 5.1. The distribution in Equation 6 worked as a 'soft' path limitation, and this may be a reason why this strategy worked so well.

Overall, this is how we obtained the abovementioned improvements, but we likely could have achieved the same performance using only a simple framework based on Equation 6.

We also evaluated the proposed method using the identification rate of the referents. The items in the figure cannot be identified using only the speech from the recordings, but gesture integration clarifies the ambiguities:

$$I = \frac{C}{C_s}, \tag{7}$$

where I is the identification rate, and C and C_s are the number of utterances with correctly identified referents, and the total number of utterances accompanied with gestures, respectively. The identification rate using the integrated recognition results was 91.7%, while the identification rate using only the speech portion of the

integrated recognition results was 20.0%, thus a 71.7% point improvement was achieved through integration.

7 Conclusions

In this paper, we introduced an integrative recognition method using accompanying speech to recognize gestures. First, we proposed a probability density of the differences in starting times between speech and the corresponding gestures to align the two. Then, we incorporated this probability into an integrative recognition method, which scored sequenced pairs of utterances and gestures using dynamic programming. This multimodal recognition method achieved more than 3% points of improvement in both speech and gesture recognition.

Note that our method could also possibly be used with other types of multimodalities, although currently, this method is specialized to the task which we have selected. A speaker-dependent, large-vocabulary, continuous speech recognizer could be used without any specific training, but a task-specific gesture recognizer would need to be constructed because there are no universal primitive units for gesture recognition corresponding to the phonemes and syllables used for speech recognition. The correspondence between modalities should also be defined for the task *a priori*. Even so, we believe that we can apply our method to any task which meets the following conditions: each of the modalities can be recognized using methods such as HMMs, the relationship between modalities can be described by constraint rules, and the timing difference between modalities can be described as a probability density. The larger the task becomes, the more difficult it is to construct such a framework, but once this is achieved, our proposed method can be applied. Application of this method to larger scale tasks is one of our future goals.

Although so far, we have only used N-best lists as intermediate expressions for our integrative method, other expressions with less information loss could also be used, such as word graphs or HMM trellises.

Endnotes

[a]Another reason to use HMMs is that the score obtained from an HMM is based on a probability, and thus the integration explained in Section 5 becomes theoretically correct.

[b]Of course, we can use other parametric discrete/continuous distributions, and one of them may achieve better performance, but pursuing such distributions is a task for future work.

[c]The N values of utterances and gestures can differ. In this paper, however, we used the same $N(20)$ for both values, as described in Section 6. This was decided through preliminary experiments.

[d]We used K-fold cross validation because we tested the HMM parameters for gesture recognition under an open data condition. This setting is different from that used for speech recognition, in which we prepared training and test data separately. Under both conditions, however, no data were used for both training and test data, and thus, the difference in the experimental setup for gestures and speech did not affect the results.

Competing interests
The authors declare that they have no competing interests.

Author details
[1] Department of Media Science, Nagoya University, Nagoya, Aichi Prefecture 464-8603, Japan. [2] Department of Information Engineering, Mie University, Mie Prefecture 514-8507, Japan.

References
1. S Oviatt, R Coulston, R Lundsford, When do we interact multimodally? Cognitive load and multimodal communication patterns, in *Proceedings of ICMI* (ACM, New York, 2004), pp. 129–136
2. B Dumas, B Signer, D Lalanne, Fusion in multimodal interactive systems: an HMM-Based algorithm for user-induced adaptation, in *Proceedings of 4th ACM SIGCHI Symposium on Engineering Interactive Computing Systems* (ACM, New York, 2012), pp. 15–24
3. S Kettebekov, M Yeasin, R Sharma, Prosody based co-analysis for continuous recognition of co-verbal gestures, in *Proceedings of ICME* (IEEE Computer Society, Washington DC, 2002), pp. 161–166
4. M Fukumoto, Y Suenaga, K Mase, Finger-pointer: pointing interface by image processing. ACM Comput. Graph. **18**(5), 633–642 (1994)
5. RA Bolt, Put-that-there: voice and gesture at the graphics interface. ACM Comput. Graph. **14**(3), 262–270 (1980)
6. P Hui, H Meng, Joint interpretation of input speech and pen gestures for multimodal human computer interaction, in *INTERSPEECH* (ISCA, Pittsburgh, 2006), pp. 1197–1200
7. S Qu, JY Chai, Salience modeling based on non-verbal modalities for spoken language understanding, in *Proceedings of ICMI* (ACM, New York, 2006), pp. 193–200
8. N Krahnstoever, S Kettebekov, M Yeasin, R Sharma, A real-time framework for natural multimodal interaction with large screen displays, in *Proceedings of ICMI* (IEEE, Piscataway, 2002), pp. 349–354
9. D Lalanne, L Nigay, P Palanque, P Robinson, J Vanderdonckt, J Ladry, Fusion engines for multimodal input: a survey, in *Proceedings of ICMI-MLMI* (ACM, New York, 2009), pp. 153–160
10. J Chai, P Hong, M Zhou, Z Prasov, Optimization in multimodal interpretation, in *Proceedings of ACL* (Association for Computational Linguistics, Stroudsburg, 2004), pp. 1–8
11. M Johnston, Finite-state multimodal parsing and understanding, in *Proceedings of COLING* (Association for Computational Linguistics, Stroudsburg, 2000), pp. 369–375
12. M Johnston, Unification-based multimodal parsing, in *Proceedings of COLING-ACL* (Association for Computational Linguistics, Stroudsburg, 1998), pp. 624–630
13. L Wu, L Oviatt, PR Cohen, Multimodal integration - a statistical view. Trans. Multimedia **1**(4), 334–341 (1999)
14. H Ban, C Miyajima, K Itou, K Takeda, F Itakura, Speech recognition using synchronization between speech and finger tapping, in *Proceedings of ICSLP* (ISCA, Pittsburgh, 2004), pp. 943–946
15. K Shinoda, Y Watanabe, K Iwata, Y Liang, R Nakagawa, S Furui, Semi-synchronous speech and pen input for mobile user interfaces. Speech Commun. **53**(3), 283–291 (2011)
16. M Miki, C Miyajima, T Nishino, N Kitaoka, K Takeda, An integrative recognition method for speech and gestures, in *Proceedings of ICMI* (ACM, New York, 2008), pp. 93–96
17. A Lee, T Kawahara, K Shikano, Julius — an open source real-time large vocabulary recognition engine, in *Proceedings of EUROSPEECH* (ISCA, Aalborg, 2001), pp. 1691–1694
18. K Maekawa, Corpus of spontaneous Japanese: its design and evaluation, in *Proceedings of SSPR* (ISCA and IEEE, Tokyo, 2003), pp. 7–12

14

ViSQOL: an objective speech quality model

Andrew Hines[1,2]*, Jan Skoglund[3], Anil C Kokaram[3] and Naomi Harte[2]

Abstract

This paper presents an objective speech quality model, ViSQOL, the Virtual Speech Quality Objective Listener. It is a signal-based, full-reference, intrusive metric that models human speech quality perception using a spectro-temporal measure of similarity between a reference and a test speech signal. The metric has been particularly designed to be robust for quality issues associated with Voice over IP (VoIP) transmission. This paper describes the algorithm and compares the quality predictions with the ITU-T standard metrics PESQ and POLQA for common problems in VoIP: clock drift, associated time warping, and playout delays. The results indicate that ViSQOL and POLQA significantly outperform PESQ, with ViSQOL competing well with POLQA. An extensive benchmarking against PESQ, POLQA, and simpler distance metrics using three speech corpora (NOIZEUS and E4 and the ITU-T P.Sup. 23 database) is also presented. These experiments benchmark the performance for a wide range of quality impairments, including VoIP degradations, a variety of background noise types, speech enhancement methods, and SNR levels. The results and subsequent analysis show that both ViSQOL and POLQA have some performance weaknesses and under-predict perceived quality in certain VoIP conditions. Both have a wider application and robustness to conditions than PESQ or more trivial distance metrics. ViSQOL is shown to offer a useful alternative to POLQA in predicting speech quality in VoIP scenarios.

Keywords: Objective speech quality; POLQA; P.853; PESQ; ViSQOL; NSIM

1 Introduction

Predicting how a user perceives speech quality has become more important as transmission channels for human speech communication have evolved from traditional fixed telephony to Voice over Internet Protocol (VoIP)-based systems. Packet-based networks have compounded the traditional background noise quality issues with the addition of new channel-based degradations. Network monitoring tools can give a good indicator of the quality of service (QoS), but predicting the quality of experience (QoE) for the end user of heterogeneous networked systems is becoming more important as transmission channels for human speech communication have a greater reliance on VoIP. Accurate reproduction of the input waveform is not the ultimate goal, as long as the user perceives the output signal as a high-quality representation of their expectation of the original signal input.

Popular VoIP applications, such as Google Hangouts and Skype, deliver multimedia conferencing over standard computer or mobile devices rather than dedicated video conferencing hardware. End-to-end evaluation of the speech quality delivery has become more complex as the number of variables impacting the signal has expanded. For system development and monitoring purposes, quality needs to be reliably assessed. Subjective testing with human listeners is the ground truth measurement for speech quality but is time consuming and expensive to carry out. Objective measures aim to model this assessment, to give accurate estimates of quality when compared with subjective tests.

PESQ (Perceptual Evaluation of Speech Quality) [1] and the more recent POLQA (Perceptual Objective Listening Quality Assessment) [2], described in ITU standards, are full-reference measures meaning they allow prediction of speech quality by comparing a reference to a received signal. PESQ was developed to give an objective estimate of narrowband speech quality and was later extended to also address wideband speech quality [3]. The newer POLQA model yields quality estimates for narrowband, wideband, and super-wideband speech and

*Correspondence: andrew.hines@dit.ie
[1] School of Computing, Dublin Institute of Technology, Kevin St, Dublin 8, Ireland
[2] Sigmedia, Department of Electronic and Electrical Engineering, Trinity College Dublin, College Green, Dublin 2, Ireland
Full list of author information is available at the end of the article

addresses other limitations in PESQ, specifically time alignment and warped speech. It is slowly gaining more widespread use, so as yet, there has been limited publication of its performance outside of its own development and conformance tests.

This work presents an alternative model, the Virtual Speech Quality Objective Listener, or ViSQOL, which has been developed to be a general full-reference objective speech quality metric with a particular focus on VoIP degradations. The experiments presented compare the performance to PESQ and POLQA and benchmarks their performance over a range of common background noises and warp, clock drift, and jitter VoIP impairments.

The early development of ViSQOL was presented in a paper introducing the model's potential to measure two common VoIP problems: clockdrift and jitter [4]. Further work developed the algorithm and mapped the model output to mean opinion score (MOS) estimates [5]. This work expands on these experiments and presents a detailed description of the algorithm and experimental results for a variety of quality degradations. The model performance is further evaluated against two more simplistic quality metrics as well as the ITU standards PESQ and POLQA.

Section 2 provides a background and sets the context for this research, giving an introduction to subjective and objective speech quality measurement and related research. Sections 3 and 4 introduce and then describe the ViSQOL model architecture. Section 5 describes five experiments, presents details of the tests undertaken and datasets used, and discusses the experimental results. Section 6 summaries the results, and Section 7 concludes the paper and suggests some areas for further model testing and development.

2 Background
2.1 Speech quality issues with Voice over IP
There are three factors associated with packet networks that have a significant impact on perceived speech quality: delay, jitter (variations in packet arrival times), and packet loss. All three factors stem from the nature of a packet network, which provides no guarantee that a packet of speech data will arrive at the receiving end in time, or even that it will arrive at all [6]. Packet losses can occur both in routers in the network or at the end point when packets arrive too late to be played out. To account for these factors and to ensure a continuous decoding of packets, a jitter buffer is required at the receiving end. The design trade-off for the jitter buffer is to keep the buffering delay as short as possible while minimizing the number of packets that arrive too late to be used. A large jitter buffer causes an increase in the overall delay and decreases the packet loss. A high delay can severely affect the quality and ease of conversation as the wait leads to annoying talker overlap. The ITU-T Recommendation G.114 [7] states that the one-way

delay should be kept below 150 ms for acceptable conversation quality. In practice somewhat larger delays can be tolerated, but in general a latency larger than 300 to 400 ms is deemed unacceptable. A smaller buffer decreases the delay but increases the resulting packet loss. When a packet loss occurs, some mechanism for filling in the missing speech must be incorporated. Such solutions are usually referred to as packet loss concealment (PLC) algorithms, see Kim et al. [8] for a more complete review. This can be done by simply inserting zeros, repeating signals, or by some more sophisticated methods utilizing features of the speech signal, e.g., pitch periods. The result of inserting zeros or repeating packets is choppy speech with highly audible discontinuities perceived as clicks. Pitch-based methods instead try finding periodic segments to repeat in a smooth periodic manner during voiced portions of speech. This typically results in high-quality concealment, even though it may sound robotic and buzzy during events of high packet loss. An example of such a pitch-period-based method is the NetEq [9] algorithm in WebRTC, an open-source platform for audio and video communication over the web [10]. NetEq is continuously adapting the playout timescale by adding or reducing pitch periods to not only conceal lost segments but also to reduce built-up delay in the jitter buffer.

Another important aspect which indirectly may affect the quality is clock drift. Whether the communication end-points are gateways or other devices, low-frequency clock drift between the two can cause receiver buffer overflow or underflow. If the clock drift is not detected accurately, delay builds up during a call, so clock drift can have a significant impact on the speech quality. For example, the transmitter might send packets every 20 ms according to its perception of time, while the receiver's perception is that the packets arrive every 20.5 ms. In this case, for every 40th packet, the receiver has to perform a packet loss concealment to avoid buffer underflow. The NetEq algorithm's timescale modification inherently adjusts for clock drift in a continuous sample-by-sample fashion and thereby avoids such step-wise concealment.

2.2 Subjective and objective speech quality assessment
Inherently, the judgement of speech quality for human listeners is subjective. The most reliable method for assessment is via subjective testing with a group of listeners. The ITU-T has developed a widely used recommendation (ITU-T Rec. P.800 [11]) defining a procedure for speech quality subjective tests. The recommendation specifies several testing paradigms. The most frequently used is the Absolute Category Rating (ACR) assessment where listeners rate the quality of speech samples into a scale of 1 to 5 (bad, poor, fair, good, and excellent). The ratings for all listeners are averaged to a single score known as a

mean opinion score (MOS). With multiple listeners rating a common minimal value of four samples per condition (spoken by two male and two female speakers), subjective testing is time consuming, expensive, and requires strict adherence to the methodology to ensure applicability of results. Subjective testing is impractical for frequent automated software system regression tests or routine network monitoring applications.

As a result, objective test methods have been developed in recent years and remain a topic of active research. This is often seen as surprising considering telephone communications have been around for a century. The advent of VoIP has introduced a range of new technological issues and related speech quality factors that require the adaptation of speech quality models [12]. Objective models are machine executable and require little human involvement for repeatable automated regression tests to be created for VoIP systems. They are useful tools for a wide audience: VoIP application and codec developers can use them to benchmark and assess changes or enhancements to their products; while telecommunications operators can evaluate speech quality throughout their system life cycles from planning and development through to implementation, optimization, monitoring, and maintenance. They are important tools for a range of research disciplines such as human computer interfaces, e.g., speech or speaker recognition, where knowledge of the quality of the test data is important in quantifying their system's robustness to noise [13]. An extensive review of objective speech quality models and their applications can be found in [14].

Objective methods can be classified into two major categories: parameter-based and signal-based methods. Parameter-based methods do not test signals over the channel but instead predict the speech quality through modeling the channel parameters. The E-model is an example of a parameter-based model. It is defined by ITU-T Recommendations G.107 [15] (narrowband version) and G.107.1 [16] (wideband version) and is primarily used for transmission planning purposes in narrowband and wideband telephone networks.

This work concentrates on the other main category, namely signal-based methods. They predict quality based on evaluation of a test speech signal at the output of the channel. They can be divided into two further subcategories, intrusive or non-intrusive. Intrusive signal-based methods use an original reference and a degraded signal, which is the output of the system under test. They identify the audible distortions based on the perceptual domain representation of two signals incorporating human auditory models. Several intrusive models have been developed during recent years. The ITU-T Recommendation P.861 (PSQM), published in 1996, was a first attempt to objectively model human listeners and predict

speech quality from subjective listener tests. It was succeeded in 2001 by P.862, commonly known as PESQ, a full-reference metric for predicting speech quality. PESQ has been widely used and was enhanced and extended over the next decade. It was originally designed and tested on narrowband signals. It improved on PSQM and the model handles a range of transmission channel problems and variations including varied speech levels, codecs, delays, packet loss, and environmental noise. However, it has a number of acknowledged shortcomings including listening levels, loudness loss, effects of delay in conversational tests, talker echo, and side tones [1]. An extension to PESQ was developed that adapted the input filters and MOS mapping to allow wideband signal quality prediction [3].

The newer POLQA algorithm, presented in ITU-T P.863 Recommendation, addresses a number of the limitations of PESQ as well as improving the overall correlation with subjective MOS scores. POLQA also implements an 'idealisation' of the reference signal. This means that it will attempt to create a reference signal weighting the perceptually salient data before comparing it to the degraded signal. It allows for predicting overall listening speech quality in two modes: narrowband (300 to 3,400 Hz) and superwideband (50 to 14,000 Hz). It should be noted that in the experiments described in this paper, POLQA was used in narrowband mode where the specification defines the estimated MOS listener quality objective output metric (MOS-LQOn, with n signifying narrowband testing) saturating at 4.5.

In contrast to intrusive methods, the idea of the single-ended (non-intrusive) signal-based method is to predict the quality without access to a reference signal. The result of this comparison can further be modified by a parametric degradation analysis and integrated into an assessment of overall quality. The most widely used non-intrusive models include Auditory Non-Intrusive QUality Estimation (ANIQUE+) [17] and ITU-T standard P.563 [18], although it is still an active area of research [19-22].

For much of the published work on speech quality in VoIP, PESQ is used as an objective metrics of speech quality, e.g., [23,24]. PESQ was originally designed with narrowband telephony in mind and did not specifically target the most common quality problems encountered in VoIP systems described in 2.1. POLQA has sought to address some of the known shortcomings of PESQ, but only a small number of recent publications, e.g., [25], have begun to evaluate the performance of POLQA for VoIP issues. PESQ is still worthy of analysis as recently published research continues to use PESQ for VoIP speech quality assessment, e.g., [26,27].

This paper presents the culmination of work from the authors [4,5,28] in developing a new objective metric of speech quality, called ViSQOL. ViSQOL has been designed to be particularly sensitive to VoIP degradation but without sacrificing wider deployability. The metric works by examining similarity in time-frequency representations of the reference and degraded speech, looking for the manifestation of these VoIP events. The new metric is compared to both PESQ and POLQA.

2.3   Benchmark models

Both ITU-T models, PESQ and POLQA, involve a complex series of pre-processing steps to achieve a comparison of signals. These deal with factors like loudness levels, temporal alignments, and delays. They also include a perceptual model that filters the signal using bandpass filters to mimic the frequency sensitivity and selectivity of the human ear. For ease of comparison with ViSQOL, block diagrams of the three models are presented in Figures 1, 2, 3, and 4. The models differ in a variety of ways beyond the fundamental distance calculations between signals, including level alignment, voice activity detection, time-alignment, and mapping from an internal metric to a MOS estimate. All three are quite complex in their implementations and more detail on PESQ and POLQA can be found in the relevant ITU-T standards. Further details on ViSQOL follows in Section 3.

When dealing with speech quality degradations that are constrained to background noise or speech enhancement algorithms attempting to counteract noise, simple SNR distance metrics may suffice. This was shown to be the case by Hu and Loizou when evaluating speech enhancement algorithms with a variety of objective quality metrics [29]. However, these metrics have difficulty with modern communications networks. Modern codecs can produce high-quality speech without preserving the input waveform. Quality measures based on waveform similarity do not work for these codecs. Comparing signals in the spectral domain avoids this problem and can produce results that agree with human judgement. The two best performing metrics from Hu and Loizou's study,

the log-likelihood ratio (LLR) and frequency domain segmental signal-to-noise ratio (fwSNRSeg) [29,30], are tested along with the specialised speech quality metrics, PESQ and POLQA, to illustrate their strengths and weaknesses.

2.4   Experimental datasets

Subjective databases used for metric calibration and testing are a key component in objective model development. Unfortunately, many datasets are not made publicly available; and those that are frequently used do not contain a realistic sample of degradation types targeting a specific application under study, or their limited size does not allow for statistically significant results. MOS scores can vary, based on culture and language, or balance of conditions in a testset, even for tests within the same laboratory [31]. The coverage of the data in terms of variety of conditions and range of perceived quality is usually limited to a range of conditions of interest for a specific research topic. A number of best practice procedures have been set out by the ITU, e.g., the ITU-T P.800 test methodology [11], to ensure statistically reliable results. These cover details such as the number of listeners, environmental conditions, speech sample lengths, and content and help to ensure that MOS scores are gathered and interpreted correctly. This work presents results from tests using a combination of existing databases where available and subjective tests carried out by the authors for assessing objective model performance for a range of VoIP specific and general speech degradations.

3   Measuring speech quality through spectrogram similarity

ViSQOL was inspired by prior work on speech intelligibility by two of the authors [32,33]. This work used a model of the auditory periphery [34] to produce auditory nerve discharge outputs by computationally simulating the middle and inner ear. Post-processing of the model outputs yield a neurogram, analogous to a spectrogram with

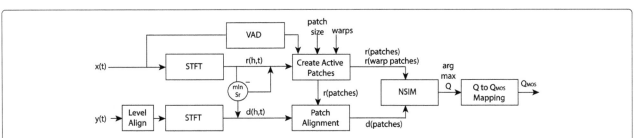

Figure 1 Block diagram of ViSQOL. High-level block diagram of the ViSQOL algorithm, also summarised in Algorithm 1. Pre-processing includes signal leveling and production of spectrogram representations of the reference and degraded signal. Similarity comparison: alignment, warp compensation, and calculating similarity scores between patches from the spectrograms. Quality prediction: patch similarity scores are combined and translated to an overall objective MOS result. Full reference MATLAB implementation available.

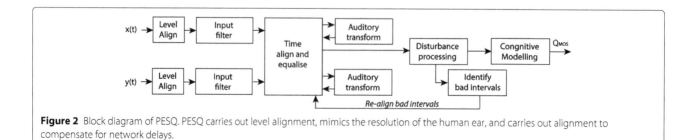

Figure 2 Block diagram of PESQ. PESQ carries out level alignment, mimics the resolution of the human ear, and carries out alignment to compensate for network delays.

time-frequency color intensity representation related to neural firing activity.

Most speech quality models quantify the degradation in a signal, i.e., the amount of noise or distortion in the speech signal compared to a 'clean' reference. ViSQOL focuses on the similarity between a reference and degraded signal by using a distance metric called the Neurogram Similarity Index Measure or NSIM. NSIM was developed to evaluate the auditory nerve discharges in a full-reference way by comparing the neurogram for reference speech to the neurogram from degraded speech to predict speech intelligibility. It was inspired and adapted for use in the auditory domain from an image processing technique, structural similarity, or SSIM [35], which was created to predict the loss of image quality due to compression artifacts. Adaptations of SSIM have been used to predict audio quality [36] and more recently have been applied in place of simple mean squared error in aeroacoustics [37]. Computation of NSIM is described below in Section 4.2.3.

While speech intelligibility and speech quality are linked, work by Voiers [38] showed that an amplitude-distorted signal that had been peak clipped did not impact intelligibility but seriously affected the quality. This phenomena is well illustrated by examples of vocoded or robotic speech where the intelligibility can be 100% but the quality is ranked as bad or poor. In evaluating the speech intelligibility provided by two hearing aid algorithms with NSIM, it was noted that while the intelligibility level was the same for both, the NSIM predicted higher levels of similarity for one algorithm over the other [39]. This suggested that NSIM may be a good indicator of other factors beyond intelligibility such as speech quality. It was necessary to evaluate intelligibility after the auditory periphery when modeling hearing impaired listeners as the signal impairment occurs in the cochlea. This paper looks at situations where the degradation occurs in the communication channel, and hence assessing the signal directly using NSIM on the signal spectrograms rather than neurograms simplifies the model. This decreased the computational complexity of the model by two magnitudes to an order comparable with other full-reference metrics such as PESQ and POLQA.

4 Algorithm description

ViSQOL is a model of human sensitivity to degradations in speech quality. It compares a reference signal with a degraded signal. The output is a prediction of speech quality perceived by an average individual. The model has five major processing stages shown in the block diagram Figure 1: pre-processing; time alignment; predicting warp; similarity comparison; and a post-process mapping similarity to objective quality. The algorithm is also summarized in Algorithm 1. For completeness, the reader should refer to the reference MATLAB source code implementation of the model available for download [40].

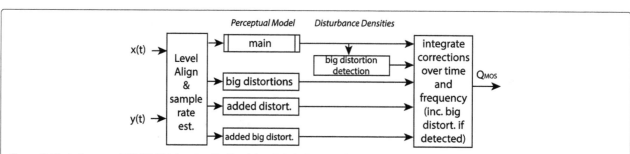

Figure 3 Block diagram of POLQA. This is a simplified high-level block diagram of POLQA. POLQA carries out alignment per frame and estimates the degraded signal sample rate. The main perceptual model (shown in panel titled 'main' in this figure and detailed in Figure 4) is executed four times with different parameters based on whether big distortions are flagged by the first model. Disturbance densities are calculated for each perceptual model and the integrated model to output a MOS estimate.

Algorithm 1 Calculate $Q_{MOS} = VISQOL(x, y)$

Require: x
Require: y
Ensure: $dBSPL(y) == dBSPL(x)$
  $r \leftarrow spectrogram(x)$
  $d \leftarrow spectrogram(y)$
  $r \leftarrow r - \arg\min r$
  $d \leftarrow d - \arg\min r$
  for $patch = 1$ to $length(r) - PATCHSIZE$ **do**
    if $VAD(r(patch)) = TRUE$ **then**
      $refpatches[\,] \leftarrow r(patch)$
      $refwarppatches[\,] \leftarrow warp(r(patch))$
    end if
    $t_d[\,] \leftarrow alignpatches(refpatches[\,], d)$
  end for
  for all $refpatches$ such that $1 \le i \le NUMPATCHES$ **do**
    for all $warps$ such that $1 \le w_i \le NUMWARPS$ **do**
      for all t_d such that $1 \le t_i \le NUMPATCHES$ **do**
        $q(i) \leftarrow nsim(refpatches(i), d(t_d(t_i))$
        $qwarp(i) \leftarrow nsim(refwarppatches(w_i), d(t_d(t_i))))$

        $q(i) \leftarrow max(q(i), qwarp(i))$
      end for
    end for
  end for
  $Q \leftarrow \sum(q(i))/NUMPATCHES$
  $Q_{MOS} \leftarrow maptomos(Q)$

4.1 Pre-processing

The pre-processing stage scales the degraded signal $y(t)$, to match the power level of the reference signal $x(t)$. Short-term Fourier transform (STFT) spectrogram representations of the reference and degraded signals are created using critical bands between 150 and 3,400 Hz for narrowband testing and including five further bands to 8,000 Hz for wideband. They are denoted r and d, respectively. A 512 sample, 50% overlap periodic

Hamming window is used for signals with 16-kHz sampling rate and a 256 sample window for 8-kHz sampling rate to keep frame resolution temporally consistent at 32-ms length with 16-ms spacing. The test spectrograms are floored to the minimum value in the reference spectrogram to level the signals with a 0-dB reference. The spectrograms are used as inputs to the second stage of the model, shown in detail on the right-hand side of Figure 1.

4.2 Feature selection and comparison

4.2.1 Time alignment

The reference signal is segmented into patches for comparison as illustrated in Figure 5. Each patch is 30 frames long (480 ms) by 16 or 21 critical frequency bands [41] (i.e., 150 to 3,400 for narrowband or 50 to 8,000 Hz for wideband signals). A simple energy threshold voice activity detector is used on the reference signal to approximately segment the signal into active patches. NSIM is used to time align the patches to ensure that the patches are aligned correctly even for conditions with high levels of background noise. Each reference patch is aligned with the corresponding area from the test spectrogram. The Neurogram Similarity Index Measure (NSIM) [33] is used to measure the similarity between the reference patch and a test spectrogram patch frame by frame, thus identifying the maximum similarity point for each patch. This is shown in the bottom pane of Figure 5 where each line graphs the NSIM similarity score over time for each patch in the reference signal compared with the example signal. The NSIM at the maxima are averaged over the patches to yield the metric for the example signal.

4.2.2 Predicting warp

NSIM is more sensitive to time warping than a human listener. The ViSQOL model exploits this by warping the spectrogram patches temporally. It creates alternative reference patches 1% and 5% longer and shorter than the

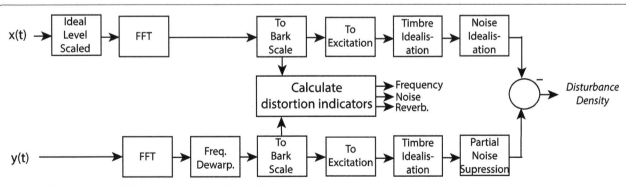

Figure 4 Block diagram of POLQA perceptual model block. The perceptual model calculates distortion indicators. An idealisation is carried out on the reference signal to remove low levels of noise and optimize timbre of the reference signal prior to the difference calculation for disturbance density estimation.

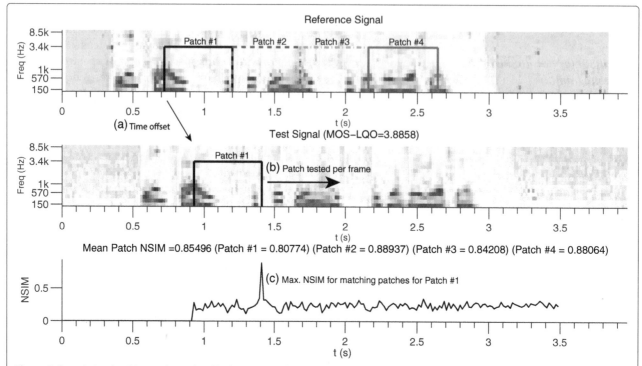

Figure 5 Speech signals with sample patches. The bottom plot shows the NSIM similarity score for each patch from the reference compared frame by frame across the degraded signal. The NSIM score is the mean of the individual patch scores given in parenthesis. **(a)** Time offset between reference and test signal. **(b)** Patch tested per frame. **(c)** Maximum NSIM for matching patches for Patch # 1.

original reference. The patches are created using a cubic two-dimensional interpolation. The comparison stage is completed by comparing the test patches to the reference patches and all of the warped reference patches using NSIM. If a warped version of a patch has a higher similarity score, this score is used for the patch. This is illustrated in Figure 6.

4.2.3 Similarity comparison

In this work, spectrograms are treated as images to compare similarity. Prior work [32,33] demonstrated that the structural similarity index (SSIM) [35] could be used to discriminate between reference and degraded images of speech to predict intelligibility. SSIM was developed to evaluate JPEG compression techniques by assessing image similarity relative to a reference uncompressed image. It exhibited better discrimination than basic point-to-point measures, i.e., relative mean squared error (RMSE). SSIM uses the overall range of pixel intensity for the image along with a measure of three factors on each individual pixel comparison. The factors, luminance, contrast, and structure, give a weighted adjustment to the similarity measure that looks at the intensity (luminance), variance (contrast), and cross-correlation (structure) between a given pixel and those that surround it versus the reference image. SSIM between two spectrograms, the reference, r, and the degraded, d, is defined with a

weighted function of intensity, l, contrast, c, and structure, s, as

$$S(r,d) = l(r,d)^\alpha \cdot c(r,d)^\beta \cdot s(r,d)^\gamma \tag{1}$$

$$S(r,d) = \left(\frac{2\mu_r\mu_d + C_1}{\mu_r^2 + \mu_d^2 + C_1} \right)^\alpha \cdot \left(\frac{2\sigma_r\sigma_d + C_2}{\sigma_r^2 + \sigma_d^2 + C_2} \right)^\beta$$
$$\times \left(\frac{\sigma_{rd} + C_3}{\sigma_r\sigma_d + C_3} \right)^\gamma \tag{2}$$

Components are weighted with α, β, and γ where all are set to 1 for the basic version of SSIM. Intensity looks at a comparison of the mean, μ, values across the two spectrograms. The structure uses the standard deviation, σ, and is equivalent to the correlation coefficient between the two spectrograms. In discrete form, σ_{rd} can be estimated as

$$\sigma_{rd} = \frac{1}{N-1} \sum_{i=1}^{N} (r_i - \mu_r)(d_i - \mu_d). \tag{3}$$

where r and d are time-frequency matrices summed across both dimensions. Full details of calculating SSIM are presented in [35].

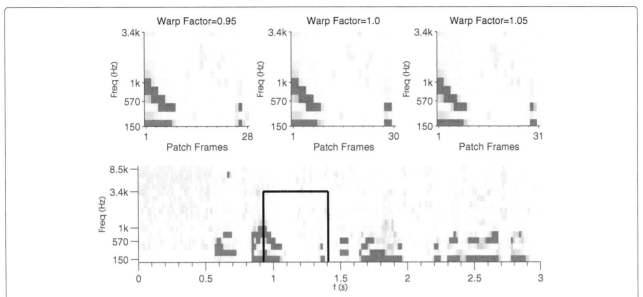

Figure 6 Patch warping. The versions of the reference patch #1 are shown: warped temporally to 0.95 times the length, un-warped (1.0 factor) and 1.05 times warped. These are compared to the degraded signal at the area of maximum similarity and adjacent frames. The highest similarity score for all warps tested is used for each given patch.

The Neurogram Similarity Index Measure (NSIM) is a simplified version of SSIM that has been shown to perform better for speech signal comparison [33] and is defined as

$$Q(r,d) = l(r,d) \cdot s(r,d) = \frac{2\mu_r \mu_d + C_1}{\mu_r^2 + \mu_d^2 + C_1} \cdot \frac{\sigma_{rd} + C_3}{\sigma_r.\sigma_d + C_3}$$

$$(4)$$

As with SSIM, each component also contains constant values $C_1 = 0.01L$ and $C_2 = C_3 = (0.03L)^2$, where L is the intensity range (as per [35]) of the reference spectrogram, which have negligible influence on the results but are used to avoid instabilities at boundary conditions, specifically where $\mu_r^2 + \mu_d^2$ is very close to zero. It was previously established that for the purposes of neurogram comparisons for speech intelligibility estimation, the optimal window size was a 3×3 pixel square covering three frequency bands and a 12.8-ms time window [32]. SSIM was further tuned, and it was established that the contrast component provided negligible value when comparing neurograms and that closer fitting to listener test data occurred using only a luminance and structural comparison [33]. Strictly, NSIM has a bounded range $-1 \leq Q \leq 1$ but for spectrograms where the reference is clean speech, the range can be considered to be $0 \leq Q \leq 1$. Comparing a signal with itself will yield an NSIM score of 1. When calculating the overall similarity, the mean NSIM score for the test patches is returned as the signal similarity estimate.

4.3 Mapping similarity to objective quality

A mapping function, roughly sigmoid in nature, is used to translate the NSIM similarity score into a MOS-LQOn score and mapped in the range 1 to 5. The mean of the third-order polynomial fitting functions for three of the ITU-T P. Supplemental 23 databases was used to create the mapping function. The database contains test results from a number of research laboratories. Results from three laboratories were used to train the mapping function (specifically those labeled A, C, and D), and laboratory O results were kept aside for metric testing and evaluation. The transfer function, $Q_{MOS} = f(z)$, where z maps the NSIM score, Q, to Q_{MOS} is described by

$$\text{clamp}(Q_{\text{MOS}}, a, b) = \begin{cases} m & \text{if } f(z) \leq m, \\ f(z) & a < f(z) \leq n \\ n & \text{if } f(z) > n \end{cases}$$

$$(5)$$

where $Q_{\text{MOS}} = az^3 + bz^2 + cz + d$, $m = 1$, $n = 5$ and the coefficients are $a = 158.7$, $b = -373.6$, $c = 295.5$ and $d = -75.3$. This transfer function is used for all data tested. A further linear regression fit was applied to the results from all of the objective metrics tested to map the objective scores to the subjective test databases used for evaluation. The correlation statistics are quoted with and without this regression fit.

4.4 Changes from early model design

An earlier prototype of the ViSQOL model was presented in prior work [4]. A number of improvements were subsequently applied to the model. Firstly, an investigation of cases with mis-aligned patches was undertaken. While NSIM is computationally more intensive than other alignment techniques such as relative mean squared error (used in [4]), it was found to be more robust [5]. Further experimentation found that while this was sufficient in medium SNR scenarios, RMSE was not robust to SNR levels less than 5 dB and resulted in mis-alignments. An example is presented in Figure 7 where a reference patch containing the utterance 'days' is shown along with the same patch from three degraded versions for the same speech sample. The RMSE remains constant for all three while the NSIM score drops in line with the perceptual MOS scores. Secondly, the warping of patches was limited to a 1% and 5% warp compared with earlier tests [4]. This was done for efficiency purposes and did not reduce accuracy.

An efficiency optimization used in the early prototype was found to reduce the accuracy of the prototype and was removed. This change was prompted by poor estimation of packet loss conditions with the earlier model for the dataset used in Experiment 4 below and is a design change to the model rather than training with a particular dataset. Specifically, the earlier model based the quality estimation on the comparison of three patches selected from the

reference signal regardless of signal duration. Removing this limitation and using a voice activity detector on the reference signal ensured that all active areas of speech are evaluated. This change ensured that temporally occurring degradations such as packet loss are captured by the model.

Finally, the intensity range, L, used by Equation 4 was set locally per patch for the results published in [5]. This was found to offset the range of the quality prediction due to dominance of the C_1 and C_3 constants in 4. By setting L globally to the intensity range of the reference spectrogram rather than each individual patch, the robustness of NSIM to MOS-LQO mapping across datasets was improved.

5 Performance evaluation

The effectiveness of the ViSQOL model is demonstrated with performance evaluation with five experiments covering both VoIP specific degradations and general quality issues. Experiment 1 expands on the results on clock drift and warp detection presented in [5] and includes a comparison with subjective listener data. Experiment 2 evaluates the impact of small playout adjustments due to jitter buffers on objective quality assessment. Experiment

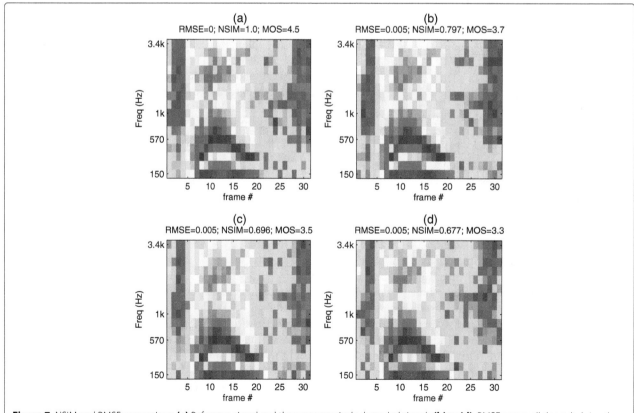

Figure 7 NSIM and RMSE comparison. **(a)** Reference signal and three progressively degraded signals **(b)** to **(d)**. RMSE scores all degraded signals equally while NSIM shows them to be progressively worse, as per the MOS results.

3 builds upon this to further analyze an open question from [28,42], where POLQA and ViSQOL show inconsistent quality estimations for some combinations of speaker and playout adjustments. Experiment 4 uses a subjectively labeled database of VoIP degradations to benchmark model performance for clock drift, packet loss, and jitter. Finally, Experiment 5 presents benchmark tests with other publicly available speech quality databases to evaluate the effectiveness of the model to a wider range of speech quality issues.

5.1 Experiment 1: clock drift and temporal warping

The first experiment tested the robustness of the three models to time warping. Packet loss concealment algorithms can effectively mask packet loss by warping speech samples with small playout adjustments. Here, ten sentences from the IEEE Harvard Speech Corpus were used as reference speech signals [43]. Time warp distortions of signals due to low-frequency clock drift between the signal transmitter and receiver were simulated. The 8-kHz sampled reference signals were resampled to create time-warped versions for resampling factors ranging from 0.85 to 1.15. This test corpus was created specifically for these tests, and a subjective listener test was carried out using ten subjects (seven males and three females) in a quiet environment using headphones. They were presented with 40 warped speech samples and asked to rate them on a MOS ACR scale. The test comprised four versions each of the ten sentences and there were ten resampling factors tested, including a non-resampled factor of 1.

The reference and resampled degraded signal were evaluated using PESQ, POLQA, and ViSQOL for each sentence at each resampling factor. The results are presented in Figure 8. They show the subjective listener test results in the top plot and predictions from the objective measures below. The resample factors from 0.85 to 1.15 along the x-axis are plotted against narrowband mean opinion scores (MOS-LQSn) for the subjective tests and narrowband objective mean opinion scores (MOS-LQOn) quality predictions for the three metrics.

The number of subjects and range of test material in the subjective tests (40 samples with ten listeners) make detailed analysis of the impact of warp on subjective speech quality unfeasible. However, the strong trend visible does allow comparison and comment on the predictive capabilities of the objective metrics.

The subjective results show a large perceived drop off in speech quality for warps of 10% to 15%, but the warps less than 5% seem to suggest a perceptible change but not a large drop in MOS-LQSn score. There is an apparent trend indicating that warp factors less than 1 yield a better quality score than those greater than 1 but further experiments with a range of speakers would be required to rule out voice variability.

The most notable results can been highlighted by examining the plus and minus 5%, 10%, and 15% warp factors. At 5%, the subjective tests point towards a perceptible change in quality, but one that does not alter the MOS-LQSn score to a large extent. ViSQOL predicts a slow drop in quality between 1% and 5%, and POLQA predicts no drop. Either result would be preferred to those of PESQ which predicts a rapid drop to just above 1 MOS-LQOn for a warp of 5%.

At 10% to 15%, the subjective tests indicate that a MOS-LQSn of 2 to 3 should be expected and ViSQOL predicts this trend. However, both POLQA and PESQ have saturated their scale and predict a minimum MOS-LQOn score of 1% from 10% warping. Warping of this scale does cause a noticeable change in the voice pitch from the reference speech but the gentle decline in quality scores predicted by ViSQOL is more in line with listeners' opinions than those of PESQ and POLQA.

The use of jitter buffers is ubiquitous in VoIP systems and often introduces warping to speech. The use of NSIM for patch alignment combined with estimating the similarity using warp-adjusted patches provides ViSQOL with a promising warp estimation strategy for speech quality estimation. Small amounts of warp (around 5% or less) are critical for VoIP scenarios, where playout adjustments are commonly employed. Unlike PESQ where small warps cause large drops in predicted quality, both POLQA and ViSQOL exhibit a lack of sensitivity for warps up to 5% that reflect the listener quality experience.

5.2 Experiment 2: playout delay changes

Short network delays are commonly dealt with using per talkspurt adjustments, i.e., inserting or removing portions of silence periods, to cope with time alignment in VoIP. Work by Pocta et al. [42] used sentences from the English speaking portion of ITU-T P Supplement 23 coded-speech database [44] to develop a test corpus of realistic delay adjustment conditions. One hundred samples (96 degraded and four references, two male and two female speakers) covered a range of 12 realistic delay adjustment conditions. The adjustments were a mix of positive and negative adjustments summing to zero (adding and removing silence periods). The conditions comprised two variants (A and B) with the adjustments applied towards the beginning or end of the speech sample. The absolute sum of adjustments ranged from 0 to 66 ms. Thirty listeners participated in the subjective tests, and MOS scores were averaged for each condition.

Where Experiment 1 investigated time warping, this experiment investigates a second VoIP factor, playout delay adjustments. They are investigated and presented here as isolated factors rather than combined in a single test. In a real VoIP system, the components would occur

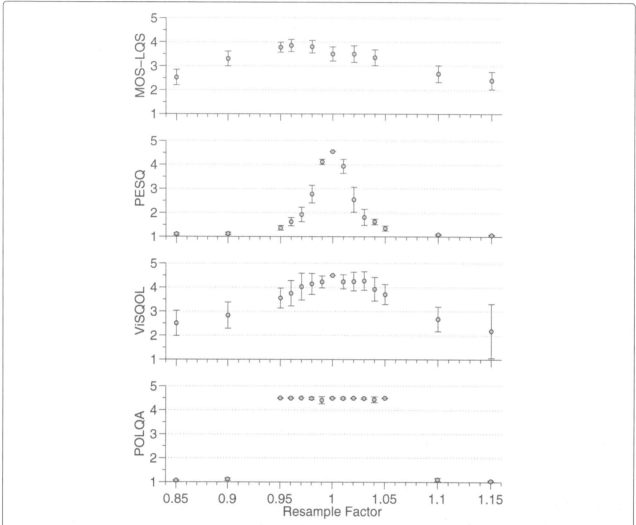

Figure 8 Experiment 1: clock drift and warp test. Subjective MOS-LQS results for listener tests with MOS-LQOn predictions below for each model comparing ten sentences for each resample factor.

together but as a practical compromise, the analysis is performed in isolation.

The adjustments used are typical (in extent and magnitude) of those introduced by VoIP jitter buffer algorithms [45]. The subjective test results showed that speaker voice preference dominated the subjective test results more than playout delay adjustment duration or location [42]. By design, full-reference objective metrics, including ViSQOL, do not qualify speaker voice difference reducing their correlation with the subjective tests.

The test conditions were compared to the reference samples for the 12 conditions, and the results for ViSQOL, PESQ, and POLQA were compared to those from the subjective tests. These tests and the dominant subjective factors are discussed in more detail in [28,42].

This database is examined here to investigate whether realistic playout adjustments that were shown to be imperceptible from a speech quality perspective are correctly disregarded by ViSQOL, PESQ, and POLQA.

The per condition results previously reported [42] showed that there was poor correlation between subjective and objective scores for all metrics tested but this was as a result of the playout delay changes not being a dominant factor in the speech quality. The results were analyzed for PESQ and POLQA [42] and subsequently for ViSQOL [28], showing MOS scores grouped by speaker and variant instead of playout condition. The combined results from both studies are presented in Figure 9. Looking at the plot of listener test results, the MOS-LQS is plotted on the y-axis against the speaker/variant on the x-axis. It is apparent from the 95% confidence interval bars that condition variability was minimal, and that there was little difference between variants. The dominant factor was the voice quality, i.e., the inherent quality

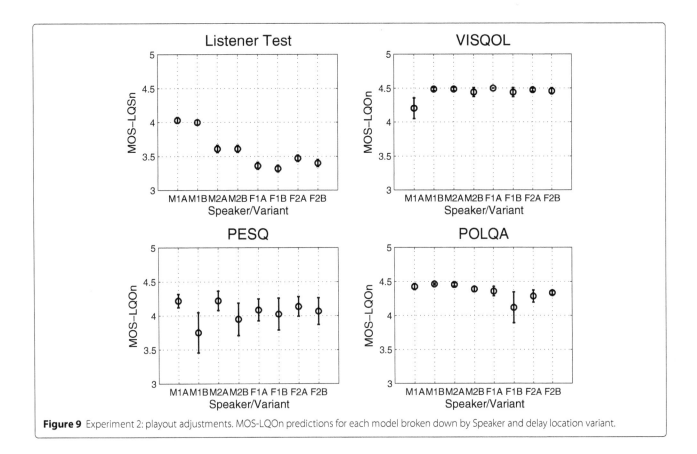

Figure 9 Experiment 2: playout adjustments. MOS-LQOn predictions for each model broken down by Speaker and delay location variant.

pleasantness of the talker's voice, and not related to transmission factors. Hence, as voice quality is not accounted for by the full-reference metrics, maximum scores should be expected for all speakers. PESQ exhibited variability across all tests, indicating that playout delay was impacting the quality predictions. This was clearly shown in [42]. The results for ViSQOL and POLQA are much more promising apart from some noticeable deviations e.g., the Male 1, Variant A (M1A) for ViSQOL; and the Female 1, Variant B (F1B) for POLQA.

5.3 Experiment 3: playout delay changes II

A follow-up test was carried out to try and establish the cause of the variability in results from Experiment 2. This test focused on two speech samples from Experiment 2 where ViSQOL and POLQA predicted quality to be much lower than was found with subjective testing.

For this experiment, two samples were examined. In the first, a silent playout adjustment is inserted in a silence period and in the second, it is inserted within an active speech segment. The start times for the adjustments are illustrated in the lower panes of Figure 10. The quality was measured for each test sentence containing progressively longer delay adjustments. The delay was increased from 0 to 40 ms in 2-ms increments. The upper panes present the results with the duration of the inserted

playout adjustment on the x-axis against the predicted MOS-LQOn from POLQA and ViSQOL on the y-axis.

ViSQOL displays a periodic variation of up to 0.5 MOS for certain adjustment lengths. Conversely, POLQA remains consistent in the second test (aside from a small drop of around 0.1 for a 40-ms delay), while in the first test, delays from 4 up to 14 ms cause a rapid drop in predicted MOS with a maximum drop in MOS-LQOn of almost 2.5. These tests highlight the fact that not all imperceptible signal adjustments are handled correctly by either model.

The ViSQOL error is down to the spectrogram windowing and the correct alignment of patches. The problems highlighted by the examples shown here occur only in specific circumstances where the delays are of certain lengths. Also, as demonstrated by the results in the previous experiment, the problem can be alleviated by a canceling effect of multiple delay adjustments where positive and negative adjustments balance out the mis-alignment.

Combined with warping, playout delay adjustments are a key feature for VoIP quality assessment. Flagging these two imperceptible temporal adjustments as a quality issue could mask other factors that actually are perceptible. Although both have limitations, ViSQOL and POLQA are again performing better than PESQ for these conditions.

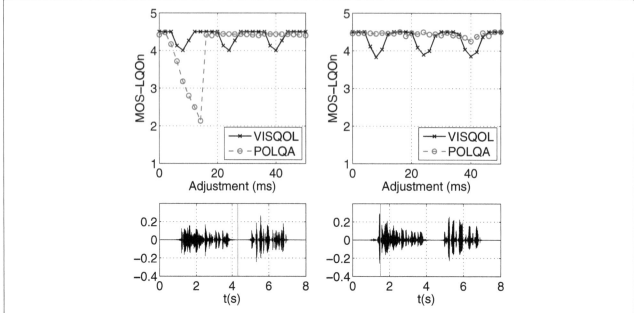

Figure 10 Experiment 3: progressive playout delays. Above, objective quality predictions for progressively increasing playout delays using two sample sentences. Below, sample signals with playout delay locations marked.

5.4 Experiment 4: VoIP specific quality test

A VoIP speech quality corpus, referred to in this paper as the GIPS E4 corpus, contains tests of the wideband codec iSAC [46] with superwideband references. The test was a MOS ACR listening assessment, performed in Native British English. Within these experiments, the iSAC wideband codec was assessed with respect to speech codec and condition. The processed sentence pairs were each scored by 25 listeners. The sentences are from ITU-T Recommendation P.501 [47] which contains two male and two female (British) English speakers sampled at 32 kHz.

For these tests, all signals were down-sampled to 8-kHz narrowband signals. Twenty-seven conditions from the corpus were tested with four speakers per condition (two males and two females). Twenty-five listeners scored each test sample, resulting in 100 votes per condition. The breakdown of conditions was as follows: 10 jitter conditions, 13 packet losses, and four clock drifts. The conditions cover real time, 20 kbps and 32 kbps versions of the iSAC codec. Details of the conditions in the E4 database are summarized in Table 1. While the corpus supplied test files containing the four speakers' sentences concatenated together for each condition, they were separated and tested individually with the objective measures. This dataset contains examples of some of the key VoIP quality degradations that ViSQOL was designed to accurately estimate as jitter, clock drift, and packet loss cause problems with time-alignment and signal warping that are specifically handed by the model design.

The results are presented in Figure 11. The scatter of conditions highlights that PESQ tended to under-predict and POLQA tended to over-predict the MOS scores for the conditions while the ViSQOL estimates were more tightly clustered. Correlation scores for all metrics are presented in Table 2.

5.5 Experiment 5: non-VoIP specific quality tests

A final experiment used two publicly available databases to give an indication of ViSQOL's more general speech quality prediction capabilities.

The ITU-T P Supplement 23 (P.Sup23) coded-speech database was developed for the ITU-T 8 kbit/s codec (Recommendation G.729) characterization tests [44]. The conditions are exclusively narrowband speech degradations but are useful for speech quality benchmarking and remain actively used for objective VoIP speech quality models, e.g., [48]. It contains three experimental datasets with subjective results from tests carried out in four labs. Experiment 3 in [44] contains four speakers (two males and two females) for 50 conditions covering a range of VoIP degradations and was evaluated using ACR. The reference and degraded PCM speech material and subjective scores are provided with the database. The English language data (lab O) is referred to in this paper as the P.Sup23 database. As stated in Section 4.3, the subjective results from the other labs (i.e., A, B, and D) were used in the model design for the similarity score to objective quality mapping function.

NOIZEUS [49] is a narrowband 8-kHz sampled noisy speech corpus that was originally developed for evaluation

Table 1 GIPS E4 database

Cond no.	Bitrate	Condition	Cond no.	Bitrate	Condition	Cond no.	Bitrate	Condition
1	Real-time	Jitter	10	20 kbps	Jitter	19	32 kbps	Clock drift
2	Real-time	Jitter	11	20 kbps	Jitter	20	32 kbps	Jitter
3	Real-time	Packet loss	12	20 kbps	Jitter	21	32 kbps	Jitter
4	Real-time	Packet loss	13	20 kbps	Jitter	22	32 kbps	Jitter
5	Real-time	Packet loss	14	20 kbps	Packet loss	23	32 kbps	Jitter
6	Real-time	Packet loss	15	20 kbps	Packet loss	24	32 kbps	Packet loss
7	Real-time	Packet loss	16	20 kbps	Packet loss	25	32 kbps	Packet loss
8	20 kbps	Clock drift	17	32 kbps	Packet loss	26	32 kbps	Packet loss
9	20 kbps	Clock drift	18	32 kbps	Clock drift	27	32 kbps	Packet loss

Tests conditions and bitrates using iSAC codec.

of speech enhancement algorithms. Mean opinion scores (MOSs) for a subset of the corpus were obtained using the ITU-T Recommendation P.835 [50] methodology for subjective evaluation. It uses three ratings for each speech sample: the quality of the speech signal alone on a 5-point scale; the intrusiveness of the background noise on a 5-point scale; and the overall signal quality as a MOS ACR. This method was designed to reduce a listener's uncertainty as to the source of the quality issue, e.g., is it the speech signal itself that has been muffled or otherwise impaired or is it a background noise or a combination of both. Further work carried out by Hu and Loizou studied the correlation between objective measures and the

subjective quality of noise-suppressed speech [29] and compared PESQ with a range of segmental SNR, LPC, and distance metrics. For the experiments in this paper, only the overall MOS scores were analyzed. Speech subjected to enhancement algorithms, as in the NOIZEUS database, was omitted from the validated scope of POLQA and PESQ. Although the NOIZEUS dataset was not included in the validation testing of POLQA, the specification does not specifically exclude voice enhancement, as was the case for PESQ [25].

Four noise types from the full NOIZEUS corpus were tested: babble, car, street, and train. Each noise type was tested with 13 speech enhancement algorithms plus the

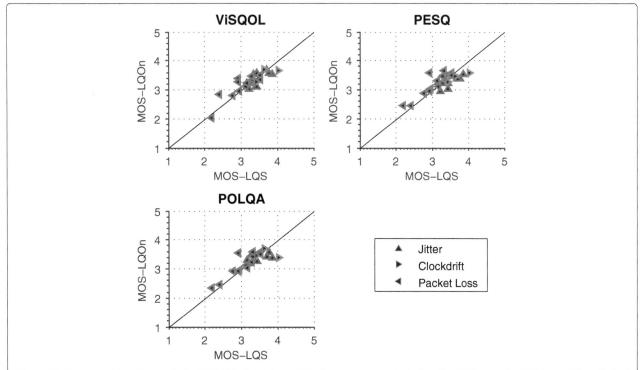

Figure 11 Experiment 4: scatter results for GIPS E4 VoIP database. Objective measures against subjective MOS scores for VoIP degradations. Plotted after linear regression fitting.

Table 2 Statistics for Experiments 4 and 5

	E4			NOIZEUS			P.Sup23		
	Pearson	Spearman	Std. err.	Pearson	Spearman	Std. err.	Pearson	Spearman	Std. err.
Without fit									
ViSQOL	0.80	0.74	0.20	0.87	0.74	0.23	0.77	0.64	0.47
PESQ	0.78	0.57	0.18	0.90	0.57	0.20	0.92	0.90	0.29
POLQA	0.81	0.65	0.26	0.77	0.65	0.29	0.96	0.96	0.20
LLR	0.25	0.27	0.20	0.88	0.27	0.22	0.44	0.18	0.65
fwSNRSeg	0.21	0.14	0.21	0.86	0.14	0.24	0.48	0.38	0.64
With linear fit									
ViSQOL	0.85	0.77	0.22	0.84	0.86	0.25	0.81	0.70	0.43
PESQ	0.78	0.57	0.26	0.90	0.88	0.20	0.92	0.90	0.29
POLQA	0.81	0.65	0.24	0.77	0.79	0.29	0.96	0.96	0.20
LLR	0.25	0.27	0.40	0.88	0.88	0.22	0.44	0.18	0.65
fwSNRSeg	0.21	0.14	0.40	0.86	0.85	0.24	0.48	0.38	0.64

noisy non-enhanced speech at two SNR levels (5 and 10 dB). This gave a total of 112 conditions (four noise types, 14 enhancement variations and two SNR levels). Thirty-two listeners rated the overall quality for each condition with 16 sentences. The MOS scores were averaged for listeners and sentences across each condition. For objective metric testing, the results were calculated in a corresponding manner, with a mean score for the 16 sentences calculated per condition.

Hu and Loizou [29] used the NOIZEUS database to evaluate seven objective speech quality measures. They also investigated composite measures by combining other measures in a weighted manner with PESQ as they did not expect simple objective measures to correlate highly with signal/noise distortion *and* overall quality. The methodology in this work follows the same experiment design and performance evaluation as Hu and Loizou [29]. They measured Pearson's correlation coefficient across the 112 conditions for each measure as well as the standard deviation of the error. For predicting overall quality, they found that PESQ generated the highest correlation of the metrics tested. Absolute values of Pearson's correlation coefficient, $|\rho|$, can be calculated using

$$\rho = \frac{\sum_i (o_i - \bar{o})(s_i - \bar{s})}{\sqrt{\sum_i (o_i - \bar{o})^2}\sqrt{\sum_i (s_i - \bar{s})^2}} \qquad (6)$$

where i is the condition index, o is the objective metric score, s is the subjective quality rating (MOS) score, and $\bar{o}$ and $\bar{s}$ are the mean values of o and s, respectively. The standard deviation of the error, $\hat{\sigma}_e$, was also measured as a secondary test,

$$\hat{\sigma}_e = \hat{\sigma}_s \sqrt{1 - \rho^2} \qquad (7)$$

where $\hat{\sigma}_s$ is the standard deviation of the subjective quality scores, and s and ρ is the correlation coefficient. The

Spearman rank correlation was also computed, replacing the quality scores o and s in 6 with their ranks. Hu and Loizou [29] split their data for training and testing. Subsequent evaluations by Kressner et al. [51] repeated the experiments using the full dataset of 1,792 speech files, which is the approach adopted in this study.

The NOIZEUS and P.Sup23 corpora were tested with ViSQOL, PESQ, POLQA, and two additional simple objective metrics, LLR and fwSNRSeg (details of which can be found in [29]). Results were averaged by condition and compared to the average MOS scores per condition. Figure 12 shows the results for each objective quality measure. The scatter shows 112 NOIZEUS conditions and 50 P.Sup23 conditions. The statistical analysis is summarised in Table 2.

As noted by Hu and Loizou in their tests [29], the two less complex metrics, LLR and fwSNRSeg, performed almost as well as PESQ in estimating the quality for the range of background noises evaluated. While they exhibit good correlation for the NOIZEUS tests, their correlation with MOS quality scores for the P.Sup23 and E4 database is much lower (see Table 2). As these are simple measures, it is understandable that while they may perform well for background noise, even if it is not homogeneous, they perform poorly when quantifying more subtle and temporally short-quality degradations such as packet loss or jitter. LLR and fwSNRSeg are simple distance metrics and do not perform any signal alignment, only signal comparison. They have no temporal alignment of signals, leveling, or other pre-processing steps before comparison. They were included in this test to highlight their limitations for VoIP speech quality conditions, and the lack of correlation in the Figure 12 scatter plots illustrates the performance variability between the difference datasets.

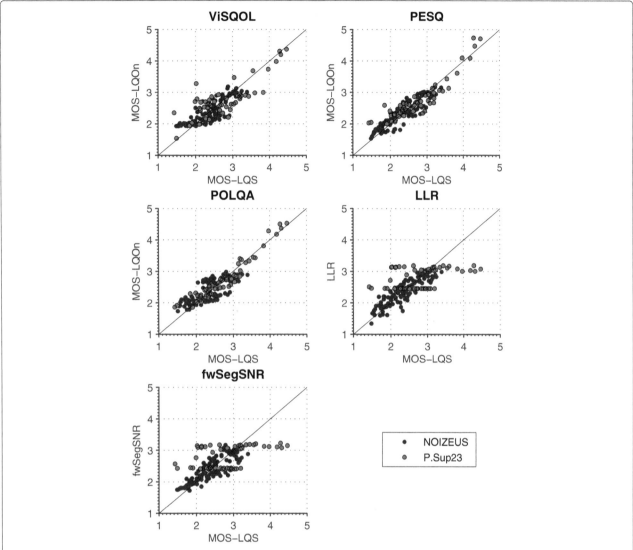

Figure 12 Experiment 5: scatter results (NOIZEUS and P.Sup23). Objective measures against subjective MOS scores for noise and other degradations using NOIZEUS and P.Sup23 Exp 3 (Lab O; English). Plotted after linear regression fitting.

6 Summary and general discussion

ViSQOL shows good correlation with the NOIZEUS database subjective listener scores. The results demonstrate ViSQOL's ability to estimate speech quality in a range of background noises and also for a range of speech enhancement conditions. The P.Sup23 tests results for ViSQOL were noticeably poorer than for the other datasets, particularly in terms of the rank correlation and standard error where both PESQ and POLQA perform significantly better. Looking at the scatter plot for ViSQOL in Figure 12, the problem appears to be for lower quality samples in the MOS range of 2 to 3 where it fails to differentiate between more severe quality degradations. This may be due to the flat region in the mapping function where the raw NSIM results are tightly clustered.

For comparison, POLQA and PESQ were tested with the same test material. The results for tests with the NOIZEUS database are consistent with the performance of PESQ reported by various other authors [29,51]. Somewhat surprisingly, POLQA did not perform as well as ViSQOL or PESQ. Examining the scatter plot for POLQA in Figure 12, the NOIZEUS conditions can be seen to cluster into two groups, with a gap in the range 2 to 2.2 on the y-axis (MOS-LQOn). Further investigation showed that this gap was not a distinction based on condition, noise type, or SNR.

The Pearson correlation between all three models and the subjective quality scores were similar for the GIPS E4 database. These results had more variability within conditions, and the confidence intervals were larger than for the conditions tested in the NOIZEUS database. However,

ViSQOL performed better in Spearman ranking correlation than either PESQ or POLQA for the GIPS E4 and NOIZEUS databases. The conformance test results carried out during the development of POLQA show that POLQA performs better than PESQ for all of the development and test conditions [2] tested during POLQA development. The results reported here show POLQA performed better than PESQ for the GIPS E4 tests in Experiment 4 but not the NOIZEUS tests in Experiment 5.

The correlation between subjective listener tests and objective predictions for all three models demonstrate an ability to predict subjective MOS scores when evaluated with unseen test corpora (Table 2). The PESQ model performed poorly in Experiment 1 testing warping (Figure 8). POLQA has addressed this design problem and predicts no degradation in perceived quality for up to 5% warping. ViSQOL deals with warping in a more gradual way than POLQA which is more in line with listener quality perceptions. For small, varied, imperceptible playout adjustments, ViSQOL and POLQA perform better than PESQ which shows a strong susceptibility to temporal alignment mismatches (Figure 9). For certain playout delay conditions, both ViSQOL and POLQA have shortcomings that were highlighted. ViSQOL can vary by up to 0.5 MOS for a range of adjustments and POLQA can by up to 2.5 MOS in certain conditions (Figure 10).

Overall, ViSQOL is a useful alternative to PESQ or POLQA as a full-reference speech quality model especially where VoIP systems are being evaluated. The algorithm design contains a number of properties that help deal with temporal and warping issues that can mask or distort the estimation of speech quality.

7 Conclusions

ViSQOL is a simple objective speech quality model based upon a mean of similarity comparisons between time-aligned, time-frequency representations of a reference and a degraded signal. Tests for a variety of conditions and VoIP-specific issues showed that it performed better than simple distance metrics and was comparable to the ITU standards, PESQ and POLQA, for wider datasets. Further work is planned with wideband speech corpora as well as for wider usage in general audio quality.

Competing interests
The authors declare that they have no competing interests.

Acknowledgements
Andrew Hines thanks Google, Inc. for support. Thanks also to Yi Hu for sharing the full listener test MOS results and enhanced test files for the NOIZEUS database.

Author details
[1] School of Computing, Dublin Institute of Technology, Kevin St, Dublin 8, Ireland. [2] Sigmedia, Department of Electronic and Electrical Engineering, Trinity College Dublin, College Green, Dublin 2, Ireland. [3] Google, Inc., 1600 Amphitheatre Parkway, CA 94043, Mountain View, USA.

References
1. ITU, Perceptual Evaluation of Speech Quality (PESQ): an objective method for end-to-end speech quality assessment of narrow-band telephone networks and speech codecs. Int. Telecomm. Union, Geneva, Switzerland, ITU-T Rec. P.862 (2001)
2. ITU, Perceptual objective listening quality assessment. Int. Telecomm. Union, Geneva, Switzerland, ITU-T Rec. P.863 (2011)
3. ITU, Wideband extension to recommendation P.862 for the assessment of wideband telephone networks and speech codecs. Int. Telecomm. Union, Geneva, Switzerland, ITU-T Rec. P.862.2 (2005)
4. A Hines, J Skoglund, A Kokaram, N Harte, in *Acoustic Echo Noise Control (IWAENC), IEEE Intl. Workshop on.* VISQOL: The Virtual Speech Quality Objective Listener (IEEE Aachen, Germany, 2012), pp. 1–4
5. A Hines, J Skoglund, A Kokaram, N Harte, in *Acoustics, Speech and Signal Processing (ICASSP), 2013 IEEE International Conference on.* Robustness of speech quality metrics to background noise and network degradations: Comparing ViSQOL, PESQ and POLQA (IEEE Vancouver, Canada, 2013), pp. 3697–3701
6. H Levy, H Zlatokrilov, The effect of packet dispersion on voice applications in IP networks. IEEE/ACM Trans. Netw. **14**(2), 277–288 (2006)
7. ITU, ITU-T One-way transmission time. Int. Telecomm. Union, Geneva, Switzerland, ITU-T Rec. G.114 (2003)
8. BH Kim, H-G Kim, J Jeong, JY Kim, VoIP receiver-based adaptive playout scheduling and packet loss concealment technique. IEEE Trans. Consum. Electron. **59**(1), 250–258 (2013)
9. WebRTC, WebRTC FAQ. (http://www.webrtc.org/)
10. WebRTC, WebRTC FAQ. (http://www.webrtc.org/architecture)
11. ITU, ITU-T Methods for subjective determination of transmission quality. Int. Telecomm. Union, Geneva, Switzerland, ITU-T Rec. P.800 (1996)
12. S Möller, R Heusdens, Objective estimation of speech quality for communication systems. Proc. of the IEEE. **101**, 1955–1967 (2013)
13. T Yamada, M Kumakura, N Kitawaki, Performance estimation of speech recognition system under noise conditions using objective quality measures and artificial voice. IEEE Trans. Audio Speech Lang. Process. **14**(6), 2006–2013 (2006)
14. S Möller, W-Y Chan, Côté, TH Falk, A Raake, M Waltermann, Speech quality estimation: models and trends. IEEE Signal Process. Mag. **28**(6), 18–28 (2011)
15. ITU, The E-model, a computational model for use in transmission planning (2009)
16. ITU, Wideband E-model. Int. Telecomm. Union, Geneva, Switzerland, ITU-T Rec. G.107.1 (2011)
17. ANSI ATIS, 0100005-2006: Auditory non-intrusive quality estimation plus (ANIQUE+): Perceptual model for non-intrusive estimation of narrowband speech quality (2006)
18. ITU, Single-ended method for objective speech quality assessment in narrow-band telephony applications. Int. Telecomm. Union, Geneva, Switzerland, ITU-T Rec. P.563 (2011)
19. L Sun, EC Ifeachor, Voice quality prediction models and their application in voip networks. IEEE Trans. Multimedia. **8**(4), 809–820 (2006)
20. TH Falk, W-Y Chan, Nonintrusive speech quality estimation using gaussian mixture models. IEEE Signal Process. Lett. **13**(2), 108–111 (2006)
21. V Grancharov, DY Zhao, J Lindblom, WB Kleijn, Low-complexity, nonintrusive speech quality assessment. IEEE Trans. Audio Speech Lang. Process. **14**(6), 1948–1956 (2006)
22. D Sharma, PA Naylor, ND Gaubitch, M Brookes, in *Proc. of the 19th European Signal Processing Conference (EUSIPCO).* Short-time objective assessment of speech quality (EURASIP Barcelona, Spain, 2011), pp. 471–475
23. Z Qiao, L Sun, E Ifeachor, in *Personal, Indoor and Mobile Radio Communications, 2008. PIMRC 2008. IEEE 19th International Symposium On.* Case study of PESQ performance in live wireless mobile voip environment (IEEE Cannes, France, 2008), pp. 1–6

24. O Slavata, J Holub, Evaluation of objective speech transmission quality measurements in packet-based networks. Comput. Stand. Interfaces. **36**, 626–630 (2014)

25. JG Beerends, C Schmidmer, J Berger, M Obermann, R Ullmann, J Pomy, M Keyhl, Perceptual Objective Listening Quality Assessment (POLQA), the third generation ITU-T standard for end-to-end speech quality measurement Part I – temporal alignment. J. Audio Eng. Soc. **61**(6), 366–384 (2013)

26. M Voznak, J Rozhon, P Partila, J Safarik, M Mikulec, M Mehic, *Predictive Model for Determining the Quality of a Call*, Proc. SPIE, vol. 9118, (Baltimore, Maryland, USA, 2014)

27. H Assem, D Malone, J Dunne, P O'Sullivan, in *Computing, Networking and Communications (ICNC), 2013 International Conference On*. Monitoring VoIP call quality using improved simplified e-model (IEEE San Diego, CA, USA, 2013), pp. 927–931

28. A Hines, P Pocta, H Melvin, in *Quality of Multimedia Experience (QoMEX), IEEE Workshop on*. Detailed analysis of PESQ and VISQOL behaviour in the context of playout delay adjustments introduced by voip jitter buffer algorithms (Klagenfurt am Wörthersee, Austria, 2013), pp. 18–22

29. Y Hu, PC Loizou, Evaluation of objective quality measures for speech enhancement. IEEE Trans. Audio Speech Lang. Process. **16**(1), 229–238 (2008)

30. PC Loizou, *Speech Enhancement – Theory and Practice*. (CRC Press, Boca Raton USA, 2007)

31. A Rix, in *Proc. Measurement of Speech and Audio Quality in Networks (MESAQIN'03)*. Comparison between subjective listening quality and P.862 PESQ score (Prague, Czech Republic, 2003)

32. A Hines, N Harte, Speech intelligibility from image processing. Speech Commun. **52**(9), 736–752 (2010)

33. A Hines, N Harte, Speech intelligibility prediction using a neurogram similarity index measure. Speech Commun. **54**(2), 306–320 (2012)

34. MSA Zilany, IC Bruce, PC Nelson, LH Carney, A phenomenological model of the synapse between the inner hair cell and auditory nerve: long-term adaptation with power-law dynamics. J. Acoust. Soc. Am. **126**(5), 2390–2412 (2009)

35. Z Wang, AC Bovik, HR Sheikh, EP Simoncelli, Image quality assessment: from error visibility to structural similarity. IEEE Trans. Image Process. **13**(4), 600–612 (2004)

36. S Kandadai, J Hardin, CD Creusere, in *Acoustics, Speech and Signal Processing, 2008. ICASSP 2008. IEEE International Conference on*. Audio quality assessment using the mean structural similarity measure (IEEE Las Vegas, NV, USA, 2008), pp. 221–224

37. D Breakey, C Meskell, Comparison of metrics for the evaluation of similarity in acoustic pressure signals. J. Sound Vibration. **332**(15), 3605–3609 (2013)

38. W Voiers, in *Acoustics, Speech, and Signal Processing, 1980. ICASSP 1980. IEEE International Conference on*. Interdependencies among measures of speech intelligibility and speech "quality", vol. 5 (IEEE Denver, CO, USA, 1980), pp. 703–705

39. A Hines, N Harte, in *Speech Perception and Auditory Disorders*, ed. by T. Dau, et al. Comparing hearing aid algorithm performance using simulated performance intensity functions (Danavox Jubilee Foundation Ballerup, Denmark, 2011), pp. 347–354

40. ViSQOL Software. http://sigmedia.tv/tools

41. ANSI, *ANSI S3.5-1997 (R2007). Methods for Calculation of the Speech Intelligibility Index*. (American National Standards Institute, New York, 1997)

42. P Pocta, H Melvin, A Hines, An analysis of the impact of playout delay adjustments introduced by VoIP jitter buffers on speech quality. Acta Acoust. united Acustica. **101**(3), 616–631 (2015)

43. IEEE, IEEE recommended practice for speech quality measurements. IEEE Trans. Audio Electroacoustics. **17**(3), 225–246 (1969)

44. ITU, ITU-T coded-speech database. Int. Telecomm. Union, Geneva, Switzerland, ITU-T Rec. P.Sup23 (1998)

45. C Hoene, H Karl, A Wolisz, A perceptual quality model intended for adaptive VoIP applications. Int. J. Commun. Syst. **19**(3), 299–316 (2005)

46. WebRTC, WebRTC FAQ. (http://www.webrtc.org/faq#TOC-What-is-the-iSAC-audio-codec-)

47. ITU, Test signals for use in telephonometry, Int. Telecomm. Union, Geneva, Switzerland, ITU-T Rec. P.501 (2012)

48. M-K Lee, H-G Kang, Speech quality estimation of voice over internet protocol codec using a packet loss impairment model. J. Acoust. Soc. Am. **134**(5), 438–444 (2013)

49. Y Hu, PC Loizou, Subjective comparison and evaluation of speech enhancement algorithms. Speech Commun. **49**(7-8), 588–601 (2007)

50. ITU, Subjective test methodology for evaluating speech communication systems that include noise suppression algorithm. Int. Telecomm. Union, Geneva, Switzerland, ITU-T Rec. P.835 (2003)

51. AA Kressner, DV Anderson, CJ Rozell, in *Applications of Signal Processing to Audio and Acoustics (WASPAA), 2011 IEEE Workshop on*. Robustness of the hearing aid speech quality index (HASQI) (IEEE New Paltz, NY, USA, 2011), pp. 209–212

15

Sparse coding of the modulation spectrum for noise-robust automatic speech recognition

Sara Ahmadi[1,2†], Seyed Mohammad Ahadi[1*], Bert Cranen[2†] and Lou Boves[2†]

Abstract

The full modulation spectrum is a high-dimensional representation of one-dimensional audio signals. Most previous research in automatic speech recognition converted this very rich representation into the equivalent of a sequence of short-time power spectra, mainly to simplify the computation of the posterior probability that a frame of an unknown speech signal is related to a specific state. In this paper we use the raw output of a modulation spectrum analyser in combination with sparse coding as a means for obtaining state posterior probabilities. The modulation spectrum analyser uses 15 gammatone filters. The Hilbert envelope of the output of these filters is then processed by nine modulation frequency filters, with bandwidths up to 16 Hz. Experiments using the AURORA-2 task show that the novel approach is promising. We found that the representation of medium-term dynamics in the modulation spectrum analyser must be improved. We also found that we should move towards sparse classification, by modifying the cost function in sparse coding such that the class(es) represented by the exemplars weigh in, in addition to the accuracy with which unknown observations are reconstructed. This creates two challenges: (1) developing a method for dictionary learning that takes the class occupancy of exemplars into account and (2) developing a method for learning a mapping from exemplar activations to state posterior probabilities that keeps the generalization to unseen conditions that is one of the strongest advantages of sparse coding.

Keywords: Sparse coding/compressive sensing; Sparse classification; Modulation spectrum; Noise robust automatic speech recognition

1 Introduction

Nobody will seriously disagree with the statement that most of the information in acoustic signals is encoded in the way in which the signal properties change over time and that instantaneous characteristics, such as the shape or the envelope of the short-time spectrum, are less important - though surely not unimportant. The dynamic changes over time in the envelope of the short-time spectrum are captured in the modulation spectrum [1-3]. This makes the modulation spectrum a fundamentally more informative representation of audio signals than a sequence of short-time spectra. Still, most approaches in speech technology, whether it is speech recognition, speech synthesis, speaker recognition, or speech coding, seem to rely on impoverished representations of the modulation spectrum in the form of a sequence of short-time spectra, possibly extended with explicit information about the dynamic changes in the form of delta and delta-delta coefficients. For speech (and audio) coding, the reliance on sequences of short-time spectra can be explained by the fact that many applications (first and foremost telephony) cannot tolerate delays in the order of 250 ms, while full use of modulation spectra might incur delays up to a second. What is more, coders can rely on the human auditory system to extract and utilize the dynamic changes that are still retained in the output of the coders. If coders are used in environments and applications in which delay is not an issue (music recording, broadcast transmission), we do see a more elaborate use of information linked to modulation spectra [4-6]. Here too, the focus is on reducing bit rates by capitalizing on the properties of the human auditory system. We are not aware of approaches to speech synthesis - where delay is not an issue - that aim to harness advantages offered by

*Correspondence: sma@aut.ac.ir
†Equal contributors
[1] Amirkabir University of Technology, Hafez 424, 15875-4413 Tehran, Iran
Full list of author information is available at the end of the article

the modulation spectrum. Information about the temporal dynamics of speech signal by means of shifted delta cepstra has proven beneficial for automatic language and speaker recognition [7].

In this paper we are concerned with the use of modulation spectra for automatic speech recognition (ASR), specifically noise-robust speech recognition. In this application domain, we cannot rely on the intervention of the human auditory system. On the contrary, it is now necessary to automatically extract the information encoded in the modulation spectrum that humans would use to understand the message.

The seminal research by [1] showed that modulation frequencies >16 Hz contribute very little to speech intelligibility. In [8] it was shown that attenuating modulation frequencies <1 Hz does not affect intelligibility either. Very low modulation frequencies are related to stationary channel characteristics or stationary noise, rather than to the dynamically changing speech signal carried by the channel. The upper limit of the band with linguistically relevant modulation frequencies is related to the maximum speed with which the articulators can move. This insight gave rise to the introduction of RASTA filtering in [9] and [10]. RASTA filtering is best conceived of as a form of post-processing applied on the output of otherwise conventional representations of the speech signal derived from short-time spectra. This puts RASTA filtering in the same category as, for example, Mel-frequency spectra and Mel-frequency cepstral coefficients: engineering approaches designed to efficiently approximate representations manifested in psycho-acoustic experiments [11]. Subsequent developments towards harnessing the modulation spectrum in ASR have followed pretty much the same path, characterized by some form of additional processing applied to sequences of short-time spectral (or cepstral) features. Perhaps somewhat surprisingly, none of these developments have given rise to substantial improvements of recognition performance relative to other engineering tricks that do not take guidance from knowledge about the auditory system.

All existing ASR systems are characterized by an architecture that consists of a front end and a back end. The back end always comes in the form of a state network, in which words are discrete units, made up of a directed graph of subword units (usually phones), each of which is in turn represented as a sequence of states. Recognizing an utterance amounts to searching the path in a finite-state machine that has the maximum likelihood, given an acoustic signal. The link between a continuous audio signal and the discrete state machine is established by converting the acoustic signal into a sequence of likelihoods that a short segment of the signal corresponds to one of the low-level states. The task of the front end is to convert the signal into a sequence of state likelihood

estimates, usually at a 100-Hz rate, which should be more than adequate to capture the fastest possible articulation movements.

Speech coding or speech synthesis with a 100-Hz frame rate using short-time spectra yields perfectly intelligible and natural-sounding results. Therefore, it was only natural to assume that a sequence of short-time spectra at the same frame rate would be a good input representation for an ASR system. However, already in the early seventies, it was shown by Jean-Silvain Liénard [12] that it was necessary to augment the static spectrum representation by so-called delta and delta-delta coefficients that represent the speed and acceleration of the change of the spectral envelope over time and that were popularized by [13]. For reasonably clean speech, this approach appears to be adequate.

Under acoustically adverse conditions, the recognition performance of ASR systems degrades much more rapidly than human performance [14]. Convolutional noise can be effectively handled by RASTA-like processing. Distortions due to reverberation have a direct impact on the modulation spectrum, and they also cause substantial difficulties for human listeners [15,16]. Therefore, much research in noise-robust ASR has focused on speech recognition in additive noise. Speech recognition in noise basically must solve two problems simultaneously: (1) one needs to determine which acoustic properties of the signal belong to the target speech and which are due to the background noise (the source separation problem), and (2) those parts of the acoustic representations of the speech signal which are not entirely obscured by the noise must be processed to decode the linguistic message (speech decoding problem).

For a recent review of the range of approaches that has been taken towards noise-robust ASR, we refer to [17]. Here, we focus on one set of approaches, guided by the finding that humans have less trouble recognizing speech in noise, which seems to suggest that humans are either better in source separation or in latching on to the speech information that is not obscured by the noise (or in both). This suggests that there is something in the auditory processing system that makes it possible to deal with additive noise. Indeed, it has been suggested that replacing the conventional short-time spectral analysis based on the fast Fourier transform by the output of a principled auditory model should improve robustness against noise. However, up to now, the results of research along this line have failed to live up to the promise [18]. We believe that this is at least in part caused by the fact that in previous research, the output of an auditory model was converted to the equivalent of the energy in one-third octave filters, necessary for interfacing with a conventional ASR back end, but without trying to capture the continuity constraints imposed by the articulatory system. In this conversion most of the additional information carried by the modulation spectrum is lost.

In this paper we explore the use of a modulation spectrum front end that is based on time-domain filtering that does not require collapsing the output to the equivalent of one-third octave filters, but which still makes it possible to estimate the posterior probability of the states in a finite-state machine. In brief, we first filter the speech signal with 15 gammatone filters (roughly equivalent to one-third octave filters) and we process the Hilbert envelope of the output of the gammatone filters with nine modulation spectrum filters [19]. The 135-dimensional (135-D) output of this system can be sampled at any rate that is an integer fraction of the sampling frequency of the input speech signal. For the conversion of the 135-D output to posterior probability estimates of a set of states, we use the sparse coding (SC) approach proposed by [20]. Sparse coding is best conceived of as an exemplar-based approach [21] in which unknown inputs are coded as positive (weighted) sums of items in an exemplar dictionary.

We use the well-known AURORA-2 task [22] as the platform for developing our modulation spectrum approach to noise-robust ASR. We will use the 'standard' back end for this task, i.e. a Viterbi decoder that finds the best path in a lattice spanned by the 179 states that result from representing 11 digit words by 16 states each, plus 3 states for representing non-speech. We expect that the effect of the additive noise is limited to a subset of the 135 output channels of the modulation spectrum analyser.

The major goal of this paper is to introduce a novel approach to noise-robust ASR. The approach that we propose is novel in two respects: we use the 'raw' output of modulation frequency filters and we use Sparse Classification to derive state posterior probabilities from samples of the output of the modulation spectrum filters. We deliberately use unadorned implementations of both the modulation spectrum analyser and the sparse coder, because we see a need for identifying what are the most important issues that are involved with a fundamentally different approach to representing speech signals and with converting the representations to state posterior estimates. In doing so we are fully aware of the risk that - for the moment - we will end up with word error rates (WERs) that are well above what is considered state-of-the-art [23]. Understanding the issues that affect the performance of our system most will allow us to propose a road map towards our final goal that combines advanced insight in what it is that makes human speech recognition so very robust against noise with improved procedures for automatic noise-robust speech recognition.

Our approach combines two novelties, *viz.* the features and the state posterior probability estimation. To make it possible to disentangle the contributions and implications of the two novelties, we will also conduct experiments in which we use conventional multi-layered perceptrons (MLPs) to derive state posterior probability estimates from the outputs of the modulation spectrum analyser. In section 4, we will compare the sparse classification approach with the results obtained with the MLP for estimating state posterior probabilities. This will allow us to assess the advantages of the modulation spectrum analyser, as well as the contribution of the sparse classification approach.

2 Method

2.1 Sparse classification front end

The approach to noise-robust ASR that we propose in this paper was inspired by [20] and [24], which introduced *sparse classification* (SCl) as a technique for estimating the posterior probabilities of the lowest-level states in an ASR system. The starting point of their approach was a representation of noisy speech signals as overlapping sequences of up to 30 speech frames that together cover up to 300 ms intervals of the signals. Individual frames were represented as Mel-frequency energy spectra, because that representation conforms to the additivity requirement imposed by the sparse classification approach. SC is an exemplar-based approach. Handling clean speech requires the construction of an exemplar dictionary that contains stretches of speech signals of the same length as the (overlapping) stretches that must be coded. The exemplars must be chosen such that they represent arbitrary utterances. For noisy speech a second exemplar dictionary must be created, which contains equally long exemplars of the additive noises. Speech is coded by finding a small number of speech and noise exemplars which, added together with positive weights, accurately approximate an interval of the original signal. The algorithms that find the best exemplars and their weights are called *solvers*; all solvers allow imposing a maximum on the number of exemplars that are returned with a weight >0 so that it is guaranteed that the result is sparse. Different families of solvers are available, but some require that all coefficients in the representations of the signals and the exemplars are non-negative numbers. Least angle regression [25], implemented by means of a version of the *Lasso* solver, can operate with representations that contain positive and negative numbers.

The SC approach sketched above is interesting for two reasons. Sequences of short-time spectra implicitly represent a substantial part of the information in the modulation spectrum. That is certainly true if the sequences cover up to 300-ms signal intervals. In addition, in [26] it was shown that it is possible to convert the weights assigned to the exemplars in a SC system to the estimates of state probabilities, provided that the frames in the exemplars are assigned to states. The latter can be accomplished by means of a forced alignment of the database from which the exemplars are selected with the states that correspond to a phonetic transcription. In actual practice, the state labels are obtained by means of a forced alignment using a conventional hidden Markov model (HMM) recognizer.

The success of the SC approach in [20,24] for noise-robust speech recognition is attributed to the fact that the speech exemplars are characterized by peaks in the spectral energy that exhibit substantial continuity over time; the human articulatory system can only produce signals that contain few clear discontinuities (such as the release of stop consonants), while many noise types lack such continuity. Therefore, it is reasonable to expect that the modulation spectra of speech and noise are rather different, even if the short-time spectra may be very similar.

In this paper we use the modulation spectrum directly to exploit the continuity constraints imposed by the speech production system. Since the modulation spectrum captures information about the continuity of the speech signal in the low-frequency bands, there is no need for a representation that stacks a large number of subsequent time frames. Therefore, our exemplar dictionary can be created by selecting individual frames of the modulation spectrum in a database of labelled speech. As in [20,24], we will convert the weights assigned to the exemplars when coding unknown speech signals into estimates of the probability that a frame in the unknown signal corresponds to one of the states.

In [20,24] the conversion of exemplar weights into state probabilities involved an averaging procedure. A frame in an unknown speech signal was included in as many solutions of the solver as there were frames in an exemplar. In each position of a sliding window, an unknown frame is associated with the states in the exemplars chosen in that position. While individual window positions return a small number of exemplars and therefore a small number of possible states, the eventual set of state probabilities assigned to a frame is not very sparse. With the single-frame exemplars in the approach presented here, no such averaging is necessary or possible. The potential downside of relying on a single set of exemplars to estimate state probabilities is that it may yield overly sparse state probability vectors.

2.2 Data
In order to provide a proof of concept that our approach is viable, we used a part of the AURORA-2 database [22]. This database consists of speech recordings taken from the TIDIGITS corpus for which participants read sequences of digits (only using the words 'zero' to 'nine' and 'oh') with one up to seven digits per utterance. These recordings were then artificially noisified by adding different types of noise to the clean recordings at different signal-to-noise ratios. In this paper we focus on the results obtained for test set A, i.e. the test set that is corrupted using the same noise types that occur in the multi-condition training set. We re-used a previously made state-level segmentation of the signals obtained by means of a forced alignment with a conventional HMM-based ASR system. These labels were also used to estimate the prior probabilities of the 179 states.

2.3 Feature extraction
The feature extraction process that we employ is illustrated in Figure 1. First, the (noisy) speech signal (sampling frequency $F_s = 8$ kHz) is analysed by a *gammatone filterbank* consisting of 15 band-pass filters with centre frequencies (F_c) spaced at one-third octave. More specifically, F_c = 125, 160, 200, 250, 315, 400, 500, 630, 800, 1,000, 1,250, 1,600, 2,000, 2,500, and 3,150 Hz, respectively. The amplitude response of an nth-order gammatone filter with centre frequency F_c is defined by

$$g(t) = a \cdot t^{n-1} \cdot \cos(2\pi F_c t + \phi) \cdot e^{-2\pi b t}. \tag{1}$$

With $b = 1.0183 \times (24.7 + F_c/9.265)$ and $n = 4$, this yields band-pass filters with equivalent rectangular bandwidth equal to 1 [27]. Subsequently, the time envelope $e_i(t)$ of the ith filter output, x_i, is computed as the magnitude of the analytic signal

$$e_i(t) = \sqrt{x_i^2 + \hat{x}_i^2}, \tag{2}$$

with $\hat{x}_i$ the Hilbert transform of x_i. We assume that the time envelopes of the outputs of the gammatone filters are a sufficiently complete representation of the input speech signal. The frequency response of the gammatone filterbank is shown in the upper part at the left-hand side of Figure 1.

The Hilbert envelopes were low-pass filtered with a fifth-order Butterworth filter (*cf.* (3)) with cut-off frequency at 150 Hz and down-sampled to 400 Hz. The down-sampled time envelopes from the 15 gammatone filters are fed into another filterbank consisting of nine modulation filters. This so-called modulation filterbank is similar to the EPSM-filterbank as presented by [28]. In our implementation of the modulation filterbank, we used one-third-order Butterworth low-pass filter with a cut-off frequency of 1 Hz, and eight band-pass filters with centre frequencies of 2, 3, 4, 5, 6, 8, 10, and 16 Hz[a].

The frequency response of an nth-order low-pass filter with gain a and cut-off frequency F_c is specified by [29]

$$H(f) = \frac{a}{1.0 + \left(\frac{f}{F_c}\right)^{2n}} \tag{3}$$

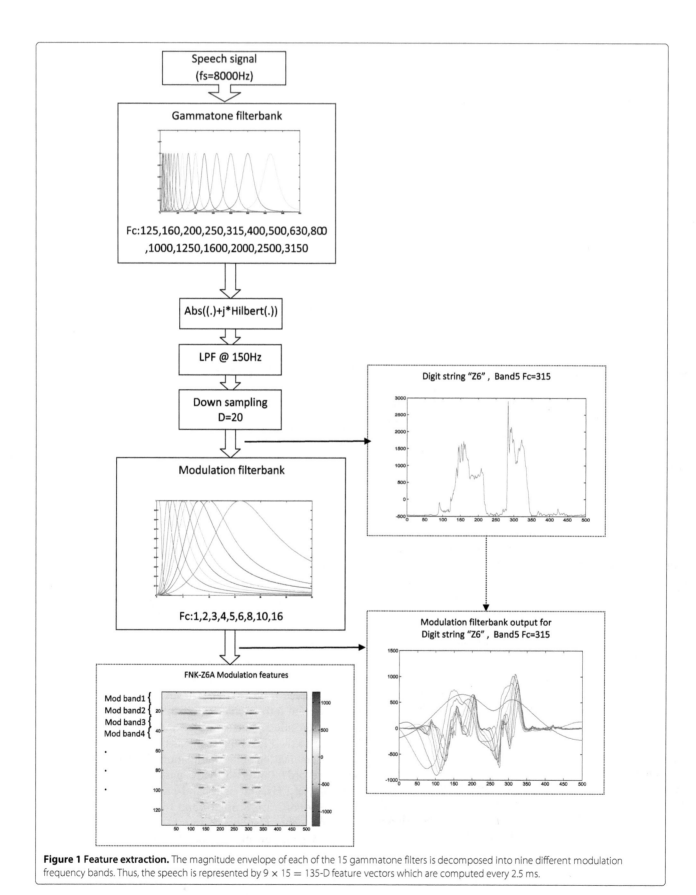

Figure 1 Feature extraction. The magnitude envelope of each of the 15 gammatone filters is decomposed into nine different modulation frequency bands. Thus, the speech is represented by 9 × 15 = 135-D feature vectors which are computed every 2.5 ms.

The complex-valued frequency response of a band-pass modulation filter with gain a, centre frequency F_c and quality factor $Q = 1$ is specified by

$$H(f) = \frac{a}{1.0 + jQ. \left(\frac{f}{F_c} - \frac{F_c}{f} \right)} \quad (4)$$

As an example, the upper panel at the right-hand side in Figure 1 shows the time envelope of the output of the gammatone filter with centre frequency at 315 Hz for the digit sequence 'zero six'. The frequency response of the complete filterbank, i.e. the sum of the responses of the nine individual filters, is shown in Figure 2. Due to the spacing of the centre frequency of the filters and the overlap of their transfer functions, we effectively give more weight to the modulation frequencies that are dominant in speech [30].

The modulation frequency filterbank is implemented as a set of frequency domain filters. To obtain a frequency resolution of 0.1 Hz with the Hilbert envelopes sampled at 400 Hz, the calculations were based on Fourier transforms consisting of 4,001 frequency samples. For that purpose we computed the complex-valued frequency response of the filters at 4,001 frequency points. An example of the ensemble of waveforms that results from the combination of the gammatone and modulation filterbank analysis for the digit sequence 'zero six' is shown in the lower panel on the right-hand side of Figure 1. The amplitudes of the $9 \times 15 = 135$ signals as a function of time are shown in the bottom panel at the left-hand side of Figure 1. The top band represents the lowest modulation frequencies (0 to 1 Hz) and the bottom band the highest (modulation filter with centre frequency $F_c = 16$ Hz).

We experimented with two different implementations of the modulation frequency filterbank, one in which we kept the phase response of the filters and the other in which we ignored the phase response and only retained the magnitude of the transfer functions. The results are illustrated in Figure 3 for clean speech and for the 5-dB signal-to-noise ratio (SNR) condition. From the second and third rows in that figure, it can be inferred that the linear phase implementation renders sudden changes in the Hilbert envelope as synchronized events in all modulation bands, while the full-phase implementation appears to smear these changes over wider time intervals. The (visual) effect is especially apparent in the right column, where the noisy speech is depicted. However, preliminary experiments indicated that the information captured in the 'visually noisy' full-phase representation could be harnessed by the recognition system: the full-phase implementation yields a performance increase in the order of 20% at the lower SNR levels compared with the performance of the linear phase implementation. However, the linear phase implementation works slightly better in clean and high SNR conditions (yielding ≈1% higher accuracies). This confirms the results of previous experiments in [31]. Therefore, all results in this paper are based on the full-phase implementation.

Another unsurprising observation that can be made from Figure 3 is that the non-negative Hilbert envelopes are turned into signals that have both positive and negative amplitude values. This will limit the options in choosing a solver in the SC approach to computing state posterior probabilities.

Figure 4 provides an extended view of the result of a modulation spectrum analysis of the utterance 'zero six'.

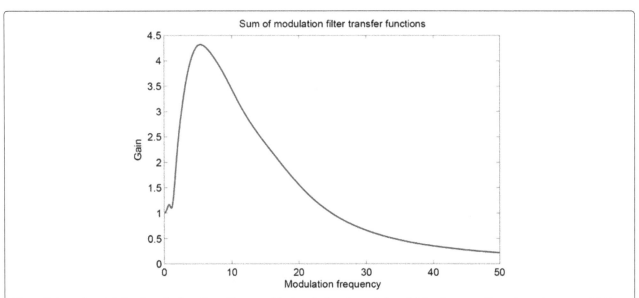

Figure 2 Sum of modulation transfer functions. The sum of the transfer functions of all modulation frequency filters gives a stronger weight to the frequencies that are known to be important for speech recognition [30].

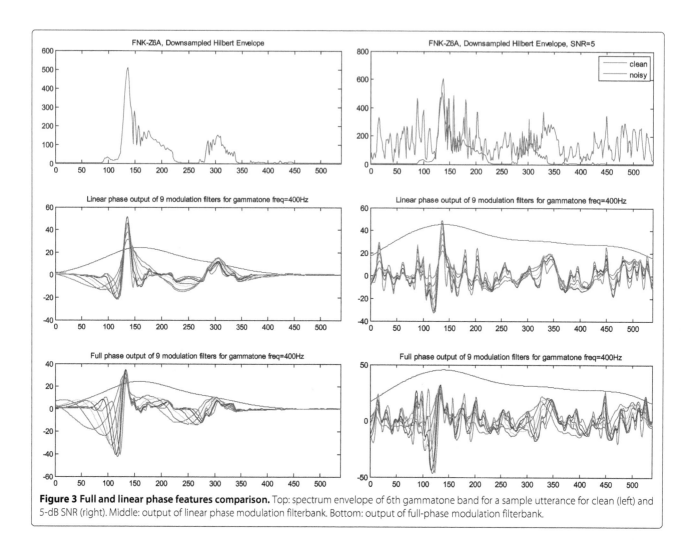

Figure 3 Full and linear phase features comparison. Top: spectrum envelope of 6th gammatone band for a sample utterance for clean (left) and 5-dB SNR (right). Middle: output of linear phase modulation filterbank. Bottom: output of full-phase modulation filterbank.

The nine heat map representations in the lower left-hand part of Figure 1 are re-drawn in such a way that it is possible to see the similarities and differences between the modulation bands. The top panel in Figure 4 shows the output amplitude of the low-pass filter of the modulation filter bank. Subsequent panels show the amplitude of the outputs of the higher modulation band filters. It can be seen that overall, the amplitude decreases with increasing band number.

Speech and background noise tend to cover the same frequency regions in the short-time spectrum. Therefore, speech and noise will be mixed in the outputs of the 15 gammatone filters. The modulation filterbank decomposes each of the 15 time envelopes into a set of nine time-domain signals that correspond to different modulation frequencies. Generally speaking, the outputs of the lowest modulation frequencies are more associated with events demarcating syllable nuclei, while the higher modulation frequencies represent shorter-term events. We want to take advantage of the fact that it is unlikely that speech and noise sound sources with frequency components in the same gammatone filter also happen to overlap completely in the modulation frequency domain. Stationary noise would not affect the output of the higher modulation frequency filters, while pulsatile noise should not affect the lowest modulation frequency filters. Therefore, we expect that many of the naturally occurring noise sources will show temporal variations at different rates than speech.

Although the modulation spectrum features capture short- and medium-time spectral dynamics, the information is encoded in a manner that might not be optimal for automatic pattern recognition purposes. Therefore, we decided to also create a feature set that encodes the temporal dynamics more explicitly. To that end we concatenated 29 frames (at a rate of one frame per 2.5 ms), corresponding to $29 \times 2.5 = 72.5$ ms; to keep the number of features within reasonable limits, we performed dimensionality reduction by means of linear discriminant analysis (LDA), with the 179 state labels as categories. The reference category was the state label of the middle frame of a 29-frame sequence. The LDA transformation matrix was

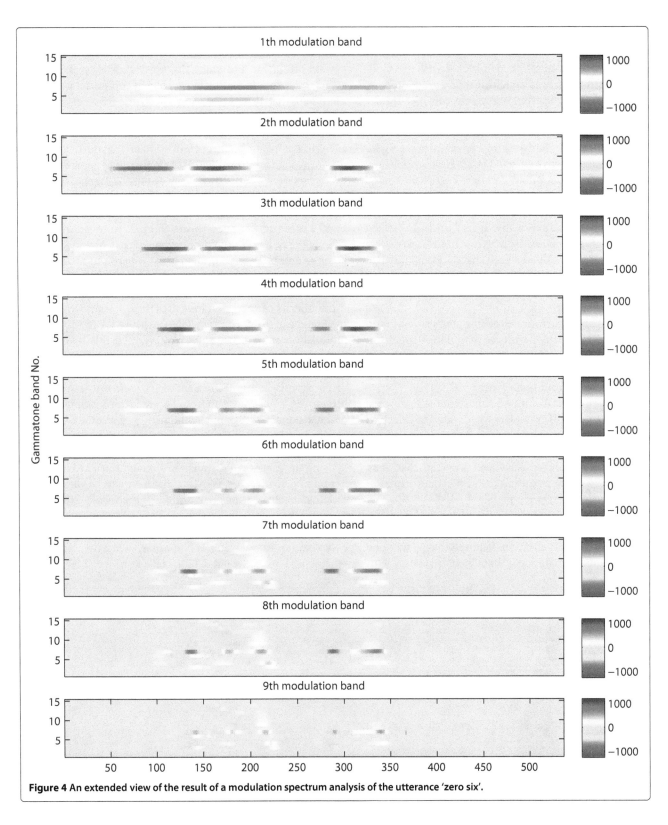

Figure 4 An extended view of the result of a modulation spectrum analysis of the utterance 'zero six'.

learned using the exemplar dictionary (*cf.*, section 2.4). The dimension of the feature vectors was reduced the 135, the same number as with single-frame features. To be able to investigate the effect of the LDA transform, we also applied an LDA transform to the original single-frame features. Here, the dimension of the transformed feature vector was limited to 135 (nine modulation bands in 15 gammatone filters).

2.4 Composition of exemplar dictionary

To construct the speech exemplar dictionary, we first encoded the clean train set of AURORA-2 with the modulation spectrum analysis system, using a frame rate of 400 Hz. Then, we quasi-randomly selected two frames from each utterance. To make sure that we had a reasonably uniform coverage of all states and both genders, 2×179 counters were used (one for each state of each gender). The counters were initialized at 48. For each selected exemplar, the corresponding counter was decremented by 1. Exemplars of a gender-state combination were no longer added to the dictionary if the counter became zero. A simple implementation of this search strategy yielded a set of 17,148 exemplars, in which some states missed one or two exemplars. It appeared that 36 exemplars had a Pearson correlation coefficient of >0.999 with at least one other exemplar. Therefore, the effective size of the dictionary is 17,091.

We also encoded the four noises in the multi-condition training set of AURORA-2 with the modulation spectrum analysis system. From the output, we randomly selected 13,300 frames as noise exemplars, with an equal number of exemplars for the four noise types.

When using LDA-transformed concatenated features, a new equally large set of exemplars was created by selecting sequences of 29 consecutive frames, using the same procedures as for selecting single-frame exemplars. In a similar vein, 29-frame noise exemplars were selected that were reduced to 135-D features using the same transformation matrix as for the speech exemplars.

2.5 The sparse classification algorithm

The use of sparse classification requires that it must be possible to approximate an unknown observation with a (positive) weighted sum of a number of exemplars. Since all operations in the modulation spectrum analysis system are linear and since the noisy signals were constructed by simply adding clean speech and noise, we are confident that the modulation spectrum representation does not violate additivity to such an extent that SC is rendered impossible. The same argument holds for the LDA-transformed features. Since linear transformations do not violate additivity, we assume that the transformed exemplars can be used in the same way as the original ones.

As can be seen in Figures 1 and 3, the output of the modulation filters contains both positive and negative numbers. Therefore, we need to use the Lasso procedure for solving the sparse coding problem, which can operate with positive and negative numbers [25]. We are not aware of other solvers that offer the same freedom. Lasso uses the Euclidean distance as the divergence measure to evaluate the similarity of vectors. This raises the question whether the Euclidean distance is a suitable measure for comparing modulation spectrum vectors. We verified this by computing the distributions of the Euclidean distance between neighbouring frames and frames taken at random time distances of >20 frames in a set of 100 randomly selected utterances. As can be seen from Figure 5, the distributions of the distances between neighbouring and distant frames hardly overlap. Therefore, we believe that it is safe to assume that the Euclidean distance measure is adequate.

Using the Euclidean distance in a straightforward manner implies that vector elements that have a large variance or large absolute values will dominate the result. Preliminary experiments showed that the modulation spectra suffer from this effect. It appeared that the difference between /u/ in *two* and /i/ in *three*, which is mainly represented by different energy levels in the 2,000-Hz

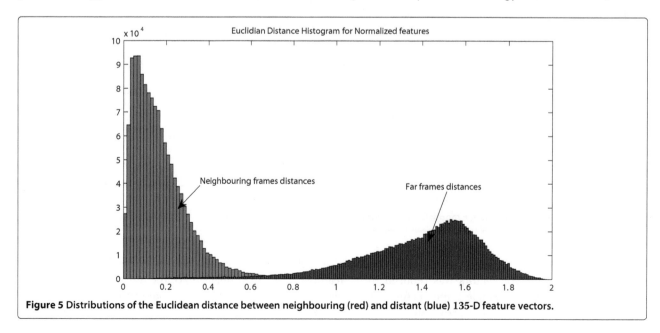

Figure 5 Distributions of the Euclidean distance between neighbouring (red) and distant (blue) 135-D feature vectors.

region, was often very small because of the absolute values of the output of the modulation filters in the gammatone filters with centre frequencies of 2,000 and 2,500 Hz which were very much smaller than the values in the gammatone filters with centre frequencies up to 400 Hz. This effect can be remedied by using a proper normalization of the vector elements. After some experiments, we decided to equalize the variance in the gammatone bands. For this purpose we first computed the variance in all 135 modulation bands in the set of speech exemplars. Then, we averaged the variance over the nine modulation bands in each gammatone filter. The resulting averages were used to normalize the outputs of the modulation filters. The effect of this procedure on the representation of the output of the modulation filters is shown in Figure 6. This procedure reduced the number of /u/ - /i/ confusions by almost a factor of 3.

2.5.1 *Obtaining state posterior estimates*
The weights assigned to the exemplars by the Lasso solver must be converted to estimates of the probability that a frame corresponds to one of the 179 states. In the sparse

classification system of [20], weights of up to 30 window positions were averaged. In our SC system, we do not have a sliding window with heavy overlap between subsequent positions. We decided to use the weights of the exemplars that approximate individual frames to derive the state posterior probability estimates. In doing so, we simply added the weights of all exemplars corresponding to a given state. The average number of non-zero elements in the activation vector varied between 15.1 for clean speech and 6.5 at −5-dB SNR. Therefore, we may face overly sparse and potentially somewhat noisy state probability estimates. This is illustrated in Figure 7a for the digit sequence '3 6 7' in the 5-dB SNR condition. The traces of state probability estimates are not continuous (do not traverse all 16 states of a word) and they include activations of other states, some of which are acoustically similar to the states that correspond to the digit sequence.

2.6 Recognition based on combinations of individual modulation bands
Substantial previous research has investigated the possibility to combat additive noise by fusing the outputs of a

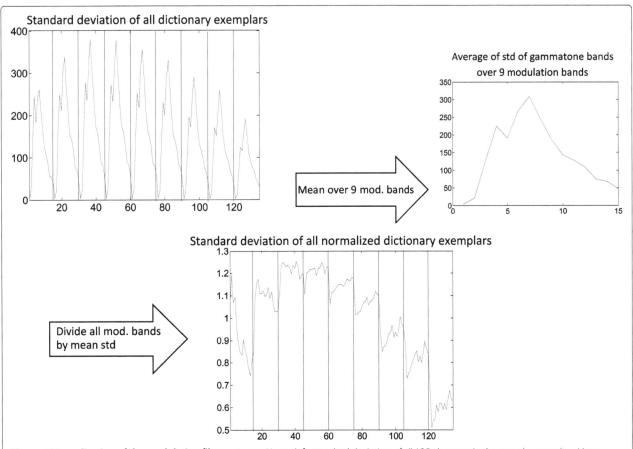

Figure 6 Normalization of the modulation filter outputs. Upper left: standard deviation of all 135 elements in the speech exemplars. Upper right: standard deviation in the gammatone filters averaged over all nine modulation filters. Lower panel: standard deviation of all 135 elements in the speech exemplars after normalization.

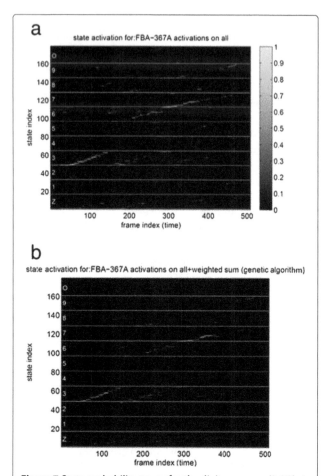

Figure 7 State probability traces for the digit sequence '3 6 7' at 5-dB SNR. (a) Traces obtained by using the activation weights of the full modulation spectrum exemplars only. The Viterbi decoder returns the incorrect sequence '3 3 7'. **(b)** Traces obtained from fusing the probability estimates obtained with the full modulation spectrum and the probability estimates obtained from nine modulation bands (weights obtained with a genetic algorithm). The Viterbi decoder now returns the correct sequence '3 6 7'.

number of parallel recognizers, each operating on a separate frequency band (*cf.*, [32] for a comprehensive review). The general idea underlying this approach is that additive noise will only affect some frequency bands so that other bands should suffer less. The same idea has also been proposed for different modulation bands [33]. In this paper we also explore the possibility that additive noise does not affect all modulation bands to the same extent. Therefore, we will compare recognition accuracies obtained when estimating state likelihoods using a single set of exemplars represented by 135-D feature vectors and the fusion of the state likelihoods estimated from the 135-D system and nine sets of exemplars (one for each modulation band) represented as 15-D feature vectors (for the 15 gammatone filters). The optimal weights for the nine sets of estimates will be obtained using a genetic algorithm with

a small set of held-out training utterances. Also, combining state posterior probability estimates from ten decoders might help to make the resulting probability vectors less sparse.

2.7 State posteriors estimated by means of an MLP

In order to tease apart the contributions of the modulation frequency features and the sparse coding, we also conducted experiments in which we used a MLP for estimating the posterior probabilities of the 179 states in the AURORA-2 task. For this purpose we trained a number of networks by means of the QuickNet software package [34]. We trained networks on clean data only, as well as on the full set of utterances in the multi-condition training set. Analogously to [35], we used 90% of the training set, i.e. 7,596 utterances for training the MLP and the remaining 844 utterances for the cross-validation. To enable a fair comparison, we trained two networks, both operating on single frames. The first network used frames consisting of 135 features; the second network used 'static' modulation frequency features extended with delta and delta-delta features estimated over a time interval of 90 ms, making for 405 input features. The delta and delta-delta features were obtained by fitting a linear regression on the sequence of feature values that span the 90-ms intervals. Actually, the 90-ms interval corresponds to the time interval covered by the perceptual linear prediction (PLP) features used in [35]. There too, the static PLP features were extended by delta and delta-delta features, making for $9 \times 39 = 351$ input nodes.

3 Results

The recognition accuracies obtained with the 135-D modulation spectrum features are presented in the top part of Tables 1 and 2 for the SC-based system. The second and third rows of Table 2 show the results for the MLP-based system. Both tables also contain results obtained previously with conventional Mel-spectrum or PLP features. Note that the results in Table 1 pertain to a single-noise condition of test set A (subway noise), while Table 2 shows the accuracies averaged over all four noise types in test set A. In experimenting with the AURORA-2 task, it is a pervasive finding that the results depend strongly on the word insertion penalty (WIP) that is used in the Viterbi back end. A WIP that yields the lowest WER in the clean condition invariably gives a very high WER in the noisiest conditions. In this paper we set aside a small development set, on which we searched the WIP that gave the best results in the conditions with SNR $\leq$ 5 dB; in these conditions the best performance was obtained with the same WIP value. Inevitably, this means that we will end up with relatively bad results in the cleanest conditions. Unfortunately, there is no generally accepted strategy for selecting the 'optimal' WIP. Since different

Table 1 Accuracy for five systems on noise type 1 (subway noise) of test set A

	Clean	20 dB	15 dB	10 dB	5 dB	0 dB	−5 dB
Sys1 (single frame)	90.51	91.00	89.53	87.69	83.76	76.76	65.31
Sys2 (single frame) (LDA transformed)	89.19	89.62	87.57	83.54	76.51	62.57	36.91
Sys3 (29 frames) (LDA transformed)	87.50	88.70	87.41	85.42	77.62	59.41	27.85
Sys4 (9 bands - GA)	89.71	90.57	89.28	87.41	84.13	77.71	63.83
Sparse coding [24] 5-frame exemplars	93.12	90.18	87.22	82.62	72.64	56.31	34.57
Sparse coding [24] 30-frame exemplars	93.21	91.86	91.53	89.62	87.47	80.01	61.61

Sys1, 135-D vectors; Sys2, LDA-transformed 135-D vectors of Sys1; Sys3, LDA-transformed 29 × 135-D vectors of 29 consecutive frames; Sys4, Sys1 plus nine recognizers operating on 15-D vectors, weights obtained from a genetic algorithm. Recognition results for noise type 1 using the sparse coding approach [20,24] using 5 and 30 frame windows are included for comparison in the bottom part.

authors make different (and not always explicit) decisions, detailed comparisons with results reported in the literature are difficult. For this paper this is less of an issue, since we are not aiming at outperforming previously published results.

3.1 Analysing the features

To better understand the modulation spectrum features, we carried out a clustering analysis on the exemplars in the dictionary, using k-means clustering. We created 512 clusters using the scikit-learn software package [36]. We then analysed the way in which clusters correspond to states. The results of the analysis of the raw features are shown in Figure 8a. The horizontal axis in the figure corresponds to the 179 states, and the vertical axis to cluster numbers. The figure shows the association between clusters and states. It can be seen that the exemplar clusters do associate to states, but there is a substantial amount of 'confusions'. Figure 8b shows the result of the same clustering of the exemplars after applying an LDA transform to the exemplars, keeping all 135 dimensions. It can be seen that the LDA-transformed exemplars result in clusters that are substantially purer. Figure 8c shows the results of the same clustering on the 135-D features obtained from the LDA transform of sequences of 29 subsequent frames. Now, the cluster purity has increased further.

Although cluster purity does not guarantee high recognition performance, from Tables 1 and 2 it can be seen that the modulation spectrum features appear to capture substantial information that can be exploited by two very different classifiers.

Table 2 Accuracies averaged over all noise types in test set A

	Clean	20 dB	15 dB	10 dB	5 dB	0 dB	−5 dB
Modulation features sparse coding 1-frame exemplar (Sys1)	90.62	90.87	89.90	88.17	84.46	76.83	59.65
Modulation features MLP 135 input nodes multi-condition	96.93	96.66	95.84	94.07	87.14	68.05	35.46
Modulation features + Δ + ΔΔ MLP 405 input nodes multi-condition	97.71	97.36	96.74	95.08	89.79	70.58	34.55
PLP + Δ and ΔΔ MLP 351 input nodes [35] multi-condition	99.08	98.89	98.45	96.89	91.80	72.80	35.67
Mel features sparse coding [24] 5-frame exemplars	93.43	90.94	89.06	84.57	75.91	58.20	32.57
Mel features sparse coding [24] 30-frame exemplars	93.68	92.53	92.02	90.78	88.01	78.93	57.11

Accuracies (averaged over all noise types in test set A) obtained with Sys1 (SC system operating on 135-D modulation spectrum features), MLP classifiers (on same features without and with Δs and ΔΔs), MLP classifier on PLP features with Δs and ΔΔs [35], SC classifier on Mel spectra [24] using 5- and 30-frame windows, respectively.

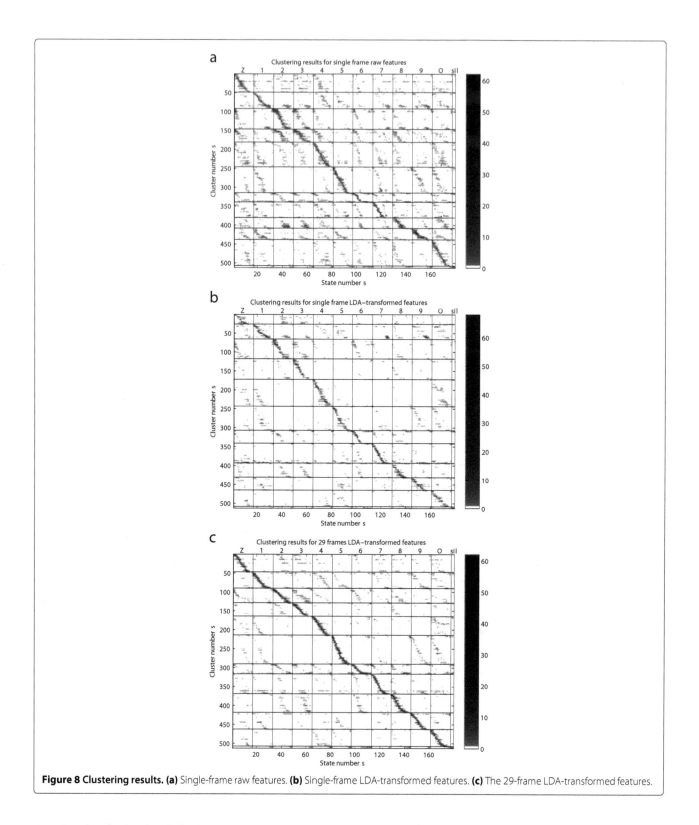

Figure 8 Clustering results. (a) Single-frame raw features. **(b)** Single-frame LDA-transformed features. **(c)** The 29-frame LDA-transformed features.

3.2 Results obtained with the SC system

Table 1 summarizes the recognition accuracies obtained with six different systems, all of which used the SC approach to estimate state posterior probabilities. Four of these systems use the newly proposed modulation spectrum features, while the remaining two describe the results using Mel-spectrum features as obtained in research done by Gemmeke [24].

From the first three rows of Table 1, it can be seen that estimating state posterior probabilities from a single frame of a modulation spectrum analysis by converting the exemplar weights obtained with the sparse classification system already yields quite promising results. Indeed, from a comparison with the results obtained with the original SC system using five-frame stacks in [24], it appears that the modulation spectrum features outperform stacks of five Mel-spectrum features in all but one condition. The conspicuous exception is the clean condition, where the performance of Sys1 is somewhat disappointing. Our Sys1 performs worse than the system in [24] that used 30-frame exemplars. From the first and second rows, it can be inferred that transforming the features such that the discrimination between the 179 states is optimized is harmful for all conditions. Apparently, the transform learned on the basis of 17.148 exemplars does not generalize sufficiently to the bulk of the feature frames. In section 4 we will propose an alternative perspective that puts part of the blame on the interaction between LDA and SC.

3.2.1   The representation of the temporal dynamics

In [20,24] the recognition performance in AURORA-2 was compared for exemplar lengths of 5, 10, 20, 30 frames. For clean speech, the optimal exemplar length was around ten frames and the performance dropped for longer exemplars; at SNR = −5 dB, increasing exemplar length kept improving the recognition performance and the optimal length found was the longest that was tried (i.e. 30). Longer windows correspond with capturing the effects of lower modulation frequencies. The trade-off between clean and very noisy signals suggests that emphasizing long-term continuity helps in reducing the effect of noises that are not characterized by continuity, but using 300-ms exemplars may not be optimal for covering shorter-term variation in the digits. From the two bottom rows in Table 1, it can be seen that going from 5-frame stacks to 30-frame stacks improved the performance for the noisiest conditions very substantially. From the second and third rows in that table, it appears that the performance gain in our system that used 29-frame features (covering 72.5 ms) is nowhere near as large. However, due to the problems with the generalizability of the LDA transform that we already encountered in Sys2, it is not yet possible to draw conclusions from this finding.

A potentially important side effect of using exemplars consisting of 30 subsequent frames in [20,24] was that the conversion of state activations to state posterior probabilities involved averaging over 30 frame positions. This diminishes the risk that a 'true' state is not activated at all. Our system approximates a feature frame as just one sum of exemplars. If an exemplar of a 'wrong' state happens to match best with the feature frame, the Lasso procedure may fill the gap between that exemplar and the feature frame with completely unrelated exemplars. This can cause gaps in the traces in the state probability lattice that represent the digits. This effect is illustrated in Figure 7a, which shows the state activations over time of the digit sequence '3 6 7' at 5-dB SNR for the state probabilities in Sys1. The initial fricative consonants /θ/ and /s/ and the vowels /i/ and /I/ in the digits '3' and '6' are acoustically very similar. For the second digit in the utterance, this results in somewhat grainy, discontinuous, and largely parallel traces in the probability lattice for the digits '3' and '6'. Both traces more or less traverse the sequence of all 16 required states. The best path according to the Viterbi decoder corresponds to the sequence '3 3 7', which is obviously incorrect.

3.2.2   Results based on fusing nine modulation bands

In Sys1, Sys2, and Sys3, we capitalize on the assumption that the sparse classification procedure can harness the differences between speech and noise in the modulation spectra without being given any specific information. In [32] it was shown that it is beneficial to 'help' a speech recognition system in handling additive noise by fusing the results of independent recognition operations on non-overlapping parts of the spectrum. The success of the multi-band approach is founded in the finding that additive noise does not affect all parts of the spectrum equally severely. Recognition on sub-bands can profit from superior results in sub-bands that are only marginally affected by the noise. Using modulation spectrum features, we aim to exploit the different temporal characteristics of speech and noise, which are expected to have different effects in different modulation bands. Therefore, we conducted an experiment to investigate whether combining the output of nine independent recognizers, each operating on a different modulation frequency band, will improve recognition accuracy. In each modulation frequency band, we have the output of all 15 gammatone filters; therefore, each modulation band 'hears' the full 4-kHz spectrum. The experiment was conducted using the part of test set A that is corrupted by subway noise.

In our experiments we opted for fusion at the state posterior probability level: We constructed a single-state probability lattice for each utterance by means of a weighted sum of the state posteriors obtained from the individual SC systems. In all cases we fused the probability estimates of Sys1, which operates with 135-D exemplars with nine sets of state posteriors from SC classifiers that each operate on 15-D exemplars. Sys1 was always given a weight equal to 1. The weights for the nine modulation band classifiers were obtained using a genetic algorithm that optimized the weights on a small development set. The weights and WIP that yielded the best results in the SNR conditions ≤5 dB were applied to all SNR conditions. The set of weights is shown in Table 3.

Table 3 Weights obtained for combining the 15 gammatone filterbands in the multi-stream analysis

F_c (Hz)	0	2	3	4	5	6	8	10	16
GA	−0.0172	−0.0921	0.0001	−0.0103	−0.223	−0.0336	−0.0072	−0.0625	0.201

GA, weights obtained with a genetic algorithm.

From row 4 (*Sys4*) in Table 1, it can be seen that fusing the state likelihood estimates from the nine individual modulation filters with the state likelihoods from the full modulation spectrum deteriorates the recognition accuracy for all but two SNRs. From Table 3 it appears that the Genetic Algorithm returns very small weights for all nine modulation bands. This strongly suggests that the individual modulation bands are not able to highlight specific information that is less easily seen in the complete modulation spectrum.

A potentially very important concomitant advantage of fusing the probability estimates from the 135-D system and the nine 15-D systems is that the fusion process may make the probability vectors less sparse, thereby reducing the risk that wrong states are being promoted. This is illustrated in Figure 7b, where it can be seen that the state probability traces obtained from the fusion of the full 135-D system and the weighted sub-band systems suffer less from competing 'ghost traces' of acoustically similar competitors that traverse all 16 states of the wrong digit: Due to the lack of consensus between the multiple classifiers, the trace for the wrong digit '3', which is clearly visible in Figure 7a, has become less clear and more 'cloud-like' in Figure 7b. As a consequence, the digit string is now recognized correctly as '3 6 7'. However, from the results in Table 1, it is clear that on average the impact of making the probability vectors less sparse by means of fusing modulation frequency sub-bands is negligible.

3.3 Results obtained with MLPs
We trained four MLP systems for computing state posterior probabilities on the basis of the modulation spectrum features, two using only clean speech and two using the multi-condition training data. We increased the number of hidden nodes, starting with 200 hidden nodes up to 1,500 nodes. In all cases the eventual recognition accuracy kept increasing, although the rate of increase dropped substantially. Additional experiments showed that further increasing the number of hidden nodes no longer yields improved recognition results. For each number of hidden nodes, we also searched for the WIP that would provide optimal results for the cross-validation set (*cf.* section 2.7). We found that the optimal accuracy in the different SNR conditions was obtained for quite different values of the WIP. Training on multi-condition data had a slight negative effect on the recognition accuracy in the clean condition, compared to training on clean data only.

However, as could be expected, the MLPs trained on clean data did not generalize to noisy data.

Table 2 shows the results obtained with SC systems operating on modulation spectrum and Mel-spectrum features and the MLP-based systems trained with multi-condition data. It can be seen that adding Δ and $\Delta\Delta$ features to the 'static' modulation spectrum features increases performance somewhat, but by no means to the extent that adding Δ and $\Delta\Delta$ features improves performance with Mel-spectrum or PLP features [12,13].

The two systems that used modulation spectrum features perform much worse on clean speech than the MLP-based system that used nine adjacent 10-ms PLP $+\Delta+\Delta\Delta$ features [37]. This suggests that the modulation spectrum features fail to capture part of the dynamic information that is represented by the speed and acceleration features derived from PLPs. Interestingly, that information is not restored by adding the regression coefficients obtained with stacks of modulation frequency features. In the noisier conditions, the networks trained with modulation frequency features derived from the multi-condition training data approximate the performance of the stacks of nine extended PLP features.

4 Discussion
In this paper we introduced a basic implementation of a noise-robust ASR system that uses the modulation spectrum, instead of the short-time spectrum to represent noisy speech signals, and sparse classification to derive state probability estimates from time samples of the modulation spectrum. Our approach differs from previous attempts to deploy sparse classification for noise-robust ASR. The first difference is the use of the modulation spectrum and the second is that the exemplars in our system are constituted by individual frames, rather than by (long) sequences of adjacent frames in [20,24], which needed such sequences to effectively cover essential information about continuity over time that comes for free in the modulation spectrum, where individual frames capture information about the dynamic changes in the short-time spectrum. Our unadorned implementation yielded recognition accuracies that are slightly below the best results in [20,24], but especially the fact that our system yielded higher accuracies in the −5-dB SNR condition than their systems with exemplars with a length of 50 ms corroborates our belief that we are on a promising track towards a novel approach to noise-robust ASR. Although all results are based on a combination of feature extraction

and posterior state probability estimation, we will discuss the features and the estimators separately - to the extent possible.

4.1 The features

In designing the modulation spectrum analysis system, a number of decisions had to be made about implementation details. Although we are confident that all our decisions were reasonable (and supported by data from the literature), we cannot claim that they were optimal. Most data in the literature on modulation spectra are based on perception experiments with human subjects, but more often than not these experiments use auditory stimuli that are very different from speech. While the results of those experiments surely provide guidance for ASR, it may well be that the automatic processing aimed at extracting the discriminative information is so different from what humans do that some of our decisions are sub-optimal. Our gammatone filterbank contains 15 one-third octave filters, which have a higher resolution in the frequencies <500 Hz than the Mel filterbank that is used in most ASR systems. However, initial experiments in which we compared our one-third octave filterbank with a filterbank consisting of 23 Mel-spaced gammatone filters, spanning the frequency range of 64 to 3,340 Hz did not show a significant advantage of the latter over the former. From the speech technology's point of view, this may seem surprising because the narrow-band filters of the one-third octave filterbank in the low frequencies may cause interactions with fundamental frequency, while the relatively broad filters in the higher frequencies cannot resolve formants. But from an auditory system's point of view, there is no such surprise, since one-third octave filters are compatible with most, if not all, outcomes of psycho-acoustic experiments. This is also true for experiments that focused on speech intelligibility [1].

For the modulation filterbank, it also holds that the design is partly based on the results of perception experiments [19]. Our modulation frequency analyser contained filters with centre frequencies ranging from 0 to 16 Hz. From [30] it appears that the modulation frequency range of interest for ASR is limited to the 2- to 16-Hz region. Therefore, here too we must ask whether our design is optimal for ASR. It might be that the spacing of the modulation filters in the frequency band that is most important for human speech intelligibility is not optimal for automatic processing. However, as with the gamma-tone filters, it is not evident why a different spacing should be preferred. It might be necessary to treat modulation frequencies ≤1 Hz, which are more likely to correspond to the characteristics of the transmission channel, different than modulation frequencies that might be related to articulation. One might think that the very low modulation frequencies would best be discarded completely in

the AURORA-2 task, where transmission channel characteristics do not play a role. However, experiments in which we did just that yielded substantially worse results. Arguably, the lowest modulation frequencies help in distinguishing time intervals that contain speech from time intervals that contain only silence or background noise. We decided to not include modulation filters with centre frequencies >16 Hz. This implies that we ignore almost all information related to the periodicity that characterizes many speech sounds. However, it is well known that the presence of periodicity is a powerful indicator of the presence of speech in noisy signals and also, in case the background noise consists of speech from one or more interfering speakers, a powerful means to separate the target speech from the background speech. In future experiments we will investigate the possibility of adding explicit information about the harmonicity of the signals to the feature set.

The experiments with the MLP classifiers for obtaining state posterior probabilities from the modulation spectrum features confirm that the modulation spectrum features capture most of the information that is relevant for speech decoding. Still, the WERs obtained with the MLPs were always inferior to the results obtained with stacks of nine conventional PLP features that include Δ and $\Delta\Delta$ features, especially in the cleanest SNR conditions. Although the modulation spectrum features are performing quite well in noisy conditions, in cleaner conditions their performance is worse than the classical PLP features. Adding Δs and $\Delta\Delta$s, computed as linear regressions over 90 ms windows, to the modulation spectrum features does not improve performance nearly as much as adding speed and acceleration to MFCC or PLP features. This suggests that our modulation spectrum features are suboptimal with respect to describing the medium-term dynamics of the speech signal. The time windows associated with the modulation frequency filters with the lowest centre frequencies is larger than 500 ms. As a consequence, time derivatives computed over a window of 90 ms for these slowly varying filter outputs is not likely to carry much additional information. We suspect that the features in the lowest modulation bands play too heavy a role. If we want to optimally exploit the redundancy in the different modulation frequency channels when part of them gets obscured by noise, information about relevant speech events (such as word or syllable onsets and offsets) should ideally be represented equally well by their temporal dynamics in all channels.

Perhaps the most striking difference between the auditory model used in this paper and the model proposed in [38] is the absence of the adaptation/compression network between the gammatone filters and the modulation frequency filters. Preliminary experiments in which we applied tenth root compression to the output of the modulation filters (rather than the gammatone filters) already showed a substantial beneficial effect. The additional high-pass filtering that is performed in the compression/adaptation network (which should only be applied to the output of the gammatone filters) is expected to have a further beneficial effect in that it implements the medium-term dynamics that we seem to be missing at the moment. Including the adaptation stage is also expected to enhance the different dynamic characteristics of speech and many noise types in the modulation frequency bands. If this expectation holds, the absence of a proper adaptation network might explain the failure of the nine band fusion system.

4.2 The classifiers

Visual inspection of traces of state activations as a function of time obtained with the SC system suggested that the similarity between adjacent feature vectors was much higher than the similarity between adjacent state activation vectors. Figure 9 shows scatter plots of the relation between the similarity between adjacent feature vectors and the corresponding state probability vectors. It can be seen that the Pearson correlation coefficient between adjacent feature frames is very high, which is what one

would expect, given the high sampling rate. It is also evident, and expected, that the variance increases as the SNR decreases. However, the behaviour of the state probability vectors is quite different. While for part of the adjacent vectors it holds that they are very similar (the pairs with a similarity close to one, represented by the points in the upper right-hand corner of the panels), it can be seen that there is a substantial proportion of adjacent state probability vectors that are almost orthogonal. We believe that this discrepancy is related to the difference between sparse coding (reconstruction of an observed modulation spectrum in terms of a linear combination of exemplars), what it is that the Lasso solver does, and sparse classification (estimating the probability of the HMM state underlying the observed modulation spectrum), which is our final goal. The frames that represent an unknown (noisy) speech signals are all decoded individually; for each frame the Lasso procedure starts from scratch. If occasionally a speech atom related to a wrong state or an atom from the noise dictionary happens to match best with an input frame, this can have a very large impact on the resulting state activation vector. Lasso can turn a close similarity between an input frame and exemplars related to the true state at the feature level into a close-to-zero probability

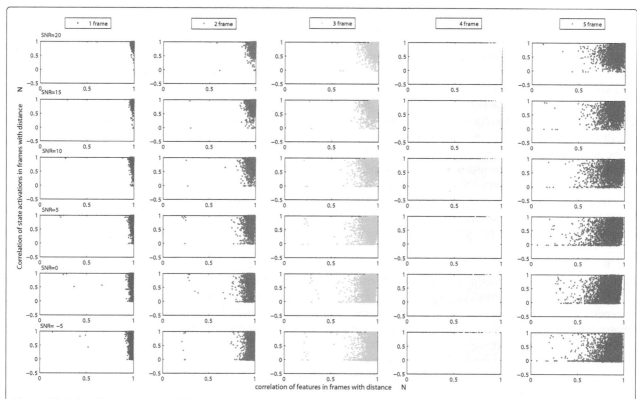

Figure 9 Relationship between the similarity between adjacent time frames and the corresponding adjacent state activation vectors.
Correlations are computed using ten randomly selected utterances. Rows, SNR conditions. Columns, time distance between frames.

of the 'correct' state in the probability vector because an exemplar related to another state (or noise) happened to match slightly better.

The substantial deterioration of the recognition performance with LDA-transformed features came as a surprise, not in the last place because we have seen that cluster purity increases after LDA transform. The fact that we see a negative effect of the transform already for clean speech suggests that the transformation matrix learned from the exemplar dictionary does not generalize well to the continuous speech data. While the correlation between the raw features in adjacent frames was very close to one in the raw features, the average Pearson correlation coefficient between adjacent frames dropped to about 0.75 after the LDA transform. The LDA transformation maximizes the differences among the 179 states, regardless of whether states are actually very similar or not. Distinguishing adjacent states in the digit word 'oh' is equally important as distinguishing the eighth state of oh from the first state of 'seven'. Exaggerating the differences between adjacent frames, because these may relate to different states, is likely to aggravate the risk that Lasso returns high activations for a wrong state because an exemplar assigned to that state happens to fit the frame under analysis best. In addition, the LDA transform affects the relations between the distributions of the features. Because we believe that the feature normalization applied to the raw modulation spectrum features yielded the best performance since it conforms with the mathematics in Lasso, we applied the same normalization to the LDA-transformed features. We did not (yet) check whether a different normalization could improve the results. The comparison between the single-frame LDA-transformed and 29-frame features that are reduced to 135-D features by means of an LDA-transform shows that adding a more explicit representation of the time context only improves the recognition accuracy in the 10- and 5-dB SNR conditions; in all other conditions, the results obtained with single-frame features are better. We believe that this finding is related to the difficulty of representing medium-term speech dynamics in the present form of the modulation spectrum features.

We experimented with LDA in order to be able to explicitly include additional information about temporal dynamics. In the present implementation, with its 400-Hz frame rate, a stack of 29 adjacent frames covers a time interval of 72.5 ms, resulting in 3,915-D feature vectors. However, the 400-Hz frame rate does not seem to be necessary. Preliminary experiments with low-pass filtering the Hilbert envelopes of the outputs of the gammatone filters with a cut-off frequency of 50 Hz and a frame rate of 100 Hz yielded equal WER results. This opens the possibility of covering time spans of about 70 ms by concatenating only nine frames. However, an experiment in which we decoded the clean speech with exemplars consisting of nine subsequent 10-ms frames did not yield accuracies better than what we had obtained with single-frame features. This corroborates our belief that the medium-term dynamics is not sufficiently captured by our modulation spectrum features.

The success of the MLP classifiers that is apparent from Table 2 shows that sparse classification is not the only way for estimating state posterior probabilities from modulation spectrum features. In fact, the MLP classifier yielded consistently better results than the SC classifier in the SNR conditions covered by the training data. However, in the 0- and −5-dB SNR conditions, which are not present in the multi-condition training, the SC classifier yielded better performance. This raises the question whether it is possible to add supervised learning to the design of an SC-based system without sacrificing its superior generalization to unseen conditions.

In [20] and [24] it is mentioned that they failed to improve the performance of their sparse coding systems by machine learning techniques in the construction of the exemplar dictionaries. However, the cause of the failure was not explained. It may well be that the situation with single-frame modulation spectrum exemplars is different from 30-frame Mel-spectrum exemplars so that clever dictionary learning might be beneficial. We have started experiments with fast dictionary learning along the lines set out in [39]. Our first results suggest that there are two quite different issues that must be tackled. The first issue relates to the cost function used in creating the optimal exemplars. Conventional approaches to dictionary learning use the difference between unknown frames and their approximation as a weighted sum of exemplars as the criterion to minimize. While this criterion is obviously valid in sparse *coding* applications, it is not the criterion of choice in sparse *classification*. In the latter application, the exemplars carry information about the states (the classes) that they represent, and this information should enter into the cost function, for example, in the form of the requirement that individual exemplars are promoted for frames that do correspond to a certain state (or set of acoustically similar states).

The second issue is that the mapping from state activations returned by some *solver* to state posterior probabilities is less straightforward than was implemented in [20] and [24] and in this paper. There is a need for including some learning mechanisms that can find the optimal mapping from a complete set of state activations to a set of state posteriors. It is quite possible that there will be interactions between enhanced dictionary learning and learning the mapping from activations to probabilities. The challenge here is to find strategies that do not fall into the trap that we have seen in our experiments with MLPs, *viz.*, that the eventual performance increases in the conditions for which training material was available but at the cost of a diminished generalization to unseen conditions.

An issue that surely needs further investigation in the construction of the dictionary is the selection of the noise exemplars. So far, noise exemplars were extracted quasi-randomly from the four noise types that were used in creating the multi-condition training set in AURORA-2. It is quite likely that the collection of noise exemplars is much more compactly distributed in the feature space than the speech exemplars because the variation in the noise signals is less than in the speech signals. The generalization to other noise types can be improved by sampling the exemplars from a wider range of noises, for example all noise types that are available in the NOISEX CD-ROM [40]. However, we think that the most important issue in the construction of the noise exemplar dictionary is the need for avoiding overlap between noise and speech exemplars. In the Lasso procedure, it is difficult - if not impossible - to enforce a preference for speech atoms over noise atoms. If a noise exemplar that is very similar to a speech exemplar happens to fit best, this may give rise to suppressing relevant speech information. It might be beneficial to not simply discard all noise exemplars activations but rather to include these, along with the activations of the speech exemplars, in a procedure that learns the mapping from activations to state posteriors that optimizes recognition performance. An approach in which all activations are used in estimating the eventual posterior probabilities would be especially important in cases where noise and speech are difficult to distinguish in terms of spectro-temporal properties, such as in babble noise or if the 'noise' consists of competing speakers. These cases will surely require additional processing, for example, aimed at tracking continuity in pitch, in addition to continuity in the modulation spectrum.

5   Conclusions

In this paper we presented a novel noise-robust ASR system that uses the modulation spectrum in combination with a sparse coding approach for estimating state probabilities. Importantly, in its present implementation, the system does not involve any form of learning/training. The best recognition accuracies obtained with the novel system are slightly below the results that have been obtained with conventional engineering systems. We have also sketched several research lines that hold the promise of improving the results and, at the same time, to advance our knowledge of those aspects of the human auditory system that are most important for ASR. We have shown that the output of a modulation spectrum analyser that does not involve any form of conversion to the equivalent of a short-time power spectrogram is able to exploit the spectro-temporal continuity constraints that are typical

for speech and which are a prerequisite for noise robust ASR. However, we also found that the representation of medium-term dynamics in the output of the modulation spectrum analyser must be improved. With respect to the sparse coding approach to estimate state posterior probabilities, we have found that there is a fundamental distinction between sparse coding, where the task is to find the optimal representation of an unknown observation in a very large dimensional space, and sparse classification, where the task is to obtain the best possible estimates of the posterior probability that an unknown observation belongs to a specific class. In this context one challenge for future research is developing a procedure for dictionary learning that uses state posterior probabilities, in addition to or rather than reconstruction error, as the cost function. The second challenge is finding a procedure for learning a mapping from state activations to state posterior probabilities that provides the same excellent generalization to unseen conditions that has been found with sparse coding.

Endnote

[a] The software used for implementing the modulation frequency analyser was adapted from Matlab code that was kindly provided by Søren Jørgensen [41]. Some choices that are somewhat unusual in speech technology, such as the 400-Hz frame rate, were kept.

Competing interests
The authors declare that they have no competing interests.

Acknowledgements
Part of this research has been funded with support from the European Commission under contract FP7-PEOPLE-2011-290000 to the Marie Curie ITN INSPIRE. We would like to thank Hugo Van hamme and Jort Gemmeke for discussing feature extraction and sparse coding issues and Søren Jørgensen for making available the Matlab code for implementing the modulation spectrum analyser. Finally, we owe thanks to two anonymous reviewers, whose comments greatly helped to improve the paper.

Author details
[1] Amirkabir University of Technology, Hafez 424, 15875-4413 Tehran, Iran.
[2] Centre for Language Studies, Radboud University Nijmegen, Erasmusplein 1, 6525HT Nijmegen, Netherlands.

References
1.   R Drullman, JM Festen, R Plomp, Effect of temporal envelope smearing on speech reception. J. Acoust. Soc. Am. **95**, 1053–1064 (1994)
2.   H Hermansky, in *Proceedings of IEEE Workshop on Automatic Speech Recognition and Understanding.* The modulation spectrum in the automatic recognition of speech (Santa Barbara, 14–17 December 1997), pp. 140–147
3.   X Xiao, ES Chng, H Li, Normalization of the speech modulation spectra for robust speech recognition. IEEE Trans. Audio Speech Lang. Process. **16**(8), 1662–1674 (2008)
4.   JK Thompson, LE Atlas, in *Proceedings IEEE International Conference on Acoustics, Speech, and Signal Processing.* A non-uniform modulation transform for audio coding with increased time resolution, vol. 5 (Hong Kong, 6–10 April 2003), pp. 397–400

5. K Paliwal, B Schwerin, K Wójcicki, Role of modulation magnitude and phase spectrum towards speech intelligibility. Speech Commun. **53**(3), 327–339 (2011)

6. R Pichevar, H Najaf-Zadeh, L Thibault, H Lahdili, Auditory-inspired sparse representation of audio signals. Speech Commun. **53**(5), 643–657 (2011)

7. PA Torres-Carrasquillo, E Singer, MA Kohler, RJ Greene, DA Reynolds, Deller Jr. J R, in *Proceedings of International Conference on Spoken Language Processing*. Approaches to language identification using gaussian mixture models and shifted delta cepstral features (Denver, 16–20 September 2002), pp. 89–92

8. T Arai, M Pavel, H Hermansky, C Avendano, Syllable intelligibility for temporally filtered LPC cepstral trajectories. J. Acoust. Soc. Am. **105**(5), 783–791 (1999)

9. H Hermansky, N Morgan, A Bayya, P Kohn, in *Proceedings of EUROSPEECH*. Compensation for the effect of the communication channel in auditory-like analysis of speech RASTA-PLP, (1991), pp. 1367–1370

10. H Hermansky, N Morgan, RASTA processing of speech. IEEE Trans. Speech Audio Process. **2**(4), 578–589 (1994)

11. H Hermansky, Speech recognition from spectral dynamics. Sadhana. **36**(5), 729–744 (2011)

12. M Mlouka, J Liénard, in *Proceedings of the 2nd Speech Communication Seminar*. Word recognition based either on stationary items or on transitions (Almquist & Wiksell International Stockholm, 1974)

13. S Furui, Cepstral analysis technique for automatic speaker verification. IEEE Trans. Acoust. Speech Signal Process. **29**(2), 254–272 (1981)

14. RP Lippmann, Speech recognition by humans and machines: miles to go before we sleep. Speech Commun. **18**(3), 247–248 (1996)

15. T Houtgast, HJM Steeneken, A review of the MTF concept in room acoustics and its use for estimating speech intelligibility in auditoria. J. Acoust. Soc. Am. **77**, 1069–1077 (1985)

16. J Rennies, T Brand, B Kollmeier, Prediction of the influence of reverberation on binaural speech intelligibility in noise and in quiet. J. Acoust. Soc. Am. **130**, 2999–3012 (2011)

17. T Virtanen, R Singh, B Raj (eds.), *Techniques for Noise Robustness in Automatic Speech Recognition*. (Wiley, Hoboken, 2012)

18. O Ghitza, Auditory models and human performance in tasks related to speech coding and speech recognition. IEEE Trans. Speech Audio Process. **2**(1), 115–132 (1994)

19. S Jørgensen, T Dau, Predicting speech intelligibility based on the signal-to-noise envelope power ratio after modulation-frequency selective processing. J. Acoust. Soc. Am. **130**(3), 1475–1487 (2011)

20. JF Gemmeke, T Virtanen, A Hurmalainen, Exemplar-based sparse representations for noise robust automatic speech recognition. IEEE Trans. Audio Speech Lang. Process. **19**(7), 2067–2080 (2011)

21. A Hurmalainen, K Mahkonen, JF Gemmeke, T Virtanen, in *International Workshop on Machine Listening in Multisource Environments*. Exemplar-based recognition of speech in highly variable noise (Florence, 1 September 2011)

22. HG Hirsch, D Pearce, in *ISCA ITRW ASR2000*. The AURORA experimental framework for the performance evaluation of speech recognition systems under noisy conditions (Paris, 18–20 September 2000), pp. 29–32

23. H Bourlard, H Hermansky, N Morgan, Towards increasing speech recognition error rates. Speech Commun. **18**, 205–231 (1996)

24. J Gemmeke, *Noise robust ASR: missing data techniques and beyond*. (PhD thesis, Radboud University, Nijmegen, 2010)

25. B Efron, T Hastie, I Johnstone, R Tibshirani, Least angle regression. Ann. Stat. **32**(2), 407–499 (2004)

26. A Hurmalainen, K Mahkonen, JF Gemmeke, T Virtanen, in *International Workshop on Machine Listening in Multisource Environments*. Exemplar-based recognition of speech in highly variable noise (Florence, 1 September 2011)

27. Glasberg B R, BCJ Moore, Derivation of auditory filter shapes from notched-noise data. Hear. Res. **47**, 103–138 (1990)

28. SD Ewert, T Dau, Characterizing frequency selectivity for envelope fluctuations. J. Acoust. Soc. Am. **108**(3), 1181–1196 (2000)

29. LR Rabiner, B Gold, *Theory and Application of Digital Signal Processing*. (Prentice-Hall, Englewood Cliffs, 1975)

30. N Kanadera, T Arai, H Hermansky, M Pavel, On the relative importance of various components of the modulation spectrum for automatic speech recognition. Speech Commun. **28**(1), 43–55 (1999)

31. N Moritz, J Anemüller, B Kollmeier, in *Proceedings IEEE International Conference on Acoustics, Speech and Signal Processing*. Amplitude modulation spectrogram based features for robust speech recognition in noisy and reverberant environments (Prague, 22–27 May 2011), pp. 5492–5495

32. C Cerisara, D Fohr, Multi-band automatic speech recognition. Comput. Speech Lang. **15**, 151–174 (2001)

33. H Hermansky, P Fousek, in *Proceedings of Interspeech*. Multi-resolution RASTA filtering for TANDEM-based ASR (Lisbon, 4–8 September 2005), pp. 361–364

34. D Johnson, D Ellis, C Oei, C Wooters, P Faerber, N Morgan, K Asanovic, ICSI Quicknet Software Package (2004). http://www.icsi.berkeley.edu/Speech/qn.html, accessed 1-June-2013

35. Y Sun, MM Doss, JF Gemmeke, B Cranen, L ten Bosch, L Boves, in *Proceedings on Interspeech*. Combination of sparse classification and multilayer perceptron for noise-robust ASR (Portland, 9–13 September 2012)

36. F Pedregosa, G Varoquaux, A Gramfort, V Michel, B Thirion, O Grisel, M Blondel, P Prettenhofer, R Weiss, V Dubourg, J Vanderplas, A Passos, D Cournapeau, M Brucher, M Perrot, E Duchesnay, Scikit-learn: machine learning in Python. J. Mach. Learn. Res. **12**(2011), 2825–2830

37. Y Sun, B Cranen, JF Gemmeke, L Boves, L ten Bosch, MM Doss, in *Proceedings on Interspeech*. Using sparse classification outputs as feature observations for noise-robust ASR (Portland, 9–13 September 2012)

38. T Dau, D Püschel, A Kohlrausch, A quantitative model of the "effective" signal processing in the auditory system. I. model structure. J. Acoust. Soc. Am. **99**(6), 3615–3622 (1996)

39. J Mairal, F Bach, J Ponce, G Sapiro, in *Proceedings of the 26th Annual International Conference on Machine Learning, ICML '09*. Online dictionary learning for sparse coding (Montreal, 14–18 May 2009), pp. 689–696

40. A Varga, HJM Steeneken, Assessment for automatic speech recognition: II NOISEX-92: a database and an experiment to study the effect of additive noise on speech recognition systems. Speech Commun. **12**(3), 247–251 (1993)

41. S Jørgensen, T Dau, Modeling speech intelligibility based on the signal-to-noise envelope power ratio. PhD thesis. Department of Electrical Engineering, Technical University of Denmark (2014)

16

SIFT-based local spectrogram image descriptor: a novel feature for robust music identification

Xiu Zhang[1], Bilei Zhu[2], Linwei Li[1], Wei Li[1,3]*, Xiaoqiang Li[4], Wei Wang[5], Peizhong Lu[1] and Wenqiang Zhang[1]

Abstract

Music identification via audio fingerprinting has been an active research field in recent years. In the real-world environment, music queries are often deformed by various interferences which typically include signal distortions and time-frequency misalignments caused by time stretching, pitch shifting, etc. Therefore, robustness plays a crucial role in music identification technique. In this paper, we propose to use scale invariant feature transform (SIFT) local descriptors computed from a spectrogram image as sub-fingerprints for music identification. Experiments show that these sub-fingerprints exhibit strong robustness against serious time stretching and pitch shifting simultaneously. In addition, a locality sensitive hashing (LSH)-based nearest sub-fingerprint retrieval method and a matching determination mechanism are applied for robust sub-fingerprint matching, which makes the identification efficient and precise. Finally, as an auxiliary function, we demonstrate that by comparing the time-frequency locations of corresponding SIFT keypoints, the factor of time stretching and pitch shifting that music queries might have experienced can be accurately estimated.

1   Introduction

With the proliferation of a huge amount of digital music, online listening, downloading, and searching have become very popular applications among end users of the Internet in the past decade. Among the applications, music identification that is capable of recognizing unknown music segments has attracted much attention from both the research community and the industry. Music identification technique relies on an audio fingerprint which is defined as a unique and compact digest characterizing and summarizing the perceptually relevant audio content. Different methods have been proposed to construct a valid fingerprint, exploiting the properties of music characteristics as in [1-3] or applying computer vision techniques on the spectrogram of music signals as in [4,5]. Audio fingerprint is used in the music identification typically following the framework described in [6]. First, the algorithm calculates fingerprints of the original music signals and stores them together with affiliated metadata into a fingerprint database; then, when presented with an unlabeled and probably distorted music segment, it extracts a fingerprint from the query audio and compares it with those in the database. If a match is found for the query fingerprint, the unlabeled music segment is identified and the associated metadata such as information concerning singers, album, lyrics, and the like is returned.

The fingerprint for music identification should be highly discriminative over a large number of distinct fingerprints, compact for ease of storing and comparing, scalable to a large database of music records or a large number of concurrent identifications, and robust against a range of environmental distortions and transmission interferences. Among the above properties, robustness plays a central role. In the real world, a person might be interested to know the lyrics or singer of a song played in a noisy environment, then she/he records a short piece of music using a mobile phone and sends it to a remote server for identification through fingerprint matching. In this circumstance, to achieve a successful matching, the extracted fingerprint must be robust against serious distortions caused by, for example, poor

*Correspondence: weili-fudan@fudan.edu.cn
[1] School of Computer Science, Fudan University, Shanghai 201203, China
[3] Shanghai Key Laboratory of Intelligent Information Processing, Fudan University, Shanghai 200433, China
Full list of author information is available at the end of the article

speakers, cheap microphones, background noise, echo, and wireless telecommunication. Moreover, many musical recordings played by TVs or radio broadcasts are often played at arbitrarily different speeds with the pitch changed or unchanged to comply with strict program schedule constraints, which constitutes the most challenging problem in the context of music identification. Specifically, such time-frequency distortions can be modeled by time scaling (or linear speed change) which modifies both duration (or speed) and pitch of music signals by resampling, time stretching (or time scale modification (TSM)) which changes only the duration using certain algorithms, and pitch shifting which merely causes the change of pitch. Roughly speaking, time scaling can be approximately deemed as the combination of time stretching and pitch shifting. Compared with other signal degradations which only influence the perceptual quality, time stretching/scaling and pitch shifting usually lead to a more significant drop of identification performance since they bring about desynchronization problems in the time and/or frequency domains.

In this paper, we extend our previous work of [7] and propose a novel music identification algorithm that is highly robust to not only common audio signal distortions but also serious time- and frequency-domain synchronization warping simultaneously. The basic idea of our algorithm follows the line of applying computer vision techniques for music identification as did in [4] and [5]. Specifically, we first convert a music signal into a two-dimensional spectrogram image, then a powerful local descriptor, i.e., scale invariant feature transform (SIFT), is computed from the image to construct a sub-fingerprint. Thanks to the stability of the SIFT feature, the proposed algorithm exhibits a high discrimination and strong robustness. To our knowledge, this is the first algorithm that can simultaneously resist the abovementioned three challenging distortions, namely time scaling, time stretching, and pitch shifting. Moreover, introducing the SIFT feature into the spectrogram image brings an auxiliary contribution to this paper, i.e., a novel method of estimating the factor-of-time stretching and pitch shifting, which provides further information on how the query music has been wrapped in time and frequency. To make the identification efficient and precise, a locality sensitive hashing (LSH)-based nearest sub-fingerprint retrieval method and a matching determination mechanism are also integrated into this algorithm.

The remainder of the paper is organized as follows. Section 2 summarizes related works. Section 3 describes the processes of spectrogram image construction and robust audio fingerprint extraction. Section 4 details the LSH-based nearest sub-fingerprint retrieval method and the matching determination mechanism for robust sub-fingerprint matching. Section 5 introduces the principle of factor estimation of time stretching and pitch shifting. Finally, robustness and identification experiments are shown in Section 6 and the whole paper is concluded in Section 7.

2 Related work

Recently, a variety of audio fingerprinting algorithms have been proposed in the literature, each with a different degree of robustness. Most of them generate audio fingerprints from spectral features and obtain enough robustness against common audio signal deformations such as audio coding and noise addition and equalization. However, only few methods exhibit a certain capability of resisting time stretching/scaling and pitch shifting, as summarized below. Philips robust hash (PRH) [8] is one of the most significant methods and is usually deemed as a milestone. By segmenting audio signals into heavily overlapped (31/32) frames and extracting a 32-bit sub-fingerprint from 33 Bark-scale frequency sub-bands of each frame according to the energy differences between sub-bands, PRH exhibits a certain robustness when audio lengths are stretched from −4% to +4%[a] on a small dataset consisting of only four music excerpts. Unfortunately, the basic idea of this algorithm makes it susceptible to even a small amount (e.g., ±1%) of frequency misalignment caused by speed change, with significantly dropped performance. To overcome the pitch-sensitive problem, the Philips authors commented that two simple methods can be utilized. One is to store the original audio and its pitch-shifted versions into the database, and the other attempts to use multiple pitch-shifted queries for each audio clip to be identified. However, the exhaustive nature makes both methods inefficient. Namely, the first needs more memory space, and the second aggravates the retrieval complexity since it needs to exhaustively search within a set of possible scaling parameters.

To enhance the speed-change robustness of PRH, several extensions of this method have been developed. In [9], the Philips authors modified their original algorithm and achieved ±6% tolerance of speed change by exploiting shift invariance of the auto-correlation function of a densely sampled power spectrum, which logarithmically portions the energy from 300 to 2,000 Hz into 512 instead of the original 33 sub-bands. Seo et al. [10] extracted fingerprints from the phase components of the Fourier-Mellin transform of locally normalized audio spectrum. In a rather small testing dataset with only four different original excerpts, scale invariance of the transform renders the fingerprints robust against pitch shifting caused by speed changes up to ±10%, and local normalization ensures the robustness against other common audio manipulations. Bellettini and Mazzini [11] replaced the original 33 Bark-scale sub-bands of PRH with the sub-band division in terms of 12-tone equal temperament (12-TET). Under the constraints of musical scale, the authors assume that generally pitch shifting will only occur on integer-multiples of semitone, and their algorithm achieves as high as +41.42% (+6 semitones) resistance against frequency misalignment by shifting the fingerprint bits. As indicated above, the major drawback of this method is that it cannot handle random pitch shifting, which lowers its value.

Motivated by the human auditory algorithm, Sukittanon et al. [12] proposed to use long-term modulation scale features for audio content identification. Combined with channel compensation and sub-band normalization techniques, this method achieves certain insensitivity to distortions such as low-bit-rate MP3 and WMA, frequency equalization, dynamic range normalization, and TSM (±5%). Whereas, experiments on pitch shifting are not reported. Seo et al. [13] first divided the audio spectrum (300 ~ 5,300 Hz) into 16 critical bands, then calculated a normalized frequency centroid for each critical band and used the 16 frequency centroids as the fingerprint of an audio frame. This fingerprint is able to resist moderate time stretching (±4%) and slight linear speed change (±1%). Malekesmaeili and Ward extracted audio fingerprints from adaptively scaled patches of the time-chroma representation, i.e., chromagram of the input audio signal [14]. The proposed fingerprint shows high robustness against tempo change and pitch shifting.

In [15], Wang described an audio fingerprinting algorithm whose ideas have been used in the famous Shazam music matching service[b]. This algorithm first identifies spectrogram peaks which are considered stable under noise and distortion. It then forms these peaks into pairs and uses the parameters of these pairs (frequencies of the peaks and the time interval between them) to generate fingerprints. Experiments show that the Wang algorithm is robust to noise addition and GSM compression, but its basic principle makes it sensitive to time and frequency synchronization distortions. In [16], Fenet et al. extended the Wang algorithm by using constant Q transform (CQT) and a new peak pair encoding mechanism. These modifications make the algorithm more robust to pitch shifting. In [17], Dupraz and Richard proposed a similar algorithm and used an ensemble of time-localized frequency peaks as the fingerprint for audio identification. By determining a constant pitch-shifting factor and multiplying all peak frequencies of the query signal by this factor prior to fingerprint matching, this method allows for promising audio identification performance with a +5% speed change.

AudioPrint [18], proposed by IRCAM, is a music recognition algorithm based on short-term and long-term frames (double-nested) short-time Fourier transform (STFT). Ramona and Peeters performed two-round improvements on this alogrithm in 2011 and 2013. In the first round, they improve the algorithm by introducing

perceptual scales for amplitude and frequency (Bark bands) and then synchronizing the stream and database frames using an onset detection algorithm [19]. In the second round, cosine filters are introduced in the short-term spectral analysis to compensate the effect of pitch shifting. A simple solution is proposed to determine the frame positions, robust to audio degradations, with nearly no additional cost [20].

As opposed to the above audio identification algorithms based on fixed-length framing plus heavy overlap, which are usually more or less susceptible to time variations, Bardeli and Kurth proposed in [21] to divide audio signals into unequal-length disjoint time intervals. The basic idea is to acquire invariance against cropping and time scaling by picking out prominent local maxima of spectral features as segmentation boundaries. Experiments demonstrate that this algorithm allows identification of audio signals time-scaled up to ±15%, which notably outperforms most fixed-length framed methods.

Spectral features characterizing local spectral or harmonic behavior of a signal serve as the basis of most existing audio fingerprinting methods. However, several other types of interesting audio features have also been investigated. For example, Kurth et al. proposed in [3] a set of time-related features that capture local tempo, rhythm, and meter characteristics of music signals. By quantizing estimated tempos into certain modular tempo classes similar to the well-known pitch chroma classes, a so-called cyclic beat spectrum (CBS) invariant with respect to tempo doubling is obtained, which endows the designed algorithm with high-identification rates even under time scaling from −21% to +26%.

In [22], Lyon proposed a machine-hearing algorithm structure, which first converts the one-dimensional sound into a two-dimensional auditory image and then extracts features from the image to work with a following trainable classifier or decision module. By using this structure, a machine-hearing problem can be transformed into a machine vision problem, and the ideas and techniques from the vision field (e.g., sparse representation, compression, multi-scale analysis, and keypoint detection) can be used to solve the machine-hearing problem. As an illustration, Lyon et al. showed in [23] that sparse-coded auditory image features degrade less in interferences than vector-quantized Mel-frequency cepstral coefficients (MFCCs). In the literature, there have been several attempts that apply computer vision techniques for music identification. In [4], Ke et al. designed an algorithm that automatically learns local descriptors from the spectrogram via pairwise boosting. In contrast, Baluja and Covell [5] first divided the spectrogram into smaller spectral images and then decomposed these images using Haar wavelet. Audio fingerprints are finally obtained by binary quantization of retained significant wavelet components. Unfortunately, the algorithm in [4] is by nature very weak to time-varying distortions and there are no related experimental results reported, and the algorithm in [5] shows only certain robustness against $\pm 10\%$ TSM and slight resistance under $\pm 2\%$ speed change.

3 Robust audio fingerprint extraction

Music signals are often contaminated by various distortions in the real-world environment. Therefore, creating highly robust feature representation is a prerequisite and challenging task for music identification. In this paper, we propose to use a SIFT local feature originating from the computer vision field for music identification. Although the link between music identification and computer vision has been made in several published algorithms such as [4] and [5], we argue that a SIFT descriptor calculated in a spectrogram image is indeed a novel and rather robust feature. The details of calculating a SIFT-based audio fingerprint are described as follows.

3.1 Spectrogram image construction

The first step of our algorithm is to construct a spectrogram image from the input music signal. This is accomplished as follows.

1) Perform STFT on the music signal to obtain the linear spectrogram, using Hanning-windowed frames of 185.76 ms (8,192 points) with a three-fourth overlap. The frame length and overlap are selected based on the following considerations. First, a long frame length endues the spectrogram with a low time resolution, which makes the representation insensitive to time variations. Second, under the framework of fixed framing, heavy overlap is a prerequisite to deal with the lack of synchronization between the short query music and the long original signal [24], since excerpts only a few seconds long are used to identify the whole audio signals. Classical PRH algorithm [8] uses an overlap up to 31/32; herein, we experimentally adopt three fourths to balance the desynchronization resistance and searching speed.

2) Quantize the linear spectrogram obtained above into 64 logarithmically spaced frequency sub-bands in terms of Equation 1 so that frequency multiplication can be reduced to addition:

$$f_i = f_{\min} \times 2^{\frac{i-1}{12}}, \tag{1}$$

where f_i is the central frequency of the ith sub-band, $i = 1, \ldots, 64$ is the sub-band index, and $f_{\min} = 318$ Hz is the minimum frequency. Therefore, the spectrogram adopted ranges from 318 to 12,101 Hz, which covers the five medium-to-high perceptually important octaves and is large enough to extract more local image features described in the next section for robust matching.

3) Convert the logarithmic spectrogram into a gray image where image features can be extracted. To achieve this end, the spectrogram is first transformed into a log-magnitude representation as follows:

$$S(i,j) = \log |X(i,j)|, \tag{2}$$

where X is the spectrogram and i and j are the frequency sub-band index and the frame index, respectively. Compared with the linear-magnitude version, the log-magnitude spectrogram reveals more about small-magnitude components where robust local features can also be extracted. After obtaining S, the spectrogram image I is then generated as:

$$I(i,j) = \frac{S(i,j) - \min(S)}{\max(S) - \min(S)} \times 255, \tag{3}$$

where $\min(S)$ and $\max(S)$ are the minimum and maximum values of S, respectively.

3.2 Relationships between audio manipulations and spectrogram image transformations

As mentioned in the introduction, time stretching, pitch shifting, and time scaling are the three most arduous audio distortions for music identification algorithms to resist. Since time scaling can be roughly deemed as the combination of time stretching and pitch shifting, in this subsection, we only take time stretching and pitch shifting into consideration and reveal that they can be distinctly described as corresponding spectrogram image transformations. Remember that time stretching merely changes the speed of an audio signal without affecting its pitch. Therefore, when an audio signal is time-stretched, its spectrogram image remains stable in the frequency axis with only the time axis lengthened or shortened, see sub-figures (a), (b1), and (c1) in Figure 1 for example. By contrast, pitch shifting just modifies the pitch of an audio signal with no influence on its duration. When an audio signal is pitch-shifted, its spectrogram image remains unchanged in the time axis with only frequency components translated upwards or downwards; see sub-figures (a), (d1), and (e1) in Figure 1 for instance.

To make things clearer, below we give some formalized explanations on the relations between pitch shifting and spectrogram image translation. Given a signal component with frequency f, its energy distributes around the sub-band with index $Y(f)$, which is calculated by inverting Equation 1 as below:

$$Y(f) = \text{Round}\left(12 \times \log_2 \frac{f}{f_{\min}} + 1\right), \tag{4}$$

where $\text{Round}(x)$ rounds x to the nearest integer. If the signal component is pitch-shifted by a factor k, which is negative when the pitch decreases and positive when the pitch increases, it will move to a new frequency $(1+k)f$, with its

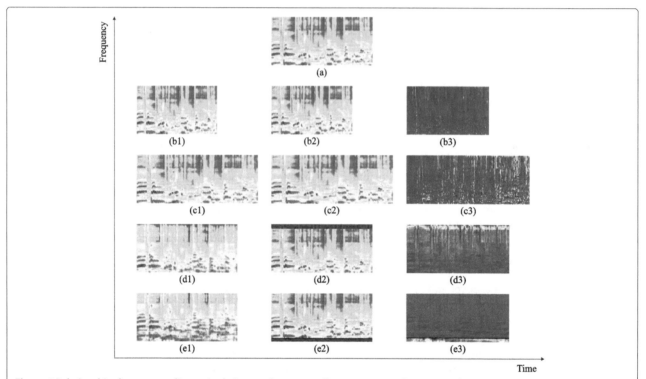

Figure 1 Relationships between audio manipulations and corresponding spectrogram image transformations. (a) is the spectrogram image of an original 10-s music clip. From the second row, the leftmost column displays spectrogram images of four audio excerpts distorted from the original clip: **(b1)** −20% time stretching, **(c1)** +20% time stretching, **(d1)** −30% pitch shifting, and **(e1)** +30% pitch shifting. The middle column displays corresponding images after spectrogram image **(a)** is modified with image transformations: **(b2)** 20% time-axis shortening, **(c2)** 20% time-axis lengthening, **(d2)** six frequency bins downshifting, and **(e2)** five frequency bins upshifting. The rightmost column **(b3, c3, d3, e3)** accordingly illustrates the differences between corresponding sub-figures of the leftmost and the middle columns. Note that warmer colors represent larger spectral differences while cooler colors represent smaller ones.

energy moved to the vicinity of the $Y((1+k)f)^{\text{th}}$ sub-band. Note that the frequency-axis hopping is independent of the absolute frequency f, as shown in Equation 5:

$$Y((1 + k)f) - Y(f) \approx \text{Round}(12 \times \log_2(1 + k)), \quad (5)$$

which means that pitch shifting applied to an audio signal can be approximately modeled as a constant vertical translation of its spectrogram determined only by coefficient k.

Figure 1 verifies the above deduction, where we can see that spectrogram images calculated from differently time-stretched or pitch-shifted audio signals exhibit high similarity with correspondingly transformed spectrogram images. For example, sub-figures (b3) and (c3) in Figure 1 are chiefly composed of cool-color components, meaning that (b1) and (c1), spectrogram images calculated from −20% and +20% time-stretched audio, possess pretty low difference with (b2) and (c2), −20% and +20% time-axis-stretched images of the original spectrogram. For another example, sub-figures (d3) and (e3) in Figure 1 are mostly composed of cool-color components, except that there are some warmer ones in the upper part of (d3) and

the lower part of (e3). As these warmer patches are rather limited, sub-figures (d1) and (e1) in Figure 1, spectrogram images calculated from −30% and +30% pitch-shifted audio, can still be correctly matched to (d2) and (e2), images translated by −6 and +5 frequency-axis bins from the original spectrogram in terms of Equation 5. To conclude, since time stretching and pitch shifting of an audio signal can be modeled by the stretch and translation of its spectrogram image, we argue that image features robust to stretch and translation should also be able to resist time stretching and pitch shifting of the original audio signal.

3.3 Robust spectrogram image feature extraction

Inspired by the machine-hearing algorithm structure of [22], the basic idea of our algorithm is to seek robust spectrogram image features for audio fingerprinting. These features should be discriminative, scalable, and, more importantly, robust to various image distortions including stretch and translation.

In order to resist stretch and translation, local spectrogram image features following the line of implicit synchronization should be more effective than global features. During these last years, local image features have received much attention because of their efficiency for several computer vision problems such as image retrieval [25,26] and object recognition [27,28]. Also, these features have found their applications in audio analysis tasks. In [29], Yu and Slotine drew inspiration from the visual classification method of [30] and proposed to extract spectrogram block matching-based features for instrument classification. In [31], Matsui et al. first extracted SIFT keypoints [27] from the spectrogram and then clustered these keypoints based on their descriptors to form a musical feature for genre classification. In [32], Kaliciak et al. first generated a set of local spectrogram patches by combining a corner detector [33] with a random points generator and then character-ized these local patches in the form of a co-occurence matrix or color moments as was done in [34]. These local patch descriptors are finally employed for music genre classification by using the 'bag-of-visual-words' approach.

3.3.1 Scale invariant feature transform (SIFT)

Among the proposed local image features, the SIFT-based features [27] are most invariant to image rotation and robust to changes in scale, illumination, and other image deformations. A typical SIFT feature extractor consists of four major stages briefly summarized as below.

- *Scale-space extrema detection*: The image is first convolved with Gaussian filters at different scales, then the difference of successive Gaussian-blurred images is taken. Potential keypoints are chosen as local maxima/minima of the Difference-of-Gaussians (DoG) that occur at multiple scales.
- *Keypoint localization*: The above detection produces too many keypoint candidates, some of which are unstable. In this step, keypoints that have low contrast are first discarded due to the sensitivity to noise and then those poorly located along edges are filtered out.
- *Orientation assignment*: Each keypoint is assigned one or more orientations based on local image gradient directions. By representing the keypoint descriptor relative to this consistent orientation, invariance to image rotation is achieved.
- *Generation of keypoint descriptor*: A set of orientation histograms are created on 4×4 pixel neighborhoods. Histograms contain eight bins each, and accordingly, a 128-dimensional ($4 \times 4 \times 8$) descriptor is obtained for each keypoint.

3.3.2 SIFT-based local spectrogram image feature extraction

In the literature, there have been a lot of different robust local image features proposed, among which the SIFT-based features possess the best results compared with other local features in the context of matching and recog-nition under various image deformations [35]. Naturally, we are inspired to employ SIFT feature extracted from the

logarithmic spectrogram image for music identification. Although SIFT feature is originally designed for object recognition in natural images, we claim that its use in the spectrogram image is feasible. According to [29], a typi-cal music piece usually involves lots of different sounds, and its spectrogram contains many partial areas with distinctive local spectral patterns. These patterns in the spectrogram can be regarded as 'objects' in a real image [31].

The output of the SIFT feature extractor is a set of key-points represented by their location, scale, orientation, and 128-dimensional descriptor (see Figure 2). The SIFT descriptor measures local image gradients and is highly distinctive between different features and robust against a corpus of image transformations. Particularly, compari-son tests carried out in [35] have shown that SIFT-based descriptors exhibit the highest matching accuracies for affine transformation such as stretch and translation com-pared with many other local descriptors. Based on these facts, we believe that the SIFT feature extracted from a spectrogram image is a good choice for music identifica-tion, especially considering that its invariance to image stretch and translation will endow the identification algo-rithm with a strong robustness against time stretching and pitch shifting.

In our method, we take the 128-dimensional SIFT descriptors calculated from the spectrogram image as sub-fingerprints of the underlying music signal. We also reserve the location of each SIFT keypoint for the esti-mation of time-stretching and pitch-shifting factor (see Section 5). The scale and orientation will not be used and are thus abandoned.

4 Robust matching of audio fingerprints

Following the procedure described in the previous section, we extract sub-fingerprints for each reference music signal and store them in the fingerprint database. When presented with an unlabeled query excerpt, we extract sub-fingerprints from it and independently match each of these sub-fingerprints against the fingerprint

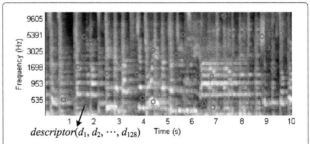

Figure 2 Illustration of SIFT local features extracted from the spectrogram image of a 10-s music excerpt. Each red circle indicates a SIFT keypoint, represented by a 128-dimensional descriptor.

database. The reference music signal which has the most matched sub-fingerprints with the query excerpt is finally returned as the identification result.

In this section, the mechanism of sub-fingerprint matching is described. It consists of two stages, i.e., nearest sub-fingerprint retrieval and matching determination.

4.1 Preliminaries of locality sensitive hashing

LSH [36] is an approximate nearest neighbor search technique that works efficiently even in high-dimensional spaces. Two 'similar' points in the original space can be hashed into a same bucket with high probability, which makes LSH appropriate to perform indexing in the retrieval task. It allows one to quickly find similar elements in large databases and has thus attracted plenty of attention from the research community. In recent years, LSH and its extensions have been successfully applied to a range of applications (e.g., [1,2,25,37,38]) and shown to significantly outperform conventional tree-based schemes such as BBF-Kd-Tree by comparison tests [39].

4.2 Nearest sub-fingerprint retrieval based on LSH

The matching of a query sub-fingerprint is performed by first retrieving its nearest neighbor, i.e., the sub-fingerprint in the fingerprint database that has minimum Euclidean distance to the query sub-fingerprint. However, audio databases in practical applications are usually large, of which corresponding fingerprint databases may contain millions of (or even more) sub-fingerprints. To find the nearest neighbor in such a large database using linear search is, in many cases, unacceptable. Also, owing to the high-dimensional SIFT-based sub-fingerprint vectors, traditional tree-like data structures succumb to the curse of dimensionality and perform no better than an exhaustive linear search.

The LSH-based nearest sub-fingerprint retrieval algorithm contains two phases: indexing and retrieval. In indexing, all the sub-fingerprints in the fingerprint database are inserted into L hash tables corresponding to L randomly selected hash functions $\{g_i, i = 1, \ldots, L\}$. Given a set of sub-fingerprints $\{\mathbf{p}\}$, each of the L hash functions is defined as:

$$g(\mathbf{p}) = (h_1(\mathbf{p}), \ldots, h_k(\mathbf{p})), \tag{6}$$

where k is the width parameter, and $\{h_j, j = 1, \ldots k\}$ are LSH functions satisfying the LSH property, i.e., sub-fingerprints that are close to each other have a higher probability to be hashed into the same bucket than sub-fingerprints that are far apart. Since our SIFT-based sub-fingerprints lie in the Euclidean space, we directly employ the LSH functions proposed in [40] as below:

$$h(\mathbf{p}) = \lfloor \frac{\mathbf{a}^{\mathrm{T}} \cdot \mathbf{p} + b}{r} \rfloor, \tag{7}$$

where $\lfloor x \rfloor$ rounds x to the nearest integer towards negative infinity, $\mathbf{a} \in \mathbb{R}^{128}$ is a random vector with elements chosen independently from a Gaussian distribution, r is a constant which is set to 2.8284 in our implementation following the suggestion of [41], and b is a real number chosen uniformly from the range of $[0, r]$.

In the retrieval phase of the nearest sub-fingerprint search algorithm, given a query sub-fingerprint $\mathbf{q}$, the algorithm iterates over the L hash tables. For each table considered, it compares $\mathbf{q}$ with the sub-fingerprints that are hashed into the same bucket as $\mathbf{q}$. The resulting nearest neighbor is identified as the compared sub-fingerprint which has the smallest Euclidean distance with $\mathbf{q}$ over the L hash tables.

4.3 Matching determination of sub-fingerprint

Using LSH, we first regroup similar elements in the fingerprint database and then, during retrieval, perform a nearest neighbor search for each of the query excerpt's sub-fingerprints within this reorganized database. Conventionally, nearest neighbors found in the database are returned as matched sub-fingerprints. However, since music signals are often distorted in a real-world environment, it is possible that a query sub-fingerprint does not have any correct counterparts in the fingerprint database so that nearest neighbors returned are actually false matches. Also, LSH is substantially an approximate similarity search algorithm; consequently, false positives do exist though very small. Considering these situations, additional measures apart from the basic LSH method must be taken to reduce the rate of false matching.

A natural way is to use a global threshold to the distance between the query sub-fingerprint and its nearest neighbor returned by LSH, rejecting those matches whose distances are larger than the threshold. However, due to the diversity of music signals, determining the threshold is an intractable problem in practical implementation. In this case, we turn to another more effective matching measure which is adopted in [27]. Given a query sub-fingerprint $\mathbf{q}$, we perform a two-nearest neighbor search using LSH and then compare the distance of the closest neighbor $\mathbf{v}$ to that of the second-closest neighbor $\mathbf{v}'$. Specifically, let $D(\cdot, \cdot)$ be the Euclidean distance between two sub-fingerprints and θ be a threshold, if:

$$D(\mathbf{q}, \mathbf{v}) < \theta \times D(\mathbf{q}, \mathbf{v}'), \tag{8}$$

sub-fingerprint $\mathbf{q}$ and $\mathbf{v}$ are judged to be matched.

5 Factor estimation of time stretching and pitch shifting

In some applications such as content-based audio authentication, it might be useful to know whether and how seriously an input music excerpt has been time-stretched or pitch-shifted [42]. In spite of this, to our knowledge, few related works have been reported in the literature. In this section, we design a novel estimation method under the framework of our audio fingerprinting algorithm.

As elaborated in the introduction, time stretching and pitch shifting applied to an audio can be equivalently reflected by time-axis stretch and frequency-axis translation of its logarithmic spectrogram, and it is natural to estimate factors of the two audio distortions by calculating factors of corresponding spectrogram image transformations. Let us take Figure 3 as an example of time-stretching factor estimation. In this figure, A and $A0$ are spectrogram images of a query music clip and its reference audio, respectively. a_1 is a stable SIFT keypoint in A and a_2 is the keypoint with minimum time-axis distance to a_1 among all the stable keypoints in A whose time-axis coordinate values are larger than that of a_1. Note that stable keypoints here refer to the SIFT keypoints for which a matched keypoint can be found in the reference audio. This matched keypoint has the smallest Euclidean distance under the constraint of Equation 8 to the stable keypoint. In Figure 3, a_{01} and a_{02} are matched keypoints of a_1 and a_2, respectively.

Given the four keypoints a_1, a_2, a_{01}, and a_{02}, a candidate of time-axis stretch factor k_t between A and $A0$ can be estimated in terms of Equation (9):

$$k_t = \frac{d_t}{d_{t0}} - 1, \tag{9}$$

where d_t is the time-axis distance between a_1 and a_2, and d_{t0} is the time-axis distance between a_{01} and a_{02}. In general, dozens of stable SIFT keypoints can be extracted from spectrogram image A, and consequently, a series of factor candidates can be computed. The median of all these candidates, $\widetilde{k_t}$, is returned as the final estimation result of the time-axis stretch factor of A and also the time-stretching factor of the original query excerpt.

Next, as shown in Figure 4, a candidate of the frequency-axis translation distance between spectrogram images of a

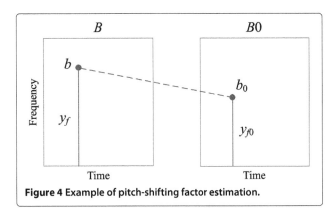

Figure 4 Example of pitch-shifting factor estimation.

query excerpt and its reference audio, B and $B0$, is simply calculated in terms of Equation 10:

$$\Delta y_f = y_f - y_{f0}, \tag{10}$$

where y_f and y_{f0} are the frequency-axis coordinate values of a pair of matched stable SIFT keypoints, b and b_0, respectively. Similarly, there exists a series of translation distance candidates, and the median, $\widetilde{\Delta y_f}$, is selected as the final result.

Remember that Equation 5 depicts the non-linear relation between the pitch-shifting factor ($\widetilde{k_f}$) of an audio signal and the frequency-axis translation distance ($\widetilde{\Delta y_f}$) of its logarithmic spectrogram image. Given $\widetilde{\Delta y_f}$ obtained as above, $\widetilde{k_f}$ can be straightly calculated according to Equation 11:

$$\widetilde{k_f} \approx 2^{\frac{\widetilde{\Delta y_f}}{12}} - 1. \tag{11}$$

6 Experimental results

To thoroughly evaluate the performance of our method, in this section, we first describe the establishment of a music database and affiliated fingerprint database, then experimentally determine several variable parameters, and finally tabulate and show the robustness and identification results. The performance of factor estimation for time stretching and pitch shifting is also presented in this section.

6.1 Database setup

To assess the proposed algorithm, we first collect a total of 10,641 music pieces of various genres such as pop, rock, disco, jazz, country music, classical music, and folk song. Each music signal is mono, 60 s long, and originally sampled at 44.1 kHz. These music pieces are then divided into two audio databases, namely DB_{train} containing 500 music pieces for parameter estimation, and DB_{test} containing 10,141 music pieces for robustness and identification testing. The affiliated fingerprint databases are called $FP\text{-}DB_{\text{train}}$ and $FP\text{-}DB_{\text{test}}$, respectively, where each

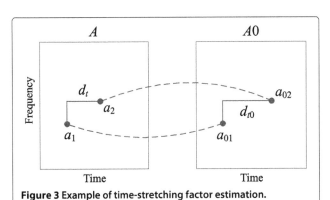

Figure 3 Example of time-stretching factor estimation.

sub-fingerprint is a 128-dimensional 8-bit integer vector extracted from the logarithmic spectrogram image using the SIFT algorithm implemented in VLFeat [43] with default setting.

Considering the large amount of high-dimensional sub-fingerprints which are found in $FP\text{-}DB_{\text{train}}$ and $FP\text{-}DB_{\text{test}}$, we index the two fingerprint databases using the LSH toolbox published by Shakhnarovich [41] (the E2LSH scheme in the toolbox is chosen) for more efficient sub-fingerprint retrieval. The indexed versions of the two fingerprint databases are denoted as $FP\text{-}DB'_{\text{train}}$ and $FP\text{-}DB'_{\text{test}}$, respectively.

As typical music identification algorithms usually identify unlabeled and distorted music fragments within the database, we also construct two query sets, i.e., QS_{train} and QS_{test}, for DB_{train} and DB_{test}, respectively. QS_{train} and QS_{test} consist of 10-s short excerpts randomly cut from distinct music pieces in DB_{train} and DB_{test}, respectively. To simulate real-world environments, all the query fragments are subjected to different audio signal distortions and synchronization attacks. The applied audio signal distortions include the following:

- *Lossy compression*: MPEG-1 layer 3 encoding/decoding at 32 kbps;
- *Echo adding*: 50% decay and 500-ms delay;
- *Equalization*: 10-band equalization with the settings of [8];
- *Noise addition*: White Gaussian noise with a signal-to-noise-ratio (SNR) of 18 dB;
- *Resampling*: Subsequent down and up sampling to 22.05 and 44.1 kHz, respectively;
- *Bandpass filtering*: Cutoff frequencies of 100 and 6,000 Hz.

The applied synchronization attacks include time stretching, pitch shifting, and time scaling. Since in the real world these three distortions mostly occur in the range of [−10%, +10%], we deform all the query clips with time stretching/scaling and pitch shifting of ±2%, ±5%, and ±10%. Meanwhile, to obtain the performance limit of the proposed algorithm, time stretching/scaling and pitch shifting out of the above range are also evaluated. To conclude, synchronization distortions we apply on the queries include the following:

- *Time stretching*: ±2%, ±5%, ±10%, ±20%, ±30%, +40%, and +50%;
- *Pitch shifting*: ±2%, ±5%, ±10%, ±20%, ±30%, ±40%, ±50%, +60%, +70%, +80%, +90%, and +100%;
- *Time scaling*: ±2%, ±5%, ±10%, ±20%, ±30%, and +40%.

Note that all the 10-s query music excerpts in the query sets are cut from corresponding original audio pieces

starting at arbitrary offsets; accordingly, all distortions performed on the queries are indeed mixed with a precedent random cropping.

6.2 Parameter estimation

There are three parameters to be tuned in the algorithm. In this sub-section, we experimentally investigate their effect on the system performance and make a suitable setting for each of them.

The first parameter to be set is the threshold θ that controls the matching determination principle described in Equation 8. Due to the constraint of θ between the nearest and the second nearest neighbors, not every query sub-fingerprint is ensured to get a matching result, no matter true or false. For a specific sub-fingerprint, bigger θ will bring about more chance to get a result returned. Accordingly, for all query sub-fingerprints, more matching results will be returned with the increase of θ; within the returned results, true matches and false matches generally increase synchronously.

In Figure 5, we increase θ from 0.1 to 1 with a step size of 0.1 and in each step calculate the correct and the false match rates of all sub-fingerprints extracted from the original and differently distorted excerpts of QS_{train} against $FP\text{-}DB_{\text{train}}$ without using LSH. More specifically, a correct (false) match rate here refers to the percentage of query sub-fingerprints for which we find correct (false) matches in the fingerprint database. A match is considered as correct if the query sub-fingerprint and its matched sub-fingerprint belong to the query excerpt and the reference audio of a same music signal, respectively. As can be seen in the figure, both the correct and the false match rates increase with the increment of θ. When $\theta < 0.8$, the false match rate increases slowly while the

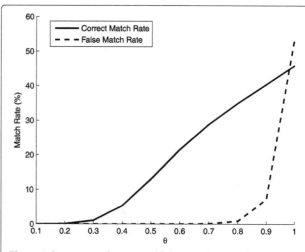

Figure 5 Correct match rates and false match rates of sub-fingerprints for different θs.

correct match rate increases significantly faster; when $\theta >$ 0.8, the false match rate becomes more notable and soon exceeds the correct match rate. Based on these observations, we set $\theta = 0.8$ in our experiment. In contrast with the results when $\theta = 1$, this setting eliminates 98.41% of the false matches at the cost of lowering 23.86% of the correct matches.

The next two parameters to be set are related to LSH, i.e., k, the width parameter, and L, the number of hash tables. They directly affect the distribution of sub-fingerprints in the fingerprint database and thus affect the efficiency of nearest sub-fingerprint retrieval. To be specific, a larger k reduces the chance of hitting sub-fingerprints that are not nearest neighbors and thus makes the nearest neighbor retrieval faster. However, this speedup is at the expense of increasing the probability of missing true nearest neighbors. In contrast, a larger L enhances the probability of finding true nearest neighbors, but it increases the time consumption at the same time. Therefore, k and L should be comprehensively considered to balance the trade-off between the retrieval accuracy and speed. In addition, increasing k and L will both lead to more memory usage. In the following, we set $k = 3$ and $L = 10$, and experiments show that this combination prevails over other values on our machine[c].

As an approximate similarity retrieval technique, LSH is aimed to accelerate the retrieval speed at the cost of slight accuracy decrease. Figure 6 compares the performance of LSH with a linear search, where hit rate indicates the percentage of query excerpts in QS_{train} and all their distorted versions which are correctly identified within DB_{train}. It is clear that the matching time for a single sub-fingerprint using LSH is significantly reduced, about 25 times faster than a linear search in our experiment environment, with only 4.7% hit rate decreases.

6.3 Robustness tests

Several groups of experiments are performed in this subsection to evaluate the robustness of the proposed music

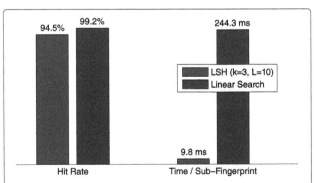

Figure 6 Comparison of accuracy and speed of music identification using LSH and linear search.

identification algorithm, using audio database DB_{test}, query set QS_{test}, and the corresponding indexed fingerprint database $FP\text{-}DB'_{test}$. The performance of each experiment is measured using the hit rate, which refers to the percentage of queries that are correctly identified within the reference database.

For comparison, identification results of the classic Shazam algorithm and state-of-the-art WavePrint [5] are also presented. The Shazam algorithm is implemented by Dan Ellis [44], and implementation of the WavePrint algorithm is available at [45].

Figure 7 compares the robustness against time stretching of the WavePrint, Shazam, and our algorithm. When there is no time stretching, the hit rates of WavePrint, Shazam, and our algorithm are 100%, 99.35%, and 100%, respectively. Under slight time stretching of $\pm 2\%$, the hit rates of WavePrint and our algorithm remain approximately 100%, and Shazam drops to around 93%. When the query is further time stretched under -5% and $+5\%$, both the WavePrint and our algorithm still maintain hit rates as high as about 99%, while the Shazam quickly drops to 60.78% and 67.7%, respectively. The reason is that the time intervals of key points, which are used to construct the fingerprint in the Shazam algorithm, are destroyed at such a level of time stretching. When queries are stretched at $\pm 10\%$, both the WavePrint and our algorithm possess hit rates above 95%. However, when stretching factor goes up to -20% and $+20\%$, the WavePrint algorithm begins to be inferior to our algorithm, with hit rates 50% vs. 96% and 80% vs. 98%, respectively. In more extreme cases where the stretch factor is bigger than $\pm 30\%$, WavePrint's hit rates quickly drop down to below 35%, while our algorithm's results remain surprisingly around 80% or above. In summary, in terms of time stretching, the Shazam, WavePrint, and our algorithm exhibit successive increased robustness, from less than $\pm 5\%$, to less than $\pm 20\%$, to bigger than $\pm 30\%$.

Identification results of differently pitch-shifted queries are shown in Figure 8. As stated in the introduction, pitch shifting of an audio signal can be equivalently modeled as the frequency-axis translation of its logarithmic spectrogram image; consequently, the translation-invariant SIFT image features introduced in the proposed algorithm bring strong robustness to the audio signal against frequency changes. Figure 8 shows that when query music fragments are pitch-shifted at different levels even up to -50% (one octave down) and $+100\%$ (one octave up), all hit rates of the proposed algorithm are still above 80%. Note that for our method, there is no linear relationship between identification results and pitch-shifting factors. For example, identification hit rates of -50% and $+100\%$ pitch-shifted queries are larger than those of nearby less distorted excerpts. In these two special cases,

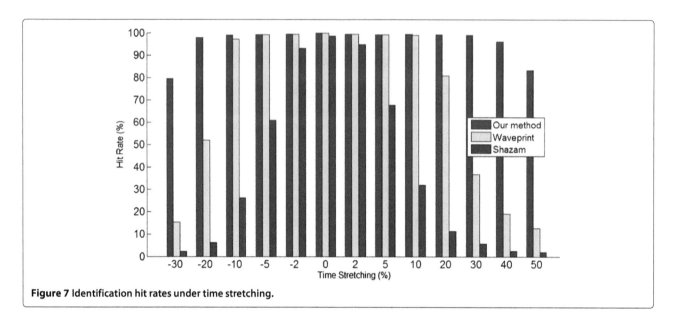

Figure 7 Identification hit rates under time stretching.

pitch shifting occurs on integer-multiples (−12 and +12) of semitone and thus causes more accurate spectrogram translations. Note that performances of the WavePrint algorithm and Shazam system are not displayed in the figure, because these algorithms are by nature very sensitive to frequency misalignments. Even for slight pitch shifting of −2% and +2%, identification hit rates are only about 72.2% and 37.3%, respectively, for WavePrint and about 11.1% and 13.3%, respectively, for Shazam. And when the distortion becomes more serious, the result gets even worse and quickly drops to near zero.

As mentioned in the introduction, time scaling can be approximately modeled as the combination of time stretching and pitch shifting. Therefore, SIFT features calculated from an audio logarithmic spectrogram image should also possess certain robustness against time scaling since they have been demonstrated to be rather stable under time stretching and pitch shifting. Figure 9 illustrates the hit rates with respect to different time-scaling levels. It shows that when music queries are deformed with a common time scaling of −10% ∼ +10%, identification results of our algorithm are pretty good, i.e., all above 98%. When the scaling gets even harder, i.e., to the factors of ±20 and +30%, our algorithm can still obtain hit rates of more than 90%, which outperforms other state-of-the-art algorithms like [3,9,10,17,21] (±6%, ±10%, +5% ±15%, −21% ∼ +26%). Finally, when the music queries are time-scaled up to −30% and +40%,

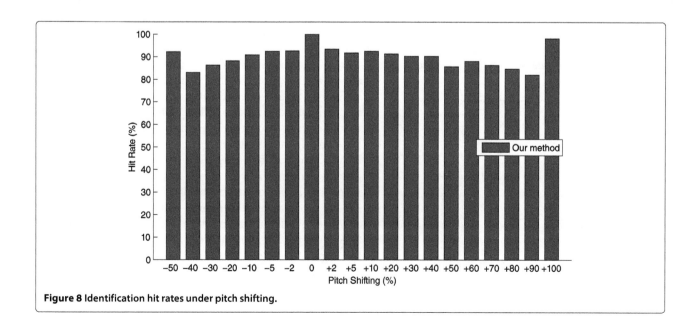

Figure 8 Identification hit rates under pitch shifting.

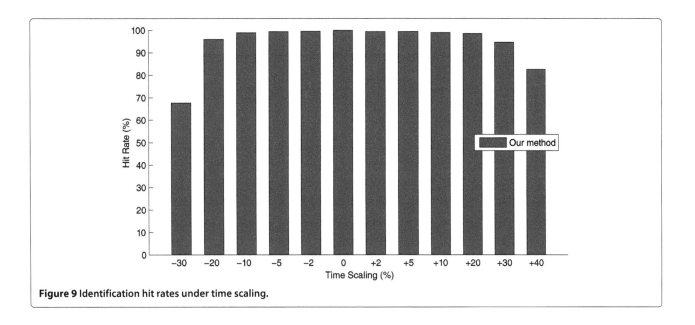

Figure 9 Identification hit rates under time scaling.

which has been beyond the scaling scope of previous algorithms' experiments, the hit rates drop to around 70% and 80%, respectively. Note that similar to the case of pitch shifting, identification results of the WavePrint algorithm and Shazam algorithm are neither illustrated in the figure. Due to poor tolerance to pitch distortions, the WavePrint algorithm only exhibits certain robustness against a time scaling of +2% (hit rate = 89.5%). The Shazam algorithm is worse, with only 9.1% and 8.7% hit rates under time scaling of −2% and +2%, respectively. And when the distortion becomes a bit more serious, both of the WavePrint's and Shazam's hit rates drop quickly to zero.

In addition to the above time- and frequency-domain synchronization distortions, music queries are often contaminated by various signal distortions in the real-world environment. Figure 10 compares the robustness against audio signal distortions of the WavePrint, Shazam, and our algorithm. Under the cases of lossy compression, noise addition, resampling, and bandpass filtering, both the WavePrint and our algorithm exhibit almost 100% hit rates. The results of Shazam are also excellent (at least 95%), only slightly weaker. In terms of equalization and echo addition, our algorithm's hit rates drop to around 90% and 80%, respectively, inferior to those of the WavePrint and Shazam. This is as expected, for the two

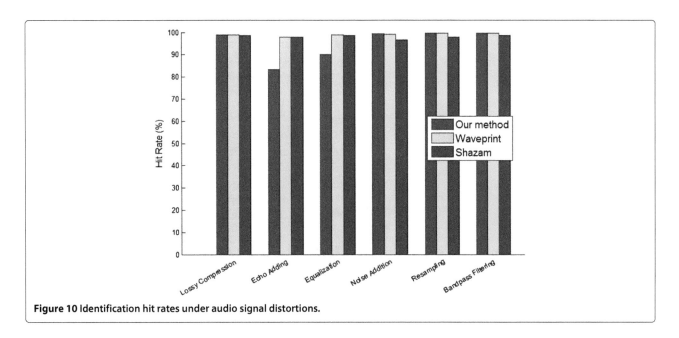

Figure 10 Identification hit rates under audio signal distortions.

distortions have greatly affected the energy distributions on spectrograms of the query excerpts and thus have more negative impact on the extraction and matching of SIFT features than other signal distortions.

In the above experiments, the source codes are written in Matlab and run on a workstation (3.2-GHz Intel Xeon CPU and 8-GB memory). The average time of extracting the SIFT features of a 10-s music query is approximately 0.23 s, which is acceptable for the identification task.

6.4 Factor estimation of time stretching and pitch shifting

In this subsection, we assess the factor estimation method of time stretching and pitch shifting proposed in Section 5. The test dataset is composed of 10-s audio excerpts randomly cut from distinct music signals in DB_{test}, and each of them is time-stretched from −30% to +50% and pitch-shifted from −50% to +100%, in accordance with the above robustness tests. After identifying the queries within DB_{test} using the proposed finger-printing algorithm, the corresponding reference music signal and query signal are compared to estimate the factor of time stretching or pitch shifting in light of Equations (9-11).

Let k_{est} be the estimated factor and k_{ref} be the reference one. The distribution of $k_{est} - k_{ref}$ is illustrated in Figure 11 for time stretching and Figure 12 for pitch shifting. As shown in the figures, our proposed method provides highly accurate factor estimation results, and more than 95% of the estimated factors are in the ±0.05 scope of the reference ones. This phenomenon actually demonstrates from a distinct aspect that treating time stretching and pitch shifting of an audio signal as the time-axis stretch and frequency-axis translation of its logarithmic spectrogram, respectively, is a reasonable way to go.

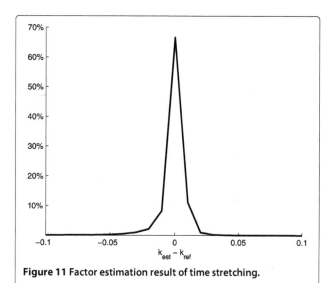

Figure 11 Factor estimation result of time stretching.

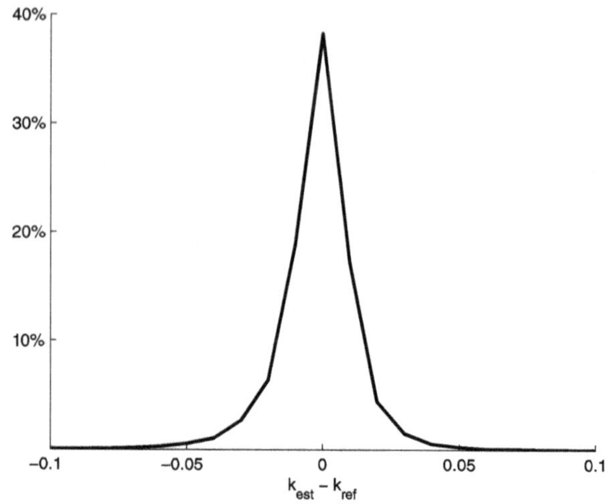

Figure 12 Factor estimation result of pitch shifting.

7   Conclusions

In this paper, a novel and robust music identification method is proposed. By combining computer vision technique, the SIFT descriptor of a spectrogram image to be exact, with locality sensitive hashing, this algorithm exhibits good performance in robustness, accuracy, and speed. What is most attractive is that even when query audio excerpts are seriously time-stretched from −30% to +50% or pitch-shifted from −50% to +100%, this method still exhibits good identification hit rates, which has been beyond all other existing algorithms, to our knowledge. Moreover, by comparing the locations of stable SIFT keypoints, a novel method is developed to estimate the distortion factor of time-stretched or pitch-shifted audio signals. In future work, we intend to combine the proposed SIFT-based feature with other spectral features to further improve the robustness under common audio signal distortions. To apply this proposed feature to other audio-related applications is also an interesting way to go.

Endnotes

[a]In this paper, positive (negative) factors of time stretching/scaling indicate the increase (decrease) of duration of a music piece. For example, +4% (−4%) time stretching/scaling lengthens (shortens) an audio signal to 104% (96%) of its original length. Similarly, positive (negative) factors of pitch shifting mean the increase (decrease) of pitch.

[b]http://www.shazam.com/.

[c]Experiments are performed on a workstation with a 3.2-GHz Intel Xeon CPU and 8-GB memory.

Competing interests
The authors declare that they have no competing interests.

Authors' information
Xiu Zhang received the B.S. degree in computer science and technology from Xidian University, Xi'an, China, in 2012. She is currently a master student in computer science at Fudan University, Shanghai, China. Her research interests include robust audio fingerprinting and audio content authentication.
Bilei Zhu received the B.S., Ph.D degree in computer science from Fudan University, Shanghai, China, in 2009 and 2014, respectively. His research interests include robust audio fingerprinting and audio sound source separation. Now he is working at SAP Labs China.
Linwei Li is currently a senior student in the Department of Physics, Fudan University, Shanghai, China. His research interests include audio fingerprint and automatic music transcription.
Wei Li received the B.S and M.S. degrees from Jilin University, China, in 1992 and 1995, respectively, both in applied physics, and the Ph.D. in computer science from Fudan University, Shanghai, China, in 2004. Since then, he has been with the School of Computer Science and Technology, Fudan University. He is currently a professor, leading the Audio Information Processing and Multimedia Information Security Laboratory. He has published 40 refereed papers in the area of audio information processing and multimedia information security including international leading journals and key conferences such as IEEE TMM, IEEE TASLP, CMJ, EURASIP JASMP, EURASIP JASP, IWDW, ACM SIGIR, and ACM Multimedia. His current research interests include audio fingerprinting, singing voice detection and separation, rhythm analysis, cover song identification, robust speaker recognition, robust audio watermarking, etc.
Xiaoqiang Li received the Ph.D. in computer science from Fudan University, Shanghai, China, in 2004. Since then, he has been with the School of Computer Engineering and Science, Shanghai University, Shanghai, China. He is now an associate professor; his research interests include image processing and analysis and multimedia information security.
Wei Wang received the Ph.D. in computer science from Fudan University, Shanghai, China, in 2012. Since then, he has been with the Naval Medical Research Institute, Shanghai, China. He is now an associate professor; his research interests include image processing and analysis and multimedia information security.
Peizhong Lu received the M.S. degree in mathematics from the University of Information Engineering, Zhengzhou, China, in 1987, and the Ph.D. degree in mathematics from the Chinese Academy of Sciences, Beijing, China, in 1998. In 1998, he joined the Department of Computer Science and Engineering, Fudan University where he is currently a professor in the field of multimedia and communication. His research interests include error-control coding for digital communication, multimedia, and information security. Dr. Lu is a member of the IEEE Information Theory Society and the Communication Society. He received the National Award for an Excellent Doctoral Dissertation in 2000.
Wenqiang Zhang received the Ph.D. in computer science from Shanghai Jiaotong University, Shanghai, China, in 2004. Since then, he has been with the School of Computer Science, Fudan University, Shanghai, China. He is now an associate professor; his research interests is multimedia information processing.

Acknowledgements
This work is supported by NSFC (61171128).

Author details
[1]School of Computer Science, Fudan University, Shanghai 201203, China. [2]SAP Labs, Shanghai 201203, China. [3]Shanghai Key Laboratory of Intelligent Information Processing, Fudan University, Shanghai 200433, China. [4]School of Computer Engineering and Science, Shanghai University, Shanghai 200444, China. [5]Naval Medical Research Institute, Shanghai 200433, China.

References
1. Y Yu, R Zimmermann, Y Wang, V Oria, Scalable content-based music retrieval using chord progression histogram and tree-structure LSH. IEEE Trans. Multimedia. **15**(8), 1969–1981 (2013)
2. Y Yu, M Crucianu, V Oria, E Damiani, in *Proceedings of ACM International Conference on Multimedia (ACM MM)*. Combining multi-probe histogram and order-statistics based LSH for scalable audio content retrieval (ACM Firenze, Italy, 2010), pp. 381–390
3. F Kurth, T Gehrmann, M Müller, in *Proceedings of the International Society for Music Information Retrieval(ISMIR)*. The cyclic beat spectrum: tempo related audio features for time-scale invariant audio identification (Victoria, Canda, 2006), pp. 35–40
4. Y Ke, D Hoiem, R Sukthankar, in *Proceedings of the, IEEE Conference on Computer Vision and Pattern Recognition (CVPR)*. Computer vision for music identification (IEEE San Diego, CA, USA, 2005), pp. 597–604
5. S Baluja, M Covell, Waveprint: efficient wavelet-based audio fingerprinting. Pattern Recognit. **41**(11), 3467–3480 (2008)
6. P Cano, E Batlle, T Kalker, J Haitsma, A review of audio fingerprinting. J. VLSI Signal Process. **41**(3), 271–284 (2005)
7. B Zhu, W Li, Z Wang, X Xue, in *Proceedings of the, ACM International Conference on Multimedia (ACM MM)*. A novel audio fingerprinting method robust to time scale modification and pitch shifting (ACM Firenze, Italy, 2010), pp. 987–990
8. J Haitsma, T Kalker, in *Proceedings of the International Society for Music Information Retrieval (ISMIR)*. A highly robust audio fingerprinting system (Paris, France, 2002), pp. 107–115
9. J Haitsma, T Kalker, in *Proceedings of the, International Conference on Acoustics, Speech, and Signal Processing (ICASSP), volume 4*. Speed-change resistant audio fingerprinting using auto-correlation (IEEE Hong Kong, China, 2003), pp. IV–728
10. JS Seo, J Haitsma, T Kalker, in *Proceedings of the IEEE Workshop on Model based Processing and Coding of Audio*. Linear speed-change resilient audio fingerprinting (IEEE Leuven, Belgium, 2002), pp. 45–48
11. C Bellettini, G Mazzini, A framework for robust audio fingerprinting. J. Commun. **5**(5), 409–424 (2010)
12. S Sukittanon, LE Atlas, JW Pitton, Modulation-scale analysis for content identification. IEEE Trans. Signal Process. **52**(10), 3023–3035 (2004)
13. JS Seo, M Jin, S Lee, D Jang, S Lee, CD Yoo, in *Proceedings of the, International Conference on Acoustics, Speech, and Signal Processing (ICASSP), volume 3*. Audio fingerprinting based on normalized spectral subband centroids (IEEE Philadelphia, Pennsylvania, USA, 2005), pp. iii–213
14. M Malekesmaeili, RK Ward, in *Proceedings of the, International Workshop on Multimedia Signal Processing (MMSP)*. A novel local audio fingerprinting algorithm (IEEE Banff, Canada, 2012), pp. 136–140
15. AL Wang, in *Proceedings of, International Society for Music Information Retrieval (ISMIR)*. An industrial strength audio search algorithm (Baltimore, Maryland, USA, 2003), pp. 7–13
16. S Fenet, G Richard, Y Grenier, in *Proceedings of International Society for Music Information Retrieval (ISMIR)*. A scalable audio fingerprint method with robustness to pitch-shifting (Miami, USA, 2011), pp. 121–126
17. E Dupraz, G Richard, in *Proceedings of the International Conference on Acoustics, Speech, and Signal Processing (ICASSP)*. Robust frequency-based audio fingerprinting (IEEE Dallas, Texas, USA, 2010), pp. 281–284
18. L Worms, *Reconnaissance dextraits sonores dans une large base de données*. (Practical lessons, Ircam, 1998)
19. M Ramona, G Peeters, in *Proceedings of the International Conference on Acoustics, Speech, and Signal Processing (ICASSP)*. Audio identification based on spectral modeling of bark-bands energy and synchronization through onset detection (IEEE Prague, Czech Republic, 2011), pp. 477–480
20. M Ramona, G Peeters, in *Proceedings of the International Conference on Acoustics, Speech, and Signal Processing (ICASSP)*. Audioprint: An efficient audio fingerprint system based on a novel cost-less synchronization scheme (IEEE Vancouver, British Columbia, Canada, 2013), pp. 818–822
21. R Bardeli, F Kurth, in *AES 25th International Conference on Metadata for Audio*. Robust identification of time-scaled audio (Springer London, UK, 2004)
22. RF Lyon, Machine hearing: an emerging field. IEEE Signal Process. Mag. **27**(5), 131–139 (2010)
23. RF Lyon, J Ponte, G Chechik, in *Proceedings of the International Conference on Acoustics, Speech, and Signal Processing (ICASSP)*. Sparse coding of auditory features for machine hearing in interference (IEEE Prague, Czech Republic, 2011), pp. 5876–5879
24. W Li, Y Liu, X Xue, in *Proceedings of the, International ACM SIGIR Conference on Research and Development in Information Retrieval*. Robust audio identification for mp3 popular music (ACM Geneva, Switzerland, 2010), pp. 627–634
25. Y Ke, R Sukthankar, L Huston, in *Proceedings of the, ACM International Conference on Multimedia (ACM MM)*. An efficient parts-based

near-duplicate and sub-image retrieval system (ACM New York, NY, USA, 2004), pp. 869–876

26. K Mikolajczyk, C Schmid, in *Proceedings of the International Conference on Computer Vision (ICCV)*. Indexing based on scale invariant interest points (IEEE Vancouver, British Columbia, Canada, 2001), pp. 525–531

27. D Lowe, Distinctive image features from scale-invariant keypoints. Int. J. Comput. Vision. **60**(2), 91–110 (2004)

28. V Ferrari, T Tuytelaars, L VanGool, Simultaneous object recognition and segmentation from single or multiple model views. Int. J. Comput. Vision. **67**(2), 159–188 (2006)

29. G Yu, JJ Slotine, in *Proceedings of the International Conference on Acoustics, Speech, and Signal Processing (ICASSP)*. Audio classification from time-frequency texture (IEEE Taipei, Taiwan, 2009), pp. 1677–1689

30. G Yu, JJ Slotine, in *Proceedings of the International Conference on Pattern Recognition (ICPR)*. Fast wavelet-based visual classification (IEEE Tampa, Florida, USA, 2008), pp. 1–5

31. T Matsui, M Goto, JP Vert, Y Uchiyama, in *Proceedings of the European Signal Processing Conference (EUSIPCO)*. Gradient-based musical feature extraction based on scale-invariant feature transform (Barcelona, Spain, 2011), pp. 724–728

32. L Kaliciak, B Horsburgh, D Song, N Wiratunga, J Pan, in *Proceedings of the Asia Information Retrieval Societies Conference (AIRS)*. Enhancing music information retrieval by incorporating image-based local features (Tianjin, China, 2012), pp. 226–237

33. J Shi, C Tomasi, in *Proceedings of the IEEE Conference on Computer Vision and Pattern Recognition (CVPR)*. Good features to track (IEEE Seattle, WA, USA, 1994), pp. 593–600

34. L Kaliciak, D Song, N Wiratunga, J Pan, in *Proceedings of the ACM International Conference on Information and Knowledge Management (CIKM)*. Novel local features with hybrid sampling technique for image retrieval (ACM Toronto, Canada, 2010), pp. 1557–1560

35. K Mikolajczyk, C Schmid, A performance evaluation of local descriptors. IEEE Trans. Pattern Anal. Machine Intelligence. **27**(10), 1615–1630 (2005)

36. P Indyk, R Motwani, in *Proceedings of the ACM Symposium on Theory of Computing*. Approximate nearest neighbors: towards removing the curse of dimensionality (ACM Dallas, Texas, USA, 1998), pp. 604–613

37. G Shakhnarovich, P Viola, T Darrell, in *Proceedings of the International Conference on Computer Vision(ICCV)*. Fast pose estimation with parameter-sensitive hashing (IEEE Nice, France, 2003), pp. 750–757

38. M Casey, M Slaney, in *Proceedings of the, International Conference on Acoustics, Speech, and Signal Processing (ICASSP), volume 4*. Fast recognition of remixed music audio (IEEE Honolulu, Hawaii, USA, 2007), pp. IV–1425

39. A Auclair, L Cohen, N Vincent, in *Proceedings of the International Workshop on Adaptive Multimedia Retrieval*. How to use SIFT vectors to analyze an image with database templates (Paris, France, 2007), pp. 224–236

40. M Datar, N Immorlica, P Indyk, VS Mirrokni, in *Proceedings of the twentieth annual symposium on Computational Geometry*. Locality-sensitive hashing scheme based on p-stable distributions (ACM Barcelona, Spain, 2004), pp. 253–262

41. G Shakhnarovich, An implementation of locality sensitive hashing algorithm (2008). http://ttic.uchicago.edu/~gregory/download.html

42. X Xue, W Li, Y Yin, in *Proceedings of the ACM International Conference on Multimedia (ACM MM)*. Towards content-based audio fragment authentication (ACM Scottsdale, AZ, USA, 2011), pp. 1249–1252

43. A Vedaldi, B Fulkerson, VLFeat: An open and portable library of computer vision algorithms (2008). http://www.vlfeat.org

44. D Ellis, Robust landmark-based audio fingerprinting (2009). http://labrosa.ee.columbia.edu/~dpwe/resources/matlab/fingerprint

45. C Sergiu, Duplicate songs detector via audio fingerprinting (2012). http://www.codeproject.com/Articles/206507/Duplicates-detector-via-audio-fingerprinting

17

Integrated exemplar-based template matching and statistical modeling for continuous speech recognition

Xie Sun[1] and Yunxin Zhao[2*]

Abstract

We propose a novel approach of integrating exemplar-based template matching with statistical modeling to improve continuous speech recognition. We choose the template unit to be context-dependent phone segments (triphone context) and use multiple Gaussian mixture model (GMM) indices to represent each frame of speech templates. We investigate two different local distances, log likelihood ratio (LLR) and Kullback-Leibler (KL) divergence, for dynamic time warping (DTW)-based template matching. In order to reduce computation and storage complexities, we also propose two methods for template selection: minimum distance template selection (MDTS) and maximum likelihood template selection (MLTS). We further propose to fine tune the MLTS template representatives by using a GMM merging algorithm so that the GMMs can better represent the frames of the selected template representatives. Experimental results on the TIMIT phone recognition task and a large vocabulary continuous speech recognition (LVCSR) task of telehealth captioning demonstrated that the proposed approach of integrating template matching with statistical modeling significantly improved recognition accuracy over the hidden Markov modeling (HMM) baselines for both TIMIT and telehealth tasks. The template selection methods also provided significant accuracy gains over the HMM baseline while largely reducing the computation and storage complexities. When all templates or MDTS were used, using the LLR local distance gave better performance than the KL local distance. For MLTS and template compression, KL local distance gave better performance than the LLR local distance, and template compression further improved the recognition accuracy on top of MLTS while having less computational cost.

Keywords: Gaussian mixture model; Template matching; KL divergence; Dynamic time warping; Large vocabulary continuous speech recognition

1 Introduction

In speech recognition, hidden Markov modeling (HMM) has been the dominant approach since it provides a principled way of jointly modeling speech spectral variations and time dynamics. However, HMM has the shortcoming of assuming the observations being independent within each state, which makes it ineffective in modeling the fine details of speech temporal evolutions that are important in characterizing nonstationary speech sounds [1]. Time derivatives of cepstral coefficients [2] are widely used to supplement time dynamic information to speech feature distributions. Trajectory model [3] introduces time-varying covariance modeling to capture temporal evolutions of speech features. Additionally, approaches like segment models [4,5] and long-contextual-span model of resonance dynamics [6] have been proposed for similar purposes.

Exemplar-based methods have the potential in addressing the deficiency of HMMs and in recent years they have drawn renewed attention in the speech recognition community [7,8], such as sparse representations (SRs) [9] and template matching [10,11]. Template-based methods make direct comparisons between a test pattern and the templates of training data via dynamic time warping (DTW), and potentially they can capture the speech dynamics better than HMMs. Template-based methods were originally used to recognize isolated words or connected digits with

* Correspondence: zhaoy@missouri.edu
[2]Department of Computer Science, University of Missouri, Columbia, MO 65211, USA
Full list of author information is available at the end of the article

good performances [12]. Until recently, template-based methods had been impractical for large tasks of speech recognition, since feature vectors of training templates need to be stored in computer memory. With today's rapid advance in computing power and memory capacity, template-based methods are investigated for large recognition tasks and promising results are reported [10,11,13-18]. However, they are still difficult to use in large vocabulary continuous speech recognition (LVCSR) due to their needs for intensive computing time and storage space. The newly proposed methods, such as template pruning and filtering [19], template-like dimension reduction of speech observations [20], and template matching in the second-pass decoding search [21], are beginning to address this problem. In general, there is a tradeoff between the costs in computation and space and the accuracy in recognition.

Considering the pros and cons of HMMs and template methods, i.e., HMM-based statistical models are effective in compactly representing speech spectral distributions of discrete states but are ineffective in representing the fine details of speech dynamics, while template matching captures well the speech temporal evolutions but demands much larger computational complexity and memory space, it appears plausible to integrate the two approaches so as to exploit their strengths and avoid their weaknesses. In the current work, we propose a novel approach of integrating exemplar-based template matching with statistical modeling. We construct triphone context-dependent phone templates to preserve the time dynamic information of phone units and use phonetic decision trees to generate templates of tied triphone units, which improves the reliability of triphone templates and covers unseen triphones by some triphone clusters. The load on memory storage is reduced by using Gaussian mixture model (GMM) indices to represent the speech frames of the templates. It is worth noting that Gaussian indices were previously used to represent speech frames in speech segmentation [22], speech separation [23], and keyword spotting [24-26]. To facilitate comparison of the templates labeled by GMM indices, we propose the local distances of log likelihood ratio (LLR) and Kullback-Leibler (KL) divergence for DTW-based template matching. To further reduce the costs of memory space and computation, we propose template selection methods to generate template representatives based on the criteria of minimum distance (MDTS) and maximum likelihood (MLTS) and we also propose a template compression method to integrate information from training templates to obtain more informative template representatives. In the recognition stage, the GMMs and the templates are used together by DTW with the proposed local distances. The proposed methods have been applied to lattice rescoring on the tasks of TIMIT [27] phone recognition and telehealth [28] large vocabulary

continuous speech recognition, and they have led to consistent error reductions over the HMM baselines.

This paper is organized as follows. In Section 2, we discuss the related work for template-based speech recognition and provide an overview of our proposed system. In Section 3, we describe the proposed methods for template construction, matching, and clustering. In Section 4, we discuss the proposed methods for template representative selection and compression. In Section 5, we present evaluation results on the task of TIMIT phone recognition and the task of telehealth LVCSR. Finally in Section 6, we give our conclusion and discuss future work.

2 Related work and system overview
2.1 Related work
Continuous speech recognition using template-based approaches has gained significant attention over the past several years. In [10], a top-down search algorithm was combined with a data-driven selection of candidates for DTW alignment to reduce search space, together with a flexible subword unit selection mechanism and a class-sensitive distance measure. On the Resource Management task, although the performance of the template matching system fell below the best published HMM results, the word error patterns of the two types of systems were found to be different and their combination was beneficial. In [13], an episodic-HMM hybrid system was proposed to exploit the ability of HMMs in producing high-quality phone graphs as well as the capability of an episodic memory in accessing fine-grained acoustic data for rescoring, where template matching was performed by DTW using the Euclidean distance. This system was evaluated on the 5k-word *Wall Street Journal* (WSJ) task and it showed a comparable performance with state-of-the-art HMM systems. In [18], prosodic information of duration, speaking rate, loudness, pitch, and voice quality was integrated with template matching through conditional random fields to improve recognition accuracy. On the Nov92 20k-word trigram WSJ task, the proposed method improved the state-of-the-art template baseline without prosodic information and led to a relative word error rate reduction of 7%. To make the template-based approach realistic for hundreds of hours of speech training data, a data pruning method was described for template-based automatic speech recognition in [19]. The pruning strategy worked iteratively to eliminate more and more templates from an initial database, and at each iteration, the feedback for data pruning was provided by the word error rate of the current model. This data pruning reduced the database size or the model size by about 30%, and consequently saved the computation time and memory usage in speech recognition. In [21], exemplar-based word-level features were investigated for large-scale speech recognition. These features were combined

with the acoustic and language scores of the first-pass model through a segmental conditional random field to rescore word lattices. Since the word lattices helped restrict the search space, the templates were not required to cover the full training data, and the templates were also filtered to a smaller set to reduce computation cost and improve robustness. Experimental results showed that the template-based approach obtained a slightly better performance than the baseline system in Voice Search and YouTube tasks.

Relative to the above-discussed efforts, our approach as proposed in the current work falls into the hybrid category, but our integration of statistical modeling and template representation and matching are tighter, since we not only rescore the lattices generated by the HMM baseline, but we also use the baseline phonetic decision tree (PDT) structures to define the tied triphone templates, representing the template frames by the GMMs and using the LLR and KL distances to measure the differences of speech frames represented in this way. In the aspect of reducing computation and memory costs, we absorb the training data information into template representatives through clustering and estimation, rather than selecting a subset of training data as the templates. On the TIMIT and telehealth tasks, we are able to show statistically significant improvements in phone and word accuracies, respectively, over the HMM baselines.

2.2 System overview

The overall architecture of the proposed template matching method is described in Figure 1. In the training stage, Viterbi alignment is performed on the training data by the baseline model to determine the phone template boundaries; using the PDT-based triphone state tying structures of the baseline system, template clustering is performed to generate tied triphone templates (Section 3.3); using the GMM codebook derived from the baseline model, the template frames are labeled by the GMMs (Section 3.1); template selection and compression are further performed to generate the template representatives (Section 4). In the test stage, the baseline model is first used to perform decoding search on a test speech utterance to generate a word lattice; the test speech frames are labeled by the GMMs in the same way as in training; template matching and best path search are then performed on the word lattice to generate the rescored sentence hypothesis (Section 3.3).

3 Template representation, matching, and clustering

3.1 Template representation

We choose the template unit to be context-dependent phone segments, the context being the immediately left and right phones of each phone segment, and we refer the context-dependent templates as triphone templates. We first carry out forced alignments of training speech data

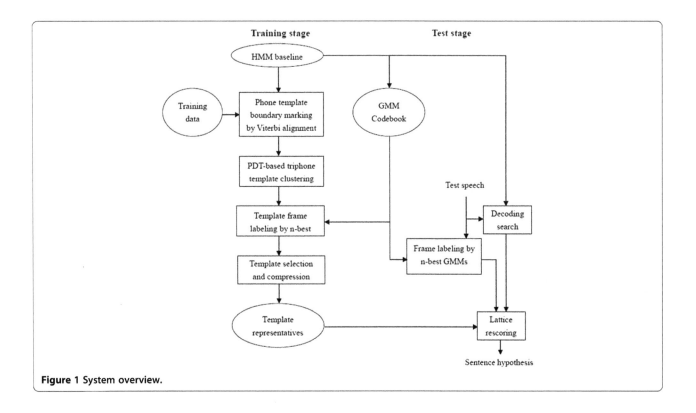

Figure 1 System overview.

with their transcriptions to obtain phone boundaries which define the phone templates. We then use a GMM codebook $\{m_1, m_2, ..., m_N\}$ that consists of the GMMs of the phonetic-decision-tree tied triphone states in the baseline HMMs to label the template frames, where N is the total number of GMMs from the HMM baseline. To do so, we compute the likelihood scores of a feature vector or frame (these two terms are used interchangeably with the understanding that a feature vector is normally extracted from a frame of data), $x_t \in R^d$ (d is the dimension of a real-valued feature vector), of a phone template by all GMMs and take the n GMMs that give the top n likelihood scores, $p(x_t|m_{1(x_t)}) \geq p(x_t|m_{2(x_t)}) \geq ... \geq p(x_t|m_{n(x_t)}) \geq ...$, to label x_t. Each GMM index is also associated with a weight $w_{k(x_t)}$ that is defined to be proportional to the likelihood score $p(x_t|m_{k(x_t)})$, with $w_{k(t)} = \frac{p(x_t|m_{k(x_t)})}{\sum_{l=1}^{n} p(x_t|m_{l(x_t)})}$ and $\sum_{k=1}^{n} w_{k(x_t)} = 1$. A template frame is therefore represented as

$$x_t \rightarrow \left\{ \begin{bmatrix} m_{1(x_t)} \\ \vdots \\ m_{n(x_t)} \end{bmatrix} \begin{bmatrix} w_{1(x_t)} \\ \vdots \\ w_{n(x_t)} \end{bmatrix} \right\}. \tag{1}$$

In general, $n << d$, and hence storing the template frames in GMM indices requires a much smaller space than storing the feature frames for the Templates.

3.2 Template matching

In using DTW to measure the dissimilarity between two speech utterances, the allowed range of speaking rate variations can be specified by local path constraints [12]. Let $d(i, j)$ denote the local distance between the ith and the jth frames of two sequences under comparison and $D(i, j)$ denote the cumulative distance between the two sequences up to the time i and j. The symmetric constraint that we adopt here is defined as

$$D(i,j) = d(i,j) + min\{D(i-1,j), D(i-1,j-1), D(i,j-1)\}. \tag{2}$$

Given a sequence S_x representing a template and a sequence S_y representing a test segment, their average frame distance is calculated as

$$\bar{D}(S_x, S_y) = \frac{1}{N} min_\varnothing \sum_{k=1}^{N} d(\varnothing_{S_x}(k), \varnothing_{S_y}(k)), \tag{3}$$

where $\varnothing_{S_x}$ and $\varnothing_{S_y}$ are the warping functions that map S_x and S_y to a common time axis, and N is the warping path length. Considering the fact that in HMM-based decoding search the acoustic score of a test segment is the sum of its frame log likelihood scores (the segment acoustic score is therefore the average frame score scaled by the length of the segment), we define the distance between the template S_x and the test segment S_y in the similar way as

$$D(S_x, S_y) = L \times \bar{D}(S_x, S_y)$$
$$= \frac{L}{N} min_\varnothing \sum_{K=1}^{N} 1d(\varnothing_{S_x}(k), \varnothing_{S_y}(k)) \tag{4}$$

where L is the length of the test segment S_y. Through scaling the average frame distance by the test segment length, the acoustic scores for different hypotheses of a test speech utterance (which in general consists of many segments) can be directly compared in template matching, as in HMM-based decoding search. Note that without the normalization by N in Equation 3, a template matching score for a speech segment would be affected by the length of the time warping path, which may vary with different templates; on the other hand, if the rescaling by L is not adopted, then the total distance on a decoding path would be dependent on the number of test segments in the path but not the lengths of these segments.

Commonly used local distances, such as Euclidean or Mahalanobis distances, compute the difference between two feature vectors directly [10], and they are thus of a feature-feature type. Let x and y represent two frames under comparison. The Euclidean distance is

$$d_{Euc}(x, y) = (x-y)'(x-y) \tag{5}$$

and the Mahalanobis distance is

$$d_{Mah}(x, y) = (x-y)'\Sigma^{-1}(x-y) \tag{6}$$

with Σ as the covariance matrix estimated from training data.

When the template frames are represented by GMM indices, the Euclidean and Mahalanobis distances are no longer suitable. One possibility is to use negated log likelihood (NLL) score as a local distance. Let x_t and $y_{t'}$ be the frames of a test segment and a training template, respectively, and assume that $y_{t'}$ is labeled by a GMM $m_{1(y_{t'})}$. The NLL distance is then

$$d_{NNL}(x_t, y_{t'}) = -\log p(x_t|m_{1(y_{t'})}). \tag{7}$$

When $y_{t'}$ is represented by n GMMs $\{m_{1(y_{t'})}, ..., m_{n(y_{t'})}\}$ with the weights $\{w_{1(y_{t'})}, ..., w_{n(y_{t'})}\}$, the NLL distance becomes

$$d_{NNL}(x_t, y_{t'}) = -\log \sum_{k=1}^{n} w_{k(y_{t'})} p(x_t|m_{k(y_{t'})}). \tag{8}$$

The NLL distance is of the feature-model type, as it does not use the information of the GMM labels on the test segment frames. The proposed log likelihood ratio and KL divergence distances make use of the GMM labels on both the test and the training frames. These two model-model distances are described below.

3.2.1 Log likelihood ratio local distance

Assuming that the test frame x_t is labeled by a GMM $m_{1(x_t)}$ and the training frame $y_{t'}$ is labeled by a GMM $m_{1(y_{t'})}$. The LLR local distance between x_t and $y_{t'}$ is then defined as follows:

$$d_{LLR}(x_t, y_{t'}) = \log \frac{p(x_t|m_{1(x_t)})}{p(x_t|m_{1(y_{t'})})}. \tag{9}$$

The LLR distance contrasts the fit score of a test frame with its best model against its fit score with the best model of the template frame, and it therefore compares the two frames indirectly through the models. The LLR distance is nonnegative when 1-best GMM is used in frame labeling. When using multiple GMM indices for speech frame representation, the nonnegativity also holds if the weights are kept uniform, but it is not guaranteed if the weights are nonuniform, where the latter is due to the fact that although the GMM scores of the numerator are not smaller than those of the denominator, a skew in the denominator's weights toward some large GMM scores may make the denominator larger than the numerator. On the other hand, since what we really need is the difference of the numerator and denominator log likelihood scores as the dissimilarity between a test frame and a template frame, while a strict-sense log likelihood ratio is not needed here as in statistic hypothesis testing, we can therefore simply take the absolute value of the log likelihood score difference as the distance measurement which is also the rectified LLR given in Equation 10:

$$d_{LLR}(x_t, y_{t'}) = \left| \log \sum_{k=1}^{n} w_{k(x_t)} p(x_t|m_{k(x_t)}) \right.$$
$$\left. - \log \sum_{k=1}^{n} w_{k(y_{t'})} p(x_t|m_{k(y_{t'})}) \right|$$
$$= \left| \log \frac{\sum_{k=1}^{n} w_{k(x_t)} p(x_t|m_{k(x_t)})}{\sum_{k=1}^{n} w_{k(y_{t'})} p(x_t|m_{k(y_{t'})})} \right| \tag{10}$$

(it is worth mentioning here that although getting a negative log likelihood ratio is a mathematical possibility, it never occurred in the experiments described in Section 5).

3.2.2 KL divergence local distance

In either the NLL distance or the LLR distance, the feature vector x_t is involved in the distance calculation. Here we consider measuring the local distance between two frames without using the feature vectors. KL divergence is widely used for measuring the difference between two probability distributions [29]. Since the frames are represented by GMM indices, the KL divergence between GMMs becomes a natural choice for indirectly measuring the dissimilarity of two frames. Because there is no closed-form expression for KL distance of GMMs, we use the Monte Carlo sampling method of Hershey and Olsen [30] to compute the divergence from a GMM m_x to a GMM m_y as

$$d(m_x \| m_y) = \frac{1}{n_s} \sum_{i=1}^{n_s} \log \frac{m_x(x_i)}{m_y(x_i)} \tag{11}$$

where the x_is are i.i.d. samples generated from the GMM m_x. Since the KL divergence is asymmetric, we further define a symmetric KL distance as

$$d_{KL}(m_x, m_y) = \frac{1}{2}(d(m_x \| m_y) + d(m_y \| m_x)). \tag{12}$$

The local distance between the two frame vectors x_t and $y_{t'}$ is then calculated as

$$d(x_t, y_{t'}) = \sum_{k=1}^{n} \sum_{l=1}^{n} w_{k(x_t)} w_{l(y_{t'})} d_{KL}(m_{k(x_t)}, m_{l(y_{t'})}). \tag{13}$$

3.3 PDT-based template clustering and matching score calculation

Considering the fact that certain triphone contexts may rarely occur or even be missing in a training set, we investigate tying triphone templates into clusters of equivalent contexts to improve the reliability of template matching as well as to handle unseen triphones in recognition. Among many possible clustering algorithms, we decide to utilize the PDT tying structures of the triphone states in the baseline HMMs directly to cluster triphone segments, since the tying structure of a phone state indicates partial similarities among triphone segments. We assume that each phone HMM has three emitting states as commonly used in HTK [31]. For the triphone templates of each monophone, we keep the three tying structures defined by the three emitting states of the corresponding phone HMM and use them jointly in template matching.

Specifically, in matching a test speech segment against a triphone arc in a word lattice, we first identify the three tied triphone clusters by answering the phonetic questions in the PDTs, and for an identified cluster i with k_i templates, we then choose $\sqrt{k_i}$ best-matching templates and average their matching scores for the test segment, and we further average the three scores of the three clusters as the matching score between the speech segment and the triphone arc. Using the square-root rule helps compress the variations of the number of templates k_i used in computing the scores, since the number often vary largely in different triphone clusters. The rule is also analogous to the K-

nearest neighbor (KNN) method where K is set as the square root of the training sample size [32].

Figure 2 illustrates the process of computing template matching score for lattice rescoring. It shows a phone lattice and a test speech segment X extracted from a speech utterance according to the start and end time of the phone arc P that has a predecessor phone P_L and successor phone P_R. Figure 3 illustrates the way that the matching scores of X with the three triphone template clusters containing $P_L - P + P_R$ are averaged to one matching score, which is used to replace the original acoustic score in the phone lattice for the phone arc P.

4 Template selection and compression

When the above-described template matching is used for lattice rescoring in LVCSR, the computation and storage overheads are still high. However, certain redundancies in the training templates can be reduced to improve computation and storage efficiency. We propose three methods of template selection and compression to address this problem. In template selection, the goal is to choose a small subset of templates as the representatives for the full set of training templates. In template compression, new GMMs are generated for labeling the frames of the selected template representatives so as to better capture the information in the training Templates.

4.1 Minimum-distance-based template selection

Agglomerative clustering [33] is a hierarchical clustering algorithm and it is widely used in pattern recognition, including speech recognition [34]. For selecting template representatives, we use the agglomerative clustering algorithm to further cluster the templates in each tied triphone cluster at a PDT leaf node, which recursively merges two closest clusters into one cluster until only one cluster is left. Given a distance function $D(C_i, C_j)$ for two clusters, the following procedure describes the algorithm for clustering m templates $\{s_1, s_2,...,s_m\}$ in a leaf node of a PDT:

1. Initialize the template set $Z_1 = \{\{s_1\}, \{s_2\}, ..., \{s_m\}\}$ with each template s_i being a cluster.
2. For $n = 2,...,m$: Obtain the new set Z_n by merging the two clusters C_i and C_j in the set Z_{n-1} with the

distance $D(C_i, C_j)$ to be the minimum among all existing distinct cluster pairs. Stop the clustering process if the number of clusters in the set Z_n drops below a threshold.

The cluster distance function $D(C_i, C_j)$ is commonly defined by the distance of their elements $D(s_x, s_y)$, and the average distance measure is adopted here [33]:

$$D(C_i, C_j) = \frac{1}{|C_i||C_j|} \Sigma_{s_x \in C_i} \Sigma_{s_y \in C_j} D(s_x, s_y). \qquad (14)$$

Note that $D(s_x, s_y)$ is the DTW distance of two templates as defined in Section 3.2, and in this step, the local distance d is the Euclidean distance of two frames.

To select a template representative for a cluster, we use the minimum distance from a template to all other templates in the cluster as the criterion, and therefore the method is called minimum distance template selection (MDTS). Given a cluster C_i, the template-to-cluster distance is defined as follows [33]:

$$D(s_x, C_i) = \sum_{\substack{s_{x'} \in C_i \\ s_x \neq s_{x'}}} D(s_x, s_{x'}), \qquad (15)$$

and the template s^* is selected as the representative for the cluster C_i if its distance to the rest of the templates in the cluster is the minimum, i.e.,

$$s^* = \mathrm{argmin}_{s_x \in C_i} D(s_x, C_i). \qquad (16)$$

The frames of the selected template representatives are subsequently indexed by their n-best GMMs according to Section 3.1.

4.2 Maximum-likelihood-based template selection

In maximum likelihood template selection, each frame of a cluster center s^* as generated by the MDTS method is relabeled by a set of GMMs that are selected by using a maximum likelihood criterion, so as to make the representative better characterize the templates in each cluster. For maximum likelihood template selection (MLTS), we

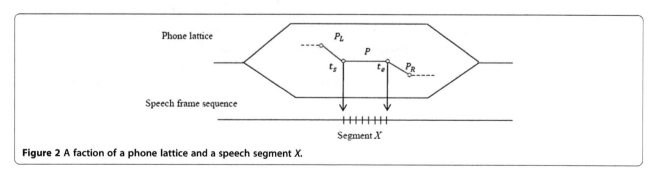

Figure 2 A faction of a phone lattice and a speech segment X.

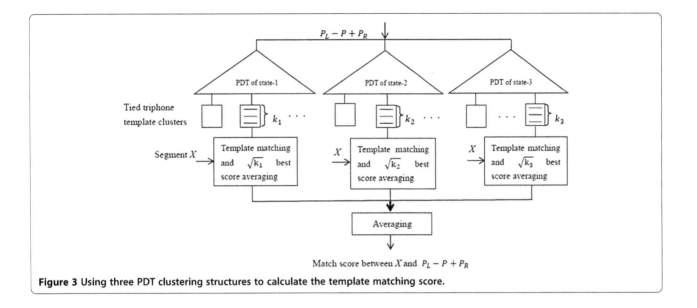

Figure 3 Using three PDT clustering structures to calculate the template matching score.

use the DTW described in Section 3.2 to align the templates in a cluster C_i to the MDTS-initialized template center s^*. Figure 4 illustrates an outcome of aligning the sequences $s_1,..., s_N$ to s^* in C_i, where the frames $x_{t_1}^{(1)},..., x_{t_N}^{(N)}$ of the sequences $s_1,..., s_N$, respectively, are aligned to the frame $x_{t_*}^{(*)}$ of the cluster center s^*. The following procedure describes the MLTS method that is applied to relabel $x_{t_*}^{(*)}$ of s^* by using the aligned frames $X = \left\{ x_{t_*}^{(*)}, x_{t_1}^{(1)},..., x_{t_N}^{(N)} \right\}$:

1. Pool the distinct GMMs which are used to label the frames in X into a local GMM set M.
2. Use the K-medoids algorithm [33] with the KL distance to partition the GMM set M into l clusters M_i, $i = 1,..., l$, where each M_i defines a subset of frames that are labeled by the GMMs in M_i.
3. For $i = 1,..., l$: Use the maximum likelihood criterion to select a GMM of M_i as the cluster center m_i^* for M_i:

$$m_i^* = \text{argmax}_{m_i^j \in M_i} \left(\sum_{x \in X_{M_i}} \log p(x|m_i^j) \right) \quad (17)$$

where m_i^j is the jth GMM in M_i.

4. For $i = 1,..., l$: Calculate the weight w_i for each GMM cluster center m_i^*, which is proportional to the likelihood of X evaluated by m_i^*, i.e., $p(X|m_i^*)$:

$$w_i = \frac{p(X|m_i^*)}{\sum_{k=1}^{l} p(X|m_k^*)} = \frac{e^{\sum_{x \in X} \log p(x|m_i^*)}}{\sum_{k=1}^{l} e^{\sum_{x \in X} \log p(x|m_k^*)}}. \quad (18)$$

After the relabeling, the frame x_t is represented by m_i^* and w_i, $i = 1,..., l$. The MLTS procedure is applied to each frame of s^*. The resulting representation of s^* has a form similar to what is described in Section 3.1, with the difference that the best-fitting n GMMs of the baseline HMMs are used to label a frame in Section 3.1, but here the template frames that are aligned to a frame of the MDTS representative are used to select a set of l GMMs to relabel the frame of the representative.

4.3 Template compression

The template compression method aims at taking in more information from the original templates for the template representatives. For each frame of a template representative, instead of selecting only one GMM and excluding the rest of the GMMs for a cluster M_i as in MLTS, here we merge the original GMMs in each cluster M_i into a new GMM and use the l new GMMs from the l clusters M_i, $i = 1,..., l$ to relabel the frame. To reduce the negative effect of outlier templates, for each GMM m_i^j in a cluster M_i, we calculate its distance to the cluster center m_i^* based on the KL distance $d_i^j = d\left(m_i^j, m_i^* \right)$. From the distances d_i^j

$$s_1 : ... x_{t_1}^{(1)} \left\{ \begin{bmatrix} m_1(x_{t_1}^{(1)}) \\ \vdots \\ m_n(x_{t_1}^{(1)}) \end{bmatrix} \begin{bmatrix} w_1(x_{t_1}^{(1)}) \\ \vdots \\ w_n(x_{t_1}^{(1)}) \end{bmatrix} \right\} ...$$

$$\downarrow \quad \vdots$$

$$\text{Center } s^* : ... x_{t_*}^{(*)} \left\{ \begin{bmatrix} m_1(x_{t_*}^{(*)}) \\ \vdots \\ m_n(x_{t_*}^{(*)}) \end{bmatrix} \begin{bmatrix} w_1(x_{t_*}^{(*)}) \\ \vdots \\ w_n(x_{t_*}^{(*)}) \end{bmatrix} \right\} ...$$

$$\uparrow \quad \vdots$$

$$s_N : ... x_{t_N}^{(N)} \left\{ \begin{bmatrix} m_1(x_{t_N}^{(N)}) \\ \vdots \\ m_n(x_{t_N}^{(N)}) \end{bmatrix} \begin{bmatrix} w_1(x_{t_N}^{(N)}) \\ \vdots \\ w_n(x_{t_N}^{(N)}) \end{bmatrix} \right\} ...$$

Figure 4 An alignment of the sequences $s_1,..., s_N$ to s^*.

of M_i, the mean $\bar{d}$ and the standard deviation σ are computed. If a GMM m_i^j is t times standard deviation away from $\bar{d}$, i.e.,

$$|d_i^j - \bar{d}| > t\sigma \tag{19}$$

then it is considered an outlier and is removed from the merging process. Suppose that after removing the outliers, there are n_G GMMs left in M_i. We first pool the component Gaussian densities from the n_G GMMs and normalize the weight of each Gaussian component by n_G. We then merge the pooled Gaussian components according to the criterion of minimum entropy increment. The entropy increase due to merging two Gaussian components $f_i \sim N(\mu_i, \Sigma_i)$ and $f_j \sim N(\mu_j, \Sigma_j)$ into $N(\mu, \Sigma)$ is defined as [35]:

$$\Delta E\left(f_i, f_j\right) = \log|\Sigma| - \frac{w_i}{w_i + w_j}\log|\Sigma_i| - \frac{w_j}{w_i + w_j}\log|\Sigma_j| \tag{20}$$

where w_i and w_j are the normalized mixture weights for f_i and f_j. The mean μ, covariance Σ, and mixture weight w of the newly generated Gaussian component are defined as

$$\Sigma = \frac{w_i}{w_i + w_j}\Sigma_i + \frac{w_j}{w_i + w_j}\Sigma_j + \frac{w_i w_j}{\left(w_i + w_j\right)^2}\left(\mu_i - \mu_j\right)\left(\mu_i - \mu_j\right)'$$

$$\mu = \frac{w_i}{w_i + w_j}\mu_i + \frac{w_j}{w_i + w_j}\mu_j$$

$$w = w_i + w_j. \tag{21}$$

The Gaussian components are merged iteratively until the number of components in M_i is below a preset threshold. The remaining Gaussian components are used to construct a new GMM, and the new GMM is used as one of the l GMMs to label the corresponding frame of the template representative.

The flowcharts of the above-discussed three template selection and compression methods are given in Figure 5. As shown in the figure, the three methods share the same template representatives that are selected from the original GMM-labeled templates. While MDTS stops here, MLTS reselects the GMM labels for the representative frames, and template compression generates new GMMs and uses them to relabel the frames of the template representatives. As are shown in the experimental results of Section 5, the refinements on the GMM labels make the template representatives more effective, and when coupled with a proper local distance they allow using only a small fraction of template representatives in lattice rescoring with little performance loss.

5 Experimental results

We performed speaker-independent phone recognition on the task of TIMIT [27] and speaker-dependent large vocabulary speech recognition on the task of telehealth captioning [28]. The experimental outcomes were measured in phone accuracy and word accuracy, respectively, for TIMIT and telehealth through aligning each phone or word string hypothesis against its reference string by using the Levenshtein distance [31].

5.1 Corpora

The TIMIT training set consisted of 3,696 sentences from 462 speakers and the standard test set included 1,344 sentences spoken by 168 speakers. The telehealth task included spontaneous speech from five doctors and the vocabulary size was 46,000. A summary of the Telehealth corpus is given in Table 1, where the word counts from the transcription texts are also listed. For a detailed description of this task, please refer to [28].

5.2 Experimental set up and lattice rescoring

For both tasks of TIMIT and telehealth, the speech features consisted of 13 MFCCs and their first- and second-order time derivatives, and crossword triphone acoustic models were trained by using HTK toolkit. In calculating a KL distance between two GMMs [30], 10,000 Monte Carlo simulation data samples were generated.

For the TIMIT dataset, the set of 39 phones was defined as in [36], and a phone bi-gram language model (LM) was used (trained from the TIMIT training speech transcripts). The HMM baseline was trained with the GMM mixture sizes of 24; and 1,189 GMMs were extracted for template construction. The total original triphone templates were 152,715 in the training set. Phone lattices were generated for each test sentence by HTK. The average number of nodes per lattice was in the order of 850, and the average number of arcs was in the order of 2,350.

For the telehealth task, speaker-dependent acoustic models were trained for five healthcare provider speakers Dr. 1 to Dr. 5. In the baseline acoustic model, each GMM included 16 Gaussian components and on average, 1,905 GMMs were extracted from the baseline HMMs of each of the five doctors. The average number of triphone templates was 181,601 per speaker for the five doctors. Trigram language models were trained on both in-domain and out-of-domain datasets, where word-class mixture trigram language models with weights obtained from a procedure of forward weight adjustment were used [37]. For each test sentence, word lattices including phone boundaries were generated by HTK. The average number of nodes per lattice was in

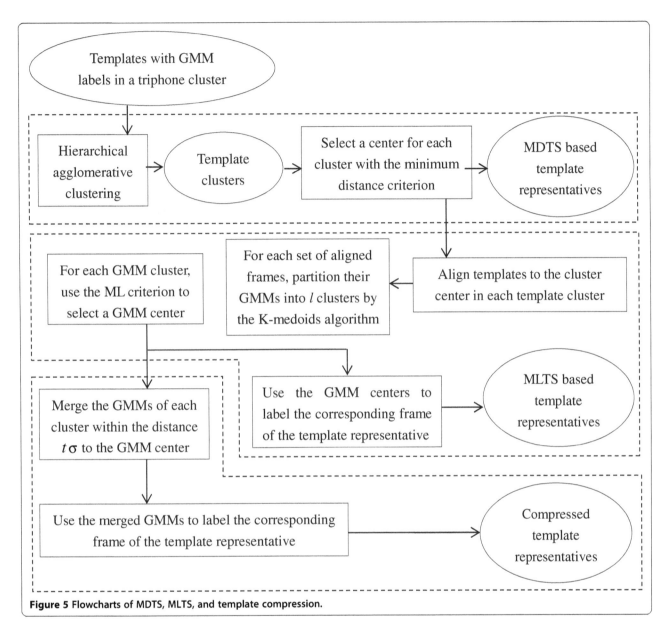

Figure 5 Flowcharts of MDTS, MLTS, and template compression.

the order of 700, and the average number of arcs was in the order of 1,950.

In rescoring a lattice, the acoustic score of each phone arc in the lattice was replaced by its corresponding triphone template matching score, where the distance

Table 1 Datasets used in the telehealth task: speech (min)/text (no. of words)

	Training set	Test set
Dr. 1	210/35,348	19.3/3,248
Dr. 2	200/39,398	29.8/5,085
Dr. 3	145/28,700	12.1/3,988
Dr. 4	180/39,148	14.3/2,759
Dr. 5	250/44,967	27.8/6,421
Total	985/187,561	103.3/21,501

score of Equation 4 was negated to become a similarity score. By using the acoustic similarity scores and the original language model scores, the best path with the largest sum of acoustic and language model log scores was searched on the lattice using dynamic programming to produce the rescored sentence hypothesis.

5.3 TIMIT phone recognition task

On the TIMIT task, we provide a detailed account of the factors in the proposed template matching methods that affect the rescoring performance, including local distances, number of GMMs employed for frame labeling, template selection, compression methods and their interactions with the local distances, and the percentage of selected template representatives. We also examine the patterns of phone error reduction and look at the cost-performance tradeoffs.

5.3.1 Local distances

In Figure 6, we compare the phone recognition performances by using the HMM baseline and the template-matching-based lattice rescoring with the local distances of Mahalanobis, NLL, LLR, and KL divergence. Except for the baseline and the Mahalanobis distance, each frame of a template or a test speech segment was labeled by 1GMM index. The HMM baseline had the phone accuracy of 72.72%. In template matching, the Mahalanobis and NLL local distances improved the baseline by merely 0.11% and 0.12% absolute, respectively, but the LLR and KL distances improved the HMM baseline by 1.30% and 0.96% absolute, respectively. The LLR distance gave higher phone accuracies than the KL distance did. This may be attributed to the fact that the KL divergence measures the difference between GMM distributions but not directly the difference between feature vectors, whereas the LLR distance contrasts the likelihood scores of two sets of GMMs for each test frame, and therefore it reflects the characteristics of the test frame more closely. Giving the superiority of the proposed LLR and KL distances, we only use these two local distances in the subsequent experiments.

5.3.2 Number of GMMs for frame labeling

In Figure 7, we show the effects of using different numbers of GMMs ($n = 1$, $n = 3$, $n = 5$, and $n = 7$) in labeling each frame of the templates. For both LLR and KL distances, the accuracy performance peaked when five GMMs were used for frame labeling, and phone accuracies of 74.51% and 74.26% were achieved for LLR and KL distances with absolute improvements of 1.79% and 1.54%, respectively, over the HMM baseline of 72.72%. The results confirmed the advantage of using multiple GMMs for frame labeling over using single GMM, as the former induced smaller quantization errors than the latter. However, using too many GMMs to represent a frame could increase confusion and reduce efficiency. We conducted significance tests on the performance difference between the '5GMMs' case and the HMM baseline. Let x_i and y_i be the phone recognition accuracy of the ith test sentence for the baseline and a proposed method, respectively. Let $t_i = y_i - x_i$ and denote the sample mean and sample variance of t_i as $\bar{t}$ and s^2 with sample size m. The Student's t test statistic is $T = \bar{t}/(s/\sqrt{m})$. In the TIMIT standard test set, $m = 1{,}344$ and $t_{m-1, 1-0.05} = 1.65$ for one-sided test. For the LLR and KL local distances, we obtained $T > t_{m-1, 1-0.05}$, and therefore our proposed template matching methods using the LLR and KL distances improved TIMIT phone recognition accuracy significantly over the HMM baseline at the significance level of 0.05. We also used two-fold cross-validation on the test set to automatically select the number of GMMs for frame labeling, and the case of 5GMM was selected in each validation set. Therefore, the result of the 5GMM case in Figure 7 also represents an open test performance. In the subsequent experiments, five GMMs were used for labeling each frame.

5.3.3 Template selection and compression

The performances of template selection and compression exhibited a dependency on the local distance measures. Here we discuss how the three methods of (1) MDTS, (2) MLTS, and (3) template compression performed when using the LLR and KL distances and show the results in Figure 8, where the number of template representatives were kept to be 20% of the total templates for the three cases (further details are discussed in Section 5.3.5). In template compression, the threshold t in Equation 19 was set to 2 for removing GMM outliers, and the number of Gaussian components in each merged GMM was 24, the same as the GMM mixture size in the baseline HMMs, with a total of 749 newly generated GMMs for the template representatives. In MDTS,

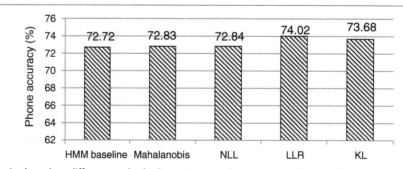

Figure 6 Phone accuracies based on different methods. Comparison on phone accuracies (percent) from the HMM baseline and the template-matching-based lattice rescoring with the local distances of Mahalanobis, NLL, LLR, and KL, where in the last three cases 1GMM was used in labeling each frame vector.

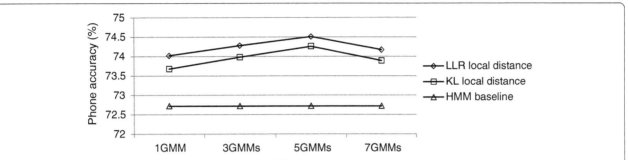

Figure 7 Lattice rescoring phone accuracy (percent) using different numbers of GMM indices for frame representation. Using multiple GMMs such as 3, 5, and 7 to label each frame can get better performance than using one single GMM. For both LLR and KL distances, the accuracy performance peaked when five GMMs were used for frame labeling.

the phone accuracies were 73.82% and 72.70% for the LLR and KL distance, respectively, and in MLTS, the phone accuracies were 74.05% and 73.07% for the LLR and the KL distance, respectively. Relative to MLTS, template compression increased absolute phone accuracy by 0.27% with the KL distance and it decreased absolute phone accuracy by 0.40% with the LLR distances. Several points worth noting in Figure 8 are discussed below.

First, MDTS worked well with the LLR distance but poorly with the KL distance, and vice versa for MLTS and template compression. In MDTS, the template representative frames were labeled in the same way as the test frames, i.e., by the best-fit GMMs of the baseline model, and in this case, a better outcome of LLR than KL is consistent with what was shown in Figure 6 for using all templates. In MLTS, however, the selected template representative frames were relabeled by GMMs to maximize the likelihood of the aligned template frames, and template compression went further by generating new GMMs from the baseline GMMs and used the new GMMs to relabel the representative frames. Because in MLTS or template compression the template representative frames were no longer labeled by the best-fit GMMs, the LLR distance that contrasted the model-frame fit

became ineffective in comparison with the KL distance that measures the distance between GMMs.

Second, relative to using all of the original templates as discussed in Section 5.3.2, using 20% template representatives that were selected by MLTS with the KL distance slightly decreased phone accuracy by 0.21% (from 74.26% to 74.05%), but using the template representatives selected by MDTS with the LLR distance significantly decreased phone accuracy by 0.69% (from 74.51% to 73.82%). This difference may be explained by the fact that MDTS simply selects a cluster center as a template representative, but MLTS further refines the GMM indices of each template representative frame to maximize the likelihood of the aligned frames in the corresponding cluster. In this way, MLTS absorbs more information from the training data into the template representatives than MDTS, and so fewer template representatives are needed in MLTS than in MDTS.

Third, with the KL distance, template compression further improved the performance over MLTS, where by using 20% template representatives, phone accuracy was actually improved by 0.06% over the case of using all templates (from 74.26% to 74.32%). This indicates that the new GMMs were more effective in labeling the

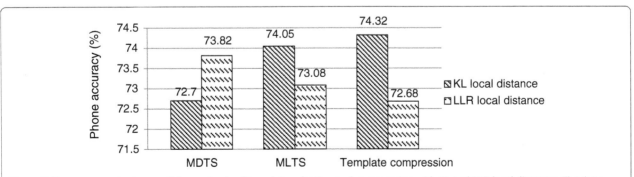

Figure 8 Phone accuracies (percent) for methods of template selection and compression with KL and LLR local distances. The three methods of template selection and compression interact with the LLR and KL local distances in different ways, and therefore each selection or compression method has its most compatible local distance. Here the number of template representatives was kept to be 20% of total templates.

Table 2 Phone accuracies (percent) from using different outlier threshold values for the compressed template representatives

Threshold $t\sigma$	1σ	2σ	3σ	∞
Accuracy (%)	73.95	74.32	73.42	70.89

template representative frames, and the exclusion of the outlier GMMs was helpful, too.

In summary, MDTS worked well with LLR distance, and MLTS and template compression worked well with KL distance. Using the respectively compatible local distances and fixing the selection percentage at 20%, template compression performed the best, MLTS the next, and MDTS the last. Specifically, the accuracy gains over the HMM baseline were 1.6% absolute by template compression with KL, 1.33% by MLTS with KL, and 1.1% by MDTS with LLR. We also conducted the Student's t test on the performance differences between each of the three methods (with respectively compatible distance) and the HMM baseline, and the three methods all significantly improved phone accuracy over the baseline at the level of $\alpha = 0.05$.

5.3.4 Evaluation on the outlier threshold t

In Table 2, we show how the threshold value t of Equation 19 for removing the GMM outliers affected the recognition performance, where the template selection method was MLTS with the KL distance, and 20% template representatives were selected. Among the four t values studied here, it is observed that $t = 2$ gave the best phone accuracy performance. Also note that when $t = \infty$, all GMMs in a cluster were used to generate compressed templates, where the existence of outliers degraded the accuracy performance significantly. Accordingly, the threshold $t = 2$ was used in all the template compression experiments.

5.3.5 Evaluation on the number of template representatives in template selection methods

In Figure 9, we show how the percentages of template representatives selected from the total templates affect

phone accuracies for MDTS and MLTS with their respectively compatible distances. The number of GMM clusters l in MLTS was set to 5, corresponding to using five GMMs to label each frame of a template representative. It is seen from the two curves that with the percentage varied from 100% down to 1%, the phone accuracies decreased for both methods. When 100% templates were used, i.e., without template selection, LLR distance performed better than KL distance, as discussed in Section 5.3.1 and Section 5.3.2. When less than 80% templates were used, MLTS performed better than MDTS since the MLTS templates generalized better than MDTS templates, as discussed in Section 5.3.3. For MDTS, when the selection percentage reduced from 100% to 60%, the phone accuracy dropped rapidly by 0.55% (from 74.51% to 73.96%), and when the selection percentage reduced from 60% to 20%, the phone accuracy reduced slowly by 0.14% (from 73.96% to 73.82%). In contrast, for MLTS, with the selection percentage reduced from 100% to 20%, the phone accuracy went down gradually by 0.21% (from 74.26% to 74.05%). Moreover, both curves went down rapidly when the selection percentage was further reduced below 20%. From Figure 9, we conclude that MLTS is more robust to using a small percentage of template representatives, and the selection percentage of 20% is a reasonable compromise between accuracy performance and computation and storage cost.

5.3.6 Phone accuracy analysis

In order to better understand the effect of the proposed template matching methods, we compare the patterns of TIMIT phone accuracies from using the methods of all templates with the KL and LLR local distances against that of the HMM baseline. Table 3 provides the phone accuracies of the five broad phone classes (vowels, semi-vowels, stops, fricatives, and nasals) and the accuracy of silence for the HMM baseline and template matching. In Figure 10, we plot the absolute phone accuracy changes

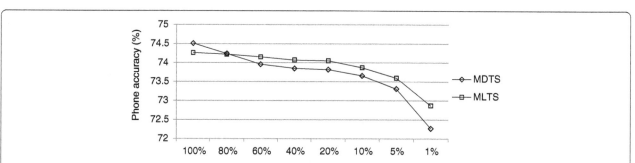

Figure 9 Phone accuracies (percent) versus the percentage of template representatives for MDTS (LLR) and MLTS (KL). For MDTS and MLTS with their respectively compatible distances, when less templates were used, worse performance was obtained. MLTS is more robust to using a small percentage of template representatives, and the selection percentage of 20% is a reasonable compromise between accuracy performance and computation and storage cost.

Table 3 Phone accuracies (percent) of vowels, semivowels, stops, fricatives, nasals, and silence

	Vowels	Semivowels	Stops	Fricatives	Nasals	Silence
HMM baseline	63.48	72.47	73.65	74.83	72.03	86.02
KL distance	68.30	76.52	73.45	72.37	72.53	85.48
LLR distance	68.32	76.85	75.65	71.95	72.66	85.57

of template matching against the HMM baseline. For the vowel class, the KL- and LLR-based template matching produced absolute phone accuracy gains of 4.82% and 4.84%, respectively, and for the semivowel class, the absolute accuracy gains were 4.05% and 4.38%, in the same order. For the stop class, template matching using the LLR distance made an absolute gain of 2.0% while using the KL distance did not help. For the fricative class, phone accuracies were decreased 2.46% and 2.88% by the KL- and LLR-based template matching, respectively. For the nasal class, there were small phone accuracy gains, and for silence, there were small accuracy degradation by template matching, but both changes were small and insignificant.

It is not surprising that the template-based methods produced the largest positive impact on semivowels (largest relative phone error reduction). Semivowels are transient sounds and templates can capture their trajectory information better than HMM. Similarly, some vowel sounds are nonstationary, such as diphthongs or vowels in strong coarticulation. Stops, having the closure and burst pattern, are nonstationary as well and often have short durations, and they are difficult to model by HMM but can be better represented by templates, as reflected in the accuracy gain by the LLR-based template matching. Fricatives are noise like and without clear trajectory patterns, and their boundaries are also difficult to determine, making template-based methods not as effective as HMMs.

5.3.7 Computation time and memory overhead

We first compare the storage space costs of the conventional and the proposed template representation methods, assuming a speech feature vector is 39 dimensional as in the baseline HMM. In conventional template methods that use Mahalanobis local distance, a speech frame is represented by a 39-dimensional vector (float), while in the proposed method a frame is labeled by n GMM indices (short integer) and $n-1$ weights (float). On a 32-bit machine and with $n=5$ in our experiments, the proposed method used 26 $(5 \times 2 + (5-1) \times 4)$ bytes per frame versus the conventional method of 156 bytes per frame, which amounts to an 83% saving in storage space. For the TIMIT dataset, there were 152,715 phone templates and the average length of a phone template was eight frames (with the frame shift of 10 ms), giving a total of 1,221,720 frames and an overhead for template storage of 30.3 MB. In template selection, the memory overhead was around 6.1 MB when 20% templates were selected to be the representatives. In template compression, the memory overhead for template storage was the same as in template selection. However, since there were 749 new GMMs for labeling the frames of the template representatives, there was an extra memory overhead of 5.4 MB.

In Table 4, we provide a comparison on the per-frame computational time for the proposed template-matching-based lattice rescoring and the HMM baseline. The computation time was divided into two parts. One part was on test-frame labeling which used GMMs from the HMM

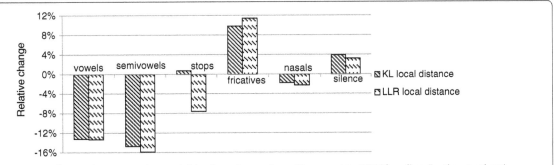

Figure 10 Phone accuracy change due to template-matching-based rescoring with respect to HMM baseline. For the vowel and semivowel classes, the KL- and LLR-based template matching obtained better performance than HMM baseline. For the stop class, template matching using the LLR distance got better phone accuracy than HMM baseline while using the KL distance did not help. For the fricative class, the phone accuracies were worse than HMM baseline for both KL- and LLR-based template matching. For the nasal class and silence, the changes between template-based methods and HMM baseline were not significant.

Table 4 Computational overhead (percent) per frame using all templates, template selection, and template compression for TIMIT phone recognition

	All templates	Template selection	Template compression
Test frame labeling overhead	40.0	40.0	22.4
Rescoring overhead	22.0	4.4	4.4
Overall computational overhead	62.0	44.4	26.8

baseline and the time was proportional to the total number of GMMs extracted from the HMMs. The other part was the rescoring time which calculated the DTW matching scores between a test segment (time marked by a phone arc on the phone lattice) and templates in a template clusters (specified by the PDTs of the phone unit). The more templates were in a template cluster, the longer the rescoring time. Since the KL distances between the GMMs were pre-calculated and the likelihood scores used in LLR distance were obtained in the test frame labeling, the time for rescoring was mainly consumed on determining the warping path in DTW, and hence for the LLR and KL distances, the rescoring times were similar (we therefore omit the local distance in Table 4). Relative to the decoding time per frame of the HMM baseline, when all templates were used, the test per-frame labeling overhead was 40% and the rescoring overhead was 22%, and hence the overall computational overhead per frame was 62.0%. In template selection, since only 20% template representatives were used, the rescoring time was reduced to 1/5 of the all-template case, and the computational overhead became 44.4%.In template compression, the number of new GMMs that were merged from the baseline GMMs was about 63% of the baseline GMMs (749 vs. 1,189), the time consumed for test frame labeling also decreased, and the computation overhead was reduced to 26.8%. Based on these numbers, we conclude that by using template representatives with a selection percentage of 20%, the costs in computation time and storage space were greatly reduced.

5.4 Large vocabulary speech recognition task
Based on the outcomes of the TIMIT phone recognition task, we only report the telehealth results for the following three cases of template matching: (1) all templates with LLR distance, (2) MLTS with KL distance, and (3) template compression with KL distance, where the cases 2 and 3 used 20% templates as the representatives and word

accuracy was averaged over the five doctors. In template compression, the number of Gaussian components in each new GMM was 16, the same as the GMMs of the baseline; the average number of GMMs generated for the compressed template representatives was 1,048 per doctor (the baseline was 1,905 GMMs per doctor). The HMM baseline was trained using crossword triphone models, with an average word accuracy of 78.43%. In Table 5, we compare the recognition word accuracies between the HMM baseline and the template-based methods. In case 1, the average word accuracy was 80.03%, which is an absolute gain of 1.6% over the baseline. In case 2, the average word accuracy was 79.40%, which is an absolute gain of 0.97% over the baseline. In case 3, the word accuracy was 79.70%, which is an absolute gain of 1.27% over the baseline. Again, we conducted a Student's t test on the word accuracy gain (averaged over the five doctors) obtained by each of the three cases over the baseline and found the performance gain in every case to be statistically significant at the level of $\alpha = 0.05$.

In Table 6, the average computation cost of the five doctors is given for the three cases. In comparison with the TIMIT phone recognition task, even though there were more GMMs to be used for test frame labeling and more templates in template clusters, the computation overhead did not increase much, especially for template selection and template compression. In addition, the memory overhead for all five doctors was around 236.2, 47.2, and 73.2 MB for using all templates, selected template representatives, and compressed template representatives, respectively. Therefore, the template-based methods, especially MLTS and template compression, are affordable for LVCSR.

5.5 Discussion
So far we have shown that representing the template frames by GMMs and using the local distance measures

Table 5 Comparison of word accuracies (percent) between the HMM baseline and the template-based methods

Speakers (no. of words)	Dr. 1 (3,248)	Dr. 2 (5,085)	Dr. 3 (3,988)	Dr. 4 (2,759)	Dr. 5 (6,421)	Average
Baselines	72.14	82.50	84.00	74.20	79.32	78.43
All templates (LLR)	73.53	84.22	85.98	75.74	80.67	80.03
MLTS (KL)	73.22	83.39	84.87	75.35	80.15	79.40
Template compression (KL)	73.55	83.61	85.21	75.71	80.39	79.70

Word accuracies (%) for HMM baselines, LLR-based all templates, and KL-based MLTS and template compression for five doctors in the telehealth task.

Table 6 Average computation overhead (percent) per frame of the five doctors

	All templates (LLR)	MLTS (KL)	Template compression (KL)
Test frame labeling overhead	43.3	43.3	23.3
Rescoring overhead	26.7	5.4	5.4
Overall computational overhead	70.0	48.7	28.7

Computational overhead per frame using LLR-based all templates and KL-based MLTS and template selection for five doctors in the telehealth task.

of LLR or KL significantly improved the accuracy performance over our HMM baselines, and the proposed methods are much more effective than the conventional template matching methods where the template frames use the original speech features. A question naturally arises is how would the proposed template-matching methods interact with an underlying acoustic model from which the GMMs are derived and the phone or word lattices are generated, and of particular interest is that as a baseline HMM system improves, whether the performance gain we have observed by the proposed template matching methods can still hold. This is a relevant issue since a baseline HMM system can be improved by using more advanced training methods and better features. Recently, a major advance has been made in using deep neural networks (DNNs) with many hidden layers for speech acoustic modeling, where the resulting DNNs learn a hierarchy of nonlinear feature detectors that can capture complex statistical patterns for speech data. For example, context-independent, pre-trained DNN/HMM hybrid architectures have achieved competitive performance in TIMIT phone recognition [38], context-dependent DNN/HMM has led to large improvements to several public domain large speech recognition tasks [39], and dumping features from deep convolutional neural networks to train GMM/HMM-based systems achieved higher accuracy performance than DNN/HMM hybrid architectures in several tasks [40].

We have investigated this issue in [41] on the TIMIT phone recognition task by performing lattice rescoring with the proposed template-matching methods on top of progressively better HMM baselines, where the test set was the same as discussed in Section 5.1. The HMM baseline system employed discriminative training, neural-network-derived phone posterior probability features, as well as ensemble acoustic models, etc. We observed that with the baseline system phone accuracy raised to 73.25%, 75.66%, 76.51%, and 77.97%, the template-matching-based lattice rescoring delivered consistent performance gains and gave phone accuracies of 74.74%, 77.27%, 77.96%, and 79.55%, respectively, where the phone accuracy of 79.55% was among the best reported results on the TIMIT continuous phoneme recognition task. For the sake of space, we omit the details of these baseline systems. For further information, please refer to [41]. The consistent performance gains support the notion that template matching improves recognition accuracy through a mechanism different from HMM. This is in agreement with the observation in [10] that the template matching system and the HMM system behave differently in word error patterns. Since our template-based methods are compatible with the GMMs trained from neural-network-derived features, it is reasonable to expect that our methods can take advantage of and add value to the advancements in this research direction.

6 Conclusions

In this paper, we have presented a novel approach of integrating template matching with statistical modeling for continuous speech recognition. The approach inherits the GMMs and the PDT state tying structures from the baseline HMMs and is therefore easily implemented. Generating template representatives and representing the frames by GMM indices make the approach extendable to LVCSR task. Based on our experimental results from the tasks of TIMIT phone recognition and telehealth LVCSR, we conclude that the proposed method of integrating template matching and statistical modeling has significantly improved the recognition performance over our HMM baselines, and the proposed template selection and compression methods have also largely saved computation time and memory space over using all templates with small losses in accuracy performance. Although in the current work we used the basic acoustic modeling techniques to train our HMM baselines, the proposed template matching methods can take advantage of and add value to more advanced GMM/HMM systems, and as such they are promising for further improving the state-of-the-art speech recognition.

Competing interests
The authors declare that they have no competing interests.

Disclosures
The work described in this paper was conducted during the first author's Ph.D. study at the University of Missouri-Columbia, USA.

Author details
[1]Nuance Communications, Inc, 1 Wayside Rd, Burlington, MA 01801, USA. [2]Department of Computer Science, University of Missouri, Columbia, MO 65211, USA.

References

1. M Ostendorf, V Digalakis, OA Kimball, From HMMs to segment models: a unified view of stochastic modeling for speech recognition. IEEE Trans on SAP **4**(5), 360–378 (1996)
2. S Furui, Speaker-independent isolated word recognition using dynamic features of speech spectrum. IEEE Trans SAP **ASSP-34**(1), 52–59 (1986)
3. H Gish, K Ng, Parametric trajectory models for speech recognition. Proc of ICSLP1 , 466–469 (1996)
4. J Glass, A probabilistic framework for segment-based speech recognition. Computer Speech and Language **17**(2–3), 13–152 (2003)
5. G Zweig, P Nguyen, A segmental CRF approach to large vocabulary continuous speech recognition, in *IEEE Workshop on Automatic Speech Recognition & Understanding* (, Merano, 2009), pp. 152–157
6. L Deng, D Yu, A Acero, A long-contextual-span model of resonance dynamics for speech recognition: parameter learning and recognizer evaluation, in *Proceedings of IEEE Workshop on Automatic Speech Recognition and Understanding* (San Juan, 2005), pp. 145–150
7. K Demuynck, D Seppi, H van Hamme, D van Compernolle, Progress in example based automatic speech recognition, in *Proceedings of IEEE International Conference on Acoustics, Speech and Signal Processing (ICASSP)* (Prague, 2011), pp. 4692–4695
8. TN Sainath, B Ramabhadran, D Nahamoo, D Kanevsky, D van Compernolle, K Demuynck, JF Gemmeke, JR Bellegarda, S Sundaram, Exemplar-based processing for speech recognition. IEEE Signal Process. Mag. **29**, 98–113 (2012)
9. TN Sainath, B Ramabhadran, S Nahamoo, S Kanevsky, A Sethy, Exemplar-based sparse representation features for speech recognition, in *Proceedings of I NTERSPEECH 2010* (Makuhari, 2010), pp. 2254–2257
10. M de Wachter, M Matton, K Demuynck, P Wambacq, R Cools, D van Compernolle, Template-based continuous speech recognition. IEEE Trans ASLP **15**(4), 1377–1390 (2007)
11. X Sun, Y Zhao, Integrate template matching and statistical modeling for speech recognition, in *Proceedings of INTERSPEECH 2010* (Makuhari, 2010), pp. 74–77
12. L Rabiner, B Juang, *Fundamentals of Speech Recognition* (Prentice Hall, Englewood Cliffs, 1993)
13. S Demange, D van Compernolle, HEAR: an hybrid episodic-abstract speech recognizer, in *Proceedings of INTERSPEECH 2009* (Brighton, 2009), pp. 3067–3070
14. L Golipour, D O'Shaughnessy, Phoneme classification and lattice rescoring based on a k-NN approach, in *Proceedings of INTERSPEECH 2010* (Makuhari, 2010), pp. 1954–1957
15. K Demuynck, K Demuynck, D Seppi, D van Compernolle, P Nguyen, G Zweig, Integrating meta-information into exemplar-based speech recognition with segmental conditional random fields, in *Proceedings of IEEE International Conference on Acoustics, Speech and Signal Processing (ICASSP)* (Prague, 2011), pp. 5048–5051
16. S Sundaram, JR Bellegarda, Latent perceptual mapping: a new acoustic modeling framework for speech recognition, in *Proceedings of INTERSPEECH 2010* (Makuhari, 2010), pp. 881–884
17. X Sun, Y Zhao, New methods for template selection and compression in continuous speech recognition, in *Proceedings of INTERSPEECH 2011* (Florence, 2011), pp. 985–988
18. D Seppi, K Demuynck, D van Compernolle, Template-based automatic speech recognition meets prosody, in *Proceedings of INTERSPEECH 2011* (Florence, 2011), pp. 545–548
19. D Seppi, D Van Compernolle, Data pruning for template-based automatic speech recognition, in *Proceedings of INTERSPEECH 2010* (Makuhari, 2010), pp. 901–904
20. S Sundaram, J Bellegarda, Latent perceptual mapping with data driven variable-length acoustic units for template-based speech recognition, in *Proceedings of IEEE International Conference on Acoustics, Speech and Signal Processing (ICASSP)* (Kyoto, 2012), pp. 4125–4128
21. G Heigold, P Nguyen, M Weintraub, V Vanhoucke, Investigations on exemplar-based features for speech recognition towards thousands of hours of unsupervised, noisy data, in *Proceedings of IEEE International Conference on Acoustics, Speech and Signal Processing (ICASSP)* (Kyoto, 2012), pp. 4437–4440
22. J Ming, Maximizing the continuity in segmentation- a new approach to model, segment and recognize speech, in *Proceedings of IEEE International Conference on Acoustics, Speech and Signal Processing (ICASSP)* (Taiwan, 2009), pp. 3849–3852
23. J Ming, R Srinivasan, D Crookes, A Jafari, CLOSE—a data-driven approach to speech separation. IEEE Trans ASLP **21**(7), 1355–1368 (2013)
24. A Garcia, H Gish, Keyword spotting of arbitrary words using minimal speech resources, in *Proceedings of IEEE International Conference on Acoustics, Speech and Signal Processing, (ICASSP), vol. 1* (Atlanta, 2006), pp. 123–127
25. T Hazen, W Shen, C White, Query-by-example spoken term detection using phonetic posteriorgram templates, in *IEEE Workshop on Automatic Speech Recognition & Understanding* (Merano, 2009)
26. Y Zhang, J Glass, Unsupervised spoken keyword spotting via segmental DTW on Gaussian posteriorgrams, in *IEEE Workshop on Automatic Speech Recognition & Understanding* (Merano, 2009)
27. L Lamel, R Kassel, S Seneff, Speech database development: design and analysis of the acoustic-phonetic corpus, in *Proceedings of the DARPA Speech Recognition Workshop*, 1989
28. Y Zhao, X Zhang, R Hu, J Xue, X Li, L Che, R Hu, L Schopp, An automatic captioning system for telemedicine, in *Proceedings of IEEE International Conference on Acoustics, Speech and Signal Processing (ICASSP)* (Toulouse, 2006), pp. 957–960
29. S Kullback, Letter to the editor: the Kullback–Leibler distance. Am. Stat. **41**(4), 338–341 (1987)
30. JR Hershey, PA Olsen, Approximating the Kullback–Leibler divergence between Gaussian mixture models, in *Proceedings of IEEE International Conference on Acoustics, Speech and Signal Processing (ICASSP), vol 4* (Hawaii, 2007), pp. 317–320
31. S Young, G Evermann, M Gales, T Hain, D Kershaw, X Liu, G Moore, J Odell, D Ollason, V Valtchev, P Woodland, *The HTK Book* (Cambridge University Engineering Department, Cambridge, 2009)
32. R Duda, P Hart, D Stork, *Pattern Classification*, 2nd edn. (Wiley, New York, 2009)
33. S Theodoridis, K Koutroumbas, *Pattern Recognition*, 3rd edn. (Academic Press, San Diego, 2006)
34. A Sankar, F Beaufays, V Digalakis, Training data clustering for improved speech recognition, in *Proceedings of EUROSPEECH* (Madrid, 1995)
35. Y Li, L Li, A greedy merge learning algorithm for Gaussian Mixture Model, in *Third International Symposium on IITA*, 2009, pp. 506–509. vol. 2, Nanchang, 21–22 November 2009
36. KF Lee, HW Hon, Speaker-independent phone recognition using hidden Markov models. IEEE Trans ASSP **37**(11), 1641–1648 (1989)
37. X Zhang, Y Zhao, L Schopp, A novel method of language modeling for automatic captioning in telemedicine. IEEE Trans ITB **11**(3), 332–337 (2007)
38. A Mohamed, G Dahl, G Hinton, Acoustic modeling using deep belief networks. IEEE Trans ASLP **20**(1), 14–22 (2012)
39. F Seide, G Li, X Chen, D Yu, Feature engineering in context-dependent deep neural networks for conversational speech transcription, in *Proceedings of IEEE Workshop on Automatic Speech Recognition & Understanding* (Hawaii, 2011), pp. 24–29
40. TN Sainath, A Mohamed, B Kingsbury, B Ramabhadran, Deep convolutional neural networks for LVCSR, in *Proceedings of IEEE International Conference on Acoustics, Speech and Signal Processing (ICASSP)* (Vancouver, 2013), pp. 8614–8618
41. X Sun, X Chen, Y Zhao, On the effectiveness of statistical modeling based template matching approach for continuous speech recognition, in *Proceedings of INTERSPEECH* (Florence, 2011), pp. 2163–2166

18

Noisy training for deep neural networks in speech recognition

Shi Yin[1,4], Chao Liu[1,3], Zhiyong Zhang[1,2], Yiye Lin[1,5], Dong Wang[1,2]*, Javier Tejedor[6], Thomas Fang Zheng[1,2] and Yinguo Li[4]

Abstract

Deep neural networks (DNNs) have gained remarkable success in speech recognition, partially attributed to the flexibility of DNN models in learning complex patterns of speech signals. This flexibility, however, may lead to serious over-fitting and hence miserable performance degradation in adverse acoustic conditions such as those with high ambient noises. We propose a noisy training approach to tackle this problem: by injecting moderate noises into the training data intentionally and randomly, more generalizable DNN models can be learned. This 'noise injection' technique, although known to the neural computation community already, has not been studied with DNNs which involve a highly complex objective function. The experiments presented in this paper confirm that the noisy training approach works well for the DNN model and can provide substantial performance improvement for DNN-based speech recognition.

Keywords: Speech recognition; Deep neural network; Noise injection

1 Introduction

A modern automatic speech recognition (ASR) system involves three components: an acoustic feature extractor to derive representative features for speech signals, an emission model to represent static properties of the speech features, and a transitional model to depict dynamic properties of speech production. Conventionally, the dominant acoustic features in ASR are based on short-time spectral analysis, e.g., Mel frequency cepstral coefficients (MFCC). The emission and transition models are often chosen to be the Gaussian mixture model (GMM) and the hidden Markov model (HMM), respectively.

Deep neural networks (DNNs) have gained brilliant success in many research fields including speech recognition, computer vision (CV), and natural language processing (NLP) [1]. A DNN is a neural network (NN) that involves more than one hidden layer. NNs have been studied in the ASR community for a decade, mainly in two approaches: in the 'hybrid approach', the NN is used to substitute for the GMM to produce frame likelihood [2], and in the 'tandem approach', the NN is used to produce long-context features that are used to substitute for or augment to short-time features, e.g., MFCCs [3].

Although promising, the NN-based approach, either by the hybrid setting or the tandem setting, did not deliver overwhelming superiority over the conventional approaches based on MFCCs and GMMs. The revolution took place in 2010 after the close collaboration between academic and industrial research groups, including the University of Toronto, Microsoft, and IBM [1,4,5]. This research found that very significant performance improvements can be accomplished with the NN-based hybrid approach, with a few novel techniques and design choices: (1) extending NNs to DNNs, i.e., involving a large number of hidden layers (usually 4 to 8); (2) employing appropriate initialization methods, e.g., pre-training with restricted Boltzmann machines (RBMs); and (3) using fine-grained NN targets, e.g., context-dependent states. Since then, numerous experiments have been published to investigate various configurations of the DNN-based acoustic modeling, and all the experiments confirmed that

*Correspondence: wangdong99@mails.tsinghua.edu.cn
[1]Center for Speech and Language Technology, Research Institute of Information Technology, Tsinghua University, ROOM 1-303, BLDG FIT, 100084 Beijing, China
[2]Center for Speech and Language Technologies, Division of Technical Innovation and Development, Tsinghua National Laboratory for Information Science and Technology, ROOM 1-303, BLDG FIT, 100084 Beijing, China
Full list of author information is available at the end of the article

the new model is predominantly superior to the classical architecture based on GMMs [2,4,6-13].

Encouraged by the success of DNNs in the hybrid approach, researchers reevaluated the tandem approach using DNNs and achieved similar performance improvements [3,14-20]. Some comparative studies were conducted for the hybrid and tandem approaches, though no evidence supports that one approach clearly outperforms the other [21,22]. The study of this paper is based on the hybrid approach, though the developed technique can be equally applied to the tandem approach.

The advantage of DNNs in modeling state emission distributions, when compared to the conventional GMM, has been discussed in some previous publications, e.g., [1,2]. Although no full consentience exists, researchers agree on some points, e.g., the DNN is naturally discriminative when trained with an appropriate objective function, and it is a hierarchical model that can learn patterns of speech signals from primitive levels to high levels. Particularly, DNNs involve very flexible and compact structures: they usually consist of a large amount of parameters, and the parameters are highly shared among feature dimensions and task targets (phones or states). This flexibility, on one hand, leads to very strong discriminative models, and on the other hand, may cause serious over-fitting problems, leading to miserable performance reduction if the training and test conditions are mismatched. For example, when the training data are mostly clean and the test data are corrupted by noises, ASR performance usually suffers from a substantial degradation. This over-fitting is particularly serious if the training data are not abundant [23].

A multitude of research has been conducted to improve noise robustness of DNN models. The multi-condition training approach was presented in [24], where DNNs were trained by involving speech data in various channel/noise conditions. This approach is straightforward and usually delivers good performance, though collecting multi-condition data is not always possible. Another direction is to use noise-robust features, e.g., auditory features based on Gammatone filters [23]. The third direction involves various speech enhancement approaches. For example, the vector Taylor series (VTS) was applied to compensate for input features in an adaptive training framework [25]. The authors of [26] investigated several popular speech enhancement approaches and found that the maximum likelihood spectral amplitude estimator (MLSA) is the best spectral restoration method for DNNs trained with clean speech and tested on noisy data. Some other researches involve noise information in DNN inputs and train a 'noise aware' network. For instance, [27] used the VTS as the noise estimator to generate noise-dependent inputs for DNNs.

Another related technique is the denoising auto-encoder (DAE) [28]. In this approach, some noises are randomly selected and intentionally injected to the original clean speech; the noise-corrupted speech data are then fed to an auto-encoder (AE) network where the targets (outputs) are the original clean speech. By this configuration, the AE will learn the denoising function in a non-linear way. Note that this approach is not particular for ASR, but a general denoising technique. The authors of [29] extended this approach by introducing recurrent NN structures and demonstrated that the deep and recurrent auto-encoder can deliver better performance for ASR in most of the noise conditions they examined.

This paper presents a noisy training approach for DNN-based ASR. The idea is simple: by injecting some noises to the input speech data when conducting DNN training, the noise patterns are expected to be learned, and the generalization capability of the resulting network is expected to be improved. Both may improve robustness of DNN-based ASR systems within noisy conditions. Note that part of the work has been published in [30], though this paper presents a full discussion of the technique and reports extensive experiments.

The paper is organized as follows: Section 2 discusses some related work, and Section 3 presents the proposed noisy training approach. The implementation details are presented in Section 4, and the experimental settings and results are presented in Section 5. The entire paper is concluded in Section 6.

2 Related work

The noisy training approach proposed in this paper was highly motivated by the noise injection theory which has been known for decades in the neural computing community [31-34]. This paper employs this theory and contributes in two aspects: first, we examine the behavior of noise injection in DNN training, a more challenging task involving a huge amount of parameters; second, we study mixture of multiple noises at various levels of signal-to-noise ratios (SNR), which is beyond the conventional noise injection theory that assumes small and Gaussian-like injected noises.

Another work related to this study is the DAE approach [28,29]. Both the DAE and the noisy training approaches corrupt NN inputs by randomly sampled noises. Although the objective of the DAE approach is to recover the original clean signals, the focus of the noisy training approach proposed here is to construct a robust classifier.

Finally, this work is also related to the multi-condition training [24], in the sense that both train DNNs with speech signals in multiple conditions. However, the noisy training obtains multi-conditioned speech data by corrupting clean speech signals, while the multi-condition training uses real-world speech data recorded in multiple noise conditions. More importantly, we hope to set up a theoretical foundation and a practical guideline for training DNNs with noises, instead of just regarding it as a blind noise pattern learner.

3 Noisy training

The basic process of noisy training for DNNs is as follows: first of all, sample some noise signals from some real-world recordings and then mix these noise signals with the original training data. This operation is also referred to as 'noise injection' or 'noise corruption' in this paper. The noise-corrupted speech data are then used to train DNNs as usual. The rationale of this approach is twofold: firstly, the noise patterns within the introduced noise signals can be learned and thus compensated for in the inference phase, which is straightforward and shares the same idea as the multi-condition training approach; secondly, the perturbation introduced by the injected noise can improve generalization capability of the resulting DNN, which is supported by the noise injection theory. We discuss these two aspects sequentially in this section.

3.1 Noise pattern learning

The impact of injecting noises in training data can be understood as providing some noise-corrupted instances so that they can be learned by the DNN structure and recognized in the inference (test) phase. From this perspective, the DNN and GMM are of no difference, since both can benefit from matched acoustic conditions of training and testing, by either re-training or adaptation.

However, the DNN is more powerful in noise pattern learning than the GMM. Due to its discriminative nature, the DNN model focuses on phone/state boundaries, and the boundaries it learns might be highly complex. Therefore, it is capable of addressing more severe noises and dealing with heterogeneous noise patterns. For example, a DNN may obtain a reasonable phone classification accuracy in a very noisy condition, if the noise does not drastically change the decision boundaries (e.g., with car noise). In addition, noises of different types and at different magnitude levels can be learned simultaneously, as the complex decision boundaries that the DNN classifier may learn provide sufficient freedom to address complicated decisions in heterogeneous acoustic conditions.

In contrast, the GMM is a generative model and focuses on class distributions. The decision boundaries a GMM learns (which are determined by the relative locations of the GMM components of phones/states) are relatively much simpler than those a DNN model learns. Therefore, it is difficult for GMMs to address heterogeneous noises.

The above argument explains some interesting observations in the DNN-based noise training in our experiments. First, learning a particular type of noise does not necessarily lead to performance degradation in another type of noise. In fact, our experiments show that learning a particular noise usually improves performances on other noises, only if the property of the 'unknown' noise is not drastically different from the one that has been learned. This is a clear advantage over GMMs, for which a significant performance reduction is often observed when the noise conditions of training and test data are unmatched.

Moreover, our experiments show that learning multiple types of noises are not only possible, but also complementary. As we will see shortly, learning two noises may lead to better performance than learning any single noise, when the test data are corrupted by either of the two noises. This is also different from GMMs, for which learning multiple noises generally leads to interference among each other.

The power of DNNs in learning noise patterns can be understood in a deeper way, from three perspectives. Firstly, the DNN training is related to feature selection. Due to the discriminative nature, the DNN training can infer the most discriminative part of the noise-corrupted acoustic features. For instance, with the training data corrupted by car noise, the DNN training process will learn that the corruption is mainly on the low-frequency part of the signal, and so the low-frequency components of the speech features are de-emphasized in the car noise condition. Learning the car noise, however, did not seriously impact the decision boundaries in other conditions in our experiments, e.g., with clean speech, probably due to the complicated DNN structure that allows to learn noise-conditioned decision boundaries. Moreover, learning car noise may benefit other noise conditions where the corruption mainly resides in low-frequency components (as the car noise), even though the noise is not involved in the training.

Secondly, the DNN training is related to perceptual classification. Thanks to the multi-layer structure, DNNs learn noise patterns gradually. This means that the noise patterns presented to the DNN inputs are learned together with the speech patterns at low levels, but only at high levels, the noise patterns are recognized and de-emphasized in the decision. This provides a large space for DNNs to learn heterogeneous noise patterns and 'memorize' them in the abundant parameters. This process also simulates the processing procedure of the human brain, where noise patterns are processed and recognized by the peripheral auditory system but are ignored in the final perceptual decision by the central neural system.

Finally, the DNN training is related to the theory of regularization. All admit that a large amount of parameters of DNNs allow great potential to learn complex speech and noise patterns and their class boundaries. If the training is based on clean speech only, however, the flexibility provided by the DNN structure is largely wasted. This is because the phone class boundaries are relatively clear with clean speech, and so the abundant parameters of DNNs tend to learn the nuanced variations of phone implementations, conditioned on a particular type of channel and/or background noise. This is a notorious over-fitting problem. By injecting random noises, the DNN training is enforced to emphasize on the most discriminative patterns of speech signals. In other words, the DNNs trained with noise injection tend to be less sensitive to noise corruptions. This intuition is supported by the noise injection theory as presented in the next section.

3.2 Noise injection theory

It has been known for two decades that imposing noises to the input can improve the generalization capability of neural networks [35]. A bunch of theoretical studies have been presented to understand the implication of this 'noise injection'. Nowadays, it is clear that involving a small magnitude of noise in the input is equivalent to introducing a certain regularization in the objective function, which in turn encourages the network converging to a smoother mapping function [36]. More precisely, with noise injection, the training favors an optimal solution at which the objective function is less sensitive to the change of the input [32]. Further studies showed that noise injection is closely correlated to some other well-known techniques, including sigmoid gain scaling and target smoothing by convolution [37], at least with Gaussian noises and multi-layer perceptrons (MLP) with a single layer. The relationships among regularization, weight decay, and noise injection, on one hand, provide a better understanding for each individual technique, and on the other hand, motivate some novel and efficient robust training algorithms. For example, Bishop showed that noise injection can be approximated by a Tikhonov regularization on the square error cost function [33]. Finally, we note that noise injection can be conducted in different ways, such as perturbation on weights and hidden units [31], though we just consider the noise injection to the input in this paper.

In order to highlight the rationale of noise injection (and so noisy training), we reproduce the formulation and derivation in [32] but migrate the derivation to the case of cross-entropy cost which is usually used in classification problems such as ASR.

First of all, formulate an MLP as a non-linear mapping function $f_\theta : \mathcal{R}^M \longmapsto \mathcal{R}^K$ where M is the input dimension and K is the output dimension, and θ encodes all the parameters of the network including weights and biases. Let $\mathbf{x} \in \mathcal{R}^M$ denote the input variables, and $\mathbf{y} \in \{0, 1\}^K$ denote the target labels which follow the 1-of-K encoding scheme. The cross-entropy cost is defined as follows:

$$E(\theta) = -\sum_{n=1}^{N}\sum_{k=1}^{K}\left\{\mathbf{y}^{(n)} lnf_k\left(\mathbf{x}^{(n)}\right)\right\} \tag{1}$$

where n indexes the training samples and k indexes the output units. Consider an identical and independent noise

$\mathbf{v}$ whose first and second moments satisfy the following constraints:

$$\mathbb{E}\{\mathbf{v}\} = 0 \quad \mathbb{E}\{\mathbf{v}^2\} = \epsilon I \tag{2}$$

where I is the M-dimensional identity matrix, and ϵ is a small positive number. Applying the Taylor series of $lnf(\mathbf{x})$, the cost function with the noise injection can be derived as follows:

$$\begin{aligned}
E_v(\theta) &= -\sum_{n=1}^{N}\sum_{k=1}^{K}\left\{\mathbf{y}_k^{(n)} lnf_k\left(\mathbf{x}^{(n)} + \mathbf{v}^{(n)}\right)\right\} \\
&\approx -\sum_{n=1}^{N}\sum_{k=1}^{K}\left\{\mathbf{y}_k^{(n)} lnf_k\left(\mathbf{x}^{(n)}\right)\right\} \\
&- \sum_{n=1}^{N}\sum_{k=1}^{K}\mathbf{y}_k^{(n)}\left\{\mathbf{v}^{(n)T}\frac{\nabla f_k\left(\mathbf{x}^{(n)}\right)}{f_k\left(\mathbf{x}^{(n)}\right)} + \frac{1}{2}\mathbf{v}^{(n)T}H_k\left(\mathbf{x}^{(n)}\right)\mathbf{v}^{(n)}\right\}
\end{aligned}$$

where $H_k(x)$ is defined as follows:

$$H_k(x) = \frac{-1}{f_k(\mathbf{x})}\nabla f_k(\mathbf{x})\nabla f_k(\mathbf{x})^T + \frac{1}{f_k^2(\mathbf{x})}\nabla^2 f_k(\mathbf{x}).$$

Since $\mathbf{v}^{(n)}$ is independent of $\mathbf{x}^{(n)}$ and $\mathbb{E}\{\mathbf{v}\} = 0$, the first-order item vanishes and the cost is written as:

$$E_v(\theta) \approx E(\theta) - \frac{\epsilon}{2}\sum_{k=1}^{K}tr\left(\tilde{H}_k\right) \tag{3}$$

where tr denotes the trace operation, and

$$\tilde{H}_k = \sum_{n \in \mathcal{C}_k} H_k\left(\mathbf{x}^{(n)}\right)$$

where $\mathcal{C}_k$ is the set of indices of the training samples belonging to the kth class.

In order to understand the implication of Equation 3, an auxiliary function can be defined as follows:

$$E(\theta, \mathbf{v}) = -\sum_{n=1}^{N}\sum_{k=1}^{K}\left\{\mathbf{y}_k^{(n)} lnf_k\left(\mathbf{x}^{(n)} + \mathbf{v}\right)\right\}$$

where $\mathbf{v}$ is a small change to the input vectors $\{\mathbf{x}^{(n)}\}$. Note that $E(\theta, \mathbf{v})$ differs from $E_v(\theta)$: $\mathbf{v}$ in $E(\theta, \mathbf{v})$ is a fixed value for all $\mathbf{x}^{(n)}$, while $\mathbf{v}^{(n)}$ in $E_v(\theta)$ is a random variable and differs for each training sample. The Laplacian of $E(\theta, \mathbf{v})$ with respect to $\mathbf{v}$ is computed as follows:

$$\begin{aligned}
\nabla^2 E(\theta, \mathbf{v}) &= tr\left\{\frac{\partial^2 E(\theta, \mathbf{v})}{\partial \mathbf{v}^2}\right\} \\
&= -tr\left\{\sum_{n=1}^{N}\sum_{k=1}^{K}\mathbf{y}_k^{(n)}H_k\left(\mathbf{x}^{(n)} + \mathbf{v}\right)\right\} \\
&= -tr\left\{\sum_{k=1}^{K}\sum_{n \in \mathcal{C}_k}H_k\left(\mathbf{x}^{(n)} + \mathbf{v}\right)\right\}. \tag{4}
\end{aligned}$$

By comparing Equations 4 and 3, we get:

$$E_v(\theta) \approx E(\theta) + \frac{\epsilon}{2}\nabla^2 E(\theta, 0). \tag{5}$$

Equation 5 indicates that injecting noises to the input units is equivalent to placing a regularization on the cost function. This regularization is related to the second-order derivatives of the cost function with respect to the input, and its strength is controlled by the magnitude of the injected noise. Since $\nabla^2 E(\theta, 0)$ is positive at the optimal solution of θ, the regularized cost function tends to accept solutions with a smaller curvature of the cost. In other words, the new cost function $E_v(\theta)$ is less sensitive to the change on inputs and therefore leads to better generalization capability. Note that this result is identical to the one obtained in [32], where the cost function is the square error.

4 Noisy deep learning

From the previous section, the validity of the noisy training approach can be justified in two ways: discriminative noise pattern learning and objective function smoothing. The former provides the ability to learn multiple noise patterns, and the latter encourages a more robust classifier. However, it is still unclear if the noisy training scheme works for the DNN model which involves a large number of parameters and thus tends to exhibit a highly complex cost function. Particularly, the derivation of Equation 5 assumes small noises with diagonal covariances, while in practice we wish to learn complex noise patterns that may be large in magnitude and fully dimensional correlated. Furthermore, the DNN training is easy to fall in a local minimum, and it is not obvious if the random noise injection may lead to fast convergence.

We therefore investigate how the noise training works for DNNs when the injected noises are large in magnitude and heterogeneous in types. In order to simulate noises in practical scenarios, the procedure illustrated in Figure 1 is proposed.

For each speech signal (utterance), we first select a type of noise to corrupt it. Assuming that there are n types of noises, we randomly select a noise type following a multinomial distribution:

$$v \sim \text{Mult}(\mu_1, \mu_2, \ldots, \mu_n).$$

The parameters $\{\mu_i\}$ are sampled from a Dirichlet distribution:

$$(\mu_1, \mu_2, \ldots, \mu_n) \sim \text{Dir}(\alpha_1, \alpha_2, \ldots, \alpha_n)$$

where the parameters $\{\alpha_i\}$ are manually set to control the base distribution of the noise types. This hierarchical sampling approach (Dirichlet followed by multinomial) simulates the uncertain noise type distributions in different operation scenarios. Note that we allow a special noise type 'no-noise', which means that the speech signal is not corrupted.

Secondly, sample the noise level (i.e., SNR). This sampling follows a Gaussian distribution $\mathcal{N}(\mu_{\text{SNR}}, \sigma_{\text{SNR}})$

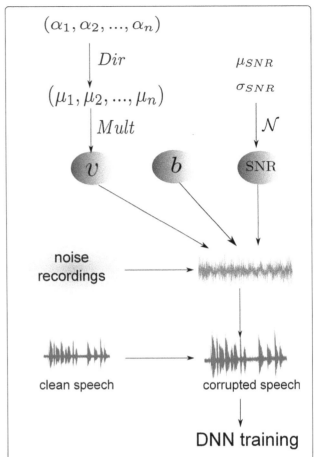

Figure 1 The noise training procedure. 'Dir' denotes the Dirichlet distribution, 'Mult' denotes the multinomial distribution, and '$\mathcal{N}$' denotes the Gaussian distribution. v is a variable that represents the noise type, b represents the starting frame of the selected noise segment, and 'SNR' is the expected SNR of the corrupted speech data.

where μ_{SNR} and σ_{SNR} are the mean and variance, respectively, and are both manually defined. If the noise type is no-noise, then the SNR sampling is not needed.

The next step is to sample an appropriate noise segment according to the noise type. This is achieved following a uniformed distribution, i.e., randomly select a starting point b in the noise recording of the required noise type and then excerpt a segment of signal which is of the same length as the speech signal to corrupt. Circular excerption is employed if the length of the noise signal is less than that of the speech signal.

Finally, the selected noise segment is scaled to reach the required SNR level and then is used to corrupt the clean speech signal. The noise-corrupted speech is fed into the DNN input units to conduct model training.

5 Experiments
5.1 Databases
The experiments were conducted with the Wall Street Journal (WSJ) database. The setting is largely standard:

the training part used the WSJ si284 training dataset, which involves 37,318 utterances or about 80 h of speech signals. The WSJ dev93 dataset (503 utterances) was used as the development set for parameter tuning and cross validation in DNN training. The WSJ eval92 dataset (333 utterances) was used to conduct evaluation.

Note that the WSJ database was recorded in a noise-free condition. In order to simulate noise-corrupted speech signals, the DEMAND noise database (http://parole.loria. fr/DEMAND/) was used to sample noise segments. This database involves 18 types of noises, from which we selected 7 types in this work, including white noise and noises at cafeteria, car, restaurant, train station, bus and park.

5.2 Experimental settings

We used the Kaldi toolkit (http://kaldi.sourceforge.net/) to conduct the training and evaluation and largely followed the WSJ s5 recipe for Graphics Processing Unit (GPU)-based DNN training. Specifically, the training started from a monophone system with the standard 13-dimensional MFCCs plus the first- and second-order derivatives. Cepstral mean normalization (CMN) was employed to reduce the channel effect. A triphone system was then constructed based on the alignments derived from the monophone system, and a linear discriminant analysis (LDA) transform was employed to select the most discriminative dimensions from a large context (five frames to the left and right, respectively). A further refined system was then constructed by applying a maximum likelihood linear transform (MLLT) upon the LDA feature, which intended to reduce the correlation among feature dimensions so that the diagonal assumption of the Gaussians is satisfied. This MLLT+LDA system involves 351 phones and 3,447 Gaussian mixtures and was used to generate state alignments.

The DNN system was then trained utilizing the alignments provided by the MLLT+LDA GMM system. The feature used was 40-dimensional filter banks. A symmetric 11-frame window was applied to concatenate neighboring frames, and an LDA transform was used to reduce the feature dimension to 200. The LDA-transformed features were used as the DNN input.

The DNN architecture involves 4 hidden layers, and each layer consists of 1,200 units. The output layer is composed of 3,447 units, equal to the total number of Gaussian mixtures in the GMM system. The cross entropy was set as the objective function of the DNN training, and the stochastic gradient descendent (SGD) approach was employed to perform optimization, with the mini batch size set to 256 frames. The learning rate started from a relatively large value (0.008) and was then gradually shrunk by halving the value whenever no improvement on frame accuracy on the development set was obtained.

The training stopped when the frame accuracy improvement on the cross-validation data was marginal (less than 0.001). Neither momentum nor regularization was used, and no pre-training was employed since we did not observe a clear advantage by involving these techniques.

In order to inject noises, the averaged energy was computed for each training/test utterance, and a noise segment was randomly selected and scaled according to the expected SNR; the speech and noise signals were then mixed by simple time-domain addition. Note that the noise injection was conducted before the utterance-based CMN. In the noisy training, the training data were corrupted by the selected noises, while the development data used for cross validation remained uncorrupted. The DNNs reported in this section were all initialized from scratch and were trained based on the same alignments provided by the LDA+MLLT GMM system. Note that the process of the model training is reproducible in spite of the randomness on noise injection and model initialization, since the random seed was hard-coded.

In the test phase, the noise type and SNR are all fixed so that we can evaluate the system performance in a specific noise condition. This is different from the training phase where both the noise type and SNR level can be random. We choose the 'big dict' test case suggested in the Kaldi WSJ recipe, which is based on a large dictionary consisting of 150k English words and a corresponding 3-gram language model.

Table 1 presents the baseline results, where the DNN models were trained with clean speech data, and the test data were corrupted with different types of noises at different SNRs. The results are reported in word error rates (WER) on the evaluation data. We observe that without noise, a rather high accuracy (4.31%) can be obtained; with noise interference, the performance is dramatically degraded, and more noise (a smaller SNR) results in more serious degradation. In addition, different types of noises impact the performance in different degrees: the white noise is the most serious corruption which causes a ten times of WER increase when the SNR is 10 dB; in contrast,

Table 1 WER of the baseline system

	Test SNR (dB)					
	5	10	15	20	25	Clean
White	77.23	46.46	21.21	9.30	5.51	4.31
Car	5.94	5.42	4.87	4.77	4.50	4.31
Cafeteria	25.33	14.27	10.07	8.38	6.88	4.31
Restaurant	46.87	22.15	13.27	9.73	7.48	4.31
Train station	34.36	12.72	6.93	5.40	4.43	4.31
Bus	13.88	8.44	6.57	5.51	4.84	4.31
Park	22.10	11.25	7.44	5.87	4.63	4.31

Values are in WER%.

the car noise is the least impactive: It causes a relatively small WER increase (37% in relative) even if the SNR goes below 5 dB.

The different behaviors in WER changes can be attributed to the different patterns of corruptions with different noises: white noise is broad-band and so it corrupts speech signals on all frequency components; in contrast, most of the color noises concentrate on a limited frequency band and so lead to limited corruptions. For example, car noise concentrates on low frequencies only, leaving most of the speech patterns uncorrupted.

5.3 Single noise injection

In the first set of experiments, we study the simplest configuration for the noisy training, which is a single noise injection at a particular SNR. This is simply attained by fixing the injected noise type and selecting a small σ_{SNR} so that the sampled SNRs concentrate on the particular level μ_{SNR}. In this section, we choose $\sigma_{SNR} = 0.01$.

5.3.1 White noise injection

We first investigate the effect of white noise injection. Among all the noises, the white noise is rather special:

it is a common noise that we encounter every day, and it is broad-band and often leads to drastic performance degradation compared to other narrow-band noises, as has been shown in the previous section. Additionally, the noise injection theory discussed in Section 3 shows that white noise satisfies Equation 2 and hence leads to the regularized cost function of Equation 5. This means that injecting white noise would improve the generalization capability of the resulting DNN model; this is not necessarily the case for most of other noises.

Figure 2 presents the WER results, where the white noise is injected during training at SNR levels varying from 5 to 30 dB, and each curve represents a particular SNR case. The first plot shows the WER results on the evaluation data that are corrupted by white noise at different SNR levels from 5 to 25 dB. For comparison, the results on the original clean evaluation data are also presented. It can be observed that injecting white noise generally improves ASR performance on noisy speech, and a matched noise injection (at the same SNR) leads to the most significant improvement. For example, injecting noise at an SNR of 5 dB is the most effective for the test speech at an SNR of 5 dB, while injecting noise at an

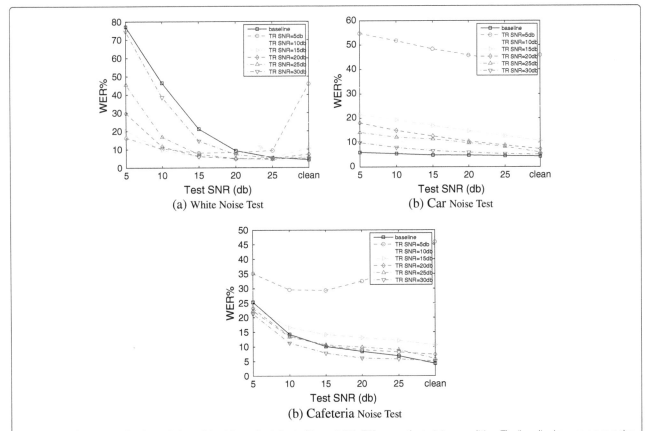

Figure 2 Performance of noisy training with white noise injected ($\sigma = 0.01$). 'TR' means the training condition. The 'baseline' curves present the results of the system trained with clean speech data, as have been presented in Table 1. **(a)** White noise test. **(b)** Car noise test. **(c)** Cafeteria noise test.

SNR of 25 dB leads to the best performance improvement for the test speech at an SNR of 25 dB. A serious problem, however, is that the noise injection always leads to performance degradation on clean speech. For example, the injection at an SNR of 5 dB, although very effective for highly noisy speech (SNR < 10 dB), leads to a WER ten times higher than the original result on the clean evaluation data.

The second and third plots show the WER results on the evaluation data that are corrupted by car noise and cafeteria noise, respectively. In other words, the injected noise in training does not match the noise condition in the test. It can be seen that the white noise injection leads to some performance gains on the evaluation speech corrupted by the cafeteria noise, as far as the injected noise is limited in magnitude. This demonstrated that the white noise injection can improve the generalization capability of the DNN model, as predicted by the noise injection theory in Section 3. For the car noise corruption, however, the white noise injection does not show any benefit. This is perhaps attributed to the fact that the cost function (Equation 1) is not so bumpy with respect to the car noise, and hence, the regularization term introduced in Equation 3 is less effective. This conjecture is supported by the baseline results which show very little performance degradation with the car noise corruption.

In both the car and cafeteria noise conditions, if the injected white noise is too strong, then the ASR performance is drastically degraded. This is because a strong white noise injection does not satisfy the small noise assumption of Equation 2, and hence, the regularized cost (Equation 3) does not hold anymore. This, on one hand, breaks the theory of noise injection so that the improved generalization capability is not guaranteed, and on the other hand, it results in biased learning towards the white noise-corrupted speech patterns that are largely different from the ones that are observed in speech signals corrupted by noises of cars and cafeterias.

As a summary, white noise injection is effective in two ways: for white noise-corrupted test data, it can learn white noise-corrupted speech patterns and provides dramatic performance improvement particularly at matched SNRs; for test data corrupted by other noises, it can deliver a more robust model if the injection is in a small magnitude, especially for noises that cause a significant change on the DNN cost function. An aggressive white noise injection (with a large magnitude) usually leads to performance reduction on test data corrupted by color noises.

5.3.2 Color noise injection

Besides white noise, in general, any noise can be used to conduct the noisy training. We choose the car noise and the cafeteria noise in this experiment to investigate the

color noise injection. The results are shown in Figures 3 and 4, respectively.

For the car noise injection (Figure 3), we observe that it is not effective for the white noise-corrupted speech. However, for the test data corrupted by car noise and cafeteria noise, it indeed delivers performance gains. The results with the car noise-corrupted data show clear advantage with matched SNRs, i.e., with the training and test data corrupted by the same noise at the same SNR, the noise injection tends to deliver better performance gains. For the cafeteria noise-corrupted data, it shows that a mild noise injection (SNR = 10 dB) performs the best. This indicates that there are some similarities between car noise and cafeteria noise, and learning patterns of car noise is useful to improve robustness of the DNN model against corruptions caused by cafeteria noise.

For the cafeteria noise injection (Figure 4), some improvement can be attained with data corrupted by both white noise and cafeteria noise. For the car noise-corrupted data, performance gains are found only with mild noise injections. This suggests that cafeteria noise possesses some similarities to both white noise and car noise: It involves some background noise which is generally white, and some low-frequency components that resemble car noise. Without surprise, the best performance improvement is attained with data corrupted by cafeteria noise.

5.4 Multiple noise injection

In the second set of experiments, multiple noises are injected when performing noisy training. For simplicity, we fix the noise level at SNR = 15 dB, which is obtained by setting $\mu_{SNR} = 15$ and $\sigma_{SNR} = 0.01$. The hyperparameters $\{\alpha_i\}$ in the noise-type sampling are all set to 10, which generates a distribution on noise types roughly concentrated in the uniform distribution but with a sufficiently large variation.

The first configuration injects white noise and car noise, and test data are corrupted by all the seven noises. The results in terms of absolute WER reduction are presented in Figure 5a. It can be seen that with the noisy training, almost all the WER reductions (except in the clean speech case) are positive, which means that the multiple noise injection improves the system performance in almost all the noise conditions. An interesting observation is that this approach delivers general good performance gains for the unknown noises, i.e., the noises other than the white noise and the car noise.

The second configuration injects white noise and cafeteria noise; again, the conditions with all the seven noises are tested. The results are presented in Figure 5b. We observe a similar pattern as in the case of white + car noise (Figure 5a): The performance on speech corrupted by any noise is significantly improved. The difference from

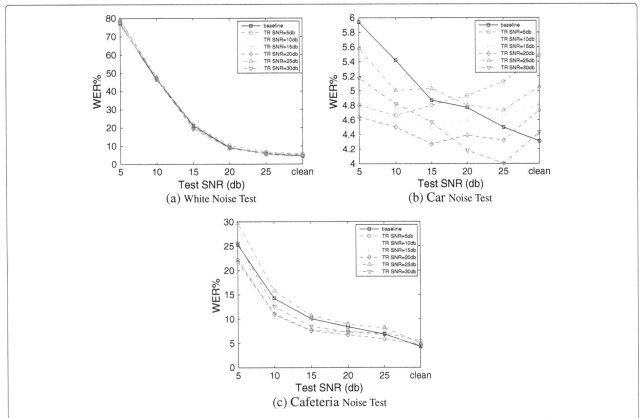

Figure 3 Performance of noisy training with car noise injected ($\sigma = 0.01$). 'TR' means the training condition. The 'baseline' curves present the results of the system trained with clean speech data, as have been presented in Table 1. **(a)** White noise test. **(b)** Car noise test. **(c)** Cafeteria noise test.

Figure 5a is that the performance on the speech corrupted by cafeteria noise is more effectively improved, while the performance on the speech corrupted by car noise is generally decreased. This is not surprising as the cafeteria noise is now 'known' and the car noise becomes 'unknown'. Interestingly, the performance on speech corrupted by the restaurant noise and that by the station noise are both improved in a more effective way than in Figure 5a. This suggests that the cafeteria noise shares some patterns with these two types of noises.

As a summary, the noisy training based on multiple noise injection is effective in learning patterns of multiple noise types, and it usually leads to significant improvement of ASR performance on speech data corrupted by the noises that have been learned. This improvement, interestingly, can be well generalized to unknown noises. In all the seven investigated noises, the behavior of the car noise is abnormal, which suggests that car noise is unique in properties and is better to be involved in noisy training.

5.5 Multiple noise injection with clean speech

An obvious problem of the previous experiments is that the performance on clean speech is generally degraded with noisy training. A simple approach to alleviate the problem is to involve clean speech in the training. This can be achieved by sampling a special 'no-noise' type together with other noise types. The results are reported in Figure 6a which presents the configuration with white + car noise and in Figure 6b which presents the configuration with white + cafeteria noise. We can see that with clean speech involved in the noisy training, the performance degradation on clean speech is largely solved.

Interestingly, involving clean speech in the noisy training improves performance not only on clean data, but also on noise-corrupted data. For example, Figure 6b shows that involving clean speech leads to general performance improvement on test data corrupted by car noise, which is quite different from the results shown in Figure 5b, where clean speech is not involved in the training and the performance on speech corrupted by car noise is actually decreased. This interesting improvement on noise data is maybe due to the 'no-noise' data that provide information about the 'canonical' patterns of speech signals, with which the noisy training is easier to discover the invariant and discriminative patterns that are important for recognition on both clean and corrupted data.

We note that the noisy training with multiple noise injection resembles the multi-condition training: Both

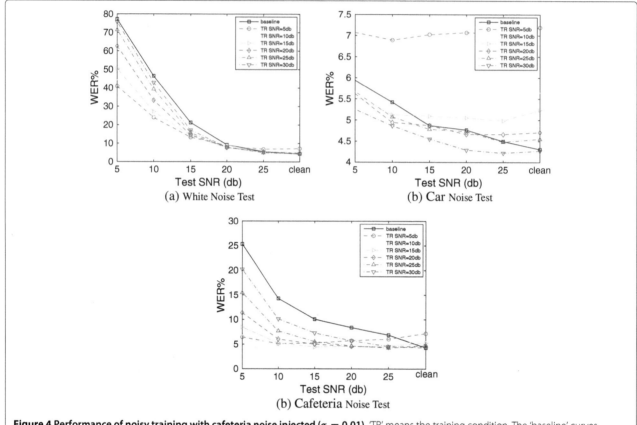

Figure 4 Performance of noisy training with cafeteria noise injected ($\sigma = 0.01$). 'TR' means the training condition. The 'baseline' curves present the results of the system trained with clean speech data, as have been presented in Table 1. **(a)** White noise test. **(b)** Car noise test. **(c)** Cafeteria noise test.

involve training speech data under multiple noise conditions. However, there is an evident difference between the two approaches: In multi-conditional training, the training data are recorded under multiple noise conditions and the noise is unchanged across utterances of the same session; in noisy training, noisy data are synthesized by noise injection, so it is more flexible in noise selection and

manipulation, and the training speech data can be utilized more efficiently.

5.6 Noise injection with diverse SNRs

The flexibility of noisy training in noise selection can be further extended by involving multiple SNR levels. By involving noise signals at various SNRs, more abundant

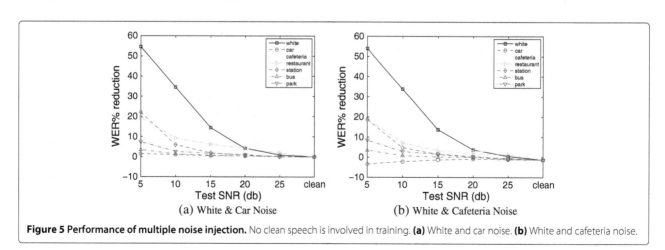

Figure 5 Performance of multiple noise injection. No clean speech is involved in training. **(a)** White and car noise. **(b)** White and cafeteria noise.

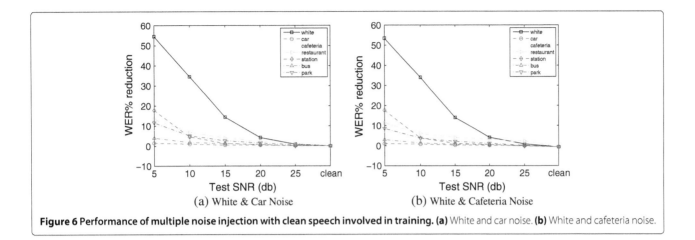

Figure 6 Performance of multiple noise injection with clean speech involved in training. **(a)** White and car noise. **(b)** White and cafeteria noise.

noise patterns can be learned. More importantly, we hypothesize that the abundant noise patterns provide more negative learning examples for DNN training, so the 'true speech patterns' can be better learned.

The experimental setup is the same as the previous experiment, i.e., fixing $\mu_{SNR} = 15$ dB and then injecting multiple noises including 'non-noise' data. In order to introduce diverse SNRs, σ_{SNR} is set to be a large value. In this study, σ_{SNR} varies from 0.01 to 50. A larger σ_{SNR} leads to more diverse noise levels and higher possibility for loud noises. For simplicity, only the results with white + cafeteria noise injection are reported, while other configurations were experimented and the conclusions are similar.

Firstly, we examine the performance with 'known noises', i.e., data corrupted by white noise and cafeteria noise. The WER results are shown in Figure 7a which presents the results on the data corrupted by white noise and in Figure 7b which presents the results on the data corrupted by cafeteria noise. We can observe that with a more diverse noise injection (a larger σ_{SNR}), the

performances under both the two noise conditions are generally improved. However, if σ_{SNR} is too large, the performance might be decreased. This can be attributed to the fact that a very large σ_{SNR} results in a significant proportion of extremely large or small SNRs, which is not consistent with the test condition. The experimental results show that the best performance is obtained with $\sigma_{SNR} = 10$.

In another group of experiments, we examine performance of the noisy-trained DNN model on data corrupted by 'unknown noises', i.e., noises that are different from the ones injected in training. The results are reported in Figure 8. We observe quite different patterns for different noise corruptions: For most noise conditions, we observe a similar trend as in the known noise condition. When injecting noises at more diverse SNRs, the WER tends to be decreased, but if the noise is over diverse, the performance may be degraded. The maximum σ_{SNR} should not exceed 0.1 in most cases (restaurant noise, park noise, station noise). For the car noise condition, the optimal σ_{SNR}

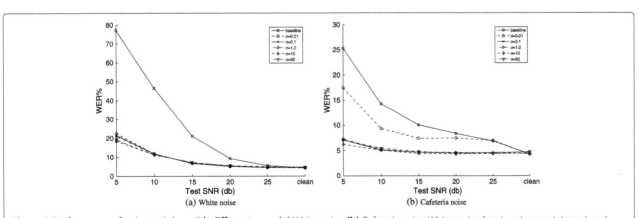

Figure 7 Performance of noise training with different σ_{SNR}. **(a)** White noise. **(b)** Cafeteria noise. White and cafeteria noises are injected, and $\mu_{SNR} = 15$ dB. For each plot, the test data are corrupted by a particular 'known' noise. The 'baseline' curves present the results of the system trained with clean speech data, as have been presented in Table 1.

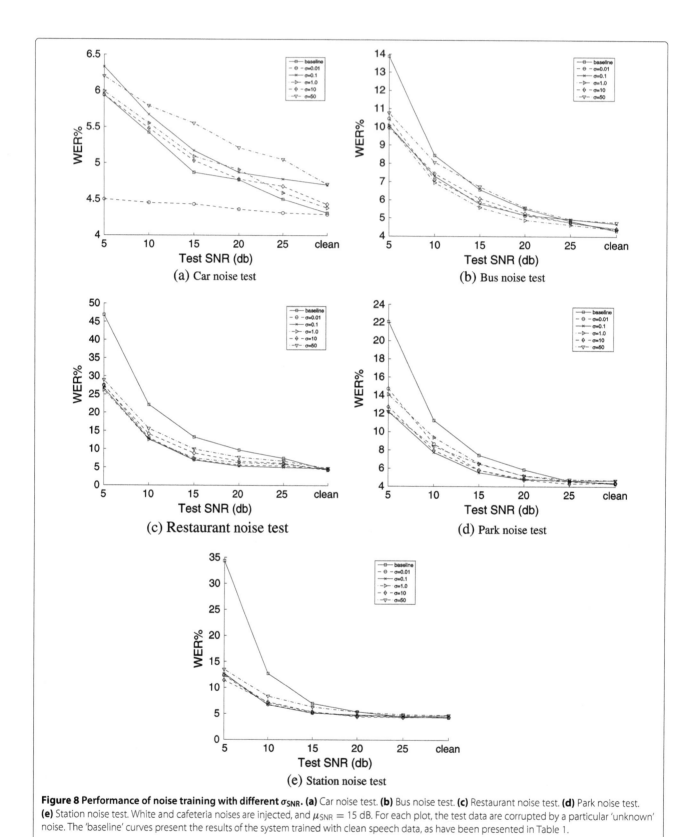

Figure 8 Performance of noise training with different σ_{SNR}. (a) Car noise test. **(b)** Bus noise test. **(c)** Restaurant noise test. **(d)** Park noise test. **(e)** Station noise test. White and cafeteria noises are injected, and $\mu_{SNR} = 15$ dB. For each plot, the test data are corrupted by a particular 'unknown' noise. The 'baseline' curves present the results of the system trained with clean speech data, as have been presented in Table 1.

is 0.01, and for the bus noise condition, the optimal σ_{SNR} is 1.0. The smaller optimal σ_{SNR} in the car noise condition indicates again that this noise is significantly different from the injected white and cafeteria noises; on the contrary, the larger optimal σ_{SNR} in the bus noise condition suggests that the bus noise resembles the injected noises.

In general, the optimal values of σ_{SNR} in the condition of unknown noises are much smaller than those in the condition of known noises. This is somewhat expected, since injection of over diverse/loud noises that are different from those observed in the test tends to cause acoustic mismatch between the training and test data, which may offset the improved generalization capability offered by the noisy training. Therefore, to accomplish the most possible gains with the noisy training, the best strategy is to involve noise types as many as possible in training so that (1) most of the noises in test are known or partially known, i.e., similar noises involved in training, and (2) a larger σ_{SNR} can be safely employed to obtain better performance. For a system that operates in unknown noise conditions, the most reasonable strategy is to involve some typical noise types (e.g., white noise, car noise, cafeteria noise) and choose a moderate noise corruption level, i.e., a middle-level μ_{SNR} not larger than 15 dB and a small σ_{SNR} not larger than 0.1.

6 Conclusions

We proposed a noisy training approach for DNN-based speech recognition. The analysis and experiments confirmed that by injecting a moderate level of noise in the training data, the noise patterns can be effectively learned and the generalization capability of the learned DNNs can be improved. Both the two advantages result in substantial performance improvement for DNN-based ASR systems in noise conditions. Particularly, we observe that the noisy training approach can effectively learn multiple types of noises, and the performance is generally improved by involving a proportion of clean speech. Finally, noise injection at a moderate range of SNRs delivers further performance gains. The future work involves investigating various noise injection approaches (e.g., weighted noise injection) and evaluating more noise types.

Competing interests
The authors declare that they have no competing interests.

Acknowledgements
This work was supported by the National Science Foundation of China (NSFC) under the Project No. 61371136 and No. 61271389. It was also supported by National Basic Research Program (973 Program) of China under Grant No. 2013CB329302 and the MESTDC PhD Foundation Project No. 20130002120011. Part of the research was supported by Sinovoice and Huilan Ltd.

Author details
[1]Center for Speech and Language Technology, Research Institute of Information Technology, Tsinghua University, ROOM 1-303, BLDG FIT, 100084 Beijing, China. [2]Center for Speech and Language Technologies, Division of Technical Innovation and Development, Tsinghua National Laboratory for Information Science and Technology, ROOM 1-303, BLDG FIT, 100084 Beijing, China. [3]Department of Computer Science and Technology, Tsinghua University, ROOM 1-303, BLDG FIT, 100084 Beijing, China. [4]School of Computer Science and Technology, Chongqing University of Posts and Telecommunications, No.2, Chongwen Road, Nan'an District, 400065 Chong Qing, China. [5]Beijing Institute of Technology, No.5 South Zhongguancun Street, Haidian District, 100081 Beijing, China. [6]GEINTRA, University of Alcalá, 28801 Alcalá de Henares, Madrid, Spain.

References
1. L Deng, D Yu, Deep learning: methods and applications. Foundations Trends Signal Process. **7**, 197–387 (2014)
2. H Bourlard, N Morgan, in *Adaptive Processing of Sequences and Data Structures, ser. Lecture Notes in Artificial Intelligence (1387)*, Hybrid HMM/ANN systems for speech recognition: overview and new research directions (USA, 1998), pp. 389–417
3. H Hermansky, DPW Ellis, S Sharma, in *Proc. of IEEE International Conference on Acoustics, Speech, and Signal Processing (ICASSP)*, Tandem connectionist feature extraction for conventional HMM systems (Istanbul, Turkey, 9 June 2000), pp. 1635–1638
4. GE Dahl, D Yu, L Deng, A Acero, in *Proc. of IEEE International Conference on Acoustics, Speech and Signal Processing (ICASSP)*, Large vocabulary continuous speech recognition with context-dependent DBN-HMMs (Prague, Czech Republic, 22 May 2011), pp. 4688–4691
5. G Hinton, L Deng, D Yu, GE Dahl, A-r Mohamed, N Jaitly, A Senior, V Vanhoucke, P Nguyen, TN Sainath, B Kingsbury, Deep neural networks for acoustic modeling in speech recognition: the shared views of four research groups. IEEE Signal Process. Mag. **29**(6), 82–97 (2012)
6. A Mohamed, G Dahl, G Hinton, in *Proc. of Neural Information Processing Systems (NIPS) Workshop Deep Learning for Speech Recognition and Related Applications*, Deep belief networks for phone recognition (Vancouver, BC, Canada, 7 December 2009)
7. GE Dahl, D Yu, L Deng, A Acero, Context-dependent pre-trained deep neural networks for large-vocabulary speech recognition. IEEE Trans. Audio Speech Lang. Process. **20**(1), 30–42 (2012)
8. D Yu, L Deng, G Dahl, in *Proc. of NIPS Workshop on Deep Learning and Unsupervised Feature Learning*, Roles of pre-training and fine-tuning in context-dependent DBN-HMMs for real-world speech recognition (Vancouver, BC, Canada, 6 December, 2010)
9. N Jaitly, P Nguyen, AW Senior, V Vanhoucke, in *Proc. of Interspeech*, Application of pretrained deep neural networks to large vocabulary speech recognition (Portland, Oregon, USA, 9–13 September 2012), pp. 2578–2581
10. TN Sainath, B Kingsbury, B Ramabhadran, P Fousek, P Novak, A-r Mohamed, in *Proc. of IEEE Workshop on Automatic Speech Recognition and Understanding (ASRU)*, Making deep belief networks effective for large vocabulary continuous speech recognition (Hawaii, USA, 11 December 2011), pp. 30–35
11. TN Sainath, B Kingsbury, H Soltau, B Ramabhadran, Optimization techniques to improve training speed of deep belief networks for large speech tasks. IEEE Trans. Audio Speech Lang. Process. **21**(1), 2267–2276 (2013)
12. F Seide, G Li, D Yu, in *Proc. of Interspeech*, Conversational speech transcription using context-dependent deep neural networks (Florence, Italy, 15 August 2011), pp. 437–440
13. F Seide, G Li, X Chen, D Yu, in *Proc. of IEEE Workshop on Automatic Speech Recognition and Understanding (ASRU)*, Feature engineering in context-dependent deep neural networks for conversational speech transcription (Waikoloa, HI, USA, 11 December 2011), pp. 24–29
14. O Vinyals, SV Ravuri, in *Proc. of IEEE International Conference on Acoustics, Speech and Signal Processing (ICASSP)*, Comparing multilayer perceptron to deep belief network tandem features for robust ASR (Prague, Czech Republic, 22 May 2011), pp. 4596–4599
15. D Yu, ML Seltzer, in *Proc. of Interspeech*, Improved bottleneck features using pretrained deep neural networks (Florence, Italy, 15 August 2011), pp. 237–240
16. P Bell, P Swietojanski, S Renals, in *Proc. IEEE International Conference on Acoustics, Speech and Signal Processing (ICASSP)*, Multi-level adaptive networks in tandem and hybrid ASR systems (Vancouver, BC, Canada, 26 May 2013), pp. 6975–6979
17. F Grezl, s Fousek P, in *Proc. of IEEE International Conference on Acoustics, Speech and Signal Processing (ICASSP)*, Optimizing bottle-neck features for LVCSR (Las Vegas, USA, 4 April 2008), pp. 4729–4732
18. P Lal, S King, Cross-lingual automatic speech recognition using tandem features. IEEE Trans. Audio Speech Lang. Process. **21**(12), 2506–2515 (2011)

19. C Plahl, R Schlüter, H Ney, in *Proc. of Interspeech*, Hierarchical bottle neck features for LVCSR (Makuhari, Japan, 26 September 2010), pp. 1197–1200

20. TN Sainath, B Kingsbury, B Ramabhadran, in *Proc. of IEEE International Conference on Acoustics, Speech and Signal Processing (ICASSP)*, Auto-encoder bottleneck features using deep belief networks (Kyoto, Japan, 25 March 2012), pp. 4153–4156

21. Z Tüske, R Schlüter, H Ney, M Sundermeyer, in *Proc. of Interspeech*, Context-dependent MLPs for LVCSR: tandem, hybrid or both? (Portland, Oregon, USA, 9 September 2012), pp. 18–21

22. D Imseng, P Motlicek, PN Garner, H Bourlard, in *Proc. of IEEE Workshop on Automatic Speech Recognition and Understanding (ASRU)*, Impact of deep MLP architecture on different acoustic modeling techniques for under-resourced speech recognition (Olomouc, Czech Republic, 8 December 2013), pp. 332–337

23. J Qi, D Wang, J Xu, J Tejedor, in *Proc. of Interspeech*, Bottleneck features based on gammatone frequency cepstral coefficients (Lyon, France, 25 August 2013), pp. 1751–1755

24. D Yu, ML Seltzer, J Li, J-T Huang, F Seide, in *Proc. of International Conference on Learning Representations (ICLR)*, Feature learning in deep neural networks - a study on speech recognition tasks (Scottsdale, Arizona, USA, 2 May 2013)

25. B Li, KC Sim, in *Proc. of IEEE International Conference on Acoustics, Speech and Signal Processing (ICASSP)*, Noise adaptive front-end normalization based on vector Taylor series for deep neural networks in robust speech recognition (Vancouver, BC, Canada, 6 May 2013), pp. 7408–7412

26. B Li, Y Tsao, KC Sim, in *Proc. of Interspeech*, An investigation of spectral restoration algorithms for deep neural networks based noise robust speech recognition (Lyon, France, 25 August 2013), pp. 3002–3006

27. ML Seltzer, D Yu, Y Wang, in *Proc. of IEEE International Conference on Acoustics, Speech and Signal Processing (ICASSP)*, An investigation of deep neural networks for noise robust speech recognition (Vancouver, BC, Canada, 6 May 2013), pp. 7398–7402

28. P Vincent, H Larochelle, Y Bengio, P-A Manzagol, in *Proc. of the 25th International Conference on Machine Learning (ICML)*, Extracting and composing robust features with denoising autoencoders (Helsinki, Finland, 5 July 2008), pp. 1096–1103

29. AL Maas, QV Le, O'Neil TM, O Vinyals, P Nguyen, AY Ng, in *Proc. of Interspeech*, Recurrent neural networks for noise reduction in robust ASR (Portland, Oregon, USA, 9 September 2012), pp. 22–25

30. X Meng, C Liu, Z Zhang, D Wang, in *Proc. of ChinaSIP 2014*, Noisy training for deep neural networks (Xi'an, China, 7 July 2014), pp. 16–20

31. G An, The effects of adding noise during backpropagation training on a generalization performance. Neural Comput. **8**(3), 643–674 (1996)

32. Y Grandvalet, S Canu, Comments on 'noise injection into inputs in back propagation learning'. IEEE Trans. Syst. Man Cybernet. **25**(4), 678–681 (1995)

33. CM Bishop, Training with noise is equivalent to Tikhonov regularization. Neural Comput. **7**(1), 108–116 (1995)

34. Y Grandvalet, S Canu, S Boucheron, Noise injection: theoretical prospects. Neural Comput. **9**(5), 1093–1108 (1997)

35. J Sietsma, RJF Dow, in *Proc. of IEEE International Conference on Neural Networks*, Neural net pruning-why and how (San Diego, California, USA, 24 July 1988), pp. 325–333

36. K Matsuoka, Noise injection into inputs in back-propagation learning. IEEE Trans. Syst. Man Cybernet. **22**(3), 436–440 (1992)

37. R Reed, RJ Marks, Seho Oh, Similarities of error regularization, sigmoid gain scaling, target smoothing, and training with jitter. IEEE Trans. Neural Netw. **6**(3), 529–538 (1995)

19

On the use of speech parameter contours for emotion recognition

Vidhyasaharan Sethu[*], Eliathamby Ambikairajah and Julien Epps

Abstract

Many features have been proposed for speech-based emotion recognition, and a majority of them are frame based or statistics estimated from frame-based features. Temporal information is typically modelled on a per utterance basis, with either functionals of frame-based features or a suitable back-end. This paper investigates an approach that combines both, with the use of temporal contours of parameters extracted from a three-component model of speech production as features in an automatic emotion recognition system using a hidden Markov model (HMM)-based back-end. Consequently, the proposed system models information on a segment-by-segment scale is larger than a frame-based scale but smaller than utterance level modelling. Specifically, linear approximations to temporal contours of formant frequencies, glottal parameters and pitch are used to model short-term temporal information over individual segments of voiced speech. This is followed by the use of HMMs to model longer-term temporal information contained in sequences of voiced segments. Listening tests were conducted to validate the use of linear approximations in this context. Automatic emotion classification experiments were carried out on the Linguistic Data Consortium emotional prosody speech and transcripts corpus and the FAU Aibo corpus to validate the proposed approach.

Keywords: Emotion recognition; Paralinguistic information; Pitch contours; Formant contours; Glottal spectrum; Temporal information; LDC emotional prosody speech corpus

1. Introduction

Human speech is an acoustic waveform generated by the vocal apparatus, whose parameters are modulated by the speaker to convey information. The physical characteristics and the mental state of the speaker also determine how these parameters are affected and, consequently, how speech conveys the intended, and on occasion unintended, information. Even though knowledge about how these parameters characterise the information is not explicitly available, the human brain is able to decipher this information from the resulting speech signal, including the emotional state of the speaker.

Information about emotional state is expressed via speech through numerous cues, ranging from low-level acoustic ones to high-level linguistic content; several approaches to speech-based automatic emotion recognition, each taking advantage of a few of these cues, have been explored [1-9]. It would be impossible to list all of them; however, approaches that use linguistic cues [10,11] are not as common as those that make use of low-level acoustic and prosodic cues. The most commonly used acoustic and prosodic features tend to be those based on cepstral coefficients, pitch, intensity and speech rate.

The standard speech production model (source-filter model) [12], widely used in speech processing literature, is the model that underpins most low-level feature extraction algorithms. However, almost universally, a simplifying assumption is made about the shape of the glottal pulses. Specifically, the glottal model is assumed to be a two-pole low-pass system (typically with both poles at unity) whose effects are 'removed' at the pre-emphasis stage of feature extraction. Section 2 explores the estimation of glottal parameters without making such an assumption.

The standard speech production model is also a short-term spectral model, and almost all low-level features tend to be short-term frame-based features incapable of capturing long-term temporal information. This shortcoming is widely recognised, and a range of approaches have been developed to overcome it, including the use of delta features (and its variants) to capture frame-to-frame temporal variations, the use of hidden Markov models to model temporal

* Correspondence: v.sethu@unsw.edu.au
The School of Electrical Engineering and Telecommunications, The University of New South Wales, Sydney, New South Wales 2052, Australia

patterns, the use of neural networks with memory and the use of functionals of sequence of frame-based parameters estimated over long segments (turns) as features. Automatic emotion recognition systems commonly address this issue in one of two ways: either by using a suitable back-end to model temporal variations of short-term features [13,14], or by capturing this information with the front-end with techniques such as contour models or using functionals of sequences of short-term features extracted from speech segments/turns [7,9,15-20]. In this paper we explore a combination of both approaches. Specifically, temporal contour patterns of pitch, the first three formant frequencies and the gains of the vocal tract at these frequencies, along with those of the glottal parameters outlined in Section 2, are used to model temporal information roughly spanning durations of voice segment, followed by a back-end based on hidden Markov models (HMMs) to model the sequences of these temporal patterns. Short-term temporal information is captured by the front-end, and longer-term temporal information is modelled by the back-end. Section 5.2 reports the results of a listening test carried out to validate the use of linear approximations of glottal parameter contours, conducted in a similar manner to a previous listening test carried out to validate the use of linear approximations to pitch contours [21]. Finally, the proposed approach has the inherent advantage that the segmentation of the speech into turns is not required since the system carries out an implicit segment-by-segment modelling of voiced speech segments.

2. The glottal source parameters

2.1. Glottal flow models

In the well-established and commonly used speech production model [12], the glottal flow that serves as the input to the vocal tract is modelled as the response of a filter. The shape of this response (glottal pulse shape) has been associated with certain characteristics of speech that are subsumed under the cover term *voice quality* [22]. The importance of appropriate glottal models in the synthesis of natural sounding speech has been well established [22,23], and the modification of glottal voice quality factors has been shown to be significant for the synthesis of emotional (expressive) speech [24].

Approximating the glottal filter model by $G(z) = 1/(1 - az^{-1})^2$, as is commonly done and is equivalent to making the assumption that the shape of the glottal pulse is always the same, may not be the best approach to take in emotion recognition systems. The incorporation of a more detailed glottal source model may be desirable and while not common, glottal parameters have been used in an emotion classification framework and were shown to be useful in distinguishing between emotional category pairs that had statistically similar pitch values [25-27].

The most popular glottal models [28-31] are time domain models that vary in the specific parameters they incorporate but share a common framework, and the spectra of the glottal flow derivatives described by all of them can be stylised by three asymptotic lines with +6 dB/oct, −6 dB/oct and −12 dB/oct slopes [32] as shown in Figure 1. Such a stylised representation allows for a very compact characterisation of the glottal flow derivative magnitude spectrum since it can be uniquely identified based on three values, specifically two corner frequencies (F_g and F_c) and the magnitude at the first corner frequency (A_g). The compact representation also lends itself to use as a feature in a classification system.

2.2. Estimation of glottal spectral parameters

While it is obvious that the use of a glottal flow (or glottal flow derivative) model results in a more accurate modelling of the speech production system when compared with the fixed two-pole approximation that is commonly utilised, the estimation of the glottal flow signal from the speech signal is not a well-defined problem and lacks an analytical solution. However, numerous techniques have been proposed over the years that are based on the properties of the glottal flow signal [33-38]. The iterative adaptive inverse filtering (IAIF) method [33] was used to estimate the glottal flow derivative in the work reported in this paper. The IAIF method can be used pitch synchronously (with variable window lengths based on pitch) or asynchronously (with fixed windows). For pitch synchronous IAIF, the DYPSA algorithm [39] has been used to detect glottal closure instants and hence identify window boundaries.

Given an estimate of the glottal flow derivative, it is proposed that the best stylised fit to its magnitude spectral envelope (Figure 1), in terms of minimum mean squared error, can be estimated via brute force search of the three-dimensional parameter space. The choice of a brute force search was made purely due to the simplicity of the search algorithm even though it is not efficient. This approach was considered acceptable since the glottal parameters themselves are the focus of the work reported in this paper and not their estimation algorithms. For any given parameter set $\{F_g, A_g, F_c\}$, the stylised glottal flow derivative magnitude spectrum, $\tilde{G}(\cdot)$, was constructed and the mean squared error between the stylised and the estimated spectra, $\hat{G}(\cdot)$, was calculated as

$$\tilde{G}_{F_g,A_g,F_c}(\zeta) = \begin{cases} A_g\text{-}20(\zeta_g\text{-}\zeta), & \zeta<\zeta_g \\ A_g\text{-}20(\zeta\text{-}\zeta_g), & \zeta_g<\zeta<\zeta_c, \\ A_g\text{-}20(\zeta_g\text{-}\zeta)\text{, -}40(\zeta\text{-}\zeta_c), & \zeta_c<\zeta<\zeta_m \end{cases}$$

$$(1)$$

where $\zeta = \log_{10}(f)$, $\zeta_g = \log_{10}(F_g)$, $\zeta_c = \log_{10}(F_c)$; A_g is the magnitude at the corner frequency in dB; $\zeta_m = \log_{10}(F_s/2)$

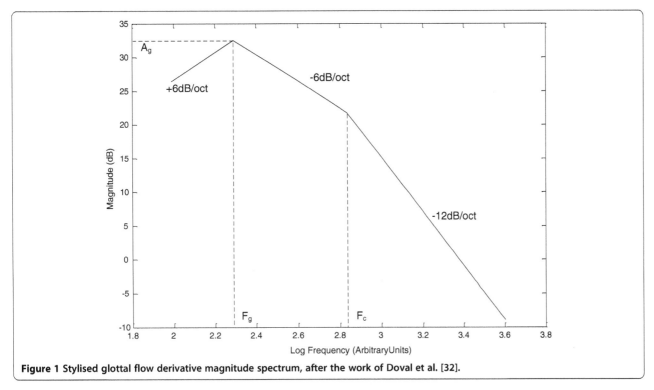

Figure 1 Stylised glottal flow derivative magnitude spectrum, after the work of Doval et al. [32].

and F_s is the sampling rate. In the experiments reported in this paper, all computations were carried out on discrete values of f, corresponding to the discrete Fourier transform coefficients computed from each frame of speech.

This mean squared error was computed for all possible combinations of F_g, A_g and F_c with the search space spanning all possible values of the three parameters with a resolution of 30 values for each parameter. The parameter set, $\{\hat{F}g, \hat{A}g, \hat{F}c\}$, that gave the lowest mean squared error was then selected as the best fit:

$$\{\hat{F}g, \hat{A}g, \hat{F}c\} = \arg \min_{Fg,Ag,Fc} \| \hat{G}(\zeta) - \tilde{G}_{Fg, Ag, Fc}(\zeta)\|_2$$

(2)

where $\|\cdot\|_2$ denotes the l_2 norm.

An overview of the glottal spectral parameter estimation method is given in Figure 2.

Visual inspection of the glottal flow spectra for a few consecutive frames and their corresponding stylised spectra indicated that even though the glottal flow spectra for the frames were not identical and had estimation errors at different points in different frames, the stylised spectra were all similar (particularly with regards to the glottal formant). This indicates that the spectrum fitting process is robust, to a certain extent, to errors in the glottal flow derivative estimation process that result from incomplete removal of the formant structure, particularly in terms of identifying the glottal formant. However, the estimation of the corner frequency, F_c, is affected to a much

larger degree by the errors and the estimated values were not very reliable. Therefore, F_c was ignored and only the glottal formant frequency and magnitudes, F_g and A_g, were used in the automatic classification results reported in this paper. These frequency domain parameters are related to the more commonly utilised time domain parameters such as the open quotient and speed quotient [32]. However, the frequency domain parameters can be obtained by fitting the linearly stylised spectrum as outlined, which is conceptually simpler than the time domain curve fitting methods required to estimate the time domain parameters.

3. Parameter contours

As previously mentioned, the study aims to capture short-term temporal information in the front-end prior to modelling longer-term information with the back-end . In this regard, the speech model parameter contours are estimated in the front-end. Parameter contours are representative of these variations over an entire utterance and are characterised by a much longer duration when compared with descriptions provided by deltas and shifted deltas. The most common and probably best studied is the pitch (F_0) contour, which is essentially pitch as a function of time, and its use in an automatic emotion recognition (AER) framework was the focus of a previous study [21]. Linear stylisation of F_0 contours [40,41] is commonly carried out, for a range of applications from speech coding to modelling dialogue acts and

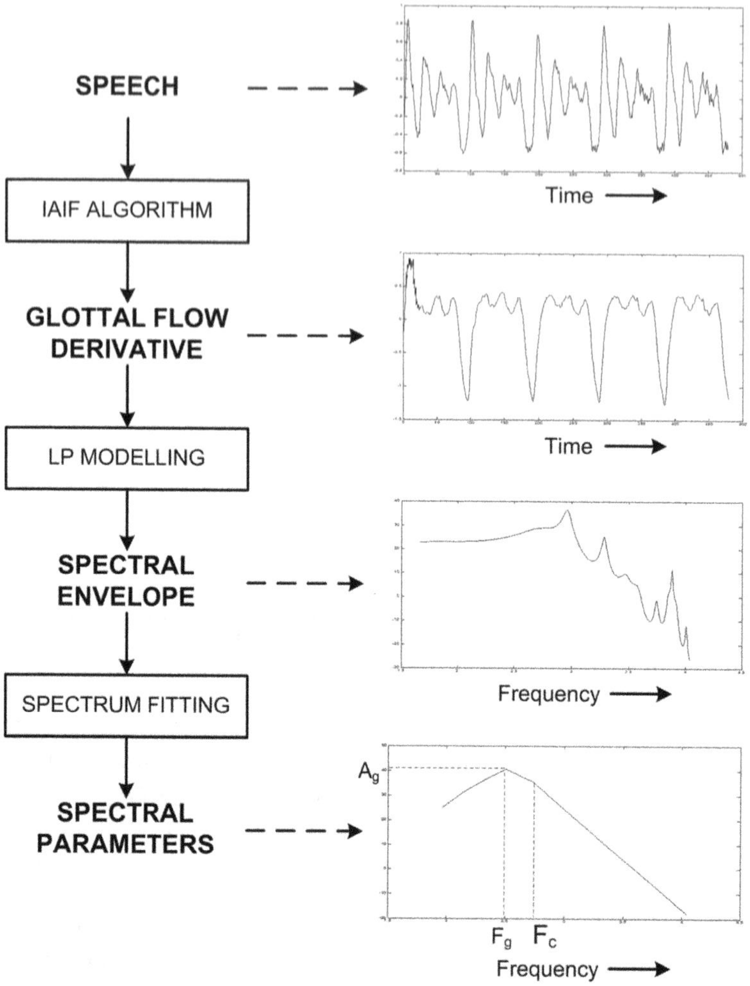

Figure 2 Overview of glottal spectral parameter estimation procedure.

speaker verification, to make them simpler to analyse, and also has the additional advantage of making their representation more compact than that of the original contour. The idea of such stylisation can be extended to the other parameters, such as the glottal formant and magnitude and formant frequencies and magnitude as well. Here we propose approximating the parameter contours in each voiced segment by a straight line that enables the representation of that contour using three parameters, namely, the slope of the line (s), the initial offset (b) and the length of the segment (τ), as shown in Figure 3. This is different from typical F_0 contour stylisation [40] since contours in each voiced segment are represented by single line segments rather than piecewise linear approximations. This is done to ensure that a single three-dimensional vector can describe an entire contour for each voiced segment. This is the simplest form of contour parameterisation, and if an AER system that makes use of such a representation outperforms a system that models the distribution of the parameter values (without taking into account any temporal information), then it is reasonable to suppose that the shape of the parameter contours contain emotion-specific information.

A small variation to the representation of the linear approximation to the contours involves the use of the value of the midpoint (m) of the contour instead of the initial values. This serves two purposes, namely: (1) In case of errors in the estimation of parameter values, particularly near the beginning of the voiced segment, the magnitude of the error in the value of the midpoint will be smaller than the error in the initial value; (2) If there are multiple errors in parameter estimation, the value of the slope can be dropped and only the value of the midpoint (which will be an estimate of the mean parameter value) can be used for a more robust but less detailed representation of the contour.

In general, any parameter that varies with time within an utterance can be linearly stylised for compact representation and ease of analysis. This paper focuses on the

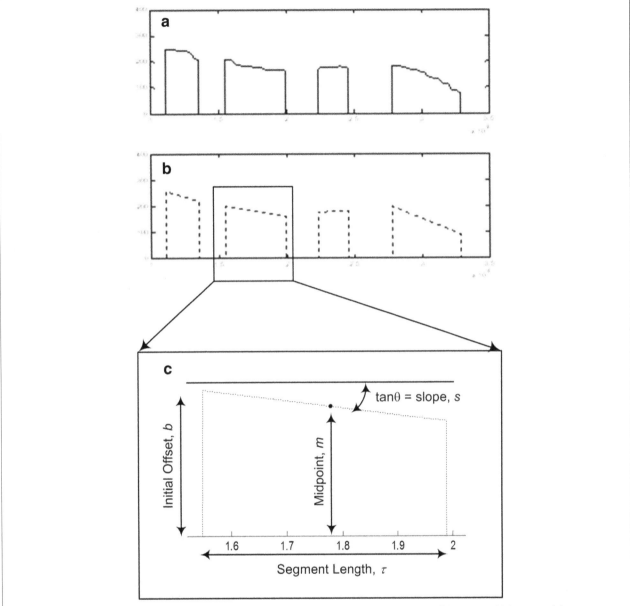

Figure 3 Approximating parameter contours. (a) Estimated F_0 contour. **(b)** Linear approximation of F_0 contour. **(c)** Linear model parameters - τ, s and b (or m).

use of the source-filter model of speech production, and consequently the contours considered are those of the parameters of this model. Specifically, the vocal tract is parameterised by the contours of the first three formant frequencies (F_1, F_2 and F_3 contours) and the contours of the magnitudes of the all-pole vocal tract spectrum at these frequencies (A_1, A_2 and A_3 contours), the glottal flow derivative (considering glottal flow and lip radiation together) by the glottal formant contours (F_g and A_g contours) and the source excitation rate using F_0 contours. Hence, an utterance can be compactly represented as a sequence of vectors, **V**:

$$\mathbf{V} = \left\{ \boldsymbol{v}^{(1)}, \boldsymbol{v}^{(2)}, ..., \boldsymbol{v}^{(N)} \right\} \tag{3}$$

where N is the number of voiced segments in the utterance, and $\boldsymbol{v}^{(i)}$ is a vector corresponding to the ith voiced segment,

$$\boldsymbol{v}^{(i)} = \begin{bmatrix} s_{F_1}^{(i)} \\ b_{F_1}^{(i)} \\ s_{F_2}^{(i)} \\ b_{F_2}^{(i)} \\ M \\ \tau^{(i)} \end{bmatrix}, \tag{4}$$

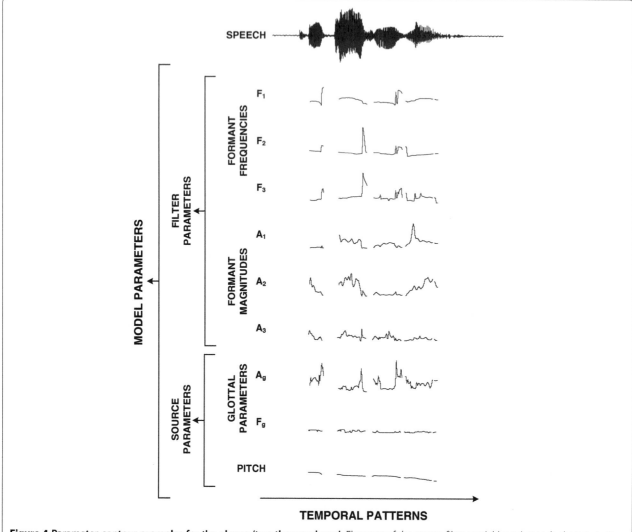

Figure 4 Parameter contour examples for the phrase 'two thousand one'. Elements of the source-filter model-based speech characterisation including glottal parameters.

where $\tau^{(i)}$ is the length of the ith voiced segment; $s_P^{(i)}$ and $b_P^{(i)}$ are the slope and initial offset (as previously mentioned, the midpoint, $m_P^{(i)}$, may be used in place of $b_P^{(i)}$ in $\boldsymbol{v}^{(i)}$) that describe the contour of parameter P in the ith voiced segment; and P is one or more of the source-filter model parameters, i.e.,

$$P \in \{F_1, F_2, F_3, A_1, A_2, A_3, F_g, A_g, F_0\} \qquad (5)$$

Note that the lengths of the contours are identical for all model parameters within each voiced segment. Hence, only one element, $\tau^{(i)}$, in each vector is required to represent the contour length. Thus, $\boldsymbol{v}^{(i)}$ is a $2K + 1$ dimensional vector, where K is the number of parameters chosen (from P) to represent each voiced segment, when slope and initial offset (or midpoint) are both used to represent a contour. If the slope values of some or all

parameters are dropped, the vector has a lower dimension. Figure 4 depicts all the parameter contours considered in this work.

4. Emotional speech corpora

The experiments reported in this paper were performed using one of two databases, namely, the Emotional Prosody Speech and Transcripts corpus (herein referred to as the LDC corpus) [42] and the German FAU Aibo corpus [43]. The two databases have significant differences, with the LDC corpus containing 'acted' emotional speech collected from seven professional actors with the speech comprising preselected, semantically neutral phrases. The Aibo corpus on the other hand contains 'elicited' emotional speech from 51 children with no restrictions on what is being said. Moreover, the emotional categories present in both corpora are different, with the

LDC corpus emphasising high-intensity 'prototypical' emotions and the Aibo corpus focussing on low-intensity 'non-prototypical' emotions. In addition, the LDC corpus contains English speech while the Aibo corpus contains German speech. A primary motivation in the choice of corpora was the significant differences between the two corpora which suggest that trends common to the experimental results obtained from both corpora are much more likely to be independent of the test data and hence more likely to be applicable to any other emotional data as well.

4.1. LDC emotional speech and transcripts corpus

The Emotional Prosody Speech and Transcripts corpus contain audio recordings, recorded at a sampling rate of 22,050 Hz, and the corresponding transcripts (word level transcripts that lack time stamps). The recordings were made by professional actors reading a series of semantically neutral utterances consisting of dates and numbers, spanning 14 distinct emotion categories, selected based on a German study [44], and a 'neutral' category that does not involve any emotional state. Of these fifteen categories, five were chosen to conduct the five-class emotion classification experiments reported in this paper. These five emotional classes are neutral, anger, happiness, sadness and boredom.

Four female and three male actors participated in the creation of this database and were provided with descriptions of each emotional context, including situational examples adapted from those used in the German study. Flashcards were used to display series of four syllable dates and numbers to be uttered in the appropriate emotional category. During the recording, the actors repeated each phrase as many times as necessary until they were satisfied that the emotion was expressed and then moved onto the next phrase. Only the last instance of each phrase was included in all the experiments reported herein. This provided about 8 to 12 utterances per speaker for each of the five emotional categories. While the phrases recorded for all emotions were not identical, they were very similar to each other and contained numerous words that were common (e.g. 'two thousand and one' and 'two thousand and twelve' or 'December second' and 'December twenty-first').

4.2. FAU Aibo emotion corpus

The German FAU Aibo Emotion Corpus [43] consists of spontaneous emotionally coloured children's speech with recordings of 51 German children (30 females and 21 males) aged between 10 and 13 from two different schools. The speech signals were recorded at a sampling rate of 48 kHz with 16-bit quantisation and then downsampled to a rate of 16 kHz. The children were given different tasks where they had to direct Sony's dog-like robot Aibo to certain objects and along given 'parcours'. They were told that they should talk to Aibo like a real dog and in particular reprimand it or praise it as appropriate. However, Aibo was remote-controlled from behind the scenes and at certain positions it was made to disobey or act in some manner not instructed by the child 'controlling' it in order to elicit an emotionally coloured response from the child. It is important to note that the real purpose of the data collection experiment, the elicitation of the emotions, was not known to the children, and none of them realised that Aibo was remote-controlled.

The recorded speech data was then annotated independently at the word level by five listeners using 11 emotional categories. The chosen units of analyses were, however, not single words but short phrases referred to as 'chunks' which were semantically and syntactically meaningful. The emotional categories assigned to each word in the chunk by all five listeners were combined heuristically to generate a single emotion label for the chunk. All classification experiments reported in this paper based on this database were setup (with regards to the training and test data sets and the performance measure) along the lines of the five-class problem set out in the INTERSPEECH 2009 Emotion Challenge [45] that made use of this database.

5. Validating linear approximations - listening test

Listening tests were conducted to determine whether linear approximations to pitch contour segments and glottal parameter contour segments retained sufficient information about the emotions being expressed. Specifically, in addition to previous results for pitch contours (F_0) which suggested that a significant amount of information was retained [21], a further listening test was conducted to determine whether linear approximations to glottal model parameter contours (F_g, A_g and F_c) were able to sufficient to retain emotion-specific information. Even though F_c contours were not used as features in the automatic classification systems used in the work reported in this paper, they cannot be ignored for speech re-synthesis since the absence of the −12 dB/oct slope would be equivalent to high-pass filtering the speech signal. With regards to linear approximations of formant contours (F_{1-3} and A_{1-3}) while they capture broad trends that may be useful in a classification scenario, if they were used in speech synthesis, the approximation errors will give rise to significant distortion and the synthesised speech would not be useful for listening tests. More complex models of formant contours will result in less error and consequently less distortion at the cost of a larger number of parameters. The use of more complex models may be investigated in the future.

5.1. Speech re-synthesis

In the work reported herein, the purpose of the speech re-synthesis procedure is to determine temporal contours of the speech production model parameters and then to re-synthesise speech from these parameter contours or their linear approximations. A synthesis method based on a non-stationary AM-FM type representation of speech, which is very close to the sinusoidal representation [46], was used. This method was chosen since all the estimated parameter contours, particularly the pitch contour, can be directly incorporated without any further processing:

$$s(t) = \sum_{k=1}^{N} V(kf(t), t) \cdot G(kf(t), t) \cdot \sin\left(\int_0^t kf(\tau)d\tau\right)$$

(6)

where $f(t)$ is the F_0 contour, N is the number of harmonics, $V(f, t)$ and $G(f, t)$ are estimates of the contributions of the vocal tract and the glottal source, respectively, towards the speech spectral magnitude (i.e. the vocal tract and glottal spectra) as a function of frequency and time.

The pitch contours were estimated using the RAPT algorithm [47], and the vocal tract and glottal spectra were estimated using the pitch synchronous IAIF algorithm [33]. The three glottal parameter contours (F_g, A_g and F_c) were estimated from the glottal spectrum as outlined in Section 2.2, and their linear approximations were obtained as described in Section 3. Based on these linear approximations, the glottal contribution to the amplitudes of the pitch harmonics, $G(f, t)$, was computed as per the stylised glottal flow derivative spectrum (Figure 1) used to estimate the glottal parameters. Thus, the parameters of the re-synthesised speech samples were identical to those of the original samples except for the glottal parameters, allowing for a subjective evaluation of the linear approximation to these parameter contours. While this speech synthesis procedure is by no means state-of-the-art, it has sufficiently high quality, as indicated by comparisons between synthesised speech (synthesised without using any linear approximations) and the original speech, which suggested that the listeners could not distinguish between the two versions [21].

It should be noted that the representation of speech as a sum of harmonic sinusoids used in this re-synthesis method holds only for voiced speech and was only applied to segments where pitch estimates were available. The unvoiced segments of the original speech samples were retained during re-synthesis. This was deemed acceptable, since the automatic emotion recognition system utilised only voiced segments, as is common with most other emotion recognition systems.

5.2. Subjective evaluation

A listening test was conducted to determine whether linear approximations to glottal parameter contours are able to retain emotion-specific information. Fourteen untrained listeners were involved in this test. For each listener, 30 speech utterances were drawn at random from the LDC corpus such that there were 6 utterances from each of the five emotions (neutral, anger, sadness, happiness and boredom). The re-synthesis method outlined in Section 5.1 was used to generate an alternative version of each of the 30 utterances using linear approximations to the glottal parameter contours. All 60 utterances were then presented to the listener in random order and for each he/she was asked to pick one out of the five emotional categories that they could associate with the utterance. Their decisions were then analysed to determine for how many of the 30 possible pairs the listener selected the same emotion for both utterances. The decisions of all 14 listeners were then combined to compute the percentage of speech samples for which listeners associated the same emotion with both the original and re-synthesised version. It should be noted that the measure of primary interest was how often listeners picked the same emotions for both versions of an utterance (one synthesised with linear approximations to parameter contours and one synthesised with actual contours) and not the actual accuracy of subjective classification since the aim of the listening tests was to validate the use of linear approximations.

The number of pairs where the listener assigned the same emotion to both versions, out of a maximum possible of 30, is given (as percentages) in Figure 5. Taken together across all 14 speakers, the same emotion was associated with both versions (re-synthesized using (6) with actual glottal parameter contours F_g, A_g and F_c and re-synthesized with linear approximations to glottal parameter contours) in 65.5% of the cases, and no individual result was poorer than 56.7%. These results suggest that the linear approximations to the glottal parameter contours are able to preserve emotion-specific information to a reasonable extent. This is in agreement with the results of a previous listening test that suggested linear approximations to pitch parameter contours preserve a significant amount of emotion-specific information [21].

In order to verify that the results reported in Figure 5 are not due to the listeners picking the same emotional label for all utterances, the distribution of how many utterances were assigned to each label was determined, and the results indicated that the distribution is not skewed severely in favour of any particular emotion. The fractions of utterances assigned to each of the five labels were 36.2% (neutral), 20% (anger), 15.7% (sadness), 10.2% (happiness) and 17.9% (boredom). It should also be noted that the

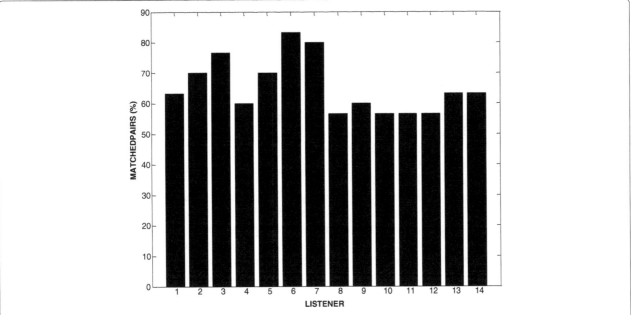

Figure 5 Percentage of pairs for which both versions were assigned the same emotion by the listener. Each listener was given 30 pairs, one version using actual contours of and one using linear approximations to F_g, A_g and F_c.

listeners were not aware that there were an equal number of samples from each of the five emotional categories.

6. Automatic classification system

6.1. The front-end

In addition to subjective evaluations, the usefulness of linear approximations to speech parameter contours to automatic classification systems was evaluated. The front-end of these systems represents the linear approximation to each parameter (P) contour in a voiced segment (i) by its slope ($s_P^{(i)}$) and initial value ($b_P^{(i)}$), as explained in Section 3. Apart from these, the length of each segment is given by a single value ($\tau^{(i)}$) and thus each voiced segment is represented by a $2K + 1$ dimensional vector, $v^{(1)}$, (where K is the number of parameters considered). Each utterance is then represented as a sequence of N such vectors, $\mathbf{V} = \left\{ v^{(1)}, v^{(2)}, ..., v^{(N)} \right\}$, (where N is the number of voiced segments in the utterance) by the front-end.

6.2. The back-end

The choice of back-end is dictated by the requirement that it should be capable of modelling utterances represented by a sequence of vectors to capture longer-term temporal information, and hence hidden Markov models (HMMs) were chosen. While this in itself is not novel, in most cases when HMMs are used in an AER system, they are utilised to directly model the temporal evolution of selected features (e.g. model pitch contours and contours of cepstral coefficients), i.e. they model

sequences of feature vectors, each one extracted from a frame of speech, spanning an utterance. There is less agreement, however, on the optimal number of states for these HMMs, with some studies suggesting four states [48,49] and others suggesting thirty-two or more [13,14]. However, in the system described in this paper, the parameters of the linear approximations to these contours describe the temporal evolution within each voiced segment, and the states of the HMM only describe the change *across different segments*. In a sense, the HMMs in the described system only model a second higher level of temporal variation instead of all the dynamic information. The number of states in each HMM determines how much of the variations in the contours between voiced segments in an utterance are modelled, which, in turn, depend on how many voiced segments are present in each utterance. A three-state HMM has sufficiently many states to model the variation in the initial, central and terminal segments of the utterance without overfitting and losing the ability to generalise. Preliminary experiments on the LDC corpus supported this choice. Each state utilised a 4-mixture Gaussian mixture model. For experiments performed on the FAU Aibo corpus, the number of states and mixtures were picked based on a preliminary search and the results are discussed in Section 7.2. All HMMs utilised in the systems proposed in this paper had linear left-right topology.

Previously, a modified feature warping technique was proposed as a means of speaker normalisation [50] and was applied to all features in experiments reported in this paper unless otherwise stated.

6.3. GMM-based classification system

In order to facilitate comparisons to help determine the significance of temporal information contained in parameter contours as opposed to the statistical distributions of parameter values, another classification system based on Gaussian mixture models (GMMs) was set up. The features used by this system are the frame-based values of the source-filter model parameters (F_0, A_g, F_g, A_{1-3}, F_{1-3}) obtained prior to approximating their contours with straight lines. The back-end of this system is a 128-mixture GMM-based classifier that models the probability distributions of the feature values (without taking into consideration any temporal dependence).

7. Experimental results

7.1. LDC corpus

The automatic classification systems setup for a five-emotion (neutral, anger, sadness, happiness and boredom) classification problem on the LDC corpus was implemented in a speaker-independent configuration. All experiments were repeated seven times in a 'leave-one-out' manner, using data from one of the seven speakers as the test set in turn, and data from the other six speakers as the training set. The accuracies reported are the means of the seven trials.

Classification experiments were performed using the HMM-based system using features based on pitch contour, glottal parameter contours and formant contours individually. In all three cases, two descriptions of the contours were used: one was the two-dimensional representation of each segment of the contour using the slope and initial value, $[s_P^{(i)}, b_P^{(i)}]$, (abbreviated as S-I henceforth) and the other a one-dimensional representation using only the value of the midpoint, $[m_P^{(i)}]$, (abbreviated as MP henceforth), where P can represent any parameter as given by Equation 5. In both descriptions the length of each voiced segment was appended as outlined in Section 6.1. The confusion matrices corresponding to these six experiments are given in Tables 1,2,3,4,5 and 6.

Emotion classification experiments were also performed using a GMM-based system with pitch, glottal parameter and formant parameter values as features in order to

compare systems that model temporal information contained in linear contour approximations to those that modelled only the statistical distributions of the parameter values. A summary of the overall accuracies obtained from these experiments is given in Table 7.

These results indicate that the contour modelling approach is better than the static distribution modelling approach for pitch and glottal parameters. Also the pitch, glottal and vocal tract parameters describe independent (based on the source-filter model) and distinct components in the speech production mechanism and are hence independent of each other. Consequently, their contours can be expected to be complementary (unless the back-end models identical information from the different parameter contours in each voiced segment). This suggests that a system, such as the HMM-based one, can be used to model all the contours by simply concatenating the contour descriptors (either slope, initial value or midpoint value or some combination of them) to form the feature vector. It should be noted that while a static modelling approach was better than the contour modelling one for vocal tract parameters, the vocal tract parameters would still contribute towards a combined system if they are complementary to pitch and glottal parameters. Such a system was constructed and its performance was evaluated on the LDC corpus. The classification accuracies obtained are reported in Table 8. This system uses the S-I description for pitch contours and the midpoint value (MP) description for glottal and vocal parameter contours, i.e. the feature vector corresponding to the ith voiced segment is

Table 2 Confusion matrix for HMM-based system using glottal parameter contours (S-I), $v^{(i)} = \left[s_{F_g}^{(i)}, b_{F_g}^{(i)}, s_{A_g}^{(i)}, b_{A_g}^{(i)} \right]$ (overall accuracy 52.6%)

	Neutral (%)	Anger (%)	Sad (%)	Happy (%)	Bored (%)
Neutral	*53.2*	0	14.9	6.4	25.5
Anger	1.4	*80.3*	0	18.3	0
Sad	16.4	3.3	*31.2*	6.6	42.6
Happy	9.6	19.2	6.9	*50.7*	13.7
Bored	13.0	1.3	31.2	9.1	*45.5*

Table 1 Confusion matrix for the HMM-based system using pitch contours (S-I), $v^{(i)} = \left[s_{F_0}^{(i)}, b_{F_0}^{(i)} \right]$ (overall accuracy 57.1%)

	Neutral (%)	Anger (%)	Sad (%)	Happy (%)	Bored (%)
Neutral	*59.6*	0	19.2	6.4	14.9
Anger	0	*78.9*	2.8	16.9	1.4
Sad	13.1	1.6	*49.2*	14.8	21.3
Happy	1.4	32.9	16.4	*43.8*	5.5
Bored	6.5	0	28.6	10.4	*54.6*

Table 3 Confusion matrix for HMM-based system using formant parameter contours (S-I), $v^{(i)} = \left[s_{F_1}^{(i)}, b_{F_1}^{(i)}, s_{F_2}^{(i)}, b_{F_2}^{(i)}, s_{F_3}^{(i)}, b_{F_3}^{(i)}, s_{A_1}^{(i)}, b_{A_1}^{(i)}, s_{A_2}^{(i)}, b_{A_2}^{(i)}, s_{A_3}^{(i)}, b_{A_3}^{(i)} \right]$ (overall accuracy 41.6%)

	Neutral (%)	Anger (%)	Sad (%)	Happy (%)	Bored (%)
Neutral	*55.3*	2.1	14.9	17.0	10.6
Anger	4.2	*46.5*	0	26.8	9.9
Sad	6.6	8.2	*32.8*	24.6	27.9
Happy	1.4	21.9	15.1	*37.0*	24.7
Bored	2.6	9.1	20.8	27.3	*40.3*

Table 4 Confusion matrix for the HMM-based system using pitch contours (MP), $v^{(i)} = \left[m_{F_0}^{(i)} \right]$ (overall accuracy 56.2%)

	Neutral (%)	Anger (%)	Sad (%)	Happy (%)	Bored (%)
Neutral	63.8	0	14.9	4.3	17.0
Anger	0	77.5	2.8	18.3	1.4
Sad	13.1	0	39.3	26.2	21.3
Happy	4.1	27.4	16.4	49.3	2.7
Bored	10.4	1.3	28.6	7.8	52.0

Table 6 Confusion matrix for HMM-based system using formant parameter contours (MP), $v^{(i)} = \left[m_{F_1}^{(i)}, m_{F_2}^{(i)}, m_{F_3}^{(i)}, m_{A_1}^{(i)}, m_{A_2}^{(i)}, m_{A_3}^{(i)} \right]$ (overall accuracy 45.0%)

	Neutral (%)	Anger (%)	Sad (%)	Happy (%)	Bored (%)
Neutral	42.6	4.3	25.5	14.9	12.8
Anger	0	66.2	8.5	16.9	8.5
Sad	6.6	8.2	37.7	11.5	36.1
Happy	8.2	19.2	19.2	37.0	16.4
Bored	3.9	7.8	29.9	18.2	40.3

given by $v^{(i)} = \left[\tau^{(i)},\ s_{F_0}^{(i)},\ b_{F_0}^{(i)},\ m_{F_g}^{(i)},\ m_{A_g}^{(i)},\ m_{F_1}^{(i)},\ m_{A_1}^{(i)}, m_{F_2}^{(i)},\ m_{A_2}^{(i)},\ m_{F_3}^{(i)},\ m_{A_3}^{(i)} \right]$.

Previously, a listening test was conducted on the LDC corpus and the results were reported in [21]. The overall accuracy obtained by 11 human listeners was 63.6%. A comparison of this accuracy to the different automatic emotion classification systems mentioned above is summarised in Table 9. In addition to determine the effect of longer-term temporal modelling afforded by the hidden Markov models, a one-state HMM system, identical in all other ways to the proposed system, was implemented and its performance is also included in Table 9. Finally, a GMM (128-mixtures)-based system, trained on mel frequency cepstral coefficients (MFCCs) and ∆MFCCs, was also implemented for comparison.

The classification accuracies obtained by the system making use of all the model parameter contours is higher than the accuracies obtained by any of the individual systems, as expected. It should also be noted that the emotion-specific classification accuracies (diagonal elements of the confusion matrix) are all higher than 55%, indicating that the system does not suffer from any inherent bias against one or more of the emotions. Moreover, the performance of the combined system compares very well with the human classification performance. Also, the automatic (GMM-based) system that did not make use of any temporal information had an overall classification accuracy of 59.0%. This system

modelled the distribution of all three component (pitch, glottal and vocal tract) parameters.

7.2. FAU Aibo corpus

Similar to the experiments performed on the LDC corpus, those performed on the FAU Aibo corpus were constructed as a five-class emotion classification problem. The emotions involved, however, were different (Anger, Emphatic, Neutral, Positive and Rest) as outlined in Section 4.2. The training and test sets for these classification experiments were taken as given in the guidelines to the INTERSPEECH 2009 Emotion Challenge [45]. Also in accordance with these guidelines, the metric used to quantify performance was the unweighted average recall (UAR) which should take into account relative imbalances in the number of occurrences of the different emotional states. However, the speaker normalisation technique employed in the experiments reported in this paper requires a priori knowledge of the distribution of speech features for each speaker (no knowledge of emotional class is required), and hence this normalisation technique could not have been applicable in the INTERSPEECH 2009 Emotion Challenge. The use of the normalisation technique was deemed acceptable since the aim of the paper is to investigate use of speech parameter contours for emotion recognition and not AER system optimisation and to make the results directly comparable to those obtained in a previous study [21] which is a precursor to the one reported in this paper.

Due to the significant differences between the two databases as outlined in Section 4, the parameters of the back-end, such as the number of states and the number

Table 5 Confusion matrix for HMM-based system using glottal parameter contours (MP), $v^{(i)} = \left[m_{F_g}^{(i)}, m_{A_g}^{(i)} \right]$ (overall accuracy 55.0%)

	Neutral (%)	Anger (%)	Sad (%)	Happy (%)	Bored (%)
Neutral	72.3	0	14.9	0	12.8
Anger	0	83.1	0	15.5	1.4
Sad	6.6	1.6	36.1	9.8	45.9
Happy	1.4	23.3	2.7	54.8	17.8
Bored	16.9	0	33.8	15.6	33.8

Table 7 Summary of overall accuracies for systems evaluated on LDC corpus

Parameter	Overall accuracy		
	HMM (S-I) (%)	HMM (MP) (%)	GMM (%)
Pitch (F_0)	57.1	56.2	46.6
Glottal (F_g, A_g)	52.6	55.0	46.6
Vocal tract (F_{1-3}, A_{1-3})	41.6	45.0	48.2

Table 8 Confusion matrix for the HMM-based system using all parameter contours, $v^{(i)} = \left[\tau^{(i)}, s_{F_0}^{(i)}, b_{F_0}^{(i)}, m_{F_g}^{(i)}, m_{A_g}^{(i)}, {}_m^{F_1(i)}, m_{A_1}^{(i)}, m_{F_2}^{(i)}, m_{A_2}^{(i)}, m_{F_3}^{(i)}, m_{A_3}^{(i)} \right]$ (overall accuracy 62.6%)

	Neutral (%)	Anger (%)	Sad (%)	Happy (%)	Bored (%)
Neutral	*55.3*	0	23.4	4.3	17.0
Anger	0	*81.7*	0	16.9	1.4
Sad	3.3	0	*57.4*	14.8	24.6
Happy	0	23.3	5.5	*60.3*	11.0
Bored	3.9	0	32.5	7.8	*55.8*

of Gaussian mixtures in each state, used in the experiments performed on the LDC corpus may not be suitable for the Aibo corpus. A preliminary search was initially performed by comparing the accuracies of the systems constructed with a different number of states (ranging from 2 to 5) and a varying number of Gaussian mixtures in each state (ranging from 2 to 10). The features used in these systems were identical to those used in the experiment used to obtain the results in Table 8, i.e. $v^{(i)} = \left[\tau^{(i)}, s_{F_0}^{(i)}, b_{F_0}^{(i)}, m_{F_g}^{(i)}, m_{A_g}^{(i)}, {}_m^{F_1(i)}, m_{A_1}^{(i)}, m_{F_2}^{(i)}, m_{A_2}^{(i)}, m_{F_3}^{(i)}, m_{A_3}^{(i)} \right]$. Consistently, the best UARs were obtained by systems using two-state HMMs. The optimal number of mixtures in each state is likely to be more dependent on feature dimensionality, but for the above-mentioned features, the highest UARs were obtained when five or six mixtures were used.

Using this back-end configuration, a series of experiments were carried out to compare the performances of systems that modelled temporal contours of pitch and glottal parameters and vocal tract parameters with the performances of systems that modelled only static distributions. GMM-based systems were used to model

Table 9 Comparison of overall accuracies obtained on LDC corpus

Classification test	Accuracy (%)
Human listeners (using 11 listeners) [21]	63.6
Automatic - using pitch contours (slope-bias)	57.1
Automatic - using glottal parameter contours (midpoint)	55.0
Automatic - using vocal tract parameter contours (midpoint)	45.0
Automatic - HMM (three-state)-based system using all model parameters	*62.6*
Automatic - HMM (one-state)-based system using all model parameters	59.3
Automatic - GMM-based system using all parameters (frame-based)	59.0
Automatic - GMM-based system using MFCC + ΔMFCC (frame-based)	51.1

Table 10 Summary of overall accuracies for systems evaluated on FAU Aibo corpus

Parameter	Overall accuracy		
	HMM (S-I) (%)	HMM (MP) (%)	GMM (%)
Pitch (F_0)	32.5	*33.3*	28.4
Glottal (F_g, A_g)	33.7	*37.4*	31.4
Vocal tract (F_{1-3}, A_{1-3})	31.6	29.9	*33.1*

distributions without taking into account temporal contours. These experiments also compared the S-I representation to the MP representation for all three parameters and the results are summarised in Table 10. This comparison is identical to the one carried out on the LDC corpus and reported in Table 7.

It can be seen that the trends observed in the LDC corpus match the ones in these results. Similar to the results in Table 7, systems that make use of temporal information (HMM-based) outperform the static system (GMM) when pitch and glottal parameters are considered, but not when vocal tract parameters are considered.

Following this comparison, another experiment was performed to determine the best feature set. This would, in turn, reveal the best performance possible given the system setup and indicate what information is utilised. The back-end was fixed as a two-state HMM with a 6-mixture GMM modelling each state and various combinations of descriptors (slope, initial and midpoint values) of the different source-filter model parameter contours (Figure 4) used as features and the UAR determined for each setup. The five highest UARs obtained and the corresponding feature sets are reported in Table 11. Table 11 also includes the UAR obtained when the standard parameter contour feature set was used by the system. In comparison, the UAR

Table 11 Top 5 UARs obtained on the Aibo corpus and the corresponding feature set utilised

Feature set $v^{(i)}$	UAR (%)
$v^{(i)} = \left[s_{F_0}^{(i)}, b_{F_0}^{(i)}, m_{F_0}^{(i)}, m_{F_g}^{(i)}, m_{A_g}^{(i)}, s_{F_1}^{(i)}, b_{F_1}^{(i)}, s_{A_1}^{(i)}, b_{A_1}^{(i)} \right]$	40.3
$v^{(i)} = \left[b_{F_0}^{(i)}, m_{F_0}^{(i)}, m_{A_g}^{(i)}, s_{F_1}^{(i)}, b_{F_1}^{(i)}, s_{A_1}^{(i)}, b_{A_1}^{(i)}, \tau^{(i)} \right]$	39.9
$v^{(i)} = \left[s_{F_0}^{(i)}, b_{F_0}^{(i)}, m_{F_g}^{(i)}, m_{A_g}^{(i)}, m_{F_1}^{(i)}, m_{A_1}^{(i)}, \tau^{(i)} \right]$	39.9
$v^{(i)} = \left[s_{F_0}^{(i)}, m_{F_0}^{(i)}, m_{A_g}^{(i)}, m_{F_1}^{(i)}, m_{A_1}^{(i)}, \tau^{(i)} \right]$	39.8
$v^{(i)} = \left[s_{F_0}^{(i)}, m_{F_g}^{(i)}, m_{A_g}^{(i)}, m_{F_1}^{(i)}, m_{A_1}^{(i)}, \tau^{(i)} \right]$	39.8
$v^{(i)} = \left[s_{F_0}^{(i)}, b_{F_0}^{(i)}, m_{F_g}^{(i)}, m_{A_g}^{(i)}, m_{F_1}^{(i)}, m_{F_2}^{(i)}, m_{F_3}^{(i)}, m_{A_1}^{(i)}, m_{A_2}^{(i)}, m_{A_3}^{(i)}, \tau^{(i)} \right]$	*37.5*

achieved by a GMM-based system jointly modelled the static distributions of pitch, glottal parameters and vocal tract parameters was 35.8% and the baseline UARs of the INTERSPEECH 2009 emotion challenge were 35.9% with dynamic modelling and 38.2% with static modelling (without any speaker normalisation).

The trends in the feature sets corresponding to the five setups reported in Table 11 are potentially more interesting than the UARs themselves. In particular, the use of one-dimensional midpoint values (MP) is better than the use of two-dimensional S-I descriptions for glottal parameter contours (F_g and A_g), and two-dimensional representations are better than one-dimensional ones for pitch contours. This is in agreement with the systems evaluated on the LDC corpus (Tables 1,2,4 and 5).

Also of interest is that these results suggest that information about the first formant is significantly more important than information about the second and third formants. However, classification tests indicated that this does not hold for the LDC corpus where dropping information about the second and third formants caused the classification accuracy to reduce from 62.6% to 57.5%. The reason for this difference in experimental results obtained from the two databases is not clear, but it could be due to the subtlety of the emotional states in the Aibo corpus or the fact that the languages spoken in both databases are different.

8. Conclusion

Commonly automatic emotion recognition systems capture spectral information with frame-based information and temporal information by either computing a range of functionals over all the frame-level features in an utterance or by using a suitable back-end to model temporal variations of these frame-level features. In this paper we explore a combined approach, extracting 'short-term' temporal information in the front-end and modelling 'longer-term' temporal information with the back-end. In particular, this paper extends the idea of modelling F_0 contours using linear approximations in each voiced segment, the focus of earlier work, to other parameters of the source-filter model to parameterise short-term temporal variations prior to segment-by-segment modelling of sequences of these parameter vectors with a back-end. The work also has the advantage of not requiring explicit separation of speech into utterances.

As part of the parameterisation process, this paper has taken a second look at the traditional source-filter model widely used in speech processing tasks and, in particular, the assumption about the vocal excitation that is inherent in common feature extraction procedures. By estimating glottal spectral parameter contours, the system is not constrained by the assumption

that the glottal spectrum can be modelled as the response of a system with a fixed transfer function. Earlier work had indicated that linear approximations to pitch contours were acceptable for the purpose of emotion classification, and another listening test conducted as part of the work reported in this paper revealed that similar approximations to glottal parameter contours were acceptable as well.

Furthermore, extending a previously developed AER system, which made use of linear approximations to pitch contours as features, to take into account linear approximations to contours of other parameters of the source-filter model as well, led to a relative increase in classification accuracy of 9.6% on the Emotional Prosody Speech and Transcripts corpus. Comparisons based on experiments using the LDC corpus revealed that an automatic emotion classification system that modelled contours outperformed one that modelled statistical distributions by 6.1% (relative) with regards to classification accuracy, and the classification accuracy of this contour-based system was comparable with human classification accuracy. The paper also includes the classification accuracies obtained when tested on the German FAU Aibo Emotion Corpus on the five-class emotion classification problem originally outlined in the INTERSPEECH 2009 Emotion Challenge. Work is currently underway on collecting an Australian speech corpus with emotional speech, and the use of the proposed contour-based features will be validated on those data in the future. Further, the choice of using linear approximations to model temporal information within voiced speech segments, while the simplest, may not be optimal and is an avenue for future work.

Competing interests
The authors declare that they have no competing interests.

References
1. R Barra, JM Montero, J Macias-Guarasa, LF D'Haro, R San-Segundo, R Cordoba, *Prosodic and segmental rubrics in emotion identification, in Proceedings of the 2006 IEEE* (International Conference on Acoustics, Speech and Signal Processing, vol. 1 (IEEE, Piscataway, 2006), 2006), p. 1
2. M Borchert, A Dusterhoft, *Emotions in speech - experiments with prosody and quality features in speech for use in categorical and dimensional emotion recognition environments, in Proceedings of 2005 IEEE International Conference on Natural Language Processing and Knowledge Engineering (IEEE NLP-KE'05)* (Piscataway, IEEE, 2005), pp. 147–151
3. M Lugger, B Yang, *An incremental analysis of different feature groups in speaker independent emotion recognition, in Proceedings of the 16th International Congress of Phonetic Sciences, Saarbruecken, August 2007* (Washington, IEEE, 2007). pp. 2149–2152
4. M Pantic, LJM Rothkrantz, Toward an affect-sensitive multimodal human-computer interaction. Proc IEEE **91**, 1370–1390 (2003)
5. D Ververidis, C Kotropoulos, Emotional speech recognition: resources, features, and methods. Speech Communication **48**, 1162–1181 (2006)
6. L Vidrascu, L Devillers, Five emotion classes detection in real-world call center data: the use of various types of paralinguistic features, in

Proceedings of International Workshop on Paralinguistic Speech - 2007. Saarbrücken **3**, 11–16 (August 2007)

7. S Yacoub, S Simske, X Lin, J Burns, Recognition of emotions in interactive voice response systems, in *Proceedings of the 8th European Conference on Speech Communication and Technology, EUROSPEECH 2003 - INTERSPEECH 2003*. Geneva **1–4**, 729–732 (September 2003)

8. D Bitouk, R Verma, A Nenkova, Class-level spectral features for emotion recognition. Speech Communication **52**, 613–625 (2010)

9. M El Ayadi, MS Kamel, F Karray, Survey on speech emotion recognition: features, classification schemes, and databases. Pattern Recognition **44**, 572–587 (2011)

10. C Lee, S Narayanan, R Pieraccini, *Combining acoustic and language information for emotion recognition, in Seventh International Conference on Spoken Language Processing* (September, Denver, 2002), pp. 873–876

11. B Schuller, A Batliner, S Steidl, D Seppi, *Emotion recognition from speech: putting ASR in the loop, in Proceedings of IEEE International Conference on Acoustics, Speech and Signal Processing, ICASSP 2009* (Piscataway, IEEE, 2009), pp. 4585–4588

12. G Fant, *Acoustic Theory of Speech Production* (Mouton, The Hague, 1960)

13. B Schuller, G Rigoll, M Lang, *Hidden Markov model-based speech emotion recognition, in Proceedings of International Conference on Acoustics* (Speech, and Signal Processing, (ICASSP'03). vol 2 2nd edn, IEEE, New York, 2003, 2003), pp. 1–4

14. A Nogueiras, A Moreno, A Bonafonte, J Mariño, *Speech emotion recognition using hidden Markov models, in Proceedings of EUROSPEECH-2001* (EUROSPEECH, Scandinavia, 2001), pp. 2679–2682

15. B Schuller, D Seppi, A Batliner, A Maier, S Steidl, *Towards more reality in the recognition of emotional speech, in Proceedings IEEE International Conference on Acoustics, Speech and Signal Processing (ICASSP 2007), Honolulu, April 2007*, vol. 4 (Piscataway, IEEE, 2007), pp. 941–944

16. B Vlasenko, B Schuller, A Wendemuth, G Rigoll, *Frame vs. turn-level: emotion recognition from speech considering static and dynamic processing, in Affective Computing and Intelligent Interaction* (Frame vs. turn-level: emotion recognition from speech considering static and dynamic processing, in Affective Computing and Intelligent Interaction, Springer Berlin, Heidelberg, 2007, 2007), pp. 139–147

17. S Planet, I Iriondo, J Socoró, C Monzo, J Adell, GTM-URL contribution to the INTERSPEECH 2009 Emotion Challenge, in *Proceedings of the 10th Annual Conference of the International Speech Communication Association (INTERSPEECH-2009)*. Brighton **6–10**, 316–319 (September 2009)

18. S Wu, TH Falk, W-Y Chan, Automatic speech emotion recognition using modulation spectral features. Speech Communication **53**, 768–785 (2011)

19. P Dumouchel, N Dehak, Y Attabi, R Dehak, N Boufaden, Cepstral and long-term features for emotion recognition, in *Proceedings of the 10th Annual Conference of the International Speech Communication Association (INTERSPEECH-2009)*. Brighton **6–10**, 344–347 (September 2009)

20. T Moriyama, S Ozawa, *Emotion recognition and synthesis system on speech, in IEEE International Conference on Multimedia Computing and Systems, 1999 vol 1*, 1st edn. (IEEE, New York, 1999), pp. 840–844

21. V Sethu, E Ambikairajah, J Epps, Pitch contour parameterisation based on linear stylisation for emotion recognition, in *Proceedings of the 10th Annual Conference of the International Speech Communication Association (INTERSPEECH-2009)*. Brighton **6–10**, 2011–2014 (September 2009)

22. DG Childers, CK Lee, Vocal quality factors: analysis, synthesis, and perception. J. Acoust. Soc. Am. **90**, 2394–2410 (1991)

23. J Cabral, S Renals, K Richmond, J Yamagishi, *Towards an improved modeling of the glottal source in statistical parametric speech synthesis, in 6th ISCA Workshop on Speech Synthesis* (Bonn, Germany, 2007)

24. C D'Alessandro, B Doval, *Voice quality modification for emotional speech synthesis, in Proceedings of the 8th European Conference on Speech Communication and Technology* (EUROSPEECH 2003 - INTERSPEECH 2003, Geneva, 2003), pp. 1653–1656

25. L He, M Lech, N Allen, On the importance of glottal flow spectral energy for the recognition of emotions in speech, in *Proceedings of the 11th Annual Conference of the International Speech Communication Association, INTERSPEECH 2010*. Makuhari, Chiba, Japan **26–30**, 2346–2349 (September 2010)

26. J Tao, Y Kang, *Features importance analysis for emotional speech classification, in Affective Computing and Intelligent Interaction* (ed. by J Tao et al, Springer Berlin, Heidelberg, 2005, 2005), pp. 449–457

27. S Rui, E Moore, JF Torres, *Investigating glottal parameters for differentiating emotional categories with similar prosodics, in IEEE International Conference*

on *Acoustics, Speech and Signal Processing, ICASSP 2009* (IEEE, New York, 2009), pp. 4509–4512

28. G Fant, J Liljencrants, Q Lin, A four-parameter model of glottal flow. STL-QPSR **4**, 1–13 (1985)

29. AE Rosenberg, Effect of glottal pulse shape on the quality of natural vowels. J. Acoust. Soc. Am. **49**, 583–590 (1971)

30. DH Klatt, LC Klatt, Analysis, synthesis, and perception of voice quality variations among female and male talkers. J. Acoust. Soc. Am. **87**, 820–857 (1990)

31. R Veldhuis, A computationally efficient alternative for the Liljencrants-Fant model and its perceptual evaluation. J. Acoust. Soc. Am. **103**, 566–571 (1998)

32. B Doval, C d'Alessandro, N Henrich. The spectrum of glottal flow models. Acta Acustica united with Acustica **92**, 1026–1046 (2006)

33. P Alku, *Glottal wave analysis with pitch synchronous iterative adaptive inverse filtering, in Proceedings of the EUROSPEECH-1991* (ICSA, Mechanicsburg, 1991), pp. 1081–1084

34. J Cabral, S Renals, K Richmond, J Yamagishi, *Glottal spectral separation for parametric speech synthesis, in Proceedings of INTERSPEECH-2008* (ICSA, Brisbane, 2008), pp. 1829–1832

35. M Frohlich, D Michaelis, HW Strube, SIM-simultaneous inverse filtering and matching of a glottal flow model for acoustic speech signals. J. Acoust. Soc. Am. **110**, 479–488 (2001)

36. L Hui-Ling, JO Smith III, *Joint estimation of vocal tract filter and glottal source waveform via convex optimization, in 1999 IEEE Workshop on Applications of Signal Processing to Audio and Acoustics* (Piscataway, IEEE, 1999), pp. 79–82

37. EL Riegelsberger, AK Krishnamurthy, *Glottal source estimation: methods of applying the LF-model to inverse filtering, in 1993 IEEE International Conference on Acoustics, Speech, and Signal Processing, ICASSP-93, vol 2*, 2nd edn. (Piscataway, IEEE, 1993). pp. 542–545

38. D Vincent, O Rosec, T Chonavel, Estimation of LF glottal source parameters based on an ARX model, in *Proceedings of INTERSPEECH 2005 - EUROSPEECH, 9th European Conference on Speech Communication and Technology*. Lisbon **4–8**, 333–336 (September 2005)

39. PA Naylor, K Anastasis, G Jon, B Mike, Estimation of glottal closure instants in voiced speech using the DYPSA algorithm. IEEE Transactions on Audio, Speech, and Language Processing **15**, 34–43 (2007)

40. D Wang, S Narayanan, Piecewise linear stylization of pitch via wavelet analysis, in *Proceedings of INTERSPEECH 2005 - EUROSPEECH, 9th European Conference on Speech Communication and Technology*. Lisbon **4–8**, 3277–3280 (September 2005)

41. S Ravuri, DPW Ellis, *Stylization of pitch with syllable-based linear segments, in IEEE International Conference on Acoustics, Speech and Signal Processing, ICASSP 2008* (Piscataway, IEEE, 2008), pp. 3985–3988

42. M Liberman, K Davis, M Grossman, N Martey, J Bell, *Emotional prosody speech and transcripts* (Linguistic Data Consortium (LDC) database, LDC catalog no. LDC2002S28, 2007). http://www.ldc.upenn.edu/Catalog/CatalogEntry.jsp?catalogId=LDC2002S28. ISBN 1-58563-237-6 (2007)

43. S Steidl, *Automatic Classification of Emotion-Related User States in Spontaneous Children's Speech* (Logos Verlag, Berlin, 2009)

44. R Banse, K Scherer, Acoustic profiles in vocal emotion expression. J. Pers. Soc. Psychol. **70**, 614–636 (1996)

45. B Schuller, S Steidl, A Batliner, *The INTERSPEECH 2009 Emotion Challenge, in INTERSPEECH-2009* (ISCA, Brighton, 2009), pp. 312–315

46. R McAulay, T Quatieri, Speech analysis/synthesis based on a sinusoidal representation. Acoustics, Speech and Signal Processing, IEEE Transactions on **34**, 744–754 (1986)

47. D Talkin, *A robust algorithm for pitch tracking (RAPT), in Speech Coding and Synthesis* (by W Kleijn, K Paliwal, Elsevier, New York, 1995), pp. 495–518

48. TL Nwe, SW Foo, LC De, Silva, Speech emotion recognition using hidden Markov models. Speech Communication **41**, 603–623 (2003)

49. R Huang, C Ma, *Toward a speaker-independent real-time affect detection system, in 18th International Conference on Pattern Recognition ICPR 2006*, vol. 1 (IEEE, New York, 2006), pp. 1204–1207

50. V Sethu, E Ambikairajah, J Epps, *Speaker normalisation for speech-based emotion detection, in 15th International Conference on Digital Signal Processing, 2007* (Piscataway, IEEE, 2007), pp. 611–614

Permissions

List of Contributors

Xiao Yao, Chiyomi Miyajima, Norihide Kitaoka and Kazuya Takeda
Graduate School of Information Science, Nagoya University, Nagoya, Aichi, Japan

Takatoshi Jitsuhiro
Graduate School of Information Science, Nagoya University, Nagoya, Aichi, Japan
Department of Media Informatics, Aichi University of Technology, Gamagori, Aichi, Japan

Tahsina Farah Sanam and Celia Shahnaz
Department of Electrical and Electronic Engineering, Bangladesh University of Engineering and Technology, Dhaka 1000, Bangladesh

Aditya Arie Nugraha and Seiichi Nakagawa
Department of Computer Science and Engineering, Toyohashi University of Technology, Toyohashi, Aichi 441-8580, Japan

Kazumasa Yamamoto
Department of Computer Science and Engineering, Toyohashi University of Technology, Toyohashi, Aichi 441-8580, Japan
Department of Information and Computer Engineering, Toyota National College of Technology, Toyota, Aichi 471-8525, Japan

Yongzhe Shi, Wei-Qiang Zhang and Jia Liu
Tsinghua National Laboratory for Information Science and Technology, Department of Electronic Engineering, Tsinghua University, 100084 Beijing, China

Michael T Johnson
Department of Electrical Engineering, Marquette University, WI 53201, Milwaukee, USA

Soheil Khorram, Hossein Sameti and Fahimeh Bahmaninezhad
Department of Computer Engineering, Sharif University of Technology, Tehran, Iran

Simon King
Centre for Speech Technology Research, University of Edinburgh, Edinburgh EH8 9LW, UK

Thomas Drugman
TCTS Lab, Faculte Polytechnique de Mons, Mons, Belgium

Yongzhe Shi, Wei-Qiang Zhang, Meng Cai and Jia Liu
Tsinghua National Laboratory for Information Science and Technology, Department of Electronic Engineering, Tsinghua University, Beijing 100084, China

Jan Staš, Jozef Juhar and Daniel Hladek
Department of Electronics and Multimedia Communications, Technical University of Košice, Park Komenskeho 13, 041 20 Košice, Slovakia

Caglar Oflazoglu and Serdar Yildirim
Computer Engineering Department, Mustafa Kemal University, Iskenderun, 31200, Hatay, Turkey

Devireddy Hanumantha Rao Naidu
Department of Mathematics and Computer Science, Sri Sathya Sai Institute of Higher Learning, Prasanthi Nilayam, Anantapur, Andhra Pradesh 515134, India

Sriram Srinivasan
Microsoft Corporation, Redmond, WA 98052, USA

Jeih-weih Hung and Hao-teng Fan
Department of Electrical Engineering, National Chi Nan University, Nantou 545, Taiwan

Hari Krishna Maganti and Marco Matassoni
Center for Information and Communication Technology, Fondazione Bruno Kessler, via Sommarive 18, Trento 38123, Italy

Hansjörg Mixdorff
Department of Computer Science and Media, Beuth University Berlin, Luxemburger Str. 10, Berlin 13353, Germany

Adrian Leemann and Volker Dellwo
Phonetic Laboratory, University of Zurich, Rämistrasse 71, Zürich 8006, Switzerland

Madoka Miki, Norihide Kitaoka, Chiyomi Miyajima and Kazuya Takeda
Department of Media Science, Nagoya University, Nagoya, Aichi Prefecture 464-8603, Japan

Takanori Nishino
Department of Information Engineering, Mie University, Mie Prefecture 514-8507, Japan

Andrew Hines
School of Computing, Dublin Institute of Technology, Kevin St, Dublin 8, Ireland
Sigmedia, Department of Electronic and Electrical Engineering, Trinity College Dublin, College Green, Dublin 2, Ireland

Jan Skoglund and Anil C Kokaram
Google, Inc., 1600 Amphitheatre Parkway, CA 94043, Mountain View, USA

Naomi Harte
Sigmedia, Department of Electronic and Electrical Engineering, Trinity College Dublin, College Green, Dublin 2, Ireland

Sara Ahmadi
Amirkabir University of Technology, Hafez 424, 15875-4413 Tehran, Iran
Centre for Language Studies, Radboud University Nijmegen, Erasmusplein 1, 6525HT Nijmegen, Netherlands

Seyed Mohammad Ahadi
Amirkabir University of Technology, Hafez 424, 15875-4413 Tehran, Iran

Bert Cranen and Lou Boves
Centre for Language Studies, Radboud University Nijmegen, Erasmusplein 1, 6525HT Nijmegen, Netherlands

Xiu Zhang, Linwei Li, Peizhong Lu and Wenqiang Zhang
School of Computer Science, Fudan University, Shanghai 201203, China

Bilei Zhu
SAP Labs, Shanghai 201203, China

Wei Li
School of Computer Science, Fudan University, Shanghai 201203, China
Shanghai Key Laboratory of Intelligent Information Processing, Fudan University, Shanghai 200433, China

Xiaoqiang Li
School of Computer Engineering and Science, Shanghai University, Shanghai 200444, China

WeiWang
Naval Medical Research Institute, Shanghai 200433, China

Xie Sun
Nuance Communications, Inc, 1 Wayside Rd, Burlington, MA 01801, USA

Yunxin Zhao
Department of Computer Science, University of Missouri, Columbia, MO 65211, USA

Shi Yin
Center for Speech and Language Technology, Research Institute of Information Technology, Tsinghua University, ROOM 1-303, BLDG FIT, 100084 Beijing, China
School of Computer Science and Technology, Chongqing University of Posts and Telecommunications, No.2, Chongwen Road, Nan'an District, 400065 Chong Qing, China

Chao Liu
Center for Speech and Language Technology, Research Institute of Information Technology, Tsinghua University, ROOM 1-303, BLDG FIT, 100084 Beijing, China
Department of Computer Science and Technology, Tsinghua University, ROOM 1-303, BLDG FIT, 100084 Beijing, China

Zhiyong Zhang, DongWang and Thomas Fang Zheng
Center for Speech and Language Technology, Research Institute of Information Technology, Tsinghua University, ROOM 1-303, BLDG FIT, 100084 Beijing, China
Center for Speech and Language Technologies, Division of Technical Innovation and Development, Tsinghua National Laboratory for Information Science and Technology, ROOM 1-303, BLDG FIT, 100084 Beijing, China

Yiye Lin
Center for Speech and Language Technology, Research Institute of Information Technology, Tsinghua University, ROOM 1-303, BLDG FIT, 100084 Beijing, China
Beijing Institute of Technology, No.5 South Zhongguancun Street, Haidian District, 100081 Beijing, China

Javier Tejedor
GEINTRA, University of Alcalá, 28801 Alcalá de Henares, Madrid, Spain

Yinguo Li
School of Computer Science and Technology, Chongqing University of Posts and Telecommunications, No.2, Chongwen Road, Nan'an District, 400065 Chong Qing, China

Vidhyasaharan Sethu, Eliathamby Ambikairajah and Julien Epps
The School of Electrical Engineering and Telecommunications, The University of New South Wales, Sydney, New South Wales 2052, Australia